The Augustan Idea in English Literature

The Augustan Idea in English Literature

Howard Erskine-Hill

Fellow of Pembroke College, Cambridge

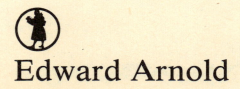

Edward Arnold

First published 1983 by
Edward Arnold (Publishers) Ltd
41 Bedford Square, London WC1B 3DQ

British Library Cataloguing in Publication Data

Erskine-Hill, Howard
   The Augustan idea in English literature
   .1. English literature—History and criticism
   2. Augustus, Emperor of Rome in literature
   I. Title
   820.9'351   PR149.A9/

ISBN 0-7131-6373-9

PR
445
.E7

Text set in 10/11 pt Times Compugraphic by Colset Private Limited, Singapore.
Printed and bound in Great Britain by Richard Clay (The Chaucer Press) Ltd,
Bungay, Suffolk

Contents

To
Nottingham University
in gratitude

Preface

When in 1975 I published *The Social Milieu of Alexander Pope* I mentioned a further piece of work which I hoped to complete, complementary to the earlier book though different in approach. *The Augustan Idea in English Literature* is the result of that work. While the earlier book approached the writings of Pope from the fields of economic, social and political history, the present one was designed to follow a more orthodox approach from the field of the history of ideas and specifically of the idea of an Augustan Age and the notions of historical pattern and process with which it has been associated. My hope is that the two studies may indeed be found complementary, at least not contradictory, or if contradictory then significantly so.

It will, however, be obvious that this is not just a book about the English eighteenth century, certainly not just about Pope. When, some twenty years ago, the book was conceived, it was always clear to me that the two great writers who would dominate it were Pope and Ben Jonson. What I did not then appreciate was the extent to which ideas of Rome's Augustan Age have been a presence in English in all periods, reaching back even to the circle of King Alfred. This realization, together with my conviction that no study of this subject could be satisfactory without discussion of Augustus himself, encouraged me to try to draw the whole contour of the Augustan Idea in English writing. I use these words with care, since what I believe emerges from the exploration is not a series of discontinuities coinciding with period divisions (conventional or otherwise) but a series of changing emphases within a relatively stable pattern of associations. This pattern had been fully assembled by the sixteenth century and remains potentially available still, but many will infer that the need for it in public writing waned with the eighteenth century.

I should add a word of explanation about my handling of foreign quotations. To be helpful to both scholar and general reader I have given major quotations from foreign languages in both original and translation, save in a few cases where the context makes the meaning clear. With verse, the original appears in the text and the translation in the footnotes. With prose this procedure is reversed. Where such quotation is intended as a background to English thought, I have often avoided modern critical editions in favour of editions available or close to the English period concerned. For the same reason I have mainly cited the older English translations. This, it should be noted, means that the English version given is not necessarily a close translation of the given original. For example, Bodin's *Six Livres de la République* is (for translation) cited in the seventeenth-century version of Richard Knolles. But Knolles's translation was built up from several editions of Bodin, in both French and Latin. My aim in these cases has been to present the foreign author in original and translation as part of the English experience. Where, on the other hand, it has seemed on balance more important to present foreign material directly to the modern reader, I have cited modern editions, and even, in the case of Augustus's *Res Gestae* in Chapter I, a source unknown between the classical era and our own time.

A few parts of this book have already appeared in earlier form: Chapter IV in A.J. Smith, ed. *John Donne: Essays in Celebration* (London, 1972); part of Chapter VI in *Renaissance and Modern Studies*, XIV (1970); Chapter VIII was given as a paper at the David Nichol Smith Seminar at Canberra in 1980; Chapter IX is a greatly expanded version of an article in *Renaissance and Modern Studies*, XI (1967); Chapter X first came out in the *Journal of the Warburg and Courtauld Institutes*, XXIII (1965). Part of Chapter XI was published in *Wolfenbütteler Forschungen*, ed. Walther Killy (Munich, 1981).

Since this book has been written over a long period, I have incurred debts to teachers, colleagues and friends in several different places. As a student at the university to which the book is dedicated, I am among the many who owe a great debt to G.R. Hibbard and J.T. Boulton in the English Department there at that time. To my friend Gilbert Sinden, SSM, I trace back interests which were to prove valuable at later stages of my work.

At the University College, Swansea, I owed an incalculable debt to Dr – now Professor – Sydney Anglo. He revealed to me a realm of Renaissance scholarship of which the literary criticism of Renaissance authors was but a part, introduced me to the tradition of the Warburg Institute, and advised me on the material of Chapter X which first appeared in the Warburg Journal. To Professor Anglo, and his wife Professor Margaret Macgowan of Sussex University, I am grateful for learned advice and unstinting scepticism offered me during the later stage of my work. Of them I may say, with Rochester, that I count their censure praise.

At Jesus College, Cambridge, Dr M.I. Finley, now Professor Sir Moses Finley, Master of Darwin, helped me begin my chapter on the Age of Augustus. The late Dr E.R. Hardy, Dean of Jesus College, answered my questions on the Fathers of the Church and showed me the importance of Orosius. Perhaps I may invoke Edward Hardy in some of his last words to me: 'Farewell and Hail – which is better than the reverse'. At that time Dr Dominic Baker-Smith, now Professor of English at the University of Amsterdam, helped me with the work on Donne which was to become Chapter IV of this book. To Dr Michael Meehan, of Flinders University of South Australia, I owe a substantial debt. His research into ideas of society and the growth of the arts in the eighteenth century (begun under my supervision) developed strikingly, and taught me a very great deal. His work, which I hope soon to see published, was of major assistance to me in Chapter IX. To Graham Storey, of Trinity Hall, I am grateful for an eminent Dickensian's discussion of the seventeenth century, and especially in the joint undergraduate seminars on seventeenth-century literature which we have run over a period of years. At the latest stage Mr Storey kindly read and commented on Chapter VII. At the same time Professor John Stevens kindly read Chapter II, and Dr Richard Gooder, of Clare College, Chapter V. My warm appreciation goes to Dr K.M. Wheeler, of St John's College, for brief but timely help with Coleridge.

At my present College Professor Ian Jack, with characteristic kindness, read through my chapters on Pope's *Imitations of Horace*. Dr Richard A. McCabe and Mr David Womersley, once pupils, now colleagues, have given me the benefit of their special knowledge of the Renaissance and the eighteenth century respectively. I am also grateful to Dr McCabe for his assistance with my quotations from Patristic and Renaissance Latin.

Because I have ventured into fields which might be thought proper to other scholars, I am especially grateful to several members of my university who have generously spent their time guiding me and helping to mitigate my ignorance. I have been privileged to be advised by Professor C.O. Brink on the poets of Augustan Rome; and by Professor Henry Chadwick on the Church Fathers. Professor P.A.M. Clemoes and my colleague Mr Colin Wilcockson went over the Old English material with me. Dr Andrew Wallace-Haddrill, of Magdalene College, Cambridge, valuably advised me on the history of the times of Augustus, and Dr Richard Hunter, of Pembroke, gave me the considerable benefit of his suggestions. Dr Patrick Sims-Williams, of St John's College, advised me on Gildas and Nennius, and Professor P. Boyde commented on those sections of my book dealing with Dante, Petrarch and Machiavelli.

To Professor Malcolm Kelsall and Professor Howard Weinbrot I am grateful for the personal warmth and friendliness with which our sometimes sharp disagreements about the eighteenth century have been discussed, in private as in public. How much I have learned from each of them will be clear from chapters IX, XI and XII, but I make general acknowledgement to them here.

I thank Cambridge University and Jesus and Pembroke Colleges for allowing me to take periodic sabbatical leave without which this book would probably never have been finished. I thank the Librarians and staff of the British Library, the Cambridge University Library, the Cambridge English Faculty Library, and the Wren Library, Trinity College, Cambridge, for their marvellous service kept up in times increasingly difficult for the world of learning.

Special thanks are due to John Davey and to Edward Arnold, for their encouragement, understanding and patience. I could not have hoped for more considerate treatment from a publisher.

My warm appreciation goes to Mrs Audrey Daughton for typing the book with so much care and skill, and to Mrs Valerie Rumbold for her generous assistance in correcting the proofs.

Finally, in at the start and there at the end, Professor George Dekker, of Stanford University, has as usual helped me in all ways, from badly needed encouragement during the slow middle stages of my work, to the amendment of phrases in the Introduction and Epilogue.

Howard Erskine-Hill
Pembroke College, Cambridge

Introduction

There are many reasons why men have remembered Gaius Octavius, later Octavianus, commonly known as the Emperor Augustus, but the most compelling is that never before had one man ruled so much of the world. His power was the power of the Roman state. This power the Greek historian Polybius compared with three famous earlier empires, Persia, Sparta and Macedonia. Their conquests were partial; those of Rome were not. Nearly the whole inhabited world, he noted, was reduced by them to obedience: and they left behind them an empire not to be paralleled in the past, unlikely to be rivalled in the future.[1] The power of Rome, like that of Augustus, was no less remarkable for duration than extent. This is one reason why modern western civilization has been and is still being shaped by our Graeco-Roman heritage. Augustus, who mediating the change from Republic to Empire was chief among those who sustained Roman rule over both east and west, holds a central position in this heritage. He has been remembered for the way in which he exploited unique opportunities, which were not purely political but involved Roman civilization. Leaving aside religious, legal and social policy, we find his name inextricably associated with contemporary achievement in poetry and architecture; indeed the relation between ruler and artist has often been a central concern within his later reputation.

The reception of Rome's Augustan Age in later civilization is surely one of the major subjects of comparative literature, though not one that has received much attention. It is an important part of a greater subject: the history of the idea of empire in the west. Far from equal to such broad and ambitious prospects, in which

> . . . *Alps* on *Alps* arise,

I hope to have contributed something to this great subject of the humanities [2] by exploring the reception of the Augustan Age of Rome in the literature of England: one of Rome's small successor states. It is in some of the earliest surviving poetry in English, from the Old English period, that we first read of what was to become a common subject of Renaissance contemplation, Roman ruins:

> Often this wall
> Stained red and gray with lichen has stood by

[1] Polybius, *Histories*, translated by Evelyn Shuckborough (London, 1889), I, pp. 1–2. The latter part of the passage summarized is conjecturally reconstructed: see Polybius, *The Histories*, ed. and tr. W.R. Paton (London, 1922), I, pp. 6–7.

[2] The other great subject, I think, is the history of the concept of free will. The first is public and historical, the second personal and philosophical.

Surviving storms while kingdoms rose and fell.
And now the high curved wall itself has fallen.[3]

– ruins not here of Rome but of a Roman city of Britain. The wall and the wide
arch of the ranged empire were remembered by the early English, and it is in the
circle of King Alfred himself, in the Old English refashioning (*c.* 890–99) of the
Historia adversus paganos of Paulus Orosius, that an image of Rome's
Augustan Age first enters English literature. A similar conception shaped one of
the finest of the medieval Nativity dramas (in the Chester Cycle) and seen as a
whole the subject is by no means confined to that period conventionally
designated 'the Augustan Age' in English writing.

This is not therefore a book about the eighteenth and later seventeenth centuries alone. The term 'Augustan' as applied to our literature has indeed its
origins in that period. They have never been fully explored, and while an
account of them is given here, I attempt to follow the subject from its medieval
beginnings through the great central period of English literature in the sixteenth,
seventeenth and eighteenth centuries. One of my chief contentions is that conscious Augustanism in English literature begins not in 1660 or 1700 but with Ben
Jonson in the last years of Elizabeth.

An attempt to trace the whole contour of the Augustan idea in English writing
may be thought to entail certain regrettable limitations. In the first place the
light and shadow of the Augustan Age are cast from a time and language
anterior to English literature. Can it be thought sensible to explore an effect
without considering its apparent cause? I have tried to solve this problem by
giving a summary account, in Chapter I, of Augustus and Augustan Rome.
Secondly the reception of the Augustan Age is a feature of European and not
merely English culture. In my account of Patristic and medieval ideas of
Augustus in Chapter II, and of Renaissance political thought in Chapter III, I
have gone some way towards drawing a European picture. It was desirable to do
so, for the Fathers of the Church, and Renaissance thinkers such as Machiavelli,
Bodin and Lipsius, entered the main stream of English thought both in their
original languages and in English translation. These sections of the book
describe stages in the story of the Augustan idea that could hardly have been told
from the English evidence alone. I have thought it worth risking the danger of
intrusion into the specialist areas of others in order to offer a more coherent and
complete account. I hope to have kept in mind the importance of continental
influence throughout the book, but I believe that once a tradition of Augustan
comparison and imitation becomes established in early seventeenth-century
England continental developments are relatively less significant than before.

The word 'Idea' in my title is not intended to suggest that the English recep-

---

[3] *A Choice of Anglo-Saxon Verse*, tr. and intro. Richard Hamer (London, 1970), p. 27. The
translation is of ll. 9–11 of 'The Ruin':

> Oft þæs wag gebad
> ræghar ond readfah rice æfter oþrum,
> ofstonden under stormum; steap geap gedreas.

(*The Exeter Book*, ed. G.P. Krapp and Elliott Van Kirk Dobbie (London, 1936); p. 227. See *Three
Old English Elegies*, ed. R.F. Leslie (Manchester, 1961), pp. 69–70.

tion of Rome's Augustan Age involved one idea alone, as it might be, for example, of peaceful empire, or of enlightened patronage of poets. 'Idea' must perforce stand for a shifting pattern of ideas, some diametrically opposed if pressed to their extreme forms. The grateful view of Virgil and Horace; the penetrating and hostile view of Tacitus; and the Christian providential view of Eusebius, each quite different from the others, are the major components of what may for the sake of brevity be termed the Augustan Idea. Separated out, they formed the arguments in a debate about the nature of Augustan Rome. Drawn together they composed a compound image in which compatibility was more evident than contradiction. Once Tacitus had been rediscovered and had begun to be assimilated it is probable that each of these views was in some measure present in the mind of anyone thinking about the Rome of Augustus. To say anything more precise than this is only possible, I believe, through the analysis of specific writings and these, it must be emphasized, tell us reliably about the minds of their authors but hardly about the mind of an age. Because one period of our literature has been known as 'the Augustan Age' it is some-times thought that to use this name implies a belief that all people of that time admired Rome's Augustan Age, or at least were constantly aware of it as an ideal, warning, or standard of judgement. The fact that many people in the six-teenth, seventeenth and eighteenth centuries demonstrably did think in these ways,[4] does not license us to generalize about the total thought of these periods. Such generalizations, common in literary criticism and based on literature alone, are quite rightly distrusted by historians. The generalizations in this book apply to no more than the evidence presented, and have no pretension to establish 'the seventeenth-century frame of mind', or the 'eighteenth-century structure of feeling'. I claim only to have traced, within the wider historical con-sciousness, a particular tradition of thought and literary practice. It may be considered a tradition of some importance, however, if only because of its link with public events, its concern with the relation of writing and rule, and its asso-ciation with authors of acknowledged stature.

To recognize a tradition clearly it is necessary to gain some perspective. A shorter book than this could have listed the chief examples in English literature of where comparisons with Augustan Rome were drawn or imitation of the Augustan writers produced. That would have been a somewhat unrewarding exercise in cultural abstraction. Every proposition is better understood by knowledge of its opposite, and every topic better appreciated by awareness of the terrain on the far side of its frontier. The Augustan idea is not only often associated with the didactic praise of other ancient and modern rulers, notably the Antonines; it is strongly linked, it will be found, with an opposite Antonian conception of experience and responsibility and conduct – this is borne out by some of the major work of both Shakespeare and Dryden. Again, a monarchical

---

[4] See the exchange of views between Vivian de Sola Pinto and Donald Greene: Pinto's 'Augustan or Augustinian? More Demythologizing Needed?' and Greene's reply, in *Eighteenth-Century Studies*, 2 (1969), pp. 291, 293–300. The broad issues are reviewed in Ch. I of Howard Weinbrot's *Augustus Caesar in 'Augustan' England* (Princeton, 1978). The evidence for the English literary use of the Augustan comparison is set forth in the following chapters; further reference to Weinbrot's opinions will be found in Ch. IX below. On the question of nomenclature, 'the Augustan Age' is, like most labels, less appropriate to some aspects of the period it is used to designate, than to others. As Weinbrot says, neutral terms, such as 'eighteenth-century' are to be preferred.

Augustan ideal was often affirmed in implicit contrast to a tradition of republican idealism. The two are as closely linked in Andrew Marvell's *Horatian Ode* as they were in the career of Augustus himself. These recognitions of how different ideas work in dialectical or symbiotic relationship with each other are in the end essential to the understanding of each separate idea. Thus I have devoted some space to Machiavelli whose political thought is in such telling contrast to the thinkers that praised Augustus. And thus I have explored at some length the relation between Antony and Caesar in *Antony and Cleopatra*. Significant too is what might be termed the penumbra of an idea in creative practice: where in Jonson an imitation of Horace fades towards Martial, or in Pope begins to gather the vehemence of Juvenal. Rightly or wrongly I have felt that I must acknowledge and explore these polarities, and attend to the delicate and unschematic frontiers of my chosen subject.

Copious as it may seem, the book is not exhaustive. The subject is so enormous that I should be rash to claim that I had assembled all the significant material in the two to three centuries which form the centre of my survey. It is my hope, at least, that all the main literary categories are represented: historical commentary; political writing; formal panegyric; dedication; the Roman play; the imitation of Augustan poets; discussion of literary and cultural achievement. I hope that, as a result, the bringing forward of further material will not gravely alter my conclusions.

This is perhaps the place, however, to add what might in any other time be a superfluous affirmation. If this book has any value it lies in its setting forth of truths about one tradition within our cultural heritage. Evidence has been presented and conclusions based on that evidence. I acknowledge the principle of truth as the end of scholarship, and have no interest in the production of subjective myth in the guise of criticism, or in the mere multiplication of readings none of which has any greater probability than the rest. Those who find value in writing of this kind have one peculiar advantage. They can never be shown to be wrong since truth, probability and the idea of an object of study are all denied by them at a would-be philosophical level. No such security is available to those who, exploring a complicated historical and literary subject, seek to make statements about the world. Their selection of evidence, analysis, judgements and conclusions are all, quite rightly, open to verification or falsification by others; they are vulnerable to challenge. But they too have a consolation. In so far as they are shown to be in the wrong, by so much is our understanding of the subject advanced. Within the procedures of empirical exploration, even surprising hypotheses may be proposed with a good conscience.

I have been aware of a further difficulty. This book has been conceived chronologically, chiefly because other methods of arrangement too easily allow hindsight to obscure the distinctness of a particular historical moment. Yet a stage-by-stage chronological narrative has – apart from some dangers of monotony – certain disadvantages in the manner in which it yields its insights. Where the critical appreciation of particular works of literature is concerned, chronological narrative flattens out the reading experience, and lifts us too easily away from the difficulties, denials and resolutions of verbal art. There are also times when the complexities of historical process demand, if they are to be properly understood, the sharpness of a proleptic or retrospective view. I have therefore attempted to vary the survey-like idiom of some parts of the book – an idiom which, properly handled, can have an excitement of its own – with other sections of more detailed critical reading: sometimes of quite short works such as Donne's *Satyre IV* or Pope's Epistle *To Addison*, sometimes of longer works such as Jonson's *Poetaster, Antony and Cleopatra*, or a major collection such as Pope's *Imitations of Horace*. Discussion of *Satyre IV* afforded the opportunity of a sudden forward look to what Pope made of it when he chose to imitate a satire of Horace (*Sat.* I, ix) through the medium of Donne. Again, the roots of the Epistle *To Addison*, on the face of it a typical neo-classical poem, go back to Petrarch and St Jerome, as the retrospective insights of an exploration of its sources reveal. Chapter IX, The Idea of an Augustan Age, surveys the eighteenth century widely, in preparation for detailed critical readings of poems by Pope in Chapters X, XI and XII. I hope that the two kinds of discussion may be found complementary. The broad patterns which these procedures reveal are briefly reviewed in the concluding pages of this Introduction.

In the Alfredian *Orosius*, Augustus, having been left heir of Julius Caesar, battles for supremacy over a reluctant Rome. According to the earlier of the two extant manuscripts he 'v gefeoht ungeferlice þurhteah', fought five battles divisively, in civil war, a statement which follows Orosius who says that at this time Augustus devoted himself to civil war: '. . . indolem suam bellis civilibus vovit'. The other, later MS, substituting 'wel cynelice' for 'ungeferlice', describes him as fighting like a king.[5] In the difference between 'ungeferlice' and 'cynelice' may, at this earliest point in the English reception of Augustus, be seen signs of two great contrasting views in the historical record. The first was to extend knowledge of his ruthless early struggle for power into a hostile and penetrating Tacitean assessment of his whole career and its effect on Rome. The second, while understanding that Augustus was never a king, recognized that he became a monarch in fact. It saw in this an example of the tendency of states towards monarchy, and in the finally victorious Augustus one of the most famous possible positive examples of how a monarch should act. The Alfredian *Orosius*, however, sets above these a third, the Patristic view that the *pax Augusta* established at the end of the civil wars was the providential preparation for the coming of the Gospel of Peace upon earth with Christ.

Each of these three views runs through the present book, and it will be seen that each has great didactic potential. The rediscovered Tacitus became almost a subversive influence in the monarchical Europe of the sixteenth, seventeenth and eighteenth centuries.[6] The second and third views, with which we shall be more concerned, lent themselves well to the development of panegyric under monarchy. From Pliny and Claudian to the eighteenth century, panegyric was a literary practice of particular importance, seeking to instruct and inspire through praise and lift the sights of both ruler and ruled to the image of a better life. Nor is this true only of formal panegyric; it is true also of all those literary

---

[5] *The Old English Orosius*, ed. Janet Bately (Early English Text Society, Supplementary series, 6; London, 1980), p. 129 (l. 10). The Lauderdale MS, which is preferred by Bately as the basis for her text and has the first reading is early tenth century and was almost certainly written at Winchester. The Cotton MS, which has the second reading, is of the first half of the eleventh century; its place of origin is unknown. Paulus Orosius, *Historia adversus paganos*, VI, xviii; Migne, *Patrologia Latina*, XXXI (Paris, 1846), p. 429.

[6] See K.C. Schellhase, *Tacitus in Renaissance Political Thought* (London, 1976).

forms in prose and verse which incorporate panegyrical features. The eighteenth-century Thomas Blackwell's *Memoirs of the Court of Augustus* is a telling borderline case: a work which strongly disapproves of Augustus, yet manages to admire the court of Augustus and can use this admiration in public praise. Panegyrical writing deserves to be taken seriously. It is quite anachronistic to regard it as by definition nothing better than the tinsel of flattery or the banality of compliment. It could sometimes be that. But a highly conventional gesture, such as the comparison of a present ruler with Augustus, changes in real meaning with the relevant context of contemporary thought about Augustus. The modern reader can also forget, as a Donne or Ben Jonson could not, what it was to be in the power of a monarch, and how far hopes for change rested with the ruler. Frances Yates is chief among those of our time who have taught us to see in the comparisons of panegyric a vision of the future. Panegyric shows us the moral and prophetic capacity of the human mind striving to ground itself in historical reality. It selects from the historical record, the better to fulfil whatever is there to be admired and used to serve the time. This is not a negligible aspect of human consciousness.

If formal panegyric is at one extreme of the tradition of the Augustan idea, and Tacitean analysis at the other, the literary imitation holds the centre. Imitation is, at the literary level, that retrieval and incorporation of what is to be admired from the past which panegyric recommends. An Augustan cultural programme starts to be fulfilled when genuine imitation of Augustan texts begins. But genuine imitation, great imitation – I have in mind above all Pope's *Imitations of Horace* – can draw from both the idealizing and the analytic extremes of the Augustan idea, and bring the modern mind into dramatic relationship with the mind from another culture. To recreate so that one can both agree and disagree, at times identify and at other times stand separate – that is the highest measure of imitation.

The Augustan idea in English can take us from the Augustus who fights 'ungeferlice' (or 'cynelice') in the Alfredian *Orosius* to the subtly inflected civilian irony of Pope's

And Nations wonder'd while they dropp'd the sword![7]

It has always encompassed the heroic (or ruthless) and civilian (or carefully calculating): where the two come together we have the ideal of Augustan maturity as it is found in the Cinna episode as set forth by Seneca in his *De Clementia*, Sir Thomas Elyot in his *Boke named the Gouernour* and Pierre Corneille in his tragedy *Cinna*. We find it in James I as Augustus in the eyes of Ben Jonson, and Charles II as Augustus in Dryden's eyes at the end of *Absalom and Achitophel*. The *princeps* who established world peace and who sought to build up the class of the *equites* against the turbulent *nobiles* to serve the state is aptly associated with civilian themes and the unashamed celebration of domestic experience. When Horace tells how he fled the field of battle leaving his shield behind, or when Carew can say:

---

[7] Alexander Pope, Epistle *To Augustus*, l. 399; *Poems*, IV, *Imitations of Horace*, ed. John Butt (London, 1939; rev. edn 1961), p. 229.

what though the German Drum
Bellow for freedome and revenge, the noyse
Concernes not us. . . .[8]

or when Pope writes:

My Life's amusements have been just the same,
Before, and after Standing Armies came

comparing the rougher world and tougher mind of Horace's:

Sæviat atque novos moveat Fortuna tumultus!
Quantum hinc imminuet?[9]

– this is a characteristic strain within the Augustan idea. More characteristic, overall, is an awareness of the practicable interdependence of private and public, the public not consuming the private, the private not blocking the public from view. This is especially clear in Pope. And in Pope, the author with whom the final chapters of this book are most concerned, it may be true to say that the chief strains within the Augustan idea find expression. Panegyric and imitation have an important place in his work. The Patristic view of the Augustan Age is felt in *Messiah* and more subtly in *Windsor Forest*. The Tacitean view of Augustus, though strongly held by some in his circle, touched him less deeply. Yet he shows his awareness of it. Tacitus and Machiavelli, through Bolingbroke, affect Pope's concern with corruption and political decline, and sometimes draw him strongly towards formal satire on the model of Juvenal. That the poets of Augustan Rome powerfully shaped Pope's work and vision is beyond dispute. His relation with Horace is especially salient.

Further than this no tidy overall patterns can be found. The value of this book will be if anywhere in its more specific formulations and in the complexities and assymetries of its material. It finds its ending not with a Conclusion but an Epilogue.

[8] *In answer of an Elegiacell Letter* . . ., ll. 96–8; *The Poems of Thomas Carew* . . ., ed. Rhodes Dunlap (Oxford, 1949), p. 77.
[9] *The Second Satire of the Second Book of Horace Paraphrased*, ll. 153–4; *Imitations of Horace*, pp. 66–7.

I   Augustus

> . . . even the best Authors . . . choose a general Air of
> a man, and according to that interpret all his Actions,
> of which, if some be so stiff and stubborn, that they
> cannot bend or writh them to any uniformity with the
> rest, they are presently imputed to dissimulation.
> *Augustus* has escapt them, for there was in him so
> apparent, sudden, and continual a variety of Actions,
> all the whole course of his life, that he is slipt away
> clear and undecided from the most hardy censurers.
> (Montaigne, 'Of the Inconstancy of Our Actions' (Tr.
> Charles Cotton)

The Rise of Octavian

Tacitus, writing some 180 years after Augustus rose to single power, declared
that Augustus then reduced the Roman Republic to despotism. His purpose,
says Syme, was 'to deny the Republic of Augustus, not to rehabilitate anarchy,
the parent of despotism.'[1] Augustus himself, in the account of his achievements
drawn up at the end of his life,[2] asserted that he 'championed the liberty of the
republic', defended it against its enemies, refused the dictatorship offered him
by Senate and the people, and indeed 'office inconsistent with the custom of our
ancestors'. These apparently conflicting claims are in great measure explained
when we consider the state of the Roman Republic into which Octavius was born
in 63 BC. Soon the structure of the old aristocratic republic was to be broken
under intolerable strains. The new provinces and mighty armies were beyond the
effective control of a government designed for a city state. Nevertheless the
party of the *optimates* in Rome, representing the old ruling families, dominating
the Senate, and supported by much of the propertied class, held resolutely to

[1]Tacitus, *Annales*, I–5: 'dominatio' is the word used, I, 3; *The Annals of Tacitus*, ed. F.R.D.
Goodyear (Cambridge, 1972), I, 49–52. Ronald Syme, *The Roman Revolution* (Oxford, 1939; rev.
edn 1951), p. 513. The present chapter is generally indebted to T. Rice Holmes, *The Architect of the
Roman Empire* (Oxford, 1928); Syme, *The Roman Revolution*; S.A. Cook, F.E. Adcock and M.P.
Charlesworth, eds., *The Cambridge Ancient History*, X: *The Augustan Empire* (Cambridge, 1952);
Ch. Wirszubski, *Libertas As a Political Idea at Rome During the Late Republic and Early Principate*
(Cambridge, 1960) and A.H.M. Jones, *Augustus* (London, 1970). Jean Béranger, *Reserches Sur
L'Aspect Ideologique du Principat* (Basle, 1953) has also been consulted.

[2]*Res Gestae*, 1, 5, 6; *Res Gestae Divi Augusti*, ed. P.A. Brunt and J.M. Moore; (Oxford, 1967),
pp. 18–21: 'rem publicam . . . in libertatem vindicavi'. Wirszubski sets in context *Res Gestae*, I,
1–2, which refer to Octavian's early action against Antony at the end of 44 BC and suggests that 'rem
publicam . . . vindicavi' was no more than a conventional way of saying: 'I worked for the public
good' (*Libertas*, p. 104).

their old forms and powers. Their conservatism denied effective solution to the enormous problems generated by Rome's success. The Italian tribes and cities, allies of Rome and sinews of her military might, were still denied Roman franchise and citizenship. The new wealth of the senatorial class, invested in land and slaves to work the land, drove out the earlier peasant proprietors, thus creating a landless proletariat whose only eventual hope of prosperity was military recruitment. For this and other reasons the loyalty and interest of the great armies of the later Republic lay rather with their commanders than with the state.

Less coherent and consistently oriented than the *optimates*, the opposing *populares* sought to remedy these ills by revolutionary measures. The combination of radical social conflict and available military power, led inexorably to civil war. From the first such civil war, in 91 BC, the Senate became but one political force in situations increasingly dominated by ambitious and powerful military commanders, who allied themselves with its declining authority only when it suited their independent purposes. Sulla, an optimate commander, used the dictatorship which he was able to secure through military power to attempt to restore the old Republic, but failed to check the decline of the Senate. Power lay with the great commanders, among whom one arose with exceptional brilliance and vision. He was a convinced and effective *populuris*, and has been described as a 'daring left-wing politician'.[3] This was Gaius Julius Caesar.

Octavius was seventeen in the year when his great uncle, Julius Caesar, having beaten his rival Pompeius at the Battle of Pharsalia, attained to the dictatorship of Rome. From among several relatives he was the favoured protégé of the childless dictator. On this connection his ambition rested, and this was the foundation of his career. But the danger of such ambition was soon brought home to him. In 44 BC, while a student at Apollonia on the Adriatic coast, he had news of Julius Caesar's assassination at the hands of Brutus and Cassius, *optimates* determined to restore the old Republic. On landing in Italy he learned that he was heir to three-quarters of Julius Caesar's estate, and had been adopted as his son.

In political terms, however, he was not even the chief heir of Caesar. 'Puer qui omnia nomini debes', Antony was to call him. The leadership of the Caesarian faction, with all its immense vested interests, passed naturally to the senior Consul and trusted lieutenant of the murdered dictator: Mark Antony himself. Once it was clear that the conservative republicans were losing control of the situation, and Brutus and Cassius were forced to leave Rome by growing hostility of the veteran soldiers and urban poor, Antony seized the initiative, implemented a number of Caesar's policies, and, while not yet breaking outright with the Republic, powerfully consolidated his position.[4] The advent in Rome of the young Octavian (the new cognomen was a mark of adoption by his uncle) could only be embarrassing to Antony, prompting him to a politically premature declaration of intent. This danger he avoided at the serious cost of a rebuff to Caesar's heir and thus offence to his veterans. Cicero, the great writer, orator and politician, who applauded the assassination, opposed Antony, and

[3]A.H.M. Jones, *Augustus*, p. 8; Rice Holmes, *The Architect of the Roman Empire*, I, pp. 1–2.
[4]Syme, *The Roman Revolution*, p. 191; Rice Holmes, *The Architect of the Roman Empire*, I, pp. 2–10; *The Augustan Empire*, pp. 2–5.

distrusted Octavian, accurately predicted trouble between the two claimants to the Caesarian interest.[5] While, during the next thirteen years, expediency repeatedly compelled them into alliance, their rivalry was the permanent feature of a period of instability and violence.

The conduct of Octavian was remarkable. 'The boy had no official standing and no troops: but he was the inheritor of a great name; many of the veterans were prepared to fight for him; and all the world has recognized that he acted with the circumspection, the caution, the astuteness, and the adroitness of an experienced politician.'[6] This true summary requires qualification. Personal loyalty and personal ambition blended in an overwhelming resolve to triumph over his 'father's' assassins and those who condoned the murder.[7] To this end he was bold as well as circumspect, especially at first when his desire for the lavish public vindication of Caesar's memory was too precipitate for the more mature political judgement of Antony. In one respect, however, Octavian was lucky in the shows he staged in memory of Caesar, for in July of 44 BC the games in honour of Venus Genetrix were marked by a comet which was taken for a sign that Caesar's soul had been received among the gods. Octavian noted it in his Autobiography (in a passage preserved by Pliny) and Virgil alludes to it in his Fifth Eclogue.[8] Octavian seems to have been capable of rashness, but his relative political impotence soon taught him to play for time; he began to establish his own military power-base, and soon became a significant third force, to form an uneasy triangle of powers with Antony and the Senate. Cicero played a double game with him and he with Cicero. Brutus recognized the great orator's mistake.[9] The time came when the Republic needed the help of Octavian against Antony; though only twenty, he then demanded the Consulship in return; when refused he seized it by force, and was temporarily master of Rome. He was now able to negotiate with Antony and his ally Lepidus from a position of some strength: the outcome was the constitutional recourse by which the three commanders became *tresviri reipublicae constituendae*, or triumvirs, a shared dictatorship of absolute powers.[10] There followed the Proscription by which, following the precedent of Sulla, but not of Caesar, the triumvirs sentenced to death a long list of those they agreed to be their public enemies, among them the great Cicero. It is sometimes thought that the young Octavian can have acquiesced only reluctantly in the deaths of 300 senators and 2,000 *equites*, but the evidence for this opinion is slim. 'Chill and mature terrorist' (Syme's phrase) probably goes too far, but he understood well enough the exceptionally ruthless times in which he strove for supremacy.[11] So did Cicero. Octavian was probably as responsible for what was done as his fellow triumvirs.

The ten years of the Triumvirate were marked by successful military action against mutual enemies, brief outbreaks of mutual hostilities, and an alternation of confrontation and reconciliation between Antony and Octavian. The last great supporters of the old Republic, Brutus and Cassius, were defeated by

[5]Rice Holmes, *The Architect of the Roman Empire*, I, pp. 5, 12; *The Augustan Empire*, pp. 8–9.
[6]Rice Holmes, I, p. 18.
[7]*The Augustan Empire*, p. 7.
[8]Jones, *Augustus*, p. 15; *Eclogae*, V, 56–7.
[9]Syme, *The Roman Revolution*, pp. 184–5.
[10]Ibid., pp. 19–20; A.H.M. Jones, *Augustus*, p. 23; Rice Holmes, I, pp. 68–71.
[11]*The Augustan Empire*, pp. 20–2; Syme, *The Roman Revolution*, p. 191.

the generalship of Antony in two large-scale battles at Philippi in Macedonia. Octavian pulled himself out of one of his periodic illnesses to join him, for the presence of Caesar's heir was important with the soldiers, and in the second action he made a substantial military contribution to the victory. A mixture of negotiation and force eventually put down Sextus Pompeius, a commander whose considerable naval power was based on Sicily. At this point Lepidus tried to secure Sicily for himself, his troops mutinied, and he was deprived of his triumviral power. In Italy, and among the armies, there was now an overwhelming desire for peace. The Pact of Brundisium, in 40 BC, which prevented hostilities between the two chief triumvirs from developing into a sustained war, 'was greeted with an outburst of jubilation by soldiers and civilians alike', and was the occasion for Virgil's Fourth Eclogue to evoke universal peace in Messianic terms.[12]

Antony and Octavian

The attitude of the two leaders is perhaps harder to construe from the detail of events than from the broad outline. Each was deeply suspicious of the other, and ready to resort to arms at any sign of a breach of their agreement. Misunderstanding caused some of the trouble, but it seems fair to say that Antony kept to the agreements more faithfully than Octavian.[13] Each sought prestige and power through military success against external enemies: Antony in his great but unsuccessful Parthian expedition, Octavian in his more modest but useful campaigns in Illyricum, which opened a road from Italy to the East. Both were rivals for the fulfilment of the Caesarian vision of Rome. The cause of the old Republic, in any sense that Brutus, Cassius or Cicero would have recognized, was dead. Octavian, young, alert, intelligent and ruthless, found no easy or complete success in anything he undertook, but consolidated his power with indomitable resolve. It is a mistake to see him as an emotionless politician. If it is hard to separate his feeling at his uncle's murder from his Caesarian ambition, it is worth noting the circumstances of his third marriage. He fell passionately in love with Livia, wife of Tiberius Nero, 'beautiful, discreet; of aristocratic Republican stock . . .'. That he now repudiated his earlier political marriage, which had become personally as well as politically repugnant, is less remarkable than the urgency with which he pressed his suit to Livia, quickly securing her divorce, and marrying her three days after she had borne a second son to her first husband. He had chosen a woman who 'throughout a devoted married life of fifty years . . . remained an influence for moderation and forgiveness'.[14] Here can be seen more clearly that driving impatience which was partly shown

[12]*The Augustan Empire*, pp. 44–5; Syme, *The Roman Revolution*, pp. 218–19. For a full modern account of the occasion and meaning of Virgil's Fourth Eclogue, see Ian M. Le M. Du Quesnay, 'Vergil's *Fourth Eclogue*', in Francis Cairns, ed., *Papers of the Liverpool Latin Seminar* (Liverpool, 1977), pp. 25–99.

[13]Octavian tried to take over Antony's legions in Gaul on the death of Calenus (*The Augustan Empire*, p. 42) and had not supplied troops for Antony's Parthian Campaign in return for Antony's naval assistance against Sextus Pompeius (ibid., pp. 53, 58; Jones, *Augustus*, p. 31); in addition Antony had reported back to Octavian deserters from his cause such as Salvidienus Rufus (ibid., p. 44).

[14]Syme, *The Roman Revolution*, pp. 229, 340; *The Augustan Empire*, pp. 56–7; Jones, *Augustus*, p. 30.

when he first came to Rome after Caesar's assassination; it is a quality which underlay his intelligent manoeuvres and alliances.

While neither of the two chief triumvirs could dispense with the other in the short term, Octavian still saw in Antony the ultimate obstacle to his ambition: to what he must have regarded as his inheritance. Antony, though an older man, seemed prepared to work on a longer time-scale. He took the measure of Octavian's touchy, decisive and determined character. Unable to destroy the younger man's inherited prestige as Caesar's heir, since the interests involved were his own power-base also, he resolved to keep terms with him over a long period, and must have hoped to strengthen his own position substantially by success in the Parthian campaign. Though he lost some turns in the power struggle, allowing or failing to prevent the fall of potential allies such as Sextus Pompeius and Lepidus, this does not, on an overall view, seem ground for thinking that his ultimate rivalry with Octavian was ever abandoned.[15] That there was indecisiveness and discontinuity in his character may, perhaps, be not so true as that, less impatiently competitive than Octavian, he was more open to experience, bringing it stage by stage to the interpretation of his Caesarian vision. Nevertheless the failure of his Parthian expedition in 36 BC, and the persuasion of his royal mistress, Cleopatra, who risked the winter seas to bring supplies for his exhausted and depleted army, convinced him that he did not have all the time in the world to achieve his end. 'Strong in the support of the plebs and the veterans', Octavian was establishing himself as the ruler of Italy, getting credit for the joint Caesarian programme of settling the soldiers on the land, and effectively controlling the supply of trained Roman troops.[16] His propaganda held out the genuine ideal, and evoked the genuine hope, of a lasting civil peace. He led the improvement and beautification of the city of Rome, and 'encouraged a steady revival of pride in the past of Italy and her religion . . .'.[17]

It was thus Antony who made the decisive break. He did so by repudiating Octavia, sister of Octavian, married to him to cement a triumviral reconciliation; by acknowledging his marriage with Cleopatra; and by staging in Alexandria two extraordinary public ceremonies, a triumph, and the Donations, which seemed to proclaim a synthesis of the Caesarian ideal with the visionary Hellenic and Eastern ambition of the great queen who was now, not only his wife, but his political partner. Antony's rôle as the guardian, and effective inheritor, of the Caesarian future, was asserted by his announcement of a marriage between Cleopatra and Julius Caesar, and of the consequent legitimacy of their son, Ptolemy Caesar, 'Caesarion', who was now made king of kings, and joint monarch with Cleopatra of Egypt and Cyprus. There could, perhaps, have been no sharper challenge to Octavian than this. To hold that Antony was now merely the Roman instrument of Cleopatra's ambition is an unnecessary inference; without abandoning his Roman rôle, which he could never afford to do, Antony was drawing to himself in partnership the wealth, power and prestige of Cleopatra, of the Hellenic East, in a challenge to Octavian for the rule of the world.[18]

---

[15]As argued in by Tarn and Charlesworth, *The Augustan Empire*, pp. 76–7.
[16]Syme, *The Roman Revolution*, p. 231; *The Augustan Empire*, pp. 32, 76.
[17]*The Augustan Empire*, pp. 83, 88–9.
[18]Syme, *The Roman Revolution*, p. 274; *The Augustan Empire*, pp. 79–83; Jones, *Augustus*, p. 35; Rice Holmes, I, pp. 36–9.

The war of propaganda preceded, and followed, the war of ships and men. It ranged from the crudest vilification to the expression of the most deeply held beliefs, entered the high art of Virgil and Horace, and in different ways and to different degrees was absorbed into historiography so that it has deeply influenced Renaissance and even modern views of the two great competitors. A modern study remarks '. . . that both the conventional portraits − of Antony as a drunken sot occasionally quitting Cleopatra's embraces for disastrous campaigns, of Octavian as a cowardly runaway, cruel and treacherous in his dealings − are due mainly to this propaganda and are wholly unreal'.[19] But since Octavian was ultimately victorious, his propaganda has lasted better. It helped him prevail, however, because it contained some elements of truth. Cleopatra was not a frenzied queen, plotting destruction to capitol and empire with her pack of squalid half-men, besotted with dreams of triumph, as Horace sang. She was a brilliant, daring and ambitious monarch, impatient of the client status of her ancient kingdom and dynasty, who was making, in essential partnership with one of the most powerful and gifted of the military successors of Julius Caesar, if not a bid for the leadership of the Roman world then at least a dramatic renovation of her Ptolemaic kingdom.[20] She would rule the East, Antony the West, in a new conception of world empire under the authority of Rome.[21] Greek as she was, Octavian only needed to focus upon what was alien in her, her country and her religion, to distort the double aspect of his competitors' design, arouse Italian patriotism, and present Antony as a traitor to Rome. Some already feared that Antony meant to change the capital city of the empire from Rome to Alexandria. In a sacrilegious bid to get to the bottom of Antony's latest intentions, Octavian compelled the Vestal Virgins to yield up Antony's will, and had it read out to the Senate. Its contents, though revealing little more than what had already been publicly implied by the Donations, fully served his purpose.[22] An oath of allegiance to Octavian was now arranged throughout Italy and the West. It seems not to have been forced, but seen as a patriotic duty, and it evoked patriotic determination in all that part of the Roman world which lay in Octavian's control, as the inevitable armed conflict with Antony approached.

By this time Octavian was already possessed of two great advantages. He was master of Italy and its supplies of Roman legionaries; and he was more closely identified than Antony with the Caesarian programme and Roman patriotism. Antony was the better general, but in Agrippa, the creator of the Italian fleet, Octavian had the more experienced naval commander. Cleopatra made an indispensable contribution to the supply of the huge land and sea forces which were being gathered against Octavian, but her partnership was a handicap as well as a help, for Antony's Roman supporters resented her presence on the campaign, and disagreed with her advice. Nevertheless, a brilliant victory by Antony could have turned the scales. But he could not easily carry the war into Italy; Cleopatra's presence there would have aroused passionate opposition, and the devastation of the land gone against him. Why he did not intercept

[19]For the artistic assimilation of such publicity in Virgil, see e.g. *Aeneid*, VIII, 685–713; and in Horace, e.g. *Carmina*, I, xxxvii. For the propaganda war generally, see Jones, *Augustus*, pp. 35–6 and *The Augustan Empire*, pp. 90–2, 97–9.

[20]Horace, *Carmina*, I, xxxvii, 6–12; *The Augustan Empire*, pp. 79–83.

[21]Syme, *The Roman Revolution*, p. 275; Jones, *Augustus*, p. 37.

[22]Jones, *Augustus*, p. 39.

Octavian's fleet as it sailed to meet him on the west coast of Greece is uncertain. Perhaps he hoped for a decisive victory by land outside Italy.

Agrippa now effected a landing in the southwest Peloponnese, capturing substantial amounts of grain and munitions bound from Egypt for Antony. Octavian, hoping to surprise an Antonian squadron near the promontory of Actium on the Gulf of Ambracia, was held off by the ships closing the mouth of the gulf, but seized and fortified its northern promontory. Informed by his scouts, Antony sailed at once for Actium and effectively fortified the southern promontory. Octavian now offered to fight on land, but Antony, waiting for his legions to concentrate, declined battle. When they came up he established an advance camp on the northern promontory; Octavian declined battle in his turn, and each manoeuvred to cut off the other from his supplies, Octavian gaining the advantage. This advantage was increased by Agrippa's capture of the ports of Leucas and Patrae, which cut Antony off from the Peloponnese, and severed his vital maritime supply-routes. Desertions to Octavian began, and hunger and malaria began to be problems in the Antonian camps. Without any major engagement having been fought the Battle of Actium was now effectively lost by Antony, whose position had become a trap. Octavian could not be compelled to fight by land; in the situation as it had developed Antony was not confident he could win by sea.

A rational assessment probably suggested that his only course was to break through the hostile fleet which barred his egress from the gulf and retreat to Egypt with his best ships and as many legionaries as possible, while the rest of his forces attempted to withdraw and rejoin him by land. This plan, advocated by Cleopatra, and communicated to Octavian in advance by a deserter, seems to have been what was eventually agreed by Antony and the queen. It was divulged to very few, presumably to prevent further desertion. Ships that could not be manned were burned; the war chest was loaded onto one of Cleopatra's ships; and (an unusual and significant step) their galleys shipped sails, though preparing for battle. On 2 September 31 BC the weather was right for the Antonian design. A considerable sea-fight was of course inevitable, but (if Antony had his way) only so much and of the kind that would allow the maximum number of ships, and above all Cleopatra's squadron with the war chest, to break through the blockade and get away. Antony placed his most formidable commanders (himself and Sosius) on the right and left respectively; Agrippa followed suit; thus the centre was likely to be an area of less fierce combat. When, to the sounding of trumpets, the Antonian fleet moved out into the calm waters of the gulf, Cleopatra's squadron was in the rear of the centre: if all went well, in the best position to break out. Since Antony now had fewer though larger ships than Agrippa, it was to his advantage to fight closer up into the gulf, where his shorter line could not be turned to admit assault in the rear. In the hope of drawing Octavian's fleet into battle, Antony, once out of shallow water, paused; but Agrippa and Octavian assessed the situation too well to be tempted. Antony had to allow himself to be drawn out, and since his ultimate aim was escape this was not without its advantages. When, at noon, the expected and necessary breeze sprang up from the sea, Antony's left advanced, followed by the centre and right. Agrippa, seeking to outflank the right, caused Antony to extend his line there, and thus create a gap in the centre. Through this relatively open water, between two and three in the afternoon, when the breeze had strengthened, and the fight seemed, but almost certainly was not, evenly balanced, Cleopatra's squadron, hitherto passive, seized the opportunity to break out for which it had been waiting, and sailed away to the Peloponnese. Though appraised of Antony's general strategy Octavian's leaders seem to have been taken by surprise. Antony transferred from his heavily engaged flagship to a smaller vessel, and followed with some other ships from his right wing. The author of the most detailed modern account of the battle concludes thus: 'To save even sixty ships out of 230 was a creditable achievement for a man embayed on a lee shore and vastly outnumbered. But Antony did better, for he seems to have extricated a few of the ships he had with him on the right . . . in military terms Antony did well to escape from a nearly hopeless position.'[23]

Virgil, Plutarch and Shakespeare have, by moral and psychological simplification, given us unforgettable dramatizations of this battle, in which the flight of the unreliable Cleopatra, followed by her passion-enslaved lover, at the height of the conflict, gave conspicuous and decisive victory to Octavian. As dusk drew on, that night, the situation must have seemed very different to Octavian himself, certain that Antony, Cleopatra, her treasure and a third of their ships had got away; certain that on shore Antony's formidable army under Canidius Crassus remained untouched; uncertain, even, whether that part of the hostile fleet which had remained fighting off Actium had been beaten. Had not his amazingly resourceful antagonist survived to challenge him in strength once again? But as Antony's position at Actium had slowly and undramatically grown into a trap, so Octavian's position now grew into victory. The remainder of the enemy fleet had surrendered or been destroyed. The veteran centurions of Antony's army now saw Octavian as the more likely victor. They knew very well the enormous value to him of their surrender. They negotiated with him for a week, got excellent terms, and were lost to Antony. 'Actium was a shabby affair . . . but in the official version of the victor . . . took on august dimensions' (said Syme). The fact remains that Antony had been outmanoeuvred and compelled to retreat.

The following summer, Octavian, having been initiated into the Eleusinian mysteries at Athens, and settled a very serious near-mutiny of troops back in Italy, moved against Antony and Cleopatra in Egypt. The latter were not without substantial forces, by land and sea, but the danger, now more than ever, was desertion. This was by no means confined to the Egyptian forces; indeed it was a more salient feature of the politically sophisticated and militarily indispensable Roman legionaries. Antony, returning from an unsuccessful action at Paraetonium, did, however, surprise and beat back Octavian's troops from the outskirts of Alexandria. Since the various recent negotiations with Octavian had come to nothing, this was now the time for the military last stand. Antony prepared to fight by both land and sea. His galleys surrendered without a fight, probably on the initiative of their commanders. The cavalry followed suit, and the infantry was defeated. Plutarch's narrative is now a reliable source. Antony's suicide was followed, after an interval of some days, by that of Cleopatra, who may at first have still hoped to win from Octavian certain

[23]John M. Carter, *The Battle of Actium: The Rise and Triumph of Augustus Caesar* (London, 1970), pp. 224, 226. My account of the battle is drawn from Chapters 15 and 16, and from Syme, *The Roman Revolution*, pp. 295–8.

advantages for her children. But after he had secured her treasure, which he desperately needed for the implementation of his home policy, she had little to offer him, unless, perhaps, her living person to display at his triumph in Rome. Certainly an effigy of Cleopatra was so displayed, but opinion is divided as to whether Octavian, capable of both ruthlessness and restraint, wished more to secure her person or her suicide. Cleopatra may have believed the former. The latter is more probable. Her death was, in any case, more than a suicide: it was a ritual triumph in which the asp, 'divine minister of the Sun-god, which raised its head on the crown of Egypt to guard the line of Re from harm', deified at the moment it killed. She died in her crown and royal robes: as one of her maids said, dying, to the guards who discovered the spectacle, 'she was descended from many kings'. To such a scene the creative imagination has had little to add; Horace acknowledged its nobility in the very ode in which he called her frenzied and drunk with fortune; Shakespeare recognized high drama when he found it in history.[24]

When we step back from the detail of these momentous events, upon which the foundation of the Augustan principate and the Augustan peace both rest, and consider their presentation in Augustan propaganda and Augustan and Renaissance high art, we may feel that some of the fundamental truths were after all recognized. Actium was a crucial victory, not because of flight by Cleopatra and Antony, but because their daring breach of the blockade did not preserve enough power and prestige to prevent subsequent desertions. Cleopatra was fatal to Antony's bid for supreme power, not because passion for her blinded his judgement, or because she was unreliable or treacherous; neither of these traditional interpretations will stand up to investigation. It was certainly because her equal partnership with Antony was deeply disturbing to Romans, even when her judgement was good, since it made Antony's particular brand of Caesarian ambition seem like a foreign threat. It gave a major propaganda advantage to Octavian. There is finally the question of the love of Cleopatra and Antony. Mention has been made of Octavian's love for Livia, since Caesar's heir has so often been presented as a mere cold politician. But Cleopatra and Antony have been seen, in propaganda, history, and literature as among the great lovers of antiquity. 'Cleopatra was neither young nor beautiful', as Syme says, but this does not rule out love. It was certainly not a case of all for love and the world well lost, as Dryden had it. Rather the claims of love, the world and necessity combined in their relation. When Antony and his exhausted and depleted army arrived back from his unsuccessful Parthian expedition, Cleopatra faithfully braved the winter navigation to bring him essential supplies. Love and her concern with Antony's political future made her faithful. When Antony staged the Donations in Alexandria, braving Roman horror at his gifts to the Egyptian queen, he did so because love and the support of Rome's greatest Eastern client-state impelled him, with its resources of treasure and grain. At Actium, Cleopatra is said to have advised breakout by

[24]For Cleopatra, see *The Augustan Empire*, pp. 109–11; Rice Holmes, I, pp. 165–6; Syme, *The Roman Revolution*, p. 274; and J.M. Carter, *The Battle of Actium*, pp. 233–4; and R.G.M. Nisbet and Margaret Hubbard, *A Commentary on Horace: Odes, Book I* (Oxford, 1970), pp. 406–21. For the love ethos of Antony and Cleopatra in life and art, see Jasper Griffin, 'Propertius and Antony', *Journal of Roman Studies*, LXVII (1977), pp. 17–26.

sea, rather than retreat by land. Antony accepted her counsel, against many of his Roman advisers, but modern historians agree that this was the best course available. The world remembered a great ambition and a great love, however the various versions have been coloured.

With the defeat of Antony, Octavian had attained that supreme power in the Roman state for which his adoption as the son of Julius Caesar had led him to strive. More important, he had secured the treasure of the Ptolemies, 'the last great accumulation of wealth in the world',[25] which, together with large fines and confiscations, at last liberated him from the importunate demands of the great military machine which had brought power to Caesar and himself, enabling him to reward the legionaries with the money or land they had been promised, without the need for wholesale expropriation of land, and consequent unrest among the landed gentry and peasantry.[26] Finally, he annexed the wealthy and powerful client-kingdom of Egypt and, since it was too good a base from which to challenge central Roman power, he did not allow it to become a senatorial province, but ruled it directly through personal representatives. Its huge surpluses of corn were essential to feed the urban proletariat of Rome, direct control of these resources being especially important in dealing with periodic famine.[27] His political pre-eminence was now placed on a firm economic foundation.

The Principate

What now happened to the Roman state can be told in diametrically opposed versions, which stand behind all the debate about Augustus in the Renaissance and after. The one surviving history (if we except the record of Augustus's own inscriptions) is by Velleius Paterculus, a senator with strong military interests. Not wholly reliable, his book has thoroughly absorbed the pro-Augustan view and is 'most useful in revealing the attitude . . . of a young man who had never known the old Republic or the civil wars'.[28] Describing the return of Octavian to Rome from Alexandria, he records the warmth of his reception, the magnificence of his triumphs and shows, and proceeds into a sequence of measured rhetoric:

> There is nothing that man can desire from the gods, nothing that the gods can grant to a man, nothing that wish can conceive or good fortune bring to pass, which Augustus on his return to the city did not bestow upon the republic, the Roman people, and the world. The civil wars were ended after twenty years, foreign wars suppressed, peace restored, the frenzy of arms everywhere lulled to rest; validity was restored to the laws, authority to the courts, and dignity to the senate; the power of the magistrates was reduced to its former limits. . . . The old traditional form of the republic was restored. Agriculture returned to the fields, respect to religion, to mankind freedom from anxiety, and to each citizen his property rights were now assured. . . . The chief

[25]*The Augustan Empire*, p. 107.
[26]Ibid., p. 106; Carter, *The Battle of Actium*, pp. 167–8.
[27]*The Augustan Empire*, pp. 303–4, 398. On the famine at Rome, see *Res Gestae*, 5; ed. cit. p. 21.
[28]Jones, *Augustus*, p. 172. But Velleius cannot be discounted as an historian. The verdict of his most recent editor (quoting Syme) is that: 'His portrayal verges on panegyric, but conveys pertinent criticism and permits a balanced estimate' (Velleius Paterculus, *The Tiberian Narrative*, ed. A.J. Woodman (Cambridge, 1977), pp. 55–6.

men of the state . . . were at the invitation of Augustus induced to adorn the city. In the case of the consulship only, Caesar was not able to have his way, but was obliged to hold that office consecutively until the eleventh time . . . but the dictatorship which the people persistently offered him, he as stubbornly refused.[29]

This is plainly uncritical enthusiasm for the official line, but it embodies some basic points: peace, order, security, republican forms, with Augustus in a position of central power but refusing the dictatorship. Not everyone saw these developments in the same light as Velleius. The old Roman aristocracy, descendants of the pre-civil war *nobiles*, must have long preserved an attitude of intelligent distaste for Augustus, and profound regret for the old Republic. This tradition is strong in Tacitus who, writing perhaps *c*. AD 116, forty-eight years after the end of the Julio-Claudian line of emperors, included mordant paragraphs on Augustus at the beginning of his *Annales*:

> When after the destruction of Brutus and Cassius there was no longer any army of the Commonwealth, when Pompeius was crushed in Sicily, and when with Lepidus pushed aside and Antonius slain, even the Julian faction had only Caesar left to lead it, then, dropping the title of triumvir, and giving out that he was a Consul, and was satisfied with a tribune's authority for the protection of the people, Augustus won over the soldiers with gifts, the populace with cheap corn, and all men with the sweets of repose, and so grew greater by degrees, while he concentrated within himself the functions of the Senate, the magistrates and the laws. He was wholly unopposed, for the boldest spirits had fallen in battle, or in the proscription, while the remaining nobles, the readier they were to be slaves, were raised the higher by wealth and promotion, so that, aggrandized by revolution, they preferred the safety of the present to the dangerous past. Nor did the provinces dislike that condition of affairs, for they distrusted the government of the Senate and the people, because of the rivalries between the leading men and the rapacity of the officials. . . .
>
> Thus the State had been revolutionized, and there was not a vestige left of the old sound morality. Stript of equality, all looked up to the commands of a sovereign without the least apprehension for the present. . . . When in advanced old age he was worn out by a sickly frame and the end was near and new prospects opened, a few spoke in vain of the blessings of freedom, but most people dreaded and some longed for war.

Incomparably more powerful and penetrating than Velleius, Tacitus is not, perhaps, less prejudiced in his general view. Liberty and equality for him refer to a narrowly aristocratic and metropolitan range of interest. But, from his

[29]*Velleius Paterculus, Compendium of Roman History* . . ., II, lxxxix; ed. and tr. F.W. Shipley, pp. 236–9. 'nihil deinde optare a dis homines, nihil dii hominibus praestare possunt, nihil voto concipi, nihil felicitate consummari, quod non Augustus post reditum in urbem rei publicae populoque Romano terrarumque orbi repraesentaverit. finita vicesimo anno bella civilia, sepulta externa, revocata pax, sopitus ubique armorum furor, restituta vis legibus, iudiciis auctoritas, senatui maiestas, imperium magistratuum ad pristinum redactum modum; . . . prisca illa et antiqua rei publica forma revocata rediit cultus agris, sacris honos, securitas hominibus, certa cuique rerum suarum posessio; . . . principes viri triumphisque et amplissimis honoribus functi adhortatu principis ad ornandam urbem inlecti sunt. consulatus tantummodo usque ad undecimum, quem continuaret Caesar, . . . impetrare [non] potuit: nam dictaturam quam pertinaciter ei deferebat populus, tam constanter repulit', *C. Vellei Patercvli ex Historiae Romanae Libris Duobus*, ed. C. Stegmann De Pritzwald (Stuttgart, 1965), p. 95. The history seems to have been written *c*. AD 30, sixteen years after the death of Augustus.

standpoint, that of 'a monarchist, from perspicacious despair of human nature', his account of Augustus's success is unrivalled, and is a tribute to the political skill of the *princeps*, as well as clear witness to the deep desire of the Roman people for peace.[30]

It will be clear from the foregoing narrative that the old Republic could not have been fully revived. Nor was its demise the particular work of Octavian; if not he, some other Caesarian figure would surely have emerged from the wreck of the older political structure. Few could have believed in a restoration of the Republic, and when in his *Res Gestae* Augustus claimed to have restored it he was not claiming to have done what Brutus and Cassius sought to do. But this does not mean that the 'restoration of the republic' was a mere publicity exercise; the decisions and measures which Octavian took after the defeat of Antony were substantial enough at the time. They must have arisen out of deep thought about recent Roman history and his present situation. Doubtless this, in its turn, took him back to conversations with his uncle, on campaign with him in Spain, or in Rome before the Ides of March. Perhaps he remembered how Julius Caesar had disapproved of Sulla's giving up the dictatorship and resolved not to adopt that course himself.[31] Still more will he have remembered Caesar himself, who had been granted the unprecedented office of dictator for life, and how soon and violently that seeming permanence had come to an end. Originally, as a very young man, he had perhaps assumed that the world empire of Rome would have to become a military monarchy. Octavian's own rise to single power had been based upon the military: yet now some new conception seemed to be required to ensure a degree of stability, not only for his own position, but for peace and order in Rome. Some way was required between the only two obvious alternatives, a theoretically possible restoration of the old Republic, and the perilously practical establishment of a second permanent dictatorship. He never so much showed the mature consideration and political judgement for which he was to be praised in the Renaissance than in the steps he now took. His solution was to institute a major shift of power between the Senate and himself, a shift to an at first temporary *de facto* monarchy in which some, but nothing like all his power was warranted by old republican offices which he held in a new way. His

[30]*Annales*, I, pp. 2–4; *The Annals and Histories by P. Cornelius Tacitus*, tr. A.J. Church and W.J. Brodribb (Chicago, 1963), pp. 1–2. 'Postquam Bruto et Cassio caesis nulla iam publica arma, Pompeius apud Siciliam oppressus, exutoque Lepido, interfecto Antonio ne Iulianis quidem partibus nisi Caesar dux reliquus, posito triumuiri nomine consulem se ferens et ad tuendam plebem tribunicio iure contentum, ubi militem donis, populum annona, cunctos dulcedine otii pellexit, insurgere paulatim, munia senatus magistratuum legum in se trahere, nullo aduersante, cum ferocissimi per acies aut proscriptione cecidissent, ceteri nobilium, quanto quis seruitio promptior, opibus et honoribus extollerentur ac nouis ex rebus aucti tuta et praesentia quam uetera et periculosa mallent. neque prouinciae illum rerum statum abnuebant, suspecto senatus populique imperio ob certamina potentium et auaritiam magistratuum. . . .

Igitur uerso ciuitatis statu nihil usquam prisci et integri moris: omnes exuta aequalitate iussa principis aspectare, nulla in praesens formidine . . . . postquam prouecta iam secectus aegro et corpore fatigabatur aderatque finis et spes nouae, pauci bona libertatis in cassum disserere, plures bellum pauescere, alii cupere' (*The Annals of Tacitus*, ed. F.R.D. Goodyear, I, pp. 49–51). Syme, *The Roman Revolution*, p. 516.

[31]Suetonius, *De Vita Caesarvm*, Divvs Ivlivs, 77; *Suetoni Tranqvilli Opera*, ed. Maximilian Ihm (Stuttgart, 1908), I, 38. Syme, *The Roman Revolution*, p. 53. On this juncture, see Wirszubski, *Libertas*, Chapter 4.

potestas transcended the annual and collegiate basis of executive power upon which republican *libertas* had rested.[32]

Three years after Actium, having purged the Senate which had grown to over a thousand through bribery and favour,[33] and having settled most immediate problems, he effectively challenged Rome to do without him, announcing that he wished to resign the special powers which he had exercised since the death of Antony. That there was prior consultation with his particular supporters in the Senate, as well as with close advisers such as Agrippa and Maecenas, is certain, and no doubt it was clear to those in his confidence that he intended a formula to emerge which would be neither dictatorship nor the abandoning of all his special powers. Above all he was anxious to avoid the impression that his position was to be permanent, and it is only in retrospect that this formula can seem merely a false façade to conceal the foundation of monarchy. Octavian cannot have been sure that events would run in the direction he wished; he desired to win solid support from a wider base than the triumphant Caesarian interest, and he did not want Rome to take for granted those benefits which could be seen to flow from his single rule. His challenge was received as he wished. His speech of resignation to the Senate was greeted with dismay, and his declared wish was denied him. A motion was carried conferring on him wide but vague powers 'in the interest of the commonwealth' but these he declined.[34] Ultimately he agreed to retain his Consulship; to exercise for ten years a special proconsular power for the unsettled provinces of the empire, which gave him control over the greater part of the armies of Rome; and to retain the tribunate, which carried some further powers, and which was symbolic expression of the link between him and the people. He was styled neither king nor dictator, but *princeps*, first citizen; and he was given the additional cognomen of Augustus, drawn from a line of the old Roman poet Ennius, which now seemed to link him with Romulus, the founder of the city of Rome. Augustus held no new office, but those offices of the old Republic which he held he held in new ways and for extended or indefinite periods, consolidating his position so firmly that four years later he was able to resign his Consulship, which he held only twice more before his death. His *auctoritas* was the major political factor in the state, obvious to all.

This then was the restoration of the Republic and the founding of the Augustan Principate. Something really was restored, because a capable senatorial class was required to assist the *princeps*, a class which could win self-respect through office and power. This was hardly inconsistent with the long-term design of establishing an effective monarchy, which (as Cassius Dio was to suggest) Augustus did not expect to be able to do in his lifetime.[35] For the rest, the desire for peace might be expected to allow these new arrangements to take root.[36]

The conflict which Augustus may have undergone in coming to these decisions was to be dramatized in long retrospect, some 250 years later, by Cassius

---

[32]Wirszubski, *Libertas*, p. 111.

[33]Suetonius, *De Vita Caesarvm*, Divvs Avgvstvs, 35; ed. cit. p. 67.

[34]Jones, *Augustus*, p. 46.

[35]Cassius Dio, *Roman History*, LII, 4; ed. and tr. Ernest Cary (London, 1917) VI, p. 85.

[36]My account of the principate is drawn from Rice Holmes, I, p. 179–86; Syme, *The Roman Revolution*, Chapters XXII–XXXIII; *The Augustan Empire*, pp. 127–32; Carter, *The Battle of Actium*, pp. 273–42; and A.H.M. Jones, *Augustus*, pp. 45–8.

Dio, when he put into the mouth of Agrippa arguments against monarchy of any kind, and arguments for monarchy (though not by name) into the mouth of Maecenas. This episode, often remembered in the Renaissance, was in the seventeenth century to be used by Corneille in his tragedy of *Cinna*. In Dio, Maecenas concludes his discourse to Augustus by advising him to avoid the title of king as ill-fated and hateful (a traditional piety since Rome had long ago expelled its kings).[37] That Augustus should not assume the style of king was elementary; but it was a major policy of his principate to avoid all such styles and honours, as dangerous to himself and bad for the self-respect of Roman citizens. Suetonius in a paragraph immediately following that which records the refusal of the dictatorship has an anecdote describing his refusal of the title or compliment of 'Lord' (which suggested the relation between master and slaves).[38] This was to be a point of great significance in Patristic writing about Augustus.

It is certain that Augustus saw himself as a renewer or second founder of Rome.[39] By legislation, precept and example he sought to perpetuate or to re-establish Roman tradition and create a powerful sense of Roman identity in men's minds. As with the whole character of his principate, it is hard to draw a line between the strictly practical in his measures, and what was designed for public effect, since each in its way was concerned with political reality. The reform of the Senate made it a more outwardly respectable as well as more useful body. The severe legislation by which Augustus attempted to rehabilitate marriage (the Lex Julia, 18 BC, subsequently modified by the Lex Papia Poppaea of AD 9) was not concerned with sexual morality, the *princeps* being as promiscuous as any, but with social morality and the preservation of the classes of patricians and *equites* through the inheritance of legitimate children, as a source for the high offices of the empire.[40] He passed sumptuary laws and, according to Suetonius, quoted a line from *Aeneid* Bk I to rebuke a crowd of men in an assembly who were wearing cloaks rather than the old fashion of the toga.[41] Both before and after he succeeded Lepidus as *Pontifex Maximus*, guardian of Roman religion, Augustus did much to revive the worship of the old Roman gods. Many temples which had grown dilapidated during the civil wars were restored, and obsolete rites and cults were revived, chiefly, perhaps, for patriotic reasons. As *Pontifex* Augustus sought to put down religious prophecies which might be harmful to the state, and selected for preservation the most valuable of the Sibylline writings. 'He revived the adoration of Venus Genetrix and built a temple to his adoptive father, who was both her reputed descendant and the deified hero of the empire';[42] he built a temple to Mars Ultor, to

[37]Cassius Dio, *Roman History*, LII, 40; ed. cit, VI, pp. 184–5. On Dio, see Fergus Millar, *Cassius Dio* (Oxford, 1964).

[38]Divvs Avgvstvs, 53; *De Vita Caesarvm*, ed. cit. p. 78.

[39]Divvs Avgvstvs, 7; ed. cit. p. 49.

[40]Rice Holmes, II, pp. 41–6; Syme, *The Roman Revolution*, pp. 444–5; *The Augustan Empire*, pp. 448–56; A.H.M. Jones, *Augustus*, pp. 131–4. There were in fact two laws on marriage in 18 BC: The *Lex Julia de adulteriis coercendis* and the *Lex Julia de maritandis ordinibus*. See J.H.W.G. Liebeschuetz, *Continuity and Change in Roman Religion* (Oxford, 1979), Ch. 2.

[41]Divvs Avgvstvs, 40, ed. cit. p. 170. Significantly enough the line (*Aeneid*, I, 282) referred to the imperial destiny of Rome.

[42]Rice Holmes, II, p. 48.

commemorate his victory over Caesar's murderers, and to be a shrine and debating chamber for military affairs; and he built the marble temple of Apollo on the Palatine, which has been called 'the most splendid of all the splendid buildings of Rome'.[43] Agrippa, for his part, built the Pantheon, dedicated to Mars and Venus, divine ancestors of the Julian line. While the new temples mingled the glorification of Caesar and of Augustus with that of Roman republican heroes and the Roman gods, Augustus was careful (probably out of genuine distaste as well as prudence) to avoid ruler-worship of himself at Rome. What the provincials did was a matter of less concern. The deification and worship in the East of Roman rulers was taken for granted even by those upper classes most hostile to the practice in Rome. By these means Augustus sought to take the worship of the old Roman gods, still alive among the common people, and reintroduce it to the more sophisticated classes as a form of piety, expressed through elaborate and ancient ritual, to the history and destiny of the Roman state.[44] It will be seen that all these measures were of a conservative kind, and were in all probability deeply felt by Augustus. But they were not measures to a conservative end, but the necessary continuity to establish a revolutionary policy.

The revival of the worship of the Roman gods, prompting the rebuilding of so many temples, involved the architectural renewal of Rome. This was an essential aspect of Augustus's renovation, and it is clear that he took personal pride in what had been achieved. Three sections in his *Res Gestae* are devoted to a recitation of the temples, aqueducts, bridges, theatre and road (the Via Flaminia) which he had constructed,[45] and Suetonius confirms the justice of his boast that he found Rome built of brick and left it in marble.[46] Both this historian and the architectural writer Vitruvius, a contemporary of Augustus, see the whole programme of building as an expression of the empire. 'I observed', wrote Vitruvius,

> that you cared not only about the common life of all men, and the constitution of the state, but also about the provision of suitable public buildings; so that the state was not only made greater through you by its new provinces, but the majesty of the empire also was expressed through the eminent dignity of its public buildings.[47]

Enough has been said to demonstrate the comprehensive nature of Augustus's bid to renew the idea of Rome. From this the nature of his concern with literature becomes clear: that aspect of his single rule which has been remembered almost as often as his crucial political rôle in the history of the world, and which has given him so prominent a place in the annals of poetry. Indeed the earliest contemporary sources for our knowledge of Augustus are poets.

[43]Ibid., II, p. 70.

[44]For Augustus's religious policy, see Rice Holmes, II, pp. 46–52; Syme, *The Roman Revolution*, pp. 446–50; *The Augustan Empire*, pp. 475–93; A.H.M. Jones, *Augustus*, pp. 144–52.

[45]*Res Gestae*, 19–21; ed. cit. pp. 26–9.

[46]*Divvs Avgvstvs*, 28; ed. cit. p. 62. It has been suggested that clay and stone render the Latin better than brick and marble, and that Augustus was speaking of the empire rather than only the city.

[47]*De Architectura*, I, 2; ed. and tr. Frank Granger (London, 1931), 3. 'Cum vero adtenderem te non solum de vita communi omnium curam publicaeque rei constitutionem habere sed etiam de opportunitate publicorum aedificiorum, ut civitas per te non solum provinciis esset aucta, verum etiam ut maiestas imperii publicorum aedificiorum egregias haberet auctoritates . . . .' (p. 2).

Princeps and Poets

Augustus was quite intelligent and well-educated enough to judge real poetic achievement on its merits. He was not without literary aspirations himself, nor the self-knowledge to abandon them with humour: 'My Ajax', he said of his unfinished tragedy, 'has fallen on his sponge'. But he wrote a work on Sicily in hexameters, and had definite views on style and diction, explicitly favouring the concise and natural, and ridiculing pedantry in old and affectation in new expressions. He called Antony a madman for writing an oratorical style to be wondered at rather than understood.[48] It is clear that Augustus would look to poetry, as he looked to religion and architecture, to help create his vision of Rome. That did not mean poets would be in fundamental agreement with him. It is also clear that he would not be content with easy propaganda alone, but with that most effective of all propaganda: the vision that is instinct in deeply felt, carefully worked and lasting art. Yet with the notable exceptions of Horace's *Carmen Saeculare*, *Carmina* Bk IV and the Letter to Augustus there is little evidence that he requested or commissioned particular works. Nor was he apparently intolerant of contemporary historians who nearly all showed a Republican bias; he is said to have called Livy a Pompeian but still been appreciative of his work.[49] What he did was to show an interest in poets, sometimes give help where it was asked, or offer it where he thought it might be needed. Generally contact was made through his eminent and trusted adviser Maecenas.

How then did the poets see Augustus? For those of the earlier generation, that of Virgil and Horace but not Ovid, the *princeps* may have had a deeper and more powerful significance even than the *Aeneid* had for him. As the years of the triumvirate drew to a close he was seen above all in the light of a peacebringer; it was to the bringer of peace, security and order to Rome that their deepest loyalty was to be paid, whoever that might be. Octavian's establishment of peace was the profoundest historical event of the time, appreciated, perhaps, all the more because it had been desired and prematurely heralded for so long. Thus the occasion of Virgil's Fourth Eclogue was the reconciliation between Antony and Octavian in 40 BC, a reconciliation which had been partly effected by the Antonian Asinius Pollio, patron and friend of the poet. This peace was marked by Pollio's taking up his suspended Consulship, hailed in the poem as the dawn of a great age of peace, and by the marriage of Antony and Octavia. The Fourth Eclogue is, as has been observed, both marriage poem and prophecy, as its allusion to Catullus's *Peleus and Thetis* makes clear.[50] There is some reason to think that Virgil grew up in a region of Caesarian sympathy, but it is quite clear from the Fourth Eclogue that his deepest positive value was independent of loyalty to any one particular person. Or let us take another famous early poem of Virgil, the First Eclogue, which makes allusion to Octavian. The occasion of the poem, as the text and both venerable critical tradition and modern investigation confirm, was a reprieve of Virgil's family by Octavian from the threat of eviction from their Mantuan farm, eviction of a kind only too common

---

[48]Suetonius, *De Vita Caesarvm*, Divvs Avgvstvs, 85–6; ed. cit. pp. 96–7.
[49]Jones, *Augustus*, p. 157.
[50]Syme, *The Roman Revolution*, pp. 219–20; L.P. Wilkinson, *The Georgics of Virgil* (Cambridge, 1969), pp. 35–9; I.M. Le M. Du Quesnay, 'Vergil's *Fourth Eclogue*' (see p. 4, n. 12 above).

as the great military commanders rewarded their veterans by settling them on the land. Through most delicate allusion of the pastoral fiction it seems to be Octavian who is thanked:

> *T.:* O Meliboee, deus nobis haec otia fecit.
> namque erit ille mihi semper deus . . . .
>
> hic illum uidi iuuenem, Meliboee, quotannis
> bis senos cui nostra dies altaria fumant.
> hic mihi responsum primus dedit ille petenti:
> 'pascite ut ante boues, pueri; submittite tauros'.[51]

Yet the whole structure of the eclogue, and indeed its echo back to the earlier Ninth Eclogue, also about eviction, balances, if it does not somewhat outweigh, the sense of wonder at deliverance by the sense of misery, even betrayal, of those who continue to be exiled from their traditional homes and traditional work. The poem is a dialogue. Tityrus can thank the youth, ever a god to him, for restoration to home and nature. Meliboeus, now an outcast, has, as the outcome of civil strife, sown his fields for a barbarian soldier; the end of the poem takes the whole weight of his indignation and misery. Thanks are rendered to Caesar, for thanks are due, but there is no evasion of injustice or suffering. 'It is', as a modern scholar has said, 'a courageous poem'.[52]

It is far from my intention to generalize about Virgil and Horace, let alone other poets, on the basis of these two poems. Yet I do believe that they give a lead in the right direction: a direction which allows us to recognize that deeply felt gratitude and genuine praise of Augustus could be expressed by the poets, while they yet retained a distance, an independence, a sympathy with suffering, which make them poets in the widest human sense. 'This implies no sycophancy or insincerity in the poet, for he and the world had much to be grateful for.'[53] Virgil had early planned to write a Roman epic, and at the beginning of Bk III of the *Georgics* seemed to announce such a poem on the deeds of Augustus. These intentions were, in a special sense, to be fulfilled in the *Aeneid*, the poem in which Augustus showed the greatest interest. In 25 BC, ill and anxious from his Spanish campaigns, Augustus wrote to Virgil at Sorrento, begging him to send him a specimen of the *Aeneid*. Virgil replied that the poem required profounder study, and that it seemed almost an aberration to have undertaken so great a task.[54] Nearly eight years later Augustus, on his return from the East, halted at

---

[51]LI. 6–7, 42–5; *P. Vergili Maronis, Opera*, ed. R.A.B. Mynors (Oxford, 1969), pp. 1–2. See Wilkinson, op. cit. pp. 24–35.

[52]Wilkinson, op. cit. p. 33. The force of the echo back to the Ninth Eclogue in l. 73 ('Now, Meliboeus graft your pears . . .') is that there the happy command: 'Graft your pears Daphnis; thy children's children shall gather fruits of thine' was associated with the star in the heavens marking the deification of Julius Caesar (ll. 46–50). Now that promise is falsified in Meliboeus's experience (see Wilkinson, op. cit. p. 33). For an interesting discussion of the patterns and balances in the whole collection of the *Eclogues*, see Brooks Otis, *Virgil: A Study in Civilized Poetry* (Oxford, 1964), Chapter IV, especially pp. 128–43; and O. Skutsch, 'Symmetry and Sense in the Eclogues', *Harvard Studies in Classical Philology*, 73 (1968), pp. 153–69. For the general rôle of the poets, see Syme, *The Roman Revolution*, pp. 459–67.

[53]W.A. Camps, *An Introduction to Virgil's Aeneid* (Oxford, 1969) p. 137.

[54]For Virgil's early epic plans, see Brooks Otis, pp. 38–40. For Augustus's request to see a specimen of the *Aeneid*, see Rice Holmes, op. cit. II, p. 8. Aelius Donatus's Life of Virgil is the ultimate source of the details mentioned here; see Camps, *Virgil's Aeneid*, pp. 115–20.

Athens and met Virgil, who accompanied him back to Italy and there died. Together with Virgil's literary executors, Augustus saved the unrevised poem from the destruction to which it was consigned in the poet's will. It is said that Virgil had chosen the second, fourth and sixth books to read to Augustus, and that when the reading took place Octavia swooned at the lines on the death of her son Marcellus in Bk VI.[55] Of the three places in the *Aeneid* in which Augustus is mentioned, only one (Bk VI) was chosen by Virgil for Augustus's early attention. The reference (ll. 791–7) is brief, yet supreme, central in the poem, and central in the whole conception of Rome which the *Aeneid* expresses: Augustus is linked with Romulus, and with Aeneas, the mythic ancestor of Julius Caesar, as a new founder of Rome, and as the restorer of an age of gold. The other references to Augustus are equally brief and crucial: to his inheriting the name of Julius Caesar and closing the doors of the Temple of Janus at the achievement of peace (I, 288–94), and to his victory at Actium (VIII, 678–81). These references could not be more significantly placed. They are, furthermore, the *foci* of other, subtler, allusions. The victory over Cleopatra seems to be recalled in Aeneas's rejection of Dido, another eastern queen who, 'pale with foreboding and death' (cf. VIII, 709 with IV, 644) nearly diverted the destiny of Rome. The celebration of Hercules by Evander in Bk VIII seems to recall Octavian's deliverance of Rome from civil war, as well as the Games, *Lusus Troiae* and Salian Hymn celebrated by Octavian to mark Julius Caesar's death. More notable still, the prophetic shield presented to Aeneas in Bk VIII not only recalled the Shield of Achilles in *The Iliad* but, inescapably, the Golden Shield commemorating the virtues of Octavian, dedicated in the Senate in 27 BC, when he proposed to relinquish his powers, and was granted the style of 'Augustus'.[56] On the other hand there is a real sense in which they are details, details in a conception of the history, tragedy and destiny of Rome which is greater than Aeneas, greater than Augustus.

Horace himself tells the story of how he fought against Octavian and Antony at the Battle of Philippi (*Ep*. II, ii, 46–52). Back in Italy he found employment as a *scriba quaestorius*, a kind of civil servant, until Maecenas became his patron. Later, Augustus invited Horace to become his private secretary, a post which the poet refused. Extracts from Augustus's letters to Horace on this matter have been preserved; they show an easy and humorous urbanity which tells that Horace's refusal was not resented, and shows something of the human relationship which underlies Horace's Letter to Augustus, that C.O. Brink has described as 'a command performance executed with great candour and skill'.[57] An invitation Horace did not refuse was to write a poem for the revived *ludi saeculares* which Augustus proposed to celebrate in 17 BC as part of his programme for the patriotic renewal of Roman religion. A commissioned poem, the *Carmen Saeculare* perhaps comes closest to telling us what Augustus most wanted from poetry when he asked for it directly. This Horatian ode is also a patriotic hymn, not for processional singing but for the end of the celebration, formed into three triads of six stanzas, with an epilogue in which the young

[55]Rice Holmes, II, pp. 37–8; Brooks Otis, *Virgil*, pp. 1–2.

[56]Camps, *Virgil's Aeneid*, pp. 98–104, 137–43.

[57]Eduard Fraenkel, *Horace* (Oxford, 1957), pp. 9–19. C.O. Brink, *Horace on Poetry; Prolegomena to the Literary Epistles* (Cambridge, 1963), p. 191.

singers acknowledge their own part. As might be expected, the hymn offers a view of Rome, recalling its mythical past in which Aeneas survived the ruin of Troy to found something greater, respectfully commending present measures (including the Augustan marriage legislation), and invoking the blessing of the gods of Rome for a new order in which the virtues might return, and from which cycles of ever better time might unfold. Formal in procedure and pattern, it shines with that starlight quality often found in Horace's greater odes when the gods, the heavens, the seas and the regions of the world form parts of a single human drama. It is notable that the patriotic conservatism of Augustus might have been thought to require a Roman hymn of much more ancient form than this. One way or another, however, Horace was encouraged to write a modern poem of his own characteristic kind. The recognition afforded by Augustus on this occasion, Fraenkel suggests, 'stirred Horace profoundly . . . the dammed up stream of his lyrics began to flow again. And so Augustus, who, two years before, had saved the *Aeneid* from destruction, was now instrumental in bringing Horace back to his true life and his true task.'[58]

A modern historian of Rome can lightly say that Horace wrote 'a few patriotic odes celebrating Augustus' but that 'the great bulk of his work . . . is purely personal'.[59] This is a point worth emphasis, but it is a little like saying that the *Aeneid* is hardly concerned with Augustus at all since it only mentions him three times. Horace was not constantly praising or addressing Augustus, but it is very hard to think that his odes and letter concerning Augustus are not, and were not to him, supremely important compositions: certainly the world of Horace's odes is as wide as the Roman world, and that imaginative range is something to do with the figure of Augustus at the centre guaranteeing its coherence. If it seems surprising that the often sceptical and ironic Horace should write odes in straight-forward praise of Augustus, it should be remembered what it must have been like to be a Roman coming through that period of civil war and proscription into an era of unity and peace, guaranteed by the triumph, political intelligence and broad human concern of one man. It is worth quoting some words of Fraenkel on this subject:

> Horace, a past master in εἰρωνεία and understatement, never lies and never pretends. In *Quo me, Bacche, rapis* he speaks of the urge which forces him to immortalize the *decus Caesaris* in tones of an overwhelming emotion and of the most genuine sincerity. From what I know of Horace I refuse to consider the possibility that in this poem he is lying or not being serious. He implies that what he is setting out to do will, if he succeeds, be the crowning triumph of his life. I believe him. I must therefore part company with those scholars who say that the Roman Odes and kindred poems are to be regarded as products of a subtle propaganda, suggested to the poet and all but forced upon him by Maecenas or somebody else.[60]

That is one side of Horace on Augustus. But stability and the policy of the *princeps* required another and very different manner, one in which, as Fraenkel says of the Letter to Augustus, 'Horace tones down what he has to say. . . . The

---

[58]Ibid. p. 382. For general discussions of the *ludi saeculares* see Rice Holmes, II, pp. 49–52 and *The Augustan Empire*, pp. 476–9.

[59]Jones op. cit. pp. 155–6.

[60]Fraenkel, op. cit. p. 260.

demand that the person and the achievements of the Princeps should be represented in a worthy manner is nothing special, not a consequence of his elevated position, but something that any ordinary citizen would have the right to insist upon. Here as before, Horace, *fidus interpres* of the intentions of Augustus, refuses to fix a gulf between the ruler and the rest of mankind.'[61]

Augustus made little attempt to stifle freedom of expression, responding to libel, lampoon or attack either by an effort to refute the charge and thus bring the author to account, or by ignoring what had been said.[62] The limits of his tolerance were, however, probably shown in the case of his treatment of Ovid. Of a later generation than Virgil and Horace, Ovid may be thought to have lacked the experience which generated some of their seriousness. He took the Augustan principate for granted, and in his brilliant and scandalous *Ars Amatoria* he ignored not only traditional respectability but the specific efforts of Augustus, as shown in his marriage legislation, to revive morality and perpetuate the family. Ovid himself may have pleased his critics better by the publication of his next work, *Remedia Amoris*, and was soon working on two more ambitious projects, the *Metamorphoses* and the *Fasti*, the latter of which must have been expected to appeal to Augustus. Then, in AD 8, with these poems still unfinished, Ovid was 'relegated' by Augustus (it was not officially exile) to a remote and barbarous outpost of the empire, Tomis in what is now Romania, and never allowed to return to Rome. What precipitated this sudden and to the sophisticated and metropolitan Ovid appalling punishment is uncertain: all we know is Ovid's own guarded statement from his *Tristia* (II, 207–8): it was a poem and a mistake. It is usually inferred that the poem was the *Ars Amatoria*, and that Ovid had in some sense been on probation since it had appeared; but this offence was decisively compounded by the mysterious error: something he saw without meaning to, a secret he could never after divulge. It is sometimes noticed that Augustus's grand-daughter, Julia, was banished from Rome for involvement in personal scandals in the same year as Ovid's relegation. From AD 450 onward, guesses have been made as to what Ovid did or saw: among the earliest were suggestions that Augustus's daughter was the poet's mistress, or that he had seen Augustus in an unnatural act with a youth. Jonson, in *The Poetaster*, may have been the first to hypothesize Ovid's participation with Julia in a blasphemous 'banquet of sense', thus linking sexual with religious offence, and giving Augustus strong grounds for the banishment of the guilty pair. But these late conjectures are of little historical value. All we can say with probability is that Augustus acted to suppress some scandal concerning his family, and that Ovid's happiness was sacrificed to keeping the secret.[63] Had it not been for this incident, the appearance of the *Metamorphoses* and the *Fasti* might well have won for Ovid the esteem of the *princeps* and the *Ars Amatoria* been forgiven.

[61]Ibid., p. 399.

[62]Rice Holmes, II, pp. 33–4; Suetonius, *De Vita Caesarvm*, Divvs Avgvstvs, 51, 55–6; ed. cit. pp. 77–8, 79–80, 210–11.

[63]Syme, *The Roman Revolution*, pp. 467–8; J.C. Thibault, *The Mystery of Ovid's Exile* (Berkeley and Los Angeles, 1964) offers a full and cautious discussion, and tabulates (a) all Ovid's statements about his offence (pp. 27–31, 131–3) and (b) all later hypotheses (pp. 24–7, 130–1, 125–9). He does not include *The Poetaster* in his survey. For Ovid generally, see Niall Rudd, *Lines of Enquiry* (London, 1977); and Ronald Syme, *History in Ovid* (Oxford, 1978).

Achievement and Death

Though interesting to literary historians, this incident was the merest detail in the great theatre of Augustus's sustained activity. Without any doubt the most striking feature of Augustus's record as *princeps* is the unflagging effort through which his economic, social, colonial, political, military, diplomatic and cultural measures reached to the frontiers of the Roman world. And while repeated military campaigns were judged necessary to consolidate frontiers, to defeat or pacify rebellions in the further provinces and to press on with the conquest of Germany, it is still true that the principate was an era of peace. This is the case partly because the appalling civil wars had now finally been brought to an end; partly because there was some real attempt to follow a policy which Virgil and Horace expressed as the ideal of Rome's destiny –

parcere subiectis et debellare superbos[64]

– in other words to overcome strong opposition by strength but make allies where possible; and partly because in 29 and again in 25 BC Rome was (save for frontier disturbances) at peace, and in 'an imposing and archaic ceremony' the gates of the Temple of Janus were closed, for only the third and fourth times in Rome's whole history.[65] In a real sense Augustus 'created an economic area characterized by an extent and peacefulness such as mankind had not previously seen. His aim was to create a corporate unity from the whole of the civilized part of the globe.'[66] The spiritual dimension of this achievement is hardly calculable. Whether on mystical or rational grounds, the fact that it was in this time of profound peace that Jesus Christ was born upon earth could not, in the centuries to come, fail to strike Christian commentators deeply. And if indeed one of Augustus's ambitious peacetime measures, the enrolment of the inhabitants of the whole empire, was carried out in Palestine when Publius Sulpicius Quirinius (St Luke's 'Syrenius') was Governor of Syria, that was another remarkable concatenation of events which suggested the hand of Providence to some.[67] The pacific dimension of Augustus's imperial policy is seen in relation to Britain where the *princeps* made no attempt to emulate and make permanent his uncle's conquest. For the time being Britain was too weak to be worth incorporating into the Roman world by force, but Augustus was in diplomatic contact with various British kings and chieftains, one of the most powerful of whom, Cunobeline, the Cymbeline of Shakespeare, and grandson of Julius Caesar's foe Cassivellaunus, may have enjoyed some kind of pragmatic alliance with Rome.[68]

Late in the principate two disastrous developments underlined the necessity for restraint. The first was a serious revolt and military mutiny in Pannonia and Dalmatia, in AD 6, which cost four years' war and an enormous military and

---

[64]*Aeneid*, Book VI, l. 853; ed. cit. p. 254. Cf. Horace, *Carmen Saeculare*, ll. 49–52.

[65]Syme, *The Roman Revolution*, p. 303; Rice Holmes, I, p. 1723; II, p. 8. *The Augustan Empire*, pp. 122, 135.

[66]*The Augustan Empire*, p. 384.

[67]Rice Holmes, II, pp. 89–90. Luke, II, 1–6. Cf. Rice Holmes, II, p. 123 for the valuation of Judaea by Quirinius in AD 6, which may have later been confused with the census (Acts, 5, 37).

[68]Rice Holmes, II, pp. 54–5.

financial effort to put down.[69] The second was the total defeat by the German chieftain Arminius of the legate of Germany, Quinctilius Varus, and the destruction of three Roman legions.[70] Both episodes stressed the shortage of reliable legionaries and the great difficulty of raising more in relatively settled and contented times. Augustus recognized the problem clearly enough, as Suetonius's report that he would 'dash his head against a door, crying: "Quintilius Varus, give me back my legions!" ' confirms.[71] He left written instructions to his successor that he should not extend the boundaries of the empire.[72]

Augustus's expressed aim that the state should be established in a firm and secure position, and that when he died the foundations he had laid should be unshaken, had been threatened from time to time by conspiracies to assassinate him, and was constantly threatened by the rapidly changing situation with regard to the succession.[73] Each point deserves brief consideration. It is obvious that Augustus, with his uncle's fate in mind, must have been constantly aware of the danger of assassination.[74] There were two attempts soon after the Battle of Actium, each discovered in time, one conspirator, Marcus Lepidus the son of the triumvir, paying for the plot with his life.[75] A later conspiracy, that of a grandson of Pompey the Great and variously named Lucius Cinna and Cnaeus Cornelius, has become much more famous but is not mentioned by modern historians, and was first related in the Dialogue on Clemency written by Seneca for the edification of the Emperor Nero.[76] According to Seneca's attractive and dramatic account, later exploited by Corneille, Augustus discovered Cinna's design, and was driven to despair that there should be yet another attempt on his life, and would have to be yet another execution. His wife Livia then urged the political wisdom of confronting Cinna with his guilt and pardoning him, which Augustus did in an effective private interview. Cinna was after this a grateful and loyal supporter of the *princeps*, attained to the Consulship, and made Augustus his sole heir.[77]

However threatened, the long life of Augustus was the most effective guarantee of the new stability of Rome, but unless very effective measures were taken nothing would be likely to stop a new outbreak of civil war on his death. As has been well argued, the nature of the principate meant that theoretically speaking there was no problem. Since Augustus was no more than first citizen, and the offices of state were filled, there *could* be no problem of succession. Practically speaking the problem was a very grave one, and Augustus's

[69]Ibid., II, pp. 111–16; *The Augustan Empire*, pp. 369–73.

[70]Rice Holmes, II, pp. 116–21; *The Augustan Empire*, pp. 373–6, 379.

[71]*De Vita Caesarvm*, Divvs Avgvstvs, 23; ed. cit. p. 58.

[72]Tacitus, *Annals*, I, xi.

[73]Suetonius, *De Vita Caesarvm,*, Divvs Avgvstvs, 28; ed. cit. pp. 62–3.

[74]Ibid., Divvs Avgvstvs, 27; ed. cit. pp. 61–2, for a lurid anecdote about his fears of assassination as a triumvir.

[75]Velleius Paterculus, *Historiae Romanae*, II, lxxxviii; ed. cit. p. 94; Rice Holmes, II, pp. 33–4.

[76]*De Clementia*, I, ix; L. Annaei Senecae, *De Beneficiis Libri VII, De Clementia, Libri II*, ed. Carolus Hosius (Leipzig, 1914), pp. 222–5.

[77]The same episode is recounted at greater length and with some changes by Cassius Dio, *Roman History*, LV, 14–22; ed. cit. pp. 426–50. Dio characteristically turns the discussion into a debate about monarchy. Cnaeus Cornelius is the name given by Dio to this possibly apocryphal conspirator.

solutions were 'incurably dynastic'.[78] He had, however, no son of his own and was, like Julius Caesar, obliged to look for a member of his family to designate his heir. His first choice was Marcus Marcellus, the son of his sister Octavia by her first marriage, the young man of brilliant promise lamented by Virgil –

> quantum instar in ipso!
> sed nox atra caput tristi circumuolat umbra.[79]

But by the time of his death in 23 BC Augustus had already considered the formidable abilities and inevitable power of Agrippa, his great general and colleague. Agrippa was by his gifts certainly the best qualified to succeed Augustus, who now hastened to marry his daughter Julia, the widow of Marcellus, to this increasingly impressive figure. Yet the *princeps* now seemed rather to favour his stepson Tiberius. Agrippa was never actually adopted; perhaps this was unnecessary; but the problem arose again on his death in 12 BC. Julia was now married to Tiberius, while her two sons by Agrippa, Gaius and Lucius, were as they grew up led to expect adoption. Once again Augustus was unfortunate. Lucius died in AD 2 and, two years later, Gaius, as the result of a treacherous wounding received while suppressing a revolt in Armenia. Augustus had now perhaps no wish, and certainly little other choice, but to adopt Tiberius as his son, and thus designate him his successor. In settling the succession on Tiberius, Augustus selected an able general and administrator, a notable intellectual and scholar, and a man whose sensibility and ambition he had frequently offended. His service to the state had already earned him high office and honours: he can only be considered an intelligent and respectable choice.[80] The future lay hidden.

Early in August of AD 14, Tiberius parted from Augustus for Illyricum, but had no sooner reached his destination that he was informed that the *princeps* was dying. He hurried back and was in time to spend a day of private conversation with Augustus before the latter allowed his attention to turn from matters of state to the more personal proprieties and felicities of dying:

> On the last day of his life he asked every now and then whether there was any disturbance without on his account; then calling for a mirror, he had his hair combed and his falling jaws set straight. After that, calling in his friends and asking whether it seemed to them that he had played the comedy of life fitly, he added the tag:
>
> > Since well I've played my part, all clap your hands
> > And from the stage dismiss me with applause.
>
> Then he sent them all off, and while he was asking some newcomers from the city about the daughter of Drusus, who was ill, he suddenly passed away as he was kissing Livia, uttering these last words: 'Live mindful of our wedlock, Livia, and farewell' . . .[81]

[78]Carter, op. cit. p. 242.

[79]*Aeneid*, VI, 865–6; ed. cit. p. 254.

[80]On the succession, see Syme, *The Roman Revolution*, Chapter XXVIII; *The Augustan Empire*, pp. 151–8 (on Gaius's death see p. 177); and Carter, *The Battle of Actium*, pp. 241–3.

[81]*Suetonius*, ed. with an English translation by J.C. Rolfe (London, 1913), I, 280. 'Supremo die identidem exquirens, an iam de se tumultus foris esset, petito speculo capillum sibi comi ac malas labantes corrigi praecepit et admissos amicos percontatus, ecquid iis uideretur minimum uitae commode transegisse, adiecit et clausulam:

It is harder to assess the character of Augustus than his achievement. So great does the discrepancy between his actions before and after Actium appear that Montaigne's remarks about the impossibility of generalization seem fully justified. But part of the difficulty arises from the radically different contexts in which we see him acting. Naturally he appears very different exposed to the world in the ruthless struggle for power after Caesar's murder than he does garbed in the dignified measures of the principate. The former view, which accords in some degree with that of Tacitus, would suggest that Octavian takes us closer to the truth than Augustus. On this interpretation the man is never anything but ruthless and intelligent. In the later and longer period of his life his intelligence showed him that ruthless measures such as the Proscriptions or the seizing of the Consulship were neither necessary nor effective means to his ends. His interests then lay in satisfying the longing of Italy for better times, or, as Tacitus would put it, for slavery. The merit of this interpretation is that it stresses one consistent trait in Augustus, which none has denied: that of political judgement. Another trait may quite uncontroversially be added to this: ambition and unflagging perseverance in pursuit of his aims. But more should be said, even if it sometimes involves inference as well as fact. Did Augustus inwardly rebel against or afterwards regret his ruthlessness before Actium? Did he become, as Seneca was to put it, wearied of cruelty?[82] It is possible that he did, and was glad when his political judgement told him that further such measures would be only self-defeating. It is probable that Augustus had more resources to his character than circumstances easily called forth: only in a situation of effective single power could all sides of his nature manifest themselves. In any case, there is no sudden *volte-face*. The Octavian of the *Eclogues* of Virgil antedates the Battle of Actium, and Virgil was not a servile flatterer. There need be no doubt that all his measures for the renovation and perpetuation of Rome and the rôle of the Roman state in the world were measures he believed in for their own sake. They helped preserve his own power, but they were not merely devices to that end. Augustus was capable of persisting for long periods with highly unpopular policies, such as those embodied in his marriage legislation. The best answer to the apparent contradictions of Augustus's career is to set Montaigne's insight of so 'continual a variety of Actions' in the context of a character whose consistent ambition and political judgement were increasingly able to recruit the many other, and latent, resources of his nature, particularly perhaps those of imagination and piety, to form in the end a true maturity, both political and personal.

The more strictly personal side of his life is easy to forget and to give it prominence involves, perhaps, trusting too much to the anecdotes of Suetonius.[83] But

ἐπεὶ δὲ πάνυ καλῶς πέπαισται‧ δότε κρότον
καὶ πάντες ἡμᾶς καρᾶς προπέμψατε.

omnibus deinde dimissis, dum aduenientes ab urbe de Drusi filia aegra interrogat, repente in osculis Liuiae et in hac uoce defecit: Liuia, nostri coniugii memor uiue, ac uale!' (Divvs Avgvstvs, 99; ed. Maximilian Ihm, I, 107).

[82]I, xi, 2; ed. cit. p. 226. Speaking of Augustus's restraint and mercy *after* the proscriptions, Perusia and Actium, Seneca says: 'Ego vero clementiam non voco lassam crudelitatem' (I, xi, 2).

[83]Suetonius is a tricky source. As secretary to the Emperor Hadrian he had access to letters and other imperial papers from the Augustan Age, some of which he quotes. He can thus be invaluable. In other respects the personal details he includes are so particular that they seem likely to be true; nor

some points are worth making. He was neither tall nor strong, but well-proportioned, with handsome features, and a remarkably bright and piercing gaze. He dressed carelessly and plainly, though in old-fashioned Roman style, and lived on the most modest scale. His long life was punctuated with serious illnesses and deep depressions, but he did not let either impair his capacity for decision. There is no reason to suppose he ever had homosexual relations, though he was sometimes accused of it, but his adulteries were frequent throughout his life. He loved to spend his spare time in gambling, as he frankly and humorously admitted in some of his letters to Tiberius. Those fragments of his personal letters which survive show him capable of warmth of manner and of a facetious sense of humour. While he often showed impatience, he did not stand on his dignity or object to disagreement or correction from others. His interest in literature is obvious, but it is worth noting that he loved the Old Comedy. He was serious about dreams and omens, certainly seems to have known fear, but could show courage when he had to. His capacity to arouse the friendship and loyalty of others was striking, though in the case of the Roman legionaries their fidelity is to be explained chiefly by their self-interest. He did not have Caesar's or Antony's feeling for soldiers, and objected to calling them 'comrades'. He was a competent but not great military commander; Agrippa and others won his important battles for him. He was high-handed in dealing with other people's personal and marital relationships, especially where his dynastic designs were at stake.[84]

It has been written that the 'assemblage of qualities and capacities that made up his personality are not such as to strike the imagination of the world'. That may be true, though on at least two occasions, when Shakespeare dramatized him as he was before the principate, in *Antony and Cleopatra*, and when Corneille dramatized him as *princeps* in *Cinna, Ou La Clemence d'Auguste* the artistic imagination has responded memorably to his character and career as understood in the Renaissance. But he is most important for his political achievement, of which the same scholar has written: 'he was the man the world needed, and may claim to have been one of the greatest servants of the human race'.[85] If to bring an end to the civil wars and to strengthen and prolong the Roman state as master of the world is to be a servant of the human race, Augustus deserves this tribute. No achievement on that scale, however, can be bought except at a price. The views of those peoples who so intrepidly fought against the Rome of Augustus are not much heard of: though Shakespeare made a fine imaginative attempt to understand them in *Cymbeline*, we inherit the Roman view. A Roman view we hear much of is that of the old Republican aristocracy, for whom Tacitus speaks. According to that view, Augustus would certainly have been a better though unsuccessful man had he attempted to restore the Republic in its old form. Unsuccessful because even Tacitus did not think it could be done. But that could only have prolonged civil war and, unless some other Caesarian figure had arisen, perhaps hastened considerably the

is he entirely uncritical of stories probably originating in Antonian propaganda (Divvs Avgvstvs, 68–71). On the other hand he does seem to have been a gatherer up of all kinds of report, so a general *caveat* is in order. Most of the following details come from Suetonius, chiefly 68–93 of Divvs Avgvstvs. For his attitude to the military, see 24–5.

[84]Rice Holmes, II, pp. 75–6.

[85]F.E. Adcock in Chapter XVIII of *The Augustan Empire*, p. 596.

collapse of the Roman world order. To see Augustus as a subverter of liberty and (in Gibbon's confident phrase) a 'subtle tyrant' is to charge him with killing what had already died. To regret the demise of the old Republic may seem natural from modern democratic assumptions, but it is in fact to identify with a narrowly aristocratic ideal, and ignore the strength of plebeian support for the monarchical revolution, even though the men of property mattered more. It is to lack understanding of the longing for peace and the blessings which peace brought, not just to Senatorial families, but all the citizens of the Roman world.[86] That is the note on which to end any discussion of the achievement of Augustus: what Pliny called 'the unthinkable majesty of Roman peace'.[87]

---

[86]See Carter, *The Battle of Actium*, pp. 237–45.
[87]T.R. Glover, writing in Chapter XVI of *The Augustan Empire*, pp. 512–13, has said: ' "The unthinkable majesty of Roman peace" (*immensa Romanae pacis maiestas*) – the four words sum up the burden of the *Aeneid*, the real meaning of the work of Augustus.'

Augustus from the Fathers to the Medieval Drama

> And it came to pass in those days, that there went out
> a decree from Caesar Augustus, that all the world
> should be taxed.
> (And this taxing was first made when Cyrenius was
> governor of Syria.)
> And all went to be taxed every one into his own city.
> And Joseph also went up from Galilee, out of the city
> of Nazareth, into Judaea, unto the city of David,
> which is called Bethlehem; (because he was of the
> house and lineage of David:)
> To be taxed with Mary his espoused wife, being great
> with child.
>
> (Luke 2, 1–5)

The Patristic Period

These verses from The Gospel According to St Luke have been as influential as
Virgil and Horace in shaping the reputation of Augustus. The information
which they impart is small, and in any case raises chronological difficulties,[1] but
the association of his name and reign with the birth of Christ has meant for
many Christians that, while it was certainly easy to think of Christ without
thinking of Augustus, it was less easy to think of Augustus without thinking of
Christ. Though not in any steady or consistent fashion, the association came to
seem providential. Perhaps it arose from the Christians' attempt to persuade
Pagans of their case. This seems to be true of one of the very earliest statements
of a providential link: the petition of Melito, Bishop of Sardis, to the Emperor
Marcus Aurelius, c. AD 177. Complaining of the harassment and persecution of
Christians in Asia, Melito asserts that:

> . . . our philosophy [i.e. Christianity] at first flourished among barbarians [i.e. Jews];
> but after it had appeared among thy peoples during the mighty principate of thy
> ancestor Augustus, it became to thy Empire especially an auspicious boon. For from
> that time the power of the Romans increased to something great and splendid. And to
> this thou hast become the successor whom men desired; yea, and such shalt thou
> continue to be, along with thy son, if thou protectest the philosophy which was nursed
> in the cradle of the Empire and saw the light along with Augustus. . . . And this is the

[1]T. Rice Holmes, *The Architect of the Roman Empire*, II, pp. 89–90; Eusebius, *The Ecclesiastical History*, Bk. IV, Ch. xxv: J.H. Lawlor and J.E.L. Oulton, eds., *The Ecclesiastical History and The Martyrs of Palestine* (London, 1927), II, pp. 52–3.

greatest proof of the fact that it was for the good that our doctrine flourished alongside of the Empire in its happy inception: that from the time of the principate of Augustus no evil has befallen it. . . . Nero and Domitian alone . . . desired to bring our doctrine into ill repute. . . . But thy pious fathers have corrected their ignorance. . . .[2]

The placatory manner of Melito pays homage to the grandeur of Rome and the happiness of the Augustan principate, but the analogy he so insistently draws appeals also to religious prudence; he does not assert that Christianity is the only true religion, but implies, sensibly enough as it may have seemed at the time, that Romans had gained from honouring it 'as they did the other religions'.[3] Might not persecution of Christianity injure the prosperity of Rome? The notion of a providential partnership not only rationalizes the past but predicts the future.

A far more aggressive Christian response to persecution was expressed twenty years later by Tertullian in his *Apology*. He roundly condemned both

---

[2]Eusebius, *The Ecclesiastical History*, ed. cit. I, pp. 132–3: he quotes at length from Melito thus preserving part of what he refers to as Melito's petition To Antoninus but which is usually known as the Apology. It can be dated by the form of its reference to the Emperor's son, Commodus, as *c.* 177 (ed. cit. II, pp. 148–9).

Τούτοις αὖθις ἐπιφέρει λέγων· «Ἡ γὰρ καθ' ἡμᾶς φιλοσοφία πρότερον μὲν ἐν βαρβάροις ἤκμασεν· ἐπανθήσασα δὲ τοῖς σοῖς ἔθνεσι κατὰ τὴν Αὐγούστου τοῦ σοῦ προγόνου μεγάλην ἀρχήν, ἐγενήθη μάλιστα τῇ σῇ βασιλείᾳ αἴσιον ἀγαθόν. Ἔκτοτε γὰρ εἰς μέγα καὶ λαμπρὸν τὸ Ῥωμαίων ηὐξήθη κράτος· οὗ σὺ διάδοχος εὐκταῖος γέγονάς τε καὶ ἔσῃ μετὰ τοῦ παιδός, φυλάσσων τῆς βασιλείας τὴν σύντροφον καὶ συναρξαμένην Αὐγούστῳ φιλοσοφίαν· ἣν καὶ οἱ πρόγονοί σου πρὸς ταῖς ἄλλαις θρησκείαις ἐτίμησαν. Καὶ τοῦτο μέγιστον τεκμήριον τοῦ πρὸς ἀγαθοῦ τὸν καθ' ἡμᾶς λόγον συνακμάσαι τῇ καλῶς ἀρξαμένῃ βασιλείᾳ, ἐκ τοῦ μηδὲν φαῦλον ἀπὸ τῆς Αὐγούστου ἀρχῆς ἀπαντῆσαι, ἀλλὰ τοὐναντίον ἅπαντα λαμπρὰ καὶ ἔνδοξα κατὰ τὰς πάντων εὐχάς. Μόνοι πάντων ἀναπεισθέντες ὑπό τινων βασκάνων ἀνθρώπων, τὸν καθ' ἡμᾶς ἐν διαβολῇ καταστῆσαι λόγον ἠθέλησαν Νέρων καὶ Δομετιανός· ἀφ' ὧν καὶ τὸ τῆς συκοφαντίας ἀλόγῳ συνηθείᾳ περὶ τοὺς τοιούτους ῥυῆναι συμβέβηκε ψεῦδος. Ἀλλὰ τὴν ἐκείνων ἄγνοιαν οἱ σοὶ εὐσεβεῖς πατέρες ἐπηνωρθώσαντο, πολλάκις πολλοῖς ἐπιπλήξαντες ἐγγράφως, ὅσοι περὶ τούτων νεωτερίσαι ἐτόλμησαν.

(J.P. Migne, *Patrologia Graeco-Latina*, XX, cc. 393–6.) Melito's Apology could have been read in English as early as 1577 in Meredith Hanmer's translation of Eusebius's *Auncient Ecclesiasticall History* . . . (London, 1577), p. 73.

[3]Lawlor and Oulton, eds., *Ecclesiastical History*, I, p. 132.

persecutions and the worship of the old gods, and pointed out the relative prominence of Christians in the Empire. But he shared with Melito the view that
Christians could bring blessings on the Roman state, and sought to refute the
claim that they were in principle disloyal to the Emperor. Here he was able to
cite the example of Augustus in a new and highly influential way:

> Augustus to whom the Empire owes its establishment because Lord is the sirname
> which wee give unto God, would not suffer his subjects to call him their Lord; yet I
> will make no difficulty to acknowledge the Emperour is my Lord, but it shall be, when
> not forced to call him my Lord, in the same sense that appertaines to my God.
>
> When I say that the Emperour is my Lord, I will not forbeare in so saying to
> preserve my liberty. This kinde of reverence makes me not his slave. For I have but one
> onely true Lord, to wit the powerfull and Eternall God, who is his God also as well as
> mine. . . . If *Augustus* would never take upon him the name of Lord, ther's less
> appearance of reason to attribute that of God unto Emperours.[4]

In this most uncompromising of early Christian apologists, Suetonius's anecdote about Augustus's refusal of the title or compliment of 'Lord' took on a new
significance. While the large issues of ruler-worship and monarchy were certainly connected with Augustus's distaste for the term, in view of its use in the
relation between master and slave, the whole matter was to him essentially one
of manners and proprieties in Rome. Tertullian for his own purposes transformed it into a major religious affirmation on the part of the founder of the
Empire. It helped him to avow his own unqualified loyalty to the 'powerful and
Eternall God' while at the same time suggesting the possibility of accommodation between the Christian Church and the Roman State.

The providential view proposed by Melito of Sardis was elaborated by Origen
in his Apology *Contra Celsum* (AD 248) and by Eusebius in his *Demonstratio
Evangelica* (*c.* AD 314–18). Each laid emphasis on how the Saviour had been
born in an era when Augustus had (as Origen said) 'made Mankind, almost, as it
were, one Body Politick' and the world enjoyed 'a Time of profound, and universal Tranquility' so that no wars impeded the spread of the gospel, Origen
stressing that a peaceful religion required a period of peace in which to grow.[5]
Eusebius noticed how old political dispensations reached their end at that time,
how with the death of Cleopatra and the dissolution of the Ptolemaic dynasty

---

[4]xxxiv; *Tertullian's Apology, Or Defence of the Christians Against the Accusations of the
Gentiles. Now made English by H[enry] B[rown] Esq.* (London, 1655), pp. 124–5. (Brown's is an
early but loose version of Tertullian, probably made from the 1635 French translation.)
'Augustus imperii formator, ne dominum quidem dici se volebat; et hoc enim dei est cognomen.
Dicam plane imperatorem dominum, sed more communi, sed quando non cogor, ut dominum dei
vice dicam. Cæterum liber sum illi; dominus enim meus unus est, Deus omnipotens et aeternus, idem
qui et ipsius. . . . Si non de mendacio erubescit adulatio ejusmodi, hominem deum appellans, timeat
saltem de infausto. Maledictum est ante apotheosiu deum Caesarem nuncupare.' (Migne,
Patrologia Latina, I, cc. 450–1.) See the *Cambridge Ancient History*, XII, *Imperial Crisis and
Recovery* (Cambridge, 1939), pp. 590–4; and Joseph Vogt, *The Decline of Rome: The Metamor-
phosis of Ancient Civilization*, 1965, tr. Janet Sondheimer (London, 1967), pp. 68–9.
[5]Origen, *Contra Celsum*, II, 30; tr. James Bellamy, Gent. (London, n.d.), p. 83. The most recent
English translation speaks of Augustus as 'the one who reduced to uniformity, so to speak, the many
kingdoms on earth so that he had a single empire' and an 'international situation' in which a 'milder
spirit prevailed' (Origen, *Contra Celsum*, tr. intro. and ed. Henry Chadwick (Cambridge, 1953; rev.
edn, 1980), p. 92.

even the kingdom of Egypt had been destroyed 'which had lasted from immemorial time, and so to say from the very beginnings of humanity'. Different forms of government were also resolved, as Eusebius argues in one of his more explicit passages:

. . . there were risings of nations against nations and cities against cities, there were countless sieges and enslavements carried through in every place and country, until the Lord and Saviour came, and concurrently with His coming, the first Roman Emperor, Augustus, conquered the nations, variety of government was almost completely ended, and peace was spread through all the world, according to the prophecy before us which expressly says of Christ's disciples: 'Wherefore they shall be glorified to the ends of the earth, and this shall be peace.'[6]

Καὶ σαφές γε, ὅτι κατὰ τὴν Αὐγούστου βασιλείαν
ὁ Ἰησοῦς γεγέννηται, τοῦ (ἵν᾽ οὕτως ὀνομάσω) ὁμαλί-
σαντος διὰ μιᾶς βασιλείας τοὺς πολλοὺς τῶν ἐπὶ γῆς.
Ἦν δὲ ἂν ἐμπόδιον τοῦ νεμηθῆναι τὴν Ἰησοῦ διδασκα-
λίαν εἰς πᾶσαν τὴν οἰκουμένην τὸ πολλὰς εἶναι βασιλείας, οὐ μόνον διὰ τὰ προειρημένα, ἀλλὰ καὶ διὰ τὸ
ἀναγκάζεσθαι στρατεύεσθαι καὶ ὑπὲρ τῶν πατρίδων
πολεμεῖν τοὺς πανταχοῦ·

(Migne, *Patrologia Graeco-Latina*, XI, c. 849.)
  [6]Eusebius, *Demonstratio Evangelica* , III, 7; VII, 2; tr. W.J. Ferrar, 2 vols. (London, 1920), I, p. 161; II, pp. 80–1.

Καίτοι τίς οὐκ ἂν θαυμάσειε, πρὸς ἑαυτῷ ἐπιλογισά-
μενος καὶ ἐνθυμηθείς, ὡς οὐκ ἀνθρώπινον ἦν τὸ μηδ᾽
ἄλλοτε ὑπὸ μίαν τὴν Ῥωμαίων γενέσθαι τὰ πλεῖστα τῆς
οἰκουμένης ἔθνη, ἀλλ᾽ ἀπὸ τῶν τοῦ Ἰησοῦ χρόνων;
Ἅμα γὰρ τῇ εἰς ἀνθρώπους αὐτοῦ παραδόξῳ ἐπιδημίᾳ
καὶ τὰ Ῥωμαίων ἀκμάσαι συνηνέχθη, τότε πρῶτον Αὐγούστου τῶν πλείστων ἐθνῶν μοναρχήσαντος, καθ᾽ ὃν,
Κλεοπάτρας ἁλούσης, ἡ κατ᾽ Αἴγυπτον τῶν Πτολεμαί-
ων διαδοχὴ λέλυτο· ἐξ ἐκείνου τε καὶ εἰς δεῦρο τὸ ἀπ᾽
αἰῶνος, καὶ ἀπ᾽ αὐτῆς, ὡς εἰπεῖν, τῆς πρώτης ἀνθρω-
πείας συστὰν Αἰγύπτου βασίλειον καθῄρητο·

.... καὶ Ἰδουμαίων, Φοινίκων τε
καὶ Σύρων, καὶ τῶν ἄλλων ἐθνῶν, ἐπανισταμένων τε
ἐθνῶν ἔθνεσι, καὶ πόλεων πόλεσι, πολιορκιῶν τε μυρί-
ων καὶ αἰχμαλωσιῶν κατὰ πάντα τόπον τε καὶ χώραν
ἐπιτελουμένων, ἐπειδὴ παρῆν ὁ Σωτὴρ καὶ Κύριος,
ὁμοῦ τῇ εἰς ἀνθρώπους αὐτοῦ παρόδῳ, πρώτου τε Ῥωμαίων Αὐγούστου τῶν ἐθνῶν ἐπικρατήσαντος, λέλυτο
μὲν ἡ πλείστη πολυαρχία, εἰρήνη δὲ διελάμβανε τὴν
σύμπασαν γῆν, τῇ μετὰ χεῖρας ἀκολούθως προῤῥήσει,
διαῤῥήδην φησάσῃ περὶ τῶν τοῦ Χριστοῦ μαθητῶν·

It will be noticed that in the hands of Origen and Eusebius the balance of the relation they discern between Christianity and the Roman state has altered. Whereas Melito, rather insecurely as it seems, prophesied benefits to the state if the Christians were left alone, Origen and Eusebius, fully conscious of the spread of their religion, are able to look back and concede the contribution of the Augustan Age to Christian providence. Eusebius does not press the providential view of Augustus in his later *Ecclesiastical History* (AD 324–5). In that ambitious work his method of persuasion is compilation rather than argument. It is, however, worth noting that when Eusebius records the birth of Christ he not only refers it (following Luke) to 'the raygne of *Augustus* the Emperour' and the enrolment when Quirinius was governor of Syria, but also, following an Eastern interest we have already seen, to 'the subiection of *Ægypt*, and the death of *Antonius* and *Cleopatra* where last of all the *Ptolomaes* in *Ægypt* ceased to beare rule'.[7] If for readers of Luke the birth of Christ and the reign of Augustus were associated, for readers of the *Ecclesiastical History* the fall of Antony and Cleopatra was likely to become part of the same providential concatenation of events.

To turn from these writers to Augustine's *De Civitate Dei* (*City of God*) is like turning to another world. In a real sense that is the truth. The previous writers take for granted and often admire the success of the Roman Empire. In one way or another they sought to establish Christianity in symbiotic relation with what, despite inner turbulence and external crises, seemed a monumental political permanence. Eusebius, indeed, had the triumph of seeing the first Christian Emperor, Constantine, achieve a power which must have seemed comparable only to that of Augustus. It was at this time that Virgil – not only the Fourth Eclogue but even the *Aeneid* – was given what must to many have seemed convincing Christian interpretation. But in the years between the completion of the *Ecclesiastical History* and the beginning of the *City of God* the political situation changed utterly. It is telling that the latter work was written between AD 410, when Rome was sacked by the Goths, and 430 when Augustine's own bishopric of Hippo was besieged by the Vandals.[8] It is hardly possible to overestimate the impact of such events on citizens of the Roman Empire. For Christians it became urgently necessary to envisage the future of their religion without Rome. For pagans it became equally necessary to question whether these disasters had not been the consequence of Rome's desertion of her original gods, and whether the falsity of Christianity had not been decisively demonstrated by its failure to save Rome from the barbarians. The *City of God* was written to refute the charges of the pagans, and reorient the Christian view of the future. Augustine 'was disturbed by the idealization of the Roman past

«Διότι νῦν μεγαλυνθήσονται ἕως ἄκρου τῆς γῆς· καὶ
ἔσται αὕτη εἰρήνη·» ᾧ συνᾴδει τὸ ἐν Ψαλμοῖς φάσκον
περὶ τοῦ Χριστοῦ λόγιον· « Ἀνατελεῖ ἐν ταῖς ἡμέραις
αὐτοῦ δικαιοσύνη, καὶ πλῆθος εἰρήνης. »

(Migne, *Patrologia Graeco-Latina*, XXII, cc. 245, 541.) See *Imperial Crisis and Recovery*, pp. 485–7, 639–45; Vogt, *The Decline of Rome*, pp. 48–50, 108–9.

[7] Bk I, ch. vii; *The Auncient Ecclesiasticall History* . . ., tr. Meredith Hanmer, ed. cit. p. 9. Vogt, *The Decline of Rome*, p. 108.

[8] Vogt, *The Decline of Rome*, pp. 105–8, 210.

which he found in fourth-century Latin antiquarians, poets and commentators on poets. He saw in them the roots of the new resistance against Christianity. . . .'[9] He sought to destroy the very foundations of the traditional pride in Rome's historical achievement.[10] Hence the paradox that while in several of the earlier Fathers, who felt a kind of loyalty to the Roman state, references to Augustus are laudatory but vague, the radical standpoint of Augustine leads him to write passages which, taken out of the context of the whole work, read like analytic secular history of a sort which Sallust or Tacitus might have liked. This is in great measure because Augustine was able to assimilate the standpoint and exploit the method of earlier Roman historians such as Sallust, who could write with a severe and pessimistic critical detachment.

Augustine reviews the history of Rome from its very foundation with Romulus. When he arrives at the period of the later Republic the question of whether Augustus usurped the ancient liberty or not is treated as a real issue:

> . . . then brake in such an inundation of depraved conditions, drawne into the state by securitie and prosperitie, that *Carthage* might justly be said to have beene a more dangerous enemy to Rome in her dissolution, then she was in her opposition. And this continued until *Augustus* his time, who (me thinkes) did not abridge the Romans of their liberty, as of a thing which they loued and prised, but as though they had vtterly despised it, and left it for the taking. Then reduced he all things vnto an imperial command, renewing and repairing the commonweale, that was become all moth-eaten and rusty with age, vice, and negligence.[11]

Manner apart, that might not seem to be so utterly different from some of the earlier Fathers' notions about Augustus. But Augustine's purpose leads him to undercut any messianic mysticism about the *princeps*, and there was no better way to do this than by recounting what had been neglected by or unknown to the earlier Fathers: the way in which Augustus had risen to power:

> Their ciuil discords . . . come downe to the other *Cæsar*, called *Augustus*, in whose raigne our Sauiour Christ was born. This *Augustus* had much ciuil wars, wherein were lost many excellent men, & *Tully* that excellent common-wealths man was one

[9]Ibid., pp. 210–14; Arnoldo Momigliano, 'Pagan and Christian Historiography in the Fourth Century' in Momigliano, ed. *The Conflict Between Paganism and Christianity in the Fourth Century* (Oxford, 1963), p. 99.

[10]Vogt, *The Decline of Rome*, p. 211.

[11]*De Civitate Dei*, Bk III, Ch. xxi; St Augustine, *The Citie of God:* . . . *Englished by J[ohn] H[ealey]* (London, 1610), pp. 139–40. '. . . ac deinde tantis malorum aggeribus obpressa Romana res publica, ut prosperitate ac securitate rerum, unde nimium corruptis moribus mala illa congesta sunt, plus nocuisse monstretur tam cito euersa, quam prius nocuerat tam diu aduersa Carthago. Hoc toto tempore usque ad Caesarem Augustum, qui uidetur non adhuc uel ipsorum opinione gloriosam, sed contentiosam et exitiosam et plane iam eneruem ac languidam libertatem omni modo extorsisse Romanis et ad regale arbitrium cuncta reuocasse et quasi morbida uetustate conlapsam ueluti instaurasse ac renouasse rem publicam;. . . .' (*S. Aurelii Augustini . . . De Civitate Dei Contra Paganos Libri XXII*, ed. J.E.C. Welldon (London, 1924), I, p. 136.) Lactantius, *Divine Institutes*, Bk VI, Ch. xv, adopts a highly critical view of the Empire, as opposed to the Republic, and speaks of Rome falling back to the government of a single ruler 'as it were revolving to a second infancy' (*The Works of Lactantius*, tr. and ed. Alexander Roberts and James Donaldson (Edinburgh, 1871); *Ante-Nicene Library*, XXI, p. 464.

amongst the rest. For C. *Cæsar*, the conqueror of *Pompey*, though hee used his victory with mercy, restoring the states and dignities to al his aduersaries: notwithstanding all this, by a conspiracy of the noblest Senators he was stabbed to death in the court, for the defence of their liberty, who held him to affect a monarchy. After this *Anthonie* (a man neither like him in meanes, nor manners, but giuen ouer to al sensuality) seemed to affect his power: whome *Tully* didde stoutly with-stand in defence of the said liberty. And then stepped vp that yonger *Caesar*, the other *Cæsar's* adopted sonne, afterwards stiled (as I said) *Augustus*: Him did *Tully* favour and confirme against *Anthony*, hoping that hee would be the man, who hauing demolished *Anthonys* pretences and powers, would re-erect the liberty of his country. But farre mistaken was he and mole-eid in this matter, for this young man whose power he hadde augmented, first of all suffered *Anthony* to cutt of *Ciceroes* head, as if it hadde beene a bargaine betweene them, and then brought that liberty which the other wrought so for, into his owne sole commaund, and vnder his owne particular subjection.[12]

Augustine's temporary adoption of a Republican viewpoint (the one figure he has a word of praise for is Cicero) enables him to see the whole sequence of events by which Augustus rose to power as a jungle of strife, ambition, intrigue and betrayal, such as no virtuous Roman, whether Christian or pagan, could take pride in. At this point Augustine is a master of the art of withering summary. Elsewhere, in a chapter in which Augustine attempts to see God's ordination of worldly events as something much beyond any easily intelligible patterns of providence, he ranks Augustus coolly among the better Roman emperors: 'he that gaue *Marius* rule, gaue *Cæsar* rule; He that gaue *Augustus* it, gaue *Nero* it: he that gaue *Vespatian* rule, or *Titus* his sonne, both sweet-natured men, gaue it also to *Domitian*, that cruel blood-sucker . . . All these did the True, sacred and only God dispose and direct as hee pleased; & if the causes be vnknowne why he did thus, or thus, is he therefore vniust?'[13]

When Augustine comes to discuss Rome's destiny in the world, however, he is not without admiration for its ideals and achievement, nor is he unwilling to suggest why God has allowed such a mighty empire to flourish so long. With

[12]Bk III, Ch. xxx, tr. Healey, p. 149. 'Crudelia bella ciuilia . . . exorta sunt . . . hinc ad alium Caesarem, qui post Augustus appellatus est, peruenerunt, quo imperante natus est Christus.
Nam et ipse Augustus cum multis gessit bella ciuilia, et in eis etiam multi clarissimi uiri perierunt, inter quos et Cicero, ille disertus artifex rei publicae regendae. Pompei quippe uictorem Gaium Caesarem, qui uictoriam ciuilem clementer exercuit suisque aduersariis uitam dignitatemque donauit, tamquam regni adpetitorem quorundam nobilium conuiratio senatorum uelut pro rei publicae libertate in ipsa curia trucidauit.
Huius deinde potentiam multum moribus dispar uitiisque omnibus inquinatus adque corruptus adfectare uidebatur Antonius cui uehementer pro eadem illa uelut patriae libertate Cicero resistebat. Tunc emerserat mirabilis indolis adulescens ille alius Caesar, illius Gai Caesaris filius adoptiuus, qui, ut dixi, postea est appellatus Augustus. Huic adulescenti Caesari, ut eius potentia contra Antonium nutriretur, Cicero fauebat, sperans eum depulsa et obpressa Antonii dominatione instauraturum rei publicae libertatem, usque adeo caecus adque inprouidus futurorum, ut ille ipse iuuenis, cuius dignitatem ac potestatem fouebat, et eundem Ciceronem occidendum Antonio quadam quasi concordiae pactione permitteret et ipsam libertatem rei publicae, pro qua multum ille clamauerat, dicioni propriae subiugaret.' (*De Civitate Dei*, ed. Welldon, I, pp. 146–7.)
[13]Bk V, Ch. xxi, tr. Healey, p. 227. 'Sic etiam hominibus: qui Mario, ipse Gaio Caesari; qui Augusto, ipse et Neroni; qui Vespasianis, uel patri uel filio, suauissimis imperatoribus, ipse et Domitiano crudelissimo. . . . Haec plane Deus unus et uerus regit et gubernat, ut placet: et si occultis causis, numquid iniustis?' (*De Civitate Dei*, ed. Welldon, I, pp. 235–6.)

frequent recourse to Sallust, and repeated quotation from that most central Augustan statement of Roman destiny, the *Aeneid*, Augustine can acknowledge how the Romans' 'love, first of liberty and afterward of soueraignty and glory, whetted them to all hard attempts. . . . For then it was honour to die bravely, or to live freely.'[14] This affirmation is certainly qualified in a number of ways, but it is never abandoned. True, love of liberty gave way to greed for the glory of domination; true, when Virgil and Sallust wrote there was dominion by corruption, and Romans abandoned the art of rule for 'deceites and trickes, to raise their glories'. Yet the ideal of Rome which Virgil put into the prophecy of Anchises, in that central book of the *Aeneid* which the poet chose to read to Augustus, and in which Augustus was praised, is allowed to stand as worthy of admiration, though not of man's ultimate loyalty:

> Tu, regere imperio populos, Romane, memento,
> (Haec tibi erunt artes) pacique imponere mores;
> Parcere subiectis & debellare superbos.

That these and the preceding four lines are quoted by Augustine, with the prefatory remark that the '*Romaines* affection of liberty and domination was a parcell of their most principall glory and lustre' shows that the Augustan ideal of Rome has been admitted to a conspicuous place in Augustine's conception of history, and was to lend it a certain Christian acceptability in the Renaissance.[15] Rome was 'comprised' in the laws of divine providence partly to punish and chastise by example 'the vicious states of other nations' but chiefly 'that the citizens of heaven in their pilgrimages vpon earth, might obserue those examples with a sober diligence, and thence gather how great care, love and respect ought to bee carried to the heavenly country for life eternall, if those men had such a deare affect to their earthly country for glory so temporall.'[16] Thus Augustine relates the city of Rome to the City of God.

With Paulus Orosius's *Historia adversus paganos* (AD 417–18) we come to the last stage of the Patristic reception of Augustus. Orosius, a refugee from the Vandals in Spain, and no very perceptive pupil of Augustine, was set by his master to compose a Christian universal history, which would in some part be an

---

[14]Bk V, Ch. xii, tr. Healey, p. 214. 'Hoc illa profecto laudis auiditas et gloriae cupido faciebat. Amore itaque primitus libertatis, post etiam dominationis et cupiditate laudis et gloriae multa magna fecerunt. . . . Tunc itaque magnum illis fuit aut fortiter mori aut liberos uiuere.' (*De Civitate Dei*, ed. Welldon, I, p. 217.)

[15]Bk V, Ch. xii, tr. Healey, p. 214.

> 'But (Romanes) be your artes, to rule, in warres,
> To make all knees to sacred peace be bow'd,
> To spare the lowely and pull downe the proud.'

'. . . uerum propterea commemorare illa uolui, ut ostenderem dominationem post libertatem sic habuisse Romanos, ut in eorum magnis laudibus poneretur.' (*De Civitate Dei*, ed. Welldon, I, pp. 217–18. See Bk.X, Ch. xxvii; ed. cit. I, p. 446, for Augustine on Virgil's Fourth Eclogue.)

[16]Bk V, Ch. xi, Healey, p. 213; V, Ch. xii, Healey, p. 216; Bk V, Ch. xvi Healey, p. 220. '. . . . uerum etiam ut ciues aeternae illius ciuitatis, quamdiu hic peregrinantur, diligenter et sobrie illa intueantur exempla et uideant quanta dilectio debeatur supernae patriae propter uitam aeternam, si tantum a suis ciuibus terrena dilecta est propter hominum gloriam.' (*De Civitate Dei*, ed. Welldon, I, p. 224.)

answer to Livy[17] and would show the world to have fared better after the coming of Christ than before. Orosius reviews the succession of the great empires of the world and, descending to his own time, bravely looks ahead to the possibility of alliance between Rome and the various barbarian peoples whose migrations he hopes were sent into the Empire in order that they might find the true religion. Rome, and the peace of Augustus, are at the centre of his historical vision, and it is remarkable that while Orosius is broadly Augustinian in his philosophy of history, he preserves nothing like Augustine's austere moral detachment when he writes about Augustus himself. He notes one or two of Augustus's fearful acts, makes a few criticisms on religious grounds, but is generally in the tradition of Origen and Eusebius.[18] Orosius, however, offers more copious discussion, gives full attention to signs and prodigies, and is assisted in his enthusiastic resolve to detect the holy patterns of providence by a fertile analogical imagination. Thus in his preamble to Bk VI, which brings his narrative up to the time of Augustus, he notes that the

> one true God . . . has chosen the weak of the world to confound the mighty and has laid the foundations of the Roman Empire by choosing a shepherd of the humblest station [Romulus]. After this empire had prospered for many years under kings and consuls and had gained the mastery of Asia, Africa and Europe, He conferred all things by His decree upon a single emperor [Augustus], who was pre-eminent in power and mercy.

Following Origen he notes how a state of great tranquility and universal peace was prepared for the coming of Christ and the spread of the gospel. The title 'Augustus', he claims, was one 'which everyone up to that time had held inviolate and one to which other rulers hitherto had not presumed': it signified 'that the assumption of the supreme power to rule the world was legitimate. From that time on the highest power of the state reposed in one man. . . . This type of government the Greeks call monarchy.' He adds that the day on which this title was conferred on Augustus was 'the same day . . . on which we observe the Epiphany . . . it was fair to have recorded this event faithfully, so that the empire of Caesar might be proven in every respect to have been prepared for the future advent of Christ.'[19]

[17]Vogt, *The Decline of Rome*, pp. 214–16; *Momigliano* in *The Conflict Between Paganism and Christianity*, p. 99.

[18]For the centrality of Augustus to Orosius's view of history, see Bk VI, Ch. i. For censure of Augustus, see e.g. VI, xviii and VII, iii. But while Orosius says that the triumvirs were tyrants, notes that Octavian 'dedicated his talents to civil wars' ('. . . indolem suam bellis civilibus vovit', Migne, *Patrologia Latina*, XXXI, 429, c. 1042) and that he joined with Antony and Lepidus, the worst crimes (including the killing of Cicero) are laid at the door of the other triumvirs (VI, xviii). The favourable trend of Orosius's discussion of Augustus is clear from these details. Where he can assimilate him into a providential scheme he does so fulsomely; where he can excuse he does so; where he can do neither he notes the unwelcome fact briefly and passes on.

[19]Bk VI, i, 20; Paulus Orosius, *Historia adversus paganos*, tr. I.W. Raymond (New York, 1963), pp. 263, 310. 'Itaque idem unus et verus Deus, in quem omnis, ut diximus, etsi ex diversis opinionibus secta concurrit, mutans regna, et disponens tempora, peccata quoque puniens, quæ infirma sunt mundi elegit, ut confundat fortia; Romanumque imperium, assumpto pauperrimi status pastore, fundavit. Hoc per reges et consules diu provectum, postquam Asiæ, Africæ atque Europæ potitum est, ad unum imperatorem, eumdemque fortissimum et clementissimum, cuncta sui ordinatione congessit.' (Migne, *Patrologia Latina*, XXXI, 365–6, cc. 986–7.) VI, xx: 'Quod

The character of Orosius's mind, which has something in common with that of Renaissance writers of panegyric, can be seen from his handling of two familiar points about Augustus: the anecdote about his being called 'lord' and the 'taxing' or census alluded to by Luke and Eusebius. Having stressed Augustus's rejection of the title of 'lord' 'on the ground that he was only a man' he goes on to give the Suetonian anecdote as though it were illustrative of a previous affirmation on the emperor's part, rather than the sole ground of the story. He proceeds to draw out the maximum possible significance from the 'facts':

> It was at this time that he who had secured universal supremacy refused to be called Lord of men, or rather dared not, when the true Lord of all mankind was born among men. It was also in this year when God had deigned to assume the appearance and nature of man, that this same Caesar, whom God had predestined for this great mystery, for the first time ordered a census to be taken of each and every province and that all men should be enrolled. In these days, then, Christ was born and His name was entered in the Roman census list immediately after His birth. This is that earliest and most famous acknowledgement which designated Caesar first of all men and the Romans lords of the world; for in the census list all men were entered individually, and in it the very Maker of all men wished to be found and enrolled as a man among men. From the very foundation of the world and the beginning of the human race an honour of this kind had never been granted. . . . Neither is there any doubt . . . that it was by the will of our Lord Jesus Christ that this City prospered, was protected, and brought to such heights of power, since to her, in preference to all others, He chose to belong when He came, thereby making it certain that He was entitled to be called a Roman citizen according to the declaration made in the Roman census list.[20]

Readers of the Gospels may well feel that Rome (in Orosius's argument) has achieved a good deal in enrolling God among its citizens. But this remarkable feat of rationalizing and interpreting depends not just on Augustus's refusal to assume a divine title (which is as much as Tertullian had claimed) but on the virtual imputation to Augustus of the knowledge of Christ ('. . . or rather dared not, when the true Lord of all mankind was born among men'). This, so far as I

nomen [Augustus] cunctis antea inviolatum, et usque ad nunc cæteris inausum dominis, tantum orbis licite usurpatum, apicem declarat imperii: atque ex eodem die summa rerum ac potestatum penes unum esse cœpit et mansit, quod Græci monarchiam vocant. Porro autem hunc esse eumdem diem, hoc est, octavum idus Januarias, quo nos Epiphania, hoc est apparitionem, sive manifestationem Dominici sacramenti observamus, nemo credentium, sive etiam fidei contradicentium, nescit.' 441–42, cc. 1052–3.)

[20]Bk VI, xxii, tr. Raymond, pp. 316–17. 'Eodemque tempore hic, ad quem rerum omnium summa concesserat, dominum se hominum appelari non passus est; immo non ausus, quo verus dominus totius generis humani inter homines natus est. Eodem quoque anno tunc primum idem Cæsar, quem his tantis mysteriis prædestinaverat Deus, censum agi singularum ubique provinciarum, et censeri omnes homines iussit, quando et Deus homo videri, et esse dignatus est. Tunc igitur natus est Christus, Romano censui statim ascriptus ut natus est. Hæc est prima illa clarissimaque professio, quæ Cæsarem omnium principem, Romanosque rerum dominos singillatim cunctorum hominum edita ascriptione signavit, in qua se et ipse, qui cum cunctos homines fecit, inveniri hominem, ascribique inter homines voluit. Quod numquam penitus ab orbe condito atque ab exordio generis humani in hunc modum . . . concessum fuit. Nec dubium . . . quod Dominus noster Jesus Christus hanc urbem nutu suo auctam defensamque, in hunc rerum apicem provexerit, cujus potissime voluit esse cum venit, dicendus utique civis Romanus, census professione Romani.' (Migne, *Patrologia Latina*, XXXI, 449, cc. 1058–9.)

am aware, is the closest any of the Fathers comes to those legends, noted by Nicephorus and Suidas in ninth and tenth-century Byzantium, according to which the advent of Christ was either revealed or enigmatically intimated to Augustus.[21] It seems probable that where Orosius's work was known it gave a powerful impetus to that final assimilation of Augustus into a Christian conception of historical providence.

In other respects Orosius can deal confidently in Christian portents. The comet which really does seem to have appeared during some of the games in honour of Julius Caesar[22] becomes in Orosius a circle like a rainbow round the sun which showed, not only that Augustus was the most powerful man in the world, but that 'it was in his time that Christ would come – He who alone had made and ruled the sun itself and the whole world.'[23] A later portent, according to Orosius, marked the triumph which Augustus was accorded after his victory over Lepidus. This was 'a spring of oil' which burst out from an inn 'on the other side of the Tiber . . . and poured forth a great stream throughout the whole day'. It prophesied Christ, whose meaning was 'anointed'; clearly Christ would come in the time of Augustus; and the flowing of the oil for a whole day meant that for the entire duration of the Roman Empire signs and prodigies would proclaim Christ, for the benefit of those who ignored the Prophets.[24] These details show that history in the hands of Orosius tended strongly towards hagiology, despite an apparent knowledge of Livy, Tacitus and Suetonius (some of whom, however, he may have read through the epitomizer Eutropius), and despite the example of some of the historical passages in Augustine.[25] Even so, his enthusiastically synthesizing mind could not assimilate all the fact that lay in his way, and his major treatment of Augustus accords very uneasily with his admission that (what as it happens was too true) Augustus crucified 6,000 masterless slaves after his victory over Pompey and Lepidus.[26] As the first Christian universal history, Orosius's work had great influence. Those who read it and accepted its claims will have seen the reign of Augustus, not just as the

[21]See the Dictionary of Suidas, first published in 1514 (Wienne, 1619), I, 487–9; and note Domenico Comparetti, *Vergil in the Middle Ages* (1895; London, 1966), pp. 173–6. The Legend of the Sybilline Prophecy of Christ's birth gained influence in the Middle Ages from a pseudo-Augustinian sermon of the fifth or sixth century, *Contra Judaeos, Paganos, et Arianos Sermo de Symbolo*. Held to be genuinely Augustinian, it concluded by quoting 27 lines of Latin hexameter, being the Erythraean Sybil's prophecy. This gave rise to the Nativity Plays of the *Ordo Prophetarum* in which a line of prophets, sometimes including Virgil, is succeeded by the Sybil. See Karl Young, *The Drama of the Medieval Church* (Oxford, 1933), II, pp. 125–71. This material does not, however, speak of a prophecy to Augustus.

[22]Jones, *Augustus*, p. 15 (quoting Pliny, *Natural History*, II, 93, who is in his turn quoting Augustus's lost Autobiography).

[23]Bk VI, xx; tr. Raymond, p. 311. '. . . cujus tempore venturus esset, qui ipsum solem solus, mundumque totum et fecisset et regeret.' (Migne, *Patrologia Latina*, XXXI, 442, c. 1053.)

[24]Bk VI, xviii, xx; tr. Raymond, pp. 306, 311. '. . . fons olei largissimus, sicut superius expressi, de taberna meritoria per totum diem fluxit.' (Migne, *Patrologia Latina*, XXXI, 442–3, cc. 1053–4.)

[25]The significance of Orosius is clear if we link two statements by Momigliano: 'Orosius gave what from a medieval point of view can be called the final Christian twist to the pagan epitome of history', ('Pagan and Christian Historiography of the Fourth Century AD', *The Conflict Between Paganism and Christianity*, (Oxford, 1963) p. 87) and 'The Roman Empire makes it possible to write universal history' ('Time in Ancient Historiography', in Arnoldo Momigliano, *Essays in Ancient and Modern Historiography* (Oxford, 1977), p. 189.

[26]Bk VI, xviii; tr. Raymond, p. 306.

centre of the history of Rome, but the centre of the history of the world under Christian providence.

The Dark Ages

Augustine and Orosius confronted in their own lifetimes those migrations of barbarian peoples which occasioned the fall of the empire in the West. To generations far in futurity, in the Renaissance and beyond, this moment was to seem a *ne plus ultra*. Before, there was civilization, a world they could understand and often admire. Faced with what followed, their rhetoric sweeps onwards over the dark backward and abysm of time to the Renaissance:

> The North by myriads pours her mighty sons,
> Great nurse of Goths, of Alans, and of Huns. . . .
>
> A *second* Deluge Learning thus o'er-run,
> And the *Monks* finish'd what the *Goths* begun.
>   At length, *Erasmus*, that *great, injur'd* Name. . . .[27]

If to a modern reader pursuing the present subject it also seems that a dark age stretches for the next 500 years − from Orosius to Alfred − there is some truth in the impression. Yet in the Gothic period under Theodoric the senatorial aristocracy was intensely conscious of the grandeur of the Roman past. Virgil and Livy were edited. Panegyrical material on Augustus survived in the epitomizer Eutropius. Augustus was also recalled with admiration in the Prologue to Vegetius's *De Re Militari*. In far-off Britain, which Gildas, writing in the sixth century, described as 'an island numb with chill ice and far removed, as in a remote nook of the world', Augustus was just remembered. Gildas does not mention him; but recounts the conquest of Britain, Boudicca's revolt, the Romanization of the island, with all its coin stamped with the image of Caesar, and writes of the spread of Christianity in the last years of Tiberius. Much stress is laid on the circumstances of the Roman withdrawal from Britain, the ills suffered both before and after being interpreted in a pattern of sin and punishment.[28] The chronicler known as Nennius, however, probably writing early in the ninth century, notes in his *Historia Brittonum* how, after the assassination of Julius Caesar, 'Octavianus Augustus' succeeded to the empire of the world. He was the only emperor to receive tribute from the Britons, according to the verse of Virgil:

> Purpurea intexit tollunt aulaea Britanni.[29]

The first English author to record the career of Augustus and characterize the Augustan Age is the anonymous member of Alfred the Great's court circle who

[27]Alexander Pope, *The Dunciad* (1743), Bk III, ll. 89–90; *An Essay on Criticism*, ll. 691–3.
[28]Theodore Mommsen, ed. *Chronica Minora, Saec. IV, V. VI. VII* (1898; new edn, 1961), III, p. 30–1. Michael Winterbottom, ed. and tr. *Gildas: The Ruin of Britain* . . . (London, 1978), p. 18. See E.A Thompson, 'Gildas and the History of Britain', *Britannia*, 10 (1979), pp. 203–26.
[29]*Chronica Minora*, III, p. 164: 'tenente Octaviano Augusto monarchiam totius mundi, et censum a Britannia ipse solus accepit, ut Virgilius ait: Purpurea intexit tollant aulea Britanni' [*Georgics*, III, 25].

sometime between 890 and 899 produced the Old English version of Orosius's *Historia adversus paganos*. Not only did he translate, but abridged, expanded and refashioned so as to make a virtually independent work. He does not stress Orosius's more polemical aim of revealing how much worse had been the state of the world before the coming of Christ than after, but uses him as a Christian account of world history. He sees that Augustus was not a king, though deriving his claim to rule a reluctant Rome from the will of Julius Caesar, and fought five battles for his inheritance. In this version, though not Orosius, Augustus gained his new name because he defeated Antony and Cleopatra in August. The Orosian portents of the ring round the sun and the fountain of oil are noted, and Augustus is said to have typified unknowingly in his acts the doctrines of the new religion which was to take its rise in his reign. Thus he called all nations together so they might learn whom they belonged to, signifying that one should be born in those days who would lead all men to a single gathering which is the life to come. The general taxation typified the truth that in future a common belief and common ethic of good works would unite mankind. The returning, freeing and crucifixion of the slaves becomes an allegory of the fate of mankind under a Christian providence: those who acknowledge their Master being redeemed, those who refuse being condemned to perdition. Following Orosius the Alfredian writer lays stress on the profound peace at the time when Christ was born and, with an eye for an expressive physical detail from his source, notes that the peace lasted so long that the locks rusted on the doors of the Temple of Janus. In the year of Christ's birth Augustus rebuilt Rome finer than it was before. On the important point of the refusal to be called Lord, the author writes that in his prosperity Augustus was temperate and humble before God ('eaðmetto wiþ God geheold'), breaking all precedent by refusing to style himself divine, and forbidding men to call him god. Later God punished Augustus for not rebuking his nephew Gaius when he neglected to worship God in Jerusalem. On a more secular note, the author records Augustus's grief at the loss of Varus and the legions.[30] Gildas, Nennius and the author of the Old English Orosius were attempting to write serious history. So was Bede, who numbered the emperors from Augustus. The fabulous history of Geoffrey of Monmouth, in the mid-twelfth century, also makes mention of Augustus; Cymbeline is said to have been brought up at his court, and Christ born in the time of their reigns.[31] The *name* 'Emperor Octovien', at least, passed into

---

[30] See *The Old English Orosius*, ed. Janet Bately (London, 1980); for authorship, pp. lxxiii–lxxxvi; date, lxxxvi–xciii; and for treatment of sources, xciii–c. For the points about Augustus mentioned above see V, xiii–VI, ii of the Old English version, ed. cit. pp. 129–35; the quoted phrase is at VI, i, 30: p. 133. There is a modern translation from the Old English by Joseph Bosworth, *King Alfred's Anglo-Saxon Version of the Compendious History of the World by Paulus Orosius* (London, 1859). See also Dorothy Whitelock, 'The Prose of Alfred's Reign' in *Continuations and Beginnings: Studies in Old English Literature*, ed. E.G. Stanley (London, 1966) pp. 89–94; and Michael Hunter, 'Germanic and Roman Antiquity: The Sense of the Past in Anglo-Saxon England', *Anglo-Saxon England*, ed. Peter Clemoes, 3 (1974), pp. 29–50. The providential interpretation of the *pax Augusta* found expression in the Christmas Day sermon of Ælfric's First Series of Catholic Homilies (*c.* 989); see *The Homilies of the Anglo-Saxon Church, The First Part, containing the Sermones Catholici, or Homilies of Ælfric*, ed. Benjamin Thorpe, 2 vols. (London, 1844–6), I, pp. 32–3.

[31] *Six Old English Chronicles*, ed. and W.J.A. Giles (London, 1896), pp. 148–9.

romance literature, but quite detached from the historical personage to whom it originally belonged.[32]

Velleius Paterculus, Plutarch, Vitruvius, Tacitus and Cassius Dio were, of course, authors lost until the Renaissance. Augustus's Autobiography was lost and has never been found, as is the case with the later books of Livy. But major texts for any account of Augustus continued to be used and studied. Virgil, Horace and Ovid were never lost; neither was Suetonius; neither was Seneca. The chief Patristic sources remained available; Orosius was in part rendered into English.[33] As to how well these authors were known, much is conjectural. Their chief importance was undoubtedly in the teaching of the Latin language.

Dante

But whenever there was aspiration to a political order transcending cities, principalities, monarchies, Rome was remembered. The imperial ideal was, periodically, capable of a measure of fulfilment. Augustus, Constantine, Justinian, Charlemagne might be recalled at such times as example and inspiration; all four are so recalled in Canto VI of Dante's Paradiso, in which Justinian himself reviews the history of Rome and its imperial successors down to the Holy Roman Empire and Dante's own lifetime.[34] It was the attempt of the Holy Roman Emperor, Henry VII, to bring his power into proportion with his titular authority and restore the universal Empire which led Dante to compose his treatise *De Monarchia* (?1309–19). 'It would be wrong to disregard the atmosphere of expectancy and anticipation which preceded and accompanied, in the whole of Italy, the journey of this Emperor who described himself as a "Rex Pacificus". . . .' Dante's passionate defence of the imperial ideal makes frequent quotation from Virgil, but draws too, among many other authorities, upon Orosius whom he may allude to as one of the twelve stars of Canto X of the Paradiso.[35] Augustus is at the centre of Dante's argument, and while his treatise is framed as a scholastic demonstration, and thus quite different from the *Historia contra paganos* in procedure, its view of Augustus is similar. Thus Dante confirms his argument that 'a Monarch is essential to the well-being of the world' by the 'noteworthy historical fact' of:

> the state of humanity which the Son of God either awaited or himself brought about when He was to become man for the salvation of men. For if we survey the ages and condition of men since the fall of our first parents . . . at no time do we see universal

[32]An example may be the 'emperour Octovyen' of l. 368 of Chaucer's *Boke of the Duchess*; see Laura A. Hibbard, *Medieval Romance in England* (1924), pp. 267–73; Lillian H. Hornstein, *Manual of the Writings in Middle English*, gen. ed. J. Burke Severs (New Haven, 1967), I, pp. 127–9. For a different view, see Russell A. Peck, 'Theme and Number in Chaucer's *Boke of the Duchess*', in A.D.S. Fowler, ed., *Silent Poetry*, (London, 1970), pp. 100, 114.

[33]R.R. Bolgar, *The Classical Heritage and its Beneficiaries* (Cambridge, 1954): for Virgil see pp. 124–6, 380, 197–8, 221, 423, 429; for Suetonius, pp. 193, 380, 407, 125, 410, 415, 423; for Seneca, pp. 125, 423. On Augustus and Latin sources available in the Old English Period, see J.D. Ogilvy, *Books Known to the English, 597–1066* (Cambridge, Mass. 1967).

[34]*Commedia*, Paradiso, VI, 1–3, 10–13. For Dante and Augustus, see A.P. d'Entrèves, *Dante as a Political Thinker* (Oxford, 1952), and C.T. Davis, *Dante and the Idea of Rome* (Oxford, 1957).

[35]U. Limentani, 'Dante's Political Thought' in U. Limentani, *The Mind of Dante* (Cambridge, 1965), p. 132; Dante, *Monarchy and Three Political Letters*, ed. Donald Nicholl and Colin Hardie (London, 1954), pp. 35, 49, 54. See too Paradiso, X, 119.

peace throughout the world except during the perfect monarchy of the immortal Augustus. The fact that mankind at that time was resting happily in universal peace is attested by all the historians and the illustrious poets. Even the recorder of Christ's gentleness [Luke] has deigned to bear witness to it. Finally Paul, also, has described that blissful state as 'the fulness of time'.[36]

'The unthinkable majesty of Roman peace' – Pliny's words, accurately conveying what Augustus had given to Italy – this above all is the significance and the ideal which Dante correctly perceived in Augustus's principate, and which he longed to see restored to the world. Further, Dante maintains that it was by right, not by usurpation, that the Roman people acquired that monarchical office over other men which is called the Empire, and draws into his argument a great part of the account of the imperial destiny of Rome in the *Aeneid*: he quotes that centrally Augustan passage about Rome's destiny to rule (Bk VI, 847–53) which we have already seen Augustine mention with approbation.[37] Having in his first Book argued that universal monarchy was necessary to the well-being of the world, and in the second that providence seemed to have vested this monarchy in the Roman people as of right, Dante devoted his third Book to the conflict between the Holy Roman Empire and the Papacy, and here had little to say directly about Augustus. In three contemporary letters, however, he deployed his conception of Augustus in direct political appeal. In 1310, when the Emperor was setting out to restore peace in Italy, Dante addressed a letter (Letter V) to its princes, senators and nobility. In opulent rhetoric he hails the dawn of a new age of peace, plenty, sunlight, freedom and justice; copious biblical allusion mingles with simplified Roman history:

> Rejoice . . . Italy, you who are now to be pitied . . . since your Bridegroom, the Consolation of the world and 'the glory of your people', the most merciful Henry, the Consecrated, Augustus and Caesar, is hastening to his wedding. . . .
> But will he have mercy on no one? Surely he will pardon all who sue for mercy, since he is Caesar. . . . Will he therefore applaud the audacities of wicked men. . . . Far be it from him, since he is Augustus; and if he is Augustus, shall he not take vengeance . . .?[38]

[36]*Monarchy*, I, xvi; tr. Nicholl and Hardie, p. 26. '. . . status videlicet illius mortalium, quem Dei Filius, in salutem hominis hominem adsumpturus, vel expectavit, vel quum voluit ipse disposuit. Nam si a lapsu primorum parentum, qui diverticulum fuit totius nostrae deviationis, dispositiones hominum et tempora recolamus; non inveniemus, nisi sub divo Augusto Monarcha, existente Monarchia perfecta, mundum undique fuisse quietum. Et quod tunc humanum genus fuerit felix in pacis universalis tranquillitate, hoc historiographi omnes, hoc poetae illustres, hoc etiam Scriba mansuetudinis Christi testari dignatus est, et denique Paulus, 'plenitudinem temporis' statum illum felicissimum appellavit' (*De Monarchia*, ed. E. Moore and W.H.V. Reade (Oxford, 1916), p. 350).

[37]*Monarchy*, II, vi; tr. Nicholl and Hardie, pp. 32, 45.

[38]*Monarchy and Three Political Letters*, p. 98. 'Laetare iam nunc miseranda Italia etiam Saracenis, quae statim invidiosa per orbem videberis, quia sponsus tuus, mundi solatium et gloria plebis tuae, clementissimus Henricus, Divus et Augustus et Caesar, ad nuptias properat. Exsicca lacrymas, et moeroris vestigia dele, pulcerrima; nam prope est qui liberabit te de carcere impiorum, qui percutiens malignantes in ore gladii perdet eos, et vineam suam aliis locabit agricolis, qui fructum iustitae reddant in tempore messis.

Sed an non miserebitur cuiquam? Immo ignoscet omnibus misericordiam implorantibus, quum sit Caesar, et maiestas eius de fonte defluat pietatis' (*Dantis Alighierii Epistolae*, ed. Paget Toynbee (Oxford, 1920; rev. edn, 1966), pp. 48–9).

On 31 March 1311, Dante wrote from exile a letter of condemnation to the citizens of Florence (Letter VI), who were refusing to acknowledge the Emperor. Here he asserts that God by His goodness 'has entrusted to the Holy Roman Empire the governance of human affairs so that mankind might have peace' and notes that 'Although this is proved by Holy Scripture and is warranted by the ancient world on the basis of reason alone, it is nevertheless no slight confirmation of the truth that, when the throne of Augustus is vacant, the whole world loses its way, the pilot and oarsmen in the ship of St Peter fall asleep, and Italy, unhappy and forsaken . . . drifts in such a battering from wind and wave as words could not express. . . .'[39] Finally, in a letter addressed to Henry himself in April of the same year (Letter VII), Dante combines Virgil and St Luke in once again reciting the argument of Orosius that Christ's birth in the reign of Augustus proved that that emperor's rule, and the world sway of Rome, was 'the most just of governments'.[40]

These writings have great importance. Dante is the first great literary figure since the fall of the Roman Empire in the West in whose thought Augustus has once again a crucial historical importance. For Dante, the reign of Augustus was a vital point of reference in mapping human history, and orienting himself in his own time. This can be said of Dante because of his adoption of an Orosian providential scheme, with Augustus at its centre, some nine centuries after the fall of the empire which Augustus had principally founded. But Dante is closer to the Roman Augustan age than this altogether acknowledges, since within the larger Christian pattern of the Orosian scheme Dante embraces, more closely than Orosius and Augustine, that poetic exposition of the destiny of Rome which Virgil wrote in the age of Augustus, and in which Augustus himself had so important a part. Limentani writes: 'The *Aeneid* of Virgil was deemed to be as historically accurate as it was poetic. It was the proof of the continuity of the nation. Virgil, the celebrator of the Roman Empire, is as much Dante's guide in the *Monarchia*, as Virgil the poet and symbol, is his guide in the *Comedy*.' A further point of interest is that *Monarchia* and the three letters, taken together, afford an example of an argued system of belief (the treatise), and the rhetorical application of those beliefs (the letters), designed to influence the world in specific political ways. The rigorous procedure of the formal defence gives way in the letters to an often quite extravagantly idealistic panegyrical mode in which copious biblical allusion and quotation sweep forward the Augustan analogy, and anticipate quite late Renaissance panegyric.[41] Yet it has more than a merely

[39]*Monarchy and Three Political Letters*, p. 103. 'Aeterni pia providentia Regis, qui dum coelestia sua bonitate perpetuat, infera nostra despiciendo non deserit, sacrosancto Romanorum imperio res humanas disposuit gubernandas, ut sub tanti serenitate praesidii genus mortale quiesceret, et ubique, natura poscente, civiliter degeretur. Hoc etsi divinis comprobatur elogiis, hoc etsi solius podio rationis innixa contestatur antiquitas, non leviter tamen veritati applaudit, quod solio Augustali vacante totus orbis exorbitat, quod nauclerus et remiges in navicula Petri dormitant, et quod Italia misera, sola, privatis arbitriis derelicta, omnique publico moderamine destituta, quanta ventorum fluctuumque concussione feratur verba non caperent . . .'. (*Epistolae*, ed. Toynbee, pp. 66–7.)

[40]*Monarchy and Three Political Letters*, p. 111. '. . . si non de iustissimi principatus aula prodiisset edictum . . .' (*Epistolae*, ed. Toynbee, p. 92.) It should be noted that the Christian interpretation of Virgil's Fourth Eclogue is used by Dante not only in the Letters, but also in *De Monarchia*, I, xi (*Monarchy and Three Political Letters*, pp. 110, 14–15).

[41]Limentani, *The Mind of Dante*, p. 122. As for later panegyric I have in mind poems such as Dryden's *Astraea Redux*.

courtly function. Dante is not just saying that Henry is another Augustus; he is another Augustus because as Holy Roman Emperor he is the true successor of Augustus.

The *Monarchia* and the three letters are not, however, Dante's full statement about Roman history and the imperial ideal. That must include the *Commedia* (1314–21), where Brutus and Cassius, last defenders of Republican Rome, are as assassins of Julius Caesar placed in the Inferno, and where Canto VI of the Paradiso gives an almost divine purview of the sweep and pace of historical evolution. Julius Caesar, Augustus and Tiberius are successive bearers of the imperial eagle of Rome. That it is Tiberius, rather than the two earlier Caesars, on whom Dante briefly concentrates, is perhaps a sign of the more deeply meditated and theological view to which the *Commedia* attains, since it was under Tiberius that Rome was the instrument of God in the supreme drama of the crucifixion. In this Canto Augustus loses the central place he has held in Dante's earlier historical exposition, assuming a necessary but subordinate part in a wider and deeper vision.[42]

The history of Dante's political vision in fourteenth- and fifteenth-century political thought in northern Italy has been explored by Hans Baron in *The Crisis of the Early Italian Renaissance*. Conflict between the republican and princely states of Italy generated opposing interpretations of Roman history, the former defending the ideal of republican liberty and asserting a link between republican Rome and republican Florence, the latter going so far as to hope that all Italy might again be united under a single monarch. So powerful was the republican feeling in Florence that many admirers of Dante were obliged to adopt an allegorical interpretation of those sections of the Inferno where Cassius and Marcus Brutus were punished. The tradition continued until the Florentine republican Donato Giannotti, in 1546, doubted the validity of such interpretation, and wished he might place Caesar where Dante had punished Brutus. On the other hand the magnetic appeal of powerful princely states such as Viscontean Milan can be seen even in the work of writers who had once glorified republican virtues. Coluccio Salutati, author of the treatise *De Tyranno*, is a case in point. What emerges clearly is the influence of contrasting forms of existing governments upon political ideals and their historical interpretation. While Augustus might find some admiration among those adhering to republican traditions, it is always in connection with the practice and theory of monarchical rule that he is accorded his highest importance. Here the Christian providential interpretation of world history, stemming from the Fathers of the Church, constituted the most majestic possible rationalization of the ideal view of Augustus.[43]

Augustus in Christian Legend

The rôle of the *princeps* in the New Testament and Patristic tradition did,

[42]Paradiso, VI, 82–90. For probable dates of the *Monarchia* and the *Commedia*, see A.M. Chiavacci Leonardi, 'La *Monarchia* di Dante alla luce della *Commedia*', *Studii Medievali*, 3rd Series, 18 (1977), pp. 147–83. For Benvenuto Rambaldi's discussion of Canto VI, see Hans Baron, *The Crisis of the Early Italian Renaissance: Civic Humanism and Republican Liberty in an Age of Classicism and Tyranny* (Princeton, 1955; rev. edn, 1966), pp. 153–6.

[43]Baron, *Crisis of the Early Italian Renaissance*, Parts One to Three.

however, carry him forward into very different forms of medieval art, and presented him to audiences very different from the readers of Dante. He figures as a character in two sequences of English Mystery plays: the Towneley Cycle and the Chester Cycle. Augustus appears in connection with the birth of Christ in each case. In the Towneley Cycle *Caesar Augustus* is a Mohammedan tyrant, who, hearing that a mightier monarch than he is about to be born, plans with his adviser Sirinius (cf. Luke 2, 1–2) to slay the child. It is a fair popular reconstruction from the Gospel, the point having been taken that Caesar Augustus was a supreme pagan ruler (a reference to Quirinius and the taxing being also worked in), and this is given vivid contemporary force by making the emperor a worshipper of Mohammed and Quirinius one of his bashaws.[44] In the beautiful Nativity drama of the Chester Cycle those traditions and legends which we have seen working to assimilate Augustus into a Christian providential scheme, have shaped a drama of a contrasting kind. The focus of attention moves between the Holy Family and the Roman Emperor, opening with the former, ending with the latter. Here Octavian first plays the supreme secular ruler, boasting of his great power, and that of Rome:

> − my name Octavian called is −
> all me aboute, full in my blisse;
> for wholly all this world, I wis,
> is ready at my owne will.
>
> No man on mould dare doe amisse
> against mee, I tell you this,
> ne no man saie that ought is his,
> but my leave be thertyll.
>
> for I halfe multeplied more
> the Citee of Rome, sith I was bore,
> then ever did any me before,
> sith I had this kingdom.
>
> for what with strength and strokes sore,
> leading lordship, lovelie lore,
> all this world nowe has bene yore
> tributary unto Rome.[45]

While, at the command of Octavian, the census is being carried out in Judaea, and taxes levied, senators come to the emperor 'from all Rome' offering to worship him as a god in reward for the blessings of his rule:

> peace hath bene long and yet is,
> no man in thy tyme lost ought of his . . .

but the emperor demurs. He is mortal, he says, whereas 'godhead askes in al thinge / tyme that hath no begininge, / ne never shall have ending; and none of these have I.'[46] He sends to the Sibyl for her advice, and she foretells the birth of

[44] *The Towneley Plays*, ed. George England and A.W. Pollard (London, 1897), pp. 78–85; *Caesar Augustus*, ll. 163–228, ed. cit. pp. 83–5.

[45] Ll. 193–208; *The Chester Plays*, Part I, ed. Herman Deimling (Oxford, 1892), pp. 112–13.

[46] Ll. 306, 337–40; ed. cit. pp. 116–17.

a baby who will bring eternal happiness. The drama now returns to Mary and
Joseph, but after the miraculous birth has taken place, the Expositor launches
into a lengthy description of the magical temple at Rome by which the state was
always warned if any hostile force threatened it. With the help of this 'temple of
peace' Rome maintained her supremacy. Now, at the moment of Christ's birth,
this temple is cast down, three suns appear in the sky, the ox and the ass worship
the holy child. Then the stage directions indicate the resumption of the drama in
its Roman aspect: '(tunc ostendant stellam, et veniet Sybill ad Imperatorem)':

> *Sibilla:*
> Sir Emperour, god the saue and see!
> looke up one height, after me!
> I tell you sicker that born is hee
> that passeth thee of power. . . .

> *Octavianus:*
> Ah! Sybbill, this is a wondrous sight,
> for yonder I see a mayden bright,
> a yonge child in her armes clight,
> a bright crosse in his head. . . .

The drama is resolved upon the theme of the worship due to Octavian.
Instructed by the Sibyl, the Emperor announces to his senators:

> Sires, senators, goes home anone,
> and warne my men every echone
> that such worship I must forgone
> as they wold doe to me.

> but this child worship each man
> with full hart, all that you can,
> for he is worthy to leeve upon,
> and that now I will see.[47]

Thus Octavian's adroit and well-meditated discretion in establishing the principate and repudiating the title of 'lord' is moulded into a nativity drama of the
conversion of Rome. This pious and potent tradition was given beautiful visual
expression, in the late fifteenth century, by the Limbourg brothers in *Les Très
Riches Heures du Duc de Berry*. Here an illumination displays a sibyl announcing the birth of Christ, while a venerable ruler, attired like a contemporary
Byzantine emperor, kneels to worship the Saviour. Between the Virgin and
Child at the top of the page, and the sibyl and Augustus at the bottom left and
right respectively, the script recounts one of those versions of the legend we have
already noticed, according to which Augustus recognizes the true God.[48] This
may be seen as a beautiful simplification of what was certainly the most
prominent feature in the medieval reputation of Augustus.

---

[47]Ll. 657–60, 665–68, 697–704; ed. cit. pp. 129–31.
[48]*Les Très Riches Heures du Duc de Berry*, intro. Jean Longnon and Raymond Cazelles (London,
1969), Plate 19 (F. 22ʳ). Another king in this illumination has, as the commentators point out, a face
resembling medals of the early Caesars.

III Augustus in Renaissance Argument

> In the life of Augustus, we behold the tyrant of the
> republic, converted, almost by imperceptible degrees,
> into the father of his country and of human kind.
> (Edward Gibbon, *The Decline and Fall of The Roman
> Empire*, Ch. XVIII)

Petrarch

It is hardly possible to speak of the Renaissance reputation of Augustus. If there
is a dominant tradition from Melito of Sardis to Dante, the Renaissance saw
opinions as opposed as those, say, of Virgil and Tacitus equally forcibly argued.
This chapter will begin and end with the literary forms of epic and panegyric. It
is not, however, in forms such as these that the complexity of Renaissance
thought about Augustus can be found. For this we must turn to more discursive
writing, able to hold a more specific historical and political content. The central
part of this chapter will therefore be devoted to a series of moral and political
works, of which Jean Bodin's *Six Livres de la République* is perhaps the most
impressive example.

It is interesting to compare Augustus's place in the *Divina Commedia* with
that accorded to him in Petrarch's unfinished Latin epic poem *Africa* (1338 ff.).
As Hans Baron points out, the period of Rome which is its subject, and the man
who is its hero, are both significantly Republican. Petrarch's poem, unlike
Dante's, was constructed on the Virgilian model, and its hero, Scipio Africanus,
is accorded in Bk II a visionary dream of Rome's final triumph over her
Carthaginian rival, her victorious subsequent expansion, the success of
Augustus against Antony and Cleopatra, and all his other victories which establish an era of peace over the world. The vision extends to the later history of
Rome: degeneration after Augustus, revival under Vespasian and Titus, final
decay and collapse before the barbarians.[1] This prominent episode of the poem
is plainly modelled on part of Bk VI of the *Aeneid*. There Aeneas's father,
Anchises, prophesied to him the future glory of Rome culminating with the
advent of its second founder, Augustus. Here it is the father of Scipio who
prophesies, and while his purview stretches as far as to the fall of Rome, and
despite Petrarch's humanist sympathy with Republican Rome, Augustus is still
the central glory of the history he foretells.[2] This episode of *Africa* resembles

---

[1] Bk II, ll. 240–58; Francesco Petrarca, *L'Africa*, ed. Nicola Festa (Florence, 1926), pp. 38–9.

[2] The episode of the *Somnium Scipionis*, as preserved in Macrobius's commentary on Cicero's *De
Republica*, VI is likely to have helped shape this section of *Africa*. Hans Baron, in *The Crisis of the
Early Italian Renaissance: Civic Humanism and Republican Liberty in an Age of Classicism and*

Canto VI of the Paradiso only in that it offers a view of Rome from Augustus to her fall, and even in this respect it lacks the extraordinary sense of the unity and headlong movement of Roman history which Canto VI of the Paradiso conveyed. It differs from Dante in the Virgilian prominence it gives Augustus; in Petrarch's poem Augustus is much more than an essential link in the chain of Christian providence. Even when we make the more difficult comparison between Petrarch's Virgilian epic and Dante's political treatise in which Augustus had prominence, we must still be struck by the great difference of presentation. Consistent with Petrarch's purpose of writing a strictly classical epic, Augustus is introduced without any reference to a Christian providential scheme; his glory is a purely Roman glory. While in *Monarchia* Dante had combined Virgilian and Orosian viewpoints, it is the Virgilian alone which survives in *Africa*. The presentation of Augustus is entirely in key with those lines in *Aeneid* VI which expound the Roman destiny to rule; emphasis is placed on his putting down of the powerful, his unification of the world under Roman rule and law, the closing of the gates of the Temple of Janus, and the long reign of peace. Into this grandly general picture an edifying touch from Suetonius is introduced as Augustus is described dying in the embraces of his dear wife.[3] There is no mention of the birth of Christ. In imitating Virgil Petrarch was not imitating the prophet of Christianity which Dante, and others before and after Petrarch, took him to have been.[4]

In this episode of *Africa* Petrarch has in effect disengaged Augustus from the framework of Christian providence and returned him to a secular history. This is in accord with the ways in which Petrarch was a Renaissance figure – a self-conscious pioneer of the revival of classical culture – but Dante was not. There is a further point. Augustus was called to the prominent place he holds in *Monarchia* by Dante's fervent idealization of the imperialist political creed, which was in turn part of his Christian conception of the world. There is a famous episode in the life of Petrarch, to which I shall revert in a later chapter, when he presented ancient coins together with his own work *De Viris Illustribus* to the Emperor Charles IV, to exhort him to emulate his imperial Roman predecessors, and to revive the ancient glory of Rome. One of these coins was a coin of Augustus.[5] Nevertheless Petrarch's attitude to the Holy Roman Empire was quite different from that of Dante. The strange Cola di Rienzo episode suggests that Petrarch also hankered after a revival of Roman republican forms; essentially what he sought was any power at all which promised to promote his ambitious conceptions of cultural revival. The Augustus of Bk II of *Africa* is not the embodiment of the one divinely sanctioned form of political rule; he is the glory of the historical achievement of Rome.[6]

Tyranny (Princeton, 1955; rev. edn, 1966), pp. 55–6, has good comments on *Africa* but rather underplays the favourable humanist presentation of Augustus himself in Scipio's dream.

[3] *Africa*, II, ll. 248–58; Suetonius, *De Vita Caesarvm*, Divvs Avgvstvs, ed. cit. I, p. 39.

[4] For a fully developed form of Christian interpretation of Virgil see the Oration to the Clergy supposed to have been delivered by the Emperor Constantine, included in certain editions of Eusebius, and in the third edition of Meredith Hanmer's English version, pp. 123–8.

[5] Petrarch, *Epistolae de Rebus Familiaribus et Variae*, ed. Fracassetti (Florence, 1859–63), II, p. 520. For a fuller discussion, see Chapter X below.

[6] On Petrarch's political views, see J.H. Whitfield, *Petrarch and the Renaissance* (Oxford, 1943), p. 36.

Petrarch's attitude to Augustus seems to link naturally with the use of the Augustan comparison in fifteenth-century panegyric upon the Florentine merchant-statesmen Cosimo and Lorenzo de Medici. Dante's concern with Augustus was universalist, providential and political; for him a new Augustus had to be the Emperor. For Petrarch, despite the Charles IV episode, this consequence was not necessary; an ideal of cultural renovation might be embodied in a figure of a very different kind. Cosimo de Medici was praised in three ways: as a republican statesman comparable to Scipio Africanus or Cicero, as an Aristotelian ruler whose influence was related to his learning, and finally by poets following the lead of Cristoforo Landino, lecturer on Virgil and Horace and commentator on Dante, as a new Maecenas and a new Augustus.[7] The title of *Pater Patriae*, conferred on Cosimo at his death, seems originally to have been given him for its republican associations. It was of course no less applicable to a man whom some praised as an Augustus. The poets Ugolini Verino and Naldo Naldi emulated the Messianic note of Virgil in hailing Cosimo as an Augustus who would bring back an Age of Gold; Fontius and Brandolini wrote of Lorenzo de Medici in the same strain.[8] If the literary origins of this praise are Virgilian, the social motives are a clear bid for patronage, and it is of great interest that, whereas republican forms of praise were used by those socially closer to the rank of the Medici family, imperial forms, the comparison with Augustus, were used by those at a lower, more professional or impoverished social level.[9] The political content is far more elusive, for the age-old motif of *laus saeculi* and hope for a new era, especially when deployed in ceremonial, panegyric and lyric poetry, is not always politically specific. Praise which may seem formally similar may differ in political implication depending on its specific historical context. If we are to draw closer to the different Renaissance conceptions of Augustus we must seek and explore more explicit literary forms.

Such forms would need to be sensitive to different viewpoints on Augustus, or at least consciously selective of one rather than another evaluation. For while the providential interpretation of Augustus continued as a potent tradition at least as far down as the time of Alexander Pope,[10] and while it is hardly true that men like Petrarch altered men's view of Augustus overnight, a more or less secular view of the *princeps* was slowly disseminated. Within the context of that view it was easier for the classical debate about Augustus to be revived and extended. Such debate was fed by a growing familiarity with some of the classical texts bearing on Augustus which had been rediscovered in the Renaissance: notably Tacitus and Cassius Dio.[11] It is probable, too, that those

[7]See Alison M. Brown, 'The Humanist Portrait of Cosimo de Medici', *Journal of the Warburg and Courtauld Institutes*, XXIV (1961), pp. 168–291. For the Latin background see L.K. Born, 'The Perfect Prince According to the Latin Panegyrists', *American Journal of Philology*, LV (1934), pp. 68–99.

[8]E.H. Gombrich, 'Renaissance and Golden Age', *Journal of the Warburg and Courtauld Institutes*, XXIV (1961), pp. 306–9.

[9]Alison Brown, art. cit. p. 207.

[10]See Francis Atterbury, *Sermons and Discourses on Several Subjects and Occasions* (London, 1723), I, pp. 102–4 (Sermon of 1694), and Pope's poetic synthesis of Virgil's Fourth Eclogue and Isaiah: *Messiah: A Sacred Eclogue* (1712).

[11]MSS of all Tacitus's surviving works were known by 1509, and much was translated into French, Italian, German and English in the sixteenth century: see R.R. Bolgar, *The Classical Heritage and its Beneficiaries* (Cambridge, 1954), pp. 356–7. MSS of Cassius Dio were recorded

aspects of *The City of God* which cast an unfavourable light on Augustus were given new attention, and not passed over as minor detail beside Augustine's more conspicuous praise of the Roman achievement at its best.[12] All this, it may fairly be conjectured, lies behind the passage from Montaigne's Essay 'On the Inconsistency of Our Actions' which stands as the epigraph to Chapter I: that professed agnosticism concerning Augustus, that readiness to consider him as an historical character of bewilderingly various behaviour, could hardly be in greater contrast with the bold outline and religious certainty of Dante's portrayal in the *Monarchia*.

Prince Literature

The sixteenth century displays a range of writing, in different measure moral, educational, historical and political, which affords the opportunity of surveying the variety of thought about Augustus during this period – the period immediately preceding the advent of the Augustan idea in imaginative literature in English. It extends from that well-defined and much used form of the manual *de regimine principum*, the book of instruction and exhortation for rulers, of which Erasmus's *Institutio principis Christiani* (1516) is an example, and Machiavelli's *Il Principe* (*c.* 1513–16) an iconoclastic counter-example, to full-length political and historical treatises, such as Bodin's *Six Livres de la République* (1576) and Justus Lipsius's *Sex Libri Politicorum* (1588–9). Yet throughout this range, from Erasmus to Bodin, from the educational humanism of Sir Thomas Elyot to the passionate concern of Gentillet with a specific historical moment, the didactic preoccupation of 'Prince Literature' is always felt.

The characteristic procedure of 'Prince Literature' is to instruct by precept and example. Celebrated or notorious rulers are cited in support of one moral point or another, especially if knowledge of such rulers happens to have come down in anecdotal form. Instances of the example of Augustus are just what one would expect to find in works like these; what is significant is their nature and relative frequency or infrequency. Erasmus's citations of Augustus are typical of the form before Machiavelli takes it up. Erasmus makes two references to the Emperor Alexander Severus, five to Augustus and six to Alexander the Great. His stance is notably cool and detached. He notes that Augustus gained the imperial throne through 'foul intrigue' yet still refused to be called 'Lord'. Augustus liked to be painted in the likeness of Apollo, yet was, along with Aristides, Epaminondas, Trajan, Antoninus Pius and Alexander Mamineas, 'one of the best leaders from the whole throng'.[13] He cites the Cinna episode out of Seneca in praise of the clemency of Augustus, and declares that rulers such as Achilles, Xerxes, Darius and Julius Caesar are 'great raging robbers' and Alexander the Great ambitious to the point of madness.[14] Despite his praise,

---

between 1421 and 1481, and he was translated into Latin by 1526 by N. Leonecimus (Bolgar, pp. 435, 470). The single MS of Velleius Paterculus was discovered in 1515.

[12]Machiavelli's discussion of the rise of Octavian, in *Discorsi*, LII, is strikingly similar to that of Augustine in Bk III, Ch. xxx of *De Civitate Dei*, though the explanation may be a common source in Plutarch's Life of Cicero.

[13]Erasmus, *Institutio principis Christiani* (1516); tr. L.K. Born (New York, 1936; 1965 reprint), pp. 176–7, 202.

[14]Ibid., pp. 172, 232, 201, 245–6.

Erasmus, by comparison with Petrarch, Dante and Orosius, does not idealize Augustus. He briefly notes the bad alongside the good, and if his verdict is on balance favourable he makes no attempt to resolve the problem of the different aspects of Augustus. The *Adagia* of Erasmus, built up in a series of collections from 1500 to the year of his death, also contained remarks about Augustus which were influential in the Renaissance. There is no question of the *princeps* being a special example: one of the best rulers of Rome, he is nevertheless one among countless historical examples selected as occasions for instruction in wisdom, expression and learning. The proverb 'Festina Lente', from the *Adagiorum Chiliades* of 1508, is an excellent example, and one remembered by later writers, notably Sir Thomas Elyot:

> . . . this proverb was a favourite with two Roman emperors, and they by far the most worthy of praise, Octavius Augustus and Titus Vespasianus. Each of them had a notable greatness of mind, and at the same time an incredible gentleness and leniency, so that they attached the affection of all by their kindliness towards the people, but they were also equally successful in dealing promptly with the greatest matters, when the situation demanded a man. Octavius, as I said, was so heartily in favour of this saying (as Aulus Gellius recounts . . .) that not only he used it often in daily speech, but often quoted it in his letters, indicating by these two words that the matter in hand was to be treated with the speed of diligence and the slowness of deliberation. Gellius thinks this can be conveyed in Latin by one word, *Matura*. For *maturare* means to do nothing over-hastily, nor later than it should be done, but at the very time. Virgil uses it in this way when he says in the *Aeneid*, book 1, *Maturate fugam*, hasten your flight.[15]

Machiavelli's *Il Principe* uses the well-understood contemporary form of 'Prince Literature' to define itself, in a highly self-conscious way, against the predominantly though not completely idealistic content of the earlier tradition. It is within this framework of literary communication that Machiavelli lays stress upon a secular *raison d'état*, and while this aspect of political relations was not neglected in relevant medieval and earlier Renaissance writing, it had perhaps never before been given such a rhetorical concentration of focus: rhetorical not in the use of high-flown periods to persuade but the terse and apparently cold form of the maxim. Now it may seem surprising that Machiavelli, concerned as he was with the problems of the new prince, and with

---

[15]'Festina Lente' in *The Adages of Erasmus: A Study With Translations*, by M.M. Phillips (Cambridge, 1964), pp. 173–4. 'Itaque non sine causa uideo factum, ut hoc Σπεῦδε βραδέως intantum arriserit duobus imperatoribus Romanis, omnium facile laudatissimis. Octauio Augusto, & Tito Vespasiano, Quorum utrique singularis quædam aderat animi magnitudo, cum incredibili quadam lenitate, facilitateque coniuncta, ut cum amabili morum popularitate omnium animos sibi deuinxerint, nihilo secius tamen pari diligentia, siquando res uirum postularet, celeriter res maximas confecerint. Octauius igitur, hoc dicto, tam impense delectatus est, quemadmodum in noctibus Atticis narrat Aulus Gellius, ut non in sermonibus modo quotidianis crebrius usurparet, uerumetiam epistolis suis frequenter insereret, admonens his duabus uocibus, ut ad rem agendam adhiberetur simul & industriæ celeritas & diligentiæ tarditas. Quod quidem Gellius Latinis existimat unico uerbo dici, Matura. Nam maturari, quod neque præpropere fiat, neque serius quàm oporteat, sed ipso in tempore. In hunc sensum usurpasse Maronem, cum ait Aeneidos libro primo: Maturate fugam.' *Erasmi Roterodami Adagiorum Chiliades Tres* . . . (Venice, 1508), f. 112ᵛ. For the significance the proverb could assume, see Edgar Wind, *Pagan Mysteries in the Renaissance* (1958; enlarged edn, London, 1968), pp. 97–112.

territories not accustomed to his rule, should neglect to derive precepts from that period of what Erasmus called 'foul intrigue' by which Augustus had risen to power, and from the long and successful period in which Augustus as a new prince subsequently consolidated the Roman state in a new form. There is no reference to Augustus in *The Prince*. It is a significant and perhaps pointed omission. Its meaning becomes more clear in the light of Machiavelli's remarks on Augustus in the *Discorsi* (c. 1513–19) and the *Dell'arte della Guerra* (*Of the Art of War*) (1519–20), but we may in any case infer that lack of reference to Augustus is one way in which *The Prince* associates itself with earlier traditions of Italian civic humanism, while marking itself off from earlier Prince literature.[16] A further inference may be hazarded: that for Machiavelli the political significance of Augustus was still firmly associated with the Christian ideal of the providential empire. Meinecke, in his broad-ranging exposition of the significance of Machiavelli, has argued that the modern West inherited from the 'Christian and Germanic Middle Ages' a new sharper sense of 'the conflict between *raison d'état* on the one hand, and ethics and law on the other . . .'; in the Augustinian view of the world the state was subordinated to a universal religion and universal moral command.[17] It is evident from the examples of Orosius and Dante that the universalist political ideal could be integrally connected with that religious and moral overstructure, that potent system of belief which, even in times when the ideal of universal empire had small political content, still led writers of Prince literature to identify the good prince with the good Christian. But it was that against which Machiavelli was writing, and 'could set about . . . analysing the essence of *raison d'état* with all the naivety of the ancient world'.[18]

Our impression of Machiavelli's view of Augustus, so far speculative, is filled out, but also complicated, when we turn to his marginally later political writings, in which Augustus *is* mentioned. Consider first, however, a passage from the *Discorsi* where the omission is just about as pointed as it could possibly be. In I, x. he discusses Julius Caesar and warns the reader not to be deceived by his apparent eminence, since those who wrote of him were either corrupted or without liberty; Caesar was worse than Catiline. After Rome had become an empire, with power in the hands of one person, how much more happy than Caesar were those who like good princes observed the laws: Titus, Nerva, Trajan, Hadrian, Antoninus and Marcus – between Nerva and Marcus, then it was that 'The times were golden.'[19] The last statement is a clear challenge to the Virgilian view of Augustus and its later Christianized versions. Augustus, by implication, cannot be admired because he completed his uncle's subversion of Roman liberty; if one must praise an emperor, one should praise (and here Machiavelli suddenly sounds the moral note of traditional Prince literature) those emperors who kept the Roman state as they found it and observed the laws. The republican stance is even more marked in the one passage of the *Discorsi* in

[16]See Hans Baron, *Crisis of the Early Italian Renaissance*, pp. 76–8, 128–9; and Allan Gilbert, *Machiavelli's Prince and its Forerunners: The Prince as a Typical Book de Regimine Principum* (Durham, North Carolina, 1938), pp. 41, 72, 90. For recent discussion, see Quentin Skinner, *The Foundations of Modern Political Thought* (Cambridge, 1978), I, *The Renaissance*, Ch. 5.

[17]Friedrich Meinecke, *Machiavellism: The Doctrine of Raison D'Etat and its Place in Modern History* (1924), tr. Douglas Scott (London, 1957), p. 28.

[18]Ibid., p. 29.

[19]*Discorsi*, I, x; *Machiavels Discourses* . . ., tr. E[dward] D[acres] (London, 1636), pp. 281–2.

which Augustus is mentioned at any length; not surprisingly Machiavelli is considering Augustus's rise to power, and he is identifying with Cicero:

> Therefore men ought in every resolution, consider the defects and dangers thereunto belonging, and not fasten on any one of them, when they can carry with them more danger, than profit, notwithstanding that they seem well to tend to the end propounded: for doing otherwise, in this case it would befall them, as it befell *Tullius*, who by going about to diminish *Marc Antonius* his power, increas'd it. For *Marc Antonius* being judged enemy of the Senate, and he having got together a great armye, a good part whereof had followed *Cesars* faction, *Tullius* to take these souldiers from him, perswaded the Senate, to set up the reputation of *Octauianus*, and send him accompanied by the Consuls, and an Armie against *Marc Antonius*, alleadging, that so soone as ere the souldiers, that followed *Marc Antonius*, should heare the name *Octauianus*, *Cesars* nephew, and that would be call'd *Cesar* too, they would forsake the other, and follow this. So that *Marcus Antonius* being dispossest of his advantages would easily be suppressed. Which fell out cleane contrary. For *Marc Antonius* got *Octauianus* to his part, who leaving *Tullius* and the Senate joyned forces with him. Which thing proov'd wholly the ruin of those great mens party. Which also it was easy to have conjectur'd: nor was that credible which *Tullius* persuaded himselfe, but hee should rather have made account, that neither that name that with so great glory had exterminated his enemyes, and gained himself the principality in Rome nor yet his heires, or adherents would ever suffer him quietly to injoy their liberty.[20]

This may seem a full revival of the Tacitean view of Augustus, Machiavelli writing in the tradition of the Roman Republican historians. But neither the surviving Tacitus, nor (the groundwork of the *Discorsi*) the surviving Livy, discusses this moment of Roman history. It seems to be in debt to Plutarch's Life of Cicero, and to Bk III, Ch. xxx, of *The City of God*.[21] Machiavelli found there just the stance and tone he needed to get into perspective that ruler who, if he were not regarded as the founder of a providential empire, was almost always regarded as a good ruler, 'one of the best . . . from the whole throng'. Against both those views, Machiavelli uncompromisingly asserts a third. It was one which in England was to attain its most forcible expression from James Harrington in the mid-seventeenth century.

---

[20]Ibid., I, lii; pp. 321–2. 'Debbono per tanto gli huomini in ogni partito considerare i diffetti & i pericoli di quello, & non gli prendere, quando vi sia più del pericoloso che dell'vtile, non ostante che ne fusse stata data sentenza conforme alla deliberation loro. Perchè facendo altrimenti, in questo caso interuerrebbe à quelli, come interuenne à Tullio, il quale volendo torre i fauori à Marc'Antonio, gliene accrebbe: perche sendo Marc'Antonio stato giudicato inimico del Senato, & hauendo quello, grande essercito insieme, adunato in bona parte, de' soldati che haueuano seguitato la parte di Cesare, Tullio per torgli questi soldati, confortò il Senato à dare riputatione ad Ottaviano, & mandarlo con l'essercito & con i Consoli contra à Marc'Antonio, allegando, che subito che i soldati che seguitauano Marc'Antonio sentissino il nome d'Ottauiano nipote di Cesare, & che si faceua chiamar Cesare, lascerebbono quello, & s'accostarabbono à costui, & così restato Marc'Antonio ignudo di fauori, sarebbe facile l'opprimerlo. La qual cosa riuscì tutta al contrario; perche Marc'Antonio si guadagnò Ottauiano, & lasciato Tullio & il Senato, si accostò à lui. La qual cosa, fù al tutto la destruttione della parte de gli Ottimati. Il che era facile à conietturare, ne si doueua credere quel che si persuase Tullio, ma tener sempre conto di quel nome che con tanta gloria hauea spenti inimici suoi, & acquistatosi il Principato in Roma, ne si douea credere mai potere, ò da suoi fautori, hauer'cosa che fusse conforme al nome libero' (*Tutte Le Opere di Nicolo Machiavelli . . . Al Santissimo et Beatissimo Padre . . . Clement VII (1550), Discorsi*, p. 92).

[21]See n. 12 above.

But we have not yet encompassed all Machiavelli's thought about Augustus. The apparently simple republican view of the *Discorsi* has another aspect, and one which helps to relate the political thinking of the later works to that of *The Prince*. In the *Discorsi* Machiavelli can remark that there are fewer commonwealths in the world now than in ancient times, and that Rome was responsible for this, since though small states and peoples had fought fiercely for their liberty when Rome was expanding, few recovered it after the Empire fell.[22] In *The Art of War* Fabritio, a participant in the dialogue, enlarges on this view, and notes how the Roman Empire absorbed into Rome and there corrupted almost all excellence, bravery and virtue in the world, thus preparing its own fall, since virtue most flourishes where there are most principalities and governments.[23] The strictly military dimension of this process is expounded with direct reference to Augustus. Arguing Machiavelli's reiterated opinion that states should have a militarily trained citizenry rather than rely on professional soldiers, Fabritio notes that:

> . . . Octavian first, and after Tiberius, minding more their own proper power, then the publike profite, began to unarme the Romaine people, to be able easely to commaunde them, and to kepe continually those same armies on the frontiers of the Empire: and bicause also they judged those, not sufficient to kepe brideled the people and the Romaine Senate, they ordeined an armie called Pretoriano, which laie hard by the walles of Rome, and was as a rocke on the backe of the same Citie. And for as much as then thei began frely to permitte, that such men as were appoincted in such exercises, should use the service of warre for their arte [i.e. be professional soldiers], streight waie the insolence of them grew, that they became fearful unto the Senate, and hurtefull to the Emperour . . . of whiche thinges proceded first the devision of the Empire, and at laste the ruine of the same.[24]

From these passages it becomes clear that the Machiavelli of the later works is not just one who prefers republican to monarchical forms of government, but one whose more fundamental affirmation is for whatever form or change most promises to create or sustain excellence, bravery and virtue: that is, in Machiavelli's potent sense, *virtù*. The monarchical super-state relying on professional soldiers, the creation of Julius Caesar and Augustus, was of all kinds of state, in Machiavelli's view, most likely to corrupt and least likely to nourish *virtù*. But, as Meinecke has observed, there was a strain of monarchism in his

---

[22]*Discorsi*, II, ii; tr. Edward Dacres, p. 336.

[23]*Dell' arte della Guerra*, II, xiii; *The Art of Warre . . . by Nicholas Machiavell and set forthe in Englishe by Peter Whitehorne* (London, 1560; Tudor Translations Series, London, 1905), pp. 93–5. Machiavelli is here in the same tradition as Leonardo Bruni; see Baron, *Crisis of the Early Italian Renaissance*, pp. 70–1.

[24]Ibid., I, iv; Whitehorne, pp. 38–9. 'Perche Ottauiano prima, & poi Tiberio, pensando più alla potenza propria, che all'vtile publico, cominciarono à disarmare il populo Romano, per poterlo facilmente comandare, & à tenere continuamente quelli medessimi esserciti alle frontiere dell'Imperio, Et perche ancora non giudicarono bastassero à tener in freno il populo & Senato Romano, ordinarono vn'essercito chiamato Pretoriano, il quale staua proprinquo alle mura di Roma, & era come vna rocca adosso à quella città. Et perche all'hora ei cominciarono liberamente à permettere, che gli huomoni deputati in quelli esserciti, usassero la militia per loro arte, ne nacque subito l'insolenza di quelli, & diuentarono formidabili al Senato & dannosi all'Imperatore . . . Dalle quali cose procedè prima, la diuisione dell'Imperio, & in vltimo, la roina di quello' (*Opere* (1550), *Dell' Arte Della Guerra*, pp. 15–16).

republican ideal, since he believed that *virtù* could be consciously nurtured as well as be, for periods, the natural possession of a people; and that in thoroughly corrupt commonwealths only the single great leader could regenerate them.[25] Thus Machiavelli's concern in *Il Principe* with how a new state under a new ruler might be established is not, in its deeper preoccupations, inconsistent with the overt republicanism of the later works. Hence too it was unthinkable that Machiavelli, with these particular concepts of *virtù* and corruption underlying his discussion, should ever derive any positive precept of his *raison d'état* from the example of Augustus. He was not as coolly analytic as his literary form sometimes suggests. In this case passionate political conviction prevented him gaining from Augustus certain appreciative political insights (the views for example, of Virgil and Horace), and even from recognizing in him the most telling example he could have hoped to conjure with in his arguments on *raison d'état*.

Machiavelli's hostility to Julius Caesar and Augustus was not therefore the result of unqualified republicanism. But admirers of the Roman Republic, and supporters of republican principles in their own time, found little to approve of in Augustus, and were unlikely to welcome panegyrical parallels between Augustus and modern rulers. For supporters of the monarchical principle, on the other hand, or for those who simply accepted monarchy as a fact of life, the reign of Augustus was richly edifying and worthy of fame.

Educational Humanism

Sir Thomas Elyot, a convinced royalist, was one of these. It is improbable that he had heard anything of Machiavelli's political writings when he wrote his *Boke Named the Governour* (1531). *Il Principe* and the *Discorsi* circulated in manuscript before their first printing in 1532.[26] Elyot's book developed from a knowledge of pre-Machiavellian Prince literature, and from the author's familiarity with the advanced humanist circle centred on the family of Thomas More. It has none of the political intensity of Machiavelli, but takes a humanistic pleasure in the arts and activities of mankind, and is at its heart an educational work. Yet it begins with a statement of monarchical theory, and the sequence of the work suggests that in opening out the education proper for a prince or magistrat Elyot is displaying the elements of the civilization which a good and wise prince will display. Elyot's argument for monarchy stresses the political advantage, and the divine and natural rightness, of the single ruler. Little is said about the advantages, or disadvantages, of monarchy in determining the succession of rule. Monarchy is the 'manner of gouernaunce [that] is best approued, and . . . moste auncient. For who can denie but that all thynge in heauen and erthe is gouerned by one god, by one perpetuall ordre, by one prouidence? One sonne ruleth ouer the day, and one Moone ouer

---

[25]Meinecke, *Machiavellism*, pp. 41–4.

[26]For a review of the composition of Machiavelli's works, see Sydney Anglo, *Machiavelli: A Dissection* (London, 1969), pp. 23–4. For MSS of Machiavelli in England, see Felix Raab, *The English Face of Machiavelli: A Changing Interpretation* (London, 1964), pp. 52–3. The point is discussed in Stanford E. Lehmberg, *Sir Thomas Elyot: Tudor Humanist* (Austin, Texas, 1960), pp. 69–70, 86–8.

the nyghte . . .'[27] Such argument by analogy, which ties metaphysical reason and rhetorical persuasion into one knot, was to be of immense importance for the next century and a half in English political and historical thought.[28] But Elyot also seeks to support his view from history: from the Old Testament, Homeric Greece, the Greek democracies, ancient and modern Italy, ancient and modern England. His remarks on Italy show him diametrically opposed to the views of Machiavelli. With surprising boldness he defends the early kings of Rome, and is so far from admiring the Republic that he attributed such stability as it had to the Senate, the creation of the kings of Rome; and its military success to its creation of '*Dictators*', temporary sovereigns, in whom there appeared 'the pristinate authoritie and maiestie of a kyng'.[29] In this picture of Roman history Augustus figures as the restorer to Rome of the most ancient, most natural and best form of government: monarchy.[30] It is hardly what Augustus thought he was restoring; and he must have seen the *de facto* monarchy as an innovation. Elyot's view is the more convincing to him because he takes for granted still the long perspectives of Christian universal history. Turning to modern times, Elyot notes the calamities suffered by Florence and Genoa 'for lacke of a continuall gouernour', whereas Ferrara and Venice (which last he cites as an example of single rule) 'seldome suffreth damage'.[31]

It is thus Augustus has place in Elyot's political theory. But he is most memorably portrayed in respect of his political, and (one might say) humanistic qualities. Most striking is Elyot's discussion of the quality of 'maturity' (the word is of Elyot's own coinage) in his chapter on the moral virtue of Prudence:

> Maturitie is a meane betwene two extremities, wherin nothing laketh or excedeth, and is in suche a state that it may neither encrease or minisshe without losinge the denomination of Maturitie. The grekes in a prouerbe do expresse it proprely in two wordes, whiche I can none otherwyse interprete in englisshe, but speede the slowly.
>
> Also of this worde Maturitie sprange a noble and preciouse sentence, recited by Salust in the bataile againe Cataline, whiche is in this maner or like, Consulte before thou enterprise any thing, and after thou hast taken counsaile, it is expedient to do it maturely.
>
> *Maturum* in latine maye be enterpreted ripe or redy, as fruite whan it is ripe, it is at the very poynte to be gathered and eaten. . . . Therfore that worde maturitie is translated to the actis of man, that whan they be done with suche moderation, that nothing in the doinge may be sene superfluous or indigent, we may say that they be maturely done. . . .
>
> In the most excellent and most noble emperour Octauius Augustus, in whom reigned all nobilitie, nothinge is more commended than that he had frequently in his mouthe this worde *Matura*, do maturely. As he sholde haue saide, do neither to moche ne to litle, to soone ne to late, to swiftly nor sloely, but in due tyme and measure.[32]

[27]*The Boke Named the Governour Deuised by Sir Thomas Elyot, Knight* . . ., I, ii; ed. H.H.S. Croft, 2 vols. (London, 1880), I, pp. 11–2. Cf. the views of Giovanni Conversino, as discussed by Baron, *Crisis of the Early Italian Renaissance*, pp. 144–5.

[28]See W.H. Greenleaf, *Order, Empiricism and Politics: Two Traditions of English Political Thought, 1550–1700* (Oxford, 1964), Chs. II and III.

[29]*The Boke Named the Governour*, I, ii; ed. Croft, I, pp. 19–20. Cf. Coluccio Salutati's view of Roman history: see Baron, *Crisis of the Early Italian Renaissance*, p. 148.

[30]*The Boke Named the Governour*, I, ii; ed. Croft, I, p. 20.

[31]Ibid., I, ii; Croft I, p. 22.

[32]Ibid., I, xxii; Croft, I, pp. 244–5.

Elyot does not, like Erasmus, comment on the dark side of Augustus's career, though it is hardly conceivable he was unaware of it.[33] But when he praises Augustus it is more than a conventional gesture. In this passage Elyot has with a humane and historical perceptiveness fastened upon a real feature of Augustus as *princeps*. If we reflect how exactly appropriate 'do maturely' (as here defined) is to Augustus's establishment of the principate, or how through his whole career the political resources of his character seem to have developed with his power to a 'ripeness', it is clear that in Elyot we have found a mind intelligently engaged with the subject: he is closer to understanding Augustus than writers such as Dante or Orosius who might be lavish of praise.

The quoted paragraphs contain what, on a reading of Elyot's whole book, it is reasonable to see as his main emphasis in writing about Augustus. It is supported by a number of specific allusions. An example of a consonant detail, twice mentioned, is Augustus's habit of relying on prepared texts and notes when he spoke in public.[34] Elyot and his Suetonian source make the relevance clear when they observe that Augustus feared saying too much or too little by speaking extempore. A more substantial point concerns the attitude of Augustus to freedom of speech: 'whanne it was shewed hym that many men in the citie had of hym unfitting words, he thought it as sufficient answere that in a free city men muste have their tunges nedes at libertie.' Elyot's argument is that patience in the face of libel brings less trouble than anger, and the best refutation is example.[35] This is a fair moralizing of the relevant passages in Suetonius, though it goes beyond the source, in the actual words attributed to Augustus.[36] More prominent than either of these points in Elyot's discussion is, as might be expected, the historically problematical Cinna episode, which Elyot takes from Seneca's *De Clementia*. It is again apparent that Elyot is giving prominence to material which supports his theme of political maturity: Augustus's very considered decision neither to ignore his information about Cinna's conspiracy, nor to execute the conspirator, but rather to confront him with his crime and then pardon him, was an admirable example for his book. It could be brought into the chapter which commended mercy in rulers, yet so handled that the political sagacity, the wise self-interest which was also the interest of the state, was apparent in the telling of the tale. Even so, a few minor changes indicate the bent of Elyot's interpretation. Seneca, at the start of his story, made brief reference to Augustus's part in the Proscriptions. This is omitted by Elyot. In outlining the political drawbacks in punishing Cinna, Elyot rather expands on the danger of an outbreak of civil war: 'effusion of the bloode of persones innumerable, and also perile of the subuersion of the empire late pacified'. Finally, in the dramatic scene in which Augustus taxes Cinna with his crime, while Seneca made him accuse the conspirator of 'parricide' (i.e. murder of Augustus, the *pater patriae*), Elyot, in a no doubt easy but nonetheless misleading translation, makes the *princeps* charge Cinna with plotting murder

[33]Erasmus had, after all, plainly alluded to the way Octavian came to power (see n. 9 above), as had Suetonius whom Elyot draws upon.

[34]*The Boke Named the Governour*, II, ii; Croft, II, p. 16. *De Vita Caesarvm*, Divvs Avgvstvs, 84; ed. Maximilian Ihm (Stuttgart, 1967), p. 95.

[35]*The Boke Named the Governour*, III, xii; Croft, II, p. 282.

[36]*De Vita Caesarvm*, Divvs Avgvstvs, 51, 54; Ihm, pp. 78, 79. Croft notes (II, p. 282) that Elyot is following Pontanus.

'of thy soueraygne lorde, whom thou oughtest to loue as thy father.[37] With engaging enthusiasm Elyot then moralizes the episode which Seneca had already shaped to edify:

> O what sufficient prayse may be gyuen to this moste noble and prudent Emperour, that in a chambre alone, without men, ordenaunce, or waipon, and perchaunce without harnes, within the space of ii houres, with wordes well couched, tempered with maiestie, nat onely vainquisshed and subdued one mortall enemie, whiche by a malignitie, engendered of a domesticall hatred, had determined to slee him, but by the same feate excluded out of the whole cite of Rome all displeasure and rencour towardes hym, so that there was nat lefte any occasion wherof mought procede any lytell suspicion of treason, whiche other wyse could nat haue hapned without slaughter of people innumerable.[38]

Elyot's purpose of moral exhortation is the more clearly seen in the way he seizes on a moral story of this kind.

Despite the clear political content of these discussions of Augustus, a reading of Elyot's book as a whole shows that this example, like those of other famous rulers, is subordinate to an overall educational, humanistic and religious purpose. Augustus was apt for Elyot's design in a number of simple moral ways. 'The noble Augustus and almost all the olde emperours made bokes in verses', Elyot notes, and again, 'the Emperor Octauius Augustus disdayned nat to read the workes of Cicero and Virgile to his children and neuewes.'[39] In speaking of the visual arts, as worthy of the practice of princes and nobility, Elyot has occasion to note that Vitruvius wrote 'of buyldyng to the emperour Augustus';[40] this is the first of many instances in English writing which associate together the names of Augustus and Vitruvius, the idea of successful rule with architectural achievement. Augustus is praised for the moderation, temperance and frugality of his later life; Elyot supports this point by narrating an episode from Suetonius in which the triumvir was severely criticized for taking part, in the guise of Apollo, in a sumptuous banquet, 'the citie of Rome at that tyme beinge vexed with a skarcitie of grayne'.[41] Like Elyot's famous story of how Prince Hal repented to the Lord Chief Justice, this anecdote also has the merit of showing how a ruler may be great enough to admit his mistakes and reform. Paradoxically, that Octavian should have participated in such an Antony-like scene, but thereafter reformed, can only have contributed to the picture of an Augustus puritanically horrified by just such scenes; an Augustus such as we are to find in Jonson's *Poetaster*.

Despite his endorsement of monarchy and admiration of the Augustan empire, Elyot does not allow them to complete his prospect of human endeavour. Worldly achievement, though a rich source of fascination and

[37]*The Boke Named the Governour*, II, vii; Croft, II, pp. 75, 77. Cf. Seneca, *De Clementia*, I, ix; ed. Hosius, pp. 222–5, where Augustus, alluding to the title 'Pater Patriae', refers to himself only as 'father'.
[38]*Boke Named the Governour*, II, vii; Croft, II, p. 78. Elyot's didactic interest in the Roman emperors extended to his later *Image of Governance compiled of the actes and sentences notable of the moste noble Emperour Alexander Seuerus . . .* (1540).
[39]Ibid., I, x; Croft, I, p. 33.
[40]Ibid., I, viii; Croft, I. p. 44.
[41]Ibid., III, xxii; Croft, II, p. 336.

edification, is set, finally, in an unworldly perspective. In order to draw from the life of Augustus a moral against ambition he almost reverses his political priorities; for Augustus

> whiche in felicitie passed all emperours, deuised often tymes with his frendes to haue resigned his autoritie. And if at that tyme the Senate had ben as well fournisshed with noble and wise personages as it was before the Ciuile warres betwene Cesar and Pompei, it is to be thought that he wolde surely haue restored the publike weale to its pristinate glorie.[42]

In the overview of the 'beginning, prosperity, and desolation' of Rome, afforded by some of the later paragraphs of his book, Elyot strikes an adroit balance between his admiration of classical learning and his religious sense of the mutability of the Roman achievement. With an almost Orosian historical sweep Elyot notes how Romulus originally chose senators and was guided by their wisdom, how Rome flourished so long as the sapience of its senate was held in respect, but how after Constantine removed it to Constantinople, and its later neglect by the folly of ignorant emperors, 'not only that most noble city . . . but also the majesty of the Empire decayed utterly,

> so that uneth a litle shadowe therof nowe remayneth; which who so beholdeth and conferreth it with Rome whan it flourished, accordinge as it is lefte in remembraunce by noble writars, he uneth kepe teares out of his eyen, beholdynge it nowe as a rotten shepecote, in comparison of that citie noble and triumphant.[43]

In both theme and emotion Elyot's humanistic prose here enters the rhetorical realm of Du Bellay's *Antiquitez de Rome*.

Bodin and Gentillet

Prince literature was not only a mode capable of evolution to meet changing circumstances, but lent itself to incorporation into the structure of works different and more ambitious in aim. This may be seen by comparing Guillaume Budé's *L'Institut du Prince* (1547) with the writings of Bodin and Gentillet. Augustus figures in Budé as an example of a good prince – praised for his moderation, modesty, political discretion, liberality to poets and learning, and for having effaced his early crimes by his later wise rule – but his example is put to fuller use in the two later writers. Innocent Gentillet's *Discours sur les moyens de bien gouverner . . . un Royaume ou autre Principauté* (1576), often known as the *Contre-Machiavel*, is an example of Prince literature with a controversial design and special contemporary application. Jean Bodin's *Les Six Livres de la République*, published in the same year, is a work of a different kind, an attempt to discern a symbolic order in the patterns of history, and to propose a theory of sovereignty within the state. Bodin's book was a major and influential work of political theory, perhaps the greatest of the sixteenth century. The reign of Augustus is of crucial concern to each author, conspicuously so in Gentillet, who proposes it as the chief of several political examples for imitation, but quite

---

[42]Ibid., III, xvi; Croft, II, pp. 300–1.
[43]Ibid., III, xxiii; Croft, II, p. 357.

clearly so in Bodin, to whom it presented a certain challenge to the historical and political understanding.

At the simplest level, Bodin shares with Elyot and Gentillet a desire to commend Augustus as a good ruler. Thus he can compare '*Marcus Antonius*, a man altogether given to riot and voluptuous pleasure', with 'the great *Augustus*, a most wise & sober prince'.[44] He is 'the Great *Augustus*', 'the most wise emperor *Augustus*', who 'surpassed all the rest that came after him . . .'.[45] At the same time, Bodin is far from simple-minded in his reception of this good example; he accords Augustus that degree of historical reality which admits doubt as to his exact actions and motives. Having in one place endorsed the proverb '*That of a craftie and subtil man is made a good king* . . .',[46] Bodin later proceeds to discuss Augustus's treatment of the conspirator Q. Gallus, who had attempted to assassinate him and been condemned for treason by the Senate, but who 'was yet by the same emperour *Augustus* (dissembling the matter as if he had thereof knowne nothing) pardoned, and so sent away vnto his brother . . . but was yet neuerthelesse vpon the way slaine, not without the secret commaundement of *Augustus* himselfe, as many men supposed . . .'. But, Bodin concludes, it is unlikely that Augustus, 'placed in so high a seat of honour and maiestie', can have chosen to stain his honour and reputation by 'secret murder'.[47] Bodin's hesitation on this point, prompted as it is by a sharp awareness of political expediency, firmly establishes Augustus in a political and historical context. A similar awareness of moral and political complexity is to be seen in Bodin's treatment of the Cinna episode. While Elyot was simply eulogistic over the prudence and magnanimity of Augustus, Bodin uses the Seneca story in a rather more tough-minded and probing discussion, which nevertheless does not dismiss the probability of a real ethical impulse in the *princeps*.[48]

We come closer to the new interest which Bodin brings to the traditional

---

[44]Guillaume Budé's *L. Institut du Prince* (Paris, 1547), ff. 35ᵛ–37ʳ; 121ʳ ; 128ʳ–130ᵛ. *The Six Bookes of a Commonweale. Written by I. Bodin a famous Lawyer, and a man of great Experience in matters of State. Out of the French and Latine Copies, done into English, by Richard Knolles* (London, 1606), IV, i, 413–14. '. . . qu' apress la fin malheureuse de Marc Antoine succeda le grand Auguste, & gouuerna l'Empire . . . tres sagement, & vertueusement . . .' (*Les Six Livres de la Republique de I. Bodin* (Paris, 1583), IV, i, 513). Knolles based his translation chiefly on the 1593 Lyon octavo edn, and on the revised Latin edn by Bodin, for Bks I–III, while using the Ober Ursel edn of 1601 for the remaining books. I have drawn my French quotations from the 1583 octavo edition. It is close to the most accurate edn (1580), and embodies Bodin's revisions of the first edn. Since the 1593 edn derives from it, it is sufficiently close to one of those used by Knolles to make it sensible to cite here. It is clear that no one French or Latin edition corresponds exactly to Knolles's English version. See Jean Bodin, *Six Bookes of a Commonweale*, ed. and intro. by K.D. Macrae (Cambridge, 1962), pp. A38–62, A80–1. For helpful views of Bodin, see Greenleaf, *Order and Empiricism*, pp. 125–6, and Quentin Skinner, *The Foundations of Modern Political Thought*, II, *The Age of Reformation*, chiefly Chs. 8–9.

[45]*Six Bookes*, IV, vi, 502; IV, iv, 487; III, i, 263. 'ce grand Auguste'; '. . . comme fit Auguste . . .'; '. . . Carquoy que l'Empereur Auguste surpassait tous les autres, qui depuis l'ont suyui . . .' (*Les Six Livres*, pp. 613, 595, 354).

[46]*Six Bookes*, II, iv, 217. 'De meschant homme bon Roy' (*Six Livres*, p. 295).

[47]*Six Bookes*, IV, vii, 521. 'Auguste dissimula de n'en rien sçavoir, & mesmes apres l'arrest de mort donné par le Senat, il luy donna sa grace, le renuoyant à son frere . . . & neantmoins il fut tué par les chemins, par le secret commandement d'Auguste, ainsi que plusieurs iugerent . . . mais la plus-part, qui auoit bonne opinion de la clemence naturelle de Cesar, & la douceur d'Auguste, n'estimoit pas qu'ils eussent voulu en vser ainsi . . .' (*Six Livres*, p. 637).

[48]*Six Bookes*, IV, i, 431. *Six Livres*, pp. 435–6.

material of Prince literature if we consider his treatment of one of the most often-repeated anecdotes about Augustus in Patristic, Medieval and Renaissance times: his refusal to be called Lord.[49] In Bodin this is at once set in the context of the three kinds of monarchy (and of the other forms of govern-ment: aristocracy and democracy) which following Aristotle he discerns in history. These are 'lawfull or royall Monarchie', 'lordly Monarchie' and 'tyran-nical Monarchie'. In a royal monarchy, which, with succession by primogeni-ture, is Bodin's preferred form and kind of government, the king obeys the laws of nature, and his subjects obey the laws of the king, enjoying their natural liberty and propriety of goods. A lordly monarch (William the Conqueror is given as an example) rules by virtue of arms and lawful war. A tyrannous monarch condemns the laws of nature and nations, and abuses his free-born subjects. Bodin finds few princes in Europe in his own time 'which call them-selues lords of the bodies and goods of their subiects, and fewer in auncient time then at this present: for *Augustus* the emperour himselfe, although he were in effect the greatest monarch in the world, yet so it was that he so abhorred to be called Lord: neither had any that held of him in fealtie and homage'.[50] Bodin is making a point of some importance about Augustus. His whole theory of history and of political forms obliges him to make a precise statement of both the real political situation and the exact constitutional status of Augustus's rule. This was the more important in that Bodin's political theory accepts the muta-tion of political forms (thus, for example, a lordly monarchy may grow into a royal one), and Augustus's long period of single rule effected the even more radical political transformation from republic to what Bodin rightly thinks of as a monarchy in effect. Here I believe that the various remarks about Augustus scattered through different parts of the *Six Livres* form an analysis of some sub-tlety. In fact Bodin is coming to terms, through historical and political analysis, with that apparently paradoxical and inconsistent character of Augustus's career which, at about the same time, was exercising the wonder of Montaigne.

Bodin sees both great political difficulty, and something like a powerful natural trend, in the transition from republic to monarchy. Thus Julius Caesar, 'desiring to chaunge into a Monarchie the free estate of the most warlike people that euer was in the world', made the mistake of pardoning his enemies.[51] Yet despite the assassination of Caesar, the two triumvirates, Pompey, Caesar and Crassus, and Augustus, Antony and Lepidus, tended inevitably towards monarchy. The second triumvirate, 'having of one popular Commonweale, made three Monarchies', first lost Lepidus, 'vnfit for gouernment'; then, 'although *Antonius* had married *Augustus* his sister, and that they two had equally diuided the empire betwixt them, and liued in countries farre distant . . .

[49]Noted, apart from authors already cited in the present study, by John of Salisbury in his *Policratus*, VIII, 19–21; see R.W. and A.J. Carlyle, *A History of Medieval Political Theory in the West* (Edinburgh and London, 1928), III, p. 145. John of Salisbury shows some of the theoretical concern with which Bodin approaches the anecdote.

[50]*Six Bookes*, II, ii, 200–1. '. . . il n'y a point de Monarchie seigneuriale, que ie sçache: & moins encores anciennement qu'à present: car mesme Auguste l' Empereur, quoy qu'il fust en effect le plus grand Monarque de la terre, si est-ce qu'il auoit en horreur qu'on appelast Seigneur: & n'y auoit point de tenures en soy & homage' (*Six Livres*, p. 275).

[51]*Six Bookes*, IV, i, 419. '. . . voulant changer en monarchie la liberté du plus belliqueux peuple qui fut onques' (*Six Livres*, p. 520).

yet rested they not long, but that the one of them was shaken out of all, by the authoritie and power of the other. Whereafter ensued the sure state of the empire, established vnder one man's gouernment.'[52] Bodin does not, however, delude himself that Augustus, in thus exercising power and authority, acted like a 'royall Monarch'. On the contrary, learning from Julius Caesar's mistakes, Augustus put to death the conspirators against his uncle, not so much for revenge as to ensure his own safety, and even after overcoming the other two triumvirs held the empire by armed might. He entrusted his legions to 'gentlemen onely, or some of the meanest of the nobilitie' and 'tooke from the people their free choice, and had the magistrats still beholden and bound vnto him . . .', 'Whereby it euidently appeareth him to haue beene a sole Monarque, and soueraigne Prince, whatsoeuer faire title of a Tribune of the people, or of a Prince, was by one or other giuen vnto him.'[53] But as Bodin had earlier observed, 'he that beareth greatest sway in the Commonweale, him men think to have the soueraigntie: but if question be made of the right, then are we to looke not what is indeed done, but what ought to be done.' It was out of regard for this distinction, Bodin seems to imply, that Augustus repudiated the title of Lord, and adopted the title of Prince, which 'signifieth no other thing but him that is first', a principality being 'but an Aristocratie, or a Democratie, having some one for chiefe or principall aboue the rest, the soueraigntie yet still remaining with the nobilitie or the people'. And it was thus that Augustus, 'by a craftie deuise hauing made himselfe but great Generall of the armie (by the name of Imperator) and Tribune of the people for the defence of their profit, (from whome for all that he had taken their libertie) . . . had taken vpon him the charge of the Commonweale for ten yeares, made that state in show and false semblant but a principalitie . . . so inuading the royal power without a Sceptre, without a Diadem, or a Crowne'.[54] At such points Bodin appears to have assimilated a Tacitean attitude towards Augustus to a degree which might seem to imperil his monarchical argument.

Yet the difference between Bodin and Tacitus – or, for that matter, Bodin

[52]*Six Bookes*, II, ii, 199. '. . . auoyent faict d'une Republique populaire trois Monarchies, qui furent reduites à deux, apres qu' Auguste eut despoillé Lepide, & les deux reünies en vne, apres la iournee Actiaque, & la suite de Marc Antoine. Par ainsi ñous tiendrons ceste resolution, que la Monarchie ne peut estre s'il y a plus d'un Prince' (*Six Livres*, p. 272).

[53]*Six Bookes*, IV, i, 419. '. . . & commettoit au gouuernement d'icelles, non pas de grands Seigneurs, mais des moins nobles . . . en effect il disposoit de tout, prenant par la main, & recommandant au peuple ceux qu'il vouloit avancer . . . En quoy il appert assez euidemment qu'il estoit seul Monarque & Prince souuerain, quelque belle qualité de Prince qu'on donnast aux vns & autres en apparence' (*Six Livres*, p. 520).

[54]*Six Bookes*, II, i, 197; II, i, 196–7 (I, x, 157). '. . . & en matiere d'estat, qui est maistre de la force, il est maistre des hommes, & des loix, & de toute la Republique: mais en termes de droit, il ne faut pas . . . auoir esgard à ce qu'on fait à Romme, mais bien a ce qu'on doit faire' (*Six Livres*, pp. 269–70); '. . . le mot de *Princeps* ne signifie autre chose que le premier, parlant proprement' (p. 269); 'Il appert donc que la Principauté n'est rien autre chose qu'une Aristocratie ou Democratie ayant quelqu'un pour president, ou premier, & neantmoins tenu de ceux qui ont la souueraineté' (p. 270). There is nothing in the 1583 text to correspond to the last part of my quotation, beginning 'by a craftie deuise . . .'. Cf. 'At in Republica Romanorum, Augustus callido commento Imperatorem se, id est exercitus ducem maximum, ac Tribunum plebis ad tuenda populi commoda, cui tamen libertatem eripuerat, & in annos decem Reipublicae curationem à Senatu penè coactus, vtî videbatur, principatum specie ac simulatione constituerat . . . regiam tamen potestatem sine sceptro, sine diademate, sine corona invaserat' (*De Republica libri sex* . . . (Paris, 1586) where, in the margin, Bodin acknowledges his source: 'Tacit. principio. lib. l.'

and Machiavelli – is that Bodin's argument is ultimately monarchical, and Augustus, however complex his situation may have been to define, however far formally and theoretically from that of royal monarch, was one of the greatest exemplars offered by history for the rightness of Bodin's political values. Thus it is that Bodin can bring one of his accounts of Augustus to an end with his statement that

> after that the subiects hauing by little and little made proofe of his iustice and wisedome, tasted of the sweetnes of long peace and assured tranquillitie, in steed of cruell and bloodie ciuill warres, and that they had to doe, rather with a father than with a lord (as saith *Seneca*) and so began to loue and reuerence him: he againe on his part discharged his guard, going as a priuat man sometimes with one man, and sometimes with another without any other companie; and so laide the foundation of that great Monarchie, with the most happie successe that euer Prince did.[55]

Bodin's view of Augustus thus combines that of Tacitus with those of Velleius Paterculus, Suetonius, and such an explicit apologist for monarchy as Cassius Dio. The means he sees with the eyes of Tacitus, the end with the eyes of the rest. And there is this threefold paradox in his account, that it does not come down to an interaction between theoretical form (aristocratic or democratic republic) and historical reality (monarchy in effect), but rather to the natural tendency in historical reality working through a proclaimed form (the principate) to evolve the best form of government by the standards of nature and experience: royal, or lawfull Monarchy. Bodin appears to be the first political thinker of the Renaissance to have given full weight to the whole range of classical sources and viewpoints on Augustus and to have formed from them a highly complex but, I believe, unified account.[56] In this account Augustan Rome was not exactly Bodin's political ideal, since it was not a royal or lawful monarchy; rather it exemplified a crucial and powerful evolution in that direction, even to the extent that Augustus, and later and more successfully the Antonines, seemed to anticipate hereditary monarchy in their attempts to settle their succession in advance.[57] From another point of view, central in Machiavelli, Bodin considers the military policy of the emperors, and concludes that whereas Augustus wisely did not discharge his forty legions but sent them to the frontiers 'to entertaine them in martiall discipline, and to preuent all occasions of ciuill warres at Rome', Constantine, by discharging the legions, 'opened a gate to barbarous nations, who inuaded the Roman empire of all

---

[55]*Six Bookes*, IV, i, 419–20. '. . . mais les subiects ayans peu à peu connu sa iustice & sagesse, & gousté la douceur d'une haute paix & tranquillité asseuree, au lieu des cruelles & sanglantes guerres ciuiles: & qu'ils auoyent à faire plustost a vn pere, qu'vn Seigneur, comme dit Seneque, ils commencerent à l'aimer & reuerer: & luy de sa part chassa ses gardes, allant tantost chez l'un, puis chez l'autre sans compagnie: & iecta les fondements de la Monarchie, auec le plus heureux succez que iamais a faict Prince' (*Six Livres*, p. 521). Bodin strengthens his view that this was the conscious policy of Augustus by twice adverting to Cassius Dio's story of Augustus consulting with Agrippa and Maecenas as to whether he should attempt to re-establish the old republic fully, or encourage an evolution in the state towards monarchy (*Six Bookes*, III, i, 263; VI, iv, 719).

[56]Bodin's vast knowledge of historiography ancient and modern may most easily be appreciated by reading ch. IV of his *Methodus ad facilem historiarum cognitionem* (1566): tr. and ed. Beatrice Reynolds (New York, 1945), pp. 41–84. He knew every source on Augustus then available, and weighed it.

[57]*Six Bookes*, VI, v, 727–8.

sides . . .'.[58] The rule of Augustus thus seemed to constitute the foundation of a future political strength, monarchy, and the recognition of how a correct military policy formed a strong shield for the state.

Thus presented, Bodin's view of Augustus may seem relatively secular and rational. But Bodin had read Orosius as well as Tacitus and Machiavelli, and could think quite as readily in terms of sacred universal history. It is not only that he can compare Moses and Augustus as fathers of their people – '. . . the best prince nothing differeth from the best father, as *Xenophon* was woont most excellently to say';[59] many, after all, read the Old Testament for its political history. It is rather that Bodin can insist that God displays to man both political institutions and the course of history 'in Harmonicall proportion . . . and also to be Harmonically gouerned'.[60] Bodin was among those Renaissance minds who found in Number Symbolism a rich source of significance for the interpretation of the world, and he devotes as much ingenuity to seeing the history of Rome and Augustus in terms of sacred numbers as Orosius did in terms of symbolic events. Seven, the number of the divine works, is the number Bodin particularly conjures with, September being consequently the most significant month. Noting that Augustus held the Olympic Games in September, when the Roman year originally began, he buttresses the importance of this by a remarkable passage in which he seeks to demonstrate that the world must have begun not in the spring but the autumn.[61] Augustus, he notes, won the mastery of the whole world at the Battle of Actium in September; in a letter to his nephew the *princeps* rejoiced that he had survived his sixty-third year, when men expected to die; and when Augustus did die it was (as it happened) in September.[62] Furthermore, from the year of Actium and the shutting of the gates of the Temple of Janus for the fourth time, to the end of the one-year reign of Augustulus, last emperor of Rome, was 496 years: seventy septeneries, with the perfect number six added. Bodin must indeed have felt that he had mastered the particular harmony of history when he was able to note that Augustulus had been slain in September.[63] This aspect of Bodin's thought is commonly neglected even by those who study sixteenth-century political theory for its own sake. Yet it is of interest in showing us how Bodin thought of history in its larger outlines, and it demonstrates how for Bodin, as in a different way for Orosius, Augustus had a place in a providential scheme.

Meinecke has seen in the work of Bodin and Gentillet two replies to the challenge of Machiavelli, each arising from the same world of French society, 'filled with civil war and struggles for State power', yet the one, Gentillet, springing from the past, the other, Bodin, 'from the future that was now coming into

[58]*Six Bookes*, V, v, p. 602. '. . . pour entretenir la discipline militaire, & chasser, le plus loing qu'il pourroit, l'occasion de guerre ciuile . . . [Constantine] cassa les legionaires: qui fut cause de faire perdre l'ancienne discipline militaire, & ouurir les portes aux ennemis, qui depuis enuahirent l'Empire Rommain de tous costés' (*Six Livres*, pp. 761–2).

[59]*Six Bookes*, II, iv, pp. 211–12. '. . . un vray père du peuple' (*Six Livres*, p. 289; cf. *De Republica*, p. 201).

[60]*Six Bookes*, VI, vi, p. 790. '. . . que l'estat Royal est Harmonique, & qu'il se doit gouuerner Harmoniquement' (*Six Livres*, p. 1056).

[61]*Six Bookes*, IV, ii, p. 440.

[62]*Six Bookes*, IV, ii, pp. 451–2.

[63]*Six Bookes*, IV, ii, pp. 463–4.

existence'.[64] In so far as Bodin proposed a sophisticated theory of the sovereignty of the state, and brought a critical and penetrating attitude to the understanding of particular historical situations, Meinecke's distinction is just. It is also true that Gentillet is closer than Bodin to the morally edifying humanistic writing of Elyot, in which it is the desired moral which tends to dictate the historical material, rather than the other way about. Viewed, on the other hand, from the point of view of the cultural spread of the Augustan Idea, Gentillet is closer than Bodin, or Elyot, to the moment when the Augustan comparison was to be a dominant feature in English panegyric, ceremonial, and related literary forms. For although in Elyot and Bodin Augustus is certainly an example cited variously for his historical, moral and political interest, there are still may others cited alongside him, whereas in Gentillet Augustus seems, among numerous citations of good princes, a conspicuous positive example offered to the reader. When we recall that this example is deliberately opposed by Gentillet to the examples and precepts of Machiavelli, and the conduct of 'our Machiavellists of Fraunce, which were authors and enterprizers of the massacres of S. Bartholomew . . .', we understand why the work of 'a religious french protestant', the Latin translation of which (1577) was dedicated to two Englishmen and praised England and Elizabeth in the Dedication, had a sympathetic reception in the two Protestant kingdoms of Britain.[65]

Gentillet, in fact, deploys the example of Augustus with less sublety and realism than Bodin, but with a greater sense of moral and political urgency. Rather than imitate Cesare Borgia, Gentillet contends, princes should copy 'the moderation of *Augustus Cæsar* in the government of the commonweale, and his dilligence to establish peace, in the whole Romane empire: For he never omitted any thing, which might bee a meane to bring all the world to peace and tranquilitie, after the civile warres, and he managed the commonweale with such moderation, as it seemed rather a civile government, than a monarchie . . .'.[66] Gentillet goes out of his way to recommend clemency, not only as a virtue in itself, but as the best means by which the ruler may protect himself, as the examples of Augustus, Vespasian, Trajan, Adrian and the Antonines showed. 'Thinkes this sot', he demands, 'that the office [of prince] is like to the office of a gally captaine, to hold his subjects in chaines . . .? . . . how much more notable and humane, is the doctrine wee learne of the life of *Augustus Cæsar*? who so much feared, that men had such an opinion of him, that he would not take away, but onely diminish the libertie of the people, that he could never abide and suffer to

[64]Meinecke, *Machiavellism*, p. 56.

[65]I quote from Simon Patricke's English translation of Gentillet's *Discours* first published in 1602 as *A Discourse Vpon The Meanes of VVel Gouerning and Maintaining in Good Peace, a Kingdome, Or Other Principalitie*. . . . That Gentillet was known in England before this translation appeared is shown by references to him in *The Politicke and Militarie Discourses of the Lord De La Noue*, tr. E.A. (London, 1587); John Case, *Sphaera Civitatis* (Oxford, 1589) and Richard Harvey, *A Theological Discourse of the Lamb of God* (London, 1590), p. 97: see N.W. Bawcutt, 'Machiavelli and Marlowe's *Jew of Malta*', *Renaissance Drama*, N.S. III (1970), pp. 12–14, 36.

[66]*Discourse*, III, vii, p. 188. '. . . la moderation d'Auguste Cesar, au gouuernement de la chose publique, & sa diligence à establir la paix en l'Empire Romain. Car il n'oublia rien pour remettre tout le monde en tranquilité apres les guerres ciuiles, & gouuerna la chose publique auec vne telle moderation, qu'il sembloit que ce fust tousiours vn estat de Republique, non de Monarchie . . .'(*Discours, Svr Les Moyens De Bien Gouuerner vn Royavme . . . Contre Nicholas Machiavel Florentin* . . . (Geneva, 1576), p. 329).

be called *Dominus* . : .'.[67] With Bodin and Gentillet, something of the political significance of this famous anecdote, if not its exact original significance, has been retrieved. Yet each puts it to slightly different use. While for Bodin it is material for his theory of the three kinds of monarchy, for Gentillet it suggests a monarchy such as he himself probably admired: a king whose power was substantially qualified by and shared with a powerful nobility, on medieval lines.[68] He is far from looking ahead to the advent of absolute monarchy, and has sufficient in common with the original republican view of Augustus to esteem 'the libertie of the people' and that aspect of government which he could term 'civile' as opposed to monarchical. Thus Gentillet's stress upon the necessity for a prince to consult both advisers and institutions culminates in the statement of an ideal of mixed government: 'Therefore was it also, that that great and wise Emperour *Augustus Cæsar*, did so communicate all the affaires of his Commonwealth with the Romane Senate, that as *Dion* saith, he made a sweet and pleasant mingled harmonie of the Monarchicall estate, with the estate of the Commonwealth.'[69] These passages perhaps give the basis for the praise of 'that good *Augustus*', 'that great Emperour *Augustus Cæsar*', which pervades Gentillet's work. Other points are, however, mentioned: Augustus knew how to tolerate slander and even treat its authors with magnanimity; he was 'a good justicier' and not only framed laws but heard causes 'and judged them their right'; he was a lover of learned men and of knowledge.[70] He condemns the Triumvirate as 'a most detestable union' but contrives to throw the main blame for the assassination of Cicero on Antony, who was then punished for this crime at Actium, 'even by *Octavius* himselfe, whom hee had induced to commit such cruelties'.[71]

A notable feature of Gentillet's work is his discussion of the relation between ruler and artist. He derides the extravagance of contemporary panegyric, and especially in eulogies at the death of Charles IX, after the Massacre of St Bartholomew. He recites some panegyrical comparisons, the ruler overthrowing more monsters than did Hercules, dying like Samson pulling down the pillars of the temple, for at such a death justice and piety died too, and asks:

I pray you is there any man of sober judgement, which doth not plainly see, that such

---

[67]*Discourse*, III, xxii, pp. 287–8. 'Et quoy? Ce sot pense-il que l'office d'vn Roy soit semblable à l'office d'vn Comite de galeres, pour tenir ses suiets enchainez, & les souetter tous les iours auec escourgees? . . . . Combien est plus notable & humaine la doctrine que nous apprenons de la vie d'Auguste Cesar? Lequel craignoit tant qu'on eust ceste opinion de luy qu'il voulust, non pas oster, mais seulement diminuer la liberté du peuple, qu'il ne vouloit aucunement estre appelé Dominus . . .' (*Discours*, p. 493).

[68]Meinecke, *Machiavellism*, pp. 54–5.

[69]*Discourse*, I, i, p. 16. 'C'est aussi pourquoy ce grand & sage Empereur Auguste Cæsar communiquoit tellement de tous afaires de la chose publique auec le Senat Romain, qu'il faisoit (comme escrit Dion) vne douce & agreable meslee de l'estàt de Monarchie auec l'estàt de la Republique' (*Discours*, p. 42). Patricke may be thought to have sounded a more Bodinian note here than his original altogether warranted.

[70]*Discourse*, I, i, p. 16; II, ii, p. 44; I, ii, p. 46; III, vii, pp. 188–9. '. . . ce bon Auguste'; '. . . ce grand Auguste Cæsar'; '. . . il estoit bon justicier . . .'; '. . . & leur faisoit droit.' Plus il estoit amateur des gens doctes & de sauoir, & leur faisoit de grands bienfaits' (*Discours*, pp. 42, 90, 329). See Greenleaf, *Order and Empiricism*, pp. 130–1.

[71]*Discourse*, III, i, pp. 154–5. '. . . vne detestable vnion'; '. . . par le moyen D'Octauius mesme, lequel il auoit induit à faire telles cruautez . . .' (*Discours*, pp. 272, 273).

speeches become rather men void of wit and understanding, by some extreame affection of flatterie, than these gallant Poets, which are drawne on and led with a generous and right Poeticall spirit? for meaning unmeasurably to praise, there escapes from them, that they speake things redounding to their dispraise: and if the dead king were alive, he would not thanke them for such praises. For a good Prince (as *Horace* saith of *Augustus*) ever rejected such foolish praises

and Gentillet loosely translates a passage from Horace, *Sat*. II, i.[72]

. . . If those goodly Poets before they had made their Epitaphs, had well read *Virgil* and *Horace*, they should have found, that these two excellent Poets writ in many places the praises of *Augustus*. But wherefore do they praise him? For that he established a good peace in all the Romane Empire, he caused justice to flourish, hee brought the people into a good repose and assurance, and reduced [led back] againe the golden world. They praise him also, because he amplified and enlarged the Romane Empire. But they speake not one word of the civile warres: nor for that he overthrew *Cassius* and *Brutus*, doe they either praise or despraise him.[73]

Gentillet considers it improper for a prince to be praised for 'cunning in arts, and the meanest mechanicall sciences' and, recalling the lines on Rome's destiny in *Aeneid* Bk VI, declares that Virgil wished princes 'should have no knowledge of the mechanicall arts: onely they should learne (sayth he) the Science well to command, to governe, to vanquish, to pardon, to make lawes and edicts, and to establish good manners and customes upon the nations under their governance'.[74] It is interesting to observe how Virgil's prophecy, which had been intended to recognize the distinctive achievement of the Roman people, has here been simply transformed into precepts for princes, and attributed directly back to Virgil.

Gentillet is often disparaged by comparison with Machiavelli and Bodin. He lacks the bold secular challenge of the one, and the breadth and subtlety of the other. His affinity with humanist Prince literature, such as Elyot's *Governour*, shows in his lack of an analytic and disinterested approach to history. But it does not therefore follow that Gentillet writes simple-minded nonsense. The humanist tradition on Augustus had a good deal of truth in it which it did not suit Machiavelli to recognize: for example, that the moderation of the *princeps* had

---

[72]*Discourse*, I, ii, p. 42 (Horace, *Sat*. II, i, ll. 17–20). 'Ie vous prie, y a-il homme de iugement rassis, qui ne voye à l'œil, que tels propos sont plustot de gens transportez d' entendement, par vne extreme affection de flaterie, que non pas de quelques gaillars Poetes, poussez d'vn gentil esprit poetique? Car en voulant demesurément louanger, il leur eschappe à dire des choses qui tendent plustot à mespris. Et si le feu Roy estoit viuant, il ne leur sauroit nul gré de telles louanges: car vn bon Prince (comme dit Horace d'Auguste) reitte tousiours ces louanges ineptes . . .' (*Discours*, p. 86).

[73]*Discourse*, I, ii, pp. 423 (Patricke gives as sidenotes at this point: '*Aenead* 6. *Hora. lib* 4. *Carm*. ode 5. 15'). 'Si ces beaux Poetes auant que faire leurs Epitaphes, eusent bien leu Virgile & Orace, ils eussent trouué que ces deux excellens Poetes escriuent en plusieures lieux, les louanges d'Auguste. Mais de quoy le louent-ils. De ce qu'il establit vne bonne paix en l'Empire Romain, fit florir la iustice, mit le peuple en repos & asseurance, ramena le siecle d'oré. Ils le louent bien aussi de ce que par les armes il amplifia l'Empire Romain: mais ils ne parlent pas vn mot des guerres ciuilles, ny de ce qu'il deffit Cassius & Brutus, ils ne le louent ny desprisent rien de cela' (*Discours*, pp. 86–7).

[74]*Discourse*, I, ii, p. 43 (Virgil, *Aeneid*, VI, ll. 847–53). '. . . il [Virgil] ne veut point qu'ils sachent les arts mechaniques, mais bien la science de commander, de gouuerner, de vaincre, de pardonner, de faire loix & edits, & d' establir bonnes moeurs & coustumes sur les nations de leur obeissance' (*Discours*, p. 88).

helped to confirm him in his new political situation, and ensured a long period of peace and stability in the world-state. Gentillet's loosely expressed concept of a royal government which shared some of its powers was not inconsistent with Bodin's thought on mixed government, and not inconsistent with the more moderate exponents of royalism in seventeenth-century England. He has been criticized for taking Machiavelli's precepts out of their context and then refuting them at length, but, as has also been observed, Machiavelli's thought is aphoristic rather than systematic, and in some ways provokes this treatment in any reply.[75] Where the relations of writer and ruler are concerned, Gentillet quite correctly distinguished between Virgil's and Horace's considered praise of Augustus, and the more extravagant forms of sixteenth-century panegyric. Gentillet's book lacks the stamp of a powerfully individual mind, but it has the strength of what must have been a widely representative synthesis of Christian-Humanist thought about the qualities of the good ruler. It is the more significant that the example of Augustus should be prominent in his work.

Botero and Lipsius

Any survey of Augustus as he figures in sixteenth-century political literature must include Giovanni Botero and Justus Lipsius. Botero's *Della ragion di Stato* (1589) represents a judicious dilution of Machiavellian insight for a world of great monarchies and the Counter-Reformation. '. . . he was just as able to satisfy the friends of the Church and of Spanish world dominion, as the admirers of the republican independence of Venice.'[76] Botero's numerous references to Augustus, 'that most judicious ruler' as at one point he calls him,[77] are for the most part neither laudatory nor hostile; they are there simply to teach the facts and procedures of politics. Despite the increasing knowledge of Tacitus at the end of the sixteenth century, a knowledge which Botero certainly shared, the debate about the *princeps* is muted indeed in this work. Justus Lipsius, the author of a great edition of Tacitus, and of commentaries on both Tacitus and Velleius Paterculus, is a figure of much more interest, for few can have studied the opposing classical viewpoints on Augustus with greater care than he.[78] Lipsius is also interesting as a man caught between the conflicting pressures and opportunities of the newly independent Protestant republic of the United Provinces, and imperial Counter-Reformation rule in his native Flanders – and for moving from one position to another with what some regarded as culpable facility. His edition of Tacitus appeared in 1574. During twelve creative years at Leyden, 1579–91, he published revised editions of Tacitus, his *Commentarii pleni in Cornelium Tacitum* (1581), *De Constantia* (1584), *Sex Libri Politicorum* (1588–9), and *Animadversiones in Velleium Paterculum*. Later, back in Flanders, he published works on Stoicism, antiquarian works on Rome, and devotional works of Roman Catholic piety. It is *De Constantia* and the

[75]Anglo, *Machiavelli*, pp. 241–2.

[76]Meinecke, *Machiavellism*, p. 67.

[77]Giovanni Botero, *The Reason of State* . . ., tr. P.J. and D.P. Waley (London, 1956), IX, ii, p. 189.

[78]See *Two Bookes of Constancie Written in Latine, by Iustus Lipsius . . . Englished by Iohn Stradling, Gentleman* (London, 1595), ed. and intro. Rudolf Kirk and C.M. Hall (New Brunswick, 1939), pp. 9–10.

Politicorum that are of special relevance to the presentation of Augustus, though only the latter is an example of Prince literature.

The design of *De Constantia*, with its tragic overview of the vicissitudes of history in the working of providence, permits the greater freedom of reference, for here Lipsius seeks to transcend rather than expound the art of politics. The intensely moving quality of his writing partly arises from his sympathy with those who suffer in political situations and great historical crises, a view contrasted in his dialogue between 'Lipsius' and 'Langius' with that which seeks wisdom from a broad survey of the ancient and modern world. In speaking of Rome he does not automatically identify with Roman rule. 'The Romanes in times past, imposed a greeuous yoke vppon the necke of the whole world, but yet a yoke that prooued wholesome in the ende; wherby Barbarisme was expelled from our mindes, as the sunne driueth away darkenesse from our eies.'[79] He is acutely aware of captivity and slavery, both in 'the auncient wars' and with the rise of a new empire of Spaniards in the 'maruellous wide new world' of the Americas;[80] in another place he speaks of the grievous tributes exacted by Julius Caesar, Antony and Octavian.[81] In a sequence defending the justice of providence he reviews the events between the breakdown of the Roman Republic and the establishment of the principate:

> Behold that Cesar, statly, A conquerour, in his own and some other folks opinion, a very god; Slaine in and of the Senate. . . . Even so Brutus loosing his life in the Phillippian fieldes for his cuntry, and with his cuntry, moueth me to compassion: But I am recomforted when I see not long after those conquering armies (as it were) before his tombe falling together by the eares betweene themselues; and Maister Antonius one of the Chiefetaines ouercome both by sea and land, among three seely women hardly finding death by that womanish hand. Where arte thou now that of late wast Lord of all the east? Leader of the Romaine Armies? Persecutor of Pompei and the common-wealth? Loe thou hangest in a rope by thy bloudy hands! Lo thou creepest into thy graue halfe aliue! Loe dying thou canste not bee withdrawne from her which was thy death! . . . . No more did that other Captain [escape punishment], who not obscurely suffered in himselfe the punishment of his youthfull misdeedes; But yet more apparantly in all his progenie. Let him be happy and mighty Cæsar, and truly *Augustus*: But with all let him haue a daughter Julia, and a neece. . . . Others let him banish out of his fauour: And with loathsomnes of these let him wish to die with fower daies hunger, and not bee able. Finally, let him liue with his *Liuia*. vnhonestlie married, vnhostlie kepte: And vpon whom he doted with vnlawfull loue, let him die a shamefull death by her meanes. In conclusion (saith *Plinie*) *He being made a god and gaining heauen . . . . let him die, and let the sonne of his enemie be his heire.*[82]

[79]*Two Bookes of Constancie . . . Englished by Iohn Stradling . . .* (London, 1595), II, xi, p. 85. 'Romani olim orbi terræ acerbum iugum imposuerunt; sed iugum salubre exitu, quod vt sol caliginem ab oculis, sic barbariem ab animis fugauit' (*Ivsti Lipsi, De Constantia Libri Dvo* (London, 1586), p. 58.

[80]*Two Bookes*, II, xxii, p. 115. 'in veterum bellis'; '. . . et novas terras delati' (*De Constantia*, pp. 79, 78).

[81]*Two Bookes*, II, xxiii, pp. 117–18.

[82]*Two Bookes*, II, xv, 96–7. 'Cæsarem illum videte, superbum, victoré, opinione sua & aliorum iam deum, in Senatu, & à Senatu, interfectum . . . . Ita Brutus in campis Philippicis, pro patriâ, & cum patriâ moriens, mihi quoq; miserationi est. sed consolor idem, cum haut longè video victores illos exercitus, velut ad eius tumulum, gladiatorio more inter se commissos. & è ducibus alterum M. Antonium, terrâ maríque victum, inter tres mulierculas, mulierosa illâ manu, ægrè mortem

The uniformly moral tone of this passage is interesting as it modulates from sympathy at the death of Brutus, horror at the death of Antony, to the studied casualness of the first reference to Augustus ('that other Captain') and the exaggeration of Augustus's family disappointment. The remark of Pliny will be used again in the seventeenth century, when writers of republican sympathy such as Boccalini and Harrington wish to disparage Augustus. Perhaps the real balance of Lipsius's view of Augustus, at least in *De Constantia*, is found when he discusses freedom of speech, judgement and religion. Making no mention of Augustus's refusal to be called Lord, Lipsius substitutes the accurate historical observation that 'that good and moderate prince Augustus had his *Flamines &* Priests in al prouinces, yea in privat houses, as a God.' 'What vanity (*Lipsius*)', Langius then observes, 'to speak ought at this day against any king? I purpose not to sail nerer this gulf . . . *for the reward of silence is void of danger*', and he concludes by quoting from the second paragraph of Tacitus's *Agricola* on the suppression of free speech and writing in the time of the Triumvirate and of Domitian.[83] The chapter closes on a note of intelligent qualification and unease.

Lipsius's remarks on Augustus in that political commonplace book the *Politicorum* may be seen as largely an expansion of his phrase: 'that good and moderate prince' in *De Constantia*. They are not, on the whole, inconsistent with what is said in the earlier work, but the purpose and form of the *Politicorum* is different, denying the mind a certain range and freedom, and bending it towards the specific consideration of the character and measures of the good ruler. In this important but more restricted context Augustus the *princeps* (not Octavian the Triumvir) seemed to embody much political wisdom, and is repeatedly mentioned with approval. Lipsius is close to Elyot's stress upon the quality of ripeness, or maturity. Thus Augustus is quoted advising the Senate that it is more profitable to a commonwealth to obey an imperfect law fully than bring in a better law by total innovation.[84] Stringing together Tacitus, Cicero, Cassius Dio and again Tacitus into one sequence of thought, Lipsius commends Augustus's judgement in establishing the principate:

> . . . in this case we must proceede gently, and in such sort, *that this globe in the commonwealth may be turned with the least noise that may be*: and slowly, and as it were by degrees, and not at one push: by the example of *Augustus*, who in the beginning of his Empire *did not execute all things immediatly, as was decreed: fearing*

inuenientem. Vbi tu es Orientis ille paulo antè dominus? lanista Romanorum exercituum? Pompej & reip. sector? En, in fune cruentis manibus pendes! en, viuus in monimentum tuum repis! en ne moriens quidem auelleris ab eâ quæ tibi morti! . . . . non item ille alter dux, qui, pœnam iuuenilium scelerum non obscurè in se luit, & clarius in omni suâ stirpe. Sit felix & magnus Cæsar, & verè Augustus: sed filiam tamen Iuliam habeat, sed nepotem. nepotes alios per fraudem per vim amittat, alios abdicet. & horum tædio, quatriduana inedia mori velit, nec possit. denique cum Livia sua uiuat, fœdè ducta, fœdè retenta: & quam turpi amore ipse periit, turpi morte per eam pereat. *In summâ*, inquit Plinius, *deus ille, cælumque . . . herede hostis sui filio excedat*, (*De Constantia*, pp. 65–6).

[83]*Two Bookes*, II, xxv, pp. 123–4. 'Inter Romanos bonus ille & moderatus Princeps Augustus, flamines & sacerdotes in prouincijs imò in domibus singulis habuit, vt Deus . . . . Quæ vanitas vel impietas si hodiè in vllo regum . . . Nec adnauigo propius hanc Scyllam . . . . *Periculo vacat silentê præmium'* (*De Constantia*, p. 84).

[84]*Sixe Bookes of Politickes or Civil Doctrine, Written in Latine by Iustus Lipsius: which doe especially concerne Principalitie. Done into English by William Iones Gentleman . . .* (London, 1594), IV, ix, p. 80.

that all things would not succeed well, if he should transpose them and change all men from their places at one time; but certaine things he disposed at the present time, and referred others to fitter opportunitie. And this is it, that *Tacitus* speaketh of him: *that he did rise by little and little, and drawe unto him the charge of the lawes, and offices.*[85]

In another place Augustus is cited in order to commend ripe deliberation and counsel in deciding on war;[86] bounty in new rulers seeking to establish themselves is elsewhere recommended on his precedent, with supporting if not reassuring quotation from Tacitus;[87] and Livia's advice to Augustus from Seneca's *De Clementia* is quoted in order to praise both the virtue and the political wisdom of clemency.[88] These references are representative. While Lipsius lays more stress than earlier writers on the wise conservatism of Augustus, the picture he offers is highly traditional. What is notable is the way the eloquent and hostile witness of Tacitus, whom Lipsius understood so well, is actually pressed into the service of a favourable view; one would never suspect from Lipsius alone that Tacitus and Cassius Dio differed in their opinion of Augustus. The *Politicorum* is witness to the monarchical assumptions inherent in Prince literature (which it takes the powerful convictions and subversive literary design of a Machiavelli to reverse); certainly it is evidence of the inescapable importance of monarchical rule in late sixteenth-century Europe, and of what looks like a growing tradition favourable to Augustus by the end of the century. A glance back to Erasmus's *Institutio* suggests this development.

Epic and Panegyric Once More

It will be right to conclude this chapter by observing some of the connections between specific discussions of Augustus and the broader imperial ideal which might be evoked with or without mention of him. Such evocations seemed especially appropriate at times when an augmentation of political power, and extended unity, or an expanded view of the world, were in prospect.[89] Ariosto, in *Orlando Furioso* (the final version of which was published in 1532), alluded to Augustus in different ways. The historical Cardinal Hyppolitus d'Este, and the descendants of the fictional Bradamant, are both associated with Augustus and a Virgilian Golden Age.[90] In another place Ariosto has sufficient poise to observe that the historical Augustus hardly measured up to Virgil's presenta-

---

[85]*Six Bookes of Politickes*, IV, ix, pp. 80–1. The original (*Politicorvm . . . Libri Sex* (Lvgdvni Batavorvm, 1589), pp. 138–9 is chiefly quotation from the Greek of Cassius Dio, 52.

[86]*Six Bookes of Politickes*, V, vi, p. 135.

[87]*Six Bookes of Politickes*, IV, viii, p. 76. 'Donabis igitur, vel Augusti exemplo: qui *Militem donis, populum annonâ, cunctos dulcedine otij pellexit*. Tacit. 1 Annal.' (*Politicorvm Libri Sex*, p. 130).

[88]*Six Bookes of Politickes*, p. 90; *Politicorum Libri Sex*, IV, x, p. 157.

[89]Cf. Gentillet, *Discourse*, I, p. 25: 'And unto this agree the doctors of the Civill law, which hold; that the emperour cannot aliene any thing of the Empires, but he is bound to increase it to his power. And from thence they drawe (but foolishly) the etymologie of that name *Augustus*, saying: The Emperors are called *Augusti*, for that they ought to encrease, and cannot diminish the Empire.' Gullaume Budé, on the other hand, had praised Augustus for halting the expansion of the empire; *L'Institut du Prince*, f121ʳ.

[90]*Orlando Furioso*, III, st. 18. The English verse translation by John Harington, dedicated to Queen Elizabeth, was published in 1591.

tion, but that his judgement in poetry made up for the evil of his proscriptions – he is, of course advising princes to be good to poets.[91] But Augustus as the embodiment of a reign of peace and justice, or as the ruler who lived down early crimes through, among other things, the discerning patronage of poets, gives way to the man who was simply the first of a line of wise and mighty Roman emperors, in the famous passage in which Andronica prophesies a new empire under Charles V, the union of the lines of Austria and Aragon, and the restoration of Astraea to her earthly throne as the new world and the old world are united under one ruler.[92] At this point Ariosto is close to Dante. In this prophecy the Augustan Empire is about to be restored. If, in Ariosto, maritime discovery is the sign of the Emperor Charles V's Augustan significance, in Luís de Camões's great Portuguese epic *Os Lusiadas* (1572) it is the very form of imperial enterprise. Yet here too Augustus, world-emperor and patron of poets, is evoked in the poem. If the seas raged when Augustus overwhelmed Antony at Actium (Jupiter tells Venus), they will rage more as the triumphant Portuguese sweep the Moslems before them.[93] Vasco da Gama's long narrative to the King of Malindi concerning the rise and explorations of the Portuguese concludes with the poet's own reflection that it was through Augustus's encouragement of Virgil that the glory of Rome became famous among men, that Portugal too has its Scipios, Caesars, Alexanders and Augustuses, the naked truth of whose achievements will be obscure without poetry, and that Augustus in his own life combined arms and arts.[94]

[91]*Orlando Furioso*, XXXV, st. 26:

Non fu sì santo né benigno Augusto
come la tuba di Virgilio suona.
L'aver avuto in poesia buon gusto
la proscrizion iniqua gli perdona.

(Ludovico Ariosto, *Orlando Furioso*, ed. Santorre Debenedetti and Cesare Segre (Bologna, 1960), p. 61.) Harington translated:

Augustus Cesar was not such a saint,
As Virgill maketh him by his description,
His loue of learning, scuseth that complaint,
That men might iustly make of his proscription . . .

(XXXV, st. 25; p. 292).

[92]*Orlando Furioso*, XV, st. 24–6; ed. cit. p. 435.

[93]Luís de Camões, *Os Lusiadas*, II, st. 53–4; ed. and intro. Frank Pierce (Oxford, 1973), p. 36.

'Nunca com Marte instruto e furioso
Se viu ferver Leucate, quando Augusto,
Nas civis áctias guerras animoso,
O capitão venceu romano injusto,
Que dos povos da Aurora e do famoso
Nilo e do Bactra scítico e robusto
A vitória trazia e presa rica,
Preso da egípcia linda e não pudica,

'Como vereias o mar fervendo aceso
Cos incêndios dos vossos; pelejando,
Levando o Idololatra e o Mouro preso,
De nações diferentes triunfando . . . .

[94]*Os Lusiadas*, V, st. 95; ed. cit. p. 131:

The epic poems of Ariosto and Camões are but two salient works in which the recall of Augustus is linked with a strong sense of present emulation and future possibility. Implicitly or explicitly, with greater or lesser appropriateness, in poems, discourses, and triumphal entries, ruler after ruler is celebrated with allusion to Augustus: the Emperor Charles V, his son Prince Philip, and Francis I, Henry II and Charles IX of France were all so treated, through what the encyclopaedic modern historian of 'La Gloire' in sixteenth-century French poetry calls 'cette comparaison banale'.[95] The comparison is certainly frequent; whether it is banal depends on what exactly it reflected in the contemporary historical context. Such aspiration could be found without specific mention of Augustus, as in the case of the Entry of Henry II into Rouen in 1550. Among the features of this elaborate celebration were a staged fight between two tribes of naked Brazilians, another between two warships upon the river, one representing France and the other Portugal, and the actual entry of the monarch into the town through a series of Triumphal arches, on the first of which stood the figure of Saturn representing the Golden Age. These features alone show connections between Virgilian prophecy, the memory of imperial Rome, and the desire of European states to expand their power into the new world. And in this case a number of military successes nearer home seemed to endorse the conventional features of the Entry, so that immediate circumstances were 'continually intruding and providing a basis for the spectacle'.[96]

The imperial ideal, in this broad sense, not necessarily involving explicit Augustan comparison, was certainly evoked in connection with Elizabethan England. It is to Frances Yates that we owe our understanding of that complex web of allusion, idealism and hope which, in the sixteenth century, linked the imperial ideal as embodied in Charles V with the cult of Queen Elizabeth as Astraea.[97] There can be no doubt that this cult, whose literary origin, like so much explicit Augustan comparison, was Virgil's Fourth Eclogue, prepared the way for what I shall argue was the first explicitly Augustan moment in English civilization at the very end of the sixteenth and beginning of the seventeenth centuries. At the same time there were important differences. It is not just that

---

Dá a terra lusitana, Scipiões,
Césares, Alexandros, e dá Augustos;
Mas não lhe dá contudo aqueles dões
Cuja falta os faz duros e robustos.
Octávio, entre as maiores oppressões,
Compunha versos doutos e venustos;
Naõ dirá Fúlvia, certo, que é mentira,
Quando a deixava António por Glafira.

Sir Richard Fanshaw's translation of *Os Lusiadas* was published in 1655.

[95]See Jean Jacquot, ed., *Les Fêtes de la Renaissance*, II (Paris, 1965), pp. 38, 95, 460. Also Françoise Joukovsky, *La Gloire Dans La Poesie Française Et Neolatine Du XVIᵉ Siècle* (Geneva, 1969), pp. 216–19. For use of the Golden Age in Latin Panegyric in the reign of Henry VII, see Sydney Anglo, 'The *British History* in Early Tudor Propaganda', *Bulletin of the John Rylands Library*, XLIV (1961), pp. 29–31.

[96]Margaret McGowan, *L'entré de Henri II à Rouen, 1550* (Amsterdam, 1973), pp. 12, 14–15, 24.

[97]Frances Yates, 'Queen Elizabeth as *Astraea*', *Journal of the Warburg and Courtauld Institutes*, X–XI (1947–8), pp. 27–82. Also: 'Charles Quint et L'Idée D'Empire' in *Les Fêtes de la Renaissance*, pp. 55–97.

there might seem, on a superficial level, to be infelicity in praising a queen as an Augustus; this, as we shall see, was in fact done, late in Elizabeth's reign, at a significant point and by a significant person. Nor is felicity of form alone sufficient to explain the identification of a virgin queen with the Virgin Astraea. As Frances Yates wrote, 'The small world of the Tudor union and the Tudor *pax*, personified in the Tudor Virgo, have here behind them the vaster European perspectives of the Habsburg union and the Habsburg *pax*; and behind these again is the august concept of Holy Roman Empire . . . both old and new worlds, under the rule of the One Monarch and the returned just virgin Astraea of a new golden age.'[98] But these perspectives were given a specifically Protestant orientation: 'She represents the return to the Constantinian, imperial Christianity, free from papal shackles, the kind of religion which Foxe regards as alone pure.'[99] This observation begins to show why Elizabeth was praised as Astraea rather than as Augustus. It was because Elizabethan England, the power of whose imperial monarchy was indeed well-established and untouched within its own borders, seemed a world separated from the world, a 'fortress built . . . Against infection and the hand of war', rather than a centrally placed and expanding world-power.[100] Giordano Bruno, writing of Elizabeth, put the point explicitly: 'I leave it to the world to judge what place she takes among all other princes for her knowledge of arts and sciences and for her fluency in all the tongues . . . if her earthly territory were a true reflection of the width and grandeur of her spirit this great Amphitrite would bring far horizons within her girdle and enlarge the circumference of her dominion to include not only Britain and Ireland but some new world, as vast as the universal frame . . .'[101] As it was, Elizabethan England was defensive rather than expansive. Queen Elizabeth as Cynthia, as Diana, as Belphoebe, as Gloriana, as Una, as Astraea, activated one part of the available imperial myth, but not, on the whole, the Augustan Idea which was central to this myth. For this the accumulated tradition concerning Augustus in sixteenth-century political literature awaited to be drawn on: when it was, it served to focus upon various dissatisfactions felt in the last years of that 'Greatest and fairest empress' whom Donne, in the fifth of his unpublished satires, addressed on the corruptions of the time.

[98]Yates, 'Queen Elizabeth as *Astraea*', p. 52.

[99]Ibid., p. 43. This is the Foxe who produced the *Actes and Monuments* (the *Book of Martyrs*). It is worth recalling that Henry VIII had assumed 'imperial' status in the religious settlement by which he repudiated the authority of the Papacy over him, and became himself the head of the English Church.

[100]Virgil, First Eclogue, ll. 64–6: 'At nos hinc alii sitientis ibimus Afros,/ pars Scythiam et rapidum cretae ueniemus Oaxen/ et penitus toto diuisos orbe Britannos'. Cf. John of Gaunt's prophecy in *Richard II*, II, i, 43–9, which seems to echo it (see Peter Ure, ed. *Richard II*, New Arden Edn (London, 1956), p. 51 (l. 45n.).

[101]Yates, 'Queen Elizabeth as *Astraea*', p. 80.

IV Courtiers out of Horace:

Donne's Satyre IV and Pope's Fourth Satire of
Dr John Donne, Dean of St Paul's, Versifyed

Belyke no Tyrantes were in Horace dayes,
And therefore Poetes freely blamed vyce.
(The poet Collingbourne, in *The Mirror for*
Magistrates)

Satyres I–III

'To my satyrs there belongs some feare . . .', Donne wrote, perhaps to Sir
Henry Wotton, perhaps at the very end of the sixteenth century.[1] This is a good,
though not total, summary of the spirit of *Satyre IV*. Yet when Donne pioneered
the Elizabethan satiric revival with his *Satire I* (*c.* 1953), he seemed to be setting
a very different kind of precedent. Based on a walk through the streets with a
ridiculous and wearisome companion, *Satyre I* may, as Milgate observes, have
been broadly influenced by the Ninth Satire of the First Book of Horace ('Ibam
forte Via Sacra . . .'): the encounter with the Talker (*garrulus* – l. 33). If we
may take *Sat*. I, ix as one pattern of Horatian satire (for Horace is certainly a
more various poet than his image in English literature often allows), other
features of Donne's poem may strike us as Horatian. It tells a short, coherent,
well-rounded story. Donne's 'humorist'-companion wishes to leave the study
for the streets, but is chidden by Donne for his 'headlong, wild uncertaine'
behaviour which respects outward appearance before inner merit. Yet the
'humorist' is contrite, and so

I shut my chamber doore, and 'Come, lets goe.'[2]

Once outside, however, Donne's reproofs are shown to have been all justified,
and are all ignored. The 'humorist's' behaviour gets more and more out of hand
until he deserts his steadier companion, and the poem comes to its comic
dénouement:

[1]*John Donne, Dean of St Paul's, Complete Poetry and Selected Prose*, ed. John Hayward
(London, 1930), p. 440.
[2]L. 52; *John Donne, The Satires, Epigrams and Verse Letters*, ed. W. Milgate (Oxford, 1967),
p. 4.

At last his Love he in a windowe spies,
And like light dew exhal'd, he flings from mee
Violently ravish'd to his lechery.
Many were there, he could command no more;
He quarrell'd, fought, bled; and turn'd out of dore
   Directly came to mee hanging the head,
   And constantly a while must keepe his bed.[3]

The progressive self-assertion of the Humorist is broadly analogous to the increasing desperation of Horace with the Talker, until each reaches its sudden reversal and conclusion. The deflation of the Humorist with words, his increasing self-assertion in the streets, and his subsequent deflation with blows, is a small triumph of comic art. As in Horace, *Sat.* I, ix, this comedy arises from a delicate balance of opposing recognitions. Horace's moral and social position, as rendered in *Sat.* I, ix, is entirely secure; yet it is precisely because of this that the importunities of the Talker yield such exquisite comic pleasure, and Horace is able to elicit so much humour from the account of his own discomfiture. In *Satyre I*, the Humorist is in a subordinate position, 'As prentises, or schooleboyes'; the superior wisdom of the speaker is unchallenged, except implicitly in its failure to make any impact upon ebullient folly. Yet, by virtue of this implicit challenge, a balance is struck in *Satyre I*, lending a degree of astringent irony to what would otherwise have been a simple union of comic perception and firm moral assurance. *Satyre I* is a precocious and not wholly unsuccessful attempt to emulate the shaped narrative, the perfect control and the finely shaped assurance of the Latin poem.

There follow, chronologically if we are to believe Drummond of Hawthornden, *Satyre II* and *Satyre III*.[4] *Satyre II* is perhaps one of the less successful of Donne's group of five formal satires. It lacks the immediate narrative and dramatic interest of *I* and *IV*, and is not united, like *Satyre III*, by the exposure of a central theological and human dilemma. The objects of Donne's attack, the abuse of poetry, law, and finally property, are united in the figure of Coscus in a largely formal sense; the union does not seem a source of dramatic or poetic life. Yet there is some effectiveness in the change of Coscus from a figure of mere ridicule to one of menace –

Shortly (as the sea) hee will compasse all our land;[5]

– and the satire abounds in strokes of vigorous and mordant wit. There is also a notable change of tone from *Satyre I*. The basic assurance of outlook, which gives rise to comedy, is here replaced by a mood of somewhat hectoring indignation. Tone and stance are different again, at the opening of *Satyre III*, and are considerably more complex:

Kinde pitty chokes my spleene; brave scorn forbids
Those teares to issue which swell my eye-lids;
I must not laugh, nor weepe sinnes, and be wise,
Can railing then cure these worne maladies?[6]

[3]L1. 106–12; *Donne, The Satires*, p. 6.
[4]Milgate, *Donne, The Satires*, p. xlvi.
[5]L. 77; ibid., p. 9.
[6]Ll. 1–4; ibid, p. 10.

Thomas Drant, in his *Medcinable Morall* . . . (1566), which it must be remembered was a verse-rendering of *The Lamentations of Jeremiah* as well as the Satires of Horace, had already set out the alternative attitudes to sin of laughter or tears:

> Therefore as it is mete for a man of god rather to wepe than to iest: and not undecent for a prophane writer to be iestyng, and merie spoken: I have brought to passe that the plaintiue Prophete *Ieremie* shoulde wepe at synne: and the pleasant poet *Horace* shoulde laugh at synne. Not one kynde of musike deliteth all passions: nor one salve for all greuances.

The easy symmetry of this resolution is not altogether sustained in Drant's own explanation. The religious hypocrisies of the sixteenth century were something unknown to Horace: 'he neuer se, yt. with the uiew of his eie, which his pensiue translator can not but everuew with the languishe of his soule'.[7] It is the very point of the opening of *Satyre III* that the alternative attitudes of laughter or tears conflict with and check one another; Donne seems both the 'prophane writer' and the 'man of god'; each rôle is necessary for a full human response to his subject. *Satyre III*, which at first develops in a free way reminiscent of a dramatic soliloquy, calls each attitude into play at different points, as it explores man's dedication of his courage to worldly ends as opposed to those of 'true religion', and the confusion of conflicting claims with which the seeker after 'true religion' must contend. The moral assurance of *Satyre I* has gone, and is replaced by the less confident but immensely stronger and more resolute aspiration towards the ideal of Truth, on its 'huge hill, / Cragged, and steep, . . .'. The speaker is strenuously engaged, with all his faculties and responses, in the midst of the conflicts which the satire exposes. *Satyre III* may merit (though not altogether for the same reasons) the term 'Tragical Satyre' which Dryden was later to apply to Juvenal.[8]

Satyre IV

Satyre IV (*c.* 1597?) brings us back to Horace. This poem has a much closer relation with the Ninth Satire of the First Book than the broad resemblances of *Satyre I*. Not only is the first half of *Satyre IV* a recognizable imitation of Horace's encounter with the Talker, but there are several small though clear echoes of Horace's text. Thus 'Towards me did runne . . .', as Donne's Courtier-Talker makes his appearance, recalls 'accurrit . . .' at the parallel point of Horace's satire.[9] Donne's 'To fit my sullennesse, . . .' (when the speaker fails to shake off the Talker) is a witty play, as Niall Rudd has observed, on Horace's '. . . ut iniquae mentis asellus . . .' (like [the ears of] a sullen ass), again at the parallel point in the Latin poem.[10] Donne's l. 94 echoes l. 4 of

---

[7]Thomas Drant, *A Medicinable Morall, that is, the two Bookes of Horace his Satyres, Englyshed accordyng to the prescription of saint Hierome . . . The Wailyngs of the Prophet hieremiah, done into Englyshe verse. Also Epigrammes* (London, 1566), To the Reader.

[8]Dryden, A Discourse Concerning Satire, l. 2225; *The Poems of John Dryden*, ed. James Kinsley (Oxford, 1958), II, p. 657.

[9]*Satyre IV*, l. 17; Horace, *Sat.* I, ix, 3.

[10]Ibid., l. 91; Horace, *Sat.* I, ix, 20. See Niall Rudd, 'Donne and Horace', *Times Literary Supplement*, 22 March 1963.

Horace, and ll. 116–17 recall ll. 10–11. The vain announcement of the Talker in Horace: 'docti sumus' (soon to be brilliantly expanded by Jonson in his *Poetaster*: 'we are a scholar, I assure thee . . . Nay, we are new turn'd *Poet* too, which is more; and a *Satyrist* too, which is more then that: I write just in thy veine, I . . . we are a prettie stoick too') is developed by Donne into an account of the Courtier-Talker's parade of linguistic accomplishment.[11] In Donne, as in Horace, the scene fills with a crowd as the poet makes his escape.[12] Trifling through these echoes might seem, they would certainly have been recognized by Donne's contemporary readers, more familiar than we are with the chief literary texts of the Roman Augustan Age. The nature of their response may perhaps be gauged by that of Pope when, in imitating Donne's poem over a century later, he correctly recognized in Donne's 'Not alone / My lonenesse is . . .' an allusion to Cicero's *De Officiis*, III, i, 1, making it more explicit in his own version.[13] The Horatian echoes are signs from Donne to his readers which acknowledge his original as a text to be remembered. In this way, whether Donne follows or departs from Horace, what he does will have a significance relative to the Latin poem. That the relationship which Donne set up was recognizable to his contemporaries may be seen from a revealing couplet in Clement Paman's seventeenth-century imitation of *Satyre IV*: *The Taverne*:

> Oh happy Donne & Horace, you h'd but one
> Deuill haunted you, but me a legion . . .[14]

The common features of *Satyre IV* and Horace, *Sat*. I, ix may be summed up as follows. In each poem the speaker is encountered in a public place by a stranger who runs and engages him in conversation. In each poem the stranger proves an intrusive and tactless talker, who praises his own accomplishment, seizes the speaker by the hand with offensive familiarity, and, because he will not be shaken off, causes the speaker to sweat with exasperation, and feel like a fool and a beast of burden. In each poem almost all the speaker says is an attempt to get rid of his unwelcome companion. In each poem a crowd fills the scene as the speaker is finally free.

Once these common features have been recognized, the many significant differences of Donne from Horace may be seen more clearly. Firstly his method is different. Horace's art in *Sat*. I, ix is above all concise. It is a model of expressive brevity. And because both narrative and dialogue are pared down to their essentials the overall shape of the encounter is made very clear. As several critics have intimated, the poem is a drama on a small scale.[15] With great skill Horace plays on his hopes of escape. Ordinary pretexts (the sick friend) fail, and the first stage

[11]Horace, *Sat*. I, ix, 7; Ben Jonson, *The Poetaster*, III, i, 23–8; *Ben Jonson*, ed. C.H. Herford and Percy and Evelyn Simpson (Oxford, 1925–50), IV, p. 234. *Satyre IV*, ll. 51–65; ed. cit. p. 16.

[12]*Satyre IV*, ll. 150–4; p. 19. Horace, *Sat*. I, ix, 77–8. Most of the detailed allusion to Horace, *Sat*. I, ix in *Satyre IV* has been pointed out by Niall Rudd, 'Donne and Horace', loc. cit.

[13]Satyre IV, ll. 67–8; p. 16. Pope, *The Fourth Satire of Dr John Donne*, l. 91. Quotations from Pope are taken from the Twickenham Edition of *The Poems of Alexander Pope*, general editor John Butt (London, 1939–61), IV, *Imitations of Horace*, ed. John Butt (London, 1939; rev. edn, 1961).

[14]Milgate, *Donne, The Satires*, p. 149.

[15]See Eduard Fraenkel, *Horace* (Oxford, 1957), pp. 113–16; Niall Rudd, *The Satires of Horace* (London, 1966), p. 75.

ends when he droops his ears like a sullen ass under a heavy load (ll. 20–1). The second stage reveals that the Talker seeks Horace's friendship and ends with the dashing of the latter's hope that the Talker would leave him to attend his case in the law court. The third and final stage then reveals that the Talker's real purpose is to get an introduction to Maecenas, whose character and household he vulgarly misunderstands. The Talker is, in effect, a would-be courtier, in the worst sense of the word. Peripeteia is introduced when Horace's friend, Aristius Fuscus, appears but refuses to save him from the Talker. This is the cruelly comic climax of the satire, immediately following which the Talker is arrested (an outcome prepared for by the legal incident at the centre of the poem), and Horace is released: 'sic me servavit Apollo'.[16] By contrast, Donne's approach to his subject is copious and exuberant. We have already seen how two words of Horace ('docti sumus') release a small fountain of comic invention in Jonson's *Poetaster*. Donne's comedy is more grotesque and dark than Jonson's but the same fertile amplification of Horace is to be seen in *Satyre IV*. Thus Donne does not start into his story, but opens with a long preamble of explosive exasperation, during the course of which a half-line ('Yet went to Court') is allowed to set the scene. The first introduction of Donne's Courtier-Talker –

> Towards me did runne
> A thing more strange, then on Niles slime, the Sunne
> E'r bred; . . .[17]

introduces no fewer than nine comparisons to convey his strangeness, and Donne launches into a denunciation of his speech before it has actually begun. The same is true of Donne's handling of the dialogue. Donne introduces a dialogue of deliberate cross-purpose, which may perhaps be seen as an extravagant comic distortion of the one interruption and change-of-subject in Horace:

> '. . . . invideat quod et Hermogenes, ego canto.'
> Interpellandi locus hic erat: 'est tibi mater,
> cognati, quis te salvo est opus?'[18]

Characteristically, Donne uses the device not once but several times.

Donne also introduces fundamental changes into the situation of Horace's satire. While these involve naturalizing his original in Donne's country and time, they go much beyond this. The Via Sacra has become the court of Queen Elizabeth. The Talker has explicitly become also a courtier, or at least a pretender to being one. Furthermore the whole theme of Maecenas and his household, which might well seem the heart of Horace's poem, has been dropped. Not only is there no parallel in *Satyre IV*, but Donne has almost reversed the positions. Thus Horace is secure in the good opinion of the noble Maecenas, an opinion which the poem encourages us to see as the just view of a disinterested as well as influential man. By this token Horace's moral and social situation is guaranteed. The Talker, on the other hand, is outside this security, and the

---

[16]I follow Rudd's analysis, *The Satires of Horace*, pp. 75–6.

[17]*Satyre IV*, ll. 17–19; p. 15.

[18]*Sat*. I, ix, 25–7: ' "Even Hermogenes might envy my singing." This was the place to break in. "Have you a mother or relations dependent on your welfare?" '

clumsiness with which he attempts to break in only emphasizes his remoteness from it. In *Satyre IV*, by contrast, the Talker is the one to be, or at least pretend to be, thoroughly conversant with the centre of power, the court, while Donne is the conscious outsider:

> He adds, 'If of court life you knew the good,
> You would leave lonenesse.' I said, 'Not alone
> My lonenesse is.'[19]

In keeping with these changes, Donne has given the conversation of his Talker a marked political aspect:

> More then ten Hollensheads, or Halls, or Stowes,
> Of triviall houshold trash he knowes; He knowes
> When the Queene frown'd, or smil'd, and he knowes what
> A subtle States-man may gather of that;[20]

Here it is possible that Donne is reaching behind Horace to the two Characters of Talkers in Theophrastus: ὁ ἀδολεσχης and ὁ λάλος .[21] Theophrastus's ὁ λάλος (Rudd translates as: 'The Loquacious Man) is full of news of the Assembly, reminiscences of speeches made there, including his own important oratorical efforts, and of tirades against 'the masses'.[22]

Perhaps Donne's most important change, however, concerns the treatment of the law. In Horace's satire the law combines with the good opinion of Maecenas in guaranteeing the poet's fundamental security. In the middle of the poem it is suggested that the leechlike Talker may have been guilty of some misdemeanour. It is his failure to answer bail which causes his arrest, and the liberation of Horace, at the end. As Niall Rudd points out, the world of law mediates between the immediate realm of the dialogue, and the more distant one of heroic warfare recalled for us through metaphor and diction. It is through the instrumentality of the law that Apollo saves Horace.[23] There has certainly been the undercurrent of something frightening in Horace's utter inability to shake off his unwelcome companion; and there is, at the end, a powerful sense of renewed security as he is saved through the public operations of his own society. The world is, after all,

[19]*Satyre IV*, ll. 86–8; p. 17.

[20]*Satyre IV*, ll. 97–100; Cf. also ll. 119–26: pp. 17–18.

[21]In the notes to his edition of Horace, *Horatii Flacci Opera Omnia* . . . (Paris, 1604), Theodorus Marcilius was to refer to these Characters of Theophrastus in connection with the *garrulus* of *Sat.* I, ix; see pp. 95–9. An edition of Theophrastus, including these Characters, and with a Latin translation, had appeared in 1527, another in 1531; and in 1592 the first of the three editions of Isaac Casaubon (see R.C. Jebb, *The Characters of Theophrastus* . . . (London, 1870; new edn by J.E. Sandys, 1909), pp. 164–5). The similarities to Horace's *garrulus* are fairly striking, apart from the general probability of Theophrastan influence on Donne. It is also probable that Donne knew, through his early friend Sir Henry Wotton, of Casaubon's preparation of the important edn of Theophrastus which he published in 1598, since Wotton had stayed with Casaubon in Geneva in 1593–4 (see R.C. Bald, *John Donne: A Life* (London, 1970), p. 284 n. 1). The explicitly Theophrastan *Character of a Dunce* (dubiously by Donne) was to be published in Overbury's *Wife* in 1622.

[22]Jebb, *The Characters of Theophrastus*, pp. 105–6. I am most grateful to Mr I.P. Davies, of Jesus College, Cambridge, for his advice concerning Theophrastus.

[23]Rudd, *The Satires of Horace*, p. 80.

an ordered and reasonable place. These important features of Horace's story have no parallel in Donne. The law certainly plays a part in *Satyre IV* – but of a very different kind. It is introduced, in the preamble, by an apparently tangential comparison: Donne's going to court and suffering for it,

> as Glaze which did goe
> To'a Masse in jest, catch'd, was faine to disburse
> The hundred markes, which is the Statutes curse,
> Before he scapt . . .²⁴

The sardonic humour of this seems to focus chiefly on Glaze, who recalls Donne's list of the ecclesiastically misled in *Satyre III*. It is, however, important that Donne himself is here, though only by analogy, made to seem vulnerable to the law. The theme is picked up again when the Courtier-Talker, 'like a priviledg'd spie', libels the conduct of the government in every aspect:

> I more amas'd then Circes prisoners, when
> They felt themselves turne beasts, felt my selfe then
> Becomming Traytor, and mee thought I saw
> One of our Giant Statutes ope his jaw
> To sucke me in;²⁵

At the end of the encounter with the Talker, Donne runs from court as one 'Who feares more actions, doth make from prison' and this seems to link with the 'Low feare' concerning which Donne communes with himself in the lines which connect the first half of *Satyre IV* with the more visionary view of the court in the second half. Even through this vision we find the theme continued, for here a gallant *protests* to a lady so much as would have had him arrested and thrown to the Inquisition at Rome: and swears so often 'by Jesu' that 'A/Pursevant would have ravish'd him away / For saying of our Ladies psalter' (ll. 212–17). When Donne finally leaves the Court, he goes 'As men which from gaoles to'execution goe' and, passing the Yeoman of the Guard, shakes with fear 'like a spyed Spie' (ll. 230–8). Throughout *Satyre IV* Donne emphasizes his sense of fundamental insecurity. This is conveyed partly through intimations that the Courtier-Talker is not what he seems (the opening description likens him to a Jesuit in disguise; while the 'priviledg'd spie' passage suggests he may be leading Donne on to betray himself), but chiefly through the constant assumption that the law is an enemy rather than a friend. The reversal of the Horatian picture could not be more striking and, in view of the echoes of Horace, *Sat*. I, ix, cannot but have been deliberate on Donne's part.

Horace's satire is autobiographical in the subtly artifical way also to be found in the satires and epistles of Pope. It may be that, in recognizing the fearful attitude towards the law in *Satyre IV*, we have come up against a fact of Donne's biography, as well as a more general response to the time. It has been suggested that Donne's satires express, if somewhat covertly, something of the viewpoint of a Roman Catholic.²⁶ Born and brought up in this religion, Donne was still a

---

²⁴*Satyre IV*, ll. 8–11; p. 14.
²⁵*Satyre IV*, ll. 129–34; p. 18.
²⁶By H.J.C. Grierson; see Bald, *Donne: A Life*, p. 70.

Catholic in 1591, but probably not when he joined the Cadiz Expedition in 1596.[27] It was probably between these dates that Donne undertook his examination of the *Disputationes* of Cardinal Bellarmine, 'the best defender of the Roman Cause'.[28] *Satyre III* (whatever date ascribed to it, 1594–5 or much later) may well seem the outcome of Donne's personal bid to 'Seeke true religion', and while it would be wrong to interpret Mirreus in that poem as a satire on the genuinely convinced Roman Catholic, such a Catholic might seem unlikely to have written the poem. *Satyre IV* has many Catholic references, but they are not all pro-Catholic and, whether pro or con, are often balanced by Protestant references.[29] If Donne is not writing as a Catholic, this does not mean that he is writing as if he had never been one. He was himself to testify, in his *Pseudo-Martyr* (1610) with what gradual deliberation he had moved away from the Roman faith (no 'violent and sudden determination'); and several commentators have observed how a Catholic awareness remained as part of his total awareness, for many years.[30] What is important here is Donne's experience of being a Catholic in a Protestant state, a member of a Church whose practices were forbidden by law. Donne's own brother had been arrested and imprisoned, in 1593, having been discovered with a priest in his chambers. The priest was condemned to death, hanged, drawn and quartered. Henry Donne died of the plague in Newgate.[31] Donne's references to 'the Statutes curse' and the 'Giant Statutes' are sufficiently intelligible in this context, and we may note that at l. 216 an early MS reads: 'Topcliff would have ravish'd him away / For saying our Ladies psalter', Richard Topcliff being the notorious priest-hunter, whose chief colleague had been responsible for the arrest of Henry Donne and his priest.[32] No such references are to be found in the free imitation of Horace, *Sat.* I, ix, published by Mathurin Régnier in 1608. His satire is thoroughly Christian and Catholic, the Talker saluting his victim while the latter is on his knees at mass, but retains the Horatian conclusion in which the satirist is saved by the law.[33] Doubtless Donne was not much less ready to allude to his Catholic background, in a Protestant state, than Horace to refer to his relation with Maecenas. Yet this should not be allowed to support an unduly restricted reading of *Satyre IV*. Of the five references in the poem which express fear of the law only two are explicitly linked with anti-Catholic legislation.[34] What, by contrast with Horace and Régnier, this poem urges upon us is the experience of fearing an unjust force in the law and operations of the established state.

The remaining differences of Donne from Horace, in the first half of *Satyre*

[27]Bald, *Donne: A Life*, p. 63; Milgate, *Donne, The Satires*, p. 139.

[28]Ibid., pp. 68–72.

[29]Cf. ll. 8–11, 241–4 with 47–8, 200–3; pp. 14, 22, 15–6, 20–1. Some such references are balanced in close pairs, e.g. ll. 55–7 and 212–18; pp. 16, 21.

[30]Bald, *Donne: A Life*, p. 67. And see, for example, E.M. Simpson, ed., *The Courtier's Library by John Donne* (London, 1930), p. 12: 'The tone of the Catalogue is indeed more anti-Protestant than we might expect from the date [*c.* 1603–11?] which I have assigned to it.' Her conclusion that Donne's Papist sympathies lingered on to some degree (pp. 12–13) seems a fair one, though here too a balance is struck by Donne.

[31]Bald, *Donne: A Life*, p. 58.

[32]Milgate, *Donne, The Satires*, p. 162; Bald, *Donne: A Life*, p. 58.

[33]Régnier, Satyre VIII, ll. 1–12, 211–24; Mathurin Régnier, *Oeuvres Complètes*; Edition critique publiée par Gabriel Raibaud (Paris, 1958), pp. 80–90.

[34]*Satyre IV*, ll. 8–11, 215–17; pp. 14, 21.

IV, are in accord with the intention and tone we have already noticed. The Sabine woman's prophecy of Horace's death from a Talker — a piece of stately mock-heroic — is dropped; so is the appearance of Horace's friend near the end of the encounter; and Donne finally gets rid of his Courtier-Talker in a shabbily ordinary way: the latter asks him for money, and the poet gives him a crown in ransom. By comparison with Horace this is a most anti-climactic ending to the encounter, but it is right, for two reasons. The asking for money is a derisive comment on the Courtier's earlier invitation to Donne to enjoy 'the good' of court life; and Donne is, unlike Horace, preparing for a different kind of climax after the encounter is over. That climax is to arise from the poet's regaining his 'wholesome solitarinesse' after the exasperation and fear of the encounter; the appearance of some 'Fuscus Aristius . . . mihi carus', however unsympathetic to the poet's plight, would have broken this necessary contrast. And indeed the episodes of Fuscus Aristius and the Sabine woman show that for Horace comedy goes almost to the heart of his situation; with Donne it is much more on the surface. Régnier was to introduce the prophecy of 'une Bohemienne' into his satire with propriety; in *Satyre IV* it would have been an intrusion.

What then is Donne's final attitude to his Courtier-Talker? Is it the rather resolute laughter recommended in his Paradox VII: *That a wise man is knowne by much Laughing*?

> A foole if he come into a Princes Court, and see a gay man leaning at the wall, so glistering, and so painted in many colors that he is hardly discernd from one of the Pictures in the Arras hangings, his body like an Ironbound chest girt in, and thicke ribbd with broad gold laces, may and commonly doth envy him, But alas! shall a wise man, which may not only not envy this fellow, but not pity him, do nothing at this monster? Yes: let him laugh.[35]

The close connection of this Paradox with *Satyre IV* is not to be doubted. Yet Donne's attitude in the poem, though it partakes of the wise laughter of the Paradox, is much more complicated. The opening description, though to the effect that the Courtier is a '*Monster*', conjures up through its exuberant amplification more fantastic shapes even than the Paradox — shapes whose appropriateness in the poem becomes clear in the second half. When Donne makes his Courtier praise 'your Apostles' as 'Good pretty linguists', he gives us something which invites sardonic ridicule, but a tremendous undercurrent of indignation is felt at the same time. Something of the same complexity is found in Donne's magnificent repartee (though here the patronizing tones of the Courtier are not, as in Pope, present to provoke anger):

> . . . I was faine to say, 'If you'had liv'd, Sir,
> Time enough to have beene Interpreter
> To Babells bricklayers, sure the Tower had stood.'[36]

---

[35]Helen Peters, ed., *Donne, Paradoxes and Problems* (Oxford, 1980), pp. 15–6. Wilbur Sanders discusses the *Paradoxes and Problemes* in connection with the Satires, in Ch. 2 of his book *John Donne's Poetry* (Cambridge, 1971). I think there is a close relation between Paradox VII and *Satyre IV*, but that the insights of the poem are more complex than those of the Paradox.

[36]*Satyre IV*, ll. 63–5; p. 16.

The comic extravagance of this conception also sizes up the Courtier effectively in Biblical terms; it tells us, perhaps, that he is not altogether a creature to be dismissed with a laugh. Once the initial exchanges are over, his conversation is by no means unmitigated nonsense. 'When the Queene frown'd, or smil'd, and . . . what / A subtle States-man may gather of that', in the atmosphere of this poem, are not altogether 'triviall houshold trash' and his subsequent remarks are in themselves so clearly a satire on court corruption that we are not surprised to notice the tones of Donne eventually taking over:

> He knowes who loves; whom; and who by poyson
> Hasts to an Offices reversion;
> He knowes who'hath sold his land, and now doth beg
> A licence, old iron, bootes, shooes, and egge-
> shels to transport; Shortly boyes shall not play
> At span-counter, or blow-point, but they pay
> Toll to some Courtier;[37]

That outrageous enjambement expresses the very acme of incredulous contempt – but whether for court gossip, or court abuse, it is hard to say. Certainly the lines have modulated into a comment by Donne at the end. It might seem that in these lines Donne recklessly takes over the Courtier's conversation as a vehicle for his satire on the court – and that that is all. But this is not so, for the subjects of the Courtier's discourse here point unmistakably ahead to the passage in which, 'like a priviledg'd spie' he libels the whole government, and terrifies his listener at the implications of the situation. There is just enough method in the Courtier's conversation to suggest that he may not be altogether what he seems; it is hinted that he talks like an intelligencer, and there the matter is left, most disturbingly and, in view of the sense of danger Donne wishes to create, most successfully, undefined. The situation is consistently dramatic. Neither in the poem, nor, at this time perhaps, in real life, has Donne the security of the mere commentator: the wise man who can just laugh. The exuberant comedy is in dialogue with fear.

Donne's Vision

It is fear which is the theme of the soliloquy to which the satire now mounts. Donne now takes his leave of Horace, *Sat*. I, ix and, given his own very different treatment of its basic situation, it is easy to see why *Satyre IV* had to continue, though Horace had solved all *his* problems with the arrest of the Talker. The somewhat anti-climactic passing of money, which ended Donne's encounter, by no means dispelled the exasperation and fear to which it had given rise, and the general sense of danger with which the writing of poetry about the court had so often been associated in sixteenth- and late fifteenth-century England. We remember Skelton, newly embarked on the 'goodly' ship 'Bouge of Court', confronted by 'Favell, full of flattery, / With fables false that well could feign a tale;' and 'Suspect, which that daily / Misdeemed each man, with face deadly

[37]Ibid., ll. 101–7; p. 17.

and pale'.[38] Wyatt in his important and successful First Satire ('Mine owne John Poyntz . . .'), while in no way scorning 'The power of them, to whom fortune hath lent / Charge over us, of right to strike the stroke', could still say: 'I am not he that can alow the state / Of high Caesar and damn Cato to die,' who 'would not live where liberty was lost'; and could oppose to the values of the court those of his personal 'liberty', retired 'in Kent and Christendom'.[39] In the 1563 edition of *The Mirror for Magistrates* appeared the plea of the unhappy poet Collingbourne:

> I thought the freedome of the auncient tymes
> Stoode styll in force. *Ridentem dicere verum*
> *Quis vetat*? . . .
>
> Belyke no Tyrantes were in Horace dayes,
> And therefore Poetes freely blamed vyce.
> Witnes theyr Satyr sharpe, and tragicke playes . . .[40]

Three years later, in the prefatory matter of Drant's *Medcinable Morall*, the perennial ideal was reaffirmed:

> The Satyrist loues Truthe, none more than he.
> An utter foe to fraude in eache degree.[41]

A simultaneous awareness of this danger and this challenge powers Donne's passage of soliloquy:

> At home in wholesome solitarinesse
> My precious soule began, the wretchednesse
> Of suiters at court to mourne, and a trance
> Like his, who dreamt he saw hell, did advance
> It selfe on mee; Such men as he saw there,
> I saw at court, and worse, and more; Low feare
> Becomes the guiltie, not th'accuser; Then,
> Shall I, nones slave, of high borne, or rais'd men
> Feare frownes? And, my Mistresse Truth, betray thee
> To th'huffing braggart, puft Nobility?
> No, no, Thou which since yesterday hast beene
> Almost about the whole world, hast thou seene,
> O Sunne, in all thy journey, Vanitie,
> Such as swells the bladder of our court?[42]

[38] *The Complete Poems of John Skelton, Laureate*, ed. Philip Henderson (London, 1931; rev. edn, 1948), p. 41.

[39] Ll. 7–9, 37–41, 80–5, 100–3; *The Collected Poems of Sir Thomas Wyatt*, ed. Joost Daalder (London, 1975), pp. 100–4.

[40] 'How Collingbourn was cruelly executed for making a foolish rime', ll. 96–101; *The Mirror for Magistrates*, ed. Lily B. Campbell (London, 1938; rev. edn, 1960), pp. 350–1. Pope knew *The Mirror for Magistrates* (see Owen Ruffhead's *Life of Pope* (London, 1769), p. 425) and was to refer to the story of Collingbourne, and also to the statutes of Edward VI and Elizabeth, when he in his turn came to discuss the dangers of writing satire: *The First Satire of the Second Book of Horace, Imitated*, ll. 145–9; *Poems*, IV p. 19.

[41] To the Reader.

[42] *Satyre IV*, ll. 155–68; p. 19.

This 'wholesome solitarinesse', prepared for, indeed longed for, in Donne's cryptic remark to the Courtier: 'Not alone / My lonenesse is', with its allusion to Cicero on the retirement of Scipio Africanus, comes with immense relief after the almost intolerable pressure of the court encounter. Yet in the freedom of this respite the mind returns again to the experience, this time fully mastering it, through the allusion to Dante, and suffusing it with an infernal hue. We may recall an entry in Donne's *Catalogus Librorum*: 'The Quintessence of Hell; or, The private apartment of Hell, in which is a discussion of the fifth region passed over by Homer, Virgil, Dante and the rest of the Papists, where, over and above the penalties and sensations of the damned, Kings are tortured by a recollection of the past'.[43] There is a comic ambiguity in this compared with the boldness and plainness of the declaration he makes in the satire:

> Such men as he saw there,
> I saw at court, and worse, and more;

which the poem's mode of sardonic exaggeration should not persuade us to pass over lightly. In the 'wholesome solitarinesse' of his retirement the moral and religious realities triumph over the temporal ones, and therefore over 'Low feare'. From this conviction springs the satirist's heroic dedication of himself to Truth despite the consequences, the emotion of which is utterly different from anything to be found in Horace, *Sat*. I, ix, though it has some affinities with the conclusion of *Sat*. II, i. The need and the energy for this dedication has, through Donne's different treatment of the situation of Horace, *Sat*. I, ix, been building up from the very beginning of *Satyre IV*. This is the centre and the climax of the poem, and is most like the 'Tragical' mode of satire already achieved by Donne in *Satyre III*. From this point the tone begins to descend once more, with the emphasis falling again on hollowness and vanity; scorn and ridicule, major weapons in Donne's satiric armoury in the first half of the poem, now come back into their own. But this central withdrawal and affirmation, which has drawn together all the leading motifs in the reflections upon court satire of Skelton, Wyatt, the *Mirror for Magistrates* author, and Drant, has structured Donne's poem, and given us, in dramatic fashion, intimations of that source of dedication and defiance which animates much of the finest satire between the Roman Lucilius and the English Pope.

' 'Tis ten a clock and past . . .' (l. 175) returns us to the court. It is hard, on the level of strict literal interpretation, to tell whether what now follows is a continuation of that 'trance / Like his, who dreamt he saw hell' which has been so crucial to Donne's satiric resolve. I am inclined to think that it is, and that the intervening lines between that and this point are another example of the eager self-anticipation, with which, at the beginning of the poem, Donne described the manner and matter of the Courtier's speech before he gave us his opening remark. Certainly once the infernal comparison has been made it is hard to forget, and this is the most important point. The comparison links readily with certain details in the latter part of the poem: 'As if the Presence were a Moschite . . .', '. . . his face be'as ill / As theirs which in old hangings whip Christ . . .',

---

[43]No. 30, *The Courtier's Library*, p. 52. Other entries in *Catalogus Librorum* relate to the Satires, e.g. No. 13 with *Satyre II*, ll. 91–6, and, more generally, No. 22 with *Satyre III*..

'. . . through the great chamber (why is it hung / With the seaven deadly sinnes?)' (ll. 199, 225–6, 231–2). Perhaps, the answer is implied, because this is like Hell. Perhaps that quality of the grotesque/fantastic, in the appearance of the original Courtier –

> A thing more strange, then on Niles slime, the Sunne
> E'er bred;

– not to mention Macrine, Glorius, and the giant Askaparts, is consonant with the same trancelike effect.

However the chief logic relating this part of *Satyre IV* to the earlier part is one of expansion. At first an individual encounter with a courtier is almost too much for the satirist, and at the sudden sight of 'All the court fill'd with more strange things then hee' he flies. After self-communing in 'wholesome solitarinesse', he is able, either literally or more probably in vision, to return and confront a full gathering of courtiers in the Presence Chamber. His renewed fortitude is not, however, a simple heroic defiance. This indeed comes first, in the central passage of soliloquy, but hard on the heels of his resolution comes a supporting – in the circumstances almost a comforting – conviction of the essential hollowness of the court. 'High borne, or rais'd men' are succeeded, if not replaced, in his awareness by 'th'huffing braggart, puft Nobility'. The stress on hollowness stretches quite far into the satire's second description of the court, and Donne's gift for remarks of sardonic realism, already deployed against the courtier, is an effective satirical resource here:

> 'For a King
> Those hose are,' cry the flatterers; And bring
> Them next weeke to the Theatre to sell;[44]

Indeed Donne's 'All are players' is a limiting judgement, lacking the philosophical resonance this famous metaphor has in More's *Utopia*, or in (the perhaps roughly contemporaneous) *As You Like It*, not to mention the forthcoming *Macbeth*. The figures of the court, at this point, are grotesque, jerking puppets. So absurd are they that even Heraclitus would laugh. Yet this reference to the Weeping Philosopher suggests an underlying conflict which is for the moment being resolutely simplified. We are reminded, as we were at the opening of *Satyre III*, of laughter and tears, the alternative attitudes to sin. In Drant 'not a thousand *Democrati*, coulde suffice to laugh' at fools that have been praised and revered, 'nor a thousand *Heracliti* be enough to wepe' at wise men discredited and profaned.[45] Donne's resolution in Paradox VII ('*Democritus* and *Heraclitus* the lovers of these extremes have beene called lovers of wisdome. Now among our wise men, I doubt not, but many would be found, who would laughe at *Heraclitus* his weeping, none which weepe at *Democritus* laughing') is further condensed at this point in *Satyre IV*.[46] The *picture* of Macrine is absurd enough to make even Heraclitus laugh; the infidel associations which are

[44]*Satyre IV*, ll. 181–3; p. 20.
[45]Drant, *A Medcinable Morall*, To the Reader.
[46]Hayward, *Donne, Complete Poetry*, pp. 343–4.

stressed immediately after ('As if the Presence were a Moschite . . .') tell us that this laughter is almost inseparable from weeping at sin.

From this point the sense of fear and horror begins to make itself felt once again. Laughter at the absurd 'protests protests protests', in the paying court to the ladies, is of no easily secure kind when followed so promptly by references to Roman Inquisitors and Elizabethan pursuivants. The portrait of Glorius, related to the 'firebrand' of Paradox VII as the Courtier is to the 'gay man . . . glistering, and . . . painted';

> if one of these hott cholerique firebrands, which nourish themselves by quarelling and kindling others spitt upon a fool but one sparke of disgrace, he like a thatcht house quickly burning, may be angry . . .[47]

is done with an especially appropriate defiant vigour:

> But here comes Glorius that will plague them both
> Who, in the other extreme, only doth
> Call a rough carelessenesse, good fashion;
> Whose cloak his spurres teare; whom he spits on
> He cares not; His ill words doe no harme
> To him; he rusheth in, as if 'Arme, arme,'
> He meant to crie. And though his face be'as ill
> As theirs which in old hangings whip Christ, yet still
> He strives to looke worse, he keepes all in awe;
> Jeasts like a licenc'd foole, commands like law.[48]

Glorius, by comparison with the summarized satiric *type* in the Paradox, is a dramatic presence; Donne's style seems to emulate 'a rough carelessenesse' here, though in fact his control is sure. The phrase 'good fashion' takes its quiet stand at the end of the third line to create a symmetry of opposites, and this sense of balance within vehement movement assures us of the continuance of Donne's judgement. But what the satire perceives morally is brilliantly conveyed in the visual detail which follows ('Whose cloak his spurres teare . . .') which at once enforces the judgement and renders the figure of Glorius immediate to the eye. A familiar balance and control may be seen in the whole portrait. On the one hand there is a reckless bravura of description ('. . . as if "Arme, arme" / He meant to crie . . .'); on the other, the pattern of the verse, frequently through skilful use of enjambement, keeps some disturbing recognitions in reserve. The manner of the contemptuous satirist seems well away with 'His ill words doe no harme', but is sharply qualified by '/ To *him*' (my italics), while the lurid and macabre comparison with those who 'in old hangings whip Christ', which we have already seen to add to the infernal atmosphere, is similarly followed up by: '. . . yet still / He strives to look worse . . .'. There is here a strange mingling of hyperbolic sarcasm and the sense of evil. The most disturbing touch of all, however, is undoubtedly the end, where another strongly symmetrical line, promising a powerful and well-rounded conclusion, associates with this barbarian, by

---

[47]Ibid., p. 344.
[48]*Satyre IV*, ll. 219–28; p. 21.

its last word, all that sense of danger from the law which this satire has cumulatively built up.

'Tyr'd, now I leave this place' (l. 229) marks not the end but the final intensification of the nightmare. Deadly sins loom from the walls, the guards stand like giants, massive in their loyalty to a sovereign whose power is not less dreadful if she has herself been absent from the vision of the court which the satirist has rendered. Amid the *grotesque* of the nightmare, the note of confidence just advances once more, as the 'Askaparts' become 'barrells of beefe, flaggons of wine', but then the motif of danger, fear and the sense of guilt felt if unearned, a motif which has run through the satire, is stressed for the last time:

I shooke like a spyed Spie . . .[49]

It is in this context, I think, that the conclusion of the satire must be read. Confident and powerful judgement upon the court, vehement and energetic ridicule, are one side only of the satirist's human response. Fear, whether, as in the central soliloquy of the satire, 'Low', or as here at the end, justified and religious, has been equally if not more emphasized, has mingled with the wit, hyperbole and exaggeration, and is the other side. This is the development, in *Satyre IV*, of those antitheses of laughter and tears which conflicted at the opening of *Satyre III*, and which had been set out schematically by Drant. The concluding appeal that 'Preachers' rather than satirists should 'Drowne the sinnes of this place' (ll. 237–41) is thus something more than the boyish 'hot flush of modest sanctimony' which a recent critic has found it, just as the poem to this point has been more than '240-odd lines . . . passionately denouncing that bladder swollen with vanity, the Court . . .'.[50] Not only has the satire been much more complex than this judgement allows but its conclusion marks the completion of an expressive structure. Donne has dramatized a double-exposure to the court, divided by a passage of self-communing which regenerates his moral strength for the second bout, but concluded by the overcoming both of his erected wit and his moral resolution to withstand.[51] In the fiction of the satire, the satirist passes his pen and his scourge over to the divine. This is his final taking of the moral measure of the court. The tone, with its '*Macchabees* modestie' (l. 242), now becomes one of controlled understatement. The final allusion, at once a graceful disclaimer of merit, an acknowledgement that his subject has in a sense been too much for him, a delicate reminder of Papist and Protestant differences, and suggestion that his views as those of a one-time Papist are urged with diffidence, nevertheless lays its chief stress on the inconspicuous but firm contention that it is the truth which the satirist has told.

Pope's 'Impertinent'

Many English translations and imitations of Horace, *Sat.* I, ix appeared between the last decade of the sixteenth century and the first decade of the

---

[49]Ibid., l. 237; p. 22.

[50]Sanders, *John Donne's Poetry*, p. 36.

[51]Sanders's view (ibid., p. 39) that 'Satirical activity of this kind . . . can have no structure beyond the episodic. . . . Most of the *Satyres* go on too long . . .' is, I think, questionable in general, but certainly wrong in respect of *Satyre IV*.

eighteenth century, but none so bold, extravagant and significant an adaptation as Donne's *Satyre IV*. One work stands out, however, partly because of intrinsic interest, partly because Pope commended it, and recalled it when he came to write his version of Donne's poem. This is John Oldham's *Imitation of Horace. Book I. – Satire IX*.[52] Oldham's poem is a genuine imitation. It follows the outline of Horace's story, ending where Horace did, and embodies all its major features. On the other hand the rendering is free in points of detail, including passages for which there is no parallel in Horace, and the situation has been transposed to the London of 1681: the Mall, Westminster Hall, Rochester recently dead, and the Popish Plot crisis just dying down. The Plot is in fact the subject of some of the most interesting lines:

> Next he begins to plague me with the *Plot*,
> Asks, whether I were known to *Oats* or not?
> '*Not I, thank Heaven! I no priest have been*:
> *Have never* Doway, *nor* St Omers *seen.*'
> '*What think you, Sir; will they* Fitz-Harris *try*?
> *Will he die, think you?*' '*Yes, most certainly.*'
> '*I mean, be hanged.*' '*Would thou wert so*, (wished I!)
> Religion came in next, tho he'd no more
> Than the *French* King, his Punk, or Confessor.
> '*Oh! the sad times, if once the King should die*!
> *Sir, are you not afraid of popery*?'
> '*No more than my superiors: why should I*?
> *I've no Estate in Abby-lands to lose.*'
> '*But Fire, and Faggot, Sir, how like you those*?'
> *Come Inquisition, anything*,' (thought I)
> *So Heav'n would bless me to get rid of thee*!
> But 'tis some comfort, that my Hell is here . . .[53]

It is convincing that this, more than topics of poetry and music, represented the current talk of the town. Furthermore the conversation of the Talker is doubly unwelcome here because it is dangerous. The Talker asks politically leading questions, and the satirist, having spotted and avoided the trap in the first ('I no priest have been . . .') is soon confronted, at that precarious turning-point in British politics when support for the succession of the Catholic Duke of York was beginning to rally, with a trap of the opposite kind ('Sir, are you not afraid of popery?'). The evasiveness of his answer only stresses the danger. It is interesting that an English imitator of Horace, *Sat*. I, ix has again responded to the Roman poem in a political way, and has underlined Horace's extreme discomfort and exasperation with the Talker by adding to it the sense of insecurity and danger. This may suggest that Oldham knew *Satyre IV* (last republished in the 1669 edition of Donne's poems) and there are other signs in the passage quoted (the wilful misunderstanding of the question about the fate of

[52]Pope marked his approval of this satire in his copy of *Oldham's Works* (1683–95) now in the British Library (pressmark: C. 45. a. 1) calling it one of 'The Most Remarkable Works in this Author'; and he echoed ll. 16–17 of it ('. . . wild to get loose . . .') at the parallel point of his imitation of *Satyre IV* of Donne (ll. 116–17); *Poems*, IV, p. 35.

[53]*An Imitation of Horace. Book I. – Satire IX*, ll. 107–24; John Oldham *Some New Pieces Never before Publish'd* (London, 1684), pp. 48–9.

those under arrest; the declaration in the last line that 'my hell is here') that this was so.[54] But whether Oldham remembered Donne or not, his poem can only have contributed to Pope's awareness of how the imitation of Horace, *Sat*. I, ix might be turned to political ends.

It is this point which ought first to be borne in mind when we ask the question: why, in 1733, did Pope choose to imitate Donne's *Satyre IV* when he might, had he so wished, have included a direct version of Horace, *Sat*. I, ix among his current *Imitations of Horace*? Pope's reasons are intimated in the Horatian epigraph he chose for his versions of Donne:

> Quid vetat, ut nosmet Lucili scripta legentes
> Quærere, num illius, num rerum dura negarit
> Versiculos natura magis factos, & euntes
> Mollius?[55]

These lines from Horace, *Sat*. I, x suggest to the reader that the relation between Horace and the earlier Roman satirist Lucilius, and that between Pope and Donne, are intended to be seen in parallel. This, coupled with the fact that much of what Horace says about Lucilius consists of praise for his wit and blame for his rough versification and poor craftsmanship, has encouraged critical investigation of the more technical differences and similarities between Donne's satires and Pope's imitations of them. Attention has been paid particularly to rough and smooth rhythm, open and closed couplets, the nature and handling of images.[56] There is, however, another aspect of the Lucilius–Donne parallel which was, if anything, more important to Pope. The poem which Pope published immediately before his version of *Satyre IV* was his imitation of Horace, *Sat*. II, i. In this satire Horace praised Lucilius for his bold attack upon vice in high places. When Pope comes to render the lines in which this tribute occurs, he departs from the procedure of Horace and assumes the rôle of Lucilius himself.[57] Horace, *Sat*. II, i, together with Pope's imitation, tell us that if indeed Pope sees Donne as the Lucilius to his Horace, it is as much because he

---

[54] It is interesting that Donne's *Ignatius His Conclave* (1611) was republished (in the original Latin) in 1680, at the height of the anti-Jesuit furore of the Popish Plot crisis, shortly after the publication of the first, and apparently after the composition of all of Oldham's own celebrated *Satires Upon the Jesuits* (1679, 1681). This might have prompted Oldham to look at Donne's Satires.

[55] Pope, *Poems*, IV, pp. 23, 129 (Horace *Sat*. I, x, 56–9): 'And as we read the writings of Lucilius, what forbids us, too, to ask whether it was himself, or the harsh nature of his material, that denied him more finished and smoother verses?' On Pope's idea of Donne as an English Lucilius, see pp. 295–7 below, and *Pope, Horatian Satires and Epistles*, ed. H.H. Erskine-Hill (Oxford, 1964), pp. 14–17.

[56] See Ian Jack's valuable essay, 'Pope and the Weighty Bullion of Dr Donne's Satires', *Publications of the Modern Languages Association*, 66 (1951), pp. 1009–22; and for a somewhat different approach, A.C. Bross, 'Alexander Pope's Revisions of John Donne's Satyres', *Xavier University Studies*, 5, 3 (1966), pp. 133–52. When in 1735 Pope published his versions of Donne's *Satyre II* and *Satyre IV* together, he invited detailed comparison by printing his original alongside them. Pope's text of Donne diverges from all previous editions (except possibly the rare 1649 edition which I have been unable to check). Perhaps Pope constructed his own text of Donne for this purpose.

[57] Horace, *Sat*. II, i, 62–79; *The First Satire of the Second Book of Horace, Imitated*, ll. 105–42. Pope, *Poems*, IV, pp. 15–19.

admired Donne's daring and dedication to truth, as because he longed to polish his rough numbers.

Pope's purpose in seeking to command and redirect the moral qualities of *Satyre IV* may be seen from the subtitle he gave his imitation, when it first appeared late in 1733: *The Impertinent, Or a Visit to the Court . . .* [58] Pope could find a pattern in Horace for much of what he wished to say about contemporary England in the third decade of the eighteenth century; he could make much of Horace's praise of a Lucilius who ' . . . primores populi arripuit . . .' (*Sat.* II, i, 69) but he could find no precedent in that many-sided poet for so direct an attack upon the court as Donne's. In the Advertisement with which Pope, two years later, was to preface his versions of Horace and Donne, he spoke of having versified the satires of Donne ' . . . *at the Desire of the Earl of* Oxford *while he was Lord Treasurer, and of the Duke of* Shrewsbury *who had been Secretary of State; neither of whom look'd upon a Satire on Vicious Courts as any Reflection on those they serv'd in.*' [59] A satire on a vicious court was thus Pope's aim, and the mildly equivocal nature of the statement quoted (though Pope versified Donne's *Satyre II* while Oxford was Treasurer there is no other evidence that he then versified *Satyre IV*) leaves us with the implication that there was a significant difference between the court of Anne and that of George II and Queen Caroline. This, with some justification, Pope firmly believed. This is not the place to enter into Pope's motives for wishing to mount an attack upon the English court at this time. Suffice to say that Pope held it to be corrupt, responsible for the prolongation in power of a corrupt and corrupting régime – that of Sir Robert Walpole – and that corruption was for Pope, not just localized maladministration that could be halted at any time but the process by which commonwealths are ruined and civilizations decay. *Satyre IV* was to be pressed into the service of a vision which had already, in Book III of the 1729 *Dunciad*, offered a prospect of the fall of earlier civilizations, and in the Epistle *To Bathurst* (published January 1733) depicted the financial corruption of contemporary Britain. [60] Thus while Pope opens his imitation in a tone of easy Horatian equanimity (remembering, perhaps, the closing lines of Horace, *Ep.* II, ii), he follows Donne in his initial attribution to the court of various sins and faults: pride, vanity, falsity and debt; and thus the moral of Donne's cryptic and sardonic allusions to Spartan drunkenness, and to Aretino, is proclaimed by Pope in rollingly clear and confident couplets:

---

[58]That Pope should have originally called his poem *The Impertinent* suggests that he was well aware of the Latin text behind *Satyre IV*. This term seems first to have been applied to Horace's *garrulus*, in English translations of *Sat.* I, ix, by Alexander Brome, who entitled his version: 'A description of an impertinent prating Fool' (*The Poems of Horace . . . Rendred into English Verse by Several Persons* (1666), p. 227). Creech followed: 'The Description of an Impertinent Fop . . .' (Thomas Creech, *The Odes, Satyrs, and Epistles of Horace. Done into English . . .* (1684), p. 410); so did Dunster: 'The Description of an Impertinent' (S. Dunster, *The Satires and Epistles of Horace, Done into English . . .* (1709), p. 95. Pope himself, in the MS note in his copy of *Oldham's Works*, refers to Oldham's version as 'The Impertinent from Hor. Sat. 9 lib. 1'.

[59]*Poems*, IV, p. 3.

[60]*The Dunciad* (1729), III, 59–110; *Epistles to Several Persons*, III (*To Allen Lord Bathurst*), ll. 25–151, 339–402. Studies which throw light on Pope's concept of corruption are: Isaac Kramnick, *Bolingbroke and His Circle* (London, 1968); Maynard Mack, *The Garden and the City* (London, 1969); and Howard Erskine-Hill, *Pope, The Dunciad* (London, 1972), Ch. 6.

> Tho' in his Pictures Lust be full display'd,
> Few are the Converts *Aretine* has made;
> And tho' the Court show *Vice* exceeding clear,
> None shou'd, by my Advice, learn *Virtue* there.[61]

Pope has certainly made himself 'exceeding clear', if he has abandoned the more subtly inflected accents of Donne.

At a later point Pope shows how well he can use Donne's poem to speak to his own time. Donne's reference to Queen Elizabeth bore witness to the awesome power of the sovereign, and the significance which might be attributed to her every gesture. Pope, with the air of an *ingénu*, follows the reference literally (as also Donne's expressive, colloquial enjambement):

> When the *Queen* frown'd, or smiled, he knows; and what
> A subtle Minister may make of that?[62]

to produce a more specific and somewhat different meaning. Queen Caroline's influence over the king was notorious, as was the fact that it was through her Walpole retained the backing of the court. In the context of the 1730s the 'subtle Minister' is Walpole himself, and 'what he makes of' Caroline's smiles or frowns is richly ambiguous. Something of what he makes of them is now detailed by Pope's Courtier-Talker, and a succession of regular end-stopped couplets provides a glib catalogue of the corruptions of the time:

> Who, having lost his Credit, pawn'd his Rent,
> Is therefore fit to have a *Government*?
> Who in the *Secret*, deals in Stocks secure,
> And cheats th'unknowing Widow, and the Poor?
> Who makes a *Trust*, or *Charity*, a job,
> And gets an Act of Parliament to rob?[63]

Pope's rhythms in this poem, though certainly more regular and rapid than those of Donne, are not without their colloquial inflexions; here, however, as Pope expands on his original, the easy symmetry of the couplets is notably appropriate to the blandness of the Courtier-Talker's delivery. The catalogue seems endless, and the satirist's expression of a moral nausea, when it comes, has more point, is more of a relief, than in Donne. Pope now comes to the 'priviledg'd spie' passage; again he is able to follow the main lines of Donne, while adding and altering in detail to give contemporary point. Walpole is again at the centre of the picture:

> Then as a licens'd Spy, whom nothing can
> Silence, or hurt, he libels the *Great Man*;
> Swears every *Place entail'd* for Years to come,
> In *Sure Succession* to the Day of Doom:
> He names the *Price* for ev'ry *Office* paid,

[61] *The Fourth Satire of Dr John Donne, Dean of St Paul's, Versifyed*, ll. 94–7; *Poems*, IV, p. 33.
[62] *The Fourth Satire of Donne*, ll. 132–3; ed. cit. p. 37. In 1735 and after, the reader would see Donne's reference to the Queen on the facing page.
[63] *The Fourth Satire of Donne*, ll. 138–43; p. 37.

And says our *Wars thrive ill*, because delay'd;
Nay hints, 'tis by Connivance of the Court,
That *Spain* robs on, and *Dunkirk's* still a Port.[64]

These were the reiterated criticisms of the Opposition to Walpole. Coming from
the Courtier, they arouse the same sense of danger in the satirist as had been
hinted at by Oldham and dramatized by Donne. But after Pope has followed
Donne almost exactly in the crucial line ('. . . methought I saw / One of our
Giant *Statutes* ope its Jaw!') he introduces his one significant change to the
story-line of Donne's poem:

In that nice Moment, as another Lye
Stood just a-tilt, the *Minister* came by.
Away he flies. He bows and bows again;
And close as *Umbra* joins the dirty Train.
Not *Fannius* self more impudently near,
When half his Nose is in his Patrons' Ear.[65]

Since 'the *Great Man*' has been alluded to so often in Pope's imitation of
Satyre IV it is appropriate that he should make this brief appearance at the
climax of the satirist's encounter with the Courtier-Talker. It is of more interest,
in Pope's context, than the passing of money would have been, though it plays
down the possibility that the Courtier-Talker was really a 'licens'd Spy'. But if
he thus appears less dangerous as an individual, he is the symptom of something
more dangerous: he is the man of no values, *Umbra*, the shade, the shadow of all
men, the creature and parasite, entirely corrupted. Pope might well compare
him with Lord Hervey (*Fannius*), the pliable go-between of Walpole and
Caroline, whose current political rôle was soon to be expressed in the Sporus
portrait of *To Arbuthnot*.[66] At this point it is clear that Pope, in deviating from
Donne, has been fully aware of Donne's Horatian original. For the Courtier-
Talker's pursuit of 'the *Great Man*' is precisely how the Talker in Horace
proposes to ingratiate himself with Maecenas ('. . . non, hodie si / exclusus
fuero, desistam; tempora quaeram, / occurram in triviis, deducam.').[67] And
this, as so often in Pope's poems, leaves us with the implied comparison between
a Roman ideal and a fallen contemporary reality. The corrupt great minister is
seen in the light of Maecenas, of whose household Horace could say to the
Talker:

     domus hac nec purior ulla est
nec magis his aliena malis; nil mi officit, inquam,
ditior hic aut est quia doctior; est locus uni
cuique suus.[68]

---

[64]Ibid., ll. 158–65; p. 39.
[65]Ibid., ll. 174–9; p. 41.
[66]*To Dr Arbuthnot*, ll. 305–33; and see the relevant notes, not only in *Poems*, IV, pp. 117–19, but
also in John Butt, ed. *An Epistle to Dr Arbuthnot* (London, 1954), pp. 36–7.
[67]*Sat*. I, ix, 57–9: 'If shut out today, I'll not give up; I'll enquire the right time; I'll meet him in the
streets; I'll escort him home.'
[68]Ibid., ll. 49–52: 'No house is cleaner or more free from such evil intrigues. It doesn't hurt me, I
say, if someone is richer or more learned than I am. Each of us has his own place.'

Christian Satire

So much for the political daring of *Satyre IV* and what Pope was able to make of this for his own time. Pope was drawn to *Satyre IV* for at least two other reasons. The first is its Christianity. The second is its wit.

In his Advertisement to his Imitations of Horace, Pope was to speak of the '*Example*' of '*Freedom in so eminent a Divine as Dr. Donne,*' which '*seem'd a proof with what Indignation and Contempt a Christian may treat Vice or Folly, in ever so low, or ever so high, a Station*'.[69] This statement prompts a question about Pope's knowledge of Donne's life. Did Pope, in some confused way, believe that Donne wrote and published his *Satyres* as an eminent divine? And was part of Pope's attraction to this Christian satirist the quiet knowledge that the form of Christianity in which Donne had been brought up was Roman Catholic? These questions cannot be answered with certainty. From the text of *Satyre IV* itself, however, Pope must have realized that it fell within the reign of Elizabeth, while if he had seen Walton's *Life* (most recently published in its complete form in 1675) he would have known at least the broad outline of Donne's career.[70] I am inclined to think that the statement in Pope's Advertisement is deliberately disingenuous: designed to suggest for satiric freedom a respectability in Donne's lifetime which it never possessed. Where Donne's early Catholicism is concerned, Warburton was later to remark: 'About this time of his life Dr. Donne had a strong propensity to Popery, which appears from several strokes in these satires';[71] and when the texts of *Satyre II* and *Satyre IV* are taken together, Ian Jack's comment that Pope must have been quick to notice features 'which suggest a Catholic background' is a fair one.[72] He adopted most of these references, and while they are not meant to proclaim a Catholic commitment on the part of the still Catholic Pope, any more than they were on the part of the no-longer Catholic Donne, they have a personal appropriateness, and somewhat strengthen that aspect of Pope's imitation, fainter than in *Satyre IV*, which emphasizes isolation and danger.

Pope would, however, almost certainly have agreed with Donne when he wrote that the Anglican and Roman churches, indeed Rome, Wittenburg and Geneva, 'are all virtuall beams of one Sun' and 'connaturall pieces of one circle'.[73] For both poets the Catholic background is subsumed in the Christian poem. Pope follows Donne in 'placing' almost every figure by means of biblical allusion. Thus the Courtier-Talker excels the apostles as a linguist, and might have translated for the builders of Babel; thus the chaplain is '*Sweeter than Sharon*' and the captain like '*Herod's* Hangdogs in old Tapestry' (ll. 76–7, 81–5, 252–3, 266–7). Donne's stress, at the centre of his satire, on 'wholesome solitarinesse' is enriched by echoes of Christian poems by Milton (*Comus*) and

[69]*Poems*, IV, p. 3.

[70]A Life was prefixed to Tonson's 1719 edition of Donne's *Poems*. It is based on Walton, but omits any reference to Donne's Papist upbringing.

[71]*The Works of Alexander Pope . . .*, ed. William Warburton (London, 1751), IV, p. 265. But Pope certainly knew of Donne's early Roman Catholicism, for he possessed and indexed a copy of *Pseudo-Martyr* (1610), in the Preface of which the fact is acknowledged (Geoffrey Keynes, *A Bibliography of the Works of John Donne* (London, 1914), p. 7).

[72]Ian Jack, 'Pope and the Weighty Bullion of Dr. Donne's Satire', p. 1017.

[73]Donne to Sir H. R. (before 1610?), *Letters to Several Persons of Honour* (London, 1651), p. 29. Cf. Pope's *Universal Prayer*.

Marvell (*The Garden*) which speak of a spiritual freedom from temptation and taint.[74] Donne's vision of the court as a court of the damned, with its allusion to Dante, its comparison of the presence chamber to a mosque, and the seven deadly sins lining the wall, is all accepted by Pope; indeed his 'See! where the *British* Youth . . .' (replacing Donne's ' 'Tis ten a clock and past . . .') more effectively assimilates the later part of the poem into the Dantesque trance to which perhaps it belongs. It is in the context of this almost medieval vision that the satirist's courageous self-dedication to Truth occurs, and Pope seeks to emulate this un-Horatian passage:

> Not *Dante* dreaming all the 'Infernal State,
> Beheld such Scenes of *Envy, Sin* and *Hate*.
> Base Fear becomes the Guilty, not the Free;
> Suits Tyrants, Plunderers, but suits not me.
> Shall I, the Terror of this sinful Town,
> Care, if a livery'd Lord or Smile or frown?
> Who cannot flatter, and detest who can,
> Tremble before a *noble Serving-Man*?
> O my fair Mistress, *Truth*! Shall I quit thee,
> For huffing, braggart, puft *Nobility*?
> Thou, who since Yesterday, has roll'd o'er all
> The busy, idle Blockheads of the Ball,
> Hast thou, O *Sun*! beheld an emptier sort . . .[75]

It is fair to say that Pope has some success. The two-line apostrophe to Truth (though altered from Donne) has a rising directness, a dramatic inflexion, and a plainness of diction ('Shall I quit thee . . .'), worthy of the tragic soliloquy-style of the earlier poet. The connectedness of the last three lines reaches this style, and 'Scenes of *Envy, Sin*, and *Hate*' strike the right note of blunt religious attack. But in other places Pope has an unfortunate tone. 'I, the Terror of this sinful Town' has an air of self-righteous complacency (Pope as John Knox, or Savonarola?) absent in those other places in his epistles and satires where he expresses an heroic personal pride. Furthermore, Pope's contempt for the nobility of the court appears to have a fair tinge of plain snobbery. On both counts, the terse strength of Donne's 'Shall I, nones slave, of high borne, or rais'd men / Fear frownes?' is far more effective.

More effective than Pope, also, is Donne's handling of the conclusion, closely connected with the Christian vision of the damned at court. This is, I think, one of the places (less frequent than a cursory reading of the poem might suggest) where Pope has simply regularized away the careful inflexions of the speaking voice. The handing over of the satirist's weapons to the preacher has lost its urgency, the final lines their subtle blend of satisfaction and caution. But Pope brings off one elegant sleight of hand, for his 'bold *Divine*' sounds very like the terms in which he was, in his Advertisement, to speak of '*so eminent a Divine as Dr*. Donne . . .'. It is possible that Pope is here doffing the mask of Pope–Donne, and yielding up his attack to the unmediated roughness and force of the Elizabethan satirist. What is very plain, however, from an examination of

---

[74]See the discussion of the passage in Maynard Mack, *The Garden and the City*, pp. 89–91.
[75]*The Fourth Satire of Donne*, ll. 192–204; p. 43.

the latter part of the later poem, is that Pope was strongly attracted to the heroic stance of this Christian satirist; that he made an intelligent and not wholly unsuccessful attempt to recreate this stance; and that this was a major reason why he sought to imitate Horace, *Sat.* I, ix, not directly, but through the mediation of *Satyre IV*.

Pope's remark to Spence that Donne had '. . . as much wit as any writer can possibly have' is celebrated, and may be supported by the very early judgement of Pope to Wycherley (10 April 1706) that 'Donne had infinitely more Wit than he wanted Versification: for the great dealers in Wit, like those in Trade, take least Pains to set off their Goods . . .'.[76] What Pope took to be the wit of Donne's *Satyres* may be said to be a vital and pervasive intelligence, seizing upon relationships through trenchant and concrete expression, often coloured by a sardonically comic exaggeration: the blood in the body of the poem, as Pope put it.[77] In this sense, much of what has already been said about the two poems has involved their wit. Since, however, much emphasis has fallen on the aspects of bold political attack and of the Christian heroic stance, it is right to conclude this essay by recognizing the comic aspect of Pope's achievement.

In speaking of the earlier part of *Satyre IV*, I suggested that it showed exuberant comedy in dialogue with fear. Donne's stress on danger and fear is felt throughout, and is necessary if (by contrast) a vivid sense of the satirist's courage and defiance is also to be conveyed. Pope saw this, for he has actually increased the number of expressions designed to convey fear (e.g. Donne's 'Tyr'd, now I leave this place . . .' becomes 'Frighted, I quit the Room . . .'). Yet this sense of fear is not convincingly conveyed in Pope's poem, partly owing to his change of the story-line, partly to his occasional note of vanity, partly to his faster and more regular metre. But chiefly this failure is the necessary opposite side of the coin to a brilliant success. In amplifying the cryptic strokes of Donne's comic wit, setting off his 'Goods' more prominently, Pope upset the balance in *Satyre IV* between mockery and fear; but he came near, in the first half of the poem, to creating a comic masterpiece. Consider what the Courtier-Talker is made to say about languages:

> Nay troth, th'*Apostles*, (tho' perhaps too rough)
> Had once a pretty Gift of Tongues enough.
> Yet these were all *poor Gentlemen*! I dare
> Affirm, 'Twas *Travel* made them what they were.'[78]

Pope had his cue from Donne's 'Nay, your Apostles were / Good pretty Linguists' especially in the word 'pretty' which has the air of a parlance at once polite and vacuous. But, expanding from this, Pope's rendering is triumphant: the mingling of blasphemy with the patronizing and empty civility of a 'polite' age, which sought to polish roughness, is itself done with such appropriately

---

[76]Joseph Spence, *Observations, Anecdotes, and Characters of Books and Men*, ed. J.M. Osborn (Oxford, 1966), item 434 (1734?); *The Correspondence of Alexander Pope*, ed. George Sherburn (Oxford, 1956), I, p. 16.

[77]*An Essay on Criticism*, ll. 303–4; *Poems*, I, p. 274. For the meaning and background of Pope's ever-memorable definition of wit (ll. 297–8), see E.N. Hooker, 'Pope on wit: The *Essay on Criticism*', *The Hudson Review*, 2 (1950), pp. 84–100.

[78]*The Fourth Satire of Donne*, ll. 76–8; p. 31.

polished rapidity of metre that the effect is quite breathtaking. The Courtier has waved a negligent hand – 'a pretty Gift of Tongues enough' – and the apostles are dismissed. Pope has not only clarified but amplified the comedy. Or again:

> Thus others Talents having nicely shown,
> He came by sure Transition to his own:
> Till I cry'd out, 'You prove yourself so able,
> 'Pity! you was not Druggerman at *Babel*:
> 'For had they found a Linguist half so good,
> 'I make no question but the *Tow'r* had stood.'
>   'Obliging Sir! for Courts you sure were made. . . .'[79]

Phrases such as 'nicely' and 'sure Transition' convey the complete control, and thus the complete security, of the satirist; he has his comic subject in the palm of his hand. The rhyme of the second couplet is brilliantly pointed, and if we regret the disappearance of Donne's 'bricklayers' we can only applaud the appearance of the fittingly exotic yet undeniably trenchant 'Druggerman'. But Pope most enriches the comedy here by making his Courtier-Talker, in insufferable vanity, take the satirist's devastating repartee for a compliment. Pope further amplifies the comedy in the satire by making additions in the spirit of his original. The comparison of the Courtier-Talker to a 'Blunderbuss' discharging a miscellaneous 'Shot of Dulness' (ll. 64–5) is not in Donne, but it has all his trenchancy, aptness and ludicrous exaggeration. And (another addition) perhaps nothing is more expressive than the civil nothingness of the following line:

> 'Oh! Sir, politely so! nay, let me dye. . . .'[80]

Pope has profited from the century of theatrical fops, from Jonson's Fastidious Brisk to Congreve's Witwoud, which elapsed between the writing of *Satyre IV* and his own time. With the possible exception of Jonson in *The Poetaster*, no English writer has made anything so richly ridiculous out of Horace's talker. A final example, comedy of a different kind, may be taken from the second half of the poem. The courtiers advance upon the ladies:

>   How each Pyrate eyes
> So weak a Vessel, and so rich a Prize!
> Top-gallant he, and she in all her Trim,
> He boarding her, she striking sail to him.[81]

The bare idea only is in Donne. The double entendre of the simile works out perfectly to each detail, the antithetical couplets perform a stylized ritual – and one of the best examples of what Rochester would have called the 'mannerly obscene' has been brought off with consummate skill.

I have tried to suggest something of the impressive human complexity of Donne's *Satyre IV*, the way it uses and changes Horace, its synthesis of classical and Christian, its tension between laughter and tears, or, more precisely,

---

[79]Ibid., ll. 80–5; pp. 31–3.
[80]Ibid., l. 112; p. 35.
[81]Ibid., ll. 228–31; p. 45.

between mockery and fear, each reined in and checked so that one does not outrun the other. I have suggested too that, far from being a shapeless and over-long denunciation, this satire possesses an expressive unifying structure.

Horace and Donne are not names very commonly linked, but *Satyre IV* belongs to a tradition of translation and imitation of the Ninth Satire of the First Book of Horace which connects it with Oldham and Pope, the latter of whom certainly recognized the dual challenge when he wrote his *The Impertinent, Or a Visit to the Court*, later entitled *The Fourth Satire of Dr John Donne, Dean of St Paul's, Versifyed*. Pope was then at a crucial stage in his poetic development. He had recently composed, in a few days, and originally as a largely unpremeditated effusion, his imitation of the First Satire of the Second Book of Horace (*To Fortescue*), with its personal identification by Pope with the bold satire of Lucilius. Dryden, in his Discourse Concerning Satire, had argued that in defining formal satire the 'Majestique way of *Persius* and *Juvenal*' should be taken into account as well as the ways of Horace.[82] Pope, in his handling of the Lucilius passage in Horace, *Sat.* II, i, began to respond to this challenge. He next proceeded to expand and enrich his satiric approach through an attempt to assimilate the qualities of Donne's sardonic yet heroic Christian satire, seeing Donne at once as an English Lucilius, and probably, one who could reach the heights of what Dryden had termed the 'Tragical Satyre' of Juvenal. A part of this attraction towards Donne was Pope's growing sense that the highest rôle of the satirical poet, and the one which his age was to warrant from him, was (far from the secure voicing of a consensus of enlightened opinion) isolated, dangerous and, partly for this reason, courageous and heroic. Pope attempted to express, though he did not manage to convey, the vivid sense of fear in *Satyre IV*; he attempted with better success the bold attack, and the lonely heroic manner of Donne's central soliloquy; and he succeeded, at some cost to the total effect he was working for, in reaping a comic harvest from Donne's satiric wit.

Brilliant and remarkable as it is, Pope's imitation of *Satyre IV* is not wholly a success; rather it is a poem of growth, a stage in that poetic development which was to culminate in *To Arbuthnot* and the two Dialogues of the Epilogue to the Satires. Yet each of the two poems considered is humanly admirable in its courage and independence: in being so intimately of its time yet so bravely against it, with all the intelligence, misgiving, principle and skill which that took. With an ideal of 'the freedome of the auncient tymes' in mind, Pope and Donne each inflected their inheritance from Horace so as to express their frequent sense of living in an age of lead or iron.

<hr />

[82]A Discourse Concerning Satire, ll. 2324–59; *The Poems of John Dryden*, II, pp. 660–1.

V The Augustan Moment

Long maist thou liue, and see me thus appeare,
As omenous a comet, from my sphaere,
Vnto thy raigne; as that did auspicate
So lasting glory to AV.GVSTVS state.
(Jonson, *Part of the King's Entertainment*, 1604)

'O Age of Rusty iron!'[1]

It is the peculiar significance of Donne's *Satyre IV*, in its confrontation of the Elizabethan court, that it should propose, then abandon and transcend, an Augustan model. This model, Horace *Sat.* I, ix, with the relation it implies between individual and state, between poet and power, is not necessarily endorsed as an ideal, but is certainly a standard by which Elizabethan London is shown to be a darker and more dangerous place than Augustan Rome. Much of the drama of the poem arises from this contrast, and it is perhaps true to say that if Horace presides over the first part of Donne's poem, it is Dante (as understood by Donne) who inspires the second. This dual awareness of an Augustan standard, and of a contemporary reality so different as to arouse only contempt, anger and fear, appears representative of the 1590s. Political historians, impressed by the brilliance of Elizabeth's political achievement, often overlook the negative testimony of late Elizabethan writers. Few of them found the Golden Age of Elizabeth as Astraea, for few found support, security, or freedom of speech. The occasion of Donne's Fifth and final Satire (*c.* 1598), a brief from Elizabeth to Lord Keeper Egerton to reform the corruption of the Star Chamber, afforded the poet an opportunity to express that painful discrepancy between an

> . . . Age of rusty iron! Some better wit
> Call it some worse name, if ought equall it;
> Th'iron Age *that* was, when justice was sold; now
> Injustice is sold dearer farre . . .

and the celebrated monarch to whom he puts and answers the question:

> Greatest and fairest Empresse, know you this?
> Alas, no more then Thames calme head doth know
> Whose meades her armes drowne, or whose corne o'rflow . . . [2]

[1]Donne, *Satyre V*, l. 35; *The Satires, Epigrams and Verse Letters*, ed. W. Milgate (Oxford, 1967), p. 23.
[2]Ibid., ll. 35–8, 28–30; Milgate, *Satires*, p. 23.

As *Satyre IV* shows, Donne did not always await a politic occasion to express criticism of Elizabethan rule, however cautiously he used poetic structures to express such criticism. His attack upon monopolies in *Satyre IV* challenged a practice which had grown up since the sixteenth year of Elizabeth's reign, and to which she had increasingly resorted as the resources of the crown failed to keep up with the cost of her foreign policy and Irish wars in a period of severe inflation. This was a widespread grievance against the crown, as the debate on it in the Queen's last parliament, in November 1601, demonstrates. When the long list of fresh patents was read out in the Commons,

> Mr. Hakewell of Lincoln's Inn stood up and asked: 'Is bread not there?' 'Bread?' quoth one. 'Bread?' quoth another. 'This voice seems strange,' quoth a third. 'No,' quoth Mr. Hakewell, 'if order be not taken for these, bread will be there before the next parliament.'

Outside there was muttering about the overthrow of monopolies and about their invasion of liberty; inside Cecil warned that 'the time was never more apt to disorder' and the conversion of sovereignty to popularity.[3] Elizabeth's masterly handling of this crisis, the 'Golden Speech' in which, with a measure of concession and a shrewd playing upon emotion, she disarmed the opposition, may have seemed to turn 'rusty iron' to the gold of restored justice, but it is also evidence of how high discontent had risen.[4] It is in this context that John of Gaunt's charge against Richard in *Richard II* (1595?), that 'this little world . . . / Is now leased out . . .' probably had contemporary relevance, and Elizabeth's enigmatic declaration to William Lambarde, after the suppression of the Essex Revolt, 'I am Richard II. know ye not that?' is pregnant with implication.[5] There can be no doubt that the 'Court-form' of the English, making '. . . of their old Queen / An ever-young, and most immortal Goddess' (Chapman's words),[6] suppressed some violently contrary recognitions which found expression at times of crisis or after her death. Essex, after his disgrace but before his attempted *coup d'état*, called the queen's mind 'as crooked as her carcase';[7] Ben Jonson, gossiping with Drummond long after, alleged that 'Queen Elizabeth never saw her self after she became old jn a true Glass. they painted her & sometymes would vermilion her nose, she had allwayes about

[3]J.B. Black, *The Reign of Elizabeth, 1558–1603* (Oxford, 1936; 2nd edn, 1959), pp. 230–2. J.E. Neale, *Queen Elizabeth* (London, 1934), gives little attention to these grievances in his eulogistic account of the Queen, pp. 382–3, but full treatment of her successful handling of the crisis.

[4]It was known as Queen Elizabeth's 'Golden Speech' then and after; Neale, *Queen Elizabeth*, pp. 382–3.

[5]*Richard II*, II, i, ll. 45, 59 and see the whole speech; *Richard II*, ed. Peter Ure, Arden Series (London, 1956), pp. 50–4; also lvii–lxii. For Elizabeth's comment to Lambarde, see Nichols, *Progresses of Queen Elizabeth* (London, 1823), III, pp. 552–3. The Queen's declaration seems to me to assert: (1) that she like Richard was an hereditary prince faced with an attempted *coup d'état* and possible deposition; and (2) that as reigning prince it was she who was reflected on, often perhaps in nothing worse than loyal warnings, by references to theatre or street representations of Richard II. The Queen was referring roundly to the many public representations of Richard II at the time of the revolt and earlier, and probably meant performances of Shakespeare's play among other representations of Richard's reign, perhaps contrived by Essex, perhaps with seditious intent.

[6]The Duke of Guise in George Chapman, *Bussy D'Ambois* (c. 1604), I, ii, ll. 10–13; ed. Nicholas Brooke, Revels Plays (London, 1964), pp. 16–17.

[7]Black, *The Reign of Elizabeth*, p. 438.

Christmas evens set dice, that threw sixes or five, & she knew not they were other, to make her win & esteame her self fortunate.'[8] Such details would have been highly suggestive to a writer so concerned with truth and flattery as Jonson.

If in much sixteenth-century political literature Augustus afforded an example of justice, truthful consultation and bounty, he was no less celebrated for the discerning patronage of truth-telling poets. Few writers if any in the later years of Elizabeth felt they had found their Maecenas or Augustus. In January 1599 Spenser, the singer of Elizabeth as Una, Belphoebe and Gloriana, who twenty years before had lamented that:

> Mecænas is yclad in claye,
> And great Augustus long ygoe is dead,

died in poverty, and though buried in Westminster Abbey was given no tomb, as the satirist Joseph Hall noted.[9] Between 1598 and 1601–2 the three Parnassus Plays were composed. With plaintive comedy they dramatize the hopeless quest for a Maecenas of several young university-trained aspirants to poetic fame. They too note the ingratitude to Spenser of 'this vnregarding soile', and all the Maecenas they find is 'a meere man of straw, a great lumpe of drousie earth.'[10] Reduced to seek employment from a London printer, or worse still from the 'basest trade' of Burbage and Kempe at the theatre, they finally resolve to become shepherds. The Augustan poets, notably Horace and Ovid, people their pilgrimage, but it is significant that the first scene of the Second Part of *The Return from Parnassus* opens with the most famous quotation from the post-Augustan satirist Juvenal ('*Difficile est, satyram non scribere . . .*' &c.), and the following affirmation: 'I, Iuuenall: thy ierking hand is good, / Not gently laying on, but fetching bloud'.[11] This reminds us that the most conspicuous development of the 1590s in non-dramatic poetry was the remarkable outburst of formal satire, pioneered by the MS satires of Donne, and breaking into print in the work of Lodge, Hall, Marston, Gilpin and others. It was writing perfectly cognizant of the example of Horace, and of the Augustan relation between prince and poet; nevertheless it is closer to the models of Juvenal and Persius. In some of these poets the denial of an Augustan parallel is quite explicit. Thus Charles Fitzgeoffrey, ringing the changes, perhaps, on the poet Collingbourne's complaint in *The Mirror for Magistrates*, can lament:

> Wel-worth *Augustus* laurel crowned times,
> Pure *Halcion* houres, *Saturnus* golden dayes,
> When worthies patronized Poets rimes,
> And Poets rimes did onlie worthies praise,
> Sdaining base *Plutus* groomes with fame to raise:

[8]Conversations with Drummond, ll. 337–42; *Ben Jonson*, ed. C.H. Herford and Percy and Evelyn Simpson (Oxford, 1925–50), I, pp. 141–2.

[9]'To Camden' (*c.* 1600), ll. 1–8; *The Poems of Joseph Hall . . .*, ed. Arnold Davenport (Liverpool, 1949; reprinted 1969), p. 105. *The Shepheards Calender*, X, 61–2.

[10]*The Second Part of the Return from Parnassus*, ll. 210–28, *First Part*, l. 225; *The Three Parnassus Plays (1598–1601)*, ed. J.B. Leishman (London, 1949), pp. 236–8, 146–7.

[11]*Second Part*, ll. 84–7; p. 225. Juvenal, I, ll. 30–1.

> When now, save mercenaryes, few do write,
> And be a Poet is be a Parasite.[12]

Two years later Hall, in the final 'byting satyre' of his *Virgidemiarum* (1597, 1598), made the same point in the heroic couplets of English satire:

> Who had but liued in *Augustus* daies
> T'had beene some honour to be crown'd with Bayes
> When *Lucan* streaked on his Marble-bed
> To think of *Caesar*, and great *Pompeys* deed. . . .[13]

The anachronistic reference to the poet Lucan (based on Juvenal, VII, ll. 79–80) reveals that Hall, throughout this satire, has in mind Juvenal's sharp comments on the Augustan poets: 'satur est cum dicit Horatius "euhoe!"'; and Virgil's muse, too, would have lost its power if the poet hadn't had a roof over his head.[14] Juvenal's question, like that of the Parnassus Plays and of Hall in this satire, is: 'Who will be a Maecenas to you today?' and Hall's poem may implicitly remind us that this particular satire of Juvenal opens with an appeal for support from the Emperor Hadrian.[15]

Augustus had been praised for allowing writers a reasonable freedom of expression. The relative political stability of the principate had allowed this tolerance, which in respecting existing freedoms had also been prudent. It was hard for Protestant England in Counter-Reformation times, to rise to this standard. Invasion, attempted or threatened, conspiracy, rumoured or real, kept the political tension high, especially as Elizabeth grew old, with the question of the succession still unsettled. Fierce legislation against Papists, strong measures to flush out itinerant Roman Catholic priests, the maintenance of a highly efficient intelligence system, mutual suspicion at court between the Essex faction and its opponents – all combined to produce a treacherous atmosphere in which even implicit criticism could seem seditious, and in which detraction flourished.[16] This atmosphere is well conveyed in Donne's *Satyre IV*. In 1599 those who, unlike Donne, had published their satires found their work called in and condemned to the fire, while at the same time restrictions on the printing of drama and history were tightened up. Marston's satires and Marlowe's *Elegies* were banned; Hall's *Virgidemiarum* was condemned and then reprieved.[17]

Especially interesting is the experience of Ben Jonson in these last years of the Queen, when writers suffered such strict restraint. Under both Elizabeth and James Jonson's career is marked by a desire to please, and an incautious but

[12]Charles Fitzgeoffry, 'Sir Francis Drake' (1596); ed. A.B. Grosart (Manchester, 1881), p. 23. See also his *Epigrammes* on poets; pp. xiv, xix, xxi and xxiii.

[13]*Virgidemiarum*, VI, ll. 205–8; *The Poems of Joseph Hall*, p. 93.

[14]Juvenal, VII, ll. 62, 69–71: 'It was a well-fed Horace who cried "Euhoe"!'

[15]Juvenal, VII, ll. 94, 1–12.

[16]Black, *The Reign of Elizabeth*, pp. 407–10, 425–6.

[17]*The Poems of Joseph Hall*, pp. xxv–vii, 293–4: Richard A. McCabe, 'Elizabethan Satire and the Bishops' Ban of 1599', *Yearbook of English Studies*, XI (1981), pp. 188–93, stresses the political motivation for the Ban, and it may be that Davies's *Epigrammes* rather than Marlowe's *Elegies* were the reason why the volume condemning both was condemned. Marlowe was, nevertheless, banned in effect.

admirable readiness to speak out – and as a consequence by a series of arrests and interrogations. His first imprisonment, from August to October 1597, was for his part in the play *The Isle of Dogs*, held by the Privy Council to contain 'very seditious & sclandrous matter'.[18] Topliffe, the informer referred to in early MSS of Donne's *Satyre IV*, was involved in his interrogation. Jonson's account of the episode (recorded by Drummond in 1619) was that: 'jn the tyme of his close Imprisonment under Queen Elizabeth his judges could gett nothing of him to all yr demands bot I and No, they placed two damn'd Villans to catch advantage of him, wt him, but he was advertised by his Keeper, of the Spies he hath ane Epigrame.'[19] Jonson was probably in danger of torture, but was eventually discharged, perhaps because the play proved more harmless than the Privy Council had feared. Undeterred by this frightening experience, Jonson evidently depicted the Queen on stage at the end of *Every Man Out of his Humour* (1599), though only in the most formal and laudatory way. Jonson had begun to refashion that late medieval mode in which a play examines the relation between prince and people by bringing them together on the stage. *Cynthia's Revels* (1600) does this quite explicitly; beneath its garb of Greek names and allusions it deploys a morality play structure in which the monarch (Cynthia) is disabused of her false courtiers. Jonson expresses his loyalty to Elizabeth through instruction and correction. His depiction of the court in III, iv unmistakably echoes that of Donne in *Satyre IV*, and we know that Jonson admired Donne's Satires from his Epigramme XCIIII commending them to the Countess of Bedford. Yet this play also includes, in praise of Elizabeth, the beautiful hymne: 'Qveene, *and* Huntresse, *chaste, and faire . . .*' and (intrusively as the monarch must have thought) justifies her treatment of Mary Queen of Scots and the recently disgraced but not yet fallen Essex.[20] Its conclusion, in which Cynthia recognizes the false guises of her courtiers, and gratefully delegates their correction to the poet Crites, an unmistakably Jonsonian *persona*, is altogether lacking in courtly tact. Its praise of Cynthia is too overdone to convince; its promotion of Crites so obvious that it betrays a kind of clumsy innocence in the author; and the whole feeling is of integrity awkwardly under stress. Sure enough, when the play was performed at court it was disliked. It was an elaborate bid for royal favour which yet adhered to staunchly independent moral judgement, proposing the ideal relation between the truth-recognizing monarch (Cynthia) and the truth-telling poet (Crites). Jonson may have taken his disappointment with bad grace. His enemy Dekker's jibe: '. . . when your Playes are misse-likt at Court, you shall not crye Mew like a Pusse-cat, and say you are glad you write out of the Courtiers Element . . .' perhaps refers to the motto which Jonson prefixed to the Quarto printing of the play: 'Quod non dant Proceres, dabit Histrio' (what the great do not give, the actor will), yet another quotation from Juvenal's Seventh Satire, that brief for neglected poets.[21] Jonson's real feelings may be gauged from the Dedication to the Court which, in the next reign, he added to the Folio edition of the play:

---

[18]*Ben Jonson*, XI, p. 574.

[19]Ibid., I, p. 139. The Epigramme is LIX, but it would seem that Epigramme CI, 'Inviting a Friend to Supper', l. 36, also alludes to one of those spies.

[20]V, vi, 1–18; xi, 1–45 (Essex: ll. 14–15; Mary ll. 16–17); *Ben Jonson*, IV, pp. 161, 176.

[21]*Ben Jonson*, IX, p. 189; Juvenal, VII, l. 90.

Jn thee, the whole Kingdome dresseth it selfe, and is ambitious to vse thee as her
glasse. . . . Jt is not pould'ring, perfuming . . . that conuerteth to a beautiful obiect:
but a mind, shining through any sute. . . . Such shalt thou find some here, euen in the
raigne of CYNTHIA (a CRITES, and an ARETE.) . . .

Thy seruant, but not slaue. . . .[22]

Jonson had attempted to hold up a 'true Glass' but had not as a result become
'belou'd Crites', nor yet Horace to an Augustus.

Thoughts of a New Reign

In his poem, *The King's Prophecy*, written to celebrate the accession of King
James VI to the English throne, Joseph Hall set down a curious reminiscence.
Recalling the gloomy predictions of what would follow the death of Elizabeth,
Hall rather now endorses the hopefulness of his own youth when (he says) he
had hailed the birth of Prince Henry, in an imitation of Virgil's Fourth Eclogue:

> How did I better long agone presage,
> (That ioyes me still I did presage so right)
> When in the wardship of my weaker age
> My puis-nè Muse presumed to recite
> The vatick lines of that *Cumean* Dame,
> (Which *Maro* falsely sung to *Pollios* name)
>
> To the deare Natals of thy princely sonne,
> O dreadest Soueraigne; in whose timely birth
> Mee seem'd I sawe this golden age begonne,
> I sawe this wearie loade of Heauen and Earth
> Freshly reuiu'd, rouze vp his fainting head,
> To see the sweete hopes this day promised.
>
> And now I liue (I wisht to liue so long
> Till I might see these golden dayes succeed,
> And solemne vow'd that mine eternall song
> Should sound thy name vnto the future seed)
> I liue to see my hopes; ô let me liue
> Till but my vowed verse might me suruiue.

If Hall had indeed (in the words of his own gloss) 'Virgil's fourth Eclogue translated and applyed to the birth of Hen. the Prince',[23] he was among the very first
to draw on the Augustan myth as a way of thinking about the new reign, when
the leading claimant should ascend Elizabeth's throne. He was far from being
the last.

In 1598 Francis Meres published his collection of sentences, similitudes and
examples entitled *Palladis Tamia, Wit's Treasury*, a commonplace book containing a comparative discourse, largely his own, 'of our English Poets, with the
Greeke, Latine and Italian Poets'. In this part of his book Meres produces, in
ambiguous manner, the Augustan comparison:

[22]Ll. 6–8, 13–15, 17–18, 24; *Ben Jonson*, IV, p. 33.
[23]Ll. 97–115; *The Poems of Joseph Hall*, p. 112.

> As the Greeke and Latine Poets haue woune immortall credit to their natiue speech, beeing encouraged and graced by liberall patrones and bountifull Benefactors: so our famous and learned Lawreat masters of England would entitle our English to far greater admired excellency, if either the Emperor *Augustus*, or *Octauia* his sister, or noble *Mecâenas* were aliue to rewarde and countenaunce them. . . .[24]

While this might seem entirely in key with the critical uses of the Augustan comparison by Fitzgeoffrey and Hall (and indeed Meres goes on to apostrophize the 'ingratefull and damned age') yet, unaware of inconsistency, he can turn his whole assessment upside down, using the very same terms:

> As noble *Mecænas* that sprung from the *Hetruscan* Kinges not only graced Poets by his bounty, but also by beeing a Poet himselfe; and as *Iames* the 6. nowe king of Scotland is not only a fauorer of Poets, but a Poet . . . so *Elizabeth* our dread soueraign and gracious Queene is not only a liberal patrone vnto Poets, but an excellent Poet herselfe. . . .[25]

It is less useful to ask what Meres is actually saying about his age in these passages (was Elizabeth a true Augustus to poets or was she not?) than to note how the syntactical and intellectual procedure of the similitude, practised throughout the book, leads him inevitably to broad cultural comparison. A scales of 'As . . .' and 'so . . .' is set up, and whether or not it balances, Augustus is certainly on one side of it. But there is also the new factor here, mentioned by Hall but not Fitzgeoffrey: the example of James VI of Scotland.

Naturally, as Elizabeth aged, poets as well as politicians turned their thoughts to King James as one of the stronger claimants to the succession. To secure this succession was the prime aim of James's diplomacy. The Queen, on the other hand, even had she been personally willing to recognize his claim, could not have afforded the consequent loss of freedom for diplomatic manoeuvre. Her pronouncements on the subject were enigmatic almost to the end. Essex entered into measures with James and accused Cecil of favouring the Spanish claimant. As speculation mounted James, already a known controversialist and poet, published his own piece of Prince literature, the *Basilikon Doron* (1599), addressed to his eldest son Prince Henry. Judged by the standard of earlier sixteenth-century works of the same kind, James's book stands up well; it is the work of a pious and decent political intelligence, taking its own mid-way between morality and expediency, at times frankly adverting to his own political inheritance in Scotland. It is unnecessary to describe the book in detail, but a few points are important. In the first place we know that James's Scottish library contained Elyot's *Boke Named the Governour* as well as Budé's *Institut du Prince* and Bodin's *Six livres de la République*.[26] James's purpose is different from Elyot's, but when he comes to discuss maturity of judgement, he is close to his predecessor:

---

[24]Francis Meres, *Palladis Tamia, Wits Treasury* (1598); Intro. Don Cameron Allen (New York, 1938), p. 278.

[25]Ibid., p. 284.

[26]G.F. Warner, 'The Library of James VI', *Publications of the Scottish History Society*, XV, Miscellany I (Edinburgh, 1893), pp. lxvi; lvi, xlii.

I need not to trouble you with the particular discourse of the foure Cardinall vertues, it is so trodden a path: but I will shortly say vnto you; make one of them, which is Temperance, Queene of all the rest within you. I meane not by the vulgar interpretation of Temperance, which only consists in *gustu & tactu*, by the moderating of these two senses: but, I meane of that wise moderation, that first commaunding your selfe, shall as a Queene, command all the affections and passions of your minde, and as a Phisician, wisely mixe all your actions according thereto.[27]

That James thought of Augustus, Elyot's prime example of maturity in a ruler, when he wrote this seems likely. It is certainly suggestive that James should bring his work to a conclusion by quoting that passage of *Aeneid* VI which was, as we have seen, almost as central to St Augustine's view of history as it was to Virgil's:

And being contente to let others excell in other things; Let it be your chiefest earthly glorie, to excel in your owne craft: according to the worthie sentence of that sublime and Heroicall Poet virgil wherein also my dictone is included;

Excudent alij spirantia mollius âera . . .

and he quotes down to 'Parcere subiectis, & debellare svperbos'. This is as James has it in the Royal MS and the edition of 1599. In the revised edition of 1603 the word 'sentence' is significantly replaced by the phrase 'counsel and charge of *Anchises* to his posteritie'.[28] This change must be seen in context of the several places in *Basilikon Doron* where James foresees the succession of his son to all three kingdoms of Britain.[29] James is for the moment Anchises prophesying the establishment of a much expanded political power. At this point James's projection of the future becomes Augustan.

Yet in the 1599 edition of *Basilikon Doron* Augustus is nowhere given as an example. Indeed James differs from Elyot and all other writers of political literature we have discussed in only rarely citing royal examples. They are chiefly Scriptural (Saul, David, the Queen of Sheba), but twice James V of Scotland is cited, once as a good and once a bad example. Alexander the Great is twice mentioned, James once speaking to Henry as Philip of Macedon spoke to Alexander.[30] It may seem probable that King James's procedure is guided by a concept of royal decorum. How true to his own regal status would it have been to have crammed his book with royal examples, ancient and modern, as the other writers of Prince literature did? Was it not enough that he was himself a monarch whose example and precepts were now being offered to his son? Certainly the absence of reference to Augustus and other Roman Emperors does not mean James thought the *princeps* unworthy of admiration. This is shown by a passage from the preface *To The Reader* which James added to his book when it was republished in 1603. Here the Scottish King excuses himself to English readers for having proposed remedies for the ills of Scotland, but nothing 'that

[27] *The Political Works of James I*, ed. C.H. McIlwain (New York, 1918; edn of 1965), p. 37.
[28] Ibid., p. 52. ΒΑΣΙΛΙΚΟΝ ΔΩΡΟΝ, Roxburghe Club (London, 1887), pp. 158–9.
[29] Ibid., pp. 22, 37. And cf. pp. 21–2: '. . . embrace the quarrell of the poore and distressed . . . thinking it your greatest honour to represse the oppressors . . .' with the last line of the passage from *Aeneid* VI.
[30] Ibid., p. 48 (and p. 34: James V).

should haue touched the sicknesses of their state, in the like sort', on the ground
that he had had no experience of England.

> I know indeed, no kingdome lackes her owne diseases, and likewise what interest I
> haue in the prosperitie of that state: for although I would be silent, my blood and
> discent doeth sufficiently proclaime it. But notwithstanding, since there is a lawfull
> Queene there presently reigning, who hath so long with so great wisedome and felicitie
> gouerned her kingdomes, as (I must in trew sinceritie confesse) the like hath not been
> read or heard of, either in our time, or since the dayes of the Romane Emperour
> *Augustus*: it could no wayes become me, farre inferiour to her in knowledge and
> experience, to be a busie-body in other princes matters. . . .[31]

This, to the best of my knowledge, is the first time an English monarch was in
the English language called an Augustus.[32] But temporal priority is less important here than the writer who makes the comparison, and the time at which he
did so. For James to praise Elizabeth through a comparison with Augustus was
a public affirmation, by the queen's probable successor, of some of his own
political values. It implied, in a way that the use of the example of Augustus in
Basilikon Doron could not have done with propriety, what the aspirations of the
future monarch would be, and thus what would be the basis of acceptable public
praise. It is evident that the whole passage has the immediate prospect of
James's succession in mind, and the balance of its observations is most adroit. It
recognizes some contemporary dissatisfaction in England (since 'no kingdome
lackes her owne diseases') yet praises the long and politically skilful reign of
Elizabeth. While James refers to the strength of his hereditary claim to the
English throne, often considered as strong or stronger than Elizabeth's, he
acknowledges her to be the 'lawfull Queene there presently reigning'. The
Augustan comparison is here central to a highly politic affirmation by James,
which in its objective as well as generous admissions bears all the marks of his
growing confidence of the succession. It may be noted that this Augustan
comparison only makes explicit what was implicit in the Virgilian conclusion of
Basilikon Doron, in the 1599 as in the 1603 edition. But this second edition was
shrewdly timed, and inevitably excited the interest of all those eager to know
better the character of their probable future ruler. This is attested by the Bishop
of Winchester, in his introductory remarks to *Basilikon Doron* in the 1616
edition of James's *Works*:

> What applause had it in the world? How did it inflame men's minds to a loue and
> admiration of his Majestie beyond measure; Insomuch that *comming out iust at the
> time his Majestie came in*, it made the hearts of his people as one man, as much to
> Honour him for his Religion and Learning, as to obey him for Title and
> Authoritie. . . . [my italics][33]

[31]Ibid., p. 11. In addition to Elyot, James may have read Lipsius on Augustus. The 1599 edition
Basilikon Doron contained a sarcastic reference to the *Constantia* of 'that proud inconstant
LIPSIUS'; ΒΑΣΙΛΙΚΟΝ ΔΩΡΟΝ, Roxburghe Club, p. 117.

[32]Latin panegyric is another matter. For Andreas Ammonius's panegyric hailing Henry VIII as a
new Augustus, see the discussion in J.D. Garrison, *Dryden and the Traditions of Panegyric*
(Berkeley, Los Angeles and London, 1975), p. 80.

[33]*The Works of The Most High and Mighty Prince, Iames . . . I*, published by Iames, Bishop of
Winton (London, 1616), Preface.

It is clearly Augustus as the exemplar of a long, stable and skilful reign that James invoked in *Basilikon Doron*, rather than Augustus the patron of poets. There were also some points in the book which must have struck a writer such as Jonson with especial interest. The manner in which James advised his son on the subject of poetry must have struck a correspondent chord in the poet.

> And because your writes will remaine as true pictures of your minde, to all posterities; let them bee free of all vncomelinesse and vn-honestie: and according to *Horace* his counsell
>
> — *Nonumquam premantur in annum.*
>
> I meane both your verse and your prose; letting first that furie and heate, wherewith they were written, coole at leasure; and then . . . reuising them ouer againe, before they bee published,
>
> — *quia nescit vox missa reuerti.*
>
> . . . And if yee write in verse, remember that it is not the principall part of a Poeme to rime right, and flowe well with many pretie words: but the chiefe commendation of a Poeme, is that when the verse shall bee shaken sundrie in prose, it shall bee found so rich in quicke inuentions . . . as it shall retaine the lustre of a Poeme. . . . And I would also aduise you to write in your owne language: for there is nothing left to be saide in Greeke and Latine alreadie . . . and besides that, it best becommeth a King to purifie and make famous his owne tongue. . . .[34]

The easy way in which James's discourse moves in and out of Horace's *Ars Poetica*, taking up the two half-lines (388, 390), the stress on deliberation, revision, the subordinate position of rhyme, and on the purification of a modern tongue, all suggests a mind in familiar contact with the Augustan Age. This period of Rome Jonson, between the dates of the first and second editions of *Basilikon Doron*, brought upon the English stage when the Children of the Chapel performed his *Poetaster*, in the Autumn of 1601.

The Poetaster

Jonson made a formal profession of his aim in writing *The Poetaster* when he put together the 'apologeticall Dialogue' once performed after the comedy, and printed in the Folio Text in 1616. He here makes particular allusion to the literary and theatrical war in which, as dramatic satirist, he had become involved, and states that he

> . . . therefore chose AVGVSTVS CAESARS times,
> When wit, and artes were at their height in *Rome*,
> To shew that VIRGIL, HORACE, and the rest
> Of those great master-spirits did not want
> Detractors, then, or practisers against them:

---

[34]*The Political Works of James I*, p. 47–8.

And by this line (although no *paralel*)
I hop'd at last they would sit downe, and blush.[35]

Though in one respect disingenuous and misleading, Jonson's statement is of great interest. The play was itself the most considerable and well publicized blow in the War of the Theatres. Jonson cannot really have thought that it would have a cooling effect. After the storm of counter-attack, however, he may well have been tempted to stress the immediate context of literary warfare rather than the wider significance of the play. It is my purpose to argue that Jonson's design to still, or more probably better, his opponents was only a part of a far more ambitious attempt, through drama, at a cultural reorientation of Britain. Where the Dialogue does not mislead is in giving us Jonson's broad assessment of Augustus: it is the Christian Humanist view, to be found in Elyot and Gentillet, which is prepared to accept the evidence of the Augustan poets and to identify the rule of Augustus with a flourishing of the arts. Despite Jonson's focus upon literary activity, and despite his knowledge of Tacitus and probably Machiavelli, it is clear that the writer of these lines is not espousing a hostile view of Augustus. Again, as we shall see, the Dialogue is reliable when it states that the play was never intended to be a '*paralel*': we must not look for a contemporary original for every character, even if two or three seem obvious; and we must not, it seems, identify Elizabeth with Augustus as the audience had been quite obviously invited to identify Elizabeth with Cynthia in *Cynthia's Revels*.

It is worth considering Jonson's probable range of sources for this play about 'AVGVSTVS CAESARS time', and the general reading which may have swayed him in his choice of setting. It is improbable that he was unfamiliar with any of the major classical sources, though it is not in every case possible to show that he knew them in 1601. The text of the play itself demonstrates the importance of Ovid, Horace, Virgil and Suetonius.[36] Donatus's life of Virgil, or traditions deriving from Donatus, provided essential material.[37] Beyond these, the extensive use Jonson was shortly to make of Tacitus, for his *Sejanus*, makes it probable that he was also then aware of the origin of the hostile tradition. (In addition, Tacitus had been in English translation since Henry Saville brought out the *Histories* and the *Agricola* in 1591, and Richard Grenawey the *Annals* and *Germania* in 1598.) Of authors favourable to Augustus, it is probable that he knew Seneca's *De Clementia*, Cassius Dio, and possible that he knew Velleius Paterculus.[38] Of relevant modern authors, it is probable that he knew Elyot's *Boke Named the Governour*, possible that he already knew Lipsius's *Politicorum*.[39] That Jonson may have known something about panegyric and political writing in later sixteenth-century France is an intriguing possibility. His reasons for choosing the times of Augustus for his drama would have been

---

[35]Ll. 101–7; *Ben Jonson*, IV, p. 320. Discussing *The Poetaster* and the War of the Theatres, George Parfitt, *Ben Jonson, Public Poet and Private Man* (London, 1976), pp. 50–1, sensibly observes that '. . . unless it can be shown that the play is *in toto* an allegorical attack . . . we have to accept that *Poetaster* is essentially a play about art'.

[36]For Suetonius see nn. 49 & 50 below. At some stage he owned the Antwerp (1578) edn; *Ben Jonson*, I, p. 267.

[37]For Donatus's life of Virgil, see Ch. I, p. 17, n. 54

[38]*Ben Jonson*, IX, p. 620 (for *De Clementia*); II, pp. 11–16 and IX, pp. 222–5 (for Dio); and IX, p. 600 (for Velleius Paterculus).

[39]Ibid., XI, p. 228, shows he knew this at a later stage.

further strengthened if he was aware of the use of the idea of a new Augustus in the Pléiade, and of the discussion of the relation between ruler and poet by Gentillet.[40] What is clear is that Jonson knew both sides of the debate about Augustus, and was as familiar with his political record as with the often-repeated fact that he had been a generous and discerning patron of poets. It is clear too that if, in *The Poetaster*, Jonson wished to offer the pattern of an ideal ruler, his choice of Augustus as the example found powerful endorsement in much sixteenth-century political literature.

The relation between ruler and writer is more centrally the focus of *The Poetaster* even than *Cynthia's Revels*. It is the culmination of a process which had begun with the confrontation of Macilente with Queen Elizabeth at the conclusion of *Every Man Out of His Humour* and developed with the more fully expounded relation between Cynthia, Arete and Crites in the *Revels*. This evolution is also notable, as I shall suggest, as an abstraction of the values enshrined in a recognizable if highly idealized Elizabeth and their reimbodiment in an Augustus whose ideal status is given in the fiction of the drama, rather than recommended through panegyric. Jonson's decision to turn to 'AVGVSTVS CAESARS times' released him from the difficulty of expressing simultaneous praise and criticism of his own ruler. It may also be true – as with *Cynthia's Revels* – that the prospect of performance by the Children of the Chapel helped Jonson write something like a moral pantomime, a precocious theatrical demonstration the very neatness and confidence of which constituted its special kind of comedy.

The action of the play concerns the relegation of Ovid, the honouring of Virgil, the vindication of Horace, and the chastisement of false poetry and false report. But it is false report – ranging from the malicious gossip of which Ovid complains in I, i, through serious detraction, to allegation of treason, all embodied in the figure of Envy who heralds the play on stage – which sets events in motion. It is at once clear that Envy does not merely concern the rivalry of writers and theatres but is the agent of danger and destruction. Envy is come, by his own announcement,

> With wrestings, comments, applications,
> Spie-like suggestions, priuie whisperings . . .

and, confronted by the *Scene* of Rome, must immediately demand: 'How might I force this to the present state?'[41] The true Prologue, who on the third sounding, banishes Envy from the stage, drives home the point:

> . . . know, 'tis a dangerous age:
> Wherein, who writes, had need present his *Scenes*
> Fortie-fold proofe against the coniuring meanes

[40]G.F. Warner, 'The Library of King James VI', pp. xxxv, lix suggest an interest in Ronsard at the Scottish court. Jonson may have heard of the taste of the Scottish court through his patron, Lord Aubigny. See n. 76 below.

[41]Ll. 24–5, 33; *Ben Jonson*, IV, p. 204. One of the fullest accounts of *The Poetaster* is to be found in O.J. Campbell's *Comicall Satyre and Shakespeare's Troilus and Cressida* (San Marino, 1959), Ch. V. Cogent in many ways, it understates the importance in the play of spies, rumour and informers, and thus of the poet as truth-teller in a healthy society.

Of base detractors, and illiterate apes,
That fill vp roomes in faire and formall shapes.[42]

To the audience of 1601 the resonances of this exchange would have been unmistakable. This is a 'Defiance to Enuie' such as Hall set the fashion for in the first two poems of his *Virgidemiarum*, and was by now associated with a publicly forbidden form of literary activity.[43] It suggests too the dangers to which the public playwright was exposed, and which Jonson had directly experienced when imprisoned on charges of slander and sedition for his part in *The Isle of Dogs*. We are reminded of the atmosphere penetrated with informers and licensed spies which Donne had explored in his Fourth Satire. The two Prologues not only raise the issues most relevant to the proper reception of the play, but like Shakespeare's prologues to *Troilus and Cressida* and *Henry IV Part 2* are '. . . suited / In like conditions as our argument': within the play we soon see spying and informing at work. Envy's question: 'How might I force this . . .?' is, as Norbert Platz has observed in a valuable article, 'posed with the utmost tactical skill from Jonson's point of view. On the one hand it seems to deny any correspondence between ancient Rome and early seventeenth-century London, but on the other it may stimulate the spectators to look for these very correspondences.'[44] In IV, iv, where the actor Histrio informs the magistrate Lupus of the properties hired by Ovid and his companions for their sacrilegious banquet, farce is finely poised against fear. In the aftermath of the Essex revolt, and the playing of *Richard II* with its deposition scene the night previous to the revolt, Lupus's reaction had obvious contemporary force: 'A *crowne*, and a *sceptre*? this is good: rebellion, now? . . . Treason, treason.'[45] The two allegations of treason in the play, one against Ovid and his fellow revellers, the other against Horace, are equally groundless, and each is recognized for what it is with the aid of comic exposure and laughter. But it is not merely a case of brushing aside the ridiculous. False allegation can have serious and unexpected consequences: in the action of the play it leads directly to the exiling of Ovid and the punishment of the Princess Julia. But this is to anticipate Jonson's treatment of Ovid in *The Poetaster*, to which we must now turn.

In the early scenes it is Ovid who engages our interest and sympathy. His enthusiastic devotion to poetry and the ideal of poetic fame is shown from the outset. Throughout the drama, whether his actions are morally endorsed or not, Ovid lives intensely in the experience of each moment. Something more, however, would have struck an alert and educated member of Jonson's audience as the first scene of the play unfolded. As Ovid recited one of his own poems, Elegy XV of his *Amores*, it would have become apparent that the English was that of Christopher Marlowe; and that, furthermore, it had been taken from the book that had been banned and burnt since 1599. Marlowe's version of the Ovid elegy, neither seditious nor erotic, had been altered by Jonson in a few minor ways 'in the direction of literalism.'[46] In this play about 'the interaction of poet

[42]Ll. 6–10; op. cit. p. 205.
[43]See n. 18 above.
[44]Norbert H. Platz, 'Ben Jonson's *Ars Poetica*: An Interpretation of *Poetaster* In Its Historical Context', *Salzburg Studies in English Literature*, 12 (1973), p. 15.
[45]IV, iv, 19–20, 43; *Ben Jonson*, IV, pp. 271–2.
[46]*Ben Jonson*, IX, p. 538.

and state'[47] Jonson's use of a banned poem by Marlowe can only be seen as a careful challenge to political authority. Careful, because the early scenes in which a young and enthusiastic devotee of poetry, Ovid, is contrasted with a humdrum and materialistic father and a self-seeking and self-important society, must be set in the context of later scenes before we can be sure what the play is saying.

Chief among such scenes is the sacrilegious banquet of IV, v in which Ovid plays Jupiter and is the leading spirit, and in which Augustus's daughter, the Princess Julia, plays Juno. Here Jonson, who has been following Ovid's own poems for an outline of this character so far, is able to use his own invention, for he now confronts the still mysterious fault which precipitated Ovid's exile, and which Ovid himself referred to but did not specify.[48] Jonson follows the traditions which supposed some connection with the Princess Julia (Augustus's daughter and granddaughter, both called Julia, were sometimes confused), but turns to an unexpected episode in Suetonius for the basis of the connection between Ovid and Julia in the play. Speaking of the recriminations between Antony and Octavian, during the triumvirate, Suetonius recounted how

> . . . much talke there was abroad of a certaine supper of his [i.e. of Octavian] more secret ywis then the rest, and which was commonly called *Dodecatheos*; at which, that their sat guests in habit of gods and goddesses, and himselfe among them adorned insteed of Apollo, not onley the letters of Antonie . . . do lay in his reproach, but also these verses without an author, so vulgarly known and rife in everie mans mouth:

> . . . Whiles Cǽsar Phoebus counterfaites profanely, and in stead,
> Of supper, new adultries makes of gods against all law. . . .[49]

Jonson joins this episode with Suetonius's slightly earlier statement that: 'His daughter and niece [i.e. granddaughter], either of them named Julia, distained with all kind of lewdness and dishonesty, he sent out of the way as banished.'[50] But Jonson turns his Suetonian source completely around, making Augustus denounce Ovid and Julia for the very impiety and licence with which, according to the historian, he had been taxed by Antony. It is possible that Jonson wished the more learned members of his audience to remember the discreditable episode from the earlier life of Augustus, and to attribute the violence of the Emperor's denunciation in IV, v to the fact that he now saw his daughter fallen into the very sins he had himself renounced. But this is probably to read more personal history and psychology into the play than the text will bear. It is more likely that we have here another case of where the pro-Augustus tradition has grown so strong that it can assimilate and convert material supporting a hostile view. We have already seen how Lipsius in his *Politicorum* manages to use Tacitus to support a favourable view of Augustus. With the licence of fictional hypothesis Jonson does the same here. Yet he may, in a general way, remember

---

[47]N.H. Platz, 'Ben Jonson's *Ars Poetica*', p. 12.

[48]Ovid, *Tristia*, II, ll. 207–8; see Chapter I, n. 59.

[49]Suetonius, *Divvs Avgvstvs*, 70; Suetonius, *Historie of the Twelve Caesars translated by Philemon Holland (Anno 1606)*, Intro. Charles Whibley, Tudor Translations Series (London, 1899), I, p. 140.

[50]Ibid., p. 135.

a recent and critical view of Augustus: that of Lipsius in *De Constantia*, who wrote that the Emperor

> . . . not obscurely suffered in himselfe the punishment of his youthfull misdeedes: But yet more apparently in all his progenie. Let him be happy and mighty Cæsar, and truly *Augustus*: But with all let him haue a daughter Iulia . . . Others let him banish out of his fauour. . . .[51]

Jonson fleshes out the ideas of Julia's lewdness and of the sacrilegious feast with dialogue which, especially in the mouths of Ovid and Julia, mounts from witty and impious bawdry to the reckless feigning of such insolence to the Emperor as might indeed seem to tremble on the brink of sedition:

Ovid: Yea, we will knocke our chin against our brest; and shake thee out of *Olympus*, into an oyster-bote, for thy scolding.

Ivli: Your nose is not long enough to doe it, Ivpiter, if all thy strumpets, thou hast among the starres; tooke thy part. And there is neuer a starre in the fore-head, but shall be a horne, if thou persist to abuse me.

Cris: A good iest, i' faith. . . .

Ovid: . . . Goe from our selfe, the great God Ivpiter, to the great Emperour, AVGVSTVS CAESAR: And command him, from vs (of whose bountie he hath receiued his sir-name, AVGVSTVS) that for a thanke-offring to our beneficence, he presently sacrifice as a dish to this banquet, his beautiful and wanton daughter IVLIA. Shee's a curst queane, tell him; and plaies the scold behind his backe. . . .

Ivli: Stay, feather-footed MERCVRY, and tell AVGVSTVS, from vs, the great IVNO SATVRNIA; if he thinke it hard to doe, as IVPITER hath com-manded him . . . that he had better doe so ten times, then suffer her to loue the well-*nosed poet*, OVID: whom he shall doe well to whip . . . for soothing her, in her follies.[52]

At this well-contrived moment Augustus, Mecœnas, Horace, Lupus and others suddenly enter. Like Mosca and Volpone, Ovid and Julia have whipped up their revelry to the point of self-destruction. It is now the response of Augustus which is important. For a moment he is ready to believe he is faced with the gods themselves, but the revellers unmask themselves as soon as they kneel to him. His fury is then such that he threatens to kill his daughter. Immediately Mecœnas and Horace intervene, and Augustus, while seeing Julia responsible for a 'pageant' which will earn other deaths, turns his attention to the humbler participants. Crispinus's admission that he is 'Your gentleman, parcell-*poet*, sir' provokes a long harangue against the abuse of the poetic vocation which culminates in the banishing of Ovid and imprisoning of Julia. The extremity of the Emperor's anger has now passed, but once again Mecœnas and Horace intervene, this time to beg forgiveness for the offenders. But Augustus is adamant, and the sentences on Ovid and Julia are not softened.

---

[51] Lipsius, *Two Bookes of Constancie*, tr. Henry Stradling (1595), II, xv, p. 96.
[52] IV, v, 116–23, 201–17; *Ben Jonson*, IV, pp. 276–9. See J.F. Kermode, 'The Banquet of Sense' *John Rylands Library Bulletin*, XLIV, pp. 73–4, 86; and A.H. King, 'The Language of the Satirized Character in Jonson's *Poetaster*' (*Lund Studies in English*, X, 1941).

The interpretation of the play at this point is in dispute. Has Augustus been a just judge and good prince in his sentence, or has he, from a distorted view of the situation which Mecoenas and Horace do not share, fallen prey to passion, and inflicted a disproportionate punishment upon Ovid?[53] Horace's view, in his angry confrontation with the informers in IV. vii, is that the banquet was, in the words of one of its own songs, '*As free from scandall, as offence*'; he tells the informers that it was 'innocent mirth, / And harmlesse pleasures, bred, of noble wit'.[54] Mecoenas expresses no disagreement with this; certainly he shares Horace's loathing of the informers. It is often assumed that Jonson cast himself as Horace in this play, and it may thus be argued that Horace always gives Jonson's view. I do not wish to deny that Horace may often speak for Jonson, but Horace is properly characterized, this is a play, and it is probable that Augustus too speaks for Jonson at times. The issue here is somewhat complex. In the first place, much of the anger of Horace and Mecoenas arises from the fact that their friends have been punished as the result of an ill-found accusation of treason. That indeed provoked the discovery of the banquet, but Augustus has punished Ovid and Julia for something else. Again, the reputation of Horace, on the record of his own work, is not one for invariable and intransigent moral exposure of vice. There are times when he has said that we must see a friend's fault in the best light possible, if we want to keep him a friend.[55] Horace's reaction in IV, vii (Mecoenas does not go so far) is a most natural and human response to what has happened. He does not wish to criticize Augustus's justice directly as he pours his wrath on the informers, and boldly states that the banquet was harmless. Horace may be right to defend his friends in this way, but Augustus may at the same time be right to punish Ovid and Julia. That Augustus is angry when he first confronts the revellers is certain; he would hardly have been human had he not been, and he himself speaks of his 'fury'. But Mecoenas and Horace are successful in their first intervention. None of the offenders is punished by death. By the time Augustus sentences Ovid and Julia his anger has been mastered, and his early staccato exclamations have subsided into connected discourse. Augustus then has been swayed by his advisers in some measure but not completely; his final sentences are not delivered at the pitch of his anger, but are, rather, a mean between what that anger originally suggested, and the total forgiveness for which Mecoenas and Horace plead. As for the justice of this, surely we only have to turn back to the dialogue of the banquet to see that the sentences are not extravagant. What court decorum of Jonson's time could possibly sanction that kind of licence between a commoner and a princess? Ovid speaks of Julia as a sexual dish for their promiscuous banquet of sense in which all may 'change their louers, and make loue to others, / As the heate of every ones bloud, / . . . shall inspire';[56] Julia responds with bawdy treble-entendre on 'the well-*nosed* poet'. Those who argue that Horace speaks invariably for Jonson in this play would have to argue that an encounter of this kind between himself and a royal princess would seem to him no more than 'innocent mirth'. This is hardly likely.

Jonson has, however, used Horace and Mecoenas to preserve our sympathy

[53]N.H. Platz, 'Ben Jonson's *Ars Poetica*', pp. 16–18.
[54]IV, vi, 41–2; *Ben Jonson*, IV, p. 284.
[55]*Sat*. I, iii, 49–54.
[56]IV, v, 31–33; *Ben Jonson*, IV, pp. 273–4.

with the two offenders. Indeed the audience has shared, as Horace and Augustus have not, the euphoric freedom of that banquet of sense – anarchic mockery mounting almost to vertigo – which brings on their downfall. This sense of involvement is evoked in a new way in IV, viii and ix in which Ovid and Julia lament their forthcoming separation and say their last farewell: it is an effective balcony scene, with Julia above at her window, and Ovid in the shadows below. Jonson strikes a successful balance of a new kind. The love of Ovid and Julia is shown to be stronger than mere sexual sampling, but it is a passion essentially of flesh and blood, and one that is heedless of morality and rank. In these scenes Jonson's verse, with a diagramatic character reinforced by the staging, and a sympathy that does not preclude moral perception, expounds an irresponsible passion:

> 'No vertue currant is, but with her stamp:
> 'And no vice vicious . . .' . . .
> 'No life hath loue in such sweet state, as this;
> 'No essence is so deare to moodie sense,
> 'As flesh, and bloud; whose quintessence is sense.
> 'Beautie, compos'd of bloud, and flesh, moues more,
> 'And is more plausible to bloud, and flesh,
> 'Then spirituall beautie can be to the spirit.[57]

While the imminent physical separation of the lovers naturally turns them, at least in their hyperbole, to the spirit, these lines, with their lingering and caressing iteration of 'flesh, and bloud . . . bloud, and flesh' and their Marlovian rejection of the spiritual order ('A god is not so glorious as a king . . .') express the heart of Ovid's human importance in this play. As one critic has rightly observed, 'Jonson is careful to show how limited are Ovid's horizons . . . he was renouncing the whole genre of Ovidian erotic poetry of which *Venus and Adonis* and *Hero and Leander* are the supreme examples . . .'.[58] It is surprising, in view of repeated attempts to find Elizabethan parallels to the classical characters of this play, that the connection between Marlowe and Ovid has not been more explored. It might be thought that the opening scene of the play proclaimed the identity, and nothing in the daring and iconoclastic career of Ovid in the play makes the link inappropriate. That Marlowe was dead by 1601 would be an objection if we were arguing that *The Poetaster* was 'a paralel': a strict, personal *roman à clef*. The argument is rather that Jonson makes Ovid express the Marlovian in the Elizabethan literary world, both the nature of his art and the nature of his life. It is a function of *The Poetaster* to propose a series of relative values, in poetry as in polity. In this series the Horatian is set above the Ovidian, as the Virgilian is to be set above the Horatian. It is the Horatian that we must next consider.

Horace is the second of the three major poets of the play to be introduced. Ovid is already well-established by the time Horace enters in III, i; a similar interval is to elapse, with similar effect, before Virgil is introduced in V, ii, as the climactic point of the play. In this respect the action of the drama is remarkably

---

[57]IV, viii, 15–16; IV, ix, 36–41; op. cit. IV, pp. 285, 287.
[58]J.B. Bamborough, *Ben Jonson* (London, 1970), p. 44.

well-paced in its conveying of a hierarchy of literary value. As Ovid was introduced in the act of composition, so too is Horace. As Ovid was presented through one of his real poems, so Horace is introduced through a poem of his own, the dramatic character of which is expanded and elaborated by Jonson. It is the same Ninth Satire of the First Book which was the basis for the first part of Donne's *Satyre IV*. It is notable that Jonson does not here draw on the latter part of Donne's poem, as he had in *Cynthia's Revels*, and that, at least in this part of *The Poetaster*, the suspicion of licensed spies that Donne had introduced into the Horatian situation, is excluded. The action of *The Poetaster* dramatizes the operations of Envy elsewhere; in these scenes Jonson is thus free to develop the comedy of Horace's poem with an altogether lighter tone than would have been appropriate in Donne's version. Jonson allows Horace much of the fundamental security that Donne's protagonist was denied. In the action and pattern of *The Poetaster* these scenes not only seem to vindicate Horace by suggesting that some of those who become his enemies (here Crispinus/Marston) start off by trying to curry favour with him, but, more important, they provide a poetic and a human mean between the ardent self-dedication of Ovid in I, i and ii and the achieved heroic of Virgil in V, ii. We can never forget that the encounter between Horace and Crispinus in III, i–iii is itself an Horatian poem: poetry is here close to the contingencies, satisfactions and exasperations of everyday life; it is unpretentious, yet flexible and poised. As in Horace, so here, the one point where it takes on real ethical force is where Horace defends the life and household of Mecoenas against the corrupt suppositions of Crispinus. The conflict is very much sharpened, in context, by Crispinus's suggestion that with his help Horace might manage to turn Virgil out of Mecoenas's favour.

These are the only scenes, in the text of the 1601 *Poetaster*, in which Horace is the dominant figure. They barely establish him as a character in his own right, but his part, and the play as a whole, were to be much strengthened by the addition, in the Folio Text, of III, v: Jonson's rendering of the First Satire of the Second Book of Horace, the dialogue between the satirist and the jurist Trebatius. Jonson's version, with its heroic couplets and fast pace, is the nearest he ever came to Pope in an imitation of Horace. The poems are two important stages within English Augustan imitation. This scene gives substance to what was otherwise a rather sketchy treatment of Horace the satirist. The issues are here formally debated, and the nature of Horace's particular talent, and of his right relation to Augustus, carefully set forth. The Emperor's martial achievements he cannot sing; his virtue in peace, his fortitude and justice, he can and will, but only on fit occasion. To do so at other times might seem flattery, which Augustus himself, 'reposed safe in his owne merit', would spurn.[59]

By the opening of Act V the play is depicting a polity from which Ovidian/Marlovian writing, with its associations of irreligion and moral licence, has been banished. The kind of writing for which Horace stands is, by its nature, exposed to slander and detraction, but if rightly understood by a just and secure prince, should be welcomed rather than proscribed. For the showing forth of Virgil and Virgilian writing which now begins, the audience has been prepared by a series of passing references. V,i mounts to the Emperor's honouring of Virgil by several stages. The first is Augustus's declaration of clemency to

---

[59]III, v, 35; *Ben Jonson*, IV, p. 258.

the two poetic offenders, Gallus and Tibullus, participants in the sacrilegious banquet, and of his high esteem for the poetic calling. The second is the poets' expression of thanks, and esteem for Augustus. The third, as Augustus turns praise away from himself, is their expression of their esteem for Virgil. The scene opens with Augustus himself, who now presides over the remainder of the play.

If anger and (as I have argued) just inflexibility marked the earlier appearance of Augustus, clemency, graciousness and familiarity mark his presence in Act V. His opening line, indeed, echoes that famous line of Virgil from *Aeneid* VI ('Parcere subiectis, et debellare superbos') which had meant so much to Christian imperialism, and which had recently concluded *Basilikon Doron*:

> We, that haue conquer'd still, to saue the conquer'd . . .

and he proceeds to a remarkable affirmation of his ideal of the fame of Rome, borne into futurity by the voice of poetry:

> Shee can so mould *Rome*, and her monuments,
> Within the liquid marble of her lines,
> That they shall stand fresh, and miraculous,
> Euen, when they mixe with innouating dust;
> In her sweet streames shall our braue *Roman* spirits
> Chace, and swim after death, with their choise deeds
> Shining on their white shoulders; and therein
> Shall *Tyber*, and our famous riuers fall
> With such attraction, that th'ambitious line
> Of the round world shall to her center shrinke,
> To heare their musicke . . .[60]

These lines, perhaps the most effective poetry in the play, are notable for the way they convey fame in images changing from the static to the mobile. The conventional contrast between the flux of time and the fixity of fame's monuments is radically modified, the point of departure being the Virgilian 'liquid marble' (cf. '. . . vivos ducent de marmore voltus': *Aeneid*, VI, 848); thereafter it is achieved fame, in both life and art, which has the flow and movement of a river, while the flux of time is by contrast mere 'innouating dust'. The 'fresh, and miraculous' does not seem to buy its longevity at the cost of full life, and when the paradox of 'liquid marble' is further developed into the image of poetry as 'sweet streames' in which 'our braue *Roman* spirits / Chace, and swim after death . . .' the winning and enjoyment of fame is more than ever like immortal physical movement, spontaneous and eternal, and not without a hint of the Marlovian sensuous. Something of what was relegated with Ovid is here readmitted as a part of Augustus's poetic ideal. The streams of poetry are made a river into which real rivers fall, sounding a music to which the round world shall listen.

In response to this speech the poets praise Augustus. Horace and Tibullus, interestingly, glance at how 'other Princes, hoisted to their thrones / By fortunes passionate and disordered power' seek not to advance but only punish

---

[60]V, i, 21–31; op. cit. IV, p. 290.

learning.[61] In view of the almost unanimous tradition, even among writers who praised Augustus, that he came to the empire by ill means, these speeches are certainly intended by Jonson as the equivocation of courtliness. Augustus *had* been hoisted to his throne by, among other things, 'fortunes passionate and disordered power' and Horace's speech *can* be construed as saying as much, though the punctuation of 1.47 on balance suggests that Horace is contrasting Augustus's rise to power with that of other princes. The sincere praise lies in what they say about how Augustus uses the power he now has. What is crucial to this issue is Augustus's reply, which more or less admits what the poets had hesitated to say:

> CAESAR, for his rule, and for so much stuffe
> As fortune puts in his hand, shall dispose it
> (As if his hand had eyes, and soule, in it)
> With worth, and iudgement.[62]

What the blind hand of fortune gives to Augustus he returns with full sight.

Virgil's arrival is now announced, and Augustus invites the other poets to express their opinion of him. He does so with interesting reference to rank, asking first Mecoenas, Gallus and Tibullus who are above Virgil in social status, then checking himself and asking Horace, '. . . that art the poorest, / And likeliest to enuy, or to detract'. Eager to elicit testimony to Virgil's intrinsic merit, Augustus has here made an error of both judgement and tact. Horace, whom we have already seen attempting to extenuate the offence of Ovid and Julia, and who has just seemed to draw a courtly veil over Augustus's rise to power, now speaks to him freely, and does not hesitate to rebuke:

> CAESAR speakes after common men, in this,
> To make a difference of me, for my poorenesse:
> As if the filth of pouertie sunke as deepe
> Into a knowing spirit, as the bane
> Of riches doth, into an ignorant soule. . . .
> But knowledge is the *nectar*, that keepes sweet
> A perfect soule, euen in this graue of sinne;
> And for my soule, it is as free, as CAESARS:
> For, what I know is due, I'le giue to all.[63]

It is an important moment, for it shows Horace, not without a touch of anger against wealth, exercising the right of the poet to correct the prince; he has certainly gone further than Crites did in *Cynthia's Revels*, and Augustus responds as the ideal ruler of Prince literature:

> Thankes, HORACE, for thy free, and holsome sharpnesse:
> Which pleaseth CAESAR more, then seruile fawnes.
> 'A flatterd prince soon turnes the prince of fooles. . . .'[64]

[61]V, i, 47–8; op. cit. IV, p. 291.
[62]V, i, 58–61; op. cit. IV, p. 291.
[63]V, i, 79–83, 88–91; op. cit. IV, p. 292.
[64]V, i, 94–6; op. cit. IV, p. 292.

This exchange also has a significant social content, for it proposes knowledge and skill as a vocation independent of rank and affording an impartial viewpoint on society. Horace, for the moment, speaks with the voice of meritocracy, of such a class of professional men as both Augustus and the Tudors had sought to expand.

In the evaluations of Virgil which now follow many of the emphases of neoclassical criticism in English are heard; above all his is a poetry not of enthusiasm but deliberation, and of total dedication in wisdom and craft. Tibullus, in course of praising the wisdom and usefulness of Virgil's works, speaks of the potential relevance of Virgil to every occasion, and Augustus picks up and endorses his meaning in possible allusion to the *Sortes Virgilianae*. This is significant preparation for the part of the *Aeneid* Virgil will actually read to Augustus and the other poets assembled. But first the moral of the earlier exchange between Augustus and Horace is acted out in the stage-business about where Virgil should sit: Virgil cannot believe that a poet 'void / Of birth, or wealth, or temporall dignity' should sit beside the Emperor on the same level; Augustus, now backed by Horace, insists on it.

That Virgil read Books IV, VI and VIII of his *Aeneid* to Augustus is a tradition of antiquity.[65] Jonson will have been aware of it. His task was then to choose a passage from these three books as relevant to the subject and design of his play as the Elegy of Ovid with which it opened and as the two Satires of Horace which form so important a part of its central sections. The section he chose was the twenty-eight lines of Book IV in which Aeneas and Dido, out hunting and caught by the storm, consummate their love in a cave. Malignant Rumour, swiftest of evils, thereafter noises it abroad. Jonson renders the passage, without significant deviations or additions, in forty-two lines.[66] The significance of Jonson's choice of this particular passage seems not to have been noticed. For a play so concerned as this is with detraction, slander and malicious informing, the passage chosen is highly appropriate. But it is not just that in a play about Rumour, a passage about Rumour is chosen. We have already been alerted by Tibullus and Augustus to look in Virgil for particular applications to any situation. The discovery and punishment of Ovid and Julia is still very recent. It is here that the indiscriminate character of Rumour is important: in Jonson, 'As couetous shee is of tales, and lies, / As prodigall of truth', while Virgil has the emphasis slightly different: 'tam ficti pravique tenax quam nuntia veri'.[67] In Virgil it is a little more plain that Rumour can announce truth as well as spread falsehood, and of course the news which eventually reaches Dido's suitor Iarbas *is* the truth. From one point of view – and it is a point of view endorsed by the *Aeneid* as a whole – Rumour really does have something bad to report. The rôle of Rumour in the downfall of Ovid and Julia is now more clear. Here too it spread falsehood yet brought out truth. Just as it is the rôle of Augustus to use with the eye of judgement what blind fortune has put into his hands, so in this affair it was his rôle to distinguish truth from falsehood in the many tongues of Rumour. Of course there is a further link between the *Aeneid* passage and the episode of Ovid and Julia. The love of Dido and Aeneas is a

---

[65]See Chapter I, p. 17, n. 54.
[66]V. ii, 56–97; *Ben Jonson*, IV, pp. 296–7. *Aeneid*, IV, 160–89.
[67]*Poetaster*, V, ii, 96–7; *Ben Jonson*, IV, p. 297; *Aeneid*, IV, 188.

guilty love, and for Aeneas a diversion in the voyage of the Trojans to found a new empire in Latium, a diversion from the path to found what was ultimately to become the empire of Augustus prophesied in Book VI. Virgil, it is sometimes considered, may have thought of Cleopatra and Egypt as he wrote of Dido and Carthage. Yet his treatment of the whole episode is fraught with human sympathy. So is Marlowe's treatment of the same subject in his *Dido Queen of Carthage*, which we are perhaps meant to recall here.[68] *The Poetaster*, at its lower literary level, presents the episode of Ovid and Julia in the same way. The lovers do not contribute to the civilization which Augustus and the whole play propose as an ideal; like Dido's their values and their love must be relegated. Yet this relegation is not seen just from the viewpoint of those who impose, or are pardoned from, the penalty. Without impairing the firmness of Jonson's moral judgement, Ovid and Julia have been allowed to make their appeal for our sympathy.

As the sacrilegious banquet mounted to its reckless climax with a mock-defiance of Augustus, only to be interrupted by Augustus at that very moment, so Virgil's recitation reaches a climax in describing the operations of Rumour, 'This monster', when at that very point in his sentence, many-tongued Rumour, or Envy, in the persons of Lupus, Tucca, Crispinus, Demetrius and Histrio, break in upon the reading. Smarting from Augustus's treatment of their allegation of treason against Ovid and Julia, and even more from Horace's bitter subsequent attack on them, they come to re-establish themselves in the favour of the Emperor with a trumped-up allegation of treason against Horace.[69] The structural symmetry of Jonson's drama here is remarkable. In the banquet scene misrule was interrupted by rule; here the positions are reversed, and the order and harmony of great poetry and a great emperor are interrupted by disorder and detraction. On this occasion Rumour reveals no fault in the accused, and the only truth to emerge concerns the character of the accusers. The epic poet Virgil now endorses the position of the satirical poet Horace. As he says to Augustus:

> 'Tis not the wholesome sharpe moralitie,
> Or modest anger of a *satyricke* spirit,
> That hurts, or wounds the bodie of a state;
> But the sinister application
> Of the malicious, ignorant, and base
> Interpreter:[70]

The high gravity which Jonson sought as Virgil read from his poem must now be abandoned, as the Emperor perceives. The comedy, which has twice reached upwards towards a higher, tragic or epic mode, now finds a lower level in the instructive farce of the closing scene of judgement and correction, in which Lupus, Demetrius, Crispinus and Tucca, are exposed and chastised. In all this the dignified figures of Virgil and Augustus are present, the former as magistrate, the latter as an approving and instructed spectator. Jonson had a good

[68] See chapter I, p. 18, n. 56.
[69] V, iii, 1–135; *Ben Jonson*, IV, pp. 297–301.
[70] V, iii, 138–42; op. cit. IV, p. 301.

basis for what he did. Suetonius recorded that the first object of Augustus in the treatment of libels was to show them to be false and afterwards to punish their authors.[71] His habit of administering justice personally[72] makes it credible that in Jonson's play he should linger to watch the correction of Crispinus. Above all Augustus had the most explicit views about the precise offence for which Crispinus, 'parcel-Poet' or poetaster, is found guilty at the end of the play.

> The eloquence that he followed was of an elegant and temperate kind; wherein he avoided unapt and unfit sentences, as also the stinking savours, as himself saith, of dark and obscure words, but took especial care how to express his mind and meaning most plainly and evidently. . . . As for those that affect new-made words, such also as use old terms past date, he loathed and rejected alike, as faulty, both the sorts of them in a contrary kind. . . . As for Marcus Antonius, he rateth him as if he were frantic, for writing that which men may rather wonder at than understand.[73]

In contriving the scene in which Crispinus is made to take 'somewhat bitter . . . but very wholesome' pills, to purge his diction in 'a light vomit', Jonson was using an idea taken from Lucian's *Lexiphanes*.[74] He was also, it is quite clear, enforcing upon the stage an Augustan judgement about writing, an opinion of Augustus himself.

If we look at the play as a whole, it may be seen that it is based on a radically new literary idea, yet in a number of ways it is reminiscent of Elizabethan drama. These two aspects are essential to one another. It has often been pointed out that Ovid's balcony scene with Julia has similarities with that of *Romeo and Juliet*, and critics have been embarrassed on Jonson's behalf. Again, Jonson's Prologue Envy recalls Shakespeare's Prologue Rumour, in *Henry IV* Part II. And while thinking of *Henry IV* we may notice how in Pantilius Tucca Jonson has given us a slippery minor Falstaff; the Falstaffian note is struck again and again in his speeches and action. Add to this the deliberate recall of Marlowe in the opening poetry of Ovid, and we can see that Jonson built his play out of many Elizabethan materials, as well as out of situations, characters and poems which were specifically Augustan.

Augustus State

As the example of a mature and discerning ruler, the Augustus of *The Poetaster* is closer to sixteenth-century Prince literature than the allusions to Augustus in sixteenth-century panegyric and ceremony. Prince literature and panegyric were, however, closely associated, as we can see from the fact that Erasmus appended panegyric verse, including versions of Pliny and Claudian, to some editions of his *Institio Principis Christiani*.[75] By the very end of Elizabeth's reign it is probable that Jonson had gleaned some knowledge of the political and cultural aspirations of the Scottish court, beyond what might be inferred from

---

[71]Suetonius, Divvs Avgvstvs, IV; *Historie of the Twelve Caesars, Translated by Philemon Holland*, pp. 128–9.
[72]Divvs Augvstvs, 33; *Historie of the Twelve Caesars*, pp. 109–10.
[73]Divvs Avgvstvs, 86; *Historie of the Twelve Caesars*, p. 152.
[74]V, iii, 393–402; *Ben Jonson*, IV, pp. 309–10.
[75]J.D. Garrison, *Dryden and the Tradition of Panegyric*, pp. 50–1.

Basilikon Doron. James sought to unite French and English poetic traditions, and anyone in a position to brief the ambitious but disappointed public poet (such an informant could have been Esmé Stuart, Lord Aubigny, Jonson's first patron) must have drawn attention to the work of Le Pléiade. The Stuart line had been celebrated in the poetry of Ronsard, in the person of Mary Queen of Scots, whom Du Bellay linked with the return of the Virgin Astraea, and James is known to have read *La Françiade*.[76] Parts of Ronsard's work were intimately linked with public ceremonial. Ronsard had himself collaborated in the design of the Royal Entry of Charles IX, in 1571, drawing on *La Françiade* is so doing. While the symbolism of this Entry, and of its conjoined Queen's Entry, is not explicitly Augustan, its use of the idea of the Trojan descent of the French monarchy points in this direction, and Frances Yates's general conclusion that 'the imperial theme could identify with the peace theme as representing the arrival of an Augustan golden age of universal peace'[77] is persuasive. What she has termed the 'wild imperialism' of the 1571 Entry may very well have provoked the discriminate judgement of Jonson; certainly he took such public ceremonial seriously, as may be seen from his engaged but at times sceptical annotations in his copy of Franciscus Modius's *Pandectae Triumphales*.[78] As the life of the old Queen drew to its close, it may have occurred to Jonson that the Augustan values he had already set forth in *The Poetaster* could, when the occasion came, find expression in public ceremonial.

After the death of Elizabeth, Jonson was among the several poets rebuked, in Chettle's strange work *England's Mourning Garment* (1603) for not praising the memory of Elizabeth; he there figures as 'our English *Horace*' and it is roundly stated that 'Of her he seems to have no Memory' (the same is said of Shakespeare and Chapman).[79] *England's Mourning Garment*, of course, welcomes James as well as mourning Elizabeth, though the stress is certainly on the latter. When eventually Jonson came to ring out the old and ring in the new, he did so with extreme brevity. In one of the songs addressed to Queen Anne, from *The Entertainment at Althrope*, he wrote: 'Long liue ORIANA / To exceed (whom shee succeeds) our late DIANA.'[80] The emphasis of this short and charming entertainment is upon uncourtly virtue; there is a playful contention between an untutored satyr and the more refined fairies in addressing the new queen, but it is the satyr to whom the burden of truth-telling is given, and he who does justice to the uncourtierlike merit of the Queen's host at Althorp, Sir Robert Spencer. In a light and glancing way this piece of Jonson's is a further 'defiance of Envy', and the satyr's words against envy are picked up in the final line of the *Entertainment* which transposes the line against Envy from the

---

[76]Helena Mennie Shire, *Song, Dance and Poetry at the Court of Scotland Under King James VI* (Cambridge, 1969), p. 95. For the use of the myths of the Golden Age and allusions to Augustus in the Pleiade, see Elizabeth Armstrong, *Ronsard and the Age of Gold*, pp. 26, 96–7 and generally.

[77]Fránces A. Yates, ed., *La ioyeuse entrée de Charles IX roy de France en Paris, 1572* (Amsterdam, 1973), p. 22.

[78]Franciscus Modius, *Pandectae Triumphales* . . . (Bruges, 1586) at present in the Library of Clare College, Cambridge. It is discussed briefly in *Ben Jonson*, XI, pp. 594–6.

[79]*England's Mourning Garment; worn here by plain Shepherds* . . ., (London, 1603), *Harleian Miscellany* (London, 1744–6), III, p. 510.

[80]Ll. 123–4; *Ben Jonson*, VII, p. 125.

Epilogue to the Queen in *Every Man Out of His Humour*. Jonson is applying a line addressed to the old Queen to the new Queen; in so doing he is quietly but firmly maintaining his own position.

The Entertainment at Althrope took place in June 1603, as Queen Anne and Prince Henry travelled south from Edinburgh to London. The new King himself had arrived in his new capital in May, and a royal entry with five triumphal arches was planned for the day of his coronation. This public triumph had then to be deferred owing to the spread of the plague in London, and eventually took place on 15 March 1604, the day James I opened his first parliament.[81] A common theme runs through *The King's Entertainment* of 1604, James's first speech from the throne in parliament, and the Speaker's answer to this speech. It is to those parts of the Royal Entry devised by Ben Jonson that we must particularly turn, to see what the author of *The Poetaster*, with its explicitly Augustan political and cultural programme, made of the task of devising a public ceremony in honour of the new monarch. The 1604 Entry has not yet been adequately studied. It was far more elaborate and splendid than that for Elizabeth in 1559. It is not my purpose to attempt a full explication of its symbolism in political context, as Sydney Anglo has done for the public spectacle of the earlier Tudor Period.[82] Rather I wish to focus upon the leading motif of Jonson's part of the *Entertainment*: the parallel of James with Augustus. Even this, clear as it is, is little discussed in the few works to consider the 1604 Entry.[83]

No elaborate rationale need, by this time, be offered for the work of Renaissance poets in panegyric, civic pageantry and masque. As the Recorder of Warwick had recited to Queen Elizabeth in 1572, speeches and pageants had, since the later Roman Empire, been devised to express, in the presence of the ruler, gratitude for benefits conferred, hopes for the future and, *laudando praecipere*, the means by which such hopes might be fulfilled. As E.W. Talbert put it in 1943, 'the voice of Jonson's masques . . . is that of the panegyric *laudando praecipere*; the sense that of precepts *de regimine principum* enlarged by the ethical–poetical *credo* of a staunch Renaissance humanist'.[84] Only the most obvious features of the *Entertainment* would have caught the attention, as the new King rode through the crowds to Westminster, but if we are to read something of Jonson's mind on this momentous occasion we must patiently attend to some of the learned detail which he was later to publish with so much care.

Ben Jonson was responsible for the first and last arches of the Entertainment.

[81]Ibid., X, p. 386.

[82]John Nichols, *The Progresses and Public Processions of Queen Elizabeth* (London, 1823), I, pp. 38–60. Sydney Anglo, *Spectacle, Pageantry and Early Tudor Policy* (Oxford, 1969). Few since C.H. Herford and the Simpsons have attempted to relate Jonson's Masques and Entertainments to his other works. Parfitt, *Ben Jonson: Public Poet and Private Man* has made a valuable start, though he seems to surmount only with difficulty the assumption that the Masques and Entertainments were meant to convey ideals rather than describe the world as it was.

[83]David M. Bergeron, *English Civic Pageantry, 1558–1642* (London, 1971), pp. 71–88, discusses the 1604 Entry but makes little attempt to explicate its historical symbolism. George Parfitt, *Ben Jonson: Public Poet and Private Man* has a few comments, pp. 67–71; but much the most interesting and refreshing so far is in Graham Parry, *The Golden Age Restor'd: The Culture of the Stuart Court, 1603–42* (Manchester, 1981), pp. 1–19, in which James's rôle as a new Augustus is mentioned.

[84]'The Interpretation of Jonson's Courtly Spectacles', *Publications of the Modern Languages Association*, 41, (1946), p. 473.

The Fenchurch Arch was the first and was a prelude to the climax of the final and (now in 1604) seventh arch, the second entrusted to him. The Fenchurch Arch pictorially represented London itself, Jonson's account of its various figures and legends being a great deal fuller than anything it would be possible to infer from the surviving pictures of the Arch itself. The Arch was probably less elaborate than Jonson's scheme. The figures of the Arch allegorically represented the British Monarchy, then in descending order, Divine Wisdom, the Genius of the City flanked by Counsel (Bouleutes) and Arms (Polemius), then the personification of the Thames. He in his turn pointed to the six daughters of the Genius of the City, 'who, in a spreading ascent, vpon several grices, helpe to beautifie both the sides'.[85] These were: Gladness, Veneration, Promptitude, Vigilance, 'louing Affectation' (*Agape*) and Unanimity. The explanation recalls first a Londinium hostile to the arms of Rome (in a passage from the *Annals* of Tacitus); then records its establishment at the Norman Conquest as 'Camera Regia'; then moves rapidly to the notion of Britain as a world in itself, 'Orbis Britannicus, Divisus Ab Orbe' with its allusion to the line in Virgil's First Eclogue. It is the line which lies behind 'this little world' of John of Gaunt's speech in *Richard II* (II, i, 45): both are to be recalled in James's speech from the throne. These words are the first of several 'legends' on the Arch drawn from the poets of Augustan Rome (though Jonson also uses Martial, Seneca, Claudian and others): the legend of Thames is from Ovid's *Amores*, and his appearance is modelled on Virgil's description of the Tiber in Book VIII of the *Aeneid*. Gladness's garb, cruze, gold cup and instruments were (though drawn from Ripa's *Iconologia*) apparently intended to recall two odes of Horace, the first (I, 27) in praise of temperate celebration, the second (I, 37) the famous congratulatory ode on Augustus's victory over Antony and Cleopatra; the legend of Veneration ('Mihi Semper Deus',) recalled the gratitude of Tityrus, in the First Eclogue, to Augustus the saviour of shepherds; the legend of Promptitude is from *Aeneid*, I and that of Vigilance from *Metamorphoses*, I.

The speeches at the Fenchurch Arch comprised an exchange between the Genius of the City (played by the great actor Edward Alleyne) and Thames, in which the Genius presented the accession of James as the fulfilment of the 'minutes, houres, weekes, months and yeares' of British history:

> Now London reare
> Thy forehead high, and on it striue to weare
> Thy choisest gems; teach thy steepe Towres to rise
> Higher with people: set with sparkling eyes
> Thy spacious windowes; and in euery street,
> Let thronging ioy, loue, and amazement meet.
> Cleaue all the ayre with showtes, and let the cry
> Strike through as long, and vniuersally,
> As thunder; for, thou now art blist to see
> That sight, for which thou didst begin to be.
> When BRVTVS plough first gaue thee infant bounds,
> And I, thy GENIVS walk't auspicious rounds
> In euery furrow; then did I forelooke,

[85]Ll. 124–5; *Ben Jonson*, VII, p. 87. John Nichols, *The Progresses, Processions and Magnificent Festivities of King James the First* . . . (London, 1828), I, pp. 325–99, gives the full description.

And saw this day mark't white in CLOTHO's booke.
The seuerall circles, both of change and sway,
Within this *Isle*, there also figur'd lay:
Of which the greatest, perfectest, and last
Was this, whose present happinesse we tast.[86]

Thames declares that he does not welcome James the less if he is silent, not competing with the seas of pomp around him, and the Genius proceeds formally to welcome the King, the Queen and the Prince. This concludes Jonson's first part of the *King's Entertainment*. The reader of his account would have been more aware than the spectator of the ceremony (in Dekker's amusing image) of 'how many paire of Latin sheets, we haue shaken & cut into shreds',[87] and in particular of that central series of quotations from, and allusions to, the Roman Augustan poets. The educated spectator might have recalled that the words most prominent on the Arch: 'PAR DOMVS HÆC COELO, SED MINOR EST DOMINO', from Martial VIII, xxxvi, were immediately preceded in their source by a line addressing Domitian as Augustus,[88] and certainly the Augustan meaning of the words of Vigilance: 'Mihi Semper Deus' would have been recognized as words in praise of Augustus in Virgil. The oratorical part of the *Entertainment*, like the Royal Entry of Charles IX, recalled the Trojan Brutus as the mythical founder of the modern nation; and it laid stress on James's accession as the great work of time, peaceful augmentation through the union of crowns (it was implied) redeeming those earlier 'circles' of sway by conquest. The implicit allying of James with Augustus in this part of the *Entertainment* is thus in harmony with the Orosian concept of Augustus as providential ruler, though Jonson's opening words in the first speech, 'Time, Fate, and Fortune haue at length conspir'd . . .' leave a little space for those more secular recognitions of how in the short term Augustus rose to power, which were admitted in *The Poetaster*.

If the Augustanism of the Fenchurch Arch was implicit, that of the Arch at Temple Bar was explicit. Indeed its rôle was the more clear through having been immediately preceded by Dekker's New World Arch, surmounted by the figure of the goddess Astraea. James was here not only 'integrated into the established state mythology';[89] he was made ready to become Augustus. Here at Temple Bar the topmost figure was the head of the god Janus, and above it the legend 'IANO QUADRIFRONTI SACRUM' proclaimed that this Arch was itself the Temple of Janus. This climactic part of Jonson's ceremony was thus to concern itself with the issues of peace and war. In his account he briefly reviews the different interpretations of the fourfrontedness of Janus (that it represents the four quarters of the world, or the four elements emerging from Chaos) before choosing the significance of Janus as the god of war and peace, of the four seasons and of the beginnings and ends of things. Both the account and the legends of the Arch draw upon Ovid's description of Janus in the *Fasti*; on a wreath round the head of the deity was a line from Martial ('Tot vultus mihi nec

---

[86]Ll. 286–93; *Ben Jonson*, VII, p. 91–2.
[87]Ibid., X, p. 388.
[88]Ll. 17–18; *Ben Jonson*, VII, p. 83. Martial, VIII, xxvi, 11: 'Haec, Auguste, tamen, quae vertica sidera pulsat . . .'
[89]Graham Parry, *The Golden Age Restor'd*, p. 16.

satis putavi') 'Signifying, that though he had four faces, yet he thought them not enough, to behold the greatnesse and glorie of that day' and beneath the head a line from the *Fasti* ('Et modo sacrifico Clvsivs ore vocor') announced that while the Janus of the open temple was called Patulcius, and of the closed temple Clusius, the spectators were to see Janus in his closed aspect: 'vpon the comming of his majestie, being to be shut, he was to be called Clvsivs.' The Temple Bar Arch was thus an acted symbol. James as a peacebringer, uniting three kingdoms by the right inherent in him, closed the doors of the Temple of Janus as he passed on to Westminster. Jonson's *Entertainment* thus plainly alluded to an event in the reign of Augustus whose fame was guaranteed by Virgil's reference to it in *Aeneid* I, the first of the three carefully placed mentions of Augustus in the poem. The spectators were thus invited to see a parallel between the accession of James and that most important event for the Christian providential view of Augustus: the closing of the Temple of Janus and the establishing of world peace. This was intimated in the '*Hexastich*' written on the Arch beneath the 'intire armes of the kingdom' and the parallel was clinched by another conspicuous feature of the Arch: two lines from Horace's address to the *princeps* in the Epistle to Augustus 'In a great freeze . . . quite along the bredth of the building', lines which, hailing the ruler as already having altars devoted to him, and being unique in history, seem a good deal more extravagant out of context than in their place in the epistle as a whole.[90]

The figures within the Temple were: Peace with Wealth at her side, and Mars grovelling at her feet with his weapons scattered; Quiet with Tumult at her feet; Liberty treading down Servitude; Safety standing above Danger; and Felicity with Unhappiness at her feet. The legend given to this last pair, the 'soule' of the emblem which together they formed, was another Augustan sentence, so familiar that its significance could be taken at a glance, and so significant that it may almost have been deemed an obligatory part of every sixteenth- and seventeenth-century royal entry from Elizabeth to William III:

REDEUNT SATVRNIA REGNA

Out of *Virgil*, to shew that now those golden times were returned againe, wherein *Peace* was with vs so aduanced, *Rest* receiued, *Libertie* restored, *Safetie* assured, and all *Blessednesse* appearing in euery of these vertues. . . .[91]

Beneath the famous words from the Fourth Eclogue were placed a line of Drances, from Book XI of the *Aeneid*, advising Turnus to make peace with Aeneas and the Trojans: 'Nulla Salvs Bello: Pacem Te Poscimvs Omnes' (l. 362). The words of Drances (not an entirely happy source) commended the acceptance of Trojan, that is Roman, destiny through peace. The theme of Trojan destiny, already touched on at the Fenchurch Arch in the allusion to Brutus, is to become more prominent at the end of the *Entertainment*.

The lines from the Epistle to Augustus afford the dramatic situation for the spoken part of the entertainment at the Temple Bar Arch. Within the arch was an altar. As the monarch approached, a flamen and the Genius of the City met at this altar, the former, roused by the tumult and finding the Ides of March

---

[90]Ll. 412–27; *Ben Jonson*, VII, p. 96.
[91]Ll. 523–7; op. cit. VII, p. 100.

come, preparing to celebrate the feast of Anna Perenna, guest of Mars, the latter checking him ('. . . these dead rites / Are long since buryed, and new power excites / More high and heartie flames.'),[92] and pointing to the inscription on the altar. This inscription ran, in part:

D.I.O.M. [Domino Iacobo Optimo Maximo]
BRITANNIARVM. IMP. PACIS.
VINDICI. MARTE. MAIORI. P.P.F.S. [Pater Patriae, Fidei Servatori]
AVGVSTO.   NOVO.   GENTIVM.   CONIVNCTARVM.   NVMINI.
TVTELARI.[93]

Like the *princeps* of the Epistle to Augustus James has an altar dedicated to him; the point is conspicuously stressed by the exchange between the Genius and the Flamen; and James is *Augustus Novus*.

Loe, there is hee,

Who brings with him a greater ANNE then shee:
Whose strong and potent vertues haue defac'd
Sterne MARS his statues, and vpon them plac'd
His, and the world's blest blessings: This hath brought
Sweet peace to sit in that bright state shee ought,
Vnbloudie, or vntroubled; hath forc'd hence
All tumults, feares, or other darke portents
That might inuade weake minds; hath made men see
Once more the face of welcome libertie:
And doth (in all his present acts) restore
That first pure world, made of the better ore.[94]

With his reference to the feast of Anna Perenna, Jonson has deployed a ponderous but smooth-working piece of classical erudition to praise Queen Anne, and to distract attention from the more familiar associations of the Ides of March. By the time he has firmly established James as Augustus he can afford to recall Julius Caesar ('And may these Ides as fortunate appeare / To thee, as they to CAESAR fatall were') and has just time to wish that James be a master of 'blind *Fortune*' (as Augustus had been in *Poetaster*) before the 'brazen gates' of the Temple swing shut, to reveal the further inscription:

IMP. IACOBVS MAX.
CÆSAR AVG. P.P.
PACE POPVLO BRITANNICO
TERRE MARIQVE PARTA
IANVM CLVSIT. S.C. [Senatus Consulto][95]

With the shutting of the gates, the assassination of Caesar, the era of Mars and the vicissitudes of Fortune are to be consigned to the past.

---

[92] Ll. 555–90; op. cit. VII, pp. 101–2.
[93] Ll. 647–51; op. cit. VII, p. 105.
[94] Ll. 589–99; op. cit. VII, p. 102.
[95] Ll. 670–4; op. cit. VII, p. 105.

After the assassination of Julius Caesar, it will be recalled, Octavian had arranged special shows in memory of his uncle at the games in honour of Venus Genetrix. At these games a comet had appeared in the sky, alluded to by Virgil in his Fifth Eclogue, and recorded by Octavian in his Autobiography in a passage which happens to have been preserved in Pliny.[96] The comet was taken as a sign that Caesar's soul had been received among the gods and that Octavian was the right heir of his uncle's single power over Rome. In other words the comet heralded the reign of Augustus. Pliny's passage was remembered by Jonson,[97] and used as the idea for that part of the *Entertainment* after the King had come through the Temple Bar Arch into the Strand. Here the 'Inuention was a Raine-bow, the Moone, Sunne, and those seuen starres, which antiquitie hath styl'd the *Pleiades*, or *Vergiliae*, aduanced betweene two magnificent Pyramid's of 70. foot in height, on which were drawne his Maiesties seuerall pedigrees *Eng.* and *Scot.*'. Here Electra, a star of the Pleiades rarely seen, was presented 'hanging in the Ayre, in figure of a Comet'.[98] Into the mouth of Electra Jonson put the final speech of the *Entertainment*. After recalling her grief at the ruin of Troy, her speech is like what we might have expected from the mouth of Astraea. Long withdrawn from sight, she has returned to grace the special day of the great king, who has confirmed peace by closing the gates of the temple of Janus, and who is to begin a reign of gold in which corruption, avarice, pride, ambition, envy, flattery, tumult, faction and discord shall not 'perturbe the musique of [his] peace'. The end of her speech drives home the Augustan parallel with clarity. Like the comet at the games of Venus Genetrix in 44 BC, recorded by Augustus himself, by Virgil and by Pliny, she hails a new providential ruler:

> This from that loud, blest *Oracle*, I sing,
> Who here, and first, pronounc'd, thee *Brit[t]aines* king.
> Long maist thou liue, and see me thus appeare.
> As omenous a comet, from my spheare,
> Vnto thy raigne; as that did auspicate
> So lasting glory to AVGVSTVS state.[99]

Jonson's *Part of the King's Entertainment* shares its imperial aspiration with sixteenth-century royal entries and allied public spectacle. Ceremonious reference to Augustus was hardly new. Yet no previous British royal entry had employed the Augustan parallel, though the closely connected myth of Astraea had been so widely used, and comparison with the Royal Entry for the coronation of Elizabeth underlines the more thoroughly dramatic, and classical, nature of Jonson's text, not to mention the slow beauty of his verse, a quality not previously achieved in British Royal Entries. Jonson was bringing British practice closer to continental precedent, but when we compare the 1604 Entry with the sixteenth-century entries on the continent, it is apparent that while all make reference to Augustus in some way, Jonson's way in the Temple Bar Arch and the spectacle in the Strand is more specific, detailed, sustained and indeed

---

[96]Virgil, *Eclogae*, V, ll. 56–66; see Chapter I, n. 8.
[97]The relevant passage from Pliny's *Natural History*, II, xxv, is cited by Jonson in his note to l. 761; *Ben Jonson*, VII, p. 109.
[98]Ll. 675–97; *Ben Jonson*, VII, p. 106.
[99]Ll. 753, 758–63; op. cit. VII, pp. 108–9.

almost antiquarian. It is very different from the more generally imperial idealism of the 1571 Entry that Ronsard devised for Charles IX. There Augustus and
the imperial peace were brought into the range of allusion, but in 1604 Jonson
had James enter into a sequence which explicitly acted out the monarch's
Augustan rôle. This is what one might expect of Jonson the classical scholar;
and what one might expect of the author of *The Poetaster* for, after all, you
cannot make a play out of 'Iam redeunt Saturnia regna' nor the hope for world
peace alone, however sincere. And, within the limits of what the highly conventionalized form of the royal entry can accommodate, it is also what one might
expect after nearly a century of serious political discussion of Augustus.

Jonson's *Entertainment* is notable in other ways. In the well-understood
laudando praecipere tradition, praise of a new monarch is there rather to
inculcate ideals and express hope, than to comment on the qualities of particular
rulers. Yet nobody who remembered the Essex Revolt, monopolies and court
flattery in the last years of Elizabeth could have entirely ignored the implication
that the Augustus who succeeded the Astraea of the New World Arch was, in a
quite special way, Prince of concord and peace.

If Jonson wished his *Entertainment* to distinguish James as Augustus from
the dead 'Astraea', he must have wished to make an even clearer distinction
between the new ruler and the *persona* of an heroic monarch yet living: Henry
IV of France. Henry IV as the Gallic Hercules, it is true, found his most ideal
significance as 'slayer of the monsters of war'[100] but the figure was obviously
appropriate to a ruler who had asserted his right to the throne of France by
armed might, and, after a long siege, entered his capital like a conqueror.[101]
Jonson's text for the 1604 Entry conspicuously avoids such comparison with
Hercules or any similar figure. James comes to his new throne and capital by
right of inheritance, unasserted by arms, and is celebrated as a king of peace. He
has without conquest brought about a new unity and an expanded realm.

Much that the 1604 Royal Entry celebrated was expressed in different ways in
James's speech from the throne to his first parliament, and in the Speaker's
reply to the King's speech. The chief burden of James's long and elaborate
address is his own significance as a bringer of peace and unity. By his accession
he has already brought to an end England's protracted war with Spain, has
established internal as well as external peace by virtue of his hereditary right. As
the seven little kingdoms of England were eventually united into one greater
kingdom, and as Wales, which was 'a great Principalitie', united with England
'added a greater strength thereto', so 'the Vnion of two ancient and famous
Kingdomes, which is the other inward Peace annexed to my Person' has created
a greater and more naturally unified kingdom still:

> now in the end and fulnesse of time vnited, the right and title of both in my Person,
> alike lineally descended of both the Crownes, whereby it is now become like a little
> World within it selfe, being intrenched and fortified round about with a naturall, and
> yet admirable strong pond or ditch, whereby all the former feares of this Nation are
> now quite cut off: The other part of the Island being euer before now not onely the

---

[100]Frances A. Yates, *Astraea: The Imperial Theme in the Sixteenth Century* (London, 1976),
p. 210. See also Corrado Vivanti, 'Henri IV, the Gallic Hercules', *Journal of the Warburg and
Courtauld Institutes*, XXX (1967), pp. 176–97.

[101]Yates, *Astraea*, p. 209.

place of landing to all strangers, that was to make inuasion here, but likewise moued by the enemies of this State. . . . What God hath conioyned then, let no man separate. I am the Husband, and the whole Isle is my lawfull Wife; I am the Head, and it is my Body; I am the Shepherd, and it is my flocke. . . . And since the successe was happie of the *Saxons* Kingdomes being conquered by the spear of *Bellona*; How much greater reason haue wee to expect a happie issue of this greater Vnion, which is onely fastened and bound vp by the wedding Ring of *Astrea*?[102]

The first speech of Genius Urbis, in Jonson's *Entertainment*, anticipated James's own emphasis upon the eventual unification of Britain as the great work of time, just as the second speech of the Genius, and the speech of Electra, anticipated his stress upon peace and justice. The image of Britain as a world divided from the world, used on the Fenchurch Arch, is taken up and expanded in the royal speech, in words remarkably reminiscent of Shakespeare's formulation, in John of Gaunt's speech in *Richard II*. The final image of the passage quoted: James coming to the throne of a united Britain, not by the spear of Bellona but the ring of Astraea, is of great interest. James thus proclaims that his right derives from legitimate hereditary succession as endorsed by justice and law. Those for whom the name Astraea recalled Elizabeth herself, however, might construe the King's words to mean that James had been Elizabeth's own eventual choice as heir. Most important, perhaps, is the use of the famous allusion as a cue. James could not say: 'I am by right of inheritance more truly your Augustus than was your "late Soueraigne of famous memory" '; he could claim to unite Britain by right of the wedding ring of Astraea, and leave his listeners to draw the appropriate conclusion.

Such a conclusion was drawn, whether by arrangement or just as an educated response to the royal speech, by the new Speaker of the House of Commons, Sir Edward Phelips. He spoke of how God,

in his divine Distribution of Kings and Kingdoms, . . . hath magnified and invested Your sacred Person, in the Imperial throne of this most victorious and happy Nation, wherein You now do, and *Nestor* like, long may, sit; not as a Conqueror, by the Sword, but as an undoubted Inheritor, by the Sceptre . . . whereby this Day, that, to foreign Enemies, and domestical Discontents, was (ill Mens Hope, and good Mens Fear) to be the Day of Blood, is now become the Day of England's settled Peace, and joyful Safety; and may well be said, This is the Day that the Lord hath made, let England rejoice and triumph in it: For that Virtue is now no Treason, nor no man wisheth the Reign of *Augustus*, nor speaketh of the first Times of *Tiberius*.[103]

It is easy for us today to underrate the basis of profound feeling and serious argument in this exchange of speeches, and hence to see in the 1604 Entry, merely an inflated blend of far-fetched comparison and implausible hope. We should therefore remember the absolute centrality of monarchy, in most states of Renaissance Europe, for the determination of war or peace abroad, of tumult or order, prosperity or hardship, oppression or freedom, at home. Rhetorical

---

[102] *The Political Works of James I*, pp. 271–3.

[103] *The Commons Journals*, I, pp. 142–9; William Cobbett, *Parliamentary History of England* (London, 1806–20), V, pp. 39–53, attributes both the two speeches of reply to Sir Edward Phelips, Speaker of the House of Commons.

exaggeration, *laudando praecipere*, was taken for granted, having a serious point beyond objective description. Such exaggeration was used to fill the space between the objective circumstances (James's accession *had* peacefully united the two crowns) and the hope for a prosperous future pushed almost to the point of the visionary. Even sceptical analysis would have to allow that James's speech arose from more than sheer vanity, that Jonson and the Speaker did not praise him merely for gain, and that the institution of monarchy bore so powerfully upon the lives of men that the immediate future could not be envisaged without a measure of make-believe. It was a part of the rôle of the public artist, such as Ronsard and Jonson, to locate and express this deep and inchoate need for hope, to shape and harmonize it with learning, and make it part of a meaningful vision of history. That is the psychological importance of the events and ceremonies of 1603–4.

Perhaps one should also insist on the intellectual respectability of what was expressed. The texts discussed above could all be glossed by reference to Jean Bodin's *Six Livres de la République*, perhaps the most impressive work of political theory of later sixteenth-century Europe. What Jonson was insisting on in the first speech of Genius Urbis and the speech of Electra, James in his image of the 'wedding Ring of *Astrea*' and the Speaker when he stressed that James came 'not as a Conqueror . . . but as an undoubted Inheritor' was that this king was a conspicuous example of what was for Bodin the highest form of ruler: not the lordly monarch, the conqueror by the sword, not the tyrant, ruling in defiance of the laws of nature and nations, but the lawful or royal monarch, succeeding by primogeniture, obeying the laws of nature, and observing the liberty of his subjects and their propriety of goods.[104] Further, Bodin did not hesitate to discern a symbolic structure in history, a structure in which Augustus had a central place as evincing more powerfully and influentially than any other example the natural tendency of states towards royal monarchy. James as Augustus thus had a special significance in the context of sixteenth-century political theory. And if even Bodin, so intimate with the *realpolitik* of Tacitus and Machiavelli, could still see nature and history as a symbolic and analogical structure, much that strikes modern ears as mere rhetoric had serious intellectual content then. James was the shepherd and the people his flock, James was Augustus and Britain a world 'divisus ab orbe': in such a conception of the created order this is not metaphor alone.

We may notice that the compliment of Sir Edward Phelips's speech implies a notion of the cyclical movement of history under providence: '. . . no man wisheth the Reign of *Augustus*, nor speaketh of the first Times of *Tiberius*'. The two reigns are in a sequence of maturation and corruption; one may look forward to a golden age of Augustus, but when that has come one can only fear the tyranny of a Tiberius. After its meridian the sun can only decline. It is a matter of judgement as to where in the pattern of the rise and fall of states one locates one's own time. Was the Augustan comparison truly more appropriate to James than to Elizabeth? When James himself praised Elizabeth with the comparison, it was in respect of the wisdom, felicity and length of her reign.[105] It has been my argument that Elizabeth was for the sixteenth and seventeenth

---

[104]See Chapter III, pp. 59–61.
[105]*Basilikon Doron*, To the Reader; *The Political Works of James I*, p. 11.

century more appropriately Astraea than Augustus (despite the intimate Virgilian connection of the two names) because Elizabethan England seemed a world apart, a defensive rather than an expansive power. Yet the 1604 Entry and James's speech to Parliament, as we have seen, laid great stress on the Virgilian image of Britain as a world divided from the world. Where did the difference lie?

Conditions for the fitness of the Augustan comparison naturally change each time it is made. To celebrate Charles II as Augustus in 1660 had much more of traditional British royalism about it because James I had been celebrated like this in 1604. In 1604 it was a more radical departure and the consequence of new circumstances. What made James's situation different from that of Elizabeth was the peaceful expansion of power resulting from the unification of all the British kingdoms under one prince. Nearly always the Augustan parallel is evoked at moments of dynastic or national expansion. At the same time the parallel with the *pax Augusta* requires either that the expansion shall have been achieved peacefully, or if by war, that the warfare be now concluded in a lasting peace. The union of the crowns provided just sufficient objective basis to warrant the Augustan comparison in 1604, and the peaceful nature of James's accession, when war had been feared, made it all the more appropriate. Even so, both Jonson in his *Entertainment* and James in his speech to Parliament were at pains to magnify as far as possible the political expansion that had taken place, and that, after all, fell somewhat short of the grounds there had been for thinking of the Emperor Charles V as a new Augustus. Thus Genius Urbis recalls the earlier 'circles, both of change and sway' in the long history of Britain, and James himself (following, perhaps, a passage in *The Boke Named the Governour*[106]) traces the slow growth of political unity in Britain from the seven warring kingdoms of England onwards. By the time the speech has taken us through all the historical stages the new unity seems much more wonderful than it would otherwise have done, and it is even then necessary to exploit to its utmost the image of Britain as a world in itself to make the parallel out. It was necessary too to stress the hereditary factors in Augustus's rise to the principate, hence Jonson's use of the comet, after the Temple Bar Arch, since the comet seemed to mark Octavian's filial relationship with a now deified Julius Caesar.

Such was the basis for the Augustan comparison in 1604, and such were some of the difficulties involved. This was the opportunity and the occasion. But the reasons why men *wished* to make the comparison were, I believe, wider and deeper. More must have been hoped for than was expressed. Jonson may serve as our example. From *The Poetaster* we know that he cared passionately that the right relation between poet and ruler be established, but we hear nothing directly about this in the text for the 1604 Entry. Others must have hoped to see the fulfilment of other positive aspects of the Augustan example. The balance of evidence is that for educated Englishmen at the turn of the sixteenth and seventeenth centuries Augustus was the Augustus of Sir Thomas Elyot, of Bodin and of Gentillet; the Augustus of Eusebius and Orosius. The counter-tradition, familiar doubtless to Jonson among others, had so far made small headway in

---

[106]Bk I, Ch. ii.

English writing, though that would soon change.[107] When men celebrated James VI and I as a new Augustus it was with a passionate desire to see, within the framework of a Christian monarchy, a better life and a higher level of civilization in Britain.

[107]See K.B. Schellhaze, *Tacitus in Renaissance Political Thought* (London 1976).

VI Shakespeare and the Emperors

> *Ant.*:   Be a child o' th' time.
> *Caes.*:   Possess it, I'll make answer.
> (*Antony and Cleopatra*, II, vii, 88–9)

Julius Cæsar

The poems of Virgil became the myth of the Julian House, and this myth Shakespeare's own allusions show that he knew. It concerns heroism, peace and justice. Shakespeare's first Roman tragedy, *Titus Andronicus*, presents the empire in a state of drastic decline. The three emperors of the drama, Titus, Saturninus and Lucius, are all linked with the myth of the Virgin Astraea, goddess of justice in Virgil's 'Messianic' Fourth Eclogue, not now returning to earth for an age of gold as in Virgil, but withdrawing to the skies as gross injustices are perpetrated and the great empire decays. Titus himself laments the departure of Astraea (IV, iii, 4), Saturninus reigns over a Rome in which an innocent virgin is brutally ravished, maimed and made dumb, while Lucius, if his hitting Virgo in the symbolic archery is to be trusted, may yet restore a fairer time again.[1] More than twenty years later, in *Antony and Cleopatra*, Shakespeare puts into the mouth of Octavian, as he prepares to fight Antony before Alexandria, a direct allusion to the Augustan peace:

> The time of universal peace is nigh.
> Prove this a prosperous day, the three-nooked world
> Shall bear the olive freely.[2]

Considering what might have been made by Shakespeare of the great providential interpretation of the *pax Augusta*, and how recently the imperial peace had been evoked in the Royal Entry of James I, it is notable now briefly and hastily this conception is here interjected, in the preparation for an engagement which Octavian does not win, and in a sequence of episodes dominated by Enobarbus's remorse at having deserted Antony. Another dramatist might perhaps have drawn the allusion, with its sense of an ideal stasis, at the end of the play, but Shakespeare rightly uses Octavian's last speech to leave our focus upon Antony and Cleopatra themselves.

[1] Frances A. Yates, *Astraea: The Imperial Theme in the Sixteenth Century* (London, 1975), pp. 74–6, makes these points in her title-chapter, the celebrated essay 'Queen Elizabeth as Astraea' originally published in the *Journal of the Warburg and Courtauld Institutes*, X (1947), pp. 27–82.

[2] The lines are noted, in connection with the idea of the Golden Age, by Frank Kermode, *The Classic* (London, 1975), p. 50.

The deeper reason, however, is surely that Shakespeare's is a dialectical imagination. He sets the ideal of Astraea against the fate of the virgin Lavinia; and he uses the ideal of the *pax Augusta* not to crown an action but to be countered by the surprising remaining resources of Antony, in military prowess and loyalty in the hearts of men. He uses, as we shall see, Octavian in the process of becoming Augustus to set against Antony. But perhaps the most evident example of Shakespeare's dialectical handling of the Augustan myth is the speech in *Julius Cæsar* by which Cassius seeks to win Brutus over to his cause.

By a bold stroke of historical and theatrical imagination Shakespeare locates the speech, as it were, off-stage: the stage on which Julius Caesar is three times offered the crown of Rome and three times refuses. Caesar puts it by, but, as Casca later explains, 'to my thinking, he would fain have had it'.[3] Twice the applause of the crowd as the crown is offered and refused breaks into Cassius's at first circumspect approach to Brutus: it lends point to the argument that Cassius puts, yet is in brilliant counterpoint to the ethos of what Cassius has to say. Caesar seems about to be the emperor of the world, while Cassius's speech is alive with the very spirit of republicanism:

> I was born free as Cæsar; so were you;
> We both have fed as well, and we can both
> Endure the winter's cold as well as he:
> For once, upon a raw and gusty day,
> The troubled Tiber chafing with her shores,
> Cæsar said to me, 'Dar'st thou, Cassius, now
> Leap in with me into this angry flood,
> And swim to yonder point?' Upon the word,
> Accoutred as I was, I plunged in
> And bade him follow; so indeed he did.
> The torrent roar'd, and we did buffet it
> With lusty sinews, throwing it aside
> And stemming it with hearts of controversy.
> But ere we could arrive the point propos'd,
> Cæsar cried, 'Help me, Cassius, or I sink.'
> I, as Æneas, our great ancestor,
> Did from the flames of Troy upon his shoulder
> The old Anchises bear, so from the waves of Tiber
> Did I the tired Cæsar. And this man
> Is now become a god, and Cassius is
> A wretched creature, and must bend his body
> If Cæsar carelessly but nod on him.

Cassius takes the measure of monarchy by responding in natural, physical and then personal ways to Caesar's imminent promotion. The whole basis of the speech is that monarchy is not an existing institution, sanctioned by gods or the laws. If it is to *be* established it will radically alter the relation of man and man. Caesar, Brutus and Cassius are all equal before Nature. Caesar's challenge to swim the Tiber (the episode is apparently Shakespeare's invention) subtly inflects the argument as the struggle against the torrent becomes touched with competition between men, and the striking word 'controversy' catches up both

---

[3]I, ii, 235–6; *Julius Caesar*, ed. T.S. Dorsch, Arden Series (London, 1955), p. 21.

ideas while seeming, at the same time, to recall the free contentions of a republic. As the story concludes Cassius and Caesar are not after all equal before Nature; Cassius is superior, and at this point, with great rhetorical effect, the great Augustan myth of Aeneas, devoted by Virgil to the founder of a *de facto* monarchy over Rome and the restorer of its peace and justice, is appropriated by Cassius: he is the Aeneas to Julius Caesar's Anchises. The effect is that of a striking displacement. Cassius as Aeneas contests the view that the heroism of the legendary Trojan pointed inexorably to Julius Caesar and Augustus.

The general shout prompts the carefully moderated comment of Brutus, which releases the full strength of Cassius's tirade:

> *Bru*: I do believe that these applauses are
> For some new honours that are heap'd on Cæsar
> *Cas*: Why, man, he doth bestride the narrow world
> Like a Colossus, and we petty men
> Walk under his huge legs, and peep about
> To find ourselves dishonourable graves.
> Men at some time are masters of their fates:
> The fault, dear Brutus, is not in our stars,
> But in ourselves, that we are underlings.
>   . . . Age, thou art shame'd!
> Rome, thou hast lost the breed of noble bloods!
> When went there by an age, since the great flood,
> But it was fam'd with more than with one man?
> When could they say, till now, that talk'd of Rome
> That her wide walks encompass'd but one man?[4]

To admit a spirit of envious competition in Cassius, as most critics of the play have done, is not necessarily to invalidate his attitude or his argument. It may be said that Shakespeare and his audience took for granted the institution of monarchy as natural and right, saw Julius Caesar as the first Roman Emperor and one of the Nine Worthies, and hence that *Julius Cæsar* like *Richard II* and *Macbeth* is a play about regicide. That such assumptions were some of the more powerful among a late-Elizabethan audience is entirely probable, but other interpretations of this period of Roman history were also abroad at the time. The monarchist Bodin recognized that the Julian House had effectively moved the government of Rome towards monarchy, while never denying the legitimacy of the republican institutions within which Julius Caesar and Augustus rose to single power. Bodin admitted the transformation of political forms. A contemporary of Shakespeare with some sympathy with Bodin's thought would have seen in Julius Caesar neither a king whose throne was sanctioned by God and the laws, nor a tyrant betraying a great republic to his own ambitions, but an enigmatic and crucial figure within the mysteries of historical evolution. The chronicler Stow considered Julius Caesar both a reigning Emperor and 'greatest traytour that ever was to the Romane State'.[5]

More obvious in the speech, however, is a strain of republican idealism for

---

[4]I, ii, 96–117, 131–9, 148–53; ed. cit. pp. 13–16.
[5]See D.S. Brewer, 'Brutus' Crime: A Footnote to *Julius Caesar*', *Review of English Studies*, N.S. 3 (1952), p. 53.

which there is no parallel in Bodin.[6] It is to the republican thought of Renaissance Italy, and in particular to Machiavelli, that we must turn for an analogue to the attitude of Cassius. There is probably no need at this time to insist that Machiavelli's works (whether yet translated into English or not) were well known in late Elizabethan England, but it is, as it happens, possible to gloss Cassius's speech with reference to the first of Machiavelli's works to be translated into English: Peter Whitehorne's translation of *The Arte of War* appeared in 1560. In a political passage at the end of Bk II (alluded to in an earlier chapter) Fabritio argues that 'in common weales, there growe more excellent men, then in kingdomes, bicause in common weales for the most part, vertue is honoured, in Kyngdomes it is helde backe: whereby groweth, that in those, vertuous men are nourished, in the other thei are extincte.' He has further argued 'that where be many dominions [i.e. states], there rise many valiaunt menne, and where be fewe, fewe.'[7] These two arguments, that republics ['common weales'] encourage human excellence more than kingdoms, and that many states encourage more excellence than few states, gives him an extremely powerful argument against a Rome which, having overcome and absorbed so many states originally independent, transformed itself into a world monarchy:

> Therefore, the Romaine Empire beyng after increased, and havyng extinguished all the common weales, and Princedomes of Europe, and of Afrike, and for the most part those of Asia, it lefte not any waie to vertue, except Rome: whereby grewe, that vertuous menne began to be as fewe in Europe, as in Asia: the which vertue, came after to the last caste: For as moche, as all the vertue beyng reduced to Roome, so sone as the same was corrupted, almoste all the worlde came to bee corrupted:[8]

---

[6] J.L. Simmons, *Shakespeare's Pagan World: The Roman Tragedies* (Hassocks, 1974), pp. 77–86, says that 'Shakespeare reveals no genuine understanding of Roman republicanism' but insists on Shakespeare's awareness of proletarian republicanism of the kind arraigned by Spenser in *Faerie Queene*, Book V, seeking to link this with the views of Cassius. His highly interesting discussion seems to me to claim too little and too much. It is right, as Simmons says, that Shakespeare's light emphasis on the Senate (whether or not stemming from Shakespeare's ignorance) is historically apt, but surely also right that Cassius and Brutus recognizably represent the spirit of Roman and Italian Renaissance republicanism. This should not be confused with any social egalitarianism. The ethos of Brutus and Cassius is aristocratic and accords with Shakespeare's sceptical treatment of the mob in the play. It is worth noting that the Cassius to whom Brutus pays such noble tribute on his death is found lying beside his bondman, i.e. slave.

[7] *The Arte of Warre Written First in Italian by Nicholas Machiavell And Set forth in English by Peter Whitehorne* (1560), in Henry Cust, ed., *Machiavelli, The Art of War . . . [and The Prince*, Tudor Translations Series, (London, 1905), p. 94.

[8] Ibid., p. 95. More remote from Shakespeare, though not necessarily beyond his ken, is Lactantius who wrote in his *Divine Institutes* that Rome entered its second childhood when the Republic reverted to monarchy (VI, xv; *Works*, tr. and ed. Alexander Roberts and James Donaldson (Edinburgh, 1871), I, p. 464). More broadly relevant and less remote are the observations of Tacitus:

'After that *Brutus* and *Cassius* were slaine, and no armes now publikely borne; *Pompey* defeated in Sicilie; *Lepidus* disarmed; *Antonie* killed; and no chiefe leader of *Iulius Caesar's* faction left, but onely *Augustus*: he would no longer be called *Triumuir*, but in shew contented with the dignitie of a Tribune to defend the people, bearing himselfe as Consul: after he had wound into the fauour of the soldiers by giftes; of the people by prouision of sustenance; and of all in generall with the sweetenes of ease and repose; by little and little taking vpon him, he drew to himselfe the affaires of the Senate; the dutie of magistrates and lawes, without contradiction of any: the stowtest by war or proscriptions alreadie spent, and the rest of the nobilitie, by how much the more seruiceable, by so much the more bettered in wealth, and advanced in honors: seing their preferment to growe by new gouern-

Whitehorn uses the word 'vertue' to translate the Machiavellian term '*virtù*' which has strong connotations of valour, energy and discipline, political integrity and independence. It is in this sense of the word, it would seem, that when Brutus, confessing that he fears Caesar will be crowned, affirms that for him the ground of honour is 'the general good', Cassius replies:

> I know that virtue to be in you, Brutus,
> As well as I do know your outward favour.[9]

Julius Cæsar may be seen to hold out several possibilities as to the interpretation of Caesar. The outcome of the drama does not demonstrate that Caesar was a king, and the conspirators' crime regicide. Neither does it demonstrate that he was a tyrant and usurper. Cut off in his hour of triumph, Caesar remains an enigma and is meant to be so: the speculations of Brutus as to how a crown might change his nature[10] are never settled. Antony calls Brutus 'the noblest Roman of them all' and declares that all the other conspirators were motivated by envy of Caesar.[11] But that same 'noblest Roman' has but just said of Cassius: 'It is impossible that ever Rome / Should breed thy fellow'.[12] Antony's verdict may thus be thought to call itself in question. What is clear is that the historical force which Julius Caesar represented, and the heirs of which by the end are Antony and Octavius, has become that tide in the affairs of men which, taken at the flood, leads on to fortune. This much is made manifest by the appearance of Caesar's ghost to Brutus and the subsequent power of that spirit, which Brutus attests to at Philippi. This would surely have been Bodin's verdict: neither king nor tyrant, Julius Caesar embodies that logic of history which was with seeming inexorability to lead on to the imperial theme and the establishment of monarchy. Like Banquo, he will be the root of a succession of monarchs.

When, in *Antony and Cleopatra*, Shakespeare returns to the subject of Rome's imperial theme, we hear no more of the cause of the old Republic. Those political arguments are laid aside as Antony and Octavius Caesar become rival emperors for the monarchy of the world. The opposing qualities with which the dialectic of the drama is now concerned belong to different categories from those of *Julius Cæsar*. Forms of government are no longer in question, but the character of the ruler and his worlds of experience are under an even more powerful focus.

---

ment, did rather choose the present state with securitie, than striue to recouer their olde with danger. . . . All was quiet in the citie; the old names of the magistrates vnchanged; the yoong men borne after the victorie at Actium, and the greatest part of the old, during the ciuill wars: how many were there which had seene the ancient forme of gouernement of the free Common-wealthe? Thus then the state of the citie turned vpside downe, there was no signe of the olde laudable customes to be seene: but contrarie, equalitie taken away, euery man endeuored to obey the prince. . . .' (*The Annales of Cornelivs Tacitvs* . . ., tr. Richard Grenawey, dedicated to the Earl of Essex (London, 1598), pp. 1–2). The situation that Tacitus describes is surely what Cassius fears.

[9] I, ii, 84, 89–90; ed. cit. pp. 12–13.
[10] II, i, 12–34; ed. cit. pp. 34–5.
[11] V, v, 68–72; ed. cit. p. 129.
[12] V, iii, 98–101; ed. cit. p. 123.

Enobarbus

Two or three years after the Royal Entry of King James in 1604, five or six years after the first performance of *The Poetaster*, Shakespeare wrote *Antony and Cleopatra*. It is unlikely that Shakespeare's presentation of Caesar – Octavian in the very process of becoming Augustus – makes no allusion to the presentation of Augustus in these texts. Whatever is the case, however, Shakespeare's dramatic conception of Caesar in relation to his great competitors, the rival emperor Antony and the queen Cleopatra, is a vital part of the reception of Augustus in the Renaissance era. More tentatively, we may also recall the words of Eusebius (in the Elizabethan translation of Meredith Hanmer), when he assigned the birth of Christ not only to the reign of Augustus, but to 'the subiection of *Ægypt*, and the death of *Antonius* and *Cleopatra*' and wonder whether in his presentation of the famous lovers Shakespeare does not engage with what seemed to him a distinctly pre-Christian experience.

A key to Shakespeare's intention in *Antony and Cleopatra* is the character of Enobarbus. For no other considerable character in the play has Shakespeare so slight a basis, as MacCallum observed. The three passing references in *The Life of Marcus Antonius* suggest a character trusted by Antony (who turned to him to address his disaffected troops during the Parthian Expedition), a man of independent judgement (he advised Antony to send Cleopatra away before Actium), and one who finally deserts his master for Caesar.[13] These are indeed salient features of Shakespeare's Enobarbus, but beyond these what manner of man he was, virtuous or libertine, grave or merry, influential or ineffective politically, in what scenes he was present, whom he knew, how he spoke – all this remained for the playwright to determine, and in so doing to help create the particular light in which he wished to view the figures, scenes and events that he accepted from his main source.

Shakespeare's decision was to make him a man of worldly shrewdness, neither a moralizer nor a libertine, but one who contributes to scene after crucial scene an air of buoyant, comradely good spirit, a sense of comic but not satiric perception, until the time comes for his anguished response to Actium, and his later more anguished realization that in deserting Antony he had violated himself. Thus in the sophisticated frivolity of the beginning of I, ii – in which major themes of the play are touched on – Enobarbus mingles naturally with the others, and proposes a health to Cleopatra.[14] Later in the same scene, when Antony condemns himself for falling prey to Cleopatra, Enobarbus is far from echoing the censure of Philo:

> *Ant.*:　Would I had never seen her!
> *Eno.*:　O, sir, you had then left unseen a wonderful piece of work, which not to have
> 　　　　been blest withal, would have discredited your travel.[15]

[13]C.F. Tucker Brooke, ed. *Shakespeare's Plutarch* (New York, 1966), II, pp. 64, 88–9, 99–100; M.W. MacCallum, *Shakespeare's Roman Plays and their Background* (London, 1910), p. 349 *et seq*. My discussion of *Antony and Cleopatra* and *Coriolanus* will, I hope, be found complementary to R.A. Brower's admirable *Hero and Saint: Shakespeare and the Graeco-Roman Heroic Tradition* (Oxford, 1971).

[14]I, ii, ll. 11–12.

[15]I, ii, 11. 150–3; pp. 20–1 of *Antony and Cleopatra*, ed. R.H. Case and M.R. Ridley, Arden Series (London, 1954) from which all quotations are taken.

The deliberate lightness of tone does not conceal his full awareness of the situation, and the serious implication that Antony could have afforded to take Cleopatra more lightly. Before the reconciliation of Antony and Caesar in II, ii, Enobarbus, in whom we have come to expect a certain detachment, is bluntly partisan for Antony; during the actual coming to terms his mocking, clear-sighted realism cannot forbear to interrupt, and his answering-back to Antony's eventual rebuke ('Go to, then: your considerate stone') contrasts strangely with Caesar's tense self-importance, and greatly enriches the human texture of the scene. In the splendid scene aboard Pompey's galley, which contrives to be at once comic and heroic, Enobarbus is at the source of the blend:

> Eno.:　There's a strong fellow, Menas.
> 　　　　(*Pointing to the Attendant who carries off Lepidus*)
> Men.:　Why?
> Eno.:　'A bears the third part of the world, man; see'st not?

and contributes to the mounting revelry:

> Eno.:　(*To Antony*) Ha, my brave emperor,
> 　　　　Shall we dance now the Egyptian Bacchanals. . . . [16]

This builds up to his exuberant mockery of Lepidus, in his dialogue of familiar understanding with Agrippa: a mockery which retains clear-sightedness while through its genial vitality it precludes moralistic judgement – even of 'a noble Lepidus'. Thereafter the tone modulates towards the approaching disaster and desertion: 'Our great navy's rigg'd' . . . 'Your ships are not well mann'd . . .' . . . 'Naught, naught, all naught . . .' . . . and the grave intimacy of his dialogue with Cleopatra at the beginning of III, xiii.[17] Inconspicuously introduced at the beginning of I, i, Enobarbus has as inconspicuously become a guide for the audience in all these scenes, but without a touch of the instructor. What he recognizes, the audience sees to be true; when he rises to laughter or revelry, the audience identifies with him; because he is so clearly involved in the fortunes of the Emperor Antony, the audience becomes so too; and when, involved but clear-sighted as he is, he refrains from explicit moral judgements such as Philo's, the audience does not dissent from the view of so winning a personality.

Intemperance

It is a feature of Shakespeare's handling of Enobarbus that he is dramatically beautifully integrated into the scenes in which he appears. His usually short speeches grow out of the scene; what he says is nearly always in harmony with or dramatic reaction to what others have said; his utterance is expressively flexible, his diction for the most part colloquial. The striking exception to this is of course his famous speech to Agrippa and Maecenas in II, ii, in which he described the first meeting of Antony with Cleopatra. Of this M.R. Ridley has written that it is 'most incongruously put into the mouth of the prosaically, however penetratingly, common-sensical Enobarbus' and implied that it is a

---

[16]II, vii, ll. 87–9, 101–2; pp. 89, 91.
[17]III, v, l. 19; III, vii, l. 34; III, x, l. 1; III, xiii, ll. 1–12; pp. 107, 115, 119, 131–2.

set-piece which, unlike the rest of the play's poetry, could stand on its own.[18] This charge may partly be answered by pointing out that if the passage could stand without the play the play could hardly stand without the passage; that Shakespeare has successfully executed the *in medias res* principle and is now giving the origin of the play's action at its centre; and that 'prosaic' is not the precise word to describe the Enobarbus of the revelry aboard Pompey's galley, of the mockery of Lepidus, or of the address to the moon in IV, ix.[19] Yet the passage has the air of a set-piece, and a conspicuous 'poetic' beauty which stands out in a play whose passages of lofty rhetoric are almost always given a human fullness and strength by their use of ordinary diction –

> O, wither'd is the garland of the war
> The soldier's pole is fall'n: *young boys and girls*
> Are level now with men. . . .[20]

We must either conclude that Shakespeare used an expedient to get the rich description from North's Plutarch into his play, or that he wished, without gross violation of character, to retain the feel of the poetic set-piece, in putting the description into the mouth of Enobarbus.

What associations would the passage from North have aroused in Shakespeare's mind, when he read it for the first time? It is a passage of almost Spenserian loveliness; not only has it a rich visual appeal in its gold, purple and silver, but a pictorial quality is specifically referred to, Cleopatra being 'attired like the goddess Venus commonly drawn in picture . . .'. Yet the visual is subtly blended with the aural, in a harmony of movement, for the silver oars 'kept stroke in rowing after the sound of the music of flutes . . .'. The sense of smell is appealed to by 'the sweet savour of perfumes' while the suggestion of texture in 'cloth of gold of tissue', and of air on the skin in the cupids fanning the wind, appeal to the tactile imagination. The description is in itself a 'banquet of sense'.[21] It is likely to have reminded Shakespeare of parts of Spenser's *Faerie Queene*, and of none more obviously than the description of Acrasia's '*Bowre of blis*' at the end of Book II. Here also, though more variously and subtly, verbal artistry has blended the different elements of sensuous appeal; here too 'the faire Enchauntresse' is attended by graceful ladies and pretty boys.[22] It is remarkable that Shakespeare, not content with the Spenserian affinities of North's description, added to its 'poetic' qualities when he remoulded it for his play, and was far from modulating it towards the speech of a prosaic captain. Thus a certain conceitedness is introduced; the winds were not 'love-sick' in North, nor the water 'amorous' of the strokes of the oars, but similar effects are found in the Bower of Bliss.[23] North did not elaborate his allusion to Venus

[18]*Antony and Cleopatra*, ed. cit. p. xlviii.

[19]Note Enobarbus's familiarity with the characteristic rhetoric of the more artificial love-sonnet; III, ii, ll. 16–17 and n., ed. cit. p. 97.

[20]IV, xv, ll. 64–6 (my italics); ed. cit. p. 186.

[21]See W.B.C. Watkin's discussion of *Antony and Cleopatra* in the chapter: 'Shakespeare's Banquet of Sense', *Shakespeare and Spenser* (Princeton, 1950), pp. 24–35.

[22]Book II, Canto XII, stanzas lxxxi–ii; Canto V, stanza xxvii; Edwin Greenlaw, C.G. Osgood and F.M. Padelford, eds., *The Works of Edmund Spenser: A Variorum Edition*; *The Faerie Queene, Book Two* (Baltimore, 1933), pp. 179, 177; 62. All quotations from Spenser are from this edition.

[23]E.g. II, XII, lxi; ed. cit. p. 174. Kenneth Muir (*Shakespeare's Sources*, I (London, 1957),

'commonly drawn in picture' but Shakespeare adds: '. . . where we see / The fancy outwork nature'; prominent in Spenser's handling of the Bower of Bliss episode is the theme of art and nature sinisterly mingling as they strive to outvie one another.[24] If in Shakespeare's handling of Enobarbus we may discern his purpose with a particular clarity, then without doubt Shakespeare deliberately retained and added to the qualities of a Spenserian poetic set-piece which the passage in North already suggested.

The Bower of Bliss is of course one of Spenser's great temptation scenes. It is characteristic of Spenser's poetic strategy in *The Faerie Queene*, for nearly always when a powerful temptation is at hand the poem modulates from narrative to descriptive, and all the poet's artistry is lavished on the creation of a *scene* – sensuously vivid yet full of moral meaning. Such scenes are dramatic too, for their impact is not only on the reader, but on the protagonist there to avoid, withstand, or overthrow. In the Bower of Bliss episode we cannot forget Guyon, overwhelmed almost by the beauty of which he has so often been fore-warned. Frequently in such temptation sequences the danger lies in the strong immediate effect of the scene. But if the protagonist is mentally able to set the scene in a wider context – of an earlier warning or ultimate purpose – then he is able to resist. Thus Guyon was in a position to remember the fate of Mordant at the hands of Acrasia, the parallel though less dire entrapment of Cymochles by Phaedria; and he had the Palmer at hand who embodied the wider and more detached understanding which preserved him – hence Guyon, the Knight of Temperance, triumphed over Acrasia and her Bower of Bliss. In this book of *The Faerie Queene* Spenser aimed again and again at the deep-grounded psychological fear of losing oneself through abandonment to pleasure; the situation to which he recurs is that of the man of action who becomes in a sense unmanned, reduced to effeminacy and effeteness, through succumbing to sexual delight. Cymochles was

> . . . a man of rare redoubted might,
> Famous throughout the world for warlike prayse,
> And glorious spoiles, purchast in perilous fight:[25]

but his love is 'that Enchaunteresse, / The vile *Acrasia*' from the 'deepe delight' of whose toils he is aroused only by the taunt that he has grown 'womanish weake', a mere 'shade' of the 'manly person' he once was.[26] Similarly the young man sleeping at Acrasia's side, when Guyon and the palmer eventually confront the Bower, 'seemd to bee

> Some goodly swayne of honourable place . . .'

in whose countenance 'grace' and 'manly sternnesse' appear, but

pp. 202–4) sees the added conceits as a masterstroke, and quotes from W.A. Edwards whom they remind of Donne. Yet the rôle of these conceits in the total effect, not to mention the omission by Shakespeare of 'all the musical instruments except the flutes, lest the more masculine howboys and viols should break the atmosphere of love and sensuousness' (p. 204), makes the comparison with Spenser more obvious.

[24]II, ii, ll. 200–1; *Faerie Queene*, II, XII, lix; ed. cit. p. 173.
[25]*Faerie Queene*, II, V, xxvi; ed. cit. p. 61.
[26]Ibid., II, V, xxvii, xxxv, xxxvi; ed. cit. p. 63–4.

His warlike armes, the idle instruments
Of sleeping praise, were hong vpon a tree,
And his braue shield, full of old moniments,
Was fowly ra'st, that none the signes might see. . . .[27]

These men have fallen prey to intemperance. Seen in one light, this is the situation of Antony at several points in the play. Shakespeare's view of the Battle of Actium, and of the relationship between the two lovers which it revealed, derives ultimately from Octavian's propagandist interpretation of the historical event. Plutarch had expressed this attitude, which might now also be termed the 'Spenserian' attitude towards Cleopatra and Antony: he speaks of the 'mischief' of Antony's love for Cleopatra, which awakened hidden vices in him, of his being 'ravished and enchanted with the sweet poison of her love'; and above all his account of how 'Antonius with much ado, [began a little to rouse himself, as if he had been wakened out of a deep sleep, and as a man may say, coming out of a great drunkenness' must have reminded Shakespeare irresistibly of Spenser.[28] Such associations were probably reinforced, in Shakespeare's mind, by the widespread moral interpretation of Antony's love for Cleopatra, as evidenced in allusions to the famous lovers in Ariosto's *Orlando Furioso*, which had helped form Spenser's poem, and in Tasso's *Gerusalemme Liberata*. The morally analogous figures to Spenser's Cymochles and Acrasia are, in Ariosto, Rogero and Alcyna, in Tasso, Rinaldo and Armida. Both Italian poets refer to Antony and Cleopatra in the context of these relationships, and Tasso, who moulds his material the most humanly and dramatically of the three, has a picture of the Battle of Actium engraved in silver and gold on the doors of Armida's palace, with Antony just turning to fly:

Antonius eeke himselfe to flight betooke,
The Empire lost to which he would aspire,
Yet fled not he, nor fight for feare forsooke,
But follow'd her, drawne on by fond desire:
Well might you see within his troubled looke,
Striue and contend, loue, courage, shame and ire;
  Oft lookt he back, oft gaz'de he on the sight,
  But oftner on his mistresse and her flight.

These poems and their English translations (*Orlando Furioso* in 1591, *Gerusalemme Liberata* in 1600) certainly stressed the moral attitude to Antony and Cleopatra, while Tasso particularly may have suggested the possibility of a more dramatic presentation of them than the rather emblem-like figures of Spenser.[29]

[27]Ibid., II, XXII, lxxix–x; ed. cit. pp. 178–9.

[28]*Shakespeare's Plutarch*, ed. cit., II, pp. 36–7; 55; 45–6. Nobody writing about Shakespeare and Spenser can ignore A.B. Potts's interesting but not always convincing *Shakespeare and the Faerie Queene* (Ithaca, 1958) which notes (pp. 199–207, especially 202 and 204) several of the Spenserian connections discussed here. But Potts discusses this predominantly secular and pagan drama in connection with *Faerie Queene*, I: the Book of Holiness. In defence of the present approach it may be noted that there are several specific allusions to temperance at crucial points in the tragedy, but none to holiness. The same is true of *Coriolanus* which Potts also discusses in connection with Book I of the *Faerie Queene*.

[29]*Orlando Furioso in English Heroical Verse*, by Iohn Harington, (London, 1591), VII, stanza 19,

It is this attitude which is so dramatically expressed by Philo at the very beginning of the play:

> Nay, but this dotage of our general's
> O'erflows the measure: those his goodly eyes,
> That o'er the files and musters of the war
> Have glow'd like plated Mars, now bend, now turn
> The office and devotion of their view
> Upon a tawny front: his captain's heart,
> Which in the scuffles of great fights hath burst
> The buckles on his breast, reneges all temper,
> And is become the bellows and the fan
> To cool a gypsy's lust.[30]

The soldierly frankness and vigour of this splendid speech counterpoints its subject ('this dotage of our general's') and enforces the criticism it makes: a criticism, be it noted, specifically of intemperance. The image of overflowing the measure, and the announcement that Antony's heart 'reneges all temper', striking us as they do at the very start of the play, tell us that intemperance is to be a major theme and link with the Spenserian implications of Enobarbus's description of Cleopatra. This way of looking at the love of Antony and Cleopatra is endorsed by Antony himself at certain points. 'I must from this enchanting queen break off', he resolves, and we must have care that the weak modern sense of 'enchanting' does not lighten the meaning for us here. Sundered from Cleopatra, Antony describes himself in his message to her as 'the firm Roman' and his manner is described by Alexas as 'Like to the time o' the year *between the extremes* / Of hot and cold . . .'; for the moment the equilibrium of temperance has been regained,[31] and the maturity managed which Erasmus had praised in Augustus. The word 'dotage', used by Philo in the first line of the play, is taken up by Scarus when he describes Antony's flight from Actium, 'like a doating mallard', and is finally owned by Antony in his self-accusation of 'fear, and doating'. He now sees himself as having 'lost command' (the phrase is kept expressively general) and sees his 'sword made weak' by Cleopatra's 'supremacy' over him.[32] When Antony is enraged at the favourable audience Cleopatra grants Thidias, he accuses her, significantly, of intemperance:

> For I am sure,
> Though you could guess what temperance should be,
> You know not what it is.[33]

This is a fine psychological stroke. Antony seems to recognize the virtue of temperance here; yet he is accusing her of that very deficiency which in himself

p. 50. *Godfrey of Bulloigne, or The Recoverie of Ierusalem. Done into English Heroicall verse, by Edward Fairefax Gent.* (London, 1600), XVI, stanzas 4–7, p. 281. I owe these references to my colleague Professor A.J. Smith, to whom I wish to make most grateful acknowledgement here.

[30] I, i, ll. 1–10; ed. cit. p. 3.

[31] I, ii, l. 125; ed. cit. p. 19; I, v, ll. 43–52; pp. 40–1 (my italics).

[32] I, i, l. 1; III, x, l. 20; III, xi, l. 15; III, xi, ll. 23, 67, 59: pp. 3, 122, 124, 124–6.

[33] III, xiii, ll. 120–2; p. 139.

has brought them to their present predicament. It is very convincing – and very ironical too, for to negotiate with Caesar at this juncture is precisely the course of action for Cleopatra which temperance enjoins. As Thidias says, and Caesar knows,

> Wisdom and fortune combating together,
> If that the former dare but what it can,
> No chance may shake it.[34]

Antony's rage puts temperance to flight at the very moment when he accuses her of lacking it, and the possibility of a delicate political negotiation to avert absolute defeat for Egypt is abruptly cut off. When this defeat becomes a reality, but before the false news of Cleopatra's death is brought to Antony, she is 'Triple-turn'd whore' and in his most trenchant and laconic expression of this mood and interpretation of himself he declares: 'The witch shall die . . .'.[35] Here indeed we feel Cleopatra as Acrasia, and Antony as some Cymochles awoken, too late, to his undoing: Ulysses in the toils of Circe.

That Antony should, at some crucial moments, make this interpretation his own shows that the moral view of his love for Cleopatra and its consequences is not merely that of outsiders and enemies to his passion. Yet their view deepens the colours in this part of the picture. Enobarbus, closest to Antony of all his supporters, who so long and with such significant effect in the play forbears judgement, judges quietly and clearly after Actium:

> *Cleo.*:   Is Antony, or we, in fault for this?
> *Eno.*:   Antony only, that would make his will
> Lord of his reason . . .
> The itch of his affection should not then
> Have nicked his captainship . . .[36]

while Scarus, who remains with Antony even after Enobarbus, could not at the scene of Actium have made a more compelling, a more undeniably true judgement:

> I never saw an action of such shame;
> Experience, manhood, honour, ne'er before
> Did violate so itself.[37]

Thus the judgement of Caesar himself cannot be ruled out of court as merely the expression of a callow and envious competitor for power, though Caesar may partly be described in this way. When in I, iv he describes Antony as 'not more manlike / Than Cleopatra' he utters a dreadfully prophetic truth; when, later in the same speech, he expands on his complaint, the ideal of temperance, unattractively presented, is central in his case:

[34]III, xiii, ll. 78–80; p. 136.
[35]IV, xii, ll. 13, 47; pp. 166, 170.
[36]III, xiii, ll. 2–8; pp. 130–1.
[37]III, x, ll. 22–4; p. 122.

> Let's grant it is not
> Amiss to tumble on the bed of Ptolemy,
> To give a kingdom for a mirth, to sit
> And keep the turn of tipling with a slave,
> To reel the streets at noon, and stand the buffet
> With knaves that smells of sweat; say this becomes, −
> As his composure must be rare indeed
> Whom these things cannot blemish, − yet must Antony
> No way excuse his foils, when we do bear
> So great weight in his lightness. If he fill'd
> His vacancy with his voluptuousness,
> Full surfeits, and the dryness of his bones
> Call on him for't. But to confound such time,
> That drums him from his sport. . . . [38]

Caesar does not like, cannot really excuse, Antony's licentious and extravagant behaviour; resentment starts from every word with which he pretends to make worldly allowance for his competitor. Even so he could forgive, if it could all be kept separate from Antony's political responsibilities − if it were mere spare-time revelry. What he says here is really what Enobarbus delicately implied; had Cleopatra been no more to Antony than 'a wonderful piece of work' which enriched his travels, then his 'dotage' would not have overflowed the measure. It is precisely this awareness of the wider context, this ability to set the assault of immediate experience in the widest perceptive − which preserved Guyon but which Antony lacks − that constitutes temperance. 'Pius Aeneas' displayed it when, almost overwhelmed by his love for Dido, he hearkened to the prompting of Mercury and followed the call to Empire.[39] In this play Shakespeare dramatizes it expressively in the different attitudes of Caesar and Antony to messengers. When a messenger from Rome intrudes upon him and Cleopatra in I, i, Antony's reaction is one of impatience and contempt − 'Grates me, the sum' − and in III, xiii he has a most important emissary from Caesar whipped. Caesar, on the other hand, is constantly receiving messages and news; when in III, vi his sister returns to him, she has scarcely greeted him before he calls her 'castaway', so up to the minute is his information, and he knows Antony has returned to Egypt before Octavia does herself.

Magnificence

Temperance, so understood, is one of the positive standards offered us by the world of the play in respect of which Antony is dramatically found wanting. The opinion that he is so is manifestly not merely the propaganda of his enemies, nor of those ignorant of, or out of sympathy with, Egypt. The Spenserian qualities of the Enobarbus description do not play us false but in conjunction with other features and details help build into the play a theme and an attitude which contribute to our understanding of Antony. Yet understanding so gained is only half the picture; Shakespeare's total treatment of Antony does not invalidate the 'Spenserian' view but includes it and renders it of just less than dominant

---

[38]I, iv, ll. 16–29; pp. 32–3.
[39]*Aeneid*, IV, 393–6.

importance. To say that Antony is intemperate but the hero of intemperance is just a start towards full appreciation. Again it is useful to look at certain details in Plutarch's narrative and ask what associations they would have had for Shakespeare. Antony, wrote Plutarch, did things that seem intolerable in other men, 'as to boast commonly, to jest with one another, to drink like a good fellow with everybody, to sit with the soldiers when they dine, and to eat and drink with them soldierlike . . .'; 'he commonly exercised himself among them . . .'; he held 'banquets and drunken feasts' and wasted expense 'upon vain light huswifes . . .'; 'in his house they did nothing but feast, dance and mask: and himself passed away the time in hearing of foolish plays, or in marrying these players, tumblers, jesters and such sort of people' – and Plutarch repeats the charge from Cicero's famous second Philippic that once, after a night of revelry, Antony was actually sick in the Senate. This was the unsavoury side of that cult of love and pleasure which (recent scholarship suggests) the historical Antony consciously pursued.[40] The mixture of licentiousness, public indignity and democratic behaviour in a man of noble qualities born to lead, must have recalled to Shakespeare's mind his own Prince Hal. Not indeed the Hal we come to know well through successive scenes of *Henry IV* 1 & 2 but the more superficially known Hal of Bolingbroke's speech in *Richard II* and of his early reference to him in the First Part of *Henry IV*, I, i: 'riot and dishonour' sums up the impression, and indeed in the younger, more self-defensive and perhaps priggish tones of Caesar, in the speech quoted above, we listen to a charge similar to that of King Henry against Hal. But of course Hal, once located amidst scenes of low riot, displays the temperance of the ruler-to-be; from his first soliloquy we know that he has constantly the long view in mind; though he keeps low company he never gives himself up to it, but somewhat coldly reveals it for what in his view it is: Falstaff flies from him and Poins at Gadshill, and Francis's simple nature makes him an easy victim. On a closer comparison the Antony of Plutarch's narrative combines qualities possessed by both Falstaff and Hotspur, the two extremes between which the temperate and long-sighted Hal steers his course to the throne. Antony had the licentiousness, the self-indulgence, the love of low and riotous company of Falstaff; but despite this he was a brave soldier, brilliant military leader, and one to whom honour was far from 'a mere scutcheon' as his reaction to Actium showed. Hotspur was the impulsive idealist, ready to reach to extremes – 'the pale fac'd moon' or 'the bottom of the deep' – for honour's sake; he is governed by the passion of the moment, lacks long views and circumspection, and is hasty with important messengers. In I, iii, where Hotspur reveals so much of his character, Worcester chides him for not being 'better temper'd'.[41] Though he creates political disorder, and though defeated by Hal in battle, Hotspur is still a character who establishes a positive value in the play. Of Falstaff in *Henry IV* 1 & 2 and *Henry V* the same may be said. While Shakespeare's imagery attests to his being a disorderly character, and this is borne out by some of his actions, he has nevertheless a rich and intelligent humanity, a wisdom not of dignity but of

---

[40]*Shakespeare's Plutarch*, II, pp. 6, 10, 14; *Oratio Philippica Secunda*, I, 63. Shakespeare could have known Cicero's *Philippics*, either in Latin, or in the French translation edited by Antoine Macault, *Les Philippiques de M.T. Ciceron . . .* (Poitiers, 1549). On Antony, see Jasper Griffin, 'Propertius and Antony', *Journal of Roman Studies*, LXVII (1977), pp. 17–26.
[41]*Henry IV, Part One*, I, iii, ll. 321–2.

indignity, which stands out against the young Henry V at the consummation of his politic and equivocal career as heir to the throne.[42]

With Antony as with Falstaff deficiency is encompassed by, is indeed not wholly separate from, a richness of positive quality. In Antony a deficiency in the Aristotelian virtue of Temperance is a part of his richness in another Aristotelian virtue: Magnificence. This balance or paradox is splendidly stated in I, i. Just as in I, ii of the First Part of *Henry IV* Hal's bantering denunciation of Falstaff through imagery of irregularity and excess is balanced by Falstaff's comic geniality, so Philo's vigorous denunciation dramatically prepares for and is balanced by the first dialogue of Antony and Cleopatra:

> *Cleo.*:　If it be love indeed, tell me how much.
> *Ant.*:　There's beggary in love that can be reckoned.
> *Cleo.*:　I'll set a bourn how far to be belov'd.
> *Ant.*:　Then thou must needs find out new heaven, new earth.[43]

The extreme effectiveness of these lines arises partly from the way they take us into the midst of their love, the 'If . . .' presupposing much that has gone before. They express a mutual absorption, yet 'dotage' does not seem a good word to describe Antony's lines, which show an energy and decisiveness in diction and rhythm; the sense of exploring new worlds through love is more akin to certain of the love poems of Donne than the besotted inertness with which the manly lovers of *Faerie Queene*, Book II, succumb to the beguilement of Acrasia.[44] Antony's utterances are expressive of Magnificence; he gives something that cannot be counted, something infinite; there is a Marlovian aspiration in his second line, though perhaps more subtle. This is Antony the Emperor who, in Plutarch's narrative, said that 'the greatness and magnificence of the Empire of Rome appeared most, not where the Romans took, but where they gave much', who in Plutarch and Shakespeare made Cleopatra mistress of half Asia Minor and proclaimed his sons – significantly named Ptolemy and Alexander – kings of kings; and the Antony who in a less grand but not less moving situation sends Enobarbus's treasure after him, when he deserts.[45]

When Antony declares:

> Let Rome in Tiber melt, and the wide arch
> Of the rang'd empire fall! Here is my space,
> Kingdoms are clay: our dungy earth alike
> Feeds beast as man; the nobleness of life
> Is to do thus . . . [46]

---

[42]The third Gloucestershire scene, V, iii, has much to do with the revival of our sympathy with Falstaff, immediately before his rejection by Hal.

[43]I, i, ll. 14–17; p. 4. To speak of a deficiency in Temperance forming the positive quality of Magnificence, in Antony, is to put in a more particular form the argument of Willard Farnham, in *Shakespeare's Tragic Frontier* (Berkeley and Los Angeles, 1950), pp. 139–205, especially 203–5.

[44]Dover Wilson has alluded to Donne in his comments on these early lines of Antony; *Antony and Cleopatra*, ed. John Dover Wilson (Cambridge, 1954), p. 142.

[45]*Shakespeare's Plutarch*, II, pp. 56, 86.

[46]I, i, ll. 33–7; pp. 5–6. Cf. 'This is the harbour that Aeneas seeks', Marlowe's *Dido, Queen of Carthage*, IV, iv, 59.

he not only declares Cleopatra's entrancing power for him, recalling perhaps Marlowe's Aeneas to Dido, but makes also a conscious choice which renders his love magnificent, since so much by comparison has become trivial. This choice proves in the end prophetic; meanwhile, though made wholeheartedly, it is not adhered to consistently: the news of Fulvia's death arouses the Roman in Antony and he returns to Italy and his affairs in 'the rang'd empire'. Yet in the scene of his reconciliation with Caesar he does not, as in those circumstances he might profitably have done, roundly condemn Cleopatra and Egypt, nor does he, now 'the firm Roman' once more, express repentance in any but a purely diplomatic way; a confident pride and colloquial directness characterize his manner:

> I learn, you take things ill which are not so:
> Or being, concern you not . . .
> > > My being in Egypt,
> Caesar, what was't to you?[47]

One brief allusion only expresses moral condemnation of himself and Cleopatra – '. . . when poisoned hours had bound me up / From mine own knowledge . . .'; his asking pardon has in it a natural pride and, unlike Caesar, a wholly unselfassertive dignity:

> > > . . . as nearly as I may
> I'll play the penitent to you. But mine honesty
> Shall not make poor my greatness. . . . [48]

Of the two emperors, Antony comes out of the scene as a man of more human stature than Caesar because he has been big enough to 'play the penitent' and too big to rail against Cleopatra or castigate himself before his rival. Antony has played the politician without seeming less the man, and the implications of the scene somewhat counterbalance the significance of his departure from Egypt, and look ahead to his return. No part of the play, however, so counterbalances the moral 'Spenserian' view of Antony and Cleopatra's love than that sequence of scenes from IV, iv to IV, xiii. It is not only that in these scenes comes Antony's magnanimous and magnificent act of sending Enobarbus's treasure after him, but also and more important that here we see Antony rising from the arms of Cleopatra and with her encouragement vindicating his profession, talent and bravery as a soldier. The impression is of an inexhaustible vitality (as Dover Wilson has affirmed of the whole play) and all the more so by contrast with the defeat at Actium. It is notable that Shakespeare is here considerably modifying his source. The scene in which Antony makes his followers 'onion-eyed' by foreseeing his defeat, and the scene in which the god Bacchus (in Shakespeare Hercules) deserts him, are both moved to *before* the successful beating back of Caesar to his camp, whereas Plutarch had placed them after. Shakespeare also considerably magnifies what was in Plutarch a very small

---

[47]II, ii, ll. 29–30, 35–6; pp. 48–9.
[48]II, ii, ll. 91–2; p. 52. Antony here displays precisely what is Aristotelian Magnanimity: having a just sense of his own great worth.

military success: a valiant sally out of the town, followed by boasting.[49] Both changes stress the unexpected reserves of valour in Antony even when under the spell of the 'enchanting queen'. And this is what in these scenes Shakespeare is most anxious to dramatize. Thus he has Antony rise and don his armour with the actual help of Cleopatra; her opening plea: 'Sleep a little', enjoining him to a 'Spenserian' inertia, is significantly brushed aside as she becomes to him 'The armourer of my heart': Antony's mood shows an heroic determination and a workmanlike vigour.[50]

> 'Tis well blown, lads.
> This morning, like the spirit of a youth
> That means to be of note, begins betimes.
> So, so; come, give me that: this way; well said.
> Fare thee well, dame, whate'er becomes of me:
> This is a soldier's kiss: rebukeable, [*Kisses her*]
> And worthy shameful check it were, to stand
> On more mechanic compliment; I'll leave thee
> Now like a man of steel.[51]

His success in the fighting before Alexandria is enhanced by the ironical implication of Agrippa's command in IV, vii: 'Retire, we have engag'd ourselves too far: / *Caesar himself has work . . .*'[52] Antony has not merely had work but has triumphed through vigour and action. His command to '. .̇ . let the queen know of our gests' has, through the choice of the last word, a chivalric, perhaps Spenserian resonance, which is wholly positive, while the word Antony uses in his assurance to Scarus a few lines later firmly drives home the point of these scenes: 'To this great fairy I'll commend thy acts . . .'[53] 'Fairy' here means 'enchantress'; Antony has already used the phrase 'enchanting queen' in the negative sense, and is shortly to call her 'witch'.[54] But commentators have pointed out positive associations too; she is after all 'this *great* fairy'; in his mood of triumph Antony needs a word which carries the sense of enchantress without imputation of evil. Spenser had applied the word in a positive sense to his *Faerie Queene*; it may be that Shakespeare wishes to remind us of Spenser here. For in these scenes Shakespeare has turned the allegory of Guyon and Acrasia upside down; Cleopatra far from beguiling Antony from his manhood, as Acrasia did Cymochles and the youth in the Bower of Bliss, has 'armoured' him 'like a man of steel' and he has returned triumphant with the spirit of youth. The language with which he welcomes her is heroic through its yoking of the poetic with the vigour of the everyday:

> My nightingale,
> We have beat them to their beds. What, girl, though grey

---

[49]*Shakespeare's Plutarch*, II, p. 118. For other significant changes in his source material in Act IV, see Geoffrey Bullough, ed., *The Narrative and Dramatic Sources of Shakespeare*, V, Roman Plays, (London, 1964), p. 245.

[50]IV, iv, ll. 1–2, 7, 15–18; pp. 151–2.

[51]IV, iv, ll. 25–33; p. 153.

[52]IV, vii, ll. 1–2 (my italics); p. 158.

[53]IV, viii, l. 12; p. 159.

[54]I, ii, ll. 125; IV, xii, l. 47; pp. 19, 170.

Do somewhat mingle with our younger brown, yet ha' we
A brain that nourishes our nerves, and can
Get goal for goal of youth.[55]

Now it is true that the final day of hostilities between Antony and Caesar is
still to come, and Antony's declaration, on the capitulation of his fleet, 'This
foul Egyptian hath betrayed me'; so that one might almost say by IV, xii that the
'Spenserian' and the 'noble' views of Antony's and Cleopatra's love are of
equal weight and truth. For the capitulation of the fleet cannot invalidate what
took place the day before; the psychological effect of Cleopatra upon Antony
can never be *simply* that of the Spenserian allegory, however much it may be
seen to partake of it. In the same way, in *Henry IV* Part 2, Falstaff, though a
self-indulgent figure increasingly associated with disease, shows up well against
Prince John on the betrayal of the rebels at Gaultree Forest, and in the nostalgic
country atmosphere of the Gloucestershire scenes reasserts his appealing
humanity. With full and impartial comprehension Shakespeare sees that both
sides of Falstaff are the truth, and it remains for him to swing our sympathies a
little one or the other way in the last episodes of Falstaff's career. Hal's rejection
of Falstaff, inevitable though it may be from a ruler, inclines our sympathies to
the old man because of its pious hypocrisy — as though Hal had ever been sufficiently out of his own control to be led astray by Falstaff! In *Antony and
Cleopatra* our sympathies are finally swung towards the 'noble' view of their
love by Antony's reaction to the false intelligence of Cleopatra's death, his
suicide, their reunion, his final death, Cleopatra's tribute to him, and her own
heroic end, a perhaps peculiarly Eastern and pagan triumph. There is something
so genuine and intimate, so full of pathos and yet so heroic too, about Antony's
address to Cleopatra from below the walls of the monument:

only
I here importune death awhile, until
Of many thousand kisses, the poor last
I lay upon thy lips.[56]

that the viewpoint from which Cleopatra seems to have beguiled Antony from
his manhood becomes not so much false as superseded; if she has, Antony has
found through her a different kind of manhood. Yet this is a manhood that
includes, though it goes beyond, the more conventional Roman heroism of
Antony's suicide, of which he makes a rhetorical if slightly self-persuading
announcement ('Not Caesar's valour hath o'enthrown Antony, / But Antony's
hath triumph'd on itself,') before he dies.[57] His Roman qualities and virtues
have never been lost, despite Actium; that he retains them and yet attains also
another kind of heroism by finding himself through intemperance and
excess — this is the final Magnificence of Antony. And this is the felicity of
Cleopatra's tribute to him after his death — a tribute made soon after she has
been shown, by Proculeius's admonition: 'O, temperance, lady!', to be finally
possessed herself by a noble intemperance:

[55] IV, viii, ll. 18–22; p. 160.
[56] IV, xv, ll. 18–21; p. 183.
[57] IV, xv, ll. 14–15; p. 183.

> For his bounty,
> There was no winter in't: an autumn 'twas
> That grew the more by reaping: his delights
> Were dolphin-like, they show'd his back above
> The element they lived in. . . . [58]

Temperance

To see the character of Caesar in the right relation to Antony, it is, I believe, useful to look ahead to the other great Roman tragedy of Shakespeare's later years: *Coriolanus*. *Coriolanus*, thought to have been written soon after *Antony and Cleopatra*, draws as heavily on Plutarch.[59] The earlier play must have been vividly in Shakespeare's mind as he wrote the later. Yet the imagined worlds of the two plays could not be more different. Indeed the difference is so great as to suggest conscious antithesis. The contrast lies first in historical period; in *Coriolanus* Rome is undergoing the painful tensions of early political and historical development. There is a claustrophobic sense of tightness and closeness; class presses upon class within the city, just as Antium presses upon Rome. Patricians and Plebeians have their fiercely self-conscious and conflicting *mores* as the cities have their conflicting ambitions. This world is stark and austere; poverty is a real factor for many, and if *Antony and Cleopatra* deals with 'crowns and crownets' Coriolanus deals with brickbats and bread. In *Antony and Cleopatra*, by contrast, we have a sense of geographical and metaphorical expansiveness; Rome has broken upon the world and opened great horizons to occident and orient. The old republican institutions can no longer contain the power and extent of the state; the precarious compromise of the Triumvirate mediates between Republic and Empire, while society too is in a state of flux, and is so far from rigid stratification that it is possible for Antony, the son of a none too wealthy private gentleman, to become one of two rival emperors of the world. Poverty and class conflict are not issues in the world of this play, such is the plenty which abounds, and Antony enjoys conspicuously good relations with his soldiers and attendants.[60] The contrast lies secondly in the characters of the two protagonists. Each, at a superficial glance, appears to be dominated by a woman, but whereas Antony's is in the end a willing alliance with Cleopatra, Coriolanus is truly dominated by his mother, Volumnia. This is at the heart of the difference between the two heroes. For Antony is rich in experience and action, while Coriolanus is a youth, narrowly intense in the strenuous but limited ethos in which his mother has reared him. Antony delights in the company of common people; Coriolanus has a pathological hatred for the Plebeians: Antony is a man of generous impulse; Coriolanus is hardly at all, and can hardly bear generosity or honour shown to himself. Antony's character is full and flexible, rich in emotional life; Coriolanus is by comparison emotionally poverty-stricken, narrow, rigid, obsessive. Antony is 'an autumn'

---

[58]V, ii, ll. 48, 86–90; pp. 197, 200–1.

[59]See *Antony and Cleopatra*, ed. cit. pp. xxiv–ix; *Coriolanus*, ed. John Dover Wilson (Cambridge, 1960), pp. i–ix; *Coriolanus*, ed. Philip Brockbank, Arden Series (London, 1976), pp. 24–9. Quotations are taken from this edn.

[60]But note as an exception (it is a special case) IV, xii, ll. 33–7; pp. 168–9.

'that grew the more by reaping'; Coriolanus is a 'boy of tears'.[61] It is a measure of Shakespeare's human and artistic achievement in these two plays that their worlds harmonize so fully with the character of their protagonists that they seem both to have moulded their respective protagonists and to express their nature. In the world of *Coriolanus* kingship is unheard of; in the world of *Antony and Cleopatra* (and in that of Demetrius, Plutarch's parallel life to his life of Antony) crowns are within the reach and within the gift of great captains. The political and personal implications of this fact are not separable; they add up to a display of Magnificence affirmed together by action, character and poetry. In *Coriolanus* action, character and poetry render that which is stark, limited and undeveloped.

Yet there is one respect in which Antony and Coriolanus are alike. Each is a study of intemperance. Again and again Coriolanus gives free rein to the emotion of violently class-conscious contempt, at the expense of that more comprehensive and balanced awareness of the whole community which Menenius expresses (in however persuasively biased a fashion) in his fable of the belly. 'He cannot temp'rately transport his honours,' notes Sicinius; it proves true, and Coriolanus will lose the Consulship unless he will return and humble himself before the Plebeians. The scene follows in which Menenius and Volumnia beg him to do this, and thus combine 'Honour and policy'.[62] He complies at length, not to his mother's pleas but her anger, and Brutus, concerting tactics with his fellow tribune, remarks: 'Being once chaf'd, he cannot / Be rein'd again to temperance . . .'; it proves true, Menenius warns: 'Nay temperately: your promise' but to no avail.[63] Coriolanus is exiled, and his hatred and contempt for the Plebeians is transferred to Rome itself. When he and Tullus Aufidius, at the head of the Volscians, return and threaten the city which cast him out, Menenius appears before him to plead for Rome. He is sent back empty-handed, and Coriolanus, turning to his new ally, declares:

This man Aufidius
Was my belov'd in Rome: yet thou behold'st.

to which Aufidius replies:

You keep a constant temper.[64]

Volumnia appears to plead for Rome; once again he responds not to her pleading but her anger; his temper proves inconstant, and he yields to the overpowering pressure of the moment. But if Antony and Coriolanus are both intemperate, they are so in opposite ways. In the *Nicomachean Ethics* Aristotle described intemperance as an excess in pleasures, and postulated a nameless vice at the opposite extreme: a deficiency in pleasures, a too weak reaction to them. Temperance was the mid-point between the two extremes.[65] Elyot wrote in

[61]*Antony and Cleopatra*, V, ii, ll. 87–8; *Coriolanus*, V, vi, l. 100. Dover Wilson (*Coriolanus*, p. xvii) has noted that Coriolanus is like and unlike Antony, but has not enlarged on the point.
[62]II, i, l. 222; III, ii, l. 42; ed. cit. pp. 165, 220.
[63]III, iii, ll. 27–8; pp. 230, 232.
[64]V, ii, ll. 90–2; p. 285.
[65]Aristotle, *Nichomachean Ethics*, III, Chs. x and xi. A brief abstract of Aristotle's *Ethics* (by

similar vein on maturity: 'a meane between two extremities, wherein nothing lacketh or excedeth'. Spenser, in Book II of his *Faerie Queene*, has Guyon expound a similar relationship in reaction to the death of Amavia and the fate of Mordant:

> Behold the image of mortalitie,
> And feeble nature cloth'd with fleshly tyre,
>   When raging passion with fierce tyrannie
>   Robs reason of her due regalitie,
>   And makes it seruant to her basest part:
>   The strong it weakens with infirmitie,
> And with bold furie armes the weakest hart;
> The strong through pleasure soonest falles, the weake through smarte.
>
> But temperance (said he) with golden squire,
> Betwixt them both can measure out a meane,
> Neither to melt in pleasures hot desire,
> Nor fry in hartlesse griefe and dolefull teene.
> Thrise happie man, who fares them both atweene.[66]

Putting Aristotle, Elyot and Spenser together, as they may have joined together in Shakespeare's mind, we have the type of a moral and psychological contrast close to that between Antony and Coriolanus. Antony, from ·the moral, 'Spenserian' viewpoint, is the strong man whose reason is fatally overcome by passion and pleasure. Coriolanus, on the other hand, is the weak heart armed with bold fury; a great fighter and a great railer, he is psychologically immature, and he falls not through a heightened sense of pleasure but a heightened sense of injury, and (finally) the inability to withstand his mother when political necessity demands he should. Once again, the contention is not that Shakespeare subordinated his creation of these two characters to an Aristotelian–Spenserian scheme; it is rather that, through the theme of temperance, the scheme may be discerned as underlying the relatively naturalistic character-portrayal, and that, once seen, it forms a point of reference by which the characters may be understood.

The suggestion that *Antony and Cleopatra* and *Coriolanus* were tragedies conceived in conscious antithesis to each other may be further supported by a consideration of the structure of Plutarch's *Lives*. *The Lives of the Noble Grecians and Romanes* are not always in simple parallel to each other. Sometimes the parallel is blended with contrast; this is the case with the lives of Coriolanus and his Greek counterpart Alcibiades. In the outline of their two careers, and in several circumstances, there is a parallel between the two, yet in personality there is a great contrast, as Plutarch himself recognized in his *Comparison of Alcibiades with Martius Coriolanus*.[67] In character Plutarch's

---

Brunetto Latini?) was translated into English by John Wilkinson as *The Ethiques of Aristotle . . .* (London, 1547). If Shakespeare knew it, it could have aroused his interest in Aristotle's ethical thought, but it gives little attention to the quality of Temperance. It stresses virtue as 'a mean between extremities', that 'there be thynges, which bee virtues, and hath no extremities in it selfe' and that 'in greate thynges the meane is called Magnificence . . .' n.p.

[66] *Faerie Queene*, II, I, lvii–iii; ed. cit. p. 17.

[67] *The Lives of the Noble Grecians & Romanes . . . by . . . Plutarke . . . Translated by James Amyot: and . . . Thomas North . . .*, 1603 (reprint: London, 1929–30), I, pp. 427–31.

Alcibiades is closer to his Antony than to Coriolanus. Thus it is interesting that at the opening of the Life of Alcibiades we should find the following observation about him:

> Now for Alcibiades beawtie, it made no matter if we speake not of it, yet I will a little touche it by the waye: for he was wonderfull fayer, being a child, a boye, and a man, and that at all times, which made him marvelous amiable, and beloved of every man. For where Euripides sayeth, that of all fayer times of the yere, the Autumne or the latter season is the fayrest: that commonly falleth not out true. And yet it proved true in Alcibiades, though in fewe other: for he was passing fayer even to his latter time, and of good temperature of bodie.[68]

In this tribute to Alcibiades's beauty it is likely that we have one origin of Cleopatra's to Antony's bounty:

> For his bounty,
> There was no winter in't: an autumn 'twas
> That grew the more by reaping.[69]

The link between Alcibiades and Antony suggests that the structural parallel-and-contrast in this pair of Plutarch's *Lives* led Shakespeare to conceive the relationship between Antony and Coriolanus, and between the two tragic worlds in which they are protagonists, in a similar way; in the sense that contrasting and facing panels of a diptych are so, *Antony and Cleopatra* and *Coriolanus* come near to being a single work of art.

If Antony and Coriolanus display two opposite kinds of intemperance (in strict Aristotelian terms intemperance and its nameless opposing vice), we may expect to find somewhere in the two plays a character or characters who are Shakespeare's human equivalents to the 'meane' of Temperance. That there is in fact no schematic, perfect centre – such as the Man of Ross in Pope's *To Bathurst* – is only what we should expect, for Shakespeare is exploring what a moral scheme amounts to in real terms. Thus Menenius in *Coriolanus* and Caesar in *Antony and Cleopatra* are not wholly admirable characters by any means. Menenius, it is true, is habitually civil to the Plebeians, and certainly knows the value of temperate self-control in a tense political situation. Yet he has really neither sympathy nor understanding for the common people (his fable is far from a fair assessment of the class-conflict of Rome) and he is perhaps most humanly sympathetic to us when his affection for the wayward hero of his own aristocratic class is being publicly repudiated. He is not the true 'meane', but he approaches it in some outward respects, and is the nearest to it that the political world of *Coriolanus* can offer.

Shakespeare's *Antony and Cleopatra* was not, as we have seen, the first occasion that Caesar Augustus was presented on the Jacobean stage. Ben Jonson, in *The Poetaster* (1601), had dramatized him as the dignified and authoritative guarantor of human order, decorum and literary values. Since Jonson paralleled Augustan Rome with the London of his own day (coming close to casting himself in the rôle of Horace) it is hard to escape the implication that the

[68]Ibid., I, p. 437.
[69]*Antony and Cleopatra*, V, ii, ll. 86–8; ed. cit. p. 200.

character of Augustus is offered as a mirror for princes and an ideal for the times. One of his most dramatic appearances in the play is in IV, iii when he breaks in upon the sacrilegious masquing arranged by the poet Ovid to find his daughter Julia taking part in this 'feast of sense'.[70] Outraged, he offers to kill Julia, banishes Ovid, and rejects Horace's plea that mercy be shown. In this scene Augustus embodies all that most opposes intemperance and licence. It is a conception which Shakespeare may well have borne in mind, and may well have combined with the picture given in the *Life of Octavius Caesar Augustus* by Simon Goulart included in the 1603 edition of North's Plutarch.[71] In this *Life* great emphasis is laid on Augustus as a bringer of order, whether in civil customs and laws, or in the military and political state of the Empire. He is endowed with some dim intimations of the birth of Christ, but his cunning and politic side is also given due weight.[72] Goulart's *Life of Augustus*, an uninspired piece of work in itself, helped Shakespeare to the complex picture he gives of the Caesar just about to become the Emperor Augustus. It is a picture which is in many ways an answer to that of Jonson, and no account of the Augustan Idea in the age of Shakespeare and Jonson can ignore it.

Shakespeare accepts the traits attributed to Augustus by Jonson and Goulart but, in a relatively rounded and naturalistic portrayal, gives them a human basis which at once modifies and fills out the picture. Youth, vulnerability, defensiveness and determination are the foundations of Caesar's character in the play. In I, iv, where Shakespeare presents *his* Augustus condemning the 'feast of sense', moral strictness ('You shall find there / A man who is the abstract of all faults . . .') is blended with an uneasy and unconvincing attempt to make worldly allowance for Antony's licence, his parenthesis in ll. 22–3 showing the real trend of his feelings.[73] As noted earlier, the standard of temperance here becomes the unattractive means by which Caesar tries to ignore Antony's leisure enjoyments but condemn his neglect of business. Caesar's defensive awareness of Antony shows throughout the speech: he protests too much that Antony is more like a woman or a boy than a man, yet he is also contemptuous of Antony's advancing years. All this bespeaks Caesar's uneasy awareness of his own youth, and is an unconscious tribute to the formidable character of Antony. This complexity of attitude is beautifully summed up in the first phrase with which Caesar refers to Antony: 'our great competitor' – he *is* formidable to Caesar, and one of whom he can only have the most acute, heightened, resentful and competitive awareness. His self-conscious and awkward dignity, which again seems very young, is finely expressed by the stiffly contorted syntax of his speech to Antony in the reconciliation scene:

> I must be laugh'd at,
> If or for nothing, or a little, I
> Should say myself offended, and with you

---

[70]*The Poetaster*, IV, v, l. 192; *Ben Jonson*, ed. Herford and Simpson, IV, p. 279.

[71]*The Lives of the Noble Grecians & Romanes* . . ., V, pp. 245–88.

[72]See, e.g. ibid., V, pp. 260–1, 265, 270–1, 280–1, 262. Octavius is *seen* to be governed by Temperance, for he would not be thought to 'lifte himselfe up above measure,' and he 'tempers' the conflicting views of Maecenas and Agrippa as to whether he should give up his principality and return all power to the Senate (pp. 261–2). He nevertheless decides to keep his power.

[73]I, iv, ll. 1–33; pp. 31–4.

Chiefly i'the world: more laugh'd at, that I should
Once name you derogately. . . . [74]

The repetition of 'laugh'd at', the stiff dignity of 'derogately', are especially expressive of painful tension in his mind. On board Pompey's galley a characteristic note is struck by Caesar when he frowns at levity in the name of 'graver business' and ruefully condemns 'the wild disguise' of drink, but the next in his splendidly expressive series of scene-openings is in III, vi: 'Contemning Rome he has done all this, and more . . .'.[75] What is striking about this speech, apart from what it tells us of Antony, is the amazing detail with which Caesar describes the acts and proclamations of his 'great competitor'. He has taken care to be minutely informed, and the information is recounted with a minuteness almost obsessive. It is here we are most aware of Caesar the master of messengers and messages; by their means he maintains his constant grasp of the total human situation in which he is to act; in their light he concerts his tactics with rapid efficiency. In this grasp of the total scene we have already recognized an essential constituent of Temperance, as understood by Spenser and Shakespeare; we may see it combine, in Caesar, with more conventional traits such as a strong moral disapproval of revelry and licence.

In effect Shakespeare has given us in Caesar our embodiment of Temperance, but with a psychological subtlety of portrayal which reduces the attractiveness of the quality, though not its evident effectiveness in the world of affairs. Caesar's condemnation of Antony's excess, and certainly his capacity to act from a grasp of the total political and human situation, both take their origin from his deeply felt resentful and competitive attitude to the older man. This is brought out with final strength at the opening of Act IV, in one of the most humanly expressive speeches of the whole play:

Cæs.:   He calls me boy, and chides as he had power
        To beat me out of Egypt. My messenger
        He hath whipt with rods, dares me to personal combat,
        Cæsar to Antony: let the old ruffian know,
        I have many other ways to die; meantime
        Laugh at his challenge.[76]

It is a cruel situation for Caesar. His 'great competitor' is virtually in his power; yet Antony has still the personal advantage in being able so to wound Caesar with words. The latter's defensive awareness of his youth is never more starkly admitted than in the first statement of this speech, nor is our sense of his vulnerable dignity ever stronger than in the third. The mask is really off in the next part of the speech; the dramatic function of the tremendously marked pause after 'die', and the unnaturalness of the word 'laugh' in the context, is to show the effort with which Caesar re-assumes the 'correct' politic attitude to Antony's challenge. Caesar's whole reaction is a kind of inverted tribute to the all-but-defeated Antony, and it is only at the very end of the scene, that, with a further unnatural effort, Caesar is able to force the appearance of magnanimity: 'Poor

[74]II, ii, ll. 30–4; pp. 48–9.
[75]III, vi, ll. 1–19; pp. 107–8.
[76]IV, i, ll. 1–5; p. 145.

Antony!'[77] Yet when he hears the news of Antony's death Caesar shows
something of a magnanimous greatness of spirit, and here Shakespeare is at
pains to distinguish an initial, rather public tribute to the dead 'competitor'
('. . . in the name lay / A moiety of the world') from a later, more personal and
much more moving one:

> O Antony,
> I have follow'd thee to this, but we do launch
> Diseases in our bodies. I must perforce
> Have shown to thee such a declining day,
> Or look on thine: we could not stall together,
> In the whole world. But yet let me lament
> With tears as sovereign as the blood of hearts,
> That thou my brother, my competitor,
> In top of all design; my mate in empire,
> Friend and companion in the front of war . . .[78]

Only the appearance of a messenger breaks off this noble rhetoric until 'some
meeter season'; but if the speech is modulating back to the conventional, there is
much in it that seems genuine. There is nothing of the politic public tribute in:
'. . . we do launch / Diseases in our bodies' and there is honest recognition in his
next statement, and in his introduction, in this context, of the word 'competitor', flanked now with warmer and more human expressions: 'brother . . .
mate in empire, / Friend and companion . . .' This speech shows something of
worth, discernment and large-spiritedness in Caesar, the sad irony being that as
long as Antony was alive and a threat to the younger competitor these qualities
could not show; this temperate politician and ruler is rarely outward-giving, and
only so to his rival when his rival is dead. In the real world of men and affairs
which Shakespeare here explores, Temperance has become close to Policy;
Caesar has still to contrive the capture of Cleopatra for his triumph at
Rome – an aim which, characteristically, he mentions briefly and but once.
That Caesar does not possess the 'vices' – which are also the magnificent positive qualities – of Antony is very clear. A thoughtful reading of *Antony and
Cleopatra* and *Coriolanus* may suggest there is less difference between the
characters of Caesar and Coriolanus. Certainly both are furious at being called
'boy' and there is a lack of emotional richness in both. The difference lies in the
intelligent control which Caesar, despite the intensity of his feelings against
Antony, keeps upon himself and his actions throughout – this and the fact that
Coriolanus never makes so generous and understanding a tribute to the
Plebeians (his real enemies rather than Aufidius) as Caesar makes to Antony.
To this extent Caesar is the 'meane' of Temperance, but an approximate
'meane' that Shakespeare discovers in the human scene which he is dramatizing,
not one that he designs in accordance with the symmetry of the Aristotelian and
Spenserian moral scheme.

   In passing judgement upon 'this pestilent plague and mischif of Cleopatra's
love' in Antony, Plutarch, wrote that: '. . . in the end, the horse of the
mind, as Plato termeth it, that is so hard of rein (I mean the unreined lust of

[77]IV, i, l. 16; p. 146.
[78]V, i, ll. 35–44; p. 191.

concupiscence) did put out of Antonius' head all honest and commendable thoughts . . .'.[79] Plato's figure, in the *Phaedrus*, is that of the charioteer driving two horses, one noble, the other ignoble. The noble horse is described as 'a lover of honour, modesty and temperance, and the follower of the true glory' but only if the other horse is compelled to behave in similar fashion will the chariot run strongly and in control.[80] The strength of unrestrained appetite only brings the chariot to grief. This image of strength through restraint, which Shakespeare has given us a very individual and profound picture of in Caesar, carries us forward to the English Augustan Era which Ben Jonson heralded in *The Poetaster*. Swift, in *The Battle of the Books*, described the Augustan poet Virgil, '. . . in shining Armour, compleately fitted to his Body; He was mounted on a dapple grey Steed, *the slowness of whose Pace, was an Effect of the highest Mettle and Vigour.*'[81] Pope, in his *Essay on Criticism*, put more explicitly what Swift meant:

'Tis more to *guide* than *spur* the Muse's Steed;
Restrain his Fury, than provoke his Speed;
The winged Courser, like a gen'rous Horse,
Shows most true Mettle when you *check* his Course.[82]

The image is at the heart of much Augustan thinking about literature, expressing as it does the ideal behind another line of Pope:

Late, very late, correctness grew our care,[83]

and accounting as it does for that change from the hyperbolical rhyming tragedies of the Restoration to the restrained tragic manner exemplified in Dryden's *All for Love*, Congreve's *Mourning Bride* and Addison's *Cato*, for Swift's early rejection of the elaborate poetic style of Dryden's odes − and for the rejection of English baroque architecture in favour of Palladianism. But the image is also at the heart of much that the English Augustans had to say about living. When Pope wrote in his Epistle *To Murray*, following another Augustan poet:

'Not to Admire, is all the Art I know,
To make men happy, and to keep them so.'[84]

he was commending temperance, not to admire, not to be carried away uncritically to extremes, not to be mastered by the experiences of life rather than master them:

[79]*Shakespeare's Plutarch*, II, pp. 55–6.
[80]*The Dialogues of Plato*, Translated by J. Jowett (Oxford, 1892), I, pp. 452, 460–1.
[81]*A Tale of a Tub . . . by Jonathan Swift*, ed. A.C. Guthkelch and David Nichol Smith (Oxford, 1920; 2nd edn, 1958), p. 246.
[82]*An Essay on Criticism*, ll. 84–7; *The Poems of Alexander Pope*, general ed. John Butt, (London, 1939–61), I (ed. E. Audra and Aubrey Williams), pp. 248–9.
[83]*To Augustus*, l. 272; *Poems*, IV, p. 219.
[84]*To Murray*, ll. 1–2; *Poems*, IV, p. 237.

> Whether we dread, or whether we desire,
> In either case, believe me, we admire;
> Whether we joy or grieve, the same the curse,
> Surpriy'd at better, or surpriz'd at worse.
> Thus good, or bad, to one extreme betray
> Th' unbalanc'd Mind, and snatch the Man away.[85]

When Pope wrote these lines what Jonson had recommended for England in *The Poetaster* had in a sense come to pass, with its particular achievements, gains and losses in the understanding of men and art: a milieu in which Pope could write of Shakespeare (in terms familiar to us from *To Murray*):

> In Tragedy, nothing was so sure to *surprise* and cause *admiration*, as the most strange, unexpected, and consequently most unnatural, events and incidents; the most exaggerated thoughts; the most absurd and bombast expression . . . yet even in these our author's wit buoys up . . . like some prince of a romance in the disguise of a shepherd or a peasant . . . [86]

and think it a defence. How fully Shakespeare understood Jonson's ideals and to what they could lead, it is hard to say, but it is certain that in *Antony and Cleopatra*, a play in which Octavian becomes Augustus, he wrote a tragedy in which hyperbole of language, far from being hollow or absurd, is endowed with the fullness and variety of everyday speech; and a tragedy which, by contrast with its interwoven Spenserian theme of Temperance, affirms that in hyperbole of action, licence, a conscious voyaging forth to the extreme, there may be, far from weakness, Magnificence.

Reconciliation

> First, her bedchamber,
> Where I confess I slept not, but profess
> Had that was well worth watching − it was hang'd
> With tapestry of silk and silver; the story,
> Proud Cleopatra when she met her Roman
> And Cydnus swell'd above the banks, or for
> The press of boats or pride.[87]

The speaker is Iachimo, his place Rome, and the time the principate of Augustus. The speech describes a banquet of sense which Iachimo has enjoyed with his eyes only. Like Antony and Cleopatra on the doors of the palace of Armida, here too the famous lovers have an emblematic significance. They suggest what Iachimo might have liked to happen − and did not. The other piece of emblematic decoration in Imogen's bedchamber − the chimney-piece carved with 'Chaste Dian bathing' − is a truer comment upon what happened. For this play is Shakespeare's *Cymbeline*, and the allusion not only reminds us of the

[85]Ibid., ll. 20–5; *Poems*, IV, pp. 237, 239.

[86]Pope, *Preface to the Works of Shakespeare*; *The Works of . . . Pope* (London, 1751; reprint of 1753), VI, p. 332.

[87]II, iv, ll. 68–71; *Cymbeline*, ed. J.M. Nosworthy, Arden Series (London, 1955; reset, 1969), pp. 65–6.

earlier Roman play, but provides a most appropriate background detail for a speech by a Roman of the reign of Augustus.

Until comparatively recently the Augustan setting of *Cymbeline* has been ignored as a mild absurdity, similar perhaps to the coast of Bohemia in *The Winter's Tale*. Yet *Cymbeline*, uniquely perhaps in Shakespeare, is full of strange disjunctions, in character, rôle, scene, setting, and even dramaturgy. It is hard to think that a play which concludes with such a protracted *tour de force* of integration has not been designedly disintegrative in the earlier acts. However this may be, the drama certainly arises out of some very extreme contrasts: primitive Britain with 'the most high and palmy state of Rome' – and for that matter the polished libertine Rome of Iachimo, the Rome of Ovid whose *Metamorphoses* (Iachimo notes) Imogen has been reading in the bedchamber scene in II, ii (ll. 44–6), with the public and martial Rome of Caius Lucius and Augustus.

Shakespeare chose for his play a period of British history, recounted with various inconsistency in Geoffrey of Monmouth, Holinshed and *The Faerie Queene*, which enabled him to focus on the earlier descendants of the first Trojan settlers of the land, and to dramatize the relation of a primitive and aggressively independent Britain with the *pax Romana* of Augustus.[88] Imogen, the royal princess, has the name of the wife of Brutus, the founder of the British Kingdom in the *British History*. Cymbeline was the British ruler brought up at the court of Augustus, alienated from Rome over the question of a British tribute, but reconciled at last after military success. A vital equilibrium, thrown out by the events in the beginning of the play, is through the fidelity of Imogen (no Cleopatra to her Roman visitor), the primitive heroism of Guiderius and Arviragus in the revival of British chivalry, and the casting off of false counsel by King Cymbeline himself, re-established by the end of the play. But the action of the drama reveals the values and capacities which are to sustain a final harmony partaking of both national independence and world empire. It is doubtless a world empire under Christian providence (the *pax Augusta* during which the Prince of Peace was born), as Holinshead and Spenser made clear.[89]

Some of these values and attitudes are seen in the prominent defiance scene at the beginning of Act III, opening with Cymbeline's question: 'Now say, what would Augustus Caesar with us?' (III, i, 1). In this disjunctive drama, the conspiratorial Queen and oafish Cloten, false pretender to the royal succession, express attitudes with which it would have been hard for a late Elizabethan or early Jacobean not to feel sympathy:

> *Queen*:   . . . A kind of conquest
> Cæsar made here, but made not here his brag
> Of 'Came, and saw, and overcame:' with shame
> (The first that ever touch'd him) he was carried

---

[88]A new approach to the play was made by Emrys Jones in his 'Stuart Cymbeline', *Essays in Criticism*, II (1961), reprinted in D.J. Palmer, ed. *Shakespeare's Later Comedies*, pp. 248–62. Certain features of Jones's discussion were carried further by Frances Yates, in Ch. 2 of her *Shakespeare's Last Plays: A New Approach* (London, 1975); see especially pp. 41–52.

[89]Holinshed, *The Chronicles of England, Scotland and Ireland* (London, 1587), I, pp. 32–3; Spenser, *The Faerie Queene*, II, X, 50–1. On the revival of chivalry, see Yates, *Shakespeare's Last Plays*, p. 49.

> From off our coast, twice beaten: and his shipping
> (Poor ignorable baubles!) on our terrible seas,
> Like egg-shells mov'd upon their surges, crack'd
> As easily 'gainst our rocks. For joy whereof
> The fam'd Cassibelan, who was once at point
> (O giglot fortune!) to master Cæsar's sword,
> Made Lud's town with rejoicing-fires bright,
> And Britons strut with courage.

'Strut' may be thought to give Cloten his cue, yet despite his bragging manner what he says is far from ridiculous:

> *Clo.*:   We have yet many among us can gripe as hard as Cassibelan: I do not say
> I am one: but I have a hand. Why tribute? Why should we pay tribute? If
> Cæsar can hide the sun from us with a blanket, or put the moon in his
> pocket, we will pay him tribute for light: else, sir, no more tribute, pray
> you now.

King Cymbeline takes up their primitive and forceful defiance to give it a more civil and sophisticated political form:

> You must know,
> Till the injurious Romans did extort
> This tribute from us, we were free. Cæsar's ambition,
> Which swell'd so much that it did almost stretch
> The sides o' th' world, against all colour here
> Did put the yoke upon's; which to shake off
> Becomes a warlike people . . . .
>
>   Say then to Cæsar,
> Our ancestor was that Mulmutius which
> Ordain'd our laws, whose use the sword of Cæsar
> Hath too much mangled; whose repair, and franchise,
> Shall (by the power we hold) be our good deed,
> Though Rome be therefore angry.[90]

The King's speech is in accord with Machiavelli's insistence on the *virtù* of independent states, faithful to the laws and principles of their founders, as against the ultimately debilitating authority of a world empire. However the final exchange, between Caius Lucius, speaking for 'Cæsar, that hath more kings his servants than / Thyself domestic officers', and Cymbeline, recalling his youth under Augustus at Rome, rounds off the scene with courtesy.

   This scene is recalled in the recognition scene at the end of Act V, after the defiance of the Queen and Cloten, unfulfilled by them, has been sustained by Guiderius, Arviragus, Belarius, and Posthumus Leonatus. While the King at last submits 'to Cæsar, / And to the Roman empire', publicly repudiating his 'wicked queen' now dead, the fact that a victorious Britain freely submits to the world empire, stresses that the alliance is now resumed not on the basis of conquest but of freedom and an ideal of civilization.

---

[90]Ll. 23–34, 41–5, 47–53, 54–9; ed. cit. pp. 75–7.

Sooth.:   The fingers of the powers above do tune
           The harmony of this peace . . . .
                              For the Roman eagle
           From south to west on wing soaring aloft,
           Lessen'd herself in the beams o' the sun
           So vanish'd; which foreshadow'd our princely eagle,
           Th'imperial Cæsar, should again unite
           His favour with the radiant Cymbeline,
           Which shines here in the west.
Cym.:   Laud we the gods,
           And let our crooked smokes climb to their nostrils
           From our blest altars. Publish we this peace
           To all our subjects. Set we forward: let
           A Roman and a British ensign wave
           Friendly together: so through Lud's town march,
           And in the temple of great Jupiter
           Our peace we'll ratify: seal it with feasts.
           Set on there! Never was a war did cease
           (Ere bloody hands were wash'd) with such a peace.[91]

Cymbeline gave Shakespeare the occasion to turn, in his last years, to a distant yet positive view of the Augustan idea. Augustus in this late play is not the ambitious opportunist of *Julius Caesar*, nor the envious but skilful political competitor of *Antony and Cleopatra*, nor the ruler-patron of *The Poetaster*. He is the embodiment of the idea of world empire, the classical icon of such a European peace as James I sought to achieve through diplomacy and marriage alliances of his children, Princess Elizabeth, Prince Henry and Prince Charles. To this royal progeny the examples of Imogen, Guiderius and Arviragus were meant to be peculiarly apt.[92]

[91]V, v, ll. 467–8, 471–86; ed. cit. p. 187.
[92]Frances Yates, *Shakespeare's Last Plays*, pp. 48–9, 53–9.

VII The Measures of These States

'Go seek the novice statesmen, and obtrude
On them some Roman-cast similitude,
Tell them of liberty, the stories fine,
Until you all grow consuls in your wine;
Or thou, Dictator of the glass, bestow
On him the Cato; this the Cicero,
Transferring old Rome hither in your talk,
As Bethlem's House did to Loreto walk.
Foul architect, that hadst not eye to see
How ill the measures of these states agree . . .'
(Andrew Marvell, *Tom May's Death*, ll. 43–52)

James as Augustus

Julius Cæsar, *Antony and Cleopatra* and *Coriolanus* offer images of the Roman state in action at different stages of its history. They do not, like *Cymbeline*, depict the world of Britain, yet the worlds they dramatize speak to the early seventeenth-century British world. *Julius Cæsar* and *Antony and Cleopatra* show the growth of a world empire into monarchy, the former weighing the human basis of monarchy and aristocratic republicanism, the latter taking the full human measure of the new Augustan ideal. *Coriolanus* shows other and contrasting ways in which the pre-eminent leader may seek to transcend yet fall victim to the state. *Cymbeline* is to these plays as Geoffrey of Monmouth (one of its sources) is to Plutarch: it renders a world of romance, yet while *Antony and Cleopatra* unfolds realms of experience in which the Augustus-to-be is humanly placed, *Cymbeline* shows the British world first resolved to be divided from the world, but restoring itself finally to the *Pax Augusta*. *Julius Cæsar*, *Antony and Cleopatra* and even *Cymbeline* explore both the *realpolitik* and the ideal of empire, and thus bear upon the situation and values of the British world. They do not however directly reflect it. We must now turn back to the kingdoms of James I, to see how a parallel between Augustan Rome and seventeenth-century Britain was used to interpret its condition through the unprecedented political changes of the period 1603–60.

It is worth asking simply how far James measured up to the Augustan standard proposed by Jonson in *The Poetaster* and the 1604 Entry. Like other Renaissance monarchs praised as Augustus, except perhaps the Emperor Charles V, James hardly wielded the might of first-century Rome. Nothing like it. Britain was not even a moderately powerful military state. But in times of expansion a small nation may sometimes develop the outlook and expanded view of a world state. Partly because James overestimated Britain's power and his influence, partly because his views on peace and religious reconciliation were ahead of his time, underestimating the deep political and religious divisions of seventeenth-century Europe, the new king did develop a world outlook of a kind. Uninterested in military expansion, from the carefully defined position of his moderate Protestantism he showed a real ecumenical drive. He saw no reason to prolong the war with Spain that he inherited from Elizabeth, and historians are agreed that his ministers secured a tough and realistic peace.[1] He sought to strengthen the peace of Europe further by means of dynastic alliance. Having made peace with Spain, his first positive alliances were with Protestant states; he joined the Protestant Union, persuading the United Provinces to do the same, and married the Princess Elizabeth to the Elector Palatine, the 'champion of militant Calvinism in Germany'.[2] However, when Spanish diplomacy then sought to neutralize Britain's Protestant stance by offering the prospects of a Spanish bride for the heir to the British throne, James saw in such a union the achievement of a European peace by political and dynastic means – not to mention pecuniary advantage, and enhanced personal prestige for himself. It is in one way to the credit of both Spain and Britain that this match never came about, since religious difficulties were so strong on both sides. It is not, however, out of such failures that an ecumenical international peace is established.

James's internationalism, then, consisted in his rejection of an embattled Protestantism in favour of an over-ambitious political flexibility, endorsed by his principled dynasticism, but hampered by a Protestantism which, if it was not fierce and narrow, was not amorphous or merely nominal either. But to implement his international values he needed to assert power abroad, and here he proved too scrupulous and theoretical, at root, perhaps, too timid, to seize his opportunities. He failed to support the Elector Palatine when the Protestants of Bohemia elected him king, for the election offended his dynastic principles. More *realpolitik* might at least have prevented the loss of the Elector's German lands, and come closer to realizing the balanced and peaceful Europe James desired.[3] With these events the Thirty Years War began, and James's pacific foreign policy gave way to the incompetent militancy of Buckingham and Prince Charles. James had fulfilled the hopes of the 1604 Entry by maintaining peace, but done so increasingly through weakness rather than strength. His internationalism proved a visionary superstructure above the real divisions of Europe, though it was not so cloudy, nor so brutally dispelled, as the pacific idealism expressed at the Royal Entry of Charles IX of France. At least Britain was not plunged into massacre and civil war in this reign. Joseph Hall said in 1613 that James 'like another *Augustus*, before the second comming of CHRIST hath becalmed the world and shut the iron gates of warre . . .'; though one commentator felt there had been a surfeit of peace:

> Some parallel'd him to Tiberius for Dissimulation, yet Peace was maintained by him as in the Time of Augustus: and Peace begot Plenty, and Plenty begot Ease and

[1]Godfrey Davies, *The Early Stuarts* (Oxford, 1937; rev. edn, 1945), pp. 46–8.
[2]Ibid., p. 51.
[3]Ibid., pp. 52–6.

Wantonness, and Ease and Wantonness begot Poetry, and Poetry swelled to that Bulk in his time, that it begot strange Monstrous Satyrs against the King's own Person, that haunted both Court and Country. . . .[4]

If we turn back for a moment from the *novus Augustus* of the 1604 Entry to the Augustus of *The Poetaster*, we turn from the idea of prince as peace-giver, to that of the prince who fosters the culture of his language and state. While the encouragement of an unservile poetry is the heart of Jonson's concern in that play, it is right for us to approach the topic of culture more broadly. The Augustus shocked into anger by Ovid's banquet of sense is a prince deeply concerned with religious belief and religious observance. Not only did men remember the legend of a Christian revelation to Augustus,[5] but, more historically, recalled that Augustus had held the office of *Pontifex Maximus*, had sifted the Sibylline writings, destroying what he thought harmful to the state, and preserving what seemed valuable; that he had revived the worship of the old Roman gods, reformed ceremonial, restored temples, and sought to establish the place of the Roman state within a renovated Roman religion.[6] James I now receives few plaudits from historians for his English reign, but his religious policy was more successful than his foreign policy, and many Anglican divines were delighted with the vigour, learning and decisiveness with which James entered into religious debate at the Conference at Hampton Court.[7] The Augustan example here was the strengthening of the link between religion and the state. This prince from Presbyterian Scotland strengthened, when he might have weakened, the alliance between episcopacy and the crown, and while the Puritans did not have the best of the Hampton Court Conference, provoking James at one point into an angry (though apparently well-argued) tirade, James was not against them in everything. His mistake was to be too bitter against them in speech, and too hasty in his attempts to force them into a conformity. Yet when in 1611 he came to appoint a new Archbishop of Canterbury, his perhaps surprising but certainly wise choice was of a low churchman who would please the Puritan interest.[8] But one achievement of James towers over all others, its beneficent religious and cultural consequences reaching into the lives of generations of men and women long after his political failures were forgotten. Its occasion arose from a request by the Puritan, Dr John Rainolds, at the Hampton Court Conference. This was the commissioning and encouraging of the King James Bible. It may fairly be said that James's own learning and enthusiasm for learning in others, qualities which astonished and delighted the divines, contributed greatly to the successful creation of the Authorized Version.[9]

If the connection between James's religious policy and his rôle as a new

---

[4]Robert Ashton, ed., *James I By His Contemporaries* (London, 1969), p. 18.

[5]See Antoine Caron's painting 'Augustus and the Sibyl', discussed and illustrated by Frances Yates, *Astraea: The Imperial Theme in the Sixteenth Century* (London, 1975), pp. 222–3 and Plate 21; and *The Works of The Most High and Mighty Prince, Iames . . . Published by Iames [Montagu] Bishope of Winton* (London, 1616), Preface.

[6]See Ch. I above, pp. 14–15.

[7]D.H. Willson, *King James I and VI* (London, 1956), pp. 201–2.

[8]Ibid., pp. 212–13 for James's complexity of motive for this appointment.

[9]Ibid., pp. 213–15.

Augustus sounds far-fetched to modern ears, it only shows that the modern literary use of the term has been allowed to grow misleadingly narrow. A contemporary of James, the courtly high churchman James Montagu, Bishop of Winchester, framed the Preface to his edition of the *Works of The Most High and Mighty Prince, King James . . .* (1616) around the parallel of James with Augustus. Recalling that many famous princes had, like James, been learned and written books, he noted that '*Octauius*, as *Suetonius* reportes, writ many *Volumes, The Historie of his owne life, Exhortations to Philosophie, Heroick Verses, Epigrams, Tragedies* and diuerse other things'. Though the 1616 edition included James's learned but not his poetic works, the reader was certainly meant to remember James's earlier fame as a royal poet. This was not, however, what Montagu most wished to stress. He chose rather to relate 'two stories not impertinent to my purpose', the first of which concerned Augustus's efforts to establish a proper canon of the writings of the 'Roman-Ethnick-Religion', destroying the dubious and preserving the true. 'I relate this *Story*', added Montagu, 'the rather for that I thinke it were a good President for our *Augustus* to follow. . . .'. It is clear from the context that Montagu was saying James had followed, and should continue to follow, this 'President'.

The other *Storie* of *Augustus* is that famous *Inscription* of his, which he made to be set up in the *Altar* of the *Capitoll* to our Sauiour Christ; of which Nicephorus makes mention; as also *Suidas* in the word *Augustus. Cæsar Augustus* being proclaimed the first *Emperour* of *Rome*, hauing done many great things and achieued great Glory and felicity, came to the *Oracle* of *Apollo*, and offering up a *Heccatomb*, which is of all others the greatest *Sacrifice*; demanded of the *Oracle*, who should rule the *Empire* after his decease; receuing no answere at all, offered up another Sacrifice, and asked with all, how it came to passe, that the *Oracle* that was wont to vse so many wordes, was now become so silent? The *Oracle* after a long pause, made this answer:

> *Me puer Hebræus, Diuos, Deus ipse gubernans*
> *Cedere sede iubet, tristemque redire sub Orcum:*
> *Aris ergo dehinc tacitus abscedito nostris.*

The *Emperour* receiuing this answere, returned to Rome, erected in the *Capitoll* the greatest *Altar* that was there, with this Inscription: *Ara primogeniti Dei.* Surely our *Augustus*, in whose dayes our Blessed *Sauiour Christ Iesus* is come to a full and perfect aage: As hee was borne in the dayes of the other, studying nothing at all to know, who shall rule the Sceptre after him (for God be praised, he is much more happie then was *Augustus* in a Blessed *Posterity* of his owne) but indeauoring, that Christ his *Kingdome*, may euer reign in his *Kingdome*, hath consulted all the *Oracles* of *God*, and hath found in them, that there is but one oneley *Altar* to be erected to the oneley Sonne of *God*, who is Blessed for euer; and therefore hath set himselfe and bestowed much paines to that Man of Sinne, *cedere sede*, and *redire sub Orcum*, that hath erected so many *Altars* Athenian-like, to unknowne Gods, making more prayers and *Supplications* to supposed *Saints*, then euer the other did to Gods they knew not.[10]

The Patristic, providential, view of the *princeps* finds here an extreme form, drawing on that potent syncretistic myth of a Christian revelation to Augustus

---

[10]*The Works of Iames . . . I*, Preface To the Reader.

which may perhaps originate in the many versions of his refusal to be called *dominus*.[11] In its analogical fertility of thought it recalls Orosius. Its courtly extravagance seeks to recognize James as defender of a faith in which Christ is now fully and purely understood ('. . . in whose dayes . . . Christ Iesus is come to a full and perfect aage') and champion against a Roman Catholicism whose many altars display a greater infidelity to the 'oneley *Altar*' than any infidelity of which the ignorance of the pagans could have been guilty. When the myth of this quite unhistorical episode (once naively and piously believed, here perhaps not quite credulously employed) is stripped away, we are left with this historical residuum: that both Augustus and James had sought to restore, order and refine the religion of their native land.

How much of an Augustus was James to the poets of his time? His real interest was established by his own authorship, and his principles of critical judgement (which look a good deal more modern than his poetic practice) by his remarks in *Basilikon Doron*. Not only was he not ignorant or contemptuous of poetry (that much could be said of Henry VIII, Edward VI and Elizabeth) but his special concern with it was a matter of record. His encouragement of Shakespeare, from the small evidence we have, appears to have been more marked than that of Elizabeth, while Jonson, whose need was greater, and whose learning no doubt additionally recommended him, had strong support from the new King. From the end of 1604 on he was regularly invited to devise masques for the court, and after 1610 James granted him an annual pension.[12] The most conspicuous example of James's determination to assist and promote a poet, that of John Donne, is in some ways a special case. It was primarily Donne the converted Papist and learned controversialist, the author of that little-remembered but once highly important treatise *The Pseudo-Martyr*, that James so earnestly sought to add to the Anglican clergy, and to promote to high rank within the church.[13] But we must not separate what a contemporary of James and Donne would have thought of as one. Was it not powerful eloquence, in the end, that the king recognized in Donne, an eloquence in which controversial learning had a part, but so had the gift and practice of poetry? This much may be allowed in favour of James I; and there is no strong evidence on the other side of the case, no Spenser left to die in poverty. It is, as we shall see, when we come to look for poems addressed to the monarch, poems with the subtle blend of independence and respect to be found in Horace's Epistle to Augustus, or indeed expressive of the attitude of Horace to Augustus in *The Poetaster*, that James fell short of the Augustan ideal which Jonson wished him to fulfil. If James liked to speak to others in homely and familiar language, he liked them to address him in terms of florid hyperbole.[14] This may have been as inimical to the composition of Horatian odes to the king as it was of Horatian epistles.

---

[11]See Ch. II, pp. 29, 36–7. Also the tenth-century Suidas's Dictionary in Greek and Latin (1489; Wienne, 1619), I, p. 488.

[12]See Glynne Wickham, 'From Tragedy to Tragi-Comedy: King Lear as Prologue', *Shakespeare Survey*, Vol. 26 (1973), pp. 33–48. C.H. Herford and Percy and Evelyn Simpson, ed., *Ben Jonson*, I, pp. 39–40, 86, 90. Barbara De Luna, *Jonson's Romish Plot* (Oxford, 1967), p. 321, places the award of the pension six years later.

[13]Bald, *John Donne: A Life*, pp. 219–22, 306–7, 377–8.

[14]D.H. Willson, *King James I and VI*, p. 168; and see Bacon's dedication of *The Advancement of Learning*, Donne's dedication of his *Pseudo-Martyr*, and Montagu's Preface to James's *Works*.

If there were failures of character, judgement or policy, these are not, as is often assumed, the whole picture of the reign. James sought peace abroad and preserved it at home. His learning was perfectly respectable by the standards of the time, and the principles he defended concerning the rôle of princes on earth and the relation of churches to monarchy were consistent with his foreign policy and embodied in a concept of a Church of England which survived even the Civil War. From the existing English versions of the Bible, and the best Greek and Hebrew scholarship, he called forth the King James Bible, and gave it to the people of Britain. With favour and financial support he sustained the long and influential literary career of Ben Jonson, during which the latter's greatest comedies were written, the court masque evolved, and a body of new poetry in the Horatian mould was composed. With ardent encouragement and speedy promotion he gave Dr John Donne, Dean of St Paul's, to London and to literature. These are not negligible achievements, and they go a long way to fulfilling some of the hopes men had when in 1604 James was hailed as a new Augustus.

The Tribe of Ben

To trace the use of the Augustan parallel in English writing it is not necessary to demonstrate the existence of a body of English poetry comparable in kind and quality to the chief poetry of Augustan Rome. Obviously no English poem even approaching the *Aeneid* was written in the reigns of James and Charles I, though the fruitful influence of the relegated Ovid still made itself felt.[15] It is enough to note that in the hands of Jonson, Carew, Herrick, Marvell, and some others, non-dramatic poetry approached the achievement of Horace in quality and kind. At this point the Augustan comparison exists not only on the level of formal compliment and programme for the future, but is in some measure fulfilled in poetic practice. It is useful to consider the poetry of the Tribe of Ben as Horatian poetry.

Jonson early invited the designation of 'the English Horace' which was subsequently to be used ironically by his enemies and sincerely by his friends. This was a myth of himself that Jonson and his friends sought to foster. If we think of some of the major forms and influences of Jonson's work we might conclude that there was a case for styling him the English Plautus (by virtue of his comedies) or the English Martial (by virtue of his *Epigrammes* and certain other poems).[16] To reflect on this point is to realize that such designations did not merely serve to acknowledge the influence of and similarity to a classical poet. If we remember the rôle of Horace in *The Poetaster* we can see that his significance was dramatically set forth in relation to society, the state and its ruler. The significance Jonson proposed for himself in seventeenth-century England

[15]See the works of the later Ovidians, especially Michael Drayton's *England's Heroical Epistles* (1597).

[16]Jonson as an 'English Horace' may be thought to have been proposed by *The Poetaster*, taken up by Dekker and others (see the Literary Record in *Ben Jonson*, XI, pp. 364–9), by Chettle in *England's Mourning Garment*, (*Harleian Miscellany*, (London, 1744–6) III, p. 510) and by the Tribe of Ben (see *Ben Jonson*, XI, pp. 334, 338, 352. The comparison with Horace was often, of course, made amidst other literary comparisons. See pp. 323, 353–4, 356 for comparisons with Plautus and Martial. It should be noted that, for writers of verse panegyric, the most popular Latin model, Claudian, himself used comparison with Augustus.

involved a particular relation between poet, monarch and society, for which Horace was the appropriate pattern. The 'English Plautus' then, though far better earned in purely literary terms than the 'English Horace', would not have served Jonson's purpose, for Plautus was a writer of Republican Rome. This objection did not apply to Martial. But there was another more severe, for to be called the 'English Martial' would sooner or later imply the existence of an English Domitian, hardly the example of a good ruler to hold up to a modern prince, and hardly the way to win that prince's favour.[17] The Horatian rôle, on the other hand, had everything to commend it. It was not, as a Virgilian rôle would have been, beyond Jonson's artistic ambitions. It implied, nevertheless, the birth of a hope for a period of supreme literary achievement in Britain, and it linked a viable and acceptable poetic rôle with a positive ideal of monarchy.

Thus we note in Jonson's poems a number of explicit Horatian imitations, relating to Horatian originals in various ways. His verse translations in imitation of Horace's *Epode 2. The praises of a countrie life*, of the First Ode of the Fourth Book, *To Venus*, the Ninth Ode of the Third Book, *The Dialogue of Horace, and Lydia*, and of *Horace, His Art of Poetrie*, all first printed in the 1640 Folio, are his final affixing of the seal to his numerous earlier and less explicit approaches to the embodiment in English verse of the Horatian example. We may instance Epigramme CI, *Inviting a Friend to Svpper*, a poem formed from three invitation epigrams of Martial (V, 78; X, 48; XI, 52), yet as a whole reminding us of the somewhat longer epistolary invitation of Horace to Torquatus (*Ep. I, 5*), and of the passage on hospitality in the Second Satire of the Second Book (ll. 118–25): Martial was here writing in the Horatian tradition, and Jonson draws on its full resources, honouring the Roman world in his very proposal, with its allusions to Virgil, Tacitus, Livy and Horace, and effectively establishing the sense of a personal independence from the dangers as well as the exasperations and luxuries of state, by its modern relevance to spies who shall not on this occasion menace 'The libertie, that wee'll enioy to night'. This sense of a modest personal independence, whether expressed through an invitation to a meal, or praise of a country life, was part of the relevance of the Horatian theme of retirement to seventeenth-century England; it is an aspect of that right relation of subject and ruler, or poet and ruler, which allows free judgement without the imputation of disloyalty. Another example of Jonson's earlier and more complex approach to Horace is *A speach according to Horace* (*The Vnder-wood*, XLIV), where three Horatian odes touching on fears of national degeneracy and the virtues of the martial calling are drawn on to form an Horatian *sermo* ('speach') on these themes.[18] It need not be stressed how much the *Beatus ille* Epode, already mentioned, pervades the Country House Poems, *To Penshvrst* and *To Sir Robert Wroth*.

Jonson established a plain and familiar style of verse, moving between satiric, philosophic and pious reflection, and deploying the closely connected forms of epigram, *sermo* and epistle. He became the master of the long, variously patterned paragraph, almost impossible for quotation to extricate from the

---

[17]Jonson had got into trouble over *Sejanus*, no doubt because of the possible implications of his portrayal of Tiberius (*Ben Jonson*, I, pp. 37–8). Relevant here is his Epigramme XXXVI.

[18]On 'Inviting a Friend to Svpper' and 'A speach according to Horace' see Wesley Trimpi, *Ben Jonson's Poems: A Study of the Plain Style* (Stanford, 1962), pp. 185–90, 165–7.

closely woven texture of the whole poem, and preserving in its gravity a wonderful poise between a generalizing wisdom and the sense of specific address. One example must serve: from the *Epistle. To Katherine Lady Aubigny*,

> Of so great title, birth, but vertue most,
>   Without which, all the rest were sounds, or lost.
> 'Tis onely that can time, and chance defeat:
>   For he, that once is good, is euer great.
> Wherewith, then, *Madame*, can you better pay
>   This blessing of your starres, then by that way
> Of vertue, which you tread? what if alone?
>   Without companions? 'Tis safe to haue none.
> In single paths, dangers with ease are watch'd:
>   Contagion in the prease is soonest catch'd.
> This makes, that wisely you decline your life,
>   Farre from the maze of custome, error, strife,
> And keepe an euen, and vnalter'd gaite:
>   Not looking by, or backe. . . .[19]

A scholar intimate with the satires and epistles of Horace, coming on these lines of Jonson for the first time, might feel the shock of their difference from the closest Horatian precedents. A scholar intimate with Renaissance English poetry in its several traditions and modes will equally feel that such lines cannot be explained or appreciated without sustained reference to the manner and matter of Horace. The point to insist on is that there are grounds here for meaningful comparative discussion; nobody is so foolish as to think that Jonson could achieve, or would seek, complete identity with Horace.

If an easier and more intimate mode than this be considered the mark of the Horatian epistle, we may turn to a poem of one of the Tribe of Ben which is among the very finest poetic epistles of the seventeenth century: Thomas Carew's *In answer of an Elegiacall Letter upon the death of the King of Sweden . . .*, written probably in 1633.

> Then let the Germans feare if *Caesar* shall,
> Or the Vnited Princes, rise, and fall,
> But let us that in myrtle bowers sit
> Vnder secure shades, use the benefit
> Of peace and plenty, which the blessed hand
> Of our good King gives this obdurate Land,
>   . . . . what though the German Drum
> Bellow for freedome and revenge, the noyse
> Concernes not us, nor should divert our joyes;
> Nor ought the thunder of their Carabins
> Drown the sweet Ayres of our tun'd Violins;
> Beleeve me friend, if their prevailing powers
> Gaine them a calme securitie like ours,
> They'le hang their Armes up on the Olive bough,
> And dance, and revell then, as we doe now.[20]

---

[19]Ll. 49–62; *Ben Jonson*, VIII, p. 118.
[20]*The Poems of Thomas Carew, With His Masque Coelum Britannicum*, ed. Rhodes Dunlap (Oxford, 1949), pp. 75, 77.

Carew's style is less weighty and sententious than Jonson's, less elaborately punctuated and pausing; his verse runs faster and, appropriate to the different social relation of writer and recipient, his 'Beleeve me friend' carries more conversational ease into the poem than does the didactic dignity of Jonson's 'Wherewith, then, *Madame*'. It is in this manner that Carew's epistle evolves the theme of Stuart peace. The failure of James's European peace policy had now been long apparent; peace had withdrawn, it seemed, into the bounds of the British world. The poem has something of the character of the political odes of Horace, looking out from a relatively secure centre onto a wider and more warlike world. What is striking here is Carew's confident defence of the British peace; a view that Jonson had more than once evoked from Horace (*A speach according to Horace, Epistle to a Friend, to persuade him to the Warres*) is rejected in favour of all that the closed Temple of Janus meant. The 'tun'd Violins' are the outward marks of a civilized peace, a 'securitie' for which the warring states of Europe are in any case striving. (Carew's attitude may be compared with his presentation of the British monarchy in his masque *Coelum Britannicum* (1633–4), and Jonson's in the 1604 Entry: it is the peaceful final goal of centuries of strife.[21]) Carew has transposed what might be thought to be an Horatian configuration. Strife in the wider world does not here arise from the resolve to establish the *pax Augusta* by arms; peace is not a centre of power but in this situation an enclave, and the warring Caesar is a foreign potentate. Yet the standpoint of the poet, lacking the political centrality of Augustan Rome, earns centrality of another kind in its assertion of the absolute value of peace, and its suggestion of war's being merely a means to the end of peace. There is in Carew's poem an air of confident and well-contented modernity, which is a further aspect of Roman Augustanism, and may be found expressed in other terms in, for example, Horace's Epistle to Augustus (ll. 1–92), Ovid's *Ars Amatoria* (III, 113–28), and perhaps in that less well-known Augustan poet, Tibullus. Carew's poem is a fine example of that complex and qualified recreation of classical patterns, which seeks less to proclaim an identity with them than to plot the course of the modern by the stars of the ancient, and of which Marvell's *Horatian Ode* is perhaps the greatest instance.

Discussion of the Jonsonian satire and epistle has already marked the importance for these writers of the Horatian ode. It is remarkable that, even when the measure of an 'Augustan Age' of English poetry is not Virgil but Horace (with Ovid and Tibullus in the background) it is so often the forms of the satire and epistle that are cited to display Augustanism. While the satires and epistles of Pope constitute beyond doubt valid grounds for calling Pope 'Augustan', it is not sufficiently insisted on in English criticism that the Augustan Horace was quite as much the Horace of the *Carmina* as of the epistles and satires. Though Pope tried his hand at the Horatian ode, none of his major poems was cast in this form, and his genius was not on the whole lyrical. The case is quite different with Jonson and his followers, who wrote major and living poems in the lyric as well as in the satiric and epistolary veins, and who thus meet more fully the challenge of the Horatian achievement. Again, two examples must suffice to make the point, though the first, Jonson's version of Horace's *Ode to Venus*

---

[21]*Coelum Britannicum*, ll. 848–76; *The Poems of Thomas Carew*, pp. 175–6. For the 1604 Entry, see Chapter V, pp. 124–8.

(*Carmina* IV, i) arguably only mounts to a full lyric power at the end, the earlier lines seeming perhaps a little antiquarian in their retention of Roman name and rite, and the overall metrical pattern a little too close to elegy. But the end of Horace's poem is in any case its most moving part: it is one of his finely withheld dramatic turns (not unlike, in its very different context, his tribute to Cleopatra at the end of I, xxvii). After praying that Venus shall no longer trouble him, a fifty-year-old man, with love but turn her attention to the young, handsome and eloquent Paullus Fabius Maximus, he finds, despite his decorous and resolute disclaiming, that love has still a hold on his heart:

> But, why, oh why, my *Ligurine*,
> Flow my thin teares, downe these pale cheeks of mine?
>   Or why, my well-grac'd words among,
> With an uncomely silence failes my tongue?
>   Hard-hearted, I dreame every Night
> I hold thee fast! but fled hence, with the Light,
>   Whether in *Mars* his field thou bee,
> Or *Tybers* winding streames, I follow thee.[22]

The sensitivity of phrasing to the Latin, in these first two lines, has been observed,[23] and the latinate syntax, despite the initial difficulty of the vocative 'Hard-hearted', ('dure'), must be accounted a triumph of expressive arrangement, with the continuous movement from 'fled hence' to the end enacting the receding of the loved one into uncertainty ('but fled hence . . . Whether . . . Or . . .') culminating in that sad, aged, unsatisfied, physical or mental pursuit. Somehow Jonson has managed, without a trace of didacticism, to confer on the emotional predicament all the weight of his didactic verse, and the result, we may well feel, touches tragedy.

For a more free relation with Horace's *Carmina*, we may turn to another of the Tribe of Ben, Robert Herrick, whose poem *His Age*, 'dedicated to his peculiar friend, M. John Wickes, under the name of Posthumous' opens by drawing on several different odes:

> 1 Ah *Posthumus*! Our yeares hence flye,
>   And leave no sound; nor piety,
>   Or prayers, or vow
>   Can keep the wrinkle from the brow:
>   But we must on,
>   As Fate do's lead or draw us; none,
>   None, *Posthumus*, co'd ere decline
>   The doome of cruell *Proserpine*.
>
> 2 The pleasing wife, the house, the ground
>   Must all be left, no one plant found
>   To follow thee,
>   Save only the *Curst-Cipresse* tree:
>   A merry mind
>   Looks forward, scornes what's left behind:

---

[22]Ll. 33–40; *Ben Jonson*, VIII, p. 293.
[23]Trimpi, *Ben Jonson's Poems*, p. 280.

> Let's live, my *Wickes*, then, while we may,
> And here enjoy our Holiday.

> 3   W'ave seen the past-best Times, and these
>   Will nere return, we see the Seas,
>   And Moons to wain;
>   But they fill up their Ebbs again:
>   But vanisht man,
>   Like to a Lilly-lost, nere can,
>   Nere can repullulate, or bring
>   His dayes to see a second Spring.

> 4   But on we must, and thither tend,
>   Where *Anchus* and rich *Tullus* blend
>   Their sacred seed:
>   Thus has *Infernall Jove* decreed;
>   We must be made,
>   Ere long, a song, ere long a shade. . . .[24]

Beginning with the opening of II, xiv ('Eheu fugaces, Postume, Postume, / labantur anni'), Herrick switches sharply to a line from I, xxviii, returns to II, xiv for the second stanza, and then moves on to IV, vii, of which the fourth stanza (ll. 13–16) is divided between Herrick's third and fourth. This passage is almost a mosaic of translation from various of Horace's odes on death, yet the poet has added, expanded and combined so skilfully that the verses read like a single lyrical effusion. This is a mark of great intimacy with the Horatian texts. We notice too within the flow of Herrick's lines, so much swifter than Jonson's, the same expressive variation in pausing and enjambement so often the response of English verse to Latin poetic syntax ('As Fate do's lead or draw us; none, / None, *Posthumus* . . .'). How far this poem sustains itself as an Horatian ode is more open to question. It continues far longer than its Horatian models, and while the poet's stance in the later stanzas can be likened to other Horatian tones, it does not really attain the power of the opening. It is notable that the odes which Herrick specifically draws on all end in confrontation with the fact of death – and end sooner. But it is the Horatian power and sadness of these stanzas which deserve notice, the way Augustan effectively speaks for the seventeenth-century English ('M. John Wickes, under the name of Posthumus'), and the fact that the poem is not exceptional in Herrick's canon. It may easily be seen that it participates in the qualities of some of Herrick's most characteristic and famous poetry, such as *Corinna's going a Maying*. Like Jonson, Herrick was a master of the lyrical as well as the plain style, and the particular aspect of Horace's *Carmina* represented by II, xiv; IV, vii and several other odes, has never perhaps been better recreated in English than by Herrick.

Poetry to the Prince

If Herrick, and to a lesser extent others of the Tribe of Ben, could respond to the Horace who sang of the seasons, youth, age and remorseless death, of love, friendship, feasting and ceremony, they did not emulate the political odes. It is

---

[24]Ll. 1–30; *The Poetical Works of Herrick*, ed. L.C. Martin (Oxford, 1956), pp. 132–3.

true to say that neither Jonson, Carew nor Herrick gives us an Horatian ode to Augustus, though they come near it once or twice. This raises the question of the poets' address to their prince in the reigns of James I and Charles I, for Horace's relation with Augustus, as embodied in his odes and epistles, must (as *The Poetaster* suggests) have been just as important to seventeenth-century poets as the challenge of his satiric, epistolary and lyrical modes.

That King James relished flattery is something Jonson is likely to have discovered early. He was probably not astonished. But, the well-known fact could only constitute a problem for a court poet such as Jonson. Not that Jonson was so little a man of the world that he did not produce some of the laudatory verse that any monarch would expect. When his *Epigrammes* were printed in the 1616 *Works* they included several in praise of the king. The fourth poem of the collection praised him as 'best of Kings' and 'best of *Poets*', asking in conclusion: 'Whom should my *Muse* then flie to, but the best / Of Kings for grace; of *Poets* for my test?' (ll. 9–10). Immediately after, a four-line epigram took up James's hopes for the union of England and Scotland in very much the terms of the king's own 1604 Speech to Parliament: 'The world the temple was, the priest a king, / The spoused paire two realmes, the sea the ring.' (ll. 3–4).[25] A later pair of epigrams, XXXV and XXXVI, first extol James as the preserver of peace, and secondly exorcize the unwelcome political associations of the Martial epigram:

To King James

Who would not be thy subiect, IAMES, to 'obay
  A Prince, that rules by'example, more than sway?
Whose manners draw, more than thy powers constraine.
  And in this short time of thy happiest raigne,
Hast purg'd thy realmes, as we haue now no cause
  Left vs of feare, but first our crimes, then lawes.
Like aydes 'gainst treasons who hath found before,
  And than in them, how could we know god more?
First thou preserued wert, our king to bee,
  And since, the whole land was preseru'd for thee.

To the Ghost of Martial

MARTIAL, thou gau'st farre nobler *Epigrammes*
  To thy DOMITIAN, than I can my IAMES:
But in my royall subiect I passe thee,
  Thou flatterd'st thine, mine cannot flatter'd bee.[26]

The first of these probably expresses well enough the general thankfulness at James's peaceful accession and early years in England, but also gives, in compressed form, James's sense of his own significance (though, if we compare l.8 with the opening of the sonnet James prefixed to *Basilikon Doron* in 1603: 'God giues not Kings the stile of *Gods* in vaine' Jonson may be thought to have somewhat muted the theme of divine right). The last line of the second epigram is very ambiguous and adroit: perhaps James is too good to allow flattery it hints, but more boldly asserts that he is so good that 'flattery' is impossible; the trick of

[25] *Ben Jonson*, VIII, p. 28.
[26] Ibid., VIII, pp. 37–8.

flattering in the very words which deny flattery is neatly executed. Jonson may have expected James to appreciate the double-take. Altogether, these epigrams told James what he might be thought to want to hear, but they do not comprise a copious laudation. Their form makes them laconic, and hyperbole seems less extravagant when it is compressed. Interspersed among the other epigrams, they give the impression of being careful and deliberate measures of praise amidst a great many other calls upon the poet's attention.

An utterly different impression is given by William Drummond of Hawthornden's *Forth Feasting*, the lengthy verse panegyric written to welcome James back to Scotland in 1617. The difference is in large measure due to the form, for this, like Jonson's *Panegyre* of 1604, is based on the panegyrics of Claudian, and could hardly be less like the Martial epigram. But even when we compare like forms, the *Panegyre* with *Forth Feasting*, we must still be struck by the greater richness and copiousness of Drummond's praise. Yet amidst so much praise and wonder, and such variety of classical ornament, the poem works towards one identification only:

> . . . That long-exil'd Astraea leaves the heaven,
> And useth right her sword, her weights holds even,
> That the Saturnian world is come again,
> Are wished effects of thy most happy reign,
> That daily peace, love, truth, delights increase . . . .

> I see an age when after many years,
> And revolutions of the slow-pac'd spheres,
> These days shall be to other far esteem'd,
> And like Augustus palmy reign be deem'd. . . .

>   Run on, great Prince, thy course in glory's way,
> The end the life, the evening crowns the day. . . .[27]

It may be right to recall that in 1616 both the works of King James and the works of Jonson had been beautifully published, the first with Montagu's Augustan parallel in the Preface, the second with the text of the 1604 Entry. On the model of Claudian, Drummond's poem endorses the Augustan comparison, but is not very Augustan in its total effect.

If we recall the different manners in which Horace addressed Augustus in the *Carmina* and the Epistle, we must feel that neither Jonson nor Drummond are especially Horatian. Surprisingly, perhaps, Drummond, writing in the tradition of Claudian, is the closer. Horace's earlier odes to Augustus convey an authentic emotion of gratitude, hope and sometimes wonder, which Jonson's laconic praise does not capture at all. Even less do these verses of Jonson and Drummond approximate to 'Horace's dignified freedom in conversing with the first man of Rome',[28] in the Epistle, and we may wonder that the 'English Horace' wrote no epistle to his Augustus. Yet Jonson did address his prince in a way different from what we have yet seen, with a comic but hardly dignified

---

[27] *The Poetical Works of William Drummond of Hawthornden* ed. W.B. Turnbull (London, 1856), pp. 133, 135.
[28] Eduard Fraenkel, *Horace* (Oxford, 1959), p. 395.

freedom, and admittedly through the interposition of a dramatic character in the well-contrived situation of a masque.

In *The Gypsies Metamorphos'd* (1621), performed before the king at Burley-on-the-Hill in Rutland and at Belvoir in August, and in an expanded version at Windsor in September 1621, a gipsy captain tells the king's fortune by reading his palm, though at first ignorant of the real identity of his client:

> Here's a Gentleman's hand.
> I'le kisse it for lucke sake, you should by this line
> Loue a horse and a hound, but no part of a swine;
> To hunt the braue stag, not so much for yor food,
> As the weale of yor bodie, and the health of yor blood.
> Y'are a man of good meanes, and haue territories store,
> Both by sea and by land, and were borne, S^r, to more,
> W^{ch} you, like a Lord and the Prince of yor Peace,
> Content wth yor hauinge, despise to increase.
> You are no great wencher, I see by yor table,
> Although yor *Mons Veneris* sayes you are able.
> You liue chaste and single, and haue buried yor wife,
> And meane not to marrie by the line of yor life.
> Whence he that coniectures yor qualitie, learnes
> You' are an honest good man, and haue care of yor barnes.
> Your *Mercuries* hill too a witt doth betoken,
> Some booke crafte you haue, and are prettie well spoken.
> But stay! in yor *Iupiters Mount*, what's here!
> A Kinge! a Monarch! what wonders appeare!
> Highe! bountifull, iust! a *Ioue* for yor parte!
> A Master of men, and that raigne in theire harte![29]

In this speech Jonson has acquired something he lacked when he wrote for Elizabeth: tact. A familiar knowledge of James the man may be brought out here without the least offence: the gipsy does not know he is reading the palm of a king, and his reading of the royal character must therefore seem the more truthful. The problem of flattery has been quite evaded; Jonson is not carrying out the task of praise, as he was in the *Epigrammes*, nor losing the man in the panegyrical mask as Drummond did. Instead there is a warm and often exquisite humour, all the more fresh and delightful if we recall the dedications to James of the *Authorized Version*, the *Advancement of Learning*, or Montagu's Preface to the royal *Works* – 'Some booke crafte you haue': the joke could not possibly be better. What Jonson has done is what, in a very different way, Dryden was to do in *Absalom and Achitophel*: first he gives us the King as a man, then the King as a king. This procedure which relates the beginning with the end of Dryden's poem is telescoped by Jonson, in *The Gypsies Metamorphos'd*, into two readings of the palm. After a song, the unassuming anapaests which revealed James as an honest good man that had care of his bairns are replaced by a more ode-like form extolling '*Iames* the iust' as a peacemaker, and this, after a dance, is succeeded by an even more ode-like fortune-telling for Prince Charles, beautifully predicting a marriage to the Spanish Infanta:

[29] Ll. 278–98; *Ben Jonson*, VII, pp. 574–5.

Shee is sister of a Starre,
One the noblest nowe that are,
        Bright *Hesper*,
Whome the *Indians* in the East
Phosphore call, and in the west
        Hight *vesper*.

Courses, even wth the sunne,
Dothe her mightie Brother runne,
        For splendor:
What can to the marriage night
More than morne and Evening light
        Attend her . . .[30]

Just for a moment Jonson's chaste lyric measure, and his use of sun and stars to envisage the whole world and a world empire, has the character of an Horatian ode.[31]

The Gypsies Metamorphos'd certainly told James some of the things he wanted to hear, but it also took a straight if affectionate look at him. In a way it goes further than Horace's 'dignified freedom' and does much to fulfil Jonson's ideal of the relation between poet and prince in which the former could speak plainly and not offend. Certainly James was not offended by this masque. On the contrary he was delighted, so much so that he increased Jonson's pension, promised him the reversion of the mastership of the revels, and was stirred to write a sonnet invoking blessings on Buckingham and his wife, who had arranged the entertainment. Thus James's 'booke crafte', here in fluent Petrarchan vein, crowned the occasion.[32]

Jonson addressed more poems to Charles I than he did to James I. One reason was that King Charles, though sporadically generous to Jonson, had not continued the pension given him by King James. These poems of Jonson are all occasional, several being requests or thanks for support; several others, which may at bottom have been similarly motivated, marked the king's or the queen's birthday, the birth of a prince expected or accomplished, or the New Year. But other members of the Tribe of Ben celebrated such occasions too, and these poems cannot be construed simply as requests. They were part of the fabric of life of King Charles's court, poems of good wishes and prayer, and they accept their occasionalness with an unpretentious grace. Among the more beautiful of such poems are Herrick's *A Pastorall upon the birth of Prince Charles* (1630) and Jonson's *A New-yeares-Gift sung to King Charles, 1635*, both in eclogue form, and both celebrating the ruler in his mythic rôle as a shepherd of peace. A different kind of poetic celebration, and one closer to a type of Horatian ode, is Carew's *New-yeares gift. To the King*, perhaps written for January 1630/31:

Looke back old *Janus*, and survey
From *Time's* birth, till this new-borne day,
All the successful season bound
With Lawrell wreathes, and Trophies crown'd;

[30]Ll. 369–80; *Ben Jonson*, VII, p. 577.
[31]Cf. *Carmina*, IV, xv, ll. 17–20.
[32]*Ben Jonson*, X, pp. 612–14.

Turne o're the Annals past, and where
Happie auspitious dayes appeare,
Mark'd with the whiter stone, that cast
On the darke brow of th'Ages past
A dazeling luster, let them shine
In this succeeding circles twine,
Till it be round with glories spread,
Then with it crowne our *Charles* his head,
That we th'ensuing yeare may call
One great continued festivall.
Fresh joyes in varied formes apply,
To each distinct captivitie. . . .
Then as a Father let him be
With numerous issue blest, and see
The faire and God-like off-spring growne
From budding starres to Suns full blowne.
Circle with peacefull Olive bowes,
And conquering Bayes, his Regall browes.
Let his strong vertues overcome,
And bring him bloodlesse Trophies home:
Strew all the pavements, where he treads
With loyall hearts, or Rebels heads;
But *Byfront*, open thou no more,
In his blest raigne the Temple'dore.[33]

If this poem seems more graceful and less strained than many of Jonson's poems to James or Charles, it may be because it does not plunge into direct praise, but yields indirect praise through adopting the form of the prayer into which so many of Horace's odes were cast. It is both a prayer and a thanksgiving for peace (Rhodes Dunlap conjectures that Carew is alluding to the King's having in the last two years made peace with Spain and France), and could not be more appropriately addressed to Janus, god of beginnings and ends as well as of peace and war. Certainly the god and temple of Janus, which formed the climax of the 1604 Entry, carried with them clear Augustan associations, and their deployment here implicitly seeks to associate Charles's new resolve to rule without warfare (and without parliament) with the *pax Augusta*. In key with this is the theme of growth to maturity; the poem proffers in little what the 1604 Entry and *Coelum Britannicum* more fully set forth: a fulfilment of 'Annals past' in the present moment of monarchy; whatever has been auspicious in the darkness of 'Ages past' is gathered into the present, circles of past years and centuries magically metamorphosed into the circles of Charles's crown which are the promise of years to come. This vision of the growth of temporal cycles into a present glory is powerfully embodied in the images with which Carew envisages the growth of Charles's children 'From budding starres to Suns full blowne'. The transposition of this remarkable image from the almost certainly earlier *Epitaph on the Lady Mary Villiers* was a stroke of high art, for in the new

---

[33]Ll. 1-16, 23-4; *The Poems of Thomas Carew*, pp. 89–90. For the date of the poem, see pp. xlii and 258. While Rhodes Dunlap suggests that the poem was written for 31 January 1630/31, when Charles had concluded peace with France and Spain, the phrase 'Rebels Heads' at l. 32 may suggest a much later date, after the King's expedition to Berwick in May and June 1639: in fact the last New Year of the poet's life.

context its merging of heavenly with terrestrial movement has new resonances; new stars have been auguries of fortunate reigns upon earth, the sun is the most common image of kingship. The classical conception of the poem, the prayer to Janus, is continued into the detail of its conclusion, with its 'Olive bowes', 'Bayes' and 'Trophies'; Carew conveys, in remarkable fashion, the mystique of Caroline kingship, but it is hard to say whether 'conquering' and 'bloodlesse' do not together begin to betray a contradiction arising, perhaps, from King Charles's situation itself, and whether the penultimate couplet struck the contemporary reader with the same sense of strain and intrusive ruthlessness that it does the modern reader.

These examples of poetry addressed to the prince have been chosen primarily to display their character and quality in relation to the several modes in which Horace addressed Augustus. My last example, like Drummond's *Forth Feasting*, again confronts us with the explicit Augustan comparison. It is Andrew Marvell's *Ad Regem Carolum Parodia*, written at the age of sixteen, and published in 1637 in a volume of poems by members of Cambridge University to congratulate Charles on the birth of the Princess Anne.[34] It is perhaps unnecessary to apologize for discussing juvenilia when the author is Marvell, and the poem the first Horatian ode of that poet.

The poem is an adaptation of the Second Ode of Horace's First Book, of all the odes to Augustus in the first three books of the *Carmina* the one Horace chose to give the prominent position of the first ode after his dedication. In its opening phrase, 'Iam satis terris . . .', it relates intimately with Book I of the *Georgics*, reminding us of Virgil's concluding prayer to the gods of Rome to bring an end to the prodigies and bloodshed of the civil wars, and allow the *iuvenis* who was now Caesar to restore the cultivation of the earth and the harmony of the world. It is also the ode in which Horace 'carried the approach to certain conceptions of the East', that is to ruler-worship, 'farther than anywhere else'.[35] May not the god Mercury, the ode suggests in prayer, assume the human form of a young man, willing to be called the avenger of Caesar? Marvell adheres exactly to the form, and as closely as he can to the very words of Horace, but there is only one Caesar in his version; the reference to Julius Caesar is omitted. Yet the *parodia* is ingeniously altered to suggest difference within parallel, and not always, perhaps, without a measure of subdued wit. The thunderstorms and flooded Tiber of Horace are replaced in Marvell by the plague, and by Cam and Granta fancifully thought to recoil from the signs of infection. In Horace sea creatures seek the mountains and fish the tops of elms; in Marvell schoolchildren are in the open fields and the scholar quits the city: fish out of water.

In Horace it is Augustus who is finally identified as the redeemer of the state; in Marvell it is King Charles. Like Horace, Marvell proceeds towards this identification by stages, and here are some of the more significant changes:

[34]*The Complete Poems of Andrew Marvell*, ed. E.S. Donno (Harmondsworth, 1972), pp. 302–3).

[35]For a discussion of these points, see Fraenkel, *Horace*, pp. 242–51 (the words quoted are at p. 249). Cf. *Georgics*, I, 498–514.

Quem vocet divum populus ruentis
Imperi rebus? Prece qua fatigent
Doctior coetus minus audientes
    Carmina coelos?

Cui dabit partes luis expiandae
Jupiter, tandem venias, precamur,
Nube candentes humeros amictus
    Auxilator.

Sive tu mavis, Erycina nostra,
Quam jocus circumvolat et Cupido,
Tuque neglectum genus et nepotes
    Auxeris ipsa.

Sola tam longam removere pestem,
Quam juvat luctus faciesque tristis,
Prolis optata reparare mole
    Sola potesque.

Sive felici Carolum figura
Parvulus princeps imitetur, almae
Sive Mariae decoret puellam
    Dulcis imago.[36]

The prayers of the Vestal Virgins are replaced by those of the 'more learned' and while Horace *asked* to whom Jupiter would assign the task of atonement Marvell refers to him who *would* expiate the pestilence. Horace momentarily envisages him as Apollo, his shining shoulders veiled in cloud, but Marvell excises all reference to 'augor Apollo'. Erycina (Aphrodite) retains her place in the text, but, in keeping with the occasion of Marvell's *parodia*, the subject of the tenth stanza is not warfare but the plague. And in a most adroit transformation

[36]Here is E.S. Donno's English translation of the quoted stanzas:

What god shall the people invoke
when the state collapses? With what prayer
may a more learned group weary the heavens,
    unheedful of their pleas?

You to whom Jove will give the role
of expiating the pestilence, come at last, we pray,
your gleaming shoulders mantled with cloud,
    our helper.

Or if you are willing, our Erycina,
whom Mirth and Love attend,
do you also aid
    your forgotten people.

You alone are able to end the long plague,
which is pleased by our mournful and sad faces;
you alone are able to renew
    our generations.

Whether a little prince shows
the happy features of Charles,
or the sweet image of Mary
    graces a daughter.   (ll. 25–44; pp. 200–2)

the eleventh stanza speaks not of the winged son of Maia (Mercury) but of the birth of a prince bearing the features of Charles I or a princess resembling his Queen. Marvell has endeavoured to keep the surface of his poem as close to that of Horace as possible, and '. . . /Sive Mariae . . .' replaces '. . . /filius Maiae . . .' in the same position.

What is the meaning of Marvell's changes? The poem, in its chosen occasion, links the plague with the expected birth of a prince or princess, and the latter event is seen, in the mysticism of compliment, as symbolically renewing the generations of the British people. Marvell is careful about his religious references. Earlier in the poem he replaced 'Iove non probante' by 'Jove comprobante', thus making it clear that the rivers only obeyed God's will. In these stanzas Marvell runs together being appointed by Jove to expiate the people's guilt, and Apollo with his shoulders clad in cloud; human or divine he is some initially unnamed minister of providence, but I do not think that the sequence of vocatives running from this point in the ode to the end makes sense unless he is ultimately to be identified with the King. In seeking to reduce the paganism of his original Marvell has allowed Jupiter to stand for God but has thus relegated Apollo. Erycina, on the other hand, could be accepted as personifying love, and she is, in any case, 'Erycina nostra': the queen herself, as the end of the penultimate stanza makes clear. The naming of Erycina accords well with the expression of hope for a renewal of the royal family, and with the very subdued 'epiphany' replacing Horace's hope that Mercury (son of Maia) would assume human form as the *iuvenis* Augustus. The address can now shift naturally from the Queen to the King (ever since 'Cui dabit . . .' the poem has really been a prayer to the monarchy itself) and the final stanza clinches the identification of Charles with Augustus, 'pater atque princeps', the third line referring again to the royal birth rather than to foreign warfare, and Horace's 'te duce, Caesar' changing to 'Te patre, Caesar' in keeping. It is I think clear that this poem, though certainly an exercise in ingenuity, is not without an alert judgement informing its pattern of differences and identities. 'Parody' on this model contains the seeds of what we call imitation in the writings of Rochester and Pope, and this poem begins to use an ode to Augustus as the measure of the kingdom.

Broadly speaking, the poetry of the Tribe of Ben meets the Horatian challenge in that it masters not only the satiric and epistolary but also the lyrical veins. There are moments when one or another poet of this school, in epistle or ode, seems utterly Horatian. The situation might possibly have yielded an English Epistle to Augustus but, in the event, it seems likely that the nature of hereditary monarchy in the Renaissance, the modes of the court and perhaps the character of James I and Charles I, combined to prevent a poet such as Jonson from striking that mean between affectionate banter and extreme praise, which Fraenkel characterized as 'dignified freedom' and which the 'English Horace' certainly admired. Generally speaking the odes of the Tribe of Ben, even when we may feel them near an Horatian manner, seem more local than the 'political' odes of Horace. The world of the *Carmina* is coterminous with the great world seen from Rome; it has a geographic grandeur –

serves iturum Caesarem in ultimos
orbis Britannos et iuvenum recens

examen Eois timendum
> partibus Oceanoque rubro —[37]

and Horace lets his imagination range out over immense distance to regions of extreme heat or cold, to extremes of wildness, or to the past or present threat of utter foreignness: Carthage, Cleopatra. As in space, so in time, Horace evokes a Roman past, historical, mythological, and, through the form of prayer, envisages the future. History, mythology, religion, knowledge of the regions of the earth and of the heavenly bodies, form the great world of time and nature in which Augustus (and sometimes younger figures of his family, Tiberius and Drusus) acts as hero, and which he holds in power, and is the guarantor of its peace. These Horatian odes are the poetry of a world-state. Other odes of Horace, above all I, ix with its *carpe diem* theme, could be woven into the lyrical poetry of the earlier English seventeenth century, but the poets of one of the small modern successor-states of Rome, in a period of declining power, could not write odes with this extensive view. Not, at least, until the mid-century, when political events had made possible the difference we shall see between Carew's *New-yeares Gift. To the King* and Marvell's *Horatian Ode*.

Tom May and Andrew Marvell

Thomas May (1595–1650) is one of the less-remembered of the Tribe of Ben. He was, however, a member of that gifted circle in the 1620s as Clarendon records; Carew wrote a commendatory poem for his comedy *The Heire* in 1622, and in 1627 Jonson himself published *To my chosen Friend*, *The learned Translator of LVCAN, Thomas May, Esquire* as a prefatory poem to the ten books of *Lucan's Pharsalia* . . . in May's version.[38] Jonson's praise is warm. What has most moved him is Lucan's poem itself, in which

> . . . neither *Pompey*'s popularitie,
> *Caesar*'s ambition, *Cato*'s libertie,
> Calme *Brutus* tenor start; but all along
> Keepe due proportion in the ample song . . .

By 'start' Jonson means start out of its place, become salient and thus unbalance the poem when it is the peculiar function of 'arts, and eloquence' to understand and preserve a mean between all those famous political combatants. Lucan has justly interpreted his subject, and so has May. Lucan, adds Jonson floridly, 'The *Sunne* translated, or the Sonne of *May*.'[39] May was ambitious as a poet as well as a translator. Three years later he published *A Continuation of the Subject of Lucan's Historicall Poem till the Death of Iulius Caesar*, of which the dedication to King Charles asserts that the author 'chose rather to fall vnder the weight of a great argument, than to present a meane one to so high a hand: your

---

[37]I, xxxv, 29–32.
'Do thou preserve our Caesar, soon to set forth against the Britons, farthest of the world! Preserve the freshly levied band of youthful soldiers who shall raise fear in Eastern parts beside the Red Sea's coast.' (*Horace, Odes and Episodes*, ed. and tr. C.E. Bennett (London, 1914), Loeb edn, p. 95.
[38]Clarendon, *Life* (1759 edn), I, 35; *The Poems of Thomas Carew*, pp. 258–9.
[39]Ll. 9–12; *Ben Jonson*, VIII, p. 395.

Maiesties renowned worth, and Heroicall vertues (the perfection of minde meeting in you with the height of Fortune) may make you securely delighted in the reading of great actions . . .'.[40]

May's *Continuation* gave him the chance to draw Augustus into his narrative. The first occasion is in connection with the love of Julius Caesar and Cleopatra, and their child Caesarion who

> Vntimely slaine, shall be in future time
> *Augustus Caesar*'s parricidall [sic] crime,
> And *Caesar*'s house with *Caesar*'s bloud shall blot;
> Thy guilt *Augustus* is that night begot,
> Which shall hereafter those rich triumphs staine,
> Which thou from *Aegypt*'s conquest shall obtaine;
> Vnlesse that flattery be taught for thee
> To wrest all natures lawes, and policy
> Of State, together with the Peace of Rome
> Alleg'd to iustifie thy bloudy doome.[41]

May's attitude here might at first seem to resemble the republican tradition, in imputing cunning and crime to Augustus, and in one sense this is true. But this does not argue republican thinking on May's part: quite the contrary. The crime he alleges is that which a proponent of monarchical divine right could be expected to perceive. Julius Caesar is seen as the founder of a monarchy, and Augustus's claim to succeed him rests on his being the (adopted) son and heir of Caesar. But if Caesar had in fact been married to Cleopatra, as Antony and Cleopatra had announced to the world, then Caesarion not Augustus was the legitimate heir to the monarchy of Rome. Hence Augustus's victory over Antony and Cleopatra was stained by a crime which, the poem implies, no reasons of *realpolitik* could justify.

This episode must, however, be set in the context of May's wider narrative which makes it abundantly clear that whatever Augustus's crimes in his rise to power, his rôle in establishing a 'happy Monarchy' over Rome was his greatest importance. In recounting Caesar's campaigns, in Bk VI, May tells how:

> A faire ostent the gods were pleas'd to shew,
> A towring Eagle long o'er Caesar flew,
> Till seeming weary, with a faire descent
> It gently perch'd on young *Octauius* tent,
> Who follow'd then his Father to the warre.
> A good presage the augurs all declare,
> And not alone to shew the warres successe,
> But young *Octauius* future happinesse:
> But not so soone, alas, could they foresee
> The full effect of this fair augury:
> How many ciuill wounds did yet remaine
> Ere Rome with patience brooke a *caesar*'s reigne,
> And for her safety be inforc'd to flye
> To great *Augustus* happy Monarchy?[42]

[40]Second edn, 1633, n.p.
[41]Bk II, n.p.
[42]Bk VI, n.p.

Thinking very much along the lines of Jonson in the 1604 Entry, or of Carew in *Coelum Britannicum*, May then tells of all the civil strife and bloodshed already suffered, and still to be suffered by Rome, that was the necessary providential preparation for Augustus: 'That Rome in those dire Tragedies might see / What horrid dangers follow'd libertie'. It is the great work of time that Augustus shall be at last 'a welcome conqueror' and May, looking beyond the chronological limit of his poem, can prophetically address him:

> Thou then anew that powerful State shalt mould,
> And long the World's high Sceptre safely hold,
> Aboue all riualls plac'd; thy god-like State
> No force shall shake; when shutting *Ianus* gate,
> Thou shalt set ope the sacred Thespian spring
> And there securely heare the Muses sing,
> Whose stately layes shall keepe thy deathlesse fame;
> And make immortal great *Augustus* name:
> Nor euer did the Arts so truly reigne,
> Nor sung the Muses in so pure a straine
> As then they did, to grace thy glorious time;
> As if the Muse before lack'd power to clime,
> Or else disdain'd her highest notes to raise,
> Till such a Monarch liu'd to give the Bayes.[43]

There can be no doubt about May's final attitude to Augustus in this poem. And nothing in Bk VI of his *Continuation* could have offended those at the Stuart court or among the Tribe of Ben who drew the Augustan comparison. Indeed the lines last quoted may have been quietly adjusted to what seemed likely to be the British situation in the 1630s. Nothing is taken from Horace's odes about the continuing martial effort of Augustus after he attained the principate. Charles's diplomacy was at this time engaged in extricating Britain from war with France and Spain, and May fully adopts the Stuart emphasis upon the peace of Augustus. As in Carew's *New-yeares gift. To the King*, the Temple of Janus is shut once more, and the prospect of civilization offered is of a flourishing of the arts in security – we note how this word is to be reiterated, in the same connection, in Carew's Epistle to Aurelian Townsend, a few years later. To anyone with some acquaintance with the Caroline court it must indeed have seemed that the arts (as opposed, perhaps, to learning) were flourishing there as never before in Britain. It is too easy for students of literature to discount the Caroline masque, and to forget that perhaps no British monarch so effectively encouraged the visual arts as Charles I.

If we put together the Caesarion episode and the Bk VI passage on Augustus, May's position can be seen as a not quite coherent approximation to that of Bodin. The dark side of Augustus's rise to power he is aware of and will not ignore, but these facts do not cancel the significance of a political career which, centrally in the history of the world, demonstrates the natural effectiveness and divine rightness of monarchical rule. The point may be referred to a more recent

---

[43]Bk VI, n.p. May later altered the lines of his poem to the republican standpoint; see R.J. Bruère, 'The Latin and English versions of Tom May's *Supplementum Lucani*', *Classical Philology*, XLIV (1949) 45–63.

work than that of Bodin, Peter Heylyn's *AVGVSTVS. Or, An Essay of those Meanes and Counsels, by which the Common-wealth of Rome was altered, and reduced unto a Monarchy*, published in 1632, but stated (with an apology for drawing Augustus 'with too much shadow') to have been 'long since written'.[44] Heylyn conveys various realistic insights into Augustus, noting, for example, how he made use of Cicero against Antony, and blending the Dio Cassius episode concerning the advice of Agrippa and Maecenas on whether the *princeps* should resign with the views of Tacitus on why the Senate suffered the principate to continue:

> Some supposed this speech [proposing resignation], not to have so much truth, as art and cunning, yet smothered their conceits, for feare of after-claps. Others were Creatures of his owne making and they hoping to rise in the fall of their Country, would not heare of a Resignation. Some few of the wiser sort, thought it not expedient, to put the Reines againe into the hands of the *Multitude*. The rest out of a sluggish and phlegmatique Constitution, chose rather the present state with securitie; than to strive to recover the old, with danger. All therefore with a joynt consent proclaime him sole *Emperor*. . . .[45]

When at a later point Heylyn states that Augustus allowed 'Liberty of speech so men would be less aware of loss of *Liberty* in the State' he is close to the spirit of Tacitus. Heylyn goes further than May in extending his criticisms of Augustus into the period of the principate itself. Yet Heylyn's purpose is not to advocate an aristocratic republic but to defend Augustus and the idea of Monarchy. Thus he writes of Augustus framing a new constitution for Rome close to that of Lacedaemon, devised by Lycurgus who had understood that the 'unmixt forme of Rule was mutable' and had established a constitution from the perfections of the three good forms, 'Reserving to the *King*, absolute Majesty; to the *Nobles*, convenient authority; to the people entire *Liberty*; all in a just and equal proportion'.[46] This had been the ideal of Gentillet. 'The Common-wealth which hee found weake and in *Rubbish*', declares Heylyn elaborating on Suetonius,[47] 'he left *Adamantine* and invincible': this is part of the panegyric upon Augustus with which the work concludes.[48] The word 'reduced' in Heylyn's title has the old meaning of 'led back to', 'restored', and this accords with the theory of history expounded at the beginning of his book, whereby 'questionlesse it fareth many times with a Commonwealth, as with the Sunne: which runneth through all the signes of the *Zodiack*, till it return to the place where its motion first began. And the *Platonicke* yeare of reducing all things to the same beginning,

---

[44]Sig. A.3. It was first published under the name of the printer, Henry Seile, and republished in Heylyn's *Cosmographie* . . . (London, 1669), as 'written many years before', 'so well entertained when it came abroad' and 'so pertinent to the Present business' (p. 38). Its reference on p. 129 to the religious conservatism of 'a late Mighty Monarch' may be to James I, in which case the date of writing may have been soon after 1625.

[45]Heylyn, *Augustus*, pp. 106–7.

[46]Ibid., pp. 120–4.

[47]Suetonius, *De Vitae Cæsarvm*, Divvs Avgvstvs, 28: '[Rome] hee beautified and set out so, as justly he made his boast, that where he found it built of bricke, hee left it all of marble.' *Historie of the Twelve Caesars*, tr. Philemon Holland, intro. Charles Whibley, Tudor Translations (London, 1899), II, p. 104.

[48]Heylyn, *Augustus*, p. 126.

continuance, and period; how false soever in the bookes of *Nature*, is in some sort true in the change of Government.'[49] As with the fabled returnings of a golden age, commonwealths periodically renew themselves by the restoration of monarchy. If the specific means whereby such restorations are brought about are sometimes cunning and criminal, that does not destroy the monarchical principle to which Heylyn and May evidently both subscribe.

Such monarchical principle, and such theory of revolutions within the state, were to be tested after King Charles, desperately short of men, money and arms, and probably not perceiving that the political conflict between crown and Parliament had begun to swing his way again, set up his standard at Nottingham, in August 1642. That Autumn, at the Battle of Edgehill, his forces threw away a major victory over the parliamentary troops, but gained a narrow one, and secured most of the subsequent strategic advantage. Just under five years later, defeated in the First Civil War and now the captive of a hostile army increasingly independent of parliament, Charles found himself back at Hampton Court. We may now contrast the attitudes of two members of the Tribe of Ben, Herrick and May, each of whom drew a Roman parallel with Augustus. Herrick's *To The King, Upon his welcome to Hampton Court* must be construed as a poetic defiance of the times by the royalist clergyman who was expelled from his living that same year, and next year was to publish his *Hesperides* with a crown on the title-page, and a dedication to the Prince of Wales.

> Welcome, *Great Cesar*, welcome now you are,
> As dearest Peace, after destructive Warre:
> Welcome as slumbers; or as beds of ease
> After our long, and peevish sicknesses.
> O *Pompe of Glory*! Welcome now, and come
> To repossess once more your long'd-for home.
> A thousand Alters smoake; a thousand thighes
> Of Beeves here ready stand for Sacrifice.
> Enter and prosper; while our eyes doe waite
> For an *Ascendent* throughly *Auspicate*:
> Under which signe we may the former stone
> Lay of our safeties new foundation:
> That done: O *Cesar*, live, and be to us,
> Our *Fate*, our *Fortune*, and our *Genius*;
> To whose free knees we may our temples tye
> As to a still protecting Deitie.
> That sho'd you stirre, we and our Altars too
> May *(Great Augustus) goe along with You.*
> *Chor.* Long live the King; and to accomplish this,
> We'l from our owne, adde far more years to his.

Perhaps no prince has been greeted as an Augustus in less august circumstances. Herrick is of course drawing on the tradition of panegyrics on the return of rulers, in which the Augustan comparison was quite common; Drummond's *Forth Feasting* was in this tradition.[50] On the face of it Herrick's defiance is to

---

[49]Ibid., pp. 20–2.
[50]*The Poetical Works of Robert Herrick*, p. 300, 561; James D. Garrison, *Dryden and the Tradition of Panegyric*, Chs. 2–3.

hold to this convention and ignore the circumstances. That is part of the poem's effect. But Herrick is also using the terms of poetry celebrating the accession or return of rulers (auguries, auspices, prophecies) to recognize a new cycle of political events. His 'eyes do waite / For an *Ascendent*': a restoration must come in which future safety shall be established on a new foundation upon the 'former stone'. Meanwhile, Charles I will still be Augustus wherever he goes.

In the same year May published his *History of the Parliament of England.* . . . Unlike Herrick he had taken the parliamentary side in the Civil War, and was by this time a public apologist for the parliamentary cause. In his account of the Battle of Edgehill, in Bk III of the *History*, as in many other parts, he draws comparisons with the history of Rome. He claims Edgehill as a parliamentary victory, but observes how the royal party nevertheless grew stronger afterwards, since all the winning side had to offer its supporters was 'free injoyment of their native Liberty'

> And how much private interest will oversway publike notions, Books of History, rather then Philosophy, will truly informe you; for concerning humane actions and dispositions, there is nothing under the Sunne which is absolutely new. Looke upon the Discourse of one Historian in that subject, DION CASSIUS, a Writer of as little bias, in the opinion of all Criticks, as any among the Antients, when he relates the last Warre about Roman Liberty, after which (as himselfe speaks) that People never againe looked back toward it. Which was the Warre of BRUTUS and CASSIUS against CÆSAR and ANTONY;. . . . Although (saith DION) before this War they had many Civill Wars, yet in others they fought who should oppress the Roman Liberty; in this War, one side fought to vindicate Liberty, the other to bring in Tyranny, yet the side of Tyranny prevailed, and drew most to it: Of what quality they were, the same Historian speaks also: The Armies of BRUTUS and CASSIUS, that stood for Liberty, consisted of the lower sort of people, and *Ex subditis Romanorum*, the other that stood for Tyranny, consisted (saith he) *Ex Romanis Nobilibus, & Fortibus*. BRUTUS and CASSIUS, two chiefe Souldiers, before the Battell making Orations, incouraged them to fight for their ancient freedome, and Roman laws. CÆSAR and ANTONY promised to their Souldiers the Estates of their Enemies. . . . Whether the parrallel will in some measure fit this occasion or not, I leave it to the Reader. . . .[51]

For Tom May, in the rapid revolution of the times, what was once 'great *Augustus* happy Monarchy' has now become simply 'Tyranny'. A Roman parallel is still drawn as a measure of the British states, but it is now between a triumphant Parliament and the 'Liberty' of the Roman Republic. For the first time, perhaps, the republican interpretation of those distant Roman events is being used to give an evaluation of recent British history.

After the First and Second Civil Wars but before the execution of the King an Augustan parallel was again deployed, this time by a royalist, to understand and derive hope from the contemporary situation by comparison with the Roman past. This was in a Summary Discourse of the Civill Warres of Rome . . ., published in 1648 by Sir Richard Fanshaw in his collection *Il Pastor Fido . . . With Additions of divers other Poems*, and dedicated to the Prince of Wales. The work is of great interest since it follows two imitations of Horatian odes (*Carm.* III, xxiv and Epode XVI) 'relating unto the Civill Warres of Rome', and is an

---

[51]Thomas May, *The History of the Parliament of England* . . . (London, 1647), Bk III, p. 30.

historical narrative that includes a blow-by-blow political commentary on *Carm*. I, xiv, translation of two famous passages from the prophecy of Anchises in *Aeneid* VI, and a concluding depiction of Augustus as a '*Mirrour of Princes*'. The whole sequence is separately addressed to the Prince of Wales, perhaps with pedagogical intent. Taken as a whole it may be thought to make explicit much that was implicit in royalist imitation of the Augustans in this period.

It is thus that Fanshaw writes of the Civil Wars of Rome:

> Yet though this war went on, and being determined by the Battell at *Philippi*, another as dismal sprang out of the ashes of it, between the Victors themselves; this same despairing *Horace* did live to see, and particularly to enjoy, other very different *times*, when the Commonwealth, after the defeat of *Mark Anthony* at the Battell of *Actium*, being now quite tired out with civill Warres, submitted her selfe to the just and peacefull Sceptre of the most Noble *Augustus*

and he quotes and translates the fifteen lines on Augustus from *Aeneid* VI, beginning with the prophetic: 'Hic vir, hic est. . . .'. Though the passage stresses the power of Augustus, it is upon another aspect of the *princeps* that Fanshaw proceeds to lay his chief emphasis:

> . . . for this *Mirrour of Princes* I have above all others ever admired, not for his great *Victories* at home or abroad (these in themselves had been but *splendid Robberies*) but for *this*, that he directed all his *studies* and *actions* to *use*, and not to *ostentation* and *glory*; nor to his *own* use, but to the use and benefit of *Mankind*, whom it was more his Ambition to *civilize* and *make happy*, than to *subject* them to his Authority.

Fanshaw praises Augustus also for valuing a plain style of writing; and in establishing the reputation of Augustus as a civilizer he quotes the passage from Velleius Paterculus – already cited in Chapter I – and concludes with the suggestion that Anchises's famous lines on the destiny of Rome ('excudent alii spirantia mollius aera. . . . parcere subiectis et debellare superbos'), quoted as we have seen by St Augustine, James VI and Ben Jonson, would have pleased Augustus himself better than the lines (791–805) which Anchises spoke specifically in his praise.[52] The Augustus that Fanshaw invokes for the guidance of the Prince of Wales in the civil wars is recognizably the Augustus of Jonson's *Poetaster*.

May's *Continuation* and *History of the Parliament* and Fanshaw's Summary Discourse are the illuminating background to a poem by Marvell not yet fully appreciated, and of great interest for any study of the Roman parallel in seventeenth-century English writing. This is *Tom May's Death*, written, perhaps, at the very end of 1650.[53] The poet who had parallelled Charles I with Augustus in his adaptation of the Second Ode of Horace's First Book, in 1637, and had just composed *An Horatian Ode upon Cromwell's Return from Ireland*, must certainly have cast an anxious as well as ironical eye upon the literary and political career of Thomas May. Indeed, the slightly later poem is,

---

[52]Sir Richard Fanshaw, *Il Pastor Fido . . . With An Addition of divers other Poems . . .* (London, 1648), pp. 299, 310, 311–12.
[53]E.S. Donno, *The Complete Poems of Andrew Marvell*, p. 241.

as several commentators have suggested,[54] an interesting guide to Marvell's method in the *Horatian Ode* itself.

Marvell's poem, in which the newly dead Tom May encounters the shade of Ben Jonson in Elysium, is a work of comedy in which literary and political concern are closely blended, and which explores with an admirable ironic poise and a detailed artistry of couplet the question of what is truly and what is falsely Roman (and who is truly and falsely laureate). As such it is the clear precursor of a kind of poem much more commonly thought of as English Augustan than any we have yet examined, a kind best exemplified by Dryden's *Mac Flecknoe* and Pope's *Dunciad*. At the same time (though this too is in common with Dryden and Pope) it draws on the comedy of the Lucianic underworld, a Stygian atmosphere once nastily exaggerated by Jonson himself in his *Famous Voyage*, and on the sophisticated political comedy of Traiano Boccalini, in his popular and much translated *Newes from Parnassus*.[55] It is also related to those poetic addresses to Jonson written by younger members of the Tribe of Ben, in which affectionate tribute had been mingled with a certain independence of judgement. The poem is truly transitional between the earlier and the later seventeenth-century Augustan.

> As one put drunk into the packet-boat,
> Tom May was hurried hence and did not know't.
> But was amaz'd on the Elysian side,
> And with an eye uncertain, gazing wide,
> Could not determine in what place he was,
> (For whence, in Stephen's Alley, trees or grass?)
> Nor where The Pope's Head, nor The Mitre lay,
> Signs by which still he found and lost his way.
> At last while doubtfully he all compares,
> He saw at hand, as he imagined, Ayres.
> Such did he seem for corpulence and port,
> But 'twas a man of much another sort;
> 'Twas Ben that in the dusky laurel shade
> Amongst the chorus of old poets layed,
> Sounding of ancient heroes, such as were
> The subjects' safety, and the rebels' fear,
> And how a double-headed vulture eats
> Brutus and Cassius, the people's cheats.[56]

The comedy plays over both figures. The telling point is May's drunken uncertainty, and it does not have to be laboured at all. Has he ever known where he was? A good question to ask of a writer who has so much compared Britain and Rome. The image of the drunkard trying to find his way home to Stephen's

[54]J.S. Coolidge, 'Marvell and Horace' in G. de F. Lord, ed., *Andrew Marvell: A Collection of Critical Essays* (Englewood Cliffs, NJ, 1968), pp. 86–8 (first published *Modern Philology*, Nov. 1965); John Wallace, *Destiny His Choice: The Loyalism of Andrew Marvell* (Cambridge, 1968), pp. 102–5. J.M. Newton, 'Marvell – moderate or immoderate or what?' *The Cambridge Quarterly*, III, 4 (Autumn 1968), pp. 393–6.

[55]For Boccalini in England see W.F. Marquatt, 'The First English Translation of Boccalini's *Raguagli di Parnaso*', *Huntington Library Quarterly*, XV (1951).

[56]Ll. 1–18; *Complete Poems*, p. 58.

Alley by the familiar tavern signs of Pope's Head and Mitre becomes a derisive summary of his political career, first so loyal to the high Anglican Charles I, then so staunch for Parliament, now quite confused. The picture of the poet, still engaged in doubtful comparing ('Whether the parrallel will in some measure fit this occasion or not, I leave it to the Reader . . .'), but this time between Stephen's Alley and Elysium, is richly comic. His confusion about places and identities, however, permits an affectionately comic introduction of Jonson. If May is blind to the real dignity of the dead laureate, his impression of a corpulent tavern keeper sounding of ancient heroes (not such a false cartoon of Old Ben) is implanted in the reader's mind. Old Ben has not lost *his* sense of political direction; his loyalism is as strong as ever, but after this introduction it is not easy to dismiss the impression of every man in his humour, of the ruling passion strong in death in each case. The last part of Ben's 'layeing' is pointed unmistakably at May's comments on Edgehill: to the monarchist Ben, Brutus and Cassius are not defenders of liberty but 'the people's cheats', *optimates* at heart (Dio and May to the contrary) while Julius Caesar and Augustus hold the true interest of the *populares*. In singing of ancient heroes, it is implied, Ben has been singing of Caesars.

At the appearance of his confused disciple Jonson restrains his own ferocity to give him a true sign of place and identity – and a reproof:

> . . . seeing May, he varied straight his song,
> Gently to signify that he was wrong.
> 'Cups more than civil of Emathian wine,
> I sing' (said he) 'and the Pharsalian Sign,
> Where the historian of the commonwealth
> In his own bowells sheathed the conquering health.'
> By this, May to himself and them was come,
> He found he was translated, and by whom,
> Yet then with foot as stumbling as his tongue
> Pressed for his place among the learned throng.
> But Ben, who knew not neither foe nor friend,
> Sworn enemy to all that do pretend,
> Rose; more than ever he was seen severe,
> Shook his gray locks, and his own bays did tear
> At this intrusion. Then with Laurel wand –
> The awful sign of his supreme command,
> At whose dread whisk Virgil himself does quake,
> And Horace patiently its stroke does take –
> As he crowds in, he whipped him o'er the pate
> Like Pembroke at the masque. . . .[57]

Jonson's rebuke (his variation of the opening lines of May's Lucan) is, perhaps oracularly, obscure. Not the Pope or the Mitre but 'the Pharsalian Sign' (he seems to say) is the sign where May first went wrong; Lucan led him astray, made him in a new sense 'historian of the commonwealth' (author of *The History of the Parliament of England*), and the warfare which may be seen as the challenge to manly self-renewal has become the means of what in Jonson's view is May's political suicide. But May, now come to himself, is not going to

[57]Ll. 19–38; op. cit. pp. 58–9.

obey authority any more. Had he deserted the royal cause to defer to a monarch of wit? The verse now catches the comic awe at Ben's assertion of his authority, the emphatic early caesura after '/Rose;' giving a breathless pause as the master prepares to bear down on his pupil, and the polished mock-alarm of 'The awful sign of his supreme command' is adroitly qualified by 'Horace patiently its stroke does take': it is funny that Ben should tyrannize over Virgil and Horace, but if the judgement and good nature of Horace can suffer it with patience then Jonson was not entirely a false Horace while he lived. The little bit of gossip at the end of the passage (Lord Pembroke failed to recognize May at a masque before the King in 1634 and broke his staff over his shoulders) shows Marvell's embarrassing intimacy (for May) with May's earlier career.

It is by now clear that the purpose of Marvell's poem is to extend into the period of the interregnum the voice and example of the dead Jonson. Had he been alive, what would he have said of such times? If times and men change, but the truth stays the same (the epigraph from the title-page of May's *History of the Parliament of England*),[58] how would the principles of Ben be expressed in the new age? It is clear too that Jonson is fully and humanly dramatized; in the lines which follow he speaks for himself:

> Far from these blessed shades tread back again
> Most servile wit, and mercenary pen,
> Polydore, Lucan, Alan, Vandal, Goth,
> Malignant poet and historian both,
> Go seek the novice statesmen, and obtrude
> On them some Roman-cast similitude,
> Tell them of liberty, the stories fine,
> Until you all grow consuls in your wine;
> Or thou, Dictator of the Glass, bestow
> On him the Cato, this the Cicero,
> Transferring old Rome hither in your talk,
> As Bethlem's house did to Loretto walk.
> Foul architect that had not eye to see
> How ill the measures of these states agree,
> And who by Rome's example England lay,
> Those but to Lucan do continue May.
> But thee nor ignorance nor seeming good
> Misled, but malice fixed and understood.
> Because some one than thee more worthy wears
> The sacred laurel, hence are all these tears?
> Must therefore all the world be set on flame,
> Because a gazette-writer missed his aim?
> And for a tankard-bearing muse must we
> As for the basket, Guelphs and Ghib'llines be?[59]

Commentators on this poem have not hesitated to attribute all these sentiments directly to Marvell,[60] but to do so is to overlook its dramatic characterization. Jonson has recognized May from the first, and has at first tried to correct him

---

[58]'Tempora mutantur. Mutantur Homines. Veritas eadem manet.'
[59]Ll. 39–62; *Complete Poems*, p. 59.
[60]Cf. Coolidge, 'Marvell and Horace', pp. 86–7, 94.

gently. Now because May has attempted to push in, Jonson has lost his temper, or is at least throwing a stately rage, in which one scornful assault follows another. This is one of those 'immodest rage[s]'[61] for which Carew and other members of the Tribe of Ben had gently chided their master, as we may surely tell from the reckless collocation of 'Polydore, Lucan, Alan, Vandal, Goth'. Jonson had once praised Lucan, and modern commentators have been hard-pressed to find something common to all these names.[62] All they have in common is Old Ben's mounting anger and will to wound. Thus, too, when the furnace of his wrath is roaring, Jonson has no hesitation in attributing May's change of politics to intelligent malice (a conclusion certainly not endorsed by Marvell's poem as a whole), malice stemming from his disappointment at not being made laureate on Jonson's death. The sheer extravagance of the similes bears out this reading. But if Ben is in a characteristic rage, this is not to say there is no reason in it. The author of *The Poetaster* may be the last person to complain about 'transferring old Rome hither' and we may infer that (in Marvell's fiction) Ben is angry because May has used Roman comparisons to support a different political side from Jonson's own. But surely in the end it is a servile facility in drawing Roman comparisons that Ben attacks. Roman ideals, whether imperial or republican, are betrayed by glib parallels between widely different situations, a glibness evidenced in May's political *volte-face*. How easy now to 'bestow / On him the Cato, this the Cicero'! A magisterial integrity emerges from Jonson's wrath, and it is this that is felt in those lines of his diatribe which are most often wrested from their context and given directly to Marvell:

> When the sword glitters o'er the judge's head,
> And fear has coward churchmen silencèd,
> Then is the poet's time, 'tis then he draws,
> And single fights forsaken virtue's cause.
> He when the wheel of empire whirleth back,
> And though the world's disjointed axle crack,
> Sings still of ancient rights and better times,
> Seeks wretched good, arraigns successful crimes.
> But thou, base man, first prostituted hast
> Our spotless knowledge and the studies chaste,
> Apostatising from our arts and us,
> To turn the chronicler of Spartacus.
> Yet was thou taken hence with equal fate,
> Before thou couldst great Charles his death relate.[63]

Through Marvell's brilliant dramatic handling of Jonson's anger, the comedy has now risen to a genuinely heroic vein and theme, those of the poet of integrity in adverse times. Ll. 67–8 seem to recall the opening of the Third Ode of Horace's Third Book ('Iustum et tenacem . . .'), and the passage is a convincing statement of what would have been Jonson's stance had he lived into the 1640s. It may, perhaps, be suggested by Fanshaw's Summary Discourse. For him, as

---

[61]Cf. Carew's 'To Ben Jonson', ll. 24; *Poems*, p. 65.
[62]Cf. E.S. Donno, ed., *Complete Poems*, p. 242. The explanation given seems unconvincing.
[63]Ll. 63–76; *Complete Poems*, p. 59–60.

for Dryden in his later years, the Roman rôle and fidelity to the monarch were inseparable, and he sings of 'forsaken virtue's cause' and 'ancient rights' when he refers to 'great Charles his death'. The course he recommends was indeed the one taken by Herrick, that other disciple of Jonson and no coward churchman, when he wrote verses to welcome the defeated Charles back to Hampton Court as an Augustus, and published them the next year. This is the climax of Marvell's poem. Now Jonson's diatribe slowly descends into a prophecy of how the dust of Chaucer and Spenser in Westminster Abbey will itself rise to expel May, whom the regicide parliament had buried there, and finally plunges into an immoderate list of underworld punishments (including that of Brutus and Cassius) which the wretched May is now to be expelled from Elysium to suffer.

Tom May's Death is by any standard a remarkable poem, but like Marvell's better known work requires delicacy of interpretation. If its comic dramatizing of the figure of Jonson is properly considered, it will be difficult to read Jonson's speech as a carefully worked out and consistent poetic *credo* of Andrew Marvell. If the quality of the verse is to be trusted, Marvell admires the heroic integrity he endows the old master with, but Ben in Elysium, like Ben on earth, is still recognizably human, and the comedy of the poem as a whole somewhat qualifies his message for the times. We cannot infer that, in new times, the only kind of poetic integrity Marvell recognized was that of the committed royalist poet; still less may we infer from Jonson's words that Marvell thought 'Roman-cast similitudes' were to be avoided.[64] Where it is plausible to see the author of *Tom May's Death* and *An Horatian Ode* endorsing the diatribe of Old Ben is in its condemnation of facile comparison that ignores the vast cultural gulf between ages and states, and its condemnation of so facile a switch of political loyalty as leaves no coherence in a man's life. Nothing of the Augustan May of the *Continuation* lasts into the republican May of the *History of the Parliament*.

The connection between *Tom May's Death* and *An Horatian Ode* is attested by the crucial phrase 'ancient rights' in each text, and by the well recognized use of Lucan (and indeed of May's Lucan) in the *Ode*. On the assumption that, in the poem on May, Jonson is speaking directly for Marvell, it has been suggested that the later poem expresses a revulsion from the position of the slightly earlier *Ode*, or even that the *Ode* is really a crypto-Royalist poem.[65] It has also been suggested, more plausibly, that while in the later poem Marvell has condemned (through the mouth of Jonson) 'extended' Roman parallels such as May deployed, in the *Ode* he has used what we might term 'local' comparisons between Britain and Rome which 'if pursued beyond the immediately obvious grounds of comparison, lead to a reminder of "How ill the measures of these states agree".'[66] The separation between Marvell and 'Jonson' in *Tom May's*

---

[64]Coolidge, 'Marvell and Horace', argues that there is a radical difference of operation between May's and Marvell's Roman similitudes, but may exaggerate the confidence and method of May's procedure.

[65]Cf. Cleanth Brooks, *English Institute Essays* (New York, 1946); L.W. Hyman, 'Politics and Poetry in Andrew Marvell', *Publications of the Modern Languages Association*, LXXIII (Dec. 1958), pp. 475–9; John Newton, 'Marvell – moderate or immoderate or what?', and 'What Do We Know About Andrew Marvell?' – 2, *Cambridge Quarterly*, III, 4 (Autumn, 1968) and II, 2, pp. 125–35.

[66]Coolidge, 'Marvell and Horace', p. 88.

Death leaves us free to explore on its merits the question of the Horatian stance of the *Horatian Ode*.[67]

Several features of the *Ode* seem salient. Unlike Marvell's earlier Horatian Ode, this does not relate to a single text of Horace but several, and in this sense is closer to an ode such as Herrick's 'Ah, *Posthumus*! Our yeares hence flye'. Further, the simple dominance of 'Caesar' in Marvell's earlier poem is here divided and qualified: once 'Caesar' is Charles I ('And Caesar's head at last/Did through his laurels blast'), once, in qualified fashion, Cromwell ('A Caesar, he, ere long to Gaul . . .'). When we find two Caesars in one ode of Horace, as we do in I, ii, the original of Marvell's own earlier Horatian ode, they are of course Julius Caesar and Augustus. Again, though Cromwell is recognized as having killed Caesar, there is no attempt to praise him or blame him as a Brutus. The *Ode* has none of May's talk of Brutus, Cassius, 'Liberty' and 'the lower sort of people' though the circumstances would have warranted it had Marvell chosen to strike that kind of republican posture. Marvell follows 'Jonson's' precepts in *Tom May's Death* thus far. Yet the *Ode* has certainly not heeded this 'Jonson's' scorn for Lucan. Not only in his opening lines, with their allusion to the youth of Ariminum preparing to defend the Republic against the invading Julius Caesar, but in the lines on the execution of Charles with their allusion to the death of Pompey, Marvell does not hesitate to draw on the poet whom 'Jonson' angrily associated with 'Alan, Vandal, Goth'. Since the *Ode* echoes phrases from May's version it is quite likely that Marvell remembered and honoured Jonson's true character of Lucan in the commendatory poem to May. If so he would have been seeking help from both Lucan and Horace to 'Keepe due proportion' in his song.[68] That 'due proportion', I believe, is not just a matter of formal composition, though it certainly is that, but also something like impartiality of judgement. In his *Continuation* May had praised Augustus's 'happy Monarchy' but in *The History of the Parliament* Augustus means 'to bring in Tyranny'. Of course political change through seventeen momentous years prevents us from easily endorsing 'Jonson's' charge that May was no more than a mercenary and malicious turncoat. But 'due proportion' forbids the simple abandonment of older loyalties in Marvell's ambitious poetic design. The Charles whom he had once sung as the father and saviour of the kingdom, by that 'ancient right', could not just be cast off, as May had cast him off, but had to be given a due prominence and hearing in the *Ode*. As Lucan had kept a 'due proportion' between Caesar, Pompey, and Cato, so Marvell would do between Charles and Cromwell. Hence, not only his reiteration of 'ancient right', 'helpless right', and allusion to 'the kingdoms old' as 'the great work of time' (a phrase recalling the presentation of the British monarchy in masque, panegyric and speech as far back as 1604), but also his gathering up all these into his noble dramatization of Charles on the 'tragic scaffold'. In this respect the *Ode* may be seen as poising itself with great care between Herrick's position in *To The King, upon his welcome to Hampton Court* (and of 'Jonson' in *Tom*

---

[67]My treatment of the *Horatian Ode* is much in debt to a public lecture delivered by Mr G.R. Hibbard at Nottingham University in 1958, especially in regard to the relation of the *Ode* to the 37th Ode of Horace's First Book; then to R.H. Syfret, 'Marvell's Horatian Ode', *Review of English Studies*, N.S. XII (May, 1961), pp. 160–72 and Coolidge, 'Marvell and Horace'.

[68]Jonson, 'To my chosen Friend, The learned Translator of Lucan . . .', l. 12; *Ben Jonson*, VIII, p. 395.

May's Death) and that of May in the *History* or, perhaps, of James Harrington in *Oceana*.[69]

The integrity of this position (striving for comprehensiveness and coherence) brings us back to Horace. The prominence Marvell gives to Lucan in the opening allusion makes it easy to think that the *Ode* is only Horatian by virtue of several local echoes of the Odes to Augustus rather than in any structural sense. Yet this seems not to be true. J.S. Coolidge, in a discussion of the *Ode*'s use of Horace which may be thought almost definitive, rightly stresses the pervasive importance in the thought of Marvell's poem of the Horatian figures of Fortune and Necessity from the Ode on Augustus, I, xv.[70] Necessity, going before Fortune, is both destroyer and builder. *Carmina* IV, v, an ode praying for the return of Augustus, has also been cited,[71] and while there seem no verbal echoes of this ode, which is also radically different in feeling from Marvell's, it must be allowed that the title *An Horatian Ode Upon Cromwell's Return* . . . prompts us to recall odes of Horace on the return of rulers and leaders. If, by his title, Marvell wished us to remember IV, v it was so that we might compare the two poems as wholes. But the ode of Horace with which Marvell's *Ode* seems to have a special relation is the Actium Ode, I, xxxvii. The point of comparison here is not just Cromwell's victory over the Irish and Augustus's over the Egyptians, though that is apt enough when each poet seems to have had in mind an untrustworthy people of alien religion. It is that uniquely among Horace's Odes I, xxxvii describes the fall of an hereditary monarch, Cleopatra, with the victory of a Caesar, Octavian, not yet but soon to be Augustus. Here several details make the parallel apt. Horace speaks of Cleopatra plotting destruction to the Capitol and empire; transferred to the British situation this is apt for a monarch of ancient line whose rule was held to have invaded the liberties of his subjects. He speaks of the corruption and sin of her followers (Antony is not mentioned by name) and this too may have seemed to Marvell a fair reflection on the court and royalist forces. The flight of Cleopatra away from Italy is compared with Charles's escape from Hampton Court to Carisbrooke: each flight leading directly to a startling and dramatic transformation as the cunning and destructive monarch arises from duplicity to face death with royal courage. Here the *Ode* is closest of all to I, xxxvii, closest of all, surely, to any one ode of Horace. Horace was not so much the partisan of Octavian that he could not pay tribute to Cleopatra on her death; that was part of the independence of the Augustan poet, and Marvell avails himself of the same generous freedom of judgement. I, xxxvii is not only linked with Marvell's *Ode* in points of detail, but in central structure: an equal drama of the opposing destinies of radically different kinds of ruler.

These three odes of Horace, like the others cited by Marvell's editors,[72] are all odes concerned with Augustus. Certain later lines in the *Ode* begin to gather implication in the light of Marvell's title and of I, xv; I, xxxvii and IV, v:

[69]See L.D. Lerner's essay, 'Marvell: *An Horatian Ode*' in John Wain, ed., *Interpretations* (London, 1955), pp. 59–74 for a discussion of some 'poised' readings in the *Ode*.
[70]Coolidge, 'Marvell and Horace', pp. 90–2.
[71]*Complete Poems*, p. 238.
[72]Ibid., p. 238.

Nor yet grown stiffer with command,
But still in the Republic's hand. . . .

And has his sword and spoils ungirt,
To lay them at the public's skirt.[73]

In another context, these might be thought to compare Cromwell's rôle merely to that of the Roman Consul, waging war abroad on behalf of the Republic. They are open to that reading, but it is interesting that the royalist theoretician Filmer, writing about the same time as Marvell, could see the Consular system as 'an apparent kind of *Monarchy*' and speak of how 'the kingly Consuls gained all the victories abroad'.[74] Filmer, of course, cannot admire the Republic, and sees Rome as reverting to its natural and right form of government under the monarchy of Augustus. Ambitious and successful consuls could become dictators, could become *Caesars*. But ll. 89–90 seem to have particular reference to the moment when Octavian, three years after Actium, attempted to resign his powers to the Senate, and in agreeing to resume them for a further period, 'restored' the Republic, established his principate, and acquired the cognomen 'Augustus'. 'Young Octavian', as Coolidge well puts it,

> had risen to power as Julius Caesar's heir and avenger. He was wholly the creature of the Caesarian mystique, of those very forces, that is, which were irresistibly battering down the ancient structure of the Roman Republic. His achievement was, first of all, to draw those forces to himself. Octavius became Caesar. His second achievement, however, was to make himself the embodiment of all the ancient ideals of Rome, of that very structure of values which the relentless tide of Caesarian power was sweeping away. Octavius Caesar became Caesar Augustus; 'the Wars and Fortunes Son' became the restorer of temples. Thus the name of 'Caesar' came to epitomize both the ancient rights and the 'forced Pow'r' that was by its origin destructive of them. It is the most ambivalent name in history, and its ambivalence corresponds to that which Marvell found in the Horatian figure of grim Necessity.[75]

It was hard to say what Octavian was before he became Augustus. After Actium his power was nameless. For Marvell it was equally uncertain what Cromwell was. He is never called Augustus in the *Ode*. Yet at every point where the 'Horatian' of the title is pursued to an analogue in Horace – and I, xxxvii is a fair analogue – Cromwell appears a potential Augustus. The *Ode* contains this subdued but sustained parallel as a 'measure of these states', and it may now be recalled that we found no evidence in *Tom May's Death* that Marvell wrote it to ridicule the sustained Roman similitude. The *Ode* is not politically simple, nor do its classical allusions point in the same direction. Marvell sought to read the signs of a political revolution, as yet unresolved, by the light of Lucan and Horace; his poem is an amalgam of differing and potentially conflicting Roman comparisons, and the different possibilities and interpretations are held in balance by its concise formal symmetries. Yet the more the relation with Horace is probed, the more the Augustan comparison seems to be offered

---

[73]Ll. 81–2, 89–90; *The Complete Poems*, p. 57.
[74]Sir Robert Filmer, *Observations Touching Forms of Government* (London, 1652); *Patriarcha . . . and Other Political Works of Sir Robert Filmer*, ed. Peter Laslett (Oxford, 1949), p. 209.
[75]Coolidge, 'Marvell and Horace', pp. 92–3.

as a new-yet-old way of thinking about the political future, and of making sense of the recent violent disruption in British history. When, thirteen years earlier, Marvell wrote his Horatian ode to Charles I he had not made anything of the *two* Caesars in his Horatian original. In *An Horatian Ode*, which like I, ii scans an old and a nascent political state across a period of civil war, Marvell took up that ultimate Horatian challenge.

There was one other way in which this challenge was now met. The Stuart emphasis on the Augustan peace, which had increasingly led to the sense of Britain as a peaceful enclave in a warring Europe, is nowhere found in the *Ode*. Its whole spirit is rather that of the stir of events, the movement of armies, of suddenly enhanced military and political possibility:

> What may not then our isle presume
> While Victory his crest does plume?
>   What may not others fear
>   If thus he crowns each year?
> A Caesar, he, ere long to Gaul. . . .[76]

That confident sense of an expanding power and world view, often associated with the Augustan comparison in the sixteenth century, is certainly felt in Marvell's poem, and is adroitly enhanced by the way in which he slips into speaking of the Irish and the Scots as though they were really as remote to him as to Augustus bound 'in ultimos / orbis Britannos':

> The Pict no shelter now shall find . . . .

– that really is made to seem worlds away. The *Ode* measures up to Horace's Roman Odes better than anything we have found in seventeenth-century English lyric poetry. Yet it still lacks one quality which many of Horace's Odes to Augustus possess: the quality of warmth.

Monarchists and Republicans

In February 1649 the 'rump' of the Long Parliament abolished the monarchy. In December 1653 a militarily encouraged political coup terminated the Nominated Parliament and drew up the Instrument of Government in which Cromwell became Lord Protector. The basis of his power was the English Army, and England ruled the rest of Britain by virtue of Cromwell's military conquests in Ireland and Scotland. Pride's Purge, the expulsion of the Rump, and the nature of the Nominated Parliament had in any case constituted a violent disruption of parliamentary legitimacy. The 'forced power' had overwhelmed parliament, and Cromwell was certainly not now 'still in the Republic's hand'. On the contrary he had, as Clarendon was to write and as many could not fail to observe, 'mounted himself into the throne of three kingdoms, without the name of king but with a greater power and authority than had ever been exercised or claimed by any king'.[77] By this time the serious

---

[76]Ll. 96–101; *Complete Poems*, p. 57.

[77]Edward, Earl of Clarendon, *The History of the Rebellion* . . . , XIV, 26; ed. W.D. Macray (Oxford, 1888), V, pp. 287–8.

pressure from the Levellers for a social revolution – in the modern sense of a leap forward to a more egalitarian society – had been defeated. The conservative social principles contended for by Cromwell and Ireton in the Army Debates were now proclaimed to Parliament by Cromwell with quasi-monarchical authority: 'We would keep up the nobility and the gentry'.[78] If we leave aside those who, at home and abroad, hoped for a Stuart Restoration, we find two other projections of the political future of Britain. One of these envisaged the hereditary principle as not only safeguarding a social conservatism but as being re-established at the highest level. Many wished Cromwell to accept the crown and to found a new royal line. This idea was seriously considered on several occasions between 1651 and 1657 when the Humble Petition and Advice asked Cromwell to assume the crown. Some sections of the Army favoured the proposal, and Cromwell himself seriously considered it. Poets such as Waller must have thought it probable.[79]

It may be seen how crucially the Augustan comparison might help a ruler in Cromwell's situation. It was, first, familiarly associated with the celebration of Stuart monarchy. Applied to Cromwell it could gloss over conflict and differences to proclaim a superficial continuity with the past. In addition several aspects of the life of Augustus, hitherto not much exploited in comparisons with British rulers, were now relevant. Cromwell, like Augustus, had risen to power on the back of an army. Cromwell, if he assumed a crown, would not hold it by inheritance as James I and Charles I had done. Augustus was the adopted heir of Julius Caesar, but this was different from descending by primogeniture from a line of kings. In fact those who had compared James I with Augustus had been at pains to mark these differences by laying great stress on his peacefulness and promising family of children. Finally, what Bodin had emphasized in *Les Six Livres*: that the rule of Augustus was central in transforming a republic into a monarchy, could be reiterated more simply in the 1650s, for it had an obvious and immediate relevance. Thus Hobbes, in *Leviathan* (1651), not only referred *en passant* to Augustus changing the Roman state into a monarchy but, interestingly enough, noted that the only offices Augustus held in effecting this change were those of Pontifex Maximus and Tribune, 'that is to say, the supreme power both in state and religion; and the succeeding emperors enjoyed the same'.[80] At another point Hobbes pointed out that the word 'heir' does not necessarily imply child, but that an heir may be declared and designated by a monarch, as the Roman emperors did their heirs.[81] Sir Robert Filmer, from his uncompromisingly royalist standpoint, could never have endorsed a Cromwellian monarchy, yet some of his remarks in *Observations Touching Forms of Government* (1652) must have given pause to less resolved minds. Having elaborated his view that the Roman Republic was 'broken and distracted into two shews of Government', the 'Popular' at home and the 'Regal' (Consular) abroad, he could pertinently add:

This is further to be considered in the Roman government, that all the time between

[78]Christopher Hill, *God's Englishman: Oliver Cromwell and the English Revolution* (Harmondsworth, 1970), p. 197.

[79]*The Poems of Edmund Waller*, ed. G. Thorn Drury (London, 1893; new edn 1901), I, p. lxi.

[80]*Leviathan . . .*, IV, 45; ed. Michael Oakshott (Oxford, 1960), p. 433.

[81]Ibid., II, 19; ed. cit. p. 128.

their Kings, and their Emperours, there lasted a continued strife, between the nobility and Commons, wherein by degrees the Commons prevailed at last, so to weaken the authority of the Consuls and the Senate, that even the last sparks of monarchy were in a manner extinguished and then instantly began the civil war, which lasted till the Regal Power was quickly brought home, and settled in monarchy.

As Filmer put it in his *Patriarcha* (written between 1635 and 1642 but not published until 1680), 'the last refuge in perils of states, is to fly to regal authority'.[82]

Still pursuing the projection of a Cromwellian monarchy, we may note that Edmund Waller's *Panegyric to the Lord Protector* must have been written between his return from exile in France in 1652 and his presentation of the poem to Cromwell and its publication in 1655. Cromwell acknowledged the poem on 13 June of that year (seeming, in his cryptic note, to thank Waller for redeeming him from the world).[83] The previous May had seen the latest suggestion that the Protector should assume the crown. In Waller's poem the parallel of Cromwell with Augustus, tentative and subdued in *An Horatian Ode*, becomes quite explicit, and in context can only be seen as a poetic bid to close the narrowing gap between Protectorate and monarchy. Though less Augustan in form than Marvell's *Ode*, *A Panegyric* draws more fully on the potential political meaning of the Augustan parallel. Its opening stanzas insist on Cromwell's success on two major counts, which together seem to make him more of an Augustus than James or Charles had ever been. The Protector has both bridled faction at home and given Britain a world rôle. He has protected the British from themselves, denied 'partial spirits' the 'liberty' to prey on their fellows (re-establishing, it is implied, a truer liberty), and he has 'Restored' (the verb is pregnant with Roman and British meaning) his 'drooping country, torn with civil hate'. At the same time Britain is now not only 'the seat of empire' in the sense that it dominates Ireland and Scotland (that strange emphasis, also in Marvell, which makes the nation-state seem more like Augustan Rome by suggesting that its subordinate kingdoms are only now acknowledging its sway), but by virtue of Cromwell's forward foreign and maritime policy has a vastly expanding power in the world. Waller's hyperbole leaps the gap between the world power of the Augustan empire and the expanding power of one of its small successor states:

> The sea's our own; and now all nations greet,
> With bending sails, each vessel of our fleet;
> Your power extends as far as winds can blow,
> Or swelling sails upon the globe may go.[84]

These are Waller's opening propositions about Cromwellian Britain. The Augustan comparison is unmistakably implied but not yet explicit. In the central sections of the poem Waller enters into more detail, and in a flight of extravagance enhances Cromwell's heroic status by suggesting that a world hidden from the conquests of Alexander had been left for Cromwell to tame: it is Scotland again, and enables the poet to return, by way of Hadrian's Wall, to

---

[82]Filmer, *Patriarcha . . .*, ed. Laslett, pp. 210, 87.
[83]*The Poems of Edmund Waller*, I, p. lxi.
[84]Ll. 17–20; op. cit. II, p. 10.

the conquests of Rome. Scottish members of Parliament now sat at Westminster;

> So kind dictators made, when they came home,
> Their vanquished foes free citizens of Rome.[85]

Reference to the proto-monarchical power of the Roman dictators carries the parallel forward to the genuine splendour of the conclusion:

> Still as you rise, the state, exalted too,
> Finds no distemper while 'tis changed by you;
> Changed like the world's great scene! when, without noise,
> The rising sun night's vulgar lights destroys.
>
> Had you, some ages past, this race of glory
> Run, with amazement we should read your story;
> But living virtue, all achievements past,
> Meets envy still, to grapple with at last.
>
> This Caesar found; and that ungrateful age,
> With losing him fell back to blood and rage;
> Mistaken Brutus thought to break their yoke,
> But cut the bond of union with that stroke.
>
> That sun once set, a thousand meaner stars
> Gave a dim light to violence, and wars,
> To such a tempest as now threatens all,
> Did not your mighty arm prevent the fall.
>
> If Rome's great senate could not wield that sword,
> Which of the conquered world had made them lord,
> What hope had ours, while yet their power was new,
> To rule victorious armies, but by you? . . . .
>
> As the vexed world, to find repose, at last
> Itself into Augustus' arms did cast;
> So England now does, with like toil oppressed,
> Her weary head upon your bosom rest.[86]

Many poems of the 1650s are poetic attempts to read the signs of the age. In times of such revolutions and uncertainty it is hardly surprising. *Tom May's Death* laughed at one writer whose reading of the signs (Pope, Mitre, Pharsalia) appeared hopelessly drunken and confused. *An Horatian Ode* was a serious attempt to read the signs, giving due weight to all claims and possibilities. On at least one occasion, *Carmina* I, ii, the original of Marvell's earlier Horatian ode, Horace had used a poem in the same way. Waller's poem is not in the direct tradition of Horace's Roman Odes, but of the verse panegyrics of Claudian. Its difference is due to its different literary descent and the clearer political situation. Waller reads the signs confidently, as they are set out in the early stanzas, and the interpretation, clinched in the simile of the stanza last-quoted, is coherent and simple. The total poem deploys the Augustan parallel to take the

[85]Ll. 95–6; *Poems*, II, p. 14.
[86]Ll. 141–60, 169–72; *Poems*, II pp. 16–17.

measure of the time and state, and concludes that a crown has certainly been earned though it may not be bestowed[87] – Augustus had been *princeps* but not king.

If we set Waller's *Panegyric* against a formally comparable English poem, such as Drummond's *Forth Feasting*, we shall see how the cloudy grandeur of the earlier poem has been replaced by a striking clarity of political insight, which tells us that parliament, like the Roman senate in the last years of the Republic, could not control its armies, and that Cromwell rose because, commanding the armies, he alone could unite the state and assert its power abroad. The clarity is, however, bought at the price of a less full interpretation of the times than Marvell gave in his *Ode*. In these stanzas Julius Caesar and Brutus do not appear to have English counterparts. They are part of the Roman background designed to show that, whatever likenesses there may or might have been between them and Cromwell (he too met envy at the last; he too 'cut the bond of union'?)[88] it is with Augustus and only with Augustus that Cromwell must now be identified.

The alternative projection of Britain's future, that of those who hoped to see a genuinely republican government evolve, may be represented by James Harrington. His *Commonwealth of Oceana*, after *Leviathan* perhaps the most significant body of new political thought in the period, appeared in 1656. This remarkable political romance, in which *Oceana* is Britain, and the Lord Archon, Olphaus Megaletor, Cromwell, proposes a political model for the country based more than any other modern state on Venice. It includes electoral procedures governed by the ballot, and the balance of property, in which Harrington saw the secret of the stability of states, and is governed by an Agrarian Law. Harrington was profoundly influenced by Italian political thought; not only by Machiavelli, who has perhaps never been so powerfully present in English political philosophy as he is in *Oceana*, but also by subsequent Italian political thinkers and historians: Donato Gianotti, Gasparo Contarini and Traiano Boccalini. It is with Machiavelli and Boccalini that we are briefly concerned here. Harrington strongly endorsed Machiavelli's view of the first emperors as betrayers of Roman liberty. He wished Cromwell to be *pater patriae* indeed, but not by founding a new monarchy. Rather he hoped that Cromwell's single power and immense prestige might be used to establish a lasting republic in Britain. *Oceana* expounds the principles of this republic, and tells how the Lord Archon resolves to give the new constitution to his country, and hand back liberty to its people. During the latter part of these transactions, after Philadelphus, Secretary of the Council, had read out in the Council the several Orders epitomizing the new Commonwealth, he happened to open a packet from his correspondent Boccalini, 'Secretary of *Parnassus*', and at once broke out in 'a violent passion of weeping'. When Lord Archon and the others ask what is the matter, Philadelphus reads aloud his News from Parnassus. It tells how Phoebus

> having taken the nature of free states into his royal consideration, and being steadily persuaded that the laws in such Governments are incomparably better . . . than in any

---

[87]LI. 181–8; *Poems*, II p. 17; Garrison, *Dryden and the Tradition of Panegyric*, pp. 126–8.
[88]See T.R. Langley, 'Abraham Cowley's "Brutus": Royalist and Republican', *Yearbook of English Studies*, VI (1976), pp. 41–52.

other . . . conceived such a loathing of their ambition and tyranny, who usurping the liberty of their native countries, become slaves to themselves . . . assembled all the senators residing in the learned court at the theater of Melpomene, where he caused Caesar the dictator to come upon the Stage, and his Sister Actia, his Nephew Augustus, Julia his daughter, with the children she had by Marcus Agrippa, Lucius, and Cajus Caesars, Agrippa Posthumus, Julia and Agrippina, with the numerous progeny which she bare unto her renowned husband Germanicus, to enter. A miserable scene in any, but most deplorable in the eies of Caesar, thus beholding what havock his prodigious ambition, not satisfied with his own bloody ghost, had made upon his more innocent Remains, even unto the total extinction of his family. . . . Now might the great soul of Caesar have been full; and yet that which powred in as much or more, was to behold that execrable race of the Claudii, having hunted, and sucked his blood with the thirst of tygars, to be rewarded with the Roman Empire, and remain in full possession of the famous patrimony: A spectacle to pollute the light of heaven.

This daunting political tableau of the punishment of usurpers is matched by a complementary scene drawn from the history of modern Italy, for

his Phaebean majesty caused to be introduced on the other side of the theater, the most illustrious and happy prince Andrea Doria, with his dear posterity, imbraced by the soft and constant arms of the city Genoa, into whose bosome, ever fruitful in her gratitude, he had dropp'd fair liberty like the dew of heaven, which when the Roman tyrant beheld, and how much more fresh that Lawrel was worn with a root in the hearts of the people, than that which hee had torn off; he fell into such horrid distortion of limbs . . . that the senators . . . covered their faces with their large sleeves.[89]

The Lord Archon takes the heavy hint of 'witty Philadelphus', observing that Caesar could not rule but by that part of man which is the beast, but that the true monarch of a commonwealth is God, since reason is her sovereign power.

This is a curious moment in *Oceana*. The political content of the passage from Boccalini is naive, its morality unsubtle. A republican providence has punished usurpers through their posterity. Harrington was too sophisticated an analyst of class and wealth in society to think that 'the liberty of their native Countryes' was an indivisible quality: too shrewd not to ask how much liberty, for whom, and at whose expense? And Boccalini was too sophisticated a neo-Machiavellian, too familiar with the monarchical Europe of the Counter-Reformation, to think long in terms of such crude moral opposites. In fact when read in context in *The News from Parnassus* the passage has something of a teasing quality. Boccalini's rôle in this delightfully fresh and intelligent work is that of the politically initiated 'fool' to the monarchs of Counter-Reformation Europe. In a mode of such prevailing degagé irony, the simplicity with which Andrea Doria is preferred to Julius Caesar is agreeably provocative: it makes a serious political point but not without a certain suggestion of news from nowhere − which indeed it is. *Oceana*, though by no means without humour, does not share this tone. Harrington wishes finally to clarify the political issues before the Lord Archon does what Augustus (so Harrington would argue) only pretended to do: give back liberty to the people. This is the function of the

[89]*The Political Works of James Harrington*, ed. G.C.A. Pocock (Cambridge, 1977), pp. 337–8.

historical tableaux from Boccalini in *Oceana*. The passage clarifies the relation between monarchical ideas and those who like Harrington advocated, not a new monarchy, but a gentry republic. That Cromwell should have responded with warmth to Waller's *Panegyric* but with suspicion to *Oceana* (which is what the scanty evidence we have suggests) would also suggest the Augustan course on which the uncrowned *princeps* of Britain considered himself bound.[90]

One reason why Harrington advocated a republic on the pattern of Venice but governed by both Ballot and Agrarian Law ('The Agrarian by the ballance of dominion preserving equality in the Root, and the ballot by an equal rotation conveying it into the branch, or exercise of soveraigne power . . .')[91] was that he believed that a state so constituted would be proof against corruption and decay. A crucial argument against the Roman Empire as a political model was that successive emperors failed to control the balance of property which alone could have preserved the state from decline. In his *Essay Upon two of Virgil's Eclogues, And Two Books of his Æneis . . .* (1658), a pedagogical work perhaps comparable to Fanshaw's Summary Discourse but written from a republican point of view, Harrington adroitly uses the First and Ninth Eclogues to support his case. Responding to the poems entirely as social documents, he uses them to show how Augustus, after his victory at Actium (as Harrington assumes), rewarded his soldiers with the lands of Cremona and Mantua 'meerly because' the inhabitants of Cremona 'had quartered his enemies, whom they were not able to resist' and, since the lands of Cremona were insufficient for his present purpose, 'diuided those of *Mantua* after the same manner, for no other reason then that *Mantua* was neerest *Cremona*'. Hence Tityrus's (Virgil's) loss of his lands, and their restoration by the god (Augustus). Harrington writes slightly though probably justly of Augustus in these remarks, but he is much more interested in how such settlements were part of a process that was fatal to the stability of Rome. His view is propounded in a series of formal queries:

1 Whether *Tarquine* made not such havock of the *Roman* Nobility, as left the advantage of the ballance of Dominion ten for one in the people? And whether this did not inevitably tend unto the generation of the Commonwealth?

2 Whether the Nobility when they overcame, under *Sylla*, held not the advantage of the ballance ten for one against the people? And whether this did not inevitably tend unto the generation of Monarchy?

3 Whether *Sylla* did not plant forty seven Legions, or one hundred and twenty thousand Veteranes in *Italy* upon Lands taken in the war? Whether this president were not followed by the *Triumvirs* first, then by *Augustus Caesar*, as in these Eclogues? and whether this were not the ballance of the *Roman* Monarchy?

4 Whether such Lands confer'd upon the Souldery came not to be called benefices, and the encumbents beneficiaries? and whether the policy of the Turkish *Timars* (a word of the same signification) be not hence derived?

5 Whether *Alexander Severus* were not the first that granted such benefices unto the next heirs of the incumbents, but upon condition they should continue to serve the Emperor in war . . .?

[90]This was the conclusion of S.B. Liljegren, in his edn of *Oceana* (Heidelberg, 1924), p. 227. Pocock, *Political Works of James Harrington*, pp. 7–14, argues that it was the printers of the book who were suspect.

[91]Ibid., p. 231.

6 Whether Constantine the Great were not the first that made these benefices . . . hereditary.

7 Whether the ballance being thus ruined, the *Roman* Empire subsisted otherwise then by stipendiating strangers or mercenaries, as the *Goths* and *Vandals*?

8 Whether this were not the means by which the *Goths* and *Vandals* came to ruine the *Roman* Empire?

9 Whether the *Goths* and *Vandals* having ruined the *Roman* Empire, did not by their policy place the over ballance of Dominion in their Nobility? and whether this were not the original of government by King, Lords, and Commons, throughout Christendom?[92]

Harrington has thus used the two Augustan poems as texts for his sermon on the instability, decline and fall of the Roman state. His overview of Roman history not only says something more interesting about Augustus than simply designating him a usurper of liberty, but clearly links Roman precedent and Roman errors with the Britain of the late 1650s. It was in the quixotic hope that Britain might cease to aspire toward the example of Augustan Rome, and instead break out of the recurring cycles of unequal power into a new political economy, that *Oceana* and its subsequent supporting pamphlets were written.

To compare James I, Charles I and Cromwell, with Augustus, however consciously within the tradition of *laudando praecipere*, required an exercise of the analogical imagination. Underlying this exercise was usually the assumption that history falls into recurrent cycles, and this view might in turn take different forms, from the poetic and mystical, often deriving from Virgil's Fourth Eclogue, to the relatively more analytic, such as Filmer's account of how Rome returned to monarchy under Augustus, or Harrington's virtually cyclical account of the vicissitudes of Rome between Tarquin and the Goths. Closely connected are notions of divinely and naturally right forms of government; both Bodin and Filmer saw a reversion to a natural and providential form of rule with the principate of Augustus, though Harrington hardly seeks this kind of metaphysical endorsement for his preferred form of government. But it is clear that analogy may be drawn, not just between two points in history but between political and metaphysical. Two pamphlets of 1659, each using analogies with Augustus, and each opposing the other in regard to its preferred form of government and to the validity of analogical thought, illustrate the issue particularly well. The first is Henry Daubeney's *Historie & Policie Re-Viewed* . . . , an elaborately structured work whose salient feature is the comparison of Cromwell with Moses. A minor feature is a series of parallels between Cromwell and Augustus: Cromwell's 'glorious perstringent aspect' is likened to that with which '*Octavianus Cæsar*' confronted the assassin 'and with the vigour (almost celestial) of his Majestick eyes, thunder-strook the villaine . . .';[93] Cromwell obeyed a dream and saved his life, like Augustus at Philippi; God protected Moses, Cromwell (the second Moses), Alexander, Julius Caesar and Augustus Caesar ('who was to be as glorious in his Victories, and a greater Instrument of Divine Wonders, than any, except this his happy Parallel'); Edmund Waller was

---

[92]*An Essay . . .*, n.p.
[93]Cf. Suetonius, *De Vitae Cæsarvm*, Divvs Avgvstvs, 79; Sir Thomas Elyot, *The Boke Named the Governour*, ed. H.H.S. Croft, III, p. 16.

the Virgil to Cromwell's Augustus.[94] Daubeney's conception of Augustus is of a traditional kind. There is no hint of the Tacitean or Machiavellian viewpoint (though he is aware of Machiavelli and advances some standard criticisms) and a quotation from Nicephorus early in the work, combined with his presentation of Augustus as an 'Instrument of Divine Wonders', shows that this author is closer to the Christian providential view than to the clear political insight of Waller.

Daubeney is, however, on the defensive in regard to the whole method of drawing parallels of this kind. Perhaps the most interesting passage is his Epistle to the Reader, where he denies that his work is 'a meer counterscarp of flattery' and asserts that it is in every part 'a solid Brestwork of truth', citing many precedents for his approach: there has been a 'compleat Parallel' between *Elias* and Dr *Luther*' and between '*Elisha*, and Mr. *Calvin*'. Not only have such parallels been made of divines, 'but many Parallels we finde in Print, between some of our late Kings, how well deserving I say not; and some of those holy Princes, and Prophets of Gods own people, as *David, Solomon, Josiah, Hezekiah*, &c. and one very expresse Parallel, between Queen *Elizabeth* of famous Memory, and that great Princesse and Prophetesse *Deborah*. Then why should not our late incomparable Prince, and Protector stand as well placed in line Parallel, with that glorious Patriarch *Moses*?'[95] Daubeney does not defend himself by the *laudando praecipere* principle, and implicitly admits that parallels between 'some of our late Kings' and princes and prophets of Scripture may have been undeserved. He is defending his procedures as a way of interpreting the times, and it was perfectly natural that men accustomed to guide their lives by the Scriptures and seek the hand of God in their own history should make such comparisons. It is not surprising that men familiar with at least the broad outlines of Roman history should do the same, and simultaneous comparison with Moses and the providential Augustus is much less extravagant in seventeenth-century terms than it may seem to us. Moses, Lycurgus and Augustus figured in the political writings of the age as lawgivers and founders of states; Moses and Augustus (the parallels need not be elaborated) could be seen as having led their people out of danger into the enjoyment of a new dispensation under God.

The second 1659 pamphlet is William Spriggs's *A Modest Plea for an Equal Common-wealth*. . . . Spriggs appears to have been a more or less Harringtonian republican; certainly he is unattracted by any kind of monarchical rule, including that exemplified in the Protector as a kind of holy *princeps*. Spriggs has a sober and sardonic manner, and dismisses those interpreting and unifying procedures of the analogical imagination, whether historical or metaphysical, as 'loose and allusive' argument:

> As for those poetical if not profane flourishes wherewith Oratours and Poets, the constant parasites of Princes, use to guild ore Monarchy, pretending it the most natural and rational of all other Forms of Government, and that whose Pattern was first shown in the Mount, or rather let down from Heaven, paralelling it with Gods *Regimen* of the Universe, which is alledg'd as it[s] prototype or first *Exemplar*,

---

[94]Daubeney, *Historie & Policie Re-viewed* . . ., pp. 13, 38, 41, and 207–8 respectively. I am indebted to Mr. R.G. Knowles of the University of Reading for drawing my attention to this work.
[95]Ibid., sig. A3–4.

and therefore to have something more of a divine right and character impres'd upon it than any other, &c.

These I say are such trite, bald and slight reasonings, that they do not merit so much respect as to receive an answer; for may we not as well by this loose and allusive way of arguing borrow a pattern from Heaven for the *Triumvirate*, that *Augustus Lepidus* and *Marc. Antony* sometime impos'd on *Rome*. Doth it not as well quadrate with the Sacred Trinity, by the triple Sceptre of whose divine providence the Empire of the world is administred, as by theirs sometime that of the *Romans*?[96]

This strikes at the root of Renaissance analogical thought. It makes a recognizably modern appeal, and if we grant his premises many of the arguments for monarchy as we have found them, for example, in Elyot and Filmer, fall to the ground. The same is true of a great part of the political thought of James I (especially the 1604 Speech from the throne). More obliquely, this view questions the providential rôle of Augustus. Logically it need not undermine the use of historical comparison to understand the times, yet the whole polemic against 'Oratours and Poets', their 'profane flourishes' and 'loose and allusive way of arguing' seems to reflect disapprovingly upon that many-stranded tradition of historical interpretation and literary practice which has been the subject of this chapter.

That tradition also includes Jonson's *Poetaster* and 1604 Entry, poems to the king by Drummond, Carew and Herrick, poems on or to Cromwell by Marvell and Waller, and much connected writing. It was a tradition perhaps doomed but not yet dead. Indeed the peculiar human and artistic interest of much courtly, satiric and dramatic writing of the Restoration period arises from the fact that its most gifted writers – Dryden above all – are both hopefully within yet cynically outside this tradition. Yet at the heart of the tradition, more vital I believe than panegyric on the model of Claudian, is the imitation of the poets of Augustan Rome, a practice which by 1660 had half its course in English letters still to run. Far from mere loose allusion, this mode constituted an intimate, precise and creative dialogue between ancient and modern, alert to difference and similarity alike, and yet rested, implicitly or explicitly, casually or deliberately, upon assumptions of historical recurrence from which analogical interpretation of the times was still a natural product, and of which Daubeney's pamphlet was an extravagant and Marvell's *Ode* a supremely intelligent manifestation. It is therefore appropriate to end this chapter, as my history reaches the year of the Stuart Restoration, with a poem on that event which is both an imitation of Horace and an Ode to Augustus, an Horatian Ode very different from Marvell's *Horatian Ode*, yet no less part of the Augustan idea as it manifested itself in English poetry.

Both Daubeney's and Spriggs's pamphlets had appeared after the death of the Lord Protector. Harrington's Olphaus Megaletor had died without establishing an equal republic; Marvell's, Waller's and Daubeney's *princeps* had not, fortunately for Britain, left behind a Tiberius in Richard Cromwell. That 'young gentleman' who 'never drew sword for the commonwealth'[97] could not control the Army. As Richard's parliament was succeeded by the recall of the

[96]William Spriggs, *A Modest Plea* . . ., p. 14.
[97]Godfrey Davies, *The Restoration*, p. 237.

Rump and his own effective abdication, more and more wanted stable civilian rule of some kind, yet civilian authority still yielded to ambitious though ill-organized military power. Government foundered, and this it is that must be remembered if we want to grasp the full contemporary force of the word 'restore'. Waller had praised Cromwell for restoring the 'drooping country, torn with civil hate'; Cromwell, it has been noted, 'was always "hugely taken with the word settlement" '.[98] Many Englishmen – all perhaps except the Levellers and principled Republicans – longed for a restoration before the Restoration, and many had hoped to see Cromwell finally bring it about. Thus beyond the precise sense of the return of the Stuarts, the word 'restoration' had deeper, more powerful, and no doubt more conflicting meanings than it is easy to express today. It had something to do with the re-establishment of civilian rule, something to do with a lasting civil order, something to do with assuring the position of the landed gentry. It had something to do with regaining contact with the past: not black reaction, but a gradual growing away from old ways rather than a violent disruption. These concerns were perhaps widely shared. For those of Clarendon's persuasion, moderate royalists, it meant the re-establishment of the rule of law under God; for dispossessed divines it meant the regaining of their benefices and the bringing back of episcopacy; for royalist exiles it meant the repossession of their estates. By comparison with all this the actual return of Charles Stuart to the throne of his fathers may seem a detail; in one sense it was. Yet the return of the King was the symbol and theoretical guarantee of all the rest, and his peaceful accession, more even than that of James I, was an event sufficiently remarkable to form a new focus of the nation's hopes.

It is the achievement of the forgotten biblical scholar and poet, Alexander Huish (1594–1668), publishing in May 1660 as 'Musa Ruralis', to have captured the deeper feeling of the word 'restore' in his close Latin and English imitations of the most mature and beautiful of all Horace's Odes to Augustus, the Fifth Ode of the Fourth Book, written when the *princeps* was expected to return to Rome after three years' absence, 16–13 BC, in Gaul and Spain.[99] An ode on Augustus's return from distant provinces of the empire, it is also retrospectively about what his 'restoration' of the republic meant to Horace. Like Marvell in *Ad Regem Carolum Parodia*, Huish presents a Latin text as close as possible to that of Horace, 'pauculis immutatis' as he says, and picks out the changed words by italicization, thus recognizing typographically the similarity and difference in his relation with the original. His English version, which I quote, is a moderately free rendering of his Latin:

> Sprung from great Kings and good, Thou of the rest,
> Great *Britanes* greatest *Steward*, hop't the best;
> Long is thy absence from thy native home:
>   Come; thy great Councell bids thee, come.
>
> Restore thy Country her lost light, good King;
> Thine own sweet face, which since like lovely Spring
> W'have hop't to see, the day hath merrier gone,
>   The Sun hath brighter, better shone.

[98]Christopher Hill, *God's Englishman*, p. 173.
[99]Eduard Fraenkel, *Horace*, pp. 440, 434.

Look how a Mother her dear Child awaits.
Who is a voyage gone beyond the *Streights*,
Whom surly winds more then a long years space
   Deteins from his sweet dwelling place;

She look's, and vow's, and pray's; and ne're gives o're;
Nor turns her face from the creeke-winding shore:
Struck so with fealty and loves holy fires,
   Thy Country Thee, her *Charles* desires.

Hoping, the Ox shall freely walk again;
Plenty and peace, Thou reigning, now shall reign;
Merchants shall without danger passe the Seas;
   Faith shall not now fear to displease.

The chast house shall with no shame be defil'd;
Manners and Laws foul sin shall tame; the Child
Like born shall yield the Mother praises true;
   And punishment all vice subdue.

Who shall need fear or forreign Enemies,
Or tumults rais'd by home-bred Sectaries,
Whiles *Charles* is safe? who shalt by help of God
   Keep peace with *Spain* and all abroad.

Each one then lying under his own Vine,
The Widow Trees shall with her branches twine;
Then to the Temple go, and pray for thee,
   And all the Royall Progenee.

With prayers all true hearts, and some in verse,
As I do now, they shall thy name rehearse,
Wishing thee glorious in thy Royall seat,
   As *France*'s *Charles*, more good, more great.

Long mayst thou live, and make long holy-day,
Good King, unto thy Country: 'tis the lay,
We fasting sing and full; at morn, at night,
   When the clear sky hath lost her light.[100]

Without infidelity to his original Huish gives his key-word: 'Restore' prominence at the opening of his second stanza. Horace's corresponding line: 'lucem redde tuae, dux bone, patriae' ('[your] light give again, good leader, to your country') yields 'Restore' for 'redde' quite naturally, but the English syntax gives it a greater prominence, and though Suetonius used Horace's word in speaking 'de reddenda reipublicae' ('of the restoration of the republic'),[101] the choice of this English word carries a wealth of contemporary political and social meaning that 'give again' would not have done. In an imitation of an ode to Augustus, it inevitably recalls the 'restoration' achieved by Augustus, perhaps too that which Waller and others hoped for from Cromwell as Augustus. Huish's line shows the peculiar advantage of being able to express this particular

[100]Musa Ruralis, *In Adventum Augustissimi Principis & Monarchiae, Caroli II . . .* [20 May] *1660. Ode. Ex Horat. Car. lib. 4. Ode 5. pauculis immutatis.* [B.L. Thomason Tracts E. 765 (12)], pp. 7–8.
[101]Horace, *Carm.* IV, v, 5; Suetonius, *De Vitae Cæsarum*, Diuus Avgvstvs, 28.

juncture of historical affairs in a poem, for the image of light, heightened here to 'lost light', may convey many different things. Salient in what it expresses must be the notion of kingship as the sun and, harmoniously with this, light as a guide that the nation has lost. Charles's return, like that of Augustus in Horace, is assimilated into a natural pattern. The image of 'lost light' carries us forward to the end of the poem, where Huish appears to be doing something different and more complex than Horace. Like Horace in his last line: 'cum sol Oceano subest' ('when the sun sinks beneath the ocean'), he seeks 'a fine diminuendo',[102] yet 'When the clear sky hath lost her light' gives us a different visual impression, and does of course recall the 'lost light' of the earlier stanza. Huish is saying a little more than (to paraphrase Horace): 'so we pray, dry at dawn, and refreshed at sunset'; is it possible that with his introduction of 'the clear sky' (not in Horace), he asks us to envisage that moment when, though the sun has set the sky still holds some light? Huish reads the political situation back into nature at the end of his poem, though he does so with delicacy, and 'the clear sky' is perhaps the poised image of a moment when the king has not yet returned but the way for his return is clear.

It is not only in the image of light that the naturalness of the ruler's return is conveyed. Fraenkel, speaking of Horace's Ode, notes how the 'solemn invocation' of its opening is succeeded ('abes nam nimium diu' − 'too long already have you been away') by a 'kind of language, direct, sad, and with a faint tinge of reproach, which a mother would use in addressing a son for whom she is longing';[103] and this anticipates the extended simile and unbroken period of stanzas 3 and 4 'within which not even the slightest pause is permissible'. Huish surely manages this development movingly. 'Long is thy absence from thy native home' has the right kind of simplicity, and as if to strengthen its bond with what is to come 'home' has been transposed from the end of stanza 3 where Horace used 'a domo', and the expanded synonym 'sweet dwelling place' inserted there instead. Huish probably allows himself too marked a pause at the end of this stanza to give Horace's full effect in which 'the endless longing is pictured in the unbroken period that seems to extend like the curve of the seashore',[104] but he has surely caught much of the feeling, whereby the curving shore seems poignantly to encompass distance in both space and time; and adds something further, for the beautiful 'creek-winding' is appropriate to the strange turnings of events in consequence of which Charles was to return. There follows 'the staccato of eight short primary sentences' like a summary, yet something very compact and solid, a primitiveness of straightness and strength, as Fraenkel has said.[105] Again, though Huish permits himself one *enjambement* that is not in Horace, that sense of bold and feelingful assertion is well conveyed.

From these assertions of a safe, prosperous and decent civil life, turned by Huish from statement of fact to assertions of hope, Horace in a characteristic movement contrasted danger on the remote frontiers of the empire from which Augustus was returning with the most intimately domestic activity. Huish,

[102]Fraenkel, *Horace*, p. 448.
[103]Ibid., p. 442.
[104]Ibid., p. 443.
[105]Ibid., p. 443.

adapting his original to English circumstances, partly breaks down this contrast, which had been equally divided between stanzas 7 and 8, substituting for the Parthian enemy 'home-bred Sectaries'. In turning Horace's 'quis ferae / bellum curet Hiberiae?' ('who would care about the war in wild Spain?') to the politically relevant 'Keep peace with Spain . . .'. Huish exploited one of those happy coincidences of reference which were to be such a sharp and startling feature of Pope's *Imitations of Horace*. We can only speculate as to the full meaning of stanza 8 for a dispossessed Anglican clergyman. Horace's lines on the serenity of working one's own land (actually a diminishing possibility in Augustan Rome) are thrown into a different light by Huish's substitution of 'Temple', that is church, for 'vina', feast, and there may have been some religious suggestiveness for him in the notion of training his own vine to the 'Widow Trees' (a very close rendering of Horace). We are reminded of his pointing of Horace's 'culpari metuit fides' ('faith shrinks from blame') by 'Faith shall not now fear to displease' which must have had religious as well as political meaning at this time. The note of prayer now mounts to a conclusion in which Horace combines solemnity with simplicity and warmth: the poet joins in the prayer of the nation, a fully communal prayer. The communal nature of Horace's verb 'dicimus' ('we pray') has already been gracefully pointed by Huish in his variation of the preceding stanza ('. . . and some in verse, / As I do now . . .') and again it seems, to me at least, that the English poem marvellously captures the blend of solemn invocation and natural simplicity and warmth that is required:

> Long mayst thou live, and make long holy-day,
> Good King, unto thy Country . . .

Huish's Horatian Ode has a simpler relation with Horace than Marvell's *Ode*. It follows one poem of Horace alone, and is more intimate with that than Marvell's *Ode* with any Horatian text. There is a deeper Horatian identification in the later poem. It is thus worth stressing that Huish's ode really is an imitation, not just a well-paced and authentic English translation in the manner of Jonson and Herrick. Huish quietly measures a distinct though not great distance from Horace: Charles is sprung from 'great Kings and good' not from 'the good gods'; 'Romulae / custos gentis' ('guardian of the race of Romulus') is brilliantly rendered by 'Great Britaine's greatest Steward' with its allusion to 'Stuart'; 'home-bred sectaries' are aligned with foreign enemies; Charles is not, like Augustus, prayed to as a god in the eighth stanza but, something much more familiar and English, he will be prayed for in the churches, which can only mean the still forbidden Book of Common Prayer. He is not compared with Hercules, since all suggestions of ruler-worship are converted, but with Charles the Great of France. These and other, more subtle, features ('the clear sky') attest to the autonomy of this imitation of Horace as an English poem. Huish's ode has neither the martial verve of Marvell's *Ode*, nor its extraordinary poetic virtuosity, nor the many-eyed alertness of its response to the revolution of the times. It does not possess the dramatic tension which arises from conflicting loyalty and the integrity which resolves to give the two conflicting figures their due. Marvell's was the ode of a nation in conflict; Huish's is more like the ode of a nation in consent. It certainly is a lesser poem than Marvell's. Yet, forgotten as it has been, it can stand comparison with Marvell's as a poem deploying the Augustan parallel as a measure of the British situation at a later and very different moment from that dramatized in *An Horatian Ode*. It is with other poems on the Restoration that Huish's Horatian ode may most revealingly be compared. If we remember Evelyn's moving reflection on the peaceful Restoration ('I stood in the Strand and beheld it, and blessed God . . .'),[106] we shall, I believe, be able to think of no poem on the Restoration which better measures up to that moment. For what the moment demanded was the warmth with which Horace could address Augustus, a quality undemanded and singularly lacking in Marvell's *Ode*, but which Huish conveys with a moving simplicity and naturalness. By comparison with it better known poems on the Restoration – Dryden's *Astraea Redux*, Waller's *To the King. Upon His Majesties Happy Return* – notable as they are, seem meretricious.

---

[106] *The Diary of John Evelyn*, ed. E.S. De Beer (Oxford, 1955), I, 246 (29 May 1660).

VIII Dryden and the Augustan Idea

> Of ancient prudence here he ruminates,
> Of rising kingdoms, and of falling states;
> What ruling arts gave great Augustus fame . . .
> (Edmund Waller, *On St James's Park* . . .)

Restoration Panegyric

The restoration of Charles II, the event which literary historians have considered as marking the beginning of an English Augustan Era, in fact marks nothing of the kind. Jonson had proposed an Augustan cultural programme before the death of Elizabeth, while to recall the English monarchs likened to Augustus is to recognize a practice which, however varying, binds the eighteenth century together with the seventeenth and sixteenth. Hitherto, perhaps, the Augustan idea had more complexity in political than in literary contexts. When used to propose a political ideal it always commended monarchy, but could adapt almost equally well to a *rex pacificus* ruling by hereditary right, as to a Cromwellian *princeps* controlling faction and an expanding empire by force of arms. When used, as Harrington used it, to warn, it could highlight the advantages of a republic. In its literary aspect the idea may be thought to comprise the values of Jonsonian literary criticism. Here it was less complex since while men were ready to challenge the example of Augustus as a political model, they did not much question the validity as literary models of Virgil and Horace. The gap between Augustan achievement and modern practice was doubtless recognized, but the evolution of literary forms whose specific life was the recognition of that space was to be the coming century's own achievement. This together with the catholic mind and eclectic practice of Dryden, one of the two or three dominant figures of the later seventeenth century, gradually imparts a new critical complexity to our concept of Augustan writing.

On the face of it, then, there was nothing notably new in Dryden's praising the restored Charles as a new Augustus in *Astraea Redux* in 1660. It was no neo-classical innovation. There was no uniquely appropriate conjuncture of events. On the other hand it should not be thought that *Astraea Redux* is just one of a hundred panegyrics conventionally hailing the returning monarch as an Augustus. While I make no claim to exhaustive investigation, the Thomason Tracts in the British Library enable us to make rough estimates at least of the writings of that time. Thomason kept nearly everything. To trace the obviously political titles he purchased between July 1659 and July 1660 is to mark the growing probability of the Restoration. Yet in the mounting wave of literary welcomes only five English poems, I believe, directly compare Charles with

Augustus: Huish's *Musa Ruralis* . . . *In Adventum Caroli II*, which we have already discussed; Thomas Higgons's *Panegyrick to the King*, Dryden's *Astraea Redux*, Thomas Pecke's *To The Most High and Mighty Monarch, Charles II* . . . , and a poem by a young Oxford scholar in his university's congratulatory volume, *Britannia Rediviva*. His name was John Locke.[1] John Evelyn, deeply moved by the Restoration as his *Diary* shows, wrote a prose panegyric to Charles II at this time. It makes no use of the parallel with Augustus, but asks, after extravagant praise of Charles, 'What then have we to do with *Augustus*, or *Titus*, with *Trajan*, *Hadrian*, *Antoninus Theodosius* or even *Constantine* himself?'[2]

In the great wave of panegyrical welcomes, as we should expect, biblical allusion overwhelms classical, though the two are so often found together. The comparison of Charles with David is more conspicuous than that with Augustus. Those who do use the Augustan comparison do so in different ways, and Dryden's poem may be seen more clearly in relation to them. Higgons's *Panegyrick* opens with an epigraph from *Aeneid* Bk II, in which Aeneas addresses the ghost of Hector: but here Hector's name has been replaced by that of Charles:

> Quæ tantæ tenuere moræ? queîs CAROLE ab oris
> Expectate venis? ut te, post multa tuorum
> Funera, post varios hominumque urbisque labores
> Defessi aspicimus![3]

This striking application of Aeneas's lines in the fall of Troy speaks of a dead warrior returned to life, a bold way of depicting the revival of monarchy, and gives the words on the death of Hector's kin an unmistakable allusion to the death of Charles I and the many supporters who died for him. The panegyric itself sets forth a pattern of political revival. The state pauses at 'the brink of ruine' and 'the wounds of Civil hate' are healed. A new ruler has arisen:

> The most Renowned Kings this fate have had,
> To mount the Throne after tempestuous times,
> And their own Vertues more conspicuous made,
> By the reflection of preceding Crimes,

---

[1]H.T. Swedenberg, Jr, 'England's Joy: *Astraea Redux* in its Setting', *Studies in Philology*, L, 1 (Jan. 1953), p. 34, has listed several 1660 poems which prophesied 'the new Augustan age of glory' (n. 4). His list does not include Huish or Locke. Equally, some items that he cites seem to contain no specific Augustan references, e.g. John Crouch, *A Mixt Poem . . .*; Thomas Forde, *A Panegyrick Upon His Sacred Majestie's Most Happy Return* (though one line refers to 'the *Golden-age*'); and Thomas Saunderson, *A Royall Loyall Poem*. Richard Brathwaite, *To His Majesty Upon His Happy Arrival* (purchased by Thomason on 12 July) offers Augustus as chief among several models for the restored king, pp. 4, 11; Thomas Mayhew, *Upon the Joyfull and Welcome Return of His Sacred Majestie . . .* repeatedly uses the form 'This, *England*, This is He', 'This, This is *He*' (pp. 6–7) in allusion to Anchises's prophetic hailing of Augustus in *Aeneid*, VI, 790–800. It is worth noting that Thomas Pecke's poem has a significant background in his *Heroick Epigrams, Upon Some Choice Passages in the Lives of the Twelve CAESARS . . .* (London, 1659).

[2]John Evelyn, *An Apologie for the Royal Party* (1659) and *A Panegyric to Charles the Second* (1661), ed. Geoffrey Keynes, Augustan Reprint Society, XXVIII (Los Angeles, 1951); *Panegyric*, p. 12.

[3]Thomas Higgons, *A Panegyrick to the King* (London, 1660), title-page.

When Rome was ruin'd with intestine hate,
Augustus took the rudder of the State.

And when Domitian's hated government
The distrest World had thrown into despair,
Trajan by Heaven was in Mercy sent,
The Ruines of the Empire to repair.
    What Trajan and Augustus did at Rome,
    England expects to see, now You are come. . . .[4]

Trajan and Augustus are now taken up into the myth of Aeneas, the exile, wanderer and founder, and the greatness of Rome is seen as the standard and spur for England, its hour come round at last to be supreme over its neighbours. Much of the excitement of expanding political power, so clear in Waller's *Panegyric* to Cromwell, is here in Higgons's *Panegyrick* to Charles. Not strictly a panegyric, Thomas Pecke's poem makes the Augustan comparison less conspicuously though no less clearly. This is really a verse essay on monarchy, which opens by seeming to hail the revolution of the Platonic Year, 'pristine shapes' and 'the *Golden Age*'. Rome split 'upon the *Rocks / Of a Free State*' and was spurious until she 'Chose Julius Caesar PATER PATRIAE'. Augustus succeeded him as his heir, and showed how monarchies 'Empires enlarge, and Cities beautifie.'[5] Locke's poem is by comparison far less political. It is Augustus the patron of poets that he remembers:

Accept these poore endeavours, till your rays
Have given new growth to our late witherd bays;
Wit too must be your Donatiue, 'tis You
Who give AUGUSTUS, must give MARO'S too.[6]

By comparison with Higgons's *Panegyrick* – and with Waller's *Panegyric* and Dryden's own *Heroique Stanza's* to Cromwell – *Astraea Redux* does not set out to convey the excitement of expanding power. While it looks back to rebellion and civil war it does not, like Thomas Pecke, deal much in debate about the forms of government. The chance to urge Charles to be good to poets is entirely left aside. The poem strikes a sober, almost chastised note for so long and elaborate a piece. While the title and totally conventional epigraph: 'Iam Redit et Virgo, Redeunt Saturnia Regna' from Virgil's Fourth Eclogue raise a clear expectation, Dryden's strategy is one of postponement as he takes us through the experience of the times with an effort at historical understanding absent from most of the panegyrical pieces of 1660:

Experienc'd Age in deep despair was lost
To see the Rebel thrive, the Loyal crost:
Youth that with Joys had unacquainted been
Envy'd gray hairs that once good days had seen. . . .

---

[4]Ibid., p. 5.
[5]Thomas Pecke, *To the Most High and Mighty Monarch, Charles II* . . . (London, 1660), n.p.
[6]*Britannia Rediviva* (Oxford, 1660), n.p. Locke's poem is 23rd in the sequence of English poems which begins with the verses ostensibly by the young Earl of Rochester.

> Yet as wise Artists mix their colour so
> That by degrees they from each other go,
> Black steals unheeded from the neighb'ring white
> Without offending the well cous'ned sight:
> So on us stole our blessed change; while we
> Th'effect did feel but scarce the manner see.[7]

The reattainment of 'time's whiter series' with the revolution of the Platonic Year and the return of justice to earth are the more effective as a vision withheld to the end, as in the recognition of a new Augustus in Charles in the well-known concluding lines.

What almost certainly established the Augustan parallel with Charles II in the imagination of educated Londoners was the series of triumphal arches erected for the King's ceremonial passage from London to Westminster for his coronation in April 1661. An account was published in the same year, *The Relation of His Majestie's Entertainment* . . . by John Ogilby, and a year later Ogilby published *The Entertainment of His Most Excellent Majestie*, a handsome folio illustrating each arch, with a learned and much expanded commentary. Evelyn, who inspected the arches the evening before the coronation, recorded in his *Diary* that they were 'of good Invention & architecture, with inscriptions.'[8] In his long-awaited edition of Ogilby's *Entertainment*, Mr R.G. Knowles is to observe that the arches, with their pictures, emblems and inscriptions comprised a programme of Augustan themes, many of which were to be echoed in the high literature of the coming century.[9]

To appreciate the 1661 Royal Entry, the last of its kind in English history, it is best to read the 1661 account (in which the character of the arches is less overlaid by learned commentary) together with the illustrations added in 1662. From these sources it is clear that there were five episodes in the *Entertainment*: four triumphal arches, with a special entertainment outside East India House, between the first arch and the second. Since Ogilby omits this from his 1662 volume it was probably not his work. The first arch, erected in Leadenhall Street and composed of the Doric Order, represented the triumph of Monarchy and Loyalty over Rebellion. The King was depicted upon it three times, and quotations from Virgil are prominent among its many legends. The third picture showed Charles landing at Dover, with the words 'Adventus Augusti' above. Panels on the eastern side of the arch showed ruins, but on the further, western side corresponding panels were 'finished, to represent the Restauration of our Happiness by His Majestie's Arrival; the Motto, "Felix Temporum Reparatio".' Here, too, Charles was called 'Restitutor Urbis' and here appeared the indispensable legend: 'Redeunt Saturnia Regna.[10] As the King

---

[7]Ll. 23–6, 125–30; *The Poems of John Dryden*, ed. James Kinsley (Oxford, 1958), I, pp. 16, 19.

[8]*The Diary of John Evelyn*, ed. E.S. De Beer (Oxford, 1955), III, p. 278.

[9]I am grateful to Mr Knowles for allowing me to read, some ten years ago, the galley proofs of his learned and admirable edition of Ogilby's *Entertainment*, still withheld from publication by the publisher, Theatrum Orbis Terrarum, of Amsterdam.

[10]John Ogilby, *The Entertainment of his Most Excellent Majesty Charles II, In His Passing through the City of London To His Coronation* . . . (London, 1662), pp. 13–42; *The Relation of His Majestie's Entertainment Passing through the City of London to His Coronation* . . . (London, 1661), pp. 2–9. Quotations are from *The Relation* unless it is stated to the contrary.

passed through this arch Rebellion was interrupted by Monarchy and fell silent in defeat.

The East India House pageant took the *Entertainment* into trade, foreign policy and, unmistakably, the world of Dryden's *Annus Mirabilis*. In aptly exotic imagery it defied the rivalry of Holland and Spain, and anticipated the theme of the arch in Cornhill, which was a Naval Arch.[11] This seems to have been composed of the Ionic and Corinthian orders, was crowned by Atlas bearing a globe surmounted by a ship under sail, and dominated by a great picture showing Charles I with the Prince of Wales viewing their ship 'The Sovereign of the Sea'. These features were tenuously linked with an Augustan parallel by the painting of the Tower of London on the south side of the arch, with the motto 'Clauduntur Belli Portae'. As Ogilby explained in 1662: 'This is in reference to the *Temple* of Janus, never shut, but in the time of *Peace*; nor opened, but in time of *War*', and he referred his readers to Virgil's account in *Aeneid*, Bk VII.[12] The actors at this arch played 'the *River* Thames; his Garment Loose, and Flowing, Colour Blew and White' and three sailors who, as the nobility approached, sang in rough measures of their hardships on the seas of the world:

> . . . We, who have rais'd, and laid the Poles,
> Plough'd Frozen Seas, and scalding Billows,
> Now stiff with cold, then scorch'd on Coals,
> Ships our Cradles, Decks our Pillows . . .

Then Thames hailed the King with lines about the trade of the City, and welcomed:

> Your blest Return! by which she is restor'd
> To all the Wealth Remotest Lands afford . . .
> Though sev'ral Nations boast their Strength on Land,
> Yet You Alone the wat'ry World command.

These stately things having been said, the sailors resumed their song, and put into a few words what a great deal in the *Entertainment* was about:

> . . . thy Royal Navy rig,
> And We'll not care a fig
> For *France*, for *France*, the *Netherlands*, nor *Spain*. . . .[13]

The third arch, in Wood Street, was of two storeys, the first in the Corinthian, the second in the Composite order. This was an Arch of Concord, its cupola surmounted by a Figure of Concord. Within the temple of this arch, the King was welcomed with a song sung by Concord, Love and Truth:

> Comes not here the King of Peace,
> Who, the stars so long fore-told,
> From all Woes should us release,
> Converting Iron-times to Gold?

[11] *The Relation*, pp. 9–11.
[12] *The Relation*, pp. 11–14; *The Entertainment*, pp. 43–110 – p. 66 for the passage quoted.
[13] *The Relation*, pp. 11, 15, 17, 18.

He was crowned with an oaken garland as 'Pater Patriae' and in the ensuing address he was again praised for having imprisoned Civil War within the Temple of Janus.[14]

The fourth and final arch in the *Entertainment* was an Arch of Plenty. It stood in Fleet Street and was composed of the Doric and (in the second storey) of the Ionic order. It was the prettiest though the least purely classical of the arches. The central Figure was that of Plenty herself, and beneath, within the architrave of the lower arch was the following inscription:

> UBERITATI AUG.
> EXTINCTO BELLI CIVILIS
> INCENDIO CLUSOQ. IANI TEMPLO,
> ARAM CELSISS. CONSTRUXIT
> S. P. Q. L.

In 1662 Ogilby drove home the point of this inscription:

> What is meant by EXTINCTO BELLI CIVILIS INCENDIO, the extinction of the Flames of Civil War, is fortunately known to us all, and may serve to explicate what follows . . . the shutting of Janus's Temple: a Rite instituted by NUMA . . . [who sought] to reform the new City, which was built by Force, and Arms, and to build it anew by Rites, Laws, and Institutions. . . . he conceiving that the fierce People might by their disaccustomance be made mild, he built a Temple to JANUS . . . the signifier of Peace, and War. . . .[15]

Bacchus, Ceres, Flora, Pomona, the Four Winds and the Four Seasons might be thought to join with Plenty as she addressed the King:

> Great Sir; the Star, which at Your Happy Birth
> Joy'd with his Beams (at Noon) the wond'ring Earth,
> Did with auspicious lustre, then presage
> The Glitt'ring Plenty of this golden Age. . . .[16]

With this deeply traditional affirmation the *Entertainment* concluded, and the restored Stuart passed on to his coronation at Westminster.

It is the character of Renaissance triumphal entries to be traditional. Their tradition is their function, which is to relate new events to a well-known pattern of history in such a way as to recall relevant examples, offer advice and express hope. Comparison with Augustus is 'cette comparaison banale'[17] only to a modern habit of mind. It would have been surprising if the 1661 Entry had not been meant to recall that of 1604. Each features prominently the return of Astraea, the power of peace and the closing of the doors of the Temple of Janus. As in 1604 Virgil is prominent as a source of quotation, though Claudian is cited more often. Nevertheless the 1661 Entry is up to date in its recognition of recent history. It is concord and peace at home, not abroad, that it celebrates.

---

[14]*The Entertainment*, pp. 111–38; *The Relation*, pp. 21–8 – p. 25 for the passage quoted.

[15]*The Entertainment*, pp. 139–65; *The Relation*, pp. 29–32. The passages quoted are at pp. 139 and 141 of *The Entertainment*.

[16]*The Relation*, p. 31.

[17]Françoise Joukovsky, *La Gloire Dans La Poesie Française* . . ., pp. 216–19.

Rebellion has been put down as maritime expansion opens up the world to Britain. The Naval Arch is new, and amidst the classicizing celebration an expanding mercantile nationalism aspires to the condition of Augustan world empire.[18]

If certain of the leading ideas of the 1661 *Entertainment* differ from 1604, so too does the artistic idiom. It does not show the inventive classicism of Jonson: Ogilby's classicism is more superficial, lacking in dramatic focus, and consisting chiefly in the large number of legends and mottoes scattered over the arches. Poetically speaking, nothing in 1661 matches the quality of Jonson's eloquence, but it may be allowed that Ogilby often aimed at a different and more popular effect. The simple lyrical style of the welcome to the 'King of Peace' or of the sailors' song at the Naval Arch must have combined visual splendour with striking scenes and something like popular utterance.

The panegyrical moment which opened with Charles's landing at Dover attained, perhaps, its finest poetic expression with Waller's poem *On St James's Park, As Lately Improved By His Majesty*, a poem which has in recent years won a measure of recognition through the telling praise of Earl Miner.[19] This is not a panegyric but a place poem. The panegyrical comparisons and insights which it holds, and which link it so clearly with poems such as *Astraea Redux*, receive a different tone through the long approach, through the park with all its mythical and social associations, to the figure of the King as ruler.

> For future shade, young trees upon the banks
> Of the new stream appear in even ranks;
> The voice of Orpheus, or Amphion's hand,
> In better order could not make them stand;
> May they increase as fast, and spread their boughs,
> As the high fame of their great owner grows!
> May he live long enough to see them all
> Dark shadows cast, and as his palace tall!
> Methinks I see the love that shall be made,
> The lovers walking in that amorous shade;
> The gallants dancing by the river's side;
> They bathe in summer, and in winter slide.[20]

The compliment to Charles in this passage, which itself mingles with images of greatness and mutability in Nature, is soon set aside for a prospect of love-making and sport, and when the King is accorded a passage of sustained praise it is not as a ruler but as a young sportsman (ll. 57–66). This greatly humanizes the royal figure, and is a refreshing evasion of the sometimes overpowering praise to be found in the formal panegyric. It is well said of this poem that what keeps it social 'is its reservation', its 'refusing to go the whole distance' towards the wholly public, 'enjoying a differing integrity'.[21] But more perhaps needs to be

---

[18]Cf. *The Relation*, pp. 11–12 with *The Entertainment*, pp. 51–3 for Ogilby's revision of the claim of Britain to sovereignty of the seas, to sovereignty of the British seas only, which must have been made with foreign policy in mind.

[19]*The Poems of Edmund Waller*, ed. G. Thorn Drury, II, pp. 40–4; Earl Miner, *The Cavalier Mode from Jonson to Cotton* (Princeton, 1971), pp. 24–37.

[20]Ll. 13–24; ed. cit. II, p. 40.

[21]Earl Miner, *The Cavalier Mode*, p. 39.

said, for it is clear that in this way the seventeenth-century English poet sought
to match the moderated manner of the Horace of the Epistle to Augustus
– where Horace, '*fidus interpres* of the intentions of Augustus, refuses to fix a
gulf between the ruler and the rest of mankind'.[22] Thus Charles is praised as a
sportsman before he is displayed as a king. But at length, at the heart of his park
which has been made to reflect both social present and mythic past, the poem
does come to the ruler:

> In such green palaces the first kings reigned,
> Slept in their shades, and angels entertained;
> With such old counsellors they did advise,
> And, by frequenting sacred groves, grew wise.
> Free from the impediment of light and noise,
> Man, thus retired, his nobler thoughts employs.
> Here Charles contrives the ordering of his states,
> Here he resolves his neighbouring princes' fates;
> What nation shall have peace, where war be made,
> Determined is in this oraculous shade;
> The world, from India to the frozen north,
> Concerned in what this solitude brings forth.[23]

The nationalistic ambitions of some of the 1660 panegyrics and of the 1661
Entry can be felt as a pressure behind these lines, but the poetic quality is
different, and the verse may rather be thought to reach after the geographical
grandeur of some of Horace's Roman Odes. The 'green palaces' of the earliest
kings, the 'sacred groves' and 'oraculous shade', the insistence on solitude and
retreat, all make kingship into a solemn mystery which the poet rather contem-
plates than actively evokes. The note deepens perceptibly as Westminster Abbey
is drawn into the circle of meditation:

> From hence he does that antique pile behold,
> Where royal heads receive the sacred gold;
> It gives them crowns, and does their ashes keep;
> There made like gods, like mortals there they sleep;
> Making the circle of their reign complete,
> Those suns of empire![24]

As the poem draws to its conclusion a more practical and day-to-day note is
struck, and the ruler is referred to with the decent freedom due to a citizen. It is
from this level that, appropriately, the poem rises to the comparison with
Augustus which is done with a notably Augustan tact and understatement.
Charles is not hailed as a new Augustus: Augustus as ruler and hero (the
princeps and Alcides were placed with careful propinquity at the opening of
Horace's Epistle to Augustus) are a part of his meditations:

> Here, free from court compliances, he walks,
> And with himself, his best adviser, talks;

[22]Eduard Fraenkel, *Horace*, p. 399.
[23]Ll. 71–82; ed. cit. II, pp. 42–3.
[24]Ll. 91–6; ed. cit. II, p. 43.

How peaceful olive may his temples shade,
For mending laws, and for restoring trade;
Or, how his brows may be with laurel charged,
For nations conquered, and our bounds enlarged.
Of ancient prudence here he ruminates,
Of rising kingdoms, and of falling states;
What ruling arts gave great Augustus fame,
And how Alcides purchased such a name.
His eyes, upon his native palace bent,
Close by, suggest a greater argument.[25]

The gravity of these lines requires comparison with the description of Charles in exile in *Astraea Redux*, and perhaps with the King's prayer upon the Fire of London in *Annus Mirabilis*, though the latter is hardly an Augustan poem. Dryden writes more boldly. Waller has here a deeper and quieter quality, marked, perhaps, by the pausing closure of his couplets though there is far more to it than that. Despite the English poet's evident differences from any poet of Augustan Rome, Waller, it may be thought, strikes a more authentically Augustan note.

What is the content of all these panegyrical comparisons? Alluding (among other rulers) to Augustus as the *exemplum* of the good prince, moderate, mature in judgement, the restorer and maintainer of peace, it derives from the positive tradition concerning Augustus that has been traced in previous chapters. That tradition goes back to Cassius Dio, Suetonius, Seneca's *De Clementia*, and to the Roman Augustan poets themselves. Equally important was the crucial position of Augustus in a Christian and providential scheme of history. This view, perennially recorded in the second chapter of Luke's Gospel, was still fully current in the 1660s, as Ogilby makes clear when he says that the Temple of Janus was shut 'after the Victory at *Actium*, about the time of the Nativity of our Saviour; and then most justly when there was an UNIVERSAL PEACE over the whole World . . .'.[26] Plenty of educated men in this period read the Fathers as well as Virgil and Horace. Francis Atterbury, friend of both Dryden and Pope, is an example. For him 'Augustan Age' seems to have had this providential meaning.[27]

The counter-tradition, going back to Tacitus and strengthening itself in Machiavelli and later Italian political thinkers, was not readily functional in panegyric. The view that the Julian House subverted the liberty and *virtù* of republican Rome was not, however, unknown to Shakespeare and Dryden, certainly not to Bolingbroke and Pope, and the panegyrists I have discussed were unlikely to be ignorant of the shadier side of Augustus. Pierre Corneille's great drama, *Cinna* (1641), the very structure of which is a move from Augustus seen as a tyrant to the Augustus who has attained to clemency, is likely to have been well known. As J.D. Garrison brings out in his admirable study *Dryden and the Tradition of Panegyric* (1975), panegyric is a form which seeks to unite ruler and ruled in the acknowledgement of certain basic values, and the sharing

[25]Ll. 115–26; ed. cit. II, p. 44.
[26]*The Entertainment*, p. 142.
[27]See his Sermon Preach'd before the Queen . . . 21 Oct. 1694, in *Sermons and Discourses . . . By Francis Atterbury, D.D.* (London, 1723), I, pp. 102–4.

of certain hopes. It draws positive examples from fame (which often means from lasting propaganda) and uses them, not to flatter, but, *laudando praecipere*, to counsel and to hold out an inspiring vision of the future. The title and epigraph of *Astraea Redux* might suggest that Dryden's poem arises directly from the Augustan Virgil's Fourth Eclogue, but, as Garrison observes, a wishful likening of the new ruler to Augustus is very much within the conventions of verse panegyric as handled by Claudian, in whose poems the *topos* of the returning age of gold is conspicuous. The end of *Astraea Redux* is really closer to the end of Claudian's Panegyric on the Fourth Consulship of Honorius than to anything in Virgil. We cannot say that the Augustan Idea came down to Dryden solely through this late Roman poet – there were as we have seen other sources – but it seems probable that the form and conventions of late Roman and of Renaissance verse panegyric decisively shaped the presence of the Augustan Idea in Dryden. Though Claudian could use the example of Augustus as a warning,[28] it is generally true that the character of panegyric itself required a positive, rather than a qualified or negative image.

Disillusion and Contrasting Conceptions

So long as the welfare of the state depended on the character of the monarch, panegyric was never an empty exercise. The hopes it expressed might be rhetorically heightened, but they were genuine and capable of genuine disappointment. This was the experience of both Evelyn and Dryden. To read the Dedicatory Epistle to *Aureng-Zebe* (1675) is to encounter deep disillusionment with Charles's court, and with the King's failure to honour the pensions he granted. The complaint is pointed through reference to 'the times of Vergil' who 'had an Augustus for his patron'.[29] Charles may be granted discrimination (he advised Dryden over *Aureng-Zebe* and praised the completed work) but his action falls short of his intelligence: 'never said a foolish thing,' etc. George McFadden's notable recent study, *Dryden the Public Writer* (1978) makes the important point that between the writing of *Annus Mirabilis* and the Exclusion Crisis Dryden was in the factions of that time never really a King's man but a Duke's man. Charles was too unsteady and self-indulgent to be the Augustus envisioned in *Astraea Redux*; the Duke, on the other hand, was a man of action and business, firm of character and grateful to his friends. McFadden tellingly observes in how many of Dryden's plays a weak and self-indulgent ruler is contrasted with a man of action, or a loyal and self-denying heir, or, as in *Aureng-Zebe*, both. This is the background, amply documented by McFadden, against which I suggest we should read *Mac Flecknoe*. This is a mock-heroic poem, and it has been firmly inculcated into us that mock-heroic does not mock the heroic but draws upon its grandeur to mock the un-heroic. I would not question this, but rather ask whether Flecknoe and Shadwell exhaust the un-heroic subjects of the poem. Satirical comedy is volatile and cannot always be pointed in one direction alone. The idea of Augustan succession (and it may be right to recall that unlike the fertile Flecknoe Augustus had no sons) is predominantly

---

[28] *Panegyricus De Sexto Consulatu Honorii Augusti*, ll. 113–21. J.D. Garrison, *Dryden and the Tradition of Panegyric*, pp. 81–2.

[29] John Dryden, *Aureng-Zebe*, ed. F.M. Link (London, 1972), p. 10.

deployed to mock the majestically mindless Flecknoe, but the satirical use of the solemn panegyrical parallels of 1660–1 seems to involve some satirical repercussion upon those ceremonies and the new Augustus whom they had celebrated:

> Now Empress *Fame* had publisht the Renown
> Of *Sh----*'s Coronation through the Town.
> Rows'd by report of Fame, the Nations meet,
> From near *Bun-Hill*, and distant *Watling-street*.
> No *Persian* Carpets spread th'Imperial way,
> But scatter'd Limbs of mangled Poets lay:
> From dusty shops neglected Authors come,
> Martyrs of Pies, and Reliques of the Bum.
> Much *Heywood*, *Shirly*, *Ogleby* there lay,
> But loads of *Sh---* almost choakt the way.
> Bilk't *Stationers* for Yeoman stood prepar'd,
> And *H----* was Captain of the Guard.[30]

The lines, with their references to the copious Ogilby, the author of the *Entertainment*, and to the tireless Heringman, printer of Dryden's own *Astraea Redux*, recall the coronation of Britain's new Augustus. 'Dusty shops' and 'neglected authors' remind us of Augustus's record as a discriminating and effective patron, adverted to by Dryden in the Epistle Dedicatory to *Aureng-Zebe* and always an integral part of the fame of Augustus. Is not Shadwell's London King Charles's capital, provocatively here called by its old Roman name of Augusta? The whole passage has a surreal quality as the productions of poets, far from winged and inspired as the poets praised by Augustus in Jonson's *Poetaster*, have become mere material objects, clogging the thoroughfare, an ecological nightmare.

Today, when we use the general term 'Augustan' we often have 'Romantic' in the back of our mind to help keep it from unprofitable vagueness. The adjective 'Augustan' seems first to have been applied to a period of English culture by Francis Atterbury in 1690,[31] but the conception of an Augustan Age is conspicuous in the Renaissance. What was the opposing conception? Some contrasted the last patrician defenders of republican liberty: Brutus, Cassius and Cato of Utica. Others contrasted the rule of Augustus with that of Tiberius, Nero and Domitian. This contrast was surely in Milton's mind when in Bk IV of *Paradise Regained* (1671) he gave, as part of the second temptation of Christ, an unforgettable portrayal of Rome. It is Rome in the last years of Tiberius: very much the Rome created by Augustus:

> On each side an imperial city stood,
> With towers and temples proudly elevate
> On seven small hills, with palaces adorn'd,
> Porches and theatres, baths, aqueducts,
> Statues and trophees, and triumphal arcs . . . .

---

[30]Ll. 94–105; *The Poems of John Dryden*, I, pp. 266.

[31]In the Preface to the Second Part of Waller's Poems; *The Poems of* Edmund Waller, ed. G. Thorn Drury, I, p. xix. It has been reprinted in 'Exhumations III', *Essays on Criticism*, XV (July 1965), pp. 288–93. See Chapter IX below, pp. 236, 244–5.

The architectural city is also the great political city:

> Thence to the gates cast round thine eye, and see
> What conflux issuing forth, or entring in,
> Pretors, proconsuls to their provinces
> Hasting or on return, in robes of state;
> Lictors and rods the ensigns of thir power,
> Legions and Cohorts, turms of horse and wings:
> Or embassies from regions far remote
> In various habits on the Appian road,
> Or on the Æmilian . . . .
>
> All Nations now to Rome obedience pay,
> To Rome's great emperour, whose wide domain
> In ample territory, wealth and power,
> Civility of manners, arts and arms,
> And long renown thou justly may'st prefer . . . .

This is the Rome of the panegyrists, far more fully and powerfully conveyed. It is the Rome meant to be recalled by educated spectators when James I in 1604 and Charles II in 1661 passed through their triumphal arches to their coronations. Nothing mars the majestic scene – save the reflection that it is Satan who speaks. The picture indeed changes somewhat as Satan outlines Christ's opportunity:

> This Emperour hath no son, and now is old,
> Old and lascivious, and from Rome retir'd
> To Capreae an Island small but strong
> On the Campanian shore, with purpose there
> His horrid lusts in private to enjoy,
> Committing to a wicked favourite
> All public cares, and yet of him suspicious,
> Hated of all, and hating. . . .

These are (in Milton's view) the ills of monarchy, the form of government which Augustus established in Rome. Christ in his contemptuous reply has only to extend the diagnosis to the Roman people as a whole: 'These thus, degenerate, by themselves enslav'd. . . .'[32]

At the start of Augustus's long principate, however, the old republic already shattered and Tiberius yet to come, the opposing conception to that of Augustus was embodied in Octavian's 'great competitors', Antony and Cleopatra, as is testified by the Thirty-Seventh Ode of the First Book of Horace, on the victory at Actium. This Ode is not untouched by Octavian's propaganda campaign against Antony, which has helped to ensure that one of the strongest traditions about Antony in Western culture has presented him as the great leader beguiled by sexual infatuation into deserting his military vocation and political responsibility. Antony himself, who it has been suggested deliberately played up to a cult of love and pleasure, gave Octavian his propaganda opportunity. He could

---

[32]Ll. 33-7, 61-9, 80-4, 90-97, 144; *The Poems of John Milton*, ed. John Carey and Alastair Fowler (London, 1968), pp. 1137-43.

be a hero of love to the Restoration, though never setting love above empire in reality. (If the most recent historian of Actium is right to say that Antony did not turn tail, but broke out of Agrippa's naval blockade, Octavian probably recognized as much at the time.[33]) This moral view of Antony is one side of Shakespeare's tragic presentation, and in the Restoration as at other times the stress on Antony and Augustus as mighty opposites was commonplace. Ogilby's commentary on his *Entertainment* comments on coins of Augustus 'where two Serpents, that is the Hostility, and Dissension of the *Roman* Empire, divided into two Factions, that of *Augustus*, and *Antony*, are separated by an intervening Victory; that of *Augustus* at *Actium*, and *Alexandria*.'[34]

By 1675 Charles may, of the two great Roman competitors, rather have seemed to resemble Antony than Augustus, an ageing king of pleasure rather than a king of policy or a king of arms. As Pope was later to put it:

> . . . *Love* was all an easie Monarch's Care;
> Seldom at *Council*, never in a *War*. . . .[35]

The Antonian celebration of the hedonistic monarch comes, as we might expect, from the pen of Rochester in one of his more libertine moments: in the Sceptre Lampoon (*c.* 1674) which mockingly and shockingly praises the sexually infatuated Charles by contrast with the politically and militarily ambitious Louis XIV, to whom Britain had just abandoned a continental war. Generally quite a lot of Rochester's more confident and less painful libertine verse – 'Upon His Drinking a Bowl' is a good example, and perhaps 'A Song of a Young Lady to Her Ancient Lover' – might usefully be termed Antonian rather than Augustan. The two words apply less well, perhaps, to the difference between Rochester's St James's Park and Waller's. If it be objected that the term hardly accommodates Rochester's development as a satirist, one may at least reply that hedonists like Rochester in his satires are usually good at seeing through the moral pretensions of other people, as is shown by Antony's own letter (quoted by Suetonius) which defends his liaison with Cleopatra by twitting Octavian on his own sexual promiscuity. In 1675, as we have seen, appeared *Aureng-Zebe* with the Augustan references in its Dedicatory Epistle. Its central figure of the Old Emperor, however, a ruler irresponsible and besotted in the pursuit of his own amorous pleasures, is Antonian rather than Augustan – the later, unheroic Antony. His relation to the character of Charles has been meticulously formulated by McFadden.[36] Early in 1676 there was presented at the Theatre Royal a much less discussed play, Lee's *Gloriana, Or the Court of Augustus Caesar*, a most interesting response to what by the late 1670s may have come to seem a hopeless Augustan aspiration. What Lee does in this sensational drama is to credit Augustus with the violent emotions, whether sexual desire or tyrannical impulse, of an Antony. Lee's Augustus is far from the politic despot of Tacitus.

---

[33] Jasper Griffin, 'Propertius and Antony', *Journal of Roman Studies*, LXVII (1977), pp. 17–26; John M. Carter, *The Battle of Actium: The Rise and Triumph of Augustus Caesar* (London, 1970), pp. 224, 226.

[34] *The Entertainment*, pp. 118–19.

[35] *An Essay on Criticism*, ll. 536–7; *The Poems of Alexander Pope*, I, p. 298.

[36] George McFadden, *Dryden the Public Writer, 1660–1685* (Princeton, 1978), Ch. 6.

While Antony himself is several times referred to, it is Augustus who early in Act I speaks like an Antony: 'Give me but one or two soft happy hours,/ And all the greatnesses of State be yours' (I, 54–5). That is hardly Augustus – even of the hostile tradition. Suetonius it was who not only quoted from Antony's letter to Octavian, but also set down the gossip about the latter's participation in a sacrilegious banquet.[37] Lee, like Jonson in *The Poetaster*, turns this round, making Ovid and Julia the sacrilegious revellers, and using the episode to dramatize the anger of Augustus. In Jonson that is a climactic moment: Lee makes of it merely the first episode of his drama which proceeds to undermine the wrath and character of the emperor by revealing his senile passions for younger women in love with younger men, the several successor figures, Caesario, Marcellus, who frequent his court. More might be said of the relation of Lee's plot to the times, but my point is made by quoting the lines with which Augustus concludes Act I:

> I, like old Saturn, must forego my Sphere,
> You're for a mad young fiery Jupiter.
> Yet this remember in your Thund'rer's reign,
> The Golden days will never come again.[38]

The problems of the last years of the principate were of course part of the inherited matter of Augustus, but if these lines didn't speak to the times in the later 1670s, nothing did.

1677 saw two new plays about Antony and Cleopatra, Sedley's and Dryden's. In *All for Love* (1677), I suggest, Dryden continued the process, seen in *Aureng-Zebe* and Lee's *Gloriana*, of exploring the Antonian monarch: the opposite term, in the cultural outlook we are examining, to the Augustan monarch. I have no wish to argue that *All for Love* is a dramatic *roman à clef* but it is an intelligible response to the court of Charles II, 'where *Love* was all an easy Monarch's Care' and, as David M. Vieth has observed, 'Restoration theatre-goers could be forgiven if they visualized Antony as the philandering Charles II, Cleopatra as a politically powerful foreign mistress like the French Duchess of Portsmouth, and Octavius as the all-conquering but personally unsoldierlike Louis XIV.'[39] Dryden needed Shakespeare because he wished to idealize Antony's love, but that does not mean, any more than in Shakespeare, that the political and moral view is laid aside. Dryden keeps something like Shakespeare's balance of judgement. Ventidius expresses the vigorous and soldierly view, but Antony himself comprehends both sides:

> When first I came to empire, I was borne
> On tides of people, crowding to my triumphs,
> The wish of nations! and the willing world
> Received me as its pledge of future peace.
> I was so great, so happy, so beloved,

---

[37]Suetonius, *De Vitæ Cæsarvm*, Divvs Augvstvs, 69, 70.
[38]*The Works of Nathaniel Lee*, ed. T.B. Stroup and A.L. Cooke (New Brunswick, 1954), p. 161.
[39]John Dryden, *All For Love*, ed. D.M. Vieth, p. xxxiii. Quotations are drawn from this edition. For Sedley's *Antony and Cleopatra: A Tragedy*, see V. de Sola Pinto, ed., *The Poetical and Dramatic Works of Sir Charles Sedley* (London, 1928), I, pp. 187–262.

Fate could not ruin me; till I took pains
And worked against my fortune . . .
My careless days and my luxurious nights
At length have wearied her, and now she's gone. . . .[40]

How well that applied to Charles, the hoped-for Augustus of a peaceful Restoration! But Antony has another wisdom: 'Give, you gods,' he says, 'Give to your boy, your Caesar, / This rattle of a globe to play withal . . .'[41] – Charles, as we have seen, had just withdrawn England from the war in which Louis was now gaining significant victories.

Absalom and Achitophel and After

The Antonian ideal has its own insights – 'He kills, and keeps his temper'[42] says Antony of Octavian at one point – but it is the sad truth that states needed Augustuses not Antonys. Charles's handling of the Exclusion Crisis, 1679–81, brought Dryden round again to Augustan panegyric because the King now seemed to be displaying the fortitude of an Aureng-Zebe and the original defiance of a Ventidius. He was standing up for his hereditary throne and thus for the Duke of York's right. *Absalom and Achitophel*, as Bernard Schilling has suggested, mediates between the monarch as a man at the beginning and the monarch as a monarch at the end.[43] The symmetrical structure of the poem is certain, and holds within it, as it were, that decision which Charles himself had made the basis of his new stand: that he had been 'easie' to a fault in the past, but would now be firm. If McFadden is right, the poem holds within it also the Laureate's conversion back into a King's man: certainly *Absalom and Achitophel* does not constitute a warning to the King as did *Aureng-Zebe* and *All for Love*. But more, I think, remains to be said about the poem's twofold presentation of Charles. It may be noted that the beginning and end amount to two different versions of the Golden Age. The first is a golden age of sexual indulgence such as is celebrated in the famous chorus of Tasso's *Aminta* –

    The goulden lawes of Nature, they
Found in their breasts; and them they did obey.

E'r one to one was, cursedly, confind:[44]

and the second a grave Virgilian Golden Age, a deliberate recall of those panegyrical hopes, expressed in *Astraea Redux* and elsewhere, more than twenty years earlier, for a new era of law, stability and peace. After the King's speech at the end it is more than ever clear that the *Pax Augusta*, whether at home or abroad, is only attained through resolution, and the concurrence that resolution can win:

---

[40]I, 299–308; ed. cit. p. 43.
[41]II, 442–4; ed. cit. p. 67.
[42]III, 66; ed. cit. p. 71.
[43]B.N. Schilling, *Dryden and the Conservative Myth* (London, 1961), pp. 289–90, 305–6.
[44]Translated by Henry Reynolds (1628), and quoted in Frank Kermode, ed., *English Pastoral Poetry* (London, 1952), pp. 81–2; *Absalom and Achitophel*, l. 4; ed. cit. I, p. 217.

> Henceforth a Series of new time began,
> The mighty Years in long Procession ran:
> Once more the Godlike *David* was Restor'd,
> And willing Nations knew their Lawfull Lord.[45]

It is also clear, I think, that the portrayal of Charles as David at that juncture of seventeenth-century history afforded Dryden a remarkable opportunity. David as the king of many concubines (II *Samuel*, 5, 13), and as the monarch appointed by the Lord, enables Dryden to bring together in one poem his insights into the Antonian monarch and his hopes for the Augustan monarch: David at the beginning and at the end of the poem. In the former are also conveyed those lurking intimations of comedy detectable, perhaps, in *All for Love*[46] and the more evident comic resources which just play upon the Augustan idea in *Mac Flecknoe*. There is something richly and comically natural (if politically disastrous) about the David who 'wide as his Command, / Scatter'd his Maker's Image through the Land.' Natural heirs are not in short supply, but in the fallen world man must live by the law; indeed living by the law provides the norm by which comic excess is perceived.

When Johnson wrote: 'What was said of Rome, adorned by Augustus, may be applied by an easy metaphor to English poetry embellished by Dryden, "lateritiam invenit, marmoream reliquit." He found it brick and he left it marble', he was recognizing both political and cultural aspects of the Augustan idea. When, in 1690, such a man as Atterbury questioned 'whether in Charles II's reign English did not come to its full perfection; and whether it has not had its Augustan age . . .'[47] he was, we may suspect, making a partly political point. Certainly after 1688 it became useful for a poet such as Dryden, who refused the Oaths to William and Mary, to discuss the political succession in terms of the literary succession, a practice that extends at least as late as *The Dunciad*.[48] In his Epistle 'To Congreve' (1693) Dryden casts himself as a deposed literary monarch, Congreve as the true heir, and Shadwell (Mac Flecknoe, we recall) as the spurious successor. In this poem the laudatory Augustan parallel is consciously displaced. Rulers are mentioned but writers are the ostensible subject. The god Janus is introduced, not because his temple is closed to betoken an Augustan peace (William's wars were of course in full spate), but in order that the dead Charles might be seen to have emulated his peaceful cultivation of Latium, a tribute which Dryden had already paid at greater length and not quite without qualification in his *Threnodia Augustalis*. Above all the architectural metaphor, which Johnson may have remembered when he wrote the tribute quoted above, is a most important expression of what the Augustan idea meant to Dryden. 'You, the best *Vitruvius*', Dryden calls Congreve, thus announcing

---

[45]Ll. 1028–31; ed. cit. I, p. 243.

[46]See A.D. Hope, '*All For Love*, or Comedy as Tragedy' in *The Cave and the Spring: Essays on Poetry* (Adelaide, 1965).

[47]See n. 27 above.

[48]For Dryden's Jacobitism, see W.J. Cameron, 'John Dryden's Jacobitism' in Harold Love, ed., *Restoration Literature: Critical Approaches* (London, 1972), pp. 277–308; and Howard Erskine-Hill, 'Literature and the Jacobite Cause', *Modern Language Studies*, IX, 3 (Fall 1979), pp. 15–28. Alan Roper, *Dryden's Poetic Kingdoms* (London, 1965), valuably discusses the procedure of political double entendre in Dryden, especially in 'To Mr. Congreve'.

that Congreve's drama is well-made, associating with it the Augustan architectural treatise dedicated to the *princeps* himself, and recalling that Augustus left Rome well-made, *marmoream reliquit*. He further recalls that Vitruvius saw the three orders of architecture as emblematic of the different stages of a civilization evolving from simplicity to sophistication. Dryden also remembers the Renaissance conviction that the Corinthian Order was the magnificent, public and royal order – 'The fair *Corinthian* Crowns the higher Space' (l. 18).[49] Congreve's work, the poem argues, embodies the strength of design and cultural sophistication of Augustan civilization, and the fact that he is called a Vitruvius only underlines the point that nobody is called an Augustus. Panegyric sought to draw together ruler, writer and community, but Dryden was an outcast from the newly established political community of the Revolution Settlement. Matthew Prior could compare William III with Augustus, and did so in his *Carmen Seculare, for the Year MDCC*.[50] It is Dryden's achievement, in the Epistle 'To Congreve', to have prepared a place for Augustus and left it ostentatiously empty.

Dryden's Last Years

And this is not entirely unlike what he does in his strange Epistle 'To Her Grace The Dutchess of Ormond', the first poem of *The Fables* (1700). For Dryden as in traditional panegyric the idea of a restoration to Augustan rule is poetically bound up with the notion of an Age of Gold and the revolution that returns the Platonic Year. These associations run from the end of *Astraea Redux* to the end of *Absalom and Achitophel*. William III could never be Augustus for Dryden, but the Duchess of Ormond was a figure around whom he could spin a poetical web of royal legitimacy, and he could make the visit of the Duke and Duchess to Ireland in 1697 an occasion for the conjuring up of all these connected panegyrical associations. Before he spoke of the succession of writers when the succession of rulers was just as much in his mind. Here, because a Tory Duchess has landed in Ireland, he once again summons up the poetry due to a restoring Augustus:

> As when the Stars, in their Etherial Race,
> At length have roll'd around the Liquid Space,
> At certain Periods they resume their Place,
> From the same Point of Heav'n their Course advance,
> And move in Measures of their former Dance;
> Thus, after length of Ages, she returns,
> Restor'd in you, and the same place adorns;
> Or you perform her Office in the Sphere,
> Born of her Blood, and make a new Platonick Year. . . .

[49]See Howard Erskine-Hill, 'Heirs of Vitruvius: Pope and the Idea of Architecture' in Howard Erskine-Hill and Anne Smith, eds., *The Art of Alexander Pope* (London, 1978), pp. 144–8, for a discussion of the theme of architecture in 'To Mr. Congreve'; and for brief remarks on architectural form in *Absalom and Achitophel* see the same author, 'John Dryden: Poet and Critic' in Roger Lonsdale, ed., *Dryden to Johnson* (London, 1971), pp. 39–40.

[50]H.B. Wright and M.K. Spears, eds., *The Literary Works of Matthew Prior* (Oxford, 1959), I, pp. 183; see also pp. 232–3.

> At Your Approach, they crowded to the Port;
> And scarcely Landed, You create a Court:
> As *Ormond's* Harbinger, to You they run;
> For *Venus* is the Promise of the Sun.
>   The Waste of Civil Wars, their Towns destroy'd,
> *Pales* unhonour'd, *Ceres* unemploy'd,
> Were all forgot; and one Triumphant Day
> Wip'd all the Tears of three Campaigns away.
> Blood, Rapines, Massacres, were cheaply bought,
> So mighty Recompense Your Beauty brought.[51]

Dryden has perhaps never written such rich and full Augustan panegyric as this, yet Augustus is absent from the text. He is literally in exile, the hidden king whom Dryden had dramatized, immediately after the Revolution, in his *Don Sebastian*.[52] Dryden rejected the Sherlockian 'providential' argument for the recognition of true kings, as another poem of the *Fables*, 'The Character of a Good Parson', shows. For the poet the Augustan idea was by this time chiefly a comprehensive notion of cultural maturity which included Stuart legitimacy. In the 'Discourse concerning Satire', however, it was possibly also a source of passing insinuations against the *de facto* ruler. This is ironical because there was surely always some awkwardness in allying the *princeps* Augustus with an hereditary *de jure* king, and the seventeenth-century poem which is able to draw the most precise historical parallel between a British ruler and Augustus is undoubtedly Waller's *Panegyric to the Lord Protector*.

This is not, I believe, quite the end of the story. Dryden was, perhaps, especially attracted in his latest years to the most comprehensive and poetic associations of the Augustan idea, simply the idea of the revolutions of the Great Year and of the loss and return of the Age of Gold. For the same reason, we may think, that Pope after writing *The Dunciad* sought even longer and more remote historical perspectives in his *Brutus* project, Dryden included in the *Fables* his version 'Of the Pythagorean Philosophy' from that Augustan poet who, though he sang the glory of Augustan Rome, has always had a peculiar position as the one of all those famous poets of the principate to be relegated by Augustus: an exiling which both Ben Jonson and Lee dramatized for the stage. For this and no doubt for other reasons there is the most remarkable sense of liberation when the poet of so many restorations, hoped for, proclaimed and imagined, yields himself to the changes and chances of this fleeting world, to the waves of Ovid's *Metamorphoses*, wave compelling wave, which do not overwhelm him but buoy him up, affording him a wide and changing view of history and nature. The poem opens on a political note – 'A King is sought to guide the growing State' – and it seems possible that the story of Myscelos into which the poem then moves appealed to Dryden because it could be read as a commentary on the departure into exile of James II. While Dryden brings his version to an end, not with Ovid's tribute to Augustus at the end of *Metamorphoses* XV but with Numa's acceptance of the Roman crown, it is in the central section in which Pythagoras expounds to Numa the doctrine of change that Dryden is able to

---

[51]Ll. 21–69; ed. cit. IV, pp. 1464–5.
[52]See Howard Erskine-Hill, 'The Providential Context', *The Times Literary Supplement*, No. 3935 (12 Aug. 1977), p. 988.

respond to a wider view of so many of those notions which had become conventional in panegyric:

> Thus are their Figures never at a stand,
> But chang'd by Nature's innovating Hand;
> All Things are alter'd, nothing is destroy'd,
> The shifted Scene, for some new Show employ'd.
>   Then to be born, is to begin to be
> Some other Thing we were not formerly: . . .
>   That Forms are chang'd I grant; that nothing can
> Continue in the Figure it began:
> The Golden Age, to Silver was debased:
> To Copper that; our Mettal came at last.
>   The Face of Places, and their Forms decay;
> And that is solid Earth, that once was Sea:
> Seas in their turn retreating from the Shore,
> Make solid Land, what Ocean was before;
> And far from Strands are Shells of Fishes found,
> And rusty Anchors fix'd on Mountain-ground: . . .[53]

It is becoming generally recognized that Dryden the translator in *The Fables* is in many respects Dryden at his greatest. Those who will read through 'Of the Pythagorean Philosophy' as a whole will perhaps agree that it is, in its kind, as good as anything Dryden ever wrote.

Was Dryden an Augustan poet? In the modern literary-historical sense the question is not, perhaps, worth asking for in this sense the word 'Augustan' is adjusted automatically: what Dryden and Pope were, 'Augustan' is. In senses of the term that would have been recognized in Dryden's time, however, a variety of answers may be given. 'Augustan' may here mean an era in which 'the arts and polite literature' and therefore language 'are at their height'.[54] Was Dryden a great poet of such an age? Dryden would probably have said not. Even allowing for the complimentary vein of 'To Mr. Congreve' and the tributes to Charles there and in *Threnodia Augustalis* as a cultivator of the times, Dryden expressed what he meant by Augustan achievement in the Vitruvian metaphor of 'To Congreve' and saw himself a precursor rather than at the meridian of 'the promis'd hour'. Another sense of 'Augustan' that would probably have been recognized in that time is similar to the sense in which younger contemporaries of Ben Jonson had called him the 'English Horace'.[55] Such a usage proposes a close resemblance to one of the poets of Augustan Rome. To call Jonson the 'English Horace' made sense since, though Horace didn't write satirical comedy, Jonson did write imitations and translations of Horace, and wrote much of himself into Horace in *The Poetaster*. Was Dryden Augustan in this sense? Here we confront Dryden's rich and eclectic late Renaissance capacity for assimilation and translation. There is indeed fine Horatian imitation and allusion in his work but his versions of Juvenal and

[53]Ll. 386–91, 398–407; ed. cit. IV, pp. 1727–8.
[54]Joseph Warton, *An Essay on the Genius and Writings of Pope*, 3rd edn, corrected (London, 1772), I, p. 162.
[55]*Ben Jonson*, ed. C.H. Herford and Percy and Evelyn Simpson, XI, p. 338.

Persius are more conspicuous and memorable. Dryden himself finally preferred Juvenal to Horace.[56] Was Dryden the English Virgil? His ambitious English version of the *Eclogues*, *Georgics* and *Aeneid* of Virgil affords some basis for the designation, against which must be set Dryden's apparent choice of Virgil as a model in *Annus Mirabilis*, a poem which surely has more in common with Camões's *Lusiads* than with the *Aeneid*.[57] At times, I think, Dryden could be genuinely Virgilian: the moment of my own choice would be the Georgic compassion with which he writes of the sufferings of the birds in the inset fable of the swallows in Part III of *The Hind and the Panther*.[58] But Dryden at the end of his career adjudged Homer more akin to his genius than Virgil.[59] Was Dryden the English Ovid? No doubt he was attracted to Ovid and imitated a variety of his work marvellously well. Yet this is but a small part of his richly various poetic output. Rarely if ever was Dryden called the English Ovid, Virgil or Horace.

Was Dryden then an Augustan because he admired the Augustan Age? That might seem nearer the mark, whether we have in mind the character of the arts or the disposition and success of the ruler. But Dryden was no simpleminded admirer of the historical Augustus. The 'Discourse Concerning Satire' – admittedly a late work – shows that Dryden was quite well aware of the less-enchanted views of Octavian's rise to world-power, and the political calculation which, it was often recognized, lay behind what purported to be his restoration, as *princeps* Augustus, of the old Republic.[60] (So was Bossuet, whose *Discours sur L'Histoire Universelle* (1681) still saw a mystical rôle for the *pax Augusta* in the unfolding of time.[61]) To this evidence we may add Dryden's presentation of Octavian in *All For Love*.

If Dryden is an Augustan poet it is because, whatever his actual historical views, he needed the ideal of Augustus, and because his expression of this ideal is not incidental but basic and indeed structural in several of his most important works: *Astraea Redux*, *Mac Flecknoe*, *Absalom and Achitophel*, 'To Congreve'. The ideal is sharply offset, not only by his acute sense of how far his

[56]'A Discourse Concerning Satire', ll. 1823–8, 2214–24, 2282–4; James Kinsley, ed., *The Poems of John Dryden*, II, pp. 647, 657, 659.

[57]'An Account of the Ensuing Poem . . .', ll. 167–70; Kinsley, I, p. 48. Sir Richard Fanshawe's translation of Camões's maritime epic had been published in 1655.

[58]Cf. *The Hind and the Panther*, Part III, ll. 595–626; Virgil, *The Georgics*, I, 199–203, 316–34, 373–514.

[59]'Preface' to *Fables Ancient and Modern*, ll. 140–3; Kinsley, IV, p. 1448. Some tributes to Dryden on his death paid him the specifically Augustan compliment: see Henry Hall, 'To the Memory of John Dryden, Esq.'; and 'To Dr Samuel Garth . . .' in *Luctus Britannici . . .* (London, 1700), pp. 20, 54.

[60]'A Discourse Concerning Satire', ll. 1987–2075; Kinsley, II, pp. 651–3. Tacitus was always an authority to hand for insinuations against a current monarch. This may have something to do with Dryden's use of Tacitus in the post-1688 period. It is suggestive that Gillyflower, the publisher of the translation of Tacitus brought out by Dryden and others in 1698, should dedicate it to a noted non-juror nobleman, William Digby, Baron Geashill.

[61]*Discours Sur L'Histoire Universelle . . . par Jacques Benigne Bossuet* (Paris, 1681), pp. 91–4. Within a few pages Bossuet can write of the horror of the Triumvirate, the sudden change from cruelty to kindness of Octavian, his success in blaming the Proscriptions on his two colleagues, the birth of Christ almost coinciding with Rome's return to monarchy under the peaceful reign of Augustus, and the friendliness and liberality of the *princeps* to Virgil and Horace, who brought Latin poetry to its perfection.

own times fell short of it, a recognition giving rise to satire, but also by the poet's perceptive and at times even sympathetic awareness of an opposite, Antonian, conception. During the twenty five years of Charles's reign Dryden saw his King in both rôles. It is the panegyrical strain in Dryden which, if anything, warrants the term Augustan. Nor is this just a euphemistic way of saying that Dryden is the English Claudian. Verse panegyric in the tradition of Claudian certainly is central in Dryden, but Augustan allusion is not actually central in Claudian. It is to be found in him, but found more in Dryden. The form of the verse panegyric, whether as in *Astraea Redux* more or less straightforwardly put to use, or used in more elaborate and innovative poetic structures to supply a vein of tribute, ironical or sincere, was for Dryden the most available mode for that Augustan comparison which chiefly could express for him the crucial importance of monarchy in a civilized polity, and the crucial relation between rule and writing, between Corinthian, Ionic and Doric, which was the mark of the mature era in the cycles of history and constituted the temple of civilization.[62]

[62]See Howard Erskine-Hill, 'Heirs of Vitruvius', *The Art of Alexander Pope*, pp. 144–8.

IX   The Idea of an Augustan Age[1]

> Doubtless, opposers of tyrannic sway,
> But pleas'd a mild Augustus to obey.
> (Lyttelton's *Epistle to Mr. Pope*, 1730)

Hume in 1760

In the autumn of 1760, within two months of the accession of King George III, David Hume, the philosopher and historian, wrote to his friend William Strahan:

> Is this new Reign to be the Augustan Age? or have the Parsons got entire Possession of the young Prince? I hear that they brag much of their Acquisition; but he seems by his Speech to be a great Admirer of his Cousin of Prussia, who surely is no Favourer or Favourite of theirs. I wonder how Kings dare be so free: They ought to leave that to their Betters; to Men who have no Dependance on the Mob, or the Leaders of the Mob. As to poor Kings they are obligd sometimes to retract and to deny their Writings.
>
> I was glad to observe what our King says, that Faction is at an End and Party Distinctions abolish'd. You may infer from this, that I think I have kept clear of Party in my History. . . .[2]

The letter testifies to the persistence of the habit of thinking about a new Augustus at the start of a new reign, and of some of the benefits traditionally associated with his name. To think about a new Augustan Age is to ask how far the new ruler values learning and the arts, and how far his reign promises to bring civil conflict to an end. Yet if we cast our mind back to the verse panegyrics of 1660 –

> Oh Happy Age! Oh times like those alone
> By Fate reserv'd for Great *Augustus* Throne!
> When the joint growth of Armes and Arts foreshew
> The World a Monarch, and that Monarch *You*.

[1]The present chapter is an expanded and modified version of my article 'Augustans on Augustanism: England, 1655–1759', in *Renaissance and Modern Studies*, XI (1967), pp. 55–83. Discussion of this subject, which till then seemed to be opening without reference to some of the chief primary sources, has since developed into a notable debate about the eighteenth-century picture of Rome's Augustan Age. I have profited from both sides of this debate to elaborate my own conclusions: the picture is certainly less simple than I once supposed, though the main thrust of my argument is the same.

[2]*The Letters of David Hume*, ed. J.Y.T. Greig (Oxford, 1932), I, p. 336 (To William Strahan, Nov. or Dec. 1760).

(the ending of Dryden's *Astraea Redux*) – we at once feel the difference of tone in Hume's familiar letter. This difference arises only in part from the difference of literary form. The great pressure of hope is not there in Hume: instead there is the confident detachment which allows him to say: 'I wonder how Kings dare be so free: they ought to leave that to their Betters . . .'. Hume plays with the notions of enlightenment and prudence – George will not be an Augustus if he is possessed by parsons, neither will he be if, like the King of Prussia, he parades irreligious views and insults all his neighbours in a series of odes and epistles, spirited if defective in language and numbers.[3] It is important to catch Hume's attitude to kings here. He sees them neither as tyrannous nor insignificant, but quite without mystique. They are vulnerable political figures ('poor Kings') but significant enough to merit strong censure if they are imprudent. If, unlike George I and II, they can achieve a status above party and faction, they may do good and be the more secure.

Hume's letter has one other notable feature: the use of the adjective 'Augustan' to apply, not to the Rome of Augustus, but to modern civilization. Striking if one comes to it from a study of the earlier seventeenth century, this usage is common in the eighteenth century, and is perhaps first to be found in the Preface to the Second Part of Waller's Poems, probably written by Francis Atterbury, and published in 1690. It is an important document of literary criticism which I shall discuss in due course. Here it helps me to delineate the strict subject of the present chapter: that body of texts, various in purpose and form, which apply the word 'Augustan' to evaluate, affirm or deny the achievement of a phase of modern British civilization. For a century or so from the year of the Atterbury Preface, such applications are to be found, and afford a unique basis for exploring the meaning of 'Augustan' to those for whom the concept was crucial. It is the purpose of the present chapter to consider this material, together with the related discussions of Augustan Rome, in order to provide a context of opinion in which to read those poetic texts of the eighteenth century which now remain for discussion.[4]

---

[3]Ibid., I, pp. 326–7 (To Lord Minto, May 1760).
[4]The debate about 'The Meaning of "Augustan" ' began with the article of that title published by J.W. Johnson in the *Journal of the History of Ideas*, XIX (1958), pp. 507–22. It ignored important material, made exaggerated claims, and dated Pope's Epistle *To Augustus* nine years too early (p. 514) but pointed out quite rightly that eighteenth-century writers did not invariably admire Augustus and his age. The hostile tradition was quite strong. This view was restated with corrections and a better range of evidence in Chs. 1 and 2 of Johnson's *The Formation of English Neo-Classical Thought* (Princeton, 1967), a lively but sketchy treatment of an enormous subject. Hostile or sceptical views of Augustus in the eighteenth century have been explored with more literary sensitivity by Malcolm Kelsall in a sequence of articles amounting to a book-length study: 'The Meaning of Addison's *Cato*', *Review of English Studies*, N.S. XVII, 6 (May 1966), pp. 149–62; 'What God, What Mortal? The *Aeneid* and English Mock-Heroic', *Arian*, VIII (1969), pp. 359–79; 'Baroque Virgil: Joseph Trapp's *Aeneid*', *Proceedings of the Virgil Society*, XII (1972–3), pp. 1–10; 'Augustus and Pope', *The Huntington Library Quarterly*, XXXIX, 2 (Feb. 1976), pp. 117–31; *Imperious Caesar, dead and turn'd to clay*, Inaugural Lecture (Cardiff, 1977), pp. 1–19; and – with R.D. Williams – 'Joseph Addison, *Pax Gulielmi Auspiciis Europae Reddita*, 1697 . . .', *Greece and Rome*, Second Series, XXVII, 1 (April 1980), pp. 48–59. This argument about the eighteenth century reached an extreme form in Howard D. Weinbrot, *Augustus Caesar in 'Augustan' England: The Decline of a Classical Norm* (Princeton, 1978), a lively, learned but often one-sided book. As Kelsall notes, it 'is written, as it were, by a brilliant prosecuting counsel' (*The Scriblerian*, IX, 1 (Autumn, 1978)), p. 40; and Michael Meehan in an exceptionally knowledgeable review says it

Broadly speaking these considerations of a new Augustan Age divide into two kinds: those which look to the immediate or further future; and those which look back to recognize or to deny an earlier phase of English Augustan achievement. The second kind are obviously more detailed and informative, and sometimes we are lucky enough to find examples of each within the work of a single writer. This is the case with Hume whose extended discussion as to why the reign of Charles II was unworthy to be considered the English Augustan Age, published in the final volume of his *History of England* (1757), helps us to a specific understanding of what Hume meant by 'Augustan Age' in his 1760 letter. I shall consider first the prospective discussions of an Augustan Age, since these are more closely connected with panegyrical times and forms so important in the later seventeenth century, whereas the retrospective discussions are a part of the developing eighteenth-century literary criticism. A preliminary word, however, must be said about Atterbury's Preface to Waller, not only because this is so far as we know the first application of the word 'Augustan' to English culture, but because it may not be entirely the retrospective literary critical essay which it appears.

A New Augustan Age in Prospect

'Waller', wrote Atterbury, 'undoubtedly stands first in the list of refiners, and, for ought I know, last too; for I question whether in Charles II's reign English did not come to its full perfection; and whether it has not had its Augustan age as

'either overlooks or acknowledges and underestimates the significance of a considerable body of writing in which an effort was made to sift the Augustan legacy for elements of value, and to sustain these in the face of generally acknowledged defects' ('The Waning of the Augustan Age', *Southern Review*, XII, 3 (Nov. 1979), pp. 285–96). I shall briefly state my own reservations.

1. Despite a wealth of evidence cited the book cannot be regarded as exhaustive (a caveat unnecessary of a book less confident in its claims). Bevil Higgons's *Historical and Critical Remarks* . . . (2nd edn, 1727) and William Godwin's *Enquirer* paper (1797) are instances which tell against its argument and are not mentioned; neither is John Gordon's *Occasional Thoughts on the Study and Character of Classical Authors* (1762) which would have supported it. The book is equally silent on tricky, middle-of-the-road cases such as the lexicographer Thomas Sheridan.

2. Many authors are glancingly mentioned on Weinbrot's side of the argument when there is strong evidence within their work for the opposite case. This is true not only of minor authors such as Vicessimus Knox, but of others ranging from the more considerable to the great: John Dennis, Nicholas Rowe, Leonard Welsted, Horace Walpole and David Hume.

3. Citation of opinions on one or the other side is not enough: critical analysis of passages in context is necessary to bring out their significance. This is not sufficiently done. (For example, denials that there was an Augustan Age in England are not necessarily evidence that Rome's Augustan Age was deplored.) Weinbrot's case also involves statements about the 'lies and collaboration' of 'the sycophantic Horace', and 'Augustus's tyranny and control of art' (pp. 141, 217). These views may be readily assessed against the picture given in a recent collection, Kitty Chisholm and John Ferguson, ed., *Rome: The Augustan Age, a Source Book* (Oxford, 1982), and the work of C.O. Brink on Horace. The other side in the debate about the eighteenth century may be seen in R. A. Brower, *Pope: The Poetry of Allusion* (Oxford, 1960); my *Pope: Horatian Satires and Epistles* (Oxford, 1964), 'The Medal Against Time: A Study of Pope's Epistle *To Mr. Addison*', *Journal of the Warburg and Courtauld Institutes*, XXVIII (1965), pp. 507–22 (see Ch. X below), 'Augustans on Augustanism', and 'Satire and Self-Portrayal: The First Satire of the Second Book of Horace, Imitated and Pope's Reception of Horace' in *Wolfenbütteler Forschungen*, ed. Walther Killy (Munich, 1981), pp. 153–71; and John Paul Russo, *Alexander Pope: Tradition and Identity* (Cambridge, Mass., 1971), among other works. The concluding chapters of the present book may be seen in this tradition though I am substantially in debt to both Weinbrot and Kelsall.

well as the Latin.'[5] What is worth noting is the year of publication: the year which seemed to show William and Mary securely settled on the throne, and the senior line of the Stuarts decisively exiled. Waller's poetry is predominantly poetry of the Stuart court. His poem on St James's Park had specifically associated Charles II and Augustus. He had died shortly before the Revolution. The Preface may make a political as well as a literary point. At a time when it would be conventional to evoke the Augustan idea in hopes for a new reign, Atterbury uses his opportunity for retrospective discussion to bid farewell to Augustan achievement with the end of a Stuart era.[6] Four years later, as it happened, Atterbury had occasion to expound his idea of the Augustan Age of Rome. In his sermon to the Queen on *The Miraculous Propagation of the Gospel*, on 21 October 1694, he cited both Tacitus and Virgil to show that there were prophecies throughout the east, shortly before the time of Christ, that a mighty prince and messiah was to be born. 'But the most Observable thing,' says Atterbury,

> . . . is, that God pitch'd upon that particular Point of Time, for the manifestation of his Gospel, when Good Sense, and Learning, and Wit, were at the highest; when the Roman Empire was in its full Glory, and, together with it, all the Arts and Sciences flourish'd: when the World enjoy'd a profound Peace, and was at Liberty to examine the Truth of an Opinion . . . Then did the Glorious Light of the Gospel shine forth . . .[7]

The providential patristic view, strengthened perhaps by Bossuet, accords with Atterbury's argument. For this churchman the state of language and learning, and the advent and propagation of the Gospel, were bound up in the positive sense of the Augustan idea – and Tacitus of all witnesses is pressed into service.

As the new century opened Matthew Prior, as we have seen, celebrated William III in the *Carmen Seculare, for the Year MDCC*. Addressed to the god Janus, and with an epigraph from Virgil's Fourth Eclogue, it is really a panegyrical hymn in free Pindaric form and a roving survey of the rulers of ancient and modern times. Augustus himself is presented with a careful balance ('And while with clemency Augustus reigned, / The monarch was adored; the city chained'), and William is implicitly warned to do better than Augustus.[8] A year later John Dennis published his treatise on *The Advancement and Reformation of Poetry*, notable, among other things, for its attempt to relate the arts under Augustus to the wider civilization and history of the time. His thesis is that the poetry of Augustan Rome flourished and failed with its religion. Augustus was 'Religious even to Superstition'. While in the violence of the triumvirate politics got the better of his nature, once he had attained sovereign power 'Policy and Nature were reconcil'd, and both of them favour'd Religion'. In the preceding

[5] *The Poems of Edmund Waller*, ed. Thorn Drury, I, p. xix.

[6] In the Preface to his translation of More's *Utopia* (1684), Gilbert Burnet claimed that the English language had by then been 'brought to a purity' under 'a Prince, who is so great a judge, that his single approbation or dislike has almost as great an authority over our language as his prerogatives gives him over our coin . . . it is to be hoped that the Essay on Poetry, which may be matched with the best pieces of its kind that even Augustus's age produced, will have a more powerful operation . . .' (pp. xliv–v).

[7] *Sermons and Discourses On Several Subjects and Occasions* (London, 1723), I, pp. 102–3.

[8] Ll. 54–5; *The Literary Works of Matthew Prior*, ed. H. Bunker Wright and Monroe K. Spears (Oxford, 1959), I, p. 163.

age of 'continual Violences', however, religion was ignored and 'that famous Commonwealth was dwindled into an Oligarchy . . .'. What then brought *Roman* Poetry to 'its utmost Heighth' in 'the glorious Reign of *Augustus*' was that art, language and religion 'were all of them in a great deal of Force together' – though Dennis does not doubt that calm after 'a fierce and tedious Tempest', the elevation arising 'from the Remains and Appearances of Liberty', the 'Appearances of their being Masters of the Universe; and lastly, the never-to-be-forgotten Bounty of a magnanimous Prince' all played their part.[9] Dennis is no fool, whatever Pope may have said. His arguments are by no means uncritical, either of the last years of the Republic or the motives and policy of Augustus. It is notable that he can advance views of this kind, while yet being apparently familiar with the *Discorsi* of Machiavelli.[10]

In 1706 there appeared both Prior's panegyrical *Ode, Humbly Inscribed to the Queen*, which presents Augustus as an ideal, with the reservation that Queen Anne has excelled him, and Nicholas Rowe's dedication of his tragedy *Ulysses* to Lord Godolphin. Rowe's Dedication is of some importance and deserves more than cursory quotation:

> To the Right Honourable
> *SIDNEY* Lord *Godolphin*,
> *Lord High-Treasurer of* England,
> *and Knight of the most Noble Order of the Garter.*
>
> *My* LORD,
>   If those Cares in which the Service of a Great QUEEN, and the Love of Your Country, have so justly Engag'd Your Lordship, would allow any Leisure to run back and remember those Arts and Studies, which were once the Grace and Entertainment of Your Lordship's Youth; I have Presumption enough to hope, that this Tragedy may, some Time or other, find an Hour to Divert Your Lordship. Poetry, which was so venerable to former Ages, as in many Places to make a Part of their Religious Worship, and every where to be had in the highest Honour and Esteem, has miserably languish'd and been despis'd, for want of that Favour and Protection which it found in the famous *Augustan* Age. Since then, it may be asserted, without any Partiality to the Present Time, it never had a fairer Prospect of lifting up its Head, and returning to its former Reputation, than now: And the best Reason can be given for it, is, that it seems to have a particular Hope from, and Dependance upon Your Lordship, and to expect all just Encouragement, when those Great Men, who have the Power to Protect it, have so Delicate and Polite a Taste and Understanding of its true Value. The Restoring and Preserving any Part of Learning is so Generous an Action in itself, that it naturally falls into Your Lordship's Province, since every Thing that may serve to Improve the Mind, has a Right to the Patronage of so Great and Universal a Genius for Knowledge as Your Lordship's. It is indeed a Piece of good Fortune, upon which I cannot help Congratulating the present Age, that there is so Great a Man, at a Time when there is so great an Occasion for him. The Divisions which Your Lordship has heal'd, the Temper which You have restor'd to our Councils, and that indefatigable Care and Diligence which You have us'd in preserving our Peace at Home, are Benefits so virtuously and so seasonably conferr'd upon Your Country, as shall draw the Praises of all Wise Men, and the Blessings of all Good Men upon Your Lordship's Name. And when those unreasonable Feuds and Animosities, which keep Faction alive, shall be bury'd in silence and forgotten, that great Publick Good shall be

[9]*The Critical Works of John Dennis*, ed. E.N. Hooker (Baltimore, 1939–43), I, pp. 246–7.
[10]Ibid., I, p. 243.

universally acknowledg'd, as the Happy Effect of Your Lordship's most equal Temper and Right Understanding. That this Glorious End may very suddenly succeed to Your Lordship's Candor and Generous Endeavours after it, must be the Wish of every good *Englishman*. I am,

> My LORD,
> Your Lordship's
> most Obedient
> Humble Servant,
> N. ROWE.[11]

The major concern to emerge explicitly from Rowe's dedication, is the concern with enlightened patronage. An appeal on behalf of poetry is being made, not indeed to the ruler herself, but to one who has 'the Power to protect it': the chief servant of a 'great QUEEN'. Poetry, one of the ancient arts of peace and a part of religious worship, was held in high honour in the 'famous *Augustan* age'; the augury of a new Augustan Age in English is the fortunate coincidence of 'Taste', 'Understanding' and 'Power' in certain 'Great Men'. This is in fact the age-old ideal of a union of intellect and strength, wisdom and power, understanding and action, of which Plato's philosopher-prince is the most famous formulation. The ideal of enlightened patronage, perpetuated to the honour of Augustus and Maecenas through the works of Virgil and Horace, is here assumed to be the main feature of an Augustan Age. This is not, however, the only point of interest in the dedication. The second half, in which Rowe praises Godolphin for having successfully healed the 'Feuds and Animosities' of political 'Faction' in the interest of the 'public Good', is entirely in keeping with the nature of the compliment and appeal made in the first half. As Augustus established an imperial peace after a world-wide war, so Godolphin in his smaller yet analogous world has brought about harmony after a period of political 'Division'. In such a period of harmony, it is implied, the arts are better able to flourish. It is also interesting to observe the traditional humanist note in the phrase 'the Restoring and Preserving any Part of Learning. . . .'. Rowe in the eighteenth century is no less conscious of taking part in a *renascentia* than the humanists of the fifteenth and sixteenth centuries. Finally, it is curious to consider the tone of the Dedication. The implausibly extravagant compliment in the middle ('. . . so Great and Universal a Genius . . .') accords ill with the transparent affectation of a familiar, gentlemanly modesty at the beginning: the writer's hope 'that this Tragedy may, some time or other, find an Hour to Divert Your Lordship'. Rowe may be thought to aim, though not in any sustained fashion, at that 'Candour and Affability' in the relation between poet and patron which Sir William Temple had noted, when he wrote: '*Augustus* was not only a Patron, but a Friend and Companion of *Virgil* and *Horace*. . . .' and which Steele was to mention, some eight years later, as characteristic of the court of Augustus.[12]

[11]Nicholas Rowe, Dedication to *Ulysses: A Tragedy*, 1706. It was produced on 22 Nov. 1705 (Nicholas Rowe, *Three Plays*, ed. J.R. Sutherland (London, 1929), pp. 41, 7). OED, in its article on 'Augustan' wrongly assigns this passage to 1704.

[12]Sir William Temple, *Essays on Ancient and Modern Learning and on Poetry*, ed. J.E. Spingarn (Oxford, 1909), p. 77; *The Spectator*, No. 280 (21 Jan. 1712), ed. D.F. Bond (Oxford, 1965), II, p. 592.

From Atterbury, Dennis and Rowe it may be seen that at the end of the seventeenth and beginning of the eighteenth centuries there were writers ready to stress a religious dimension to the ideal of an Augustan age. While less enchanted and more secular views of the Augustan principate were readily available – both Tacitus and Machiavelli had comparatively recently been newly translated into English[13] – this religious emphasis accords with and may have influenced much Augustan poetry in the reign of Anne. In his *Messiah*, Pope like Atterbury uses the notion that Virgil's Fourth Eclogue was responding to the Sybilline prophecies of Christ: thus Isaiah and Virgil are boldly brought together in a way consistent with the ancient Christian interpretation of Virgil, not because Pope believed the tradition, but rather as a conscious poetic essay in the combination of Christian and classical, religious and poetic, to produce an Augustan poem. Pope's handling of sustained prophetic utterance is, no doubt, more like ode than eclogue, and owes much to Dryden's *Ode to Ann Killigrew* and St Cecilia Odes. When we turn from the *Messiah* to Pope's *Windsor Forest* and other poetry written to celebrate the Peace of Utrecht we find this rhapsodic utterance still there, but tempered now in the acclamation of a new peace in the world rather than of the coming of the Kingdom of Christ. The long last passage of *Windsor Forest*, which Pope added to the earlier part of the poem between 1710 and 1713, draws strongly on the seventeenth-century panegyrical tradition: indeed it is to the allegorical figure of the Thames (who it will be recalled played a part in the Royal Entries of 1604 and 1661) that Pope gives the concluding prophetic speech. The Queen has already been compared to an Augustus in all but name:

> At length great ANNA said – Let Discord cease!
> She said, the World obey'd, and all was *Peace*![14]

The conclusion of David's speech was similarly treated, in *Absalom and Achitophel*. Almost immediately following, a line taken from *Annus Mirabilis* prompts us to realize that Pope is reworking that vision of a new and more spacious city, at the heart of a world-wide but peaceful commercial empire, which had been the culmination of Dryden's poem.[15] We are not surprised therefore that Pope follows Dryden in introducing the ancient Roman name for London: *Augusta*. Both poets imply that the name has a new significance as well as an old; both are depicting the revival of a Roman creation:

> Behold! *Augusta's* glitt'ring Spires increase,
> And Temples rise, the beauteous Works of Peace.[16]

Taken as a whole Pope's place poem reaches its final level of prophetic utterance

---

[13]*The Works of the Famous Nicolas Machiavel . . . newly and faithfully Translated into English* [by Henry Neville] (London, 1675); *The Annals and History of Cornelius Tacitus: His Account of the Antient Germans, and the Life of Agricola. Made English by Several Hands* (London, 1698), of which Dryden translated *Annals*, I.

[14]Ll. 327–8; *Poems*, I, pp. 181.

[15]*Annus Mirabilis*, stanzas 288–304. Pope echoes l. 295 of Dryden's poem at l. 330 of *Windsor Forest*. *The Poems of John Dryden*, ed. James Kinsley, I, p. 93.

[16]Ll. 336, 377–8; *Poems*, pp. 182, 187.

with great skill, for the personified Thames of the conclusion is still the geographical and historical river which runs through the time and space of the whole work. It is at the end that Pope conveys that sense of extension, of universality, and of the favour of heaven which was (in different measure) expressed at the panegyrical moments of 1604 and 1660–6. With *Messiah* in his mind, Pope presses the prophecy almost to millenial vision:

> The Time shall come, when free as Seas or Wind
> Unbounded *Thames* shall flow for all Mankind . . . .

> Oh stretch thy Reign, fair *Peace*! from Shore to Shore,
> Till Conquest cease, and Slav'ry be no more:[17]

It is the association of Augustan Age and Golden Age, the informing idea of Virgil's Fourth Eclogue and one recalled by Dryden in *Astraea Redux* and *Absalom and Achitophel*, which here gives the Augustan idea its religious dimension. Pope as 'Laureate of Peace'[18] expresses it at the end of *Windsor Forest*, not only in the phrase '*Albion's* Golden Days' but in the whole atmosphere, half of prophecy, half of acclamation.

It would be wrong to attribute this kind of effect to the poetic character and views of Pope alone. Much peace poetry of this time strikes the same almost millenial note – a little-known example is Bevil Higgons's *Poem on the Glorious Peace of Utrecht*, inscribed in 1713 to the Earl of Oxford, and interesting because its author, fourteen years later, was to set out very clearly his understanding of what was meant by an English Augustan Age.

The purpose of Pope's panegyrical prophecy, like the leading seventeenth-century panegyrics, and Rowe's more explicit Dedication to *Ulysses*, was to express a hopeful belief in the early attainment of a new Augustan Age in Britain. Yet all the more ambitious of Pope's earlier poems, *An Essay on Criticism, The Temple of Fame, Windsor Forest* – even *The Rape of the Lock* in its heroi-comically allusive fashion – display a great historical range of the imagination. The same is true of his Epistle *To Mr Addison* (1720) – which I shall consider in detail in the next chapter. In many ways, it could not be more clearly an Augustan poem, but is so from a late Renaissance point of vantage. In its compliment to Addison and the statesman James Craggs it announces a new Augustan achievement, but this gains its drama from the fact that the poem is really about Rome as a whole, its triumphs, its fall and its living legacy.

In 1721 Tamworth Reresby is another who senses a contemporary Augustan achievement in Britain. He takes up Atterbury's and Dennis's concern with the condition of the language: 'As the Age of *Augustus* surpass'd a great many others in Letters, Arts, and Politeness; so did its Language: And at this Time, whilst we excel the vainest and proudest Nations in all Sort of Learning; so is our Language more copious and expressive than the so much admir'd *French*, *Italian*, and *Spanish* . . .'. This note of cultural chauvinism does not prevent the recognition that such a happy condition cannot last. Nor does his approving

---

[17]Ll. 397–8, 407–8; *Poems*, I, pp. 190–2.

[18]L. 424; *Poems*, I, p. 193. See G. Wilson Knight who, in *Laureate of Peace: On the Genius of Alexander Pope* (London, 1954) was one of the first in our time to respond to this aspect of Pope's work.

quotation of Paterculus in praise of Augustus ('Plain dealing is recall'd to the Bar . . .') mean that he is unaware what 'a mean and degenerate Race' of rulers was to follow.[19]

These remarks by Reresby are only items in his collection of verse and prose, translated or original. Leonard Welsted's volume, *Epistles and Odes* . . . (1724) comprises something very like an explicit Augustan manifesto. The dedicatory dissertation 'On the Perfection of the English Language', the Epistle to the Duke of Chandos, and the translations from the end of Ovid's *Metamorphoses*, Bk XV, including passages on the deification of Julius Caesar and on the reign of Augustus, all reinforce one another in the delineation of an Augustan literary ideal. The Dissertation shows brief recognition of the complementary effects of liberty and peace in the maturing of the arts: 'at the *Restoration* it was, that Poetry and polite Arts began to spring up: In the Reign of *William* the Third, the Founder of *English* liberty, they acquir'd great Strength and Vigour' and, though temporarily checked by political tempests, will in 'the present Calm' advance to 'that *Standard* or Perfection, which denominates a Classical Age'. The specific model for this 'Standard or Perfection' is revealed in Welsted's panegyrical epistle to Chandos:

> No more neglected shall the Lyre remain;
> Thou, CHANDOS, shalt improve its heavenly Strain:
> Thy smiles already in the Dawn I see,
> And *England* many POLLIOS boasts in Thee;
> To every Art thy generous Cares extend,
> But, chiefly, shalt thou be the Poet's Friend.
> Th'approaching Times my raptured Thought engage;
> I see arise a New *Augustean* Age:
> Here, stretch'd at ease, beneath the Beechen Boughs,
> The Sylvan Poet sings his faithful Vows;
> Others, retiring from the Vulgar Throng,
> At leisure meditate an Epic Song;
> Or chuse the Worthies of a former Age,
> With all their Pomp of Grief to fill the Stage;
> While, here, Historians BRUNSWIC'S Praise sustain,
> Record his Deeds, and lengthen out his Reign.[20]

That Welsted's volume celebrates and appeals to the current Whig establishment – other of his writings address Walpole in explicitly Augustan terms and beg support for a new translation of Horace – was not, perhaps, the sole ground on which it is unlikely to have impressed Pope. Welsted's conception of 'a New *Augustean* Age' is altogether too easy. Pope's imagination has to work for the Augustan moment, in the confrontation of decay, destruction and the struggle of the generations to revitalize their heritage: not so here. Nevertheless Welsted's fluent prose and verse outline an ideal of liberty, peace and patronage encouraging arts of the chief Augustan kinds, that is certainly serious in itself. Further, we should not underestimate Welsted's eclecticism: he was one of the

---

[19]Tamworth Reresby, *A Miscellany of Ingenious Thoughts and Reflections* (London, 1721), pp. 10, 376–7.

[20]Leonard Welsted, *Epistles and Odes, &c. Written on Several Subjects With a Translation of Longinus's Treatise on the Sublime* (London, 1724), pp. vii–viii, pp. 44–5.

chief propagandists of Longinus (whom he here translated) in the earlier eighteenth century.

In 1726 Dennis, in course of praising the greatness of the dramatic arts, wrote that '*Augustus Caesar*, as famous for the Arts of Peace as his Success in War, renown'd for the wholesome Laws he enacted, and for his reforming the Manners of the People . . . found it easier to make himself Emperor of the World, than a great Dramatick Poet.[21] It will be seen that the ideal of the Augustan Age retained enough vitality for it to be evoked, in the traditional way, on the accession of George II. Laurence Eusden did his duty as Poet Laureate; Richard Savage, in an elaborate poem *Sacred to the Glorious Memory of our Late Most Gracious Sovereign Lord King George* . . . announced:

> But mark! – AUGUSTUS, still above thy Rage [that of death],
> Steps forth to give a second, GOLDEN AGE.[22]

Pope, of course, marked the auspicious accession of George Augustus in his own inimitable way – and one year later. The 1728 *Dunciad*, like the two later versions, incorporates much material that would have reminded its readers of royal entries. Not only did it include, on its first page, that disingenuous imitation of Dryden:

> Still *Dunce the second reigns like Dunce the first*?

with a dagger suggesting to the unskilful reader that this was a *quotation*. (The simple-minded reader's suspicion that somehow the line refers to George II and George I is supported when in the 1729 version the imitation is traced to its source in Dryden's crypto-Jacobite Epistle 'To Mr. Congreve'.) Not only that. The hailing of the new Augustus in Bk III, including the by now familiar pane-gyrical formula 'This, this is he' from *Aeneid* VI, is here again:

> This, this is He, foretold by ancient rhymes,
> Th' Augustus born to bring Saturnian times;
> Beneath his reign, shall Eusden wear the bays . . . .

and since Eusden was the real laureate under King George Augustus, it is by no means clear that this mock-Augustus of *The Dunciad* is Tibbald, all Tibbald, and nothing but Tibbald, even though 'Mr. *Tibbald* was made *Hero* of This Poem'.[23] As in *Mac Fleckno*, the spirit of Rabelais or perhaps the spirit of Lucian has pushed in between the ideal of the original Augustus and the

---

[21]Dennis, 'The Stage Defended . . .', *Critical Works*, II, p. 320.

[22]Ll. 117–18; *The Poetical Works of Richard Savage*, ed. Clarence Tracy (Cambridge, 1962), p. 86.

[23]Cf. l. 6 of the 1728 *Dunciad*; *Poetical Works*, ed. Herbert Davis (Oxford, 1966), p. 725, with l. 6 of *The Dunciad Variorum* (1729); *Poems*, V, p. 61. Dryden's line: 'Still Tom the Second reigns, like Tom the First', alluding in the first place to Thomas Shadwell and Thomas Rymer who at the Revolution supplanted Dryden in his offices as Laureate and Historiographer Royal, also carried an anti-Williamite innuendo (see Derek Roper, *Dryden's Poetic Kingdoms* (London, 1965), pp. 138–9). See Bk III, ll. 317–19; *Poems*, V, pp. 186, 187 (l. 319n).

purported new Augustus, like the figure of the anti-masque whom no pretensions can fool. Meanwhile the serious tradition of Augustan panegyric continued, and is fully exemplified when Samuel Boyse, in avowed imitation of Prior, celebrated the Georgian peace in *The Olive: An Heroic Ode. Occasion'd By the Auspicious Success of His Majesty's Counsels, and His Majesty's Most Happy Return 1736–37*. This is one of the latest full-dress panegyrics, on a proper panegyrical occasion, in English literature. It was an appeal for patronage by a poet desperately in need of support, but the talent that made the appeal was not negligible:

> While thus beneath our greater Cæsar's sway
>   Domestic jars, and foreign broils suppress'd
> Britain beholds to gentler toils give way,
>   And cultivates the nobler arts of rest:
> While he, Augustus-like, with godlike hand
>   Bids the refolding gates of Janus close!
> And makes the glory of his wide command,
>   To give his people and the world repose:
> The Muse, that sees with joy the storm subside,
> Hangs up her lyre to peace, with grateful honest pride![24]

It is certainly interesting that the same year should see the publication of Boyse's *Ode* and Pope's Epistle *To Augustus*. It is instructive to compare them.

A New Augustan Age in Retrospect

To turn now to the second kind of evidence in which the word 'Augustan' is applied to English writing, retrospective discussion of an earlier period, we must look first at Atterbury's influential Preface to Waller. It is good enough to deserve extensive quotation.

> The reader needs to be told no more in commendation of these Poems, than that they are Mr. Waller's; a name that carries everything in it that is either great or graceful in poetry. He was, indeed, the parent of English verse, and the first that showed us our tongue had beauty and numbers in it. Our language owes more to him than the French does to Cardinal Richelieu, and the whole Academy. A poet cannot think of him without being in the same rapture Lucretius is in when Epicurus comes in his way.
>
> > Tu pater, es rerum inventor; tu patria nobis
> > Suppeditas præcepta; tuisque ex, Inclute! chartis,
> > Floriferis ut apes in saltibus omnia libant,
> > Omnia nos itidem depascimur aurea dicta,
> > Aurea! perpetua semper dignissima vita!
>
> The tongue came into his hands like a rough diamond: he polished it first, and to that degree, that all artists since him have admired the workmanship, without pretending to mend it. Suckling and Carew, I must confess, wrote some few things smoothly enough; but as all they did in this kind was not very considerable, so it was a little later than the earliest pieces of Mr. Waller. He undoubtedly stands first in the list

---

[24]Alexander Chalmers, ed., *Works of the English Poets* . . . (London, 1810), XIV, p. 591.

of refiners, and, for aught I know, last too; for I question whether in Charles II's reign English did not come to its full perfection; and whether it has not had its Augustan age as well as the Latin. It seems to be already mixed with foreign languages as far as its purity will bear; and, as chemists say of their menstruums, to be quite sated with the infusion. But posterity will best judge of this. In the meantime, it is a surprising reflection, that between what Spenser wrote last, and Waller first, there should not be much above twenty years' distance; and yet the one's language, like the money of that time, is as current now as ever; whilst the other's words are like old coins, one must go to an antiquary to understand their true meaning and value. Such advances may a great genius make, when it undertakes anything in earnest!

Some painters will hit the chief lines and masterstrokes of a face so truly, that through all the differences of age the picture shall still bear a resemblance. This art was Mr. Waller's: he sought out, in this flowing tongue of ours, what parts would last, and be of standing use and ornament; and this he did so successfully, that his language is now as fresh as it was at first setting out. Were we to judge barely by the wording, we could not know what was wrote at twenty, and what at fourscore. He complains, indeed, of a tide of words that come in upon the English poet, and overflows whatever he builds; but this was less his case than any man's that ever wrote; and the mischief of it is, this very complaint will last long enough to confute itself; for though English be mouldering stone, as he tells us there, yet he has certainly picked the best out of a bad quarry.[25]

Atterbury is not speaking here of '. . . an "Augustan" condition of linguistic attainment in England . . .' in any narrow sense.[26] To proclaim that a language has come to an *Augustan* perfection is to imply it has done so in and through the work of a great author or authors. Waller is at the centre of the Augustan achievement that Atterbury describes. The crucial sentence begins: 'He Waller undoubtedly stands first in the list of refiners, and, for aught I know, last too; for I question . . .' and it is plain that those qualities which Atterbury ascribes to Waller's artistry with words are judged fit to qualify him for the title 'Augustan'. The opening tribute to Waller is indeed remarkable enough, with its culmination in the glowing enthusiasm of Lucretius's lines in praise of Epicurus.[27] Few passages of Roman poetry express so powerfully the spirit of a new birth, the shining forth of light, understanding and achievement, the sense of Donne's 'And now good morrow to our waking souls . . .' but on a greater scale, than that from which these lines were taken. It is useful to look at the opening lines (the beginning of Book III of *De Rerum Natura*):

E tenebris tantis tam clarum extollere lumen
qui primus potuisti inlustrans commoda vitae,
te sequor. . . .[28]

Again the ideas of a renaissance and an Augustan age are integral parts of the same concept. On what grounds did Atterbury pay Waller this

[25]*The Poems of Edmund Waller*, I, pp. xii–xiv.

[26]J.W. Johnson, 'The Meaning of "Augustan" ', p. 508. George Sherburn, in 'The Restoration and the Eighteenth Century' perhaps the first to notice the important use of 'Augustan' in this Preface (*A Literary History of England*, ed. A.C. Baugh (New York, 1948)), p. 699, did not suggest so limited a meaning.

[27]Lucretius, *De Rerum Natura*, III, 9–13.

[28]Ibid., III, 1–3.

tremendous – and to most modern minds undeserved – compliment? The greater part of the Preface is in fact a reply to this question, and the brief, fundamental answer is that in Atterbury's eyes Waller brought form where there had been formlessness, permanence where there had been impermanence, the essential where before there had been mixture and confusion. Waller showed '. . . our tongue had beauty and numbers in it' and did so through a mastery of modes both 'great' and 'graceful': of an elevated public manner (as for example in his *Panegyric to my Lord Protector*) and one lighter and more intimate (his lyrics and complimentary pieces).

When we look further into the passage quoted, we find that it is Atterbury's use of simile and metaphor which tells us most about the meaning of his terms; indeed it is the imagery of this Preface which makes it a remarkable and valuable critical document. Poets of this age are so often praised by their contemporaries for being 'polished' that the word has become hackneyed, and the quality praised a seemingly insipid virtue. But a diamond owes its whole brightness and beauty to being polished; the comparison of the language before Waller to a rough diamond brings the proper meaning out of the word: to 'polish', in this context, is to make manifest a latent value and beauty. The word 'refiner', a little further on, connects with the simile of the diamond and continues the train of thought. Again, the term 'refined', like 'polished', has since become worn and weak; but here it is plain that Atterbury refers to the actual process of refining, extracting from dross what is essential and valuable, taking a noble and durable metal from the ore.[29] The next simile, that of the chemists and their menstruums, seems to confirm that these implications of the word 'refine' were intended, and makes explicit the ideal, already implied, of the purity of the individual language. This ideal does not involve simply the exclusion of recent foreign elements. Rather it is a concentration upon the essential character of the language, which is connected, in turn, with natural and frequent use, as the next simile makes clear. Though Spenser's last work and Waller's first are chronologically close, the language of the last survives like current coin, while that of Spenser (who, as Jonson remarked, 'for affecting the ancients, writ no language') seems as strange to modern eyes as ancient money. Because Waller did not indulge any personal or poetic idiosyncrasy in his choice of expression, but chose rather what Jonson recommended when he wrote: 'Pure and neat Language I love, yet plaine and customary', his words survive like current coin.[30] Atterbury's meaning is deepened by the last two important images in the passage: those of painting and building. The theme of the mutable and the durable, already expressed in the image of the coins, now becomes dominant. To speak of the essential character of a language, which the great poet must discern and make manifest, is perhaps meaninglessly metaphysical; yet Atterbury renders his argument persuasive, even convincing, by introducing the

---

[29]Cf. Sir William Temple, *On Poetry*, ed. cit. pp. 68–9: 'Yet, in this new Dress [rhyme as used in the early Renaissance], Poetry was not without some Charms, especially those of Grace and Sweetness, and the Oar began to shine in the Hands and Works of the first Refiners', and Pope, Epistle *To Augustus*, ll. 276–81; *Poems*, IV, p. 219.

[30]*Timber: or, Discoveries*, ll. 1870–1; *Ben Jonson*, ed. Herford and Simpson, VIII, p. 620. An interesting earlier discussion of the English language, using many of the same terms and metaphors as Atterbury, is '*Vindex Anglicus*: Or, the Perfections of the *English* Language defended and asserted' (1644), *Harleian Miscellany* (London, 1744–6), II, pp. 33–7.

metaphor of the painter who can depict on his canvas not merely the actual appearance of a face at a given time (as a writer might use the language indiscriminately) but its 'chief lines, and masterstrokes' which express character. Thus though the flesh of a face may fill out or thin, new lines come, hair recede, the constant portrait of the changing countenance will remain permanent and true. So it is with the Augustan poet's artistry in language. This is what Joseph Warton was to mean when, some sixty-five years later, he spoke of how '. . . Boccace and Petrarch polished, and fixed the standard of, the Italian language'.[31] Waller and Atterbury shared anxiety at the formlessness and impermanence of the Enlish tongue. Atterbury calls it a 'flowing tongue', in this sense, and alludes a little later to Waller's own lines:

> Poets that lasting marble seek,
> Must carve in Latin, or in Greek;
> We write in sand, our language grows,
> And, like the tide, our work o'erflows.[32]

To this overflowing 'tide of words' (something at once shapeless, shifting, yet destructive) Atterbury opposes the image of building; those parts of the language which would 'last' and 'be of standing use and ornament', the best stone 'out of a bad quarry', are the materials for a structured and formed poetic architecture which may withstand time as Virgil and Horace have done.[33]

> Our lines reformed, and not composed in haste,
> Polished like marble, would like marble last.[34]

The parallel between architecture and a new Augustan achievement in poetry is not to be found in Atterbury and Waller alone; Rymer and Dryden himself discuss literature in these terms – it is a significant part of the critical consciousness of the time.[35] The next paragraph of the Preface after the passage quoted, if less closely relevant to the meaning of the term 'Augustan', nevertheless bears on the subject. Atterbury is here concerned with Waller's reformation of the numbers of English poetry, but once again we are shown how Waller drew order and grace out of a shifting formlessness. He found a poetry '. . . made up almost entirely of monosyllables; which, when they come together . . . are certainly the most harsh, untuneable things in the world'.

Besides, their verses ran all into one another, and hung together, throughout a whole

---

[31]Joseph Warton, *Essay on the Genius and Writings of Pope* (3rd edn corrected, London, 1772), I, pp. 193–4.

[32]'Of English Verse', ll. 13–16; *Poems*, II, p. 70.

[33]*The Poems of Edmund Waller*, I, pp. xx.

[34]*Prologue to 'The Maid's Tragedy'*, ll. 11–12; *Poems*, II, p. 96.

[35]Cf. Rymer, *A Short View of Tragedy*: 'One would not talk of rules, or what is regular with *Shakespear*, or any followers in the Gang of the *Strouling* Fraternity; but it is lamentable that *Ben* Johnson, his Stone and his Tymber, however otherwise of value, must lye a miserable heap of ruins, for want of Architecture, or some Son of *Vitruvius*, to joyn them together' *The Critical Works of Thomas Rymer*, ed. C.A. Zimansky (New Haven, 1956), p. 172; Dryden, 'To My Dear Friend, Mr Congreve', ll. 11–19 (*Poems*, II, p. 582); and Dennis, *The Advancement and Reformation of Poetry Critical Works*, I, p. 203.

copy, like the hooked atoms that compose a body in Des Cartes. There was no distinction of parts, no regular stops, nothing for the ear to rest upon; but as soon as the copy began, down it went like a larum, incessantly; . . . so that really verse, in those days, was but downright prose tagged with rhymes.[36]

Waller created greater harmony by the introduction of polysyllables, he harmonized pauses in the sense with the natural stops of the verse, and brought to the prominence of the line-end forceful words, often verbs, '. . . in which we know the life of language consists'.[37] The 'dance of words' thus created possessed in Atterbury's eyes both more form and more life than could previously be found in English verse. This is a classic apology for the Augustan use of the heroic couplet. It also shows with vividness, clarity and detail what one critic of sensitivity and intelligence understood by an 'Augustan' achievement of English poetry; we need not agree with his judgement of Waller to see that the terms in which he assesses this poet have a certain grandeur and resonance of their own (the analogue of divine creation is seldom remote) and that they are fundamental to some of the chief convictions of the age.

One who disagreed with Atterbury's assessment was Jonathan Swift. In his *Proposal for Correcting the English Tongue* (1711) he deprecated the literary achievement of Charles II's reign, and preferred the times of James and Charles I. In his *Thoughts on Various Subjects* (written sometime between 1711 and 1745) he put his view more specifically: 'The *Epicureans* began to spread at *Rome* in the Empire of *Augustus*, as the *Socinians*, and even the *Epicureans* too, did in England, towards the end of King *Charles* II's Reign; which is reckoned, although very absurdly, our *Augustan* Age.' Swift, it may seem, assumed the religious criterion for an Augustan Age which Dennis had already proposed. Oldmixon, however, in his *Reflections on Dr Swift's Letter* (1712) reaffirmed that the Restoration was the 'Augustan Age of English poetry'.[38]

A more comprehensive assessment of Charles II's time as the English Augustan Age was published by Bevil Higgons in 1726, in answer to a parallel Gilbert Burnet had drawn between Charles II and the Emperor Nero (this was the same Burnet who had paralleled Charles with Augustus in 1684, in the preface to his translation of More's *Utopia*):

The Author would have been more lucky in his Choice, and have drawn a juster Parallel, if he had compared this Prince with the fortunate Predecessor of this infamous Tyrant. Such a Comparison would have given a better Opinion of his Judgement, as well as his Justice, and have made him concur with the greater Part of the World, who have always allowed and called the Times of King CHARLES II the *Augustan Age* of *England*, so great was the resemblance of Genius and Manners. Both these great Princes were invited to Empire after long and bloody civil Wars, whose Wounds they equally healed with the same pacifick Hands; they both alike pardoned their greatest Enemies, and both met with the same Returns; *England* had her *Cinnas* as well as *Rome*. The great Events of the Reigns were equally auspicious. They both saw their Capital Cities rebuilt with greater Magnificence; they both

[36]*Poems of Edmund Waller*, I, p. xxi.

[37]Ibid., I, xxi–ii.

[38]*Proposal for Correcting the English Tongue, &c.* ed. Herbert Davis and Louis Landa (Oxford, 1957), pp. 9–10, 249. John Oldmixon, *Reflections on Dr Swift's Letter* (London, 1712), p. 19.

reformed the Rudeness and Manners of the Age, and introduced a politeness and Elegance unknown before, not more by their Encouragement, than Example. The Purity of the *Latin* and *English* Tongues are owing to the Care and Improvement of those two Monarchs. The noblest Wits and diviner Poets flourished in their Times; Arts and Sciences sprung and bloomed in the Sun-shine of their warm Influence; the Muses and Graces attended them to the Throne, and vanished when they departed; as whatever was Noble and Great at *Rome*, was owing to *Augustus Caesar*, so all that are illustrious at this Day among us in the nobler Sciences, had their Birth or Education under the auspicious Star of Charles II. In short, they both vanquished all Difficulties with the same Felicity, and after long, peaceful, and prosperous Reigns, dyed equally lamented by their Subjects. The only Difference between them was in Extent of Command, in the greatness of Empire, and not of the Men.[39]

Higgons is engaging in historical and political controversy. He wishes to retrieve and vindicate from Burnet an idealized image of the later Caroline Era. He evidently has no fear that comparison with Augustus might open King Charles to criticism from those who did not admire the *princeps*. He is as confident in this as in his general designation of the Restoration as the English Augustan Age. The long and fruitful peace he can praise Charles II for establishing is doubtless the panegyrical ideal of peace for which he had hoped when he addressed his poem on the Peace of Utrecht to Lord Oxford, at the end of the reign of Queen Anne. It involves civil concord, great architectural achievement, purification of the language, a flourishing of both arts and sciences. This is the comprehensive cultural ideal of an Augustan Age in England, assumed by several later writers who, in the point of fact, would deny that such an age was to be found in Charles's reign, if it could be found at all.

The Spread of a Tacitean View

Between 1726 and 1756 there were, to the best of my knowledge, no serious applications of the term 'Augustan' to English culture, though Lord Hervey, the court Whig and original of Pope's Sporus, wrote in his *Memoirs* that there was no 'similitude between the two princes who presided in the Roman and English Augustan ages besides their names, for George Augustus neither loved learning nor encouraged men of letters, nor were there any Mæcenases about him. There was another very material difference too between these two Augustuses. For as personal courage was the only quality necessary to form a great prince which the one was suspected to want, so I fear it was the only one the other was ever thought to possess.'[40] However these thirty years are notable for the spread of the hostile view of Augustus in English writing, a development which must ultimately have affected the proposal of the Augustan Age as a model for emulation. The ruthless early career of Octavian was, of course, clear in some of the earliest classical sources, such as Seneca's *De Clementia*, and Jonson showed that he knew it in *The Poetaster* itself.[41] Further, a critical or

[39]Bevil Higgons, *Historical and Critical Remarks on Bishop Burnet's History of His Own Time, Second Edition with Additions* (London, 1727) p. 295.

[40]John, Baron Hervey of Ickworth, *Some Materials Towards Memoirs of the Reign of King George II*, ed. Romney Sedgwick (London, 1931), p. 261.

[41]*Ben Jonson*, IV, p. 291. And Jonson uses Tacitus in *Sejanus*.

hostile view of the Augustan principate had been available as soon as Tacitus was recovered and Machiavelli known. The panegyric writers of the seventeenth century are unlikely to have been ignorant of these unfavourable perspectives: what determined their writing was the contemporary importance of the institution of monarchy, and the need (in order to advise and request through praise) for a really famous monarchical example, capable of appealing in religious and cultural as well as directly political ways. At the same time there arose in monarchical late Renaissance Italy a Lucianic form designed to undermine (among other things) ideas of monarchical grandeur and probity. Associated with the name of Traiano Boccalini and often called dialogues of the dead, it shaped some of the most intelligent and playful political satire of the seventeenth and eighteenth centuries, though it is more often disrespectful than radical. We have already seen Harrington's anti-Augustan use of Boccalini in *Oceana*; Pope had in his library the republican Earl of Monmouth's translation of *Advertisements from Parnassus* (3rd edn, 1675),[42] and, as Howard Weinbrot has rightly pointed out, would have found an effective anti-Augustan satire in the same form when he came to edit the *Works* of the late John Sheffield, Duke of Buckingham, first published in 1723.[43] Augustus emerges from this dialogue with little probity or dignity though it must be allowed that Buckingham made more out of Augustus's sex life than the proscription of Cicero. Later in the century Pope's friend Lyttelton, who can both praise and blame Augustus, presents him pretty favourably in his *Dialogues of the Dead*.[44]

More hard-hitting and historical were Trenchard and Gordon's *Cato's Letters* (1720–3), Lewis Crusius's *Lives of the Roman Poets* (1726), and Thomas Gordon's *Discourses on Tacitus* (1728). The latter were taken up by Henry St John, Viscount Bolingbroke, one of Pope's most admired friends, and used in some of his attacks on Walpole and George Augustus published in his opposition journal *The Craftsman*. During its great decade of influence, 1726–36, *The Craftsman* can be found both favourable and hostile to Augustus. Middleton's *Life of Cicero* (1741) commended a republican view to its readers, and Pope's friend Spence, both in his Oxford Lectures on Poetry in the early 1730s and his *Polymetis* (1747) took a qualified view of the *Aeneid* stressing those political aspects of it that were acceptable to and meant to be acceptable to Augustus himself. To say with Spence that the *Aeneid* was a political poem would not, of course, be to say anything very surprising to eighteenth- or seventeenth-century ears. The point, perhaps, is that under the two Georges the idea of court poetry had become devalued in England, and the more the Augustan poets were drawn into that category the more complicated became the admiration for them that most writers wished to express. All these sources, some totally anti-Augustan like the *Discourses on Tacitus*, some mixed like *The Craftsman*, have been fully expounded in their anti-Augustan tendency by Howard Weinbrot in *Augustus Caesar in 'Augustan' England*. They form a significant and indeed major feature of eighteenth-century literary civilization; and while there is no reason after the publication of Professor Weinbrot's study for me to expound each

[42]Maynard Mack, 'Pope's Books: A Biographical Survey With A Finding List', No. 22; in Maximilian E. Novak, ed., *English Literature in the Age of Disguise* (London, 1977), p. 239.

[43]Howard D. Weinbrot, *Augustus Caesar in 'Augustan' England*, pp. 80–2.

[44]George, Baron Lyttelton, *Dialogues of the Dead* (London, 1760), pp. 67–74, 100–2, 153–66.

such source in turn, it is no part of my purpose to play down their significance. Taken together their tendency is to reinforce the tradition that had formed from Tacitus, Machiavelli and Harrington. In their view the Augustan principate, in artfully beguiling the Romans from the spirit and reality of their old republican institutions, and in appeasing them merely by the appearance of a restored republic, sowed the seeds of the corruption and decline of Rome. The paradox of the change of behaviour from Octavian to Augustus, which had so challenged Montaigne, was thus resolved, not in Dennis's formulation of 'Policy and Nature . . . reconcil'd', but in the recognition of a cunning mask of moderation designed to conceal from a war-weary people the steady advance of a cruel despotism. The broad view of the rise and fall of Rome available to Machiavelli, Harrington and their followers made it easier for them than it was for Tacitus simply to associate the vigour of Rome with its republican period, and to see the Julian House as betraying the Republic rather than as a new political force arising out of its collapse. Since, as Spence and others recognized, the high art of a Virgil did praise the Julian House; and since the *Aeneid*, though without any narrowing of human sympathy, implicitly commended the Augustan principate, the great poetry of the Augustan Age could be seen as embarrassingly involved in the establishment of despotism. Bolingbroke adopted Machiavelli's account of the vigour and corruption of states as a weapon against the Whig hegemony, and this seemed to associate the temporarily repressed but latently vigorous elements of the British constitution with republican rather than imperial Rome. Yet it is also clear that Bolingbroke agreed with Machiavelli in thinking that in the decline of states only a prince could arrest the decay. Thus in the last analysis neither ruled out a pragmatic resort to monarchy.

In any balanced account of Augustans on Augustanism, however, there is one writer who deserves to be singled out from the general movement in political writing and historiography just summarized. This is Thomas Blackwell the younger, whose remarkable *Memoirs of the Court of Augustus* appeared in 1753, 1755 and (Volume III completed by John Mills) 1763. 'The first effect which this book has on the reader', said Dr Johnson, 'is that of disgusting him with the Author's vanity.' Author of the important *Enquiry into the Life and Writings of Homer* (1735), and appointed by George II as Principal of Marischal College, Aberdeen in 1748, Blackwell was more interested to trace the founts of artistic creativity in an heroic society than in the patronage of a stable monarchy; more inclined to rehearse the aggressive Whig ideology which generations of eighteenth-century Whigs sought to fasten upon the events of 1688–9 than to look for an Augustan reconciliation under a Patriot King. The *Memoirs of the Court of Augustus*, which deserve a fuller critical discussion than can be offered here, are a highly readable blend of *belles lettres* and serious historiography, not unmixed with trenchant and personal colloquialism. In his partisan manner he can brand the politics of the last years of Anne as 'a crazy Start of a squint-ey'd Faction in the end of a female Reign'.[45] So much for the golden ideal of *Windsor Forest*! He has fully absorbed and perhaps simplified the Tacitean view; and there is nothing of a providential or religious mystique about his Augustus, who is considered throughout in a tone of aggressive

---

[45]*Memoirs of the Court of Augustus*, I, p. 151. Johnson's comment is to be found in his *Works*, ed. Arthur Murphy (London, 1810), II, pp. 375.

realism. On the other hand a modern historian would probably consider that Blackwell exaggerated the possibilities of preserving the late Republic and over-idealized the last republicans. Johnson spoke of his 'furious and unnecessary zeal for liberty' and wondered 'why anyone but a schoolboy in his declamation should whine over the commonwealth of Rome, which grew great only by the misery of the rest of mankind'. Blackwell calls Octavian after Philippi 'the young Savage' and of the period after Actium he can write:

> In the subsequent Age, when the Slavery entailed on a brave People by the Pride of one Man [Julius Caesar], and their own Corruption, had produced its *natural* effect; when their Minds debased, and their Understandings blinded; they gave into that dastardly Opinion of FATE and FORTUNE — and very naturally. For in an *absolute Government*, VIRTUE meets not with its proper Reward.[46]

The third volume can compare Augustus's concern for Romans with the solicitude 'a *West India* Planter has for his Negroes' (the refusal of the title *dominus* was nothing to Blackwell and Mills) and can go on to remark that 'all his boasted Marble Structures put together were not worth the Life of one brave Inhabitant of the old brick Buildings, of whom he had massacred Thousands . . .'.[47] Yet Blackwell did see the Age of Augustus as a happy time. In the measured summary with which he concludes his second volume he divides the conduct of Octavian-Augustus into three phases: the first in which under the direction of Cicero 'he acted the *Patriot* and the *Republican*'; the second 'when he play'd the *Tyrant* and the *Triumvir*'; and the third 'when he became the *Prince* and *Parent* of the *Roman* People'. What was for Blackwell the tragedy of the Principate was nevertheless the 'happy Period' which, with the victory at Actium, 'broke forth into broad Day'.[48]

Standing in this 'broad Day' are 'the Poets of the *Augustan* Age' — 'our Imagination immediately presents us with VIRGIL and HORACE . . . And great Men they were; sufficient to illustrate any Period of Time, or grace the Reign of any Prince.'[49] This is a striking tribute as we come to it towards the end of Blackwell's second volume and recall how much he prefers the great centuries of the Republic before the monarchy founded by Augustus. Blackwell's discussion of Maecenas and the poets in Vol. II includes the ideal of intelligent patronage in its full force but with a new inflection. In his narrative the humane and intelligent Maecenas recruited the poets in 'the great Design of taming the savage Cesar'. The very ode of Horace (*Carm*. I, ii) which the young Marvell had amended to address to Charles I is boldly expounded by Blackwell to show how 'the artful Poet' performed his task. He candidly recalls his own youthful indignation at this poem — 'An Officer of *M. Brutus* to fawn upon the young *Cesar*!' in order to warn his readers away from a superficial reaction. 'Let us not injure HORACE so far as to imagine that he flattered for any *mean* Interest of his *own*: that he wanted Favours from *Cesar* either for himself or his Friends, and renounced his Honour and Patriot Principles to obtain them. No — he

---

[46]*Memoirs*, II, p. 194. Johnson, *Works*, II, pp. 379, 377.
[47]Ibid., III, pp. 376–7.
[48]Ibid., II, p. 256.
[49]Ibid., II, p. 256.

refused Favours – he flattered for the PUBLIC GOOD – to reform a Prince who had the Lives of thousands in his power.'[50] It is in these terms that the Blackwell–Mills Vol. III can argue that 'what we loosely term the Stile of the *Augustan Age*, was not *formed* under *Augustus*. It was formed under the Common-Wealth, during the high struggles for Liberty . . .'.[51] This immensely influential argument, which ratified in terms of Roman republican values a continuing admiration of the Augustan poets, was fully consonant with Blackwell's characteristic emphasis upon the arts as a product of their society as a whole. Thrown into a simplified form it allowed people, if they so wished, to detach a literary Augustan Age which they might admire from a reign of Augustus about which they might feel at the best equivocal.

In his second volume Blackwell shows that he understands very well the art of literary imitation from one language to another: the selection of what could be most happily expressed in the language of the imitator, and the 'Characters and Sentiments' of the original for application to '*modern Life* and *Manners*'. Virgil, Boileau and Pope are all praised as 'perfect Masters' in these respects.[52] Consistently with this Blackwell writes about Roman history with British history always in mind. Section II is called; 'The Plan of the Consular Government – compared with the British Constitution' and his discourse sometimes modulates into direct and complimentary address to his dedicatee, as it does here to Henry Pelham:

> To whom therefore could a DRAUGHT of the *Roman Empire* (a State founded on Freedom) be so fitly addressed, and to whose Judgement could a COMPARISON of its *Constitution* with *our own* be so properly submitted, as to the Man who has the genuine Honour of leading in the Councils of such a Nation as *Great Britain*? Let me not ill deserve his Goodness in reviewing the DRAUGHT, by concealing such Condescension, or suppressing the Pride justly inspired by Mr PELHAM'S Approbation. Encouraged by these, SIR! I proceed to give the History of a COURT, which, by turning from a Course of Violence and Oppression to the *Maxims* you pursue, and to the *Moderation* you practise, became beneficent and humane; and, if not strictly virtuous in private Life, at least decent in Public, and eminent in Politeness and Learning.[53]

It will be seen that this is panegyric, and that, even though Blackwell is anticipating some of his characteristic arguments concerning the Augustan Age, he is still praising and advising through the application of the Augustan idea. In the following paragraph he praises Augustus for his patronage of 'Men of Learning and Genius' and those same men for retrieving him from 'Vice and Misery in the Flower of his life . . .'.[54] The power of this traditional comparison and standard is strong indeed when we find it in the pages of Blackwell. But the *Memoirs of the Court of Augustus* is a strongly panegyrical work in other ways. A traditional Whig who can praise John Hampden and Algernon Sidney, Blackwell views with unfeigned satisfaction the prospect in the north of Britain where, in

[50]Ibid., II, pp. 256–7.
[51]Ibid., III, p. 467.
[52]Ibid., II, pp. 262–3.
[53]Ibid., I, p. 199.
[54]Ibid., I, p. 199.

the aftermath of the 1745 Jacobite Rebellion, 'thro' the Courage and Conduct of a Royal Leader, Peace now reigns . . .'. This praise of the Duke of Cumberland leads to praise of the King, and as in true panegyric this praise is a celebration of all the values upon which, in the view of the panegyrist, the well-being of the community rests: ' "A supreme Magistrate, governing according to Law . . . the Father of a free People . . . is one of the most exalted among Men:" And such a Character, and such a King hath the whole Tenor of his Reign approved GEORGE II to have been to *Great Britain*. Every Step of his Government, – every Treaty he has made, every War he has waged, every Alliance he has contracted, shew him firm to the *Protestant* cause, and true to the Interests of his *People*. . . . Deservedly does *such* a Prince reign in the Hearts of the worthiest of his Subjects . . .'.[55]

The significance of Blackwell's work is in demonstrating the great hold that admiration of the Augustan poets had over the minds of the educated. To have gone so far down the road to outright hostility to Augustus, and yet have produced an account of Horace and Virgil which accords them, if anything, an even more positive moral rôle than in traditional appreciations, was a striking resolution of what was for many in the eighteenth century coming to be the difficult paradox of the Augustan Age. Blackwell used two major attitudes of his time to construct his argument: first an increasing admiration for the Republic, which yielded the point that Virgil and Horace were really republican products; secondly, a continuing understanding of the moral rôle of panegyric, which could thus stress the most admirable aspect of court poetry.

The character and direction of Blackwell's argument, together with his love of British applications, would have been clear to his contemporaries by 1756, when Hume ridiculed his love of giving English equivalents for Latin names, and professed, perhaps sincerely, to think that such a work could have no merit.[56] It was not, however, until the third volume of the *Memoirs* that an explicit comparison was made between the Augustan Age and the reign of Charles II. 'Let not therefore *Virgil* or *Horace*, or *Valgius* or *Varus*, be looked upon as *courtbred* Poets under *Augustus*: no more than Milton, Waller and Cowley were under Charles II.'[57] Meanwhile, in 1756, there had appeared the first volume of Joseph Warton's *Essay on the Genius and Writings of Pope*, containing in response to the following couplet from Pope's *Essay on Criticism*:

> When *Love* was all an easie Monarch's Care;
> Seldom at *Council*, never in a *War*:

a paragraph of excellent terseness and asperity:

> The dissolute reign of Charles II justly deserved the satirical proscription in this passage. Under the notion of laughing at the absurd austerities of the Puritans, it became the mode to run into the contrary extreme, and to ridicule real religion and unaffected virtue. The king, during his exile, had seen and admired the splendor of the court of Louis XIV and endeavoured to introduce the same luxury into the English court. The common opinion, that this was the Augustan age in England, is excessively

[55]Ibid., I, pp. 150–4.
[56]*The Letters of David Hume*, I, p. 230.
[57]*Memoirs*, III, p. 468.

false. A just taste was by no means yet formed. What was called SHEER WIT, was alone studied and applauded. Rochester, it is said, had no idea that there could be a better poet than Cowley. The king was perpetually quoting HUDIBRAS. The neglect of such a poem as the Paradise Lost, will forever remain a monument of the bad taste that prevailed. It may be added, that the progress of philological learning, and of what is called the belles lettres, was perhaps obstructed by the institution of the Royal Society; which turned the thoughts of men of genius to physical enquiries. Our style in prose was but beginning to be polished: although the diction of Hobbes is sufficiently pure; which philosopher, and not the FLORID Spratt, was the classic of that age. If I was to name a time, when the arts and polite literature, were at their height in this nation, I should mention the latter end of King William, and the reign of Queen Anne.[58]

Striking here is the positive sense of the word 'Augustan' which Warton assumes in conveying his disapproval of the Restoration: what he means by 'the Augustan age in England' is a time 'when the arts and polite literature, were at their height in this nation . . .'. Notable too is his reference to the fact that the Augustan designation of Charles II's reign had become 'common opinion' – this has its implications for an interpretation of Pope's Epistle *To Augustus*. Where 'Augustus' himself is concerned, Warton sees the King as having failed to take a lead – or rather as having given only a brief and false one. Charles is seen simply as a symptom of a prevailing bad taste, and this is based on literary standards alone. Far from sharing Bevil Higgons's comprehensive approval of the whole civilization of the reign, Warton sees the Royal Society as an obstacle to the advance of letters. *Paradise Lost* was neglected while 'SHEER WIT' was applauded to excess: if Jonson wished to relegate the Ovidian from his literary commonwealth, Warton would like to relegate wit and *Hudibras*. Since Milton and Hobbes are singled out for praise it may be right to note that each of these flourished during the Commonwealth. While it is not surprising that Warton should condemn the neglect of *Paradise Lost*, it is curious that for him this condemns that age as less than Augustan. He might, after all, have advanced the more important argument that the age was Augustan because it produced *Paradise Lost* – produced it in the way Blackwell thought the Augustan Age produced Virgil. Warton cannot have doubted why *Paradise Lost* was neglected: political reasons and his own second sentence say it all. More than curious, it may be thought, is the fact that the age Warton calls Augustan includes none of those poets whom in the controversial dedication of his book he considers 'In the first class': 'our only three sublime and pathetic poets; Spenser, Shakespeare, Milton'.[59] The writers Warton considered to comprise the English Augustan Age were (as is made clear in a later passage): 'Dryden, Tillotson, Temple, Pope, Addison, Garth, Congreve, Rowe, Prior, Lee, Swift, Bolingbroke, Atterbury, Boyle, Locke, Newton, Clarke, Kneller, Thornhill, Jarvas, Meade, Friend'.[60] Possibly Warton presupposes that an Augustan age must be an age of general achievement in the arts and polite literature, that one great poet does not make an age Augustan, while several civilized and successful poets do. As Goldsmith was to write, 'In that period of

[58]*An Essay on the Genius and Writings of Pope* (3rd edn), I, pp. 161–2.
[59]Ibid., I, p. xi.
[60]Ibid., I, p. 192.

British glory [the age of Anne], though no writer attracts our attention singly, yet, like stars lost in each others brightness, they have cast such a lustre on the age in which they lived, that their minutest transactions will be attended to by posterity . . .'.[61] Yet the Augustan Age of Rome had both qualifications. It is perhaps more likely that we have here the beginning of that significant shift in the meaning of the word 'Augustan' which occurred between the eighteenth and the twentieth centuries: the change from a primarily evaluative word (for a standard not equalled in other periods) to a primarily descriptive word (for a pre-eminent achievement of a certain kind but not necessarily of the highest kind). Such a distinction would be consistent with Warton's critical thinking as a whole – including his reservations about Virgil expressed elsewhere[62] but if it were intended here it has not been rationalized and made explicit.

In the final volume of his *History of England* (1757) Hume agreed with Warton that Charles II's reign was in no sense 'our augustan age'. He is even more contemptuous of the received opinion than Warton, but his more detailed discussion is both more thoughtful and more traditional in political and literary attitude. The literary criticism of so great a figure as Hume warrants an extensive quotation:

> This age was far from being so favorable to polite literature as to the sciences. Charles, tho' fond of wit, tho' possessed himself of a considerable share of it, tho' his taste of conversation seems to have been sound and just; served rather to corrupt than improve the poetry and eloquence of his time. When the theatres were opened at the restoration, and freedom was again given to pleasantry and ingenuity; men, after so long an abstinence, fed on these delicacies with less taste than avidity, and the coarsest and most irregular species of wit was received by the court as well as by the people. The productions at that time represented on the theatre were such monsters of extravagance and folly; so utterly devoid of all reason or even common sense; that they would be the disgrace of English literature, had not the nation made atonement for its former admiration of them, by the total oblivion to which they are now condemned. The duke of Buckingham's Rehearsal, which exposed these wild productions, seems to be a piece of ridicule carried to excess; yet in reality the copy scarcely equals some of the absurdities, which we meet with in the originals.
>
> This severe satyre, together with the good sense of the nation, corrected, after some time, the extravagancies of the fashionable wit; but the productions of literature still wanted much of that correctness and delicacy, which we so much admire in the antients, and in the French writers, their judicious imitators. It was indeed during this period chiefly, that that nation left the English behind them in the productions of poetry, eloquence, history, and other branches of polite letters; and acquired a superiority, which the efforts of English writers, during the subsequent age, did more successfully contest with them. The arts and sciences were imported from Italy into this island as early as into France; and made at first more surprising advances. Spencer, Shakespear, Bacon, Johnson were much superior to their contemporaries, who flourished in that kingdom. Milton, Waller, Denham, Cowley, Harvey were at least equal to their cotemporaries. The reign of Charles the second, which some preposterously represent as our augustan age, retarded the progress of polite literature in this island; and it was then found, that the immeasurable licentiousness, which was indulged or rather applauded at court, was more destructive to the refined arts than

---

[61]*An Account of the Augustan Age of England*; *The Collected Works of Oliver Goldsmith*, ed. Arthur Friedman (Oxford, 1965), I, p. 498.

[62]*The Works of Virgil*, ed. Joseph Warton (London, 1753).

even the cant, nonsense, and enthusiasm of the preceding period.

Most of the celebrated writers of this age remain monuments of genius, perverted by indecency and bad taste; but none more than Dryden, both by reason of the greatness of his talents and the gross abuse which he made of them. His plays, excepting a few scenes, are utterly disfigured by vice or folly or both: His translations appear too much the offspring of haste and hunger: Even his fables are ill-chosen tales, conveyed in an incorrect, tho' spirited versification. Yet amidst this great number of loose productions, the refuse of our language, there are found some small pieces, his Ode to St Cecilia, the greatest part of Absalom and Achitophel, and a few more, which discover so great genius, such richness of expression, such pomp and variety of numbers, that they leave us equally full of regret and indignation, on account of the inferiority or rather great absurdity of his other writings.

The very name of Rochester is offensive to modest ears; yet does his poetry discover such energy of style and such poignancy of satyre, as give ground to imagine what so fine a genius, had he fallen in a more happy age and followed better models, was capable of producing. The antient satyrists often used great liberty in their expressions; but their freedom no more resembles the licence of Rochester, than the nakedness of an Indian does that of a common prostitute.

[In two further paragraphs Hume discusses Wycherley, Otway, Buckingham, Mulgrave, Dorset, Roscommon, Halifax and Temple; he then turns to Butler.]

Tho' Hudibras was published, and probably composed, during Charles's reign, Butler may justly, as well as Milton, be thought to belong to the foregoing period. No composition abounds so much as Hudibras in strokes of just and inimitable wit; yet are there many performances, which give us as great or greater entertainment on the whole perusal. The allusions are often dark and far-fetched; and tho' scarce any author was ever able to express his thoughts in so few words, he often employs too many thoughts on one subject, and thereby becomes prolix after an unusual manner. It is surprizing how much erudition Butler has introduced with so good a grace into a work of pleasantry and humor: Hudibras is perhaps one of the most learned compositions, that is to be found in any language. The advantage, which the royal cause received from this poem, in exposing the fanaticism and false pretensions of the former parliamentary party, was prodigious. The King himself had so good taste as to be highly struck with the merit of the work, and had even got a great part of it by heart: Yet was he either so careless in his temper, or so little endowed with the virtue of liberality, or, more properly speaking, of gratitude, that he allowed the author, who was a man of virtue and probity, to live in obscurity and dye in want. Dryden is an instance of a negligence of the same kind. His Absalom sensibly contributed to the victory, which the Tories obtained over the Whigs, after the exclusion Parliaments: Yet could not this merit, aided by his great genius, procure him an establishment, which might exempt him from the necessity of writing for bread. Otway, tho' a profest Royalist, could not even procure bread by his writings; and he had the singular fate of dying literally of hunger. These incidents throw a great stain on the memory of Charles, who had discernment, loved genius, was liberal of money, but attained not the praise of true generosity.[63]

Hume's arguments against those who considered the reign of Charles II an English Augustan Age are partly moral and partly aesthetic. In each case the example set by the restored monarch is seen to be at the heart of this failure in civilization. Despite his admiration of the court of France, in his years of exile, Charles failed to use his apparent discrimination to restrain the fashionable excesses of taste in the Restoration theatre. Either his taste was in fact no better

[63]David Hume, *The History of Great Britain* (Edinburgh, 1757), II, pp. 452–4.

than the *mores* of his court and capital, in which case he lacked the critical judgement of the patron of Virgil and Horace, or (as Hume rather hints) he did not bother to exert the influence of his better judgement, in which case his failure was chiefly moral. Certainly moral was his failure to reward adequately poets such as Dryden and Butler who had on many occasions devoted their literary talent to his political purposes. On these specific counts, Hume considers Charles II unworthy of the Augustan compliment twice paid him by the most gifted poet of that age.[64] An Augustan Age, according to Hume, is the joint product of natural talent and the right conditions for this talent to develop. What might 'so fine a genius' as Rochester have achieved, 'had he fallen in a more happy age'? The responsibility of those who strive consciously for a new Augustan era is to provide, economically, socially and intellectually, the right context for genius. Genius itself only heaven or fortune can provide; it is thus an Augustan Age, in the passages from Dryden and Pope here discussed, is seen to be the creation of human action and judgement and of divine favour. In this interesting and perceptive passage from Hume the question of patronage was of prime importance.

This is also the case with the discussion of Augustanism in England, in Goldsmith's *Enquiry into the Present State of Polite Learning in Europe* (1759), where he sees Lord Somers as having fulfilled the rôle of the Augustan patron. In his time, wrote Goldsmith,

> . . . the link between patronage and learning was entire . . . all who deserved fame were in a capacity of attaining it. When the great Somers was at the helm, patronage was fashionable among our nobility. The middle ranks of mankind, who generally imitate the Great, then followed their example; and applauded from fashion, if not from feeling. I have heard an old poet of that glorious age say, that a dinner with his lordship, has procured him invitations for the whole week following: that an airing in his patron's chariot, has supplied him with a citizen's coach on every future occasion. For who would not be proud to entertain a man who kept so much good company?
>
> But this link now seems entirely broken. Since the days of a certain prime minister of inglorious memory, the learned have been kept pretty much at a distance.

Goldsmith also discussed the Augustan Age in England in *The Bee* for 24 November 1759. Goldsmith adds to Hume's discussion of patronage the point that in the reign of William and Anne there seemed to be

> . . . a just balance between patronage and the press. Before it, men were little esteemed whose only merit was genius; and since, men who can prudently be content to catch the public, are certain of living without dependance. But the writers of the period of which I am speaking, were sufficiently esteemed by the great, and not rewarded enough by booksellers, to set them above independance. Fame consequently then was the truest road to happiness; a sedulous attention to the mechanical business of the day makes the present never-failing resource.

[64]There is room for a more charitable view of Charles II, such as that expressed by James Sutherland in 'The Impact of Charles II on Restoration Literature', *Restoration and Eighteenth-Century Literature*, ed. Carroll Camden (London, 1963), pp. 251–63, especially 254. Whatever his faults the King was able to establish genuine human contact with many of the writers of his time, and was able to inspire sympathy and loyalty. The relation between monarch and poet implied by the first twenty-two lines of *Absalom and Achitophel* was something valuable and rare.

It is notable that Goldsmith follows Hume in denying the Augustan quality of the reign of Charles II, and Warton in identifying it with the reigns of William and Anne. Goldsmith is doubtless much influenced by the two earlier writers. He absorbs their ideas, but only on the question of patronage has much to offer that is his own.[65]

Hume's discussion of Charles II as an Augustan monarch raises the general question of literary standards. What meaning ought we to infer from phrases such as Rowe's in compliment to Godolphin: '. . . so Delicate and Polite a Taste and Understanding . . .' from Warton's term 'a just taste', or from Hume's saying of Charles: '. . . his taste in conversation seems to have been sound and just . . .'? In expressing his own judgement, Hume made at least some points clear. A sound taste would not commend extravagance and licentiousness, but it would recognize and appreciate 'richness of expression', 'pomp and variety of numbers' in Dryden; 'energy of style', 'poignancy of satire' in Rochester; 'just and inimitable wit' in Butler. His use of the phrase 'correctness and delicacy' is linked with an admiration for the ancients and of 'the French writers, their judicious imitators'. Except perhaps for a personal delight in the wit of Butler's *Hudibras*, there is nothing here inconsistent with the neo-classical criticism which dominated the greater part of the eighteenth century – one notes the confident first-person plural in which he speaks of admiration for the ancients and their imitators in seventeenth-century France. Equally, there is nothing which would conflict with the aesthetic values expounded in the Atterbury Preface – even though Waller is allowed no special prominence in Hume's discussion. To Atterbury, Warton and Hume, it is plain, regularity, refinement, polish, purity of language, were strong and positive virtues. Atterbury's Preface shows us the original life of these terms. To all three, also, it was important that an author should guard against waywardness and excess by founding his work on the broad ground of common experience. Reproof by Warton of an excessive pursuit of 'Sheer Wit', by Hume of licentious extravagance, Atterbury's stress on using those parts of a language which will remain fresh and current – all these judgements spring from the same principle: one which also underlies Jonson's statement, in the *Discoveries*: '*Custome* is the most certaine Mistresse of Language, as the publicke stampe makes the current money . . . now nothing is good that is naturall: Right and naturall language seemes to have least of the wit in it; that which is writh'd and tortur'd, is counted the more exquisite' and Pope's adjuration in *An Essay on Criticism* (with which the critical parts of the *Discoveries* have so much in common) that writers should: 'First follow NATURE', and that readers should remember: 'Tis not a *Lip*, or *Eye*, we Beauty call, / But the joint Force and full *Result* of all'.[66] It would certainly be forcing the argument to suggest that all this is implied by Hume's comparatively playful question in 1760: 'Is this new Reign to be the Augustan Age?' but it is quite reasonable to suppose that he meant what he had so recently explained in the last volume of his *History of England*.

[65]Oliver Goldsmith, *Enquiry into the Present State of Polite Learning in Europe*, ch. X, and *An Account of the Augustan Age of England*, *The Bee* (24 November, 1759); *Collected Works*, I, pp. 310–11, 499.

[66]*Timber: or, Discoveries*, ll. 1926–7, 575–8; *Ben Jonson*, VIII, pp. 622, 581. *An Essay on Criticism*, ll. 68, 245–6; *Poems*, I, pp. 246, 267–8.

Convenient though it might be to find in the later eighteenth century the waning of an Augustan ideal, the English evidence is very mixed. We must distinguish senses, different occasions and purposes, and of course differences of opinion. The historians, however, generally agree in presenting Augustus himself through the viewpoint of Tacitus. To deplore the means by which Octavian rose to single power was of course deeply traditional, but those historians whose plan included this phase of his career now generally expanded on it. Where the influence of Tacitus is felt is in the view that the Augustan principate, though outwardly successful and happy, was a subtle tyranny, buying its stability at the cost of the later decline and fall of the Roman Empire. As we might expect after Goldsmith's use of 'Augustan' to praise certain periods of English civilization, his *Roman History from the Foundation of the City of Rome to the Destruction of the Western Empire* (1769) is the least overtly hostile, is indeed often appreciative, but his analysis is still Tacitean.[67] Pope's friend Nathaniel Hooke, in his *Roman History from the Building of Rome to the Ruin of the Commonwealth* (1738–71) shows a bias towards the *populares* and a scepticism as to the liberty defended by Cicero. Nevertheless he regards the Augustan principate as ending liberty for both senate and people. Adam Ferguson's *History of the Roman Republic* (1783) – and indeed Ferguson's other writings – extend his hostility to the political Augustus to the cultural values for which he considered that era had come to stand. It is however to Gibbon that we should turn for a formidable summary of the trend:

> The tender respect of Augustus for a free constitution which he had destroyed can only be explained by an attentive consideration of the character of that subtle tyrant. A cool head, an unfeeling heart, and a cowardly disposition prompted him at the age of nineteen to assume the mask of hypocrisy, which he never afterward laid aside. With the same hand, and probably with the same temper, he signed the proscription of Cicero and the pardon of Cinna. His virtues, and even his vices, were artificial; and according to the various dictates of his interest, he was at first the enemy, and at last the father, of the Roman world. When he framed the artful system of the Imperial authority, his moderation was inspired by his fears. He wished to deceive the people by an image of civil liberty, and the armies by an image of civil government.
> . . . Augustus was sensible that mankind is governed by names; nor was he deceived in his expectation that the senate and people would submit to slavery, provided they were respectfully assured that they still enjoyed their ancient freedom. A feeble senate and enervated people cheerfully acquiesced in the pleasing illusion, as long as it was supported by the virtue, or even by the prudence, of the successors of Augustus. It was a motive of self-preservation, not a principle of liberty, that animated the conspirators against Caligula, Nero and Domitian. They attacked the person of the tyrant, without aiming their blow at the authority of the emperor.[68]

These paragraphs are the English consummation of the tradition of Tacitus and Machiavelli.

The literary consequences of such a view are another matter. Gibbon's view of Augustus is apparent in his very earliest work: it could hardly be stronger

---

[67]*Roman History* (London, 1769), II, pp. 95–119.

[68]*The History of the Decline and Fall of the Roman Empire*, ed. J.B. Bury (London, 1896; rev. edn, 1909), I, p. 78.

there, if less splendidly expressed. But this did not lead him to develop the view, already proposed by Spence and others, that the *Aeneid* was written to help ratify the new monarchy. For Gibbon Virgil was republican in spirit, and commenting on the presentation of Aeneas and the Etruscans, he can exclaim: 'Milton himself, I mean the Milton of the Commonwealth, could not have asserted with more energy the daring pretensions of the people, to punish as well as to resist a Tyrant . . . the Republic was subverted, but the minds of the Romans were still Republican.'[69] Thomas Sheridan could argue in his *British Education* (1756) that while 'it was in the reign of Augustus, after the form of government had been changed, that the arts appeared in their highest lustre at Rome', 'the artists themselves were all bred up during the most remarkable period of the Republick whose last blaze was it's brightest . . .'.[70] In the Preface of his *Complete Dictionary of the English Language* (1780) he could use the term 'Augustan' positively, and say: 'There was a time, and that at no very distant period, which may be called the Augustan age of England, I mean during the reign of Queen Anne, when English was the language spoken at court' and derived consequent advantage. Since 'the accession of a foreign family to the throne', however, English gave way to French at court.[71] Lord Kames, dedicating his *Elements of Criticism* to George III in 1761, had a splendid opportunity to hope that the young English monarch would be a new Augustus. Patronage by 'wise Princes' is specifically commended, but the only classical example adduced is that of 'ancient Greece'.[72] With the occasion so very appropriate, the absence of the traditional gesture is notable.

A year later John Gordon's *Occasional Thoughts . . .* suggests some significant shifts of taste and thought. He argues that in human life, we first see best, then imagine, finally understand. Fine writing is superficial, like seeing. If then 'the days of *fine writing* be over with us, there will not be much reason to lament – place them under one of our *famous Queens*, or in *Charles* the second's reign, it will not be a matter of much import: for an age of *fine writing*, and of *just* reasoning are certainly if not two opposite, at least two extremely different things. It would be difficult, I suppose, to produce from all antiquity two Writers, who should equal *Tacitus* and *Lucian*, in point of good sense; though it is certain, the first did not write in the *Augustan* age, nor the last in the *Attic* Greek. . . .' Very amusingly he goes on to give his notion of the Augustan

---

[69]See Gibbon's *Essai sur l'étude de la littérature* (composed *c.* 1758–9) for the views that Augustus was a bloodstained tyrant, but that the *Georgics* were written to support his policy of reconciliation and settlement (including the settlement of veterans) on the land: 'Les hardis vétérans n'avoient acheté leurs possessions que par une guerre sanglante, et leurs frequens actes de violence montroient assez qu'ils se croient toujours les armes à la main. Qu'y avoit-il alors de plus assorti à la douce politique d'August, que d'employer les chants harmonieux de son ami, pour les reconciler à leur nouvel état?' (*Miscellaneous Works*, ed. John, Lord Sheffield (London, 1814), IV, pp. 35, 89–90). The quoted comment on the *Aeneid*, which develops the paradox, is from *Critical Observations on the Sixth Book of the Aeneid* (1770); *The English Essays of Edward Gibbon*, ed. Patricia B. Craddock (Oxford, 1972), p. 139.

[70]Thomas Sheridan, *The British Education: Or, The Source of the Disorders of Great-Britain* (London, 1756), p. 394. Sheridan also praises 'the long and peaceable reign of Augustus, his great liberality and nice discernment' (p. 395).

[71]*A Complete Dictionary of the English Language* (2nd edn, London, 1789), Preface.

[72]Henry Home, Lord Kames, *Elements of Criticism* (7th edn, Edinburgh, 1788), Preface (December 1761), pp. v, vii.

age of Rome: 'I am not, I own, Antiquarian enough to prove this in every instance; but when I read, as I do in *Pliny*, ''that the first man, who found out the art of clipping or shearing (*totendi*) trees and groves, was one *Cn. Matius* Kt. a friend of the Emperor *Augustus*;'' — I cannot help forming to my self an idea of an Augustan age, in which everything should appear extremely terse and neat, though at the same time extremely contrary to nature.'[73] Well might he say this, for he believed in and admired Ossian. A taste for Ossian is a good test of wider views. For the young Vicessimus Knox, whose *Essays Moral and Literary* appeared in 1778, Ossian was 'nonsensicall jargon'. Knox considers the earlier eighteenth century, then the middle and later decades, and makes clear what he means by 'Augustan'. For him it is a route to natural beauty. He commends Dryden and Pope for aiming at 'the models of the Augustan age. Their imitation was successful. Their times were captivated with their writings, and every susceptible reader acknowledged, that the nearer they approached the antients, the more they abounded in all the simple graces of natural beauty.' 'At this period,' he affirms, 'the English poetry arrived at that standard of perfection, in the admiration of which, mankind have agreed for the space of seventeen hundred years; and to which, after the slight deviation of caprice, they have constantly recurred with reiterated ardour.' In the middle of the century, however, 'love of novelty was impatient for supplies . . .'. As a result there arose the taste for Gray, Mason, Ossian and the Gothic. This taste prevailed before 'that which now begins to dawn upon us, and to promise a revival of pure Attic and Augustan wit'. What prompted this burst of optimism were Goldsmith's *Traveller* and *Deserted Village*. Perhaps Goldsmith's own positive use of the word 'Augustan' to designate a period of English excellence suggested Knox's use of the term. His discussion is of some significance in the evolution of English literary critical terminology. Only in the loosest sense, after all, are Dryden and Pope like Virgil and Horace. Neither are Virgil and Horace notable for wit in the sense that Pope and Dryden are. Yet Knox confidently assigns the term 'Augustan' to them, and to Goldsmith, while quite clear in his mind that neither Ossian, not Gray's odes, nor even his *Elegy*, are 'Augustan'. The criteria seem to be wit, clarity of design and naturalness of diction.[74]

John Pinkerton, *Letters of Literature, By Robert Heron, Esq.* (1785) has both Goldsmith, Gordon and Warton in his mind when he comes to consider the idea of an Augustan age. The paradox of designating as our Augustan age a period which does not contain the poets we most admire is met head on: 'The superior good sense and observation of the English hath taught them to fix no Augustan age for their country. May her Augustan age be a *sœculum sœculorum*! The names of Chaucer, of Shakspere, of Milton, of Gray, are as remote as those of Bacon and Newton: centuries elapse between them. Nature, it would seem, according to the *inventers* of these Augustan ages, illuminates other countries by constellations of pretty stars; but in Britain concentrates the rays of many into one, which dazzles her rival nations with a *luxury of light*.'[75] Goldsmith's image of 'Stars lost in each others brightness' could not have been

---

[73]John Gordon, *Occasional Thoughts on the Study and Character of Classical Authors* (London, 1762), pp. 37, 40–1.
[74]*Essays Moral and Literary* (London, 1778), pp. 93–7.
[75]*Letters of Literature* (London, 1785), pp. 158–61.

more tellingly turned. Gordon's perception of how inadequate it was to look for one period only in which the arts and learning came to a height is here emphatically endorsed.

Our survey of the uses of the word 'Augustan' may reasonably end with instances from William Godwin and from Coleridge. Four years after the publication of the *Enquiry Concerning Political Justice* (1793), three years after *Caleb Williams*, Godwin discussed the great periods of English literature in a paper in *The Enquirer* (1797):

> The age which, next after that of queen Elizabeth, has obtained the suffrage of the critics, is that of Charles the second. This was a period adorned with the writings of Milton, Dryden, Butler and Otway; and perhaps deserves above all others to be styled the golden age of English poetry. Fanciful observers found a certain resemblance between it and the age of Augustus, the literary glory of which has sometimes been represented as owing to this circumstance, that its wits were bred up in their youth in the lap of republican freedom, and afterwards in their riper age received that polish which is to be derived from the splendour and refinement of a court. Just so, the scene amidst which the wits of King Charles's days passed their boyish years, was that of civil war, of regicide, or of unrestrained republican speculation; which was succeeded by the manners of a gay and licentious court, grafting the shoots of French refinement, upon the more vigorous and luxuriant plant of English growth. It is easy to trace in the adventurous sallies of the authors of this period, the remnant and tincture of republican audaciousness. The principle however here intended to be established is, that, if our poetry never appeared to greater advantage, our prose at least was as yet unformed and rude.[76]

Surprising as this may seem from Godwin, it is a valuable synthesis. It is a comprehensive historical and literary account of the period, like those of Higgons, Warton and Hume. It aptly connects the widespread argument about residual liberty with the character of Restoration poetry. And we see that, whatever Godwin's views on the political justice of the principate, 'the Age of Augustus' is still an age of 'literary glory'.

In the *Morning Post* of the 21, 25, 29 September and 2 October 1802, Coleridge drew a striking parallel between late republican Rome and the republican France of that year, with Napoleon Bonaparte as First Consul. As with the use of the Augustan parallel in the mid-seventeenth century, Coleridge's purpose here is chiefly to *understand* the historical process. 'Some resemblance does really exist' – and not only because revolutionary France has garbed itself in the names and offices of republican Rome: 'its Consuls, its Tribunes, its Senate, its Proconsular Provinces' and so on. Coleridge does not admire Rome's change under Augustus when 'the Government was organized into a masked and military despotism (a despotism with a frightful half-mask on its face), when the sovereign power was repeatedly and ostentatiously affirmed to reside in the people, but the right of exercising it suspended for ever . . .' and in a sober footnote he considers that Napoleon possessed 'many of the good, and some of the bad, traits' of Julius Caesar, Augustus and Tiberius. He shows Augustus's 'close application to public business, and his encouragement of the

---

[76]William Godwin, *The Enquirer. Reflections on Education, Manners, and Literature* (Dublin, 1797), pp. 402–3.

liberal arts, and great public works'; but also 'his constitutional coldness and politic craft'. As Coleridge develops his fascinating case that the historical process in France though similar is yet much more precarious, Napoleon is seen to fall short of the Roman experience: 'We have so long connected the names of Brutus and Cassius with the word Liberty, that we have forgotten that, by the Roman populace, they were considered as leaders of the senatorian aristocracy – Caesar was the child and champion of Jacobinism. But Bonaparte is to the Jacobins what the senate was to the popular faction at Rome. . . . [At Rome] The total extinction of popular liberty was not, as at present in France, effected at a blow . . .'. Under Augustus 'the utmost freedom, both in writing and speaking, was practised without danger. He was regarded with veneration, both by the people and the senate . . .' at the end of his rule 'his character was truly that of the father of his country'.[77] It is with Tiberius, finally, that Coleridge makes the parallel go home. Coleridge's discussion resembles, in a number of respects, a modern view of the establishment of the principate: 'Rome *could* not continue free . . . France *is* not free . . .'.[78] Like several of the late eighteenth-century writers considered in this chapter, Coleridge holds views of considerable complexity. He deprecates the process that began with Augustus, yet he cannot roundly condemn the age as a whole: 'The commencement of the public slavery in Rome was in the most splendid aera of human genius. Any unusually flourishing period of the arts and sciences in any country, is, even to this day, called the Augustan age of that country.'[79] Coming from this man, at that time, and in the context of these essays, this statement is a powerful witness to the survival through the eighteenth century of the ideal view of the arts and learning of Augustan Rome.

In attempting to sum up what the British eighteenth century thought about the idea of an Augustan Age it is right to start with a few reservations. No period ever thinks only one thing on a subject: it is rare for one person ever to think one thing only on a subject, even at one time. It is useful to recall Corneille's *Cinna, ou la Clémence d'Auguste* (1641). Nothing written against Augustus in the eighteenth century was more hostile than the charges of the conspirators against him early in *Cinna*, and Corneille had much the same classical sources and traditions available to him as did the eighteenth century. Yet as the drama unfolds, through shift of viewpoint, maturing of policy and change of heart the clement monarch emerges from the ruthless triumvir and usurper. Knowledge of the tradition from Tacitus did not prevent Corneille coming to a very different final presentation of Augustus. Of course the diverse eighteenth-century discussions of Augustus hardly resemble an integrated drama. Yet *Cinna* does serve to show that a series of Tacitean observations does not entail in a writer an attitude of total and permanent hostility.

Distinctions must also be made between the occasions and the kinds of work in which discussions of the Augustan Age appear. It was possible, in poems, dedications and even essays, to adduce the example of Augustus and Maecenas in recommending patronage of learning and the arts, while yet thinking that in

[77] *The Collected Works of Samuel Taylor Coleridge* (Bollingen Edition): *Essays on His Times*, ed. David Erdman (London, 1978), I, pp. 315, 312, 314, 336.
[78] Ibid., p. 336.
[79] Ibid., p. 318.

the long run the Augustan principate sowed the seeds of decline. Goldsmith is a case in point. Pope may have been another. Under a monarchy it was possible to find Augustus a positive and telling example, while also thinking that the Augustan poets went too far in his praise. Nearly always poets and panegyrists felt free to select positive features from the historical record and trust their readers not to mistake an obvious intention. In most cases they did not expect consistency and comprehensiveness to be demanded. In a telling exchange in 1706 between Granville and Bolingbroke about the use of classical comparison, Granville thought it might be allowed to be local: 'Caesar', for example, does not mean 'tyrant' unless the writer says so. Since Granville was here defending the easier practice, it may be thought that he spoke for the majority.[80]

This fragmented and diverse procedure makes it hard for us to generalize, let alone demonstrate the rise or fall of a general view. A few things can be said with certainty. The first is that the eighteenth century in Britain saw no absolute change of opinion about Augustan Rome. There had never been a time when everybody admired it and there was not now. The second is that the eighteenth century and the very end of the seventeenth stand out through their reiterated attempts to claim or to deny an English Augustan Age. Thirdly the positive sense of the word 'Augustan' was used all through the century from Atterbury in 1690 to Coleridge in 1802. I have not found a negative use, though one may well come to light. Fourthly, in both Britain and France there was a movement in historiography and related works towards the Tacitean view of Augustus himself – and indeed beyond it to a point where Voltaire, in 1770–2, could call Augustus 'un monstre adroit et heureux' and Virgil and Horace poets 'des âmes serviles'.[81] We may thus see eighteenth-century discussions of Augustus and 'Augustan' as a loose and disjointed debate in which may be discerned, among other movements and half-movements, a more or less coherent thrust by historians towards Gibbon's account of Augustan Rome. That this diffusion, not discovery, of the Tacitean view was a real development is attested by the frequency with which, from the middle decades on, we encounter the argument of residual liberty, so well calculated to rescue the Augustan poets from too close an association with Augustus himself. This is consonant with the emergence of a largely literary sense of 'Augustan' – Warton, Vicessimus Knox, perhaps Coleridge – which was also useful to those who, like Blackwell and Gibbon, did not wish to give Virgil and Horace up to a 'subtle tyrant'. Yet there seems to have been no decisive move away from the older and more comprehensive sense of 'Augustan', designating a political, social and aesthetic culture, nor was the early preoccupation with an 'Augustan' condition of the language forgotten in the later eighteenth century.

The question of political viewpoint has been most interestingly raised by Professor Weinbrot. In his view where royalism lingered, Augustus and his sycophantic court poets were longest admired: where it did not, they were not.[82]

---

[80]See Elizabeth Handasyde, *Granville the Polite: The Life of George Granville Lord Lansdowne, 1666–1735* (Oxford, 1933), pp. 96–7: '. . . if I should say my Lord Marlborough fought like a Lion, it might be told me I say he fought like a beast, If I should compare him to Caesar, I might be told that also is a reflection, for Caesar fought to enslave his country . . . it would be impossible to use any allusion at all.'

[81]*Questions sur l'encyclopédie* (Geneva, 1770–2), II, pp. 351–2.

[82]*Augustus Caesar in 'Augustan' England*, pp. 230–41. Note on pp. 230 and 236 marks of the Whig Interpretation of History.

Does the eighteenth century constitute an inexorable movement towards representative government and republicanism? It had indeed seen, by its end, republics set up in France and in America, one of which was to survive without interruption into our own time. But the danger of retrospective interpretation is great, if very natural. There seems to have been little principled republicanism in eighteenth-century Britain, though there were some republican writers, notably Tom Paine, at the very end of the period. No doubt the great bulk of the writers cited in this chapter were more or less automatically monarchist. And to be specific, the Bolingbroke who drew on Gordon's *Discourses on Tacitus* to attack George II was the Bolingbroke who later wrote *The Idea of a Patriot King* and dallied with Jacobitism in the 1730s. The Voltaire who was later to write of 'un monstre adroit et heureux' composed the proclamation for Charles Edward Stuart's projected invasion of Britain in 1744.[83] Blackwell was powerfully monarchist, though he believed, like the Tory Bolingbroke, in a mixed constitution. Loyal subjects of kings looked quite sincerely to republican Rome as a fount of patriotism and *virtù*. This much can safely be said: where monarchy was important, the example of Augustus, whether ideal or warning, was likely to be relevant. Weinbrot's striking demonstration that under Napoleon French historiography (or at least one historian, but that era *was* brief and active) turned back to approval of Augustus is relevant here. So is Napoleon's original disappointment at the fifth act of *Cinna*: apparently he found the clemency of Augustus an anti-climax.[84]

[83]Eveline Cruickshanks, *Political Untouchables: The Tories and the '45* (London, 1979), p. 97.
[84]*Memoires de Madame de Rémusat* (Paris, 1880), I, p. 279. When he saw it performed, however, he detected policy in Augustus's clemency, and admired the end in so far as he could think Cinna deceived.

X   The Medal Against Time: Pope's Epistle To Mr. Addison

> I have known an Emperor quite hid under a crust of
> dross, who after two or three days cleansing has
> appeared with all his Titles about him as fresh and
> beautiful as at his first coming out of the Mint.
>
> (Addison, *Dialogues on Medals*, I)

The Wastes of Time

Of the several ways of exploring the literary culture of an age, a broad survey of
a specific topic, such as the theme of an English Augustan Age, is one. Yet even
when the particular propositions involved have not been abstracted to form a
case but set in their contexts, and even when easy generalization is avoided, such
a presentation of a literary age will mislead if it is not complemented by detailed
criticism of particular works of art. Only that, it may be thought, can do justice
to the imaginative reach, the intensities, and (often) failures of the creative
effort of the time. As the more broad-ranging chapters earlier in this book were,
I hope, sharpened and offset by detailed critical discussion of specific works
(Donne's *Satyre IV*, *The Poetaster*, *Antony and Cleopatra* among others), ·so
here we must contract our survey until it shrinks into a poem. Yet this particular
poem, however, Pope's Epistle *To Mr. Addison, Occasion'd by his Dialogues
on Medals* (1720), broadens our sights through its very concentration. As it
unfolds it becomes clear how in the early decades of the eighteenth century
'Augustan' is subsumed in the notion of a new Golden Age – which is to say
that this poem has strong affinities with Pope's *Messiah* and *Windsor
Forest* – and as it unfolds we may see how the very life and light of the poem are
drawn from its roots in the early Renaissance and even from the Fathers of the
Church.

The reason for this is that awareness of Augustan Rome, and of the great preceding periods of Hellenistic and Greek culture, provided, in post-classical
times, a challenge and a model for Renaissance endeavour. The goal of this
endeavour, and its fulfilment, was the achievement of a new Augustan Age,
though this did not necessarily mean that Augustan Rome was seen with
uncritical eyes. The idea of a Renaissance and the idea of an Augustan Age may
be, though not invariably, integral parts of the same concept. Any writer, who
looks on himself as a new Augustan, is likely to attach special importance to the
fallen civilizations of classical antiquity, and to the means by which they may be
renewed. From the time of Ben Jonson, English poets, in different ways and to
different degrees, saw themselves as emulating the poets of the Roman

Augustan Age.[1] Contemporaries of Pope could feel that the English Augustan Age was either about to reach its zenith or was but a little way declined from it.[2] Alexander Pope himself, at some points in his career, thought of himself as an English Augustan.[3]

There are three places in Pope's writings where he discusses the fall of Rome, the Middle Ages and the Renaissance. These are: the concluding passage of *An Essay on Criticism* (1711), *To Mr. Addison, Occasioned by his Dialogues on Medals* (1720), and the greater part of Bk III of the *Dunciad* (1728–43). The *Dunciad* passage, appropriate to Pope's subject in that poem, enlarges most upon the fall of Rome and its usurpation by the Dark Ages; a Renaissance in Britain is hinted at in one line only, while the ultimate triumph of Dulness is hailed, with powerful irony, as a kind of Renaissance in reverse.[4] By contrast,

---

[1]See Chs. V & VI passim. Cleveland had addressed Jonson as the 'English *Horace*' (Jonson, *Works*, ed. C.H. Herford and Percy and Evelyn Simpson, 1925–52, XI, p. 338) and Crites, in Dryden's *An Essay of Dramatic Poesy*, recognized him as 'a professed imitator of Horace' (*Essays of John Dryden*, ed. W.P. Ker, 1900, I, p. 43). Sir Thomas Higgons, in his 'Ode on the Death of Mr. *Abraham Cowley*' (1667), reflected that: 'If he had flourish'd when *Augustus* sway'd, / Whose peaceful Sceptre the whole World obey'd, / Account of him *Mecoenas* would have made' and Sir John Denham went further: '*Horace* his wit and *Virgil*'s state, / He did not steal, but emulate' (*The Works of Mr. Abraham Cowley*, Ninth Edition (London, 1700), n.p.). Oldham, on his death, was hailed by Thomas Andrews as: '*Virgil* in judgement, *Ovid* in Delight, / An easy Thought with a *Meonian* Flight; / Horace in Sweetness, Juvenal in Rage' (*The Remains of Mr. Oldham in Verse and Prose* (London, 1687), n.p.), while the death of Waller, in 1687, was received with even more fulsome praise, involving even grander comparisons with Augustan Rome and Ancient Greece. Sir Thomas Higgons is once more lavish of comparison: '*Athens* and *Rome*, when Learning flourish'd most, / Could never such a Finish'd Poet boast: / Whose matchless softness in the *English* Tongue / Outdoes what *Horace*, or *Anacreon* sung', but he is supported by no less a person than the neo-classical critic Thomas Rymer, who affirmed that Waller 'This Northern Speech refin'd to that degree, / Soft *France* we scorn, nor envy *Italy*: / But for a fit Comparison must seek / In *Virgil*'s Latin, or in *Homer*'s Greek' (*Poems to the Memory of . . . Edmund Waller . . . By Several Hands* (London, 1688), ll. 5–8, p. 1; ll. 62–5, p. 7).

[2]See Ch. IX passim.

[3]Pope never explicitly speaks of himself as such, but comes close to it in the Advertisement to his *Epistle to Augustus* (1737): '*The Reflections of* Horace, *and the Judgements past in his Epistle to* Augustus, *seem'd so seasonable to the present Times, that I could not help applying them to the use of my own Country*' (*The Poems of Alexander Pope*, IV, p. 191). Pope's literary ideals are often Augustan (cf. *An Essay on Criticism* (1711) ll. 643–86; *Poems*, I, pp. 311–17) and he strove to follow Walsh's advice to be the first great 'correct' English poet (Joseph Spence, *Anecdotes, Observations, and Characters, of Books and Men*, ed. J.M. Osborn (Oxford, 1966), I, item 73), that is, to obey the precepts and emulate the practice of the Ancients in general and the Roman Augustans in particular. In different ways Pope did indeed emulate both Virgil and Horace. His *Pastorals* and *Messiah* are in the mode of Virgil's *Eclogues*; his *Windsor Forest* of the *Georgics*; his *Homer* of the *Aeneid*. Virgilian epic is also powerfully recalled in *The Rape of the Lock. An Essay on Criticism* is in a mode deriving ultimately from Horace's *Ars Poetica*, though Vida and Boileau do of course intervene. Pope plays an Augustan rôle, perhaps most clearly, in his *Imitations of Horace*, where, as in the writing, so in the very printing, the reader is invited to witness the parallel-and-contrast that the poet sets up between himself and his own age, and Horace and Augustan Rome.

[4]The whole of Settle's prophecy in *The Dunciad*, Bk III, is relevant to Pope's conception of barbarism and of the Dark Ages; especially important passages are *Dunciad* (1729): III, ll. 65–130, 315–56 (*Poems*, V, pp. 156–61, 186–93). It is l. 117 which alludes to the Renaissance in Britain, while ll. 315–18, 329, 335 in particular, with their deeply ironical echoes of Virgil's Fourth Eclogue and of Pope's own *Messiah*, confirm the poet's conceit of the inverted Renaissance.

the first of the passages mentioned, that in *An Essay on Criticism*, dismisses the whole of the Middle Ages with confident expedition:

> Thus long succeeding Criticks justly reign'd,
> *Licence* repress'd, and *useful Laws* ordain'd;
> *Learning* and *Rome* alike in Empire grew,
> And *Arts* still *follow'd* where her *Eagles flew*;
> From the same Foes, at last, both felt their Doom,
> And the same Age saw *Learning* fall, and *Rome*.
> With *Tyranny*, then *Supersticion* join'd,
> As that the *Body*, this enslav'd the Mind;
> Much was *Believ'd*, but little *understood*,
> And to be *dull* was constru'd to be *good*;
> A *second* Deluge Learning thus o'er-run,
> And the *Monks* finish'd what the *Goths* begun.
>   At length, *Erasmus*, that *great, injur'd Name*,
> (The *Glory* of the Priesthood, and the *Shame*!)
> *Stemm'd* the *wild Torrent* of a *barb'rous Age*,
> And drove those *Holy Vandals* off the Stage.
>   But see! each *Muse*, in *Leo*'s Golden Days,
> *Starts* from her Trance, and trims her wither'd Bays!
> *Rome*'s ancient *Genius*, o'er its *Ruins* spread,
> Shakes off the *Dust*, and rears its rev'rend Head!
> Then *Sculpture* and her *Sister-Arts* revive;
> *Stones* leap'd to *Form*, and *Rocks* began to *live*;
> With *sweeter Notes* each *rising Temple* rung;
> A *Raphael* painted, and a *Vida* sung![5]

It is in the context of this historical view that Pope's concerns in *To Mr. Addison* must be seen. This epistle is less well known than the two passages just cited. Apart from the establishing of its text and the details of its composition, little scholarly or critical attention has been paid to it.[6] Yet the ideas it expresses throw light on Pope's Augustanism, and it is in itself a brilliantly accomplished poem. It is my purpose here to discuss its content and its form in relation to the relevant background of ideas.

In his *Dialogues Upon the Usefulness of Ancient Medals*, which Pope's epistle was designed to introduce, Addison advances three chief arguments against those who think numismatics a merely pedantic pastime. In the first

---

[5]Ll. 681–704; *Poems*, I, pp. 316–20. Pope then proceeds to describe how the Renaissance, driven from Rome, moved North over the Alps to France, and gained just a foothold ('among the *sounder Few*' – l. 719) in Britain.

[6]For details of the composition and publication of the epistle see *Poems*, VI, pp. 205–6. All but ll. 5–10, 63–72 were probably written in 1713, and the poem was certainly intended to be prefixed, as was eventually the case, to Addison's *Dialogues Upon the Usefulness of Ancient Medals*. It had this place of honour in the great 1721 edition of Addison's *Works* (I, pp. 431–3) and was printed with other important epistles in Vol. II of the 1735 edition of Pope's *Works*, and of subsequent editions until his death. In Warburton's edition of Pope's *Works* (London, 1751) it appeared as a fifth *Moral Essay*. Clearly it had been hard to fit the poem into the new arrangement of Pope's epistles in that edition, and its tenuous connection with the *Moral Essays* proper was exploited as a last resort (*Works*, ed. William Warburton, 1751, III, pp. 294–9). In the big Twickenham Edition the epistle is banished to the volume of minor poems. It deserves a more significant status. This was accorded it in the single-volume Twickenham Edition of Pope's *Poems* (ed. John Butt, 1963, pp. 215–16).

place the coins of an ancient civilization afford sure evidence of its political history: the names, dates, acts, and even appearance of its rulers. Secondly, coins may convey information on other aspects of antiquity; they may bear images of buildings and statues long since destroyed, or of ancient weapons, or fashions of dress. Finally, the allegorical personages depicted on Greek or Roman coins may illustrate and illuminate passages from the ancient poets, as the poetry may help to explain the coins.[7] The assumption underlying all these arguments, which even Cynthio, the sceptic of the dialogues, never seriously questions, is the familiar humanist one: that it is a thing of value in itself to study, and be familiar with, all aspects of our classical heritage. Addison's subject in these dialogues might have led one to expect, at some point, a sustained lament at the fall of Rome, or at least a mood of regret at the passing away of ancient grandeur. On the contrary; the tone is equable to the point of monotony throughout.

Pope, on the other hand, opens his prefatory poem by evoking the broad vista of Rome in its ruins, seen down the long perspectives of time; his lofty rhetoric is designed to arouse in his readers the emotion of pity.

> See the wild Waste of all-devouring years!
> How Rome her own sad Sepulchre appears,
> With nodding arches, broken temples spread!
> The very Tombs now vanish'd like their dead!
> Imperial wonders rais'd on Nations spoil'd[8]

Pope's lines have the authority of a traditional view; the presentation of time in the first line is a commonplace in literature, albeit an impressive one,[9] while the second line suggests community of thought and feeling with Du Bellay, in his *Antiquitez de Rome* (1559). Pope uses the same figure that Du Bellay had employed in the third sonnet:

> Nouveau venu, qui cherches Rome en Rome,
>   Et rien de Rome en Rome n'apperçois,
>   Ces vieux palais, ces vieux arcz que tu vois,
>   Et ces vieux murs, c'est ce que Rome on nomme.
> Voy quel orgueil, quelle ruine: et comme
>   Celle qui mist le monde sous les lois,
>   Pour donter tout, se donta quelquefois,
>   Et devint proye au temps, qui tout consomme.
> Rome de Rome est le seul monument. . . .[10]

---

[7]Much of the longest of the three dialogues (Addison, *Miscellaneous Works*, ed. A.C. Guthkelch (Oxford, 1914) II, pp. 299–376 – all subsequent references are to this edition) is devoted to this last subject; it was to be taken up in greater detail, and in a more ambitious series of dialogues, by Joseph Spence in his *Polymetis* (London, 1747). There is a short account of this work in Austin Wright, *Joseph Spence: A Critical Biography*, (Chicago, 1950), Ch. V.

[8]Ll. 1–5; *Poems*, VI, p. 202.

[9]Cf. Du Bellay, *Antiquitez de Rome*, 1559, Sonnet III, and Spenser's version (*The Ruines of Rome: by Bellay*, (1591), III); also *Antiquitez*, VII, VIII, XXVII; Spenser, *Faerie Queene*, VII, vii, 47; Shakespeare, Sonnets XII (l. 10), XV (l. 11), XIX, LXIV and LXV.

[10]Ll. 1–9. Du Bellay, *Poésies Françaises et Latines*, ed. E. Courbet (Paris, 1918), II, p. 267. Spenser, in his *Ruines of Rome*, rendered the figure: 'Rome now of Rome is th'onely Funerall'. It is

In Du Bellay, as in Pope, the traditional meditation and lament at the passing away of grandeur and the omnipotence of time is lent immediacy and force by the scene presented. Both poets have been stirred by the ambition and power of the Roman Empire, Du Bellay perhaps more than Pope, and Du Bellay is, I think, the more eloquent on the subject. It is easy to find an earlier example of the same attitude. Petrarch, who devoted so much energy and eloquence to the cause of restoring Rome's past glory, could compose the following exchange between Joy and Reason:

> G. Sum Romanus Imperator, mundi dominus. R. Fuit quando id dici propè ueraciter poterat, quorsum uero redierint res uides . . . Non est amplius gaudii materia Romanum Imperium, sed humanæ fragilitatis & fortunæ uariantis indicium.[11]

The conceit of Rome as its own sepulchre, or monument, goes back earlier still, as Pope probably realized; it is used in two different places by St Jerome, writing contemporaneously with the final break-up of the Roman Empire. 'Vera sententia est': wrote Jerome, in the preface to the third book of his commentary on *Ezekiel*:

> Omnia orta occidunt, et aucta senescunt. Et alibi: Nihil est enim opere et manu factum, quod non conficiat et consumat vetustas. Quis crederet ut totius orbis exstructa victoriis Roma corrueret, ut ipsa suis populis et mater fieret et sepulcrum. . . .[12]

Pope does in a sense span the centuries with his description of the ruins of Rome; the reader who is attentive to the allusive mode of his poetry here cannot but feel, behind its concise summary, the accumulated testimony of 'what oft was thought'. The echo of Jerome in particular, a conscious inheritor of the imperial civilization and a contemporary witness of Rome's fall, seems to confer a special historical and human authenticity upon what Pope has to say.

In the lines which follow, Pope may be seen as expanding upon the concise, central words of Du Bellay's sonnet; 'Voy quel orgueil, quelle ruine:' yet more perhaps than in Du Bellay moral appraisal from a Christian standpoint enters into Pope's description of the 'Imperial wonders' of Ancient Rome. The part played by despoiled nations and by slavery, including the labour of persecuted early Christians, is not forgotten; upon this suffering Rome's glory was built.[13]

---

a striking and memorable conceit. That it too may have become a commonplace is suggested by the fact that James Howell uses it in a letter from Rome, in his *Epistolae Ho-Elianae* (London, 1645). His source was certainly either Du Bellay or Spenser, since the whole argument of Sonnet XVIII of the *Antiquitez* appears, unacknowledged, in another part of the same letter. (James Howell, *Epistolae Ho-Elianae: The Familiar Letters*, Bk I, Sect. I, Letter xxxviii; *To Sir* William St John, *Knight, from* Rome. Ed. Joseph Jacobs (London, 1890), pp. 85–6).

[11]*De Remediies utriusque Fortunae*, I, xcvi (*Opera*, (Basle, 1554) p. 99).

[12]Migne, *Patrologia Latina*, XXVI, c. 75. The other place where Jerome speaks of Rome as the sepulchre of its own people was first noticed in this connection by Joseph Warton (*The Works of Alexander Pope, Esq.*, (London, 1797), III, p. 303; *Poems*, VI, p. 206); it is from Epistola CXXX: *Ad Demetriadem*, 5 (Migne, *Patrologia Latina*, XXII, c. 1109).

[13]Ll. 5–10 were added to the poem in 1726 (*Poems*, VI, p. 205); they subtilize Pope's attitude to Rome, as already expressed, into one more balanced and human. Pope was always on his guard against magnificence raised at the expense of the less fortunate (see George Sherburn, ed., *The*

The emotion of pity, aroused by earlier lines, is modified by Pope's suggestion that Rome suffered a chastisement of imperial hubris, and in the following couplet compassion is blended with ironic perception:

> Fanes, which admiring Gods with pride survey,
> Statues of Men, scarce less alive than they;[14]

It is the unexpected introduction of the word 'less', in the second line of the couplet, which at a stroke reduces the Roman pantheon to the level of men long dead and disregarded. At this point one is much aware of the Christian poet writing of pagan Rome.[15] Christianity, however, is far from being exempt from Pope's critical appraisal; he had offended his fellow Catholics by his references to monkish barbarism in *An Essay on Criticism*,[16] but his condemnation of Christian philistinism is even more explicit here:

> Some felt the silent stroke of mould'ring age,
> Some hostile fury, some religious rage;
> Barbarian blindness, Christian zeal conspire,
> And Papal piety, and Gothic fire.[17]

Pope's rhetoric serves him well in these lines; the antithetic patterning of the verse becomes progressively more marked, the juxtaposition of apparent opposites, and the implication of their actual affinity, progressively more bold; the total effect is expressive of a fine critical detachment on the part of the poet. The concluding lines of the epistle's first paragraph serve both to re-emphasize the theme of mutability and to introduce the central problem of the whole poem: how may the knowledge and spirit of Rome be transmitted, through the wastes of time, into posterity?

> Perhaps, by its own ruins sav'd from flame,
> Some bury'd marble half preserves a name;
> That Name the learn'd with fierce disputes pursue,
> And give to Titus old Vespasian's due.[18]

Correspondence of Alexander Pope (Oxford, 1956), II, p. 239; also *To Bathurst*, ll. 219–33; *Poems*, III–ii, pp. 2, 108).

[14]Ll. 9–10: *Poems*, VI, p. 203. Warburton's note is apposite, though it perhaps exaggerates the effect of Pope's lines: 'By these Gods he means the Tyrants of Rome, to whom the Empire raised Temples. The epithet, *admiring* conveys a strong ridicule; that passion, in the opinion of Philosophy, always conveying the ideas of ignorance and misery, which can never approach the Deity.

> Nil admirari prope res est una, Numici,
> Solaque quae possit facere at servare beatum.

Admiration implying our ignorance of other things; *pride*, our ignorance of ourselves.' (*Works*, ed. Warburton, 1751; quoting here from the revised edition of 1766, III, p. 357).

[15]The original title of Pope's imitation of Virgil's Fourth Eclogue was 'Messiah. A Sacred Eclogue, *compos'd of several Passages of Isaiah the Prophet*. Written in Imitation of Virgil's Pollio.' (*Poems*, I, p. 103.) Pope is not an Augustan at the expense of being a Christian.

[16]*Correspondence*, ed. Sherburn, I, pp. 118–19; also *An Essay on Criticism*, ll. 687–96; *Poems*, I, pp. 204–5.

[17]Ll. 11–14; *Poems*, p. 203.

[18]Ll. 15–18; *Poems*, pp. 203, 206.

Remnants of History

An emblem in Ripa's *Iconologia* depicts History as a winged female; she writes in a book borne on the shoulders of Saturn who, carrying a scythe, walks close at her side. Beneath her right foot is a rectangular form, symbol of constancy.[19] Saturn, with his scythe, is here the personification of time, whose capacity to destroy has been overcome and controlled by the Art of History. Pope, when he speaks of 'the wild Waste of all-devouring years', presents time as a force of disorder, sterility and destruction. This presentation is the more appropriate, from Pope's viewpoint, because the particular lapse of time he has in mind is that between the fall of Rome and the revival of learning. It is worth noticing that the metaphors Pope employed for the Middle Ages in *An Essay on Criticism*, a '*second* Deluge' and a '*wild Torrent*', are also images of disorder and destruction, though that of the deluge has further implications.[20] History, then, is one feature of those 'images of men's wits and knowledges', which, as Bacon wrote,

> remain in books, exempted from the wrong of time and capable of perpetual renovation. Neither are they fitly to be called images, because they generate still, and cast their seeds in the minds of others . . . So that if the invention of the ship was thought so noble, which carrieth riches and commodities from place to place . . . how much more are letters to be magnified, which as ships pass through the vast seas of time, and make ages so distant to participate of the wisdom, illuminations, and inventions, the one of the other?[21]

As history is a branch of learning, so antiquities is a branch of history;[22] the paragraph on it in *The Advancement of Learning* suggests the closeness of Pope's thought to that of Bacon:

> Antiquities, or Remnants of history, are, as was said, *tanquam tabula naufragii*, when industrious persons, by an exact and scrupulous diligence and observation, out of monuments, names, words, proverbs, traditions, private records and evidences . . . do save and recover somewhat from the deluge of time.[23]

By the word 'monuments' Bacon understood: buildings, statues, inscriptions, coins, and the like. Du Bellay, having compared Rome to a harvest mown and stacked, might well liken the antiquary to 'le gleneur' gathering the remains 'De ce qui va tumbant apres le moissoneur'.[24] Addison said nothing new when he

---

[19]*Iconologia*, (Padua, 1611), pp. 234–5. See Rudolf Wittkower, 'Chance, Time and Virtue', *Journal of the Warburg and Courtauld Institutes*, I, 318, for the significance of the rectangular form. See also *Iconologia: Or, Moral Emblems, by Caesar Ripa* . . . (London, 1709), pp. 38–9, where this form is missing, and where the book is replaced by a shield.

[20]Ll. 690, 695: *Poems*, I, pp. 317, 319.

[21]*Of The Advancement of Learning*, I; *Works*, ed, Spedding, Ellis and Heath, (London, 1857–74), III, p. 318.

[22]For full discussion of the distinction between History and Antiquities see Arnaldo Momigliano, 'Ancient History and the Antiquarian', *Journal of the Warburg and Courtauld Institutes*, XIII, pp. 285–315.

[23]*Of The Advancement of Learning*, II; ed. cit., III, p. 334. Here, as in *An Essay on Criticism* (see n. 5 above), the image of the 'deluge' seems to suggest an almost universally obliterating power but one which, nevertheless, expresses the will of God. The implication may be that everything necessary for humanity survived the Dark Ages, just as Noah and his ark survived the Flood.

[24]*Antiquitez de Rome*, Sonnet XXX, l. 14; ed. cit., II, p. 280.

pointed out the value of coins as historical evidence. Enea Vico, in his *Discorsi sopra le Medaglie de gli Antichi* (1555), and Antonio Agustín, in his *Dialogos de medallas* (1587), were among the first to put forward the same view; it was to become a commonplace among historians and antiquaries.[25] When, in the seventeenth and eighteenth centuries, historians came to think that non-literary evidence from the past was more reliable than literary, medals assumed an even greater historical importance.[26] A representative expression of this view may be found in Charles Patin's *Histoire des Médailles* (1665), a treatise which Pope and Addison may have known.[27] In the second chapter of this work, *De l'usage des Médailles*, Patin affirms

> c'est l'Histoire, qui estoit appellée par un Ancien, la messagère de l'antiquité, & la maistresse de la vie, qui nous inspire tousjours de noble sentimens, et qui nous fait connoistre l'experience des regles qui doivent former nostre Philosophie morale. Cette Histoire ne s'apprend pas seulement dans les Livres, car d'une part ils ne disent pas tout ce que nous devons sçavoir, & de l'autre il se faut bien donner de garde de croire tout ce qu'ils nous disent: Il faut recourir aux pieces qui la justifient, à qui la malice et l'ignorance des hommes n'a pû donner d'atteinte: Il en faut croire les monumens du temps, dont les Medailles sont les marques les plus asseurées, et les plus frequentes.[28]

In another place in his treatise Patin points out that medals outlast statues and

[25]Hubert Goltz (1526–83), the antiquarian, spent several years surveying the medals in the cabinets of the European collectors, before commencing his series of major works on the antiquities and history of the ancient world. A passage in which he refers to his *Historia Siciliae et Magnae Graeciae* (1576) conveys the importance of medals to his task, and also his sense of excitement and discovery in the work. (*Thesaurus rei antiquariae*, (Antwerp, 1579), Epistola Dedicatoria, n.p.). Cf. Addison, *Dialogue I*; ed. cit., II, p. 291. 'You see here the copies of such Ports and triumphal Arches as there are not the least traces of in the places where they once stood. You have here the models of several ancient Temples, though the Temples themselves, and the Gods that were worshipped in them, are perished many hundred years ago. Or if there are still any foundations or ruines of former edifices, you may learn from Coins what was their Architecture when they stood whole and entire. These are buildings which the *Goths* and *Vandals* could not demolish, that are infinitely more durable than stone or marble, and will perhaps last as long as the earth itself. They are in short so many real monuments of Brass.'

[26]See Momigliano, 'Ancient History and the Antiquarian', *Journal of the Warburg and Courtauld Institutes*, XIII, pp. 295–307. John Evelyn put the case succinctly when he wrote of '. . . these small pieces of Metal, which seem to have broken and worn out the very Teeth of Time, that devours and tears in pieces all things else.' (*Numismata, A Discourse of Medals, Antient and Modern* (London, 1697), p. 2.)

[27]The full title of the work, on first publication, was: *Introduction à l'histoire par la connoissance des medailles*. It was reprinted in 1667, translated into Latin in 1683, and reprinted in 1695 (from which edition I quote) under the title of *Histoire des Médailles*. The eighteenth-century numismatist De la Bastie described this treatise as 'propre à en donner les notions générales, & à faciliter l'étude de cette Science [Numismatics] . . . Ces Traductions & ces Editions différentes, prouvent asséz combien un Livre de cette expéce, étoit regardé comme nécessaire. Cependant on trouva l'Ouvrage de Patin un peu trop abregé . . .' (Louis Jobert, *La Science des Médailles . . . avec des Remarques Historiques et Critiques* [by J. Bimard de la Bastie] (Paris, 1739), I, pp. xvi–xvii). Addison, in his *Dialogues*, alludes to Patin on medals, but it is not clear to which work he refers (*Miscellaneous Works*, II, p. 285).

[28]*Histoire des Médailles* (Paris, 1695), pp. 11–12. See also Louis Jobert, *La Science des Médailles* (Paris, 1693); reference is to the English translation, as *The Knowledge of Medals* (London, 1697), p. 66. Subsequent references are to this edition.

buildings, and are able, alone, to bear the image of such monuments into modern times. Addison makes the same point.[29]

This is the context of thought in which Pope, continuing his epistle, introduces the subject of medals.

> Ambition sigh'd; She found it vain to trust
> The faithless Column and the crumbling Bust;
> Huge moles, whose shadow stretched from shore to shore,
> Their ruins ruin'd, and their place no more!
> Convinc'd, she now contracts her vast design,
> And all her Triumphs shrink into a Coin:
> A narrow orb each crouded conquest keeps,
> Beneath her Palm here sad Judaea weeps,
> Here scantier limits the proud Arch confine,
> And scarce are seen the prostrate Nile or Rhine,
> A small Euphrates thro' the piece is roll'd,
> And little Eagles wave their wings in gold.[30]

What is the precise character of Pope's personified Ambition? Emphasis is laid less upon a desire for ever-greater conquests than upon a desire to be remembered by posterity, a desire that her conquests should achieve lasting fame. In this respect she comes close to Ripa's Historia, and it is interesting to note that Ripa derived his personification from the Roman figure of Writing Victory, to be found both on columns and coins.[31] One such coin is illustrated and discussed by Addison in his *Dialogues*, and would thus be known to Pope.[32] Pope's 'Ambition' is the desire to 'make history' in both senses of the term. Yet Rome's very *ruins* must undergo a second process of destruction (Du Bellay has the same thought) and even their sites will be forgotten.[33] Only medals will remain.

A successful ambiguity governs the meaning of the next line. The dominant sense of the word 'contract' is of course to restrict, to draw in; the word 'shrink', in the line following, confirms this as Pope's primary meaning. The 'vast design' is thus the Roman Empire itself which must be reduced to the dimensions of a coin, that its fame may be transmitted to posterity. There is at the same time a secondary meaning of the word 'contract' which also contributes to the meaning of the poem. Here the sense is to establish, with the implication behind it of bargain and agreement.[34] The 'vast design' is here the stratagem by which 'devouring Time' is foiled, and by which the essential knowledge of what humanity achieved in Rome is conveyed to distant ages and lands. It is however the startling diminution effect, taking its origin from the primary sense of 'contract', which occupies the remainder of the present passage, and which is perhaps the one really dazzling piece of poetic artifice in the epistle. The abstract

---

[29]*Histoire des Médailles*, pp. 1–3; Addison, *Dialogues*, I; *Miscellaneous Works*, II, p. 291.

[30]Ll. 19–30; *Poems*, VI, p. 203.

[31]See L.D. Ettlinger, 'The Pictorial Source of Ripa's Historia', *Journal of the Warburg and Courtauld Institutes*, XIII, pp. 322–3.

[32]It is in fact the second of the two medals engraved by Addison (*Miscellaneous Works*, II, pp. 370–2; Series III, Nos. 13 and 14) to which Pope may be alluding in his reference to 'sad Judaea' in l. 26 (*Poems*, VI, p. 203).

[33]*Antiquitez de Rome*, Sonnet VII, ll. 9–11; ed. cit., II, p. 269.

[34]Both senses of the word are given as current in the earlier eighteenth century by OED.

terms of l. 23 are succeeded by the spectacular visual effect of: 'And all her Triumphs shrink into a Coin', which so boldly juxtaposes the great and the minute: a live procession, celebrating an imperial victory, transformed into a graven emblem. The sense of diminution is made more poignant by the phrase 'narrow orb' with which the next line begins. Here too a successful ambiguity has been employed. Primarily, the phrase refers to the medal: the narrow circle which is now the surviving vestige and proof of Roman glory. The very coupling of the words 'narrow' and 'orb', however, has something of a surprise effect, and prompts one to think of the great orb: the world itself. The allusion, as Warburton rightly noted, is to 'the pompous title of *Orbis Romanus*, which the Romans gave to their Empire'.[35] Jerome himself, writing of the sack of Rome in 410, used this 'title' with a mixture of irony and sorrow: 'Romanus orbis ruit, et tamen cervix nostra erecta non flectitur' and elsewhere without irony, he wrote that 'in una Urbe totus orbis interiit . . .'.[36] The secondary level of meaning thus reinforces our sense of the startling transformation which it is the purpose of this whole passage to express. A third level of meaning lies in the traditional function of the circle as a symbol for eternity, a point fully discussed and illustrated by Addison in his *Dialogues*.[37] In particular Addison speaks of 'the globe' as a proper 'emblem of Eternity'; it is therefore most unlikely that Pope did not intend his 'orb' to have this significance.[38] On this level, therefore, the reference is firstly to the 'vast design' of Rome itself, a city, empire and world sometimes held to be eternal,[39] and secondly to the vast yet chastising design whereby the pride and glory of Rome *has* succeeded in defying 'the wrong of time' and in perpetuating itself in the minds of posterity.[40] The vaunted and the actual 'eternity' of Rome are thus simultaneously alluded to by the single image. All three levels of meaning here contribute to the poet's purpose. Pope has, in one image, brilliantly contrived to compress a sense both of what Rome once was, and has since become. The transformation and diminution effect, from *orbis Romanus* to medal, is completed in this image; Pope has, as it were, succeeded in contracting the 'Waste of all-devouring years' which separates his own age from Rome's original glory, and has superimposed Renaissance upon Antiquity. The hand of the poet who could parallel the arming of an epic hero

[35]*Works*, ed. Warburton (rev. edn, 1766), III, p. 358. See also Obadiah Walker, *The Greek and Roman History Illustrated by Coins and Medals* (London, 1692) pp. 139–40.

[36]Epistola LX: *Ad Heliodorum*; *Commentariorum in Ezechielem Prophetam*: Liber Primus. Migne, *Patrologia Latina*, XXII, c. 600; XXVI, c. 16.

[37]*Dialogues*, II; *Miscellaneous Works*, II, pp. 311–19.

[38]Ibid., II, pp. 318–19. See also Obadiah Walker, *The Greek and Roman History*, p. 80.

[39]See Fig. 154 of *Iconologia: or, Moral Emblems*, by Caesar Ripa . . . (London, 1709), an English emblem book based on but not identical with Ripa's *Iconologia*, for an emblem of 'Rome Eternal': 'A Figure standing with a Helmet; in her left Hand a Spear, with a triangular Head; in her right a Globe, upon which stands a Bird with a long Beak; a little Shield at her Feet; and a Serpent in a Circle denotes *Eternity*. The Bird is the *Phoenix*, out of whose Ashes springs another' (pp. 39–40).

[40]Cf. Du Bellay, *Antiquitez de Rome*, Sonnet XXVII: 'Ces vieux fragmens encor servent d'examples. / Regarde apres, comme de jour en jour / Rome fouillant son antique sejour, / Se rebastist de tant d'oeuvres divines' (ll. 8–11); ed. cit. II, p. 279), and Charles Patin, *Histoire des Medailles*: 'La Magnificence de leurs Temples, la beauté de leurs Arcs triomphaux . . . passent aujourd'hui pour des chef-d'oeuvres inimitables. Cependant le Temps jaloux de leur gloire a derobé ce qu'ils avoyent de plus precieux, & il acheve, tous les jours de rüiner ce que le fer et le feu nous en ont laissé de reste. Peu de Statues ont evités ces mesmes disgraces, les Medailles seules ont esté sauvées de ce débris, & leurs nombres les a conservées jusques à nous' (pp. 2–3).

with a fashionable Queen Anne belle at her toilet is here much in evidence.[41]

It was important for Pope's purpose, as will shortly be shown, that the 'narrow orb' of the medal should not be allowed to seem a dead, fragmentary thing, an inert remnant of past grandeur which has fortuitously survived. Pope has already given the medal a miniature completeness by calling it a 'narrow *orb*' [my italics] and has thus precluded the idea that it is a mere fragment. He has suggested, rather, that it is the essence of Roman achievement in miniature. The remainder of this passage imparts a sense of life and movement to the medal, miniature though it is. They are 'crouded' conquests that the scantier limits of the coin confine; 'sad Judaea' is alive and weeping; the natural movement of the Euphrates has not been halted, and the eagles, most common of all emblems of Roman rule, can still wave their wings. All the precision, sensitivity and delight, with which Pope, in *The Rape of the Lock*, described the beauty of small objects, is lavished here upon the final couplet of the passage, in many ways the central couplet of the epistle.

A small Euphrates thro' the piece is roll'd,
And little Eagles wave their wings in gold.[42]

The Soul of the Medal

Bacon spoke, as we have seen, of the writings of men as able 'to generate still, and cast their seeds in the minds of others', and to pass thus, through 'the vast seas of time', to distant ages.[43] Du Bellay likened the student of Roman antiquities to the gleaner of scattered grain, after the harvest; and in another sonnet he declares that 'Ces vieux fragmens encor servent d'examples' and proceeds to describe how Rome is reviving itself from its own ruins.[44] If the spirit of Rome is to be reborn in men's minds, it is clear that its antiquities must not only be authentic historical evidence; they must also have the power to inspire. Thus the necessity, in Pope's epistle, for the medal to be made to seem alive.

In his insistence on the 'living' property of medals, Pope is recognizing in old coins a power attributed to them long before their importance as reliable historical evidence was argued by Enea Vico and Antonio Agustín. Two centuries earlier, Petrarch, in his letter to Laelius, described how he had presented Roman coins, with his *De Viris Illustribus*, to the Emperor Charles IV. After describing his exhortation to the Emperor to emulate, in his deeds, the lives of the illustrious Romans, Petrarch told how an expression of favour and approbation animated the face of the monarch.

That my utterance met with his ready approval was clearly shown by the sparkle of his eye and the inclination of his august head; and it seemed to me that the time had come to carry out something which I had long planned. Following up the opportunity afforded by my words, I presented him with some gold and silver coins, which I held

---

[41] *The Rape of the Lock*, Canto I, ll. 121–48; *Poems*, II, pp. 155–8.
[42] Ll. 29–30; *Poems*, VI, p. 203.
[43] See n. 21 above.
[44] *Antiquez de Rome*, Sonnet XXX, ll. 12–14; Sonnet XXVII (lines quoted in n. 40 above); ed. cit., II, pp. 280, 279.

very dear. They bore the effigies of some of our rulers, – one of them, a most lifelike head of Caesar Augustus, – and were inscribed with exceedingly minute ancient characters. 'Behold, Caesar, those whose successor you are,' I exclaimed, 'those whom you should admire and emulate, and with whose image you may well compare your own. To no one but you would I have given these coins, but your rank and authority induces me to part with them. I know the name, the character, and the history, of each of those who are there depicted, but you have not merely to know their history, you must follow in their footsteps; – the coins should, therefore, belong to you.' Thereupon I gave him the briefest outline of the great events in the life of each of the persons represented, adding such words as might stimulate his courage and his desire to imitate their conduct. He exhibited great delight, and seemed never to have received a present which afforded him more satisfaction.

Coins were presented to the Emperor Charles IV expressly to reinforce the gift of *De Viris Illustribus*, to inspire him to meet the challenge of their great deeds by emulation. The coins were for the Emperor alone because, though others might be instructed by them, only he was in a position to vie with the famous figures they depicted. Centrally significant here is that one coin bears the head of Augustus, and that the image is noted to be lifelike almost to the breath. The presentation of the coins has its due place in Petrarch's rhetorical strategy, the purpose of which is not primarily to instruct the Emperor, but to inspire him to *act* (tuum est non modo nosse sed sequi).[45]

That this famous episode was remembered in the earlier eighteenth century is shown by the *Preface de l'Éditeur* of J. Bimard de la Bastie to the 1739 edition of Louis Jobert's *La Science des Médailles*. 'Le goût pour les Médailles Antiques', wrote de la Bastie,

> a commencé à la renaissance des bonnes études. Petrarque, le Restaurateur des Lettres, ne se contenta pas de remasser autant d'Ouvrages des Auteurs anciens, qu'il lui fut possible d'en trouver; il rechercha avec le même empressement les Médailles Antiques, & il crut ne pouvoir offrir à l'Empereur Charles IV. un présent plus agréable & plus digne d'un grand Prince, que de lui donner quelques Médailles Impériales en or, & en argent.[46]

[45] J.H. Robinson and H.W. Rolfe, eds., *Petrarch: The First Modern Scholar and Man of Letters* (New York, 1898), pp. 371–2. 'Quod dictum serenis oculorum radiis et augustæ frontis læto probavit assensu. Itaque peropportunam aggredi visum est, quod iamdudum facere meditabar. Sumpta igitur ex verbis occasione, aliquot sibi aureas argenteasque nostrorum principium effigies, minutissimis ac veteribus litteris inscriptas, quas in deliciis habebam, dono dedi, in quibus et Augusti Cæsaris vultus erat pene spirans: et ecce, inquam, Cæsar, quibus successisti, ecce quos imitari studeas et mirari, ad quorum formam atque imaginem te componas, quos præter te unum, nulli hominum daturus eram; tua me movit auctoritas. Licet enim horum ego mores et nomina et res gestas norim, tuum est non modo nosse sed sequi; tibi itaque debebantur. Sub hoc singulorum vitæ summam multa brevitate perstringens, quos potui ad virtutem atque ad imitandi studium aculeos verbis immiscui, quibus ille vehementer exhileratus, nec ullum gratius accepisse munusculum visus est.' (*Epistolae De Rebus Familiaribus et Variae*, ed. Fracassetti (Florence, 1859–63), II, p. 520).

[46] *La Science des Medailles: Nouvelle ed.* (Paris, 1739). This treatise was first published in 1692, was reprinted in 1693, published in Latin in 1695 and in English in 1697 as *The Knowledge of Medals*. A second English edition appeared in 1715. Addison is almost certain to have known this work, since his *Guardian* paper No. 96 (*The Error in Distributing Modern Medals*) was appended to this second English edition (pp. 152–6). Pope is likely to have known it for the same reason (in ll. 53–62 of *To Mr. Addison* he seems to allude to *Guardian*, No. 96) though possibly not before the poem was first drafted. De la Bastie described the treatise in his Preface to the 1739 edition, as 'le meilleur qu'on ait fait jusqu'à présent, pour rendre l'étude de ces Monumens Antiques plus facile,

The power of medals to inspire emulation is in fact fully recognized by Charles Patin in his *Histoire des Médailles*; he discusses it in a number of places, and clearly considers its effect to be similar to that of History Painting – with the exception that the medal is also the proof of what it depicts.[47] Louis Jobert, in his *La Science des Médailles*, suggests another aspect of the living and inspiring quality of medals when he notes how faithfully they reflect the level of civilization – Augustan or barbarous – in which they were coined.[48] It is suggested even more strongly when Jobert allows his exposition of the Figure and Legend of a medal to lead him into using the human metaphor of the body and the soul. 'It seems as if the Ancients', wrote Jobert,

> had designed to make Images and Emblems of their Medals; the One for the Common People, and those of duller Apprehensions; the Other for People of Quality, and the more refined Wits. Images to represent the Faces and Heads of Princes; Emblems their Virtues and Great Atchievements. Thus the Legend is to be looked upon as the Soul of the Medal, and the Figures as the Body; and just so it is in the Emblem, where the Device has the place of the Soul without which we could never understand what the Figures were designed to teach us.[49]

The comparison between medals and emblems, like that of Patin between medals and History Painting, makes it finally clear that the medal's living power to inspire is intimately related to the idea of the persuasive and transforming power of the visual image.[50] As late as 1709 a work purporting to be an English translation of Ripa's *Iconologia* could be introduced in the following terms:

plus utile, & plus agréable' (p. xviii). It is noteworthy that De la Bastie, in an anecdote in his Preface, seems to recall the imagined power of medals to inspire to greatness: 'Alphonse Roi d'Arragon & de Naples, Prince plus célèbre encore par son amour pour les Lettres que par ses Victoires, fit chercher avec soin des Médailles dans toute l'Italie, & il plaça la suite qu'il en avoit formée, & qui étoit asséz considérable pour ce tems-là, dans une casette d'yvoire qu'il faisoit porter par-tout avec lui' (I, p. iv). The English translator was probably Obadiah Walker, whose own treatise *The Greek and Roman History Illustrated by Coins and Medals*, was published in 1692.

[47] E.g. pp. 14–15; p. 269 (*Epistre au Roy*); pp. 6–7.

[48] *The Knowledge of Medals*, p. 30: 'Nothing shews the desolation of the Empire more than the Universal loss of all good Arts, which appears in this of Engraving, which is no more than a miserable scratching of the Metal'; p. 31: 'The small care the Emperors took of their Medals after the first three Centuries, may be very well admired. For after that time, we find not one footstep of the *Roman* Majesty; there being none but little medals without Relief or Thickness, till *Theodosius*'s time; and after the Division of the Empire when he died, nothing but Misery and Poverty. No more curious Heads or Reverses, the Characters, Language, Figures, and Legend all barbarous; so that no body troubled themselves to collect them, and they are thereby become almost as scarce as they are deformed.' Cf. Addison, *Dialogues*, III; *Miscellaneous Works*, II, p. 392.

[49] *The Knowledge of Medals*, p. 78. The passage continues: 'As for instance, we see on a Medal of *Augustus* two Hands joyned, clasping a *Caduceus* betwixt two *Cornucopia*'s; this is the Body; the word *Pax* there engraven, is to denote the Peace which that Prince had given to the State, by reconciling it to *M. Antony*, which had restored Felicity and Plenty to it. Whereas those very two Hands on the Medals of *Balbinus* and *Pupienus* have this Legend, *Amor mutus Augustorum*, expressing thereby the good Understanding between the two Colleagues in governing the Empire.' (p. 79). The metaphor of the soul and body for the Legend and Figure is common in the literature of devices; see, e.g., Thomas Blount, *The Art of Making Devices, . . . First Written in French by Henry Estienne* . . . (London, 1646), pp. 11, 13 and 18; Camden's *Remaines of a Greater Worke, Concerning Britaine* . . . (London, 1605), p. 158; Samuel Daniel, *The Worthy Tract of Paulus Iovius* (London, 1585), n.p.

[50] For a full exposition and historical account of this doctrine, see E.H. Gombrich, 'Icones Symbolicae: The Visual Image in Neo-Platonic Thought', *Journal of the Warburg and Courtauld Institutes*, XI, pp. 163–88, especially 174.

Here you will find abundance of Figures and Emblems of every thing imaginable; accompanied with curious and solid Morals, owing to very learned Authors. The understanding Peruser of this Book will meet therein Things not only to divert the Mind, but to instruct it, and fo *inspire him* [my italics] with the Love of Virtue, and Hatred of Vice; and to regulate his Manners, Behaviour and Conduct.[51]

It is from this vital background of attitudes towards the medal that the next lines of Pope's Epistle spring. In these lines the medal is fully humanized:

The Medal, faithful to its charge of fame,
Thro' climes and ages bears each form and name:
In one short view subjected to your eye
Gods, Emp'rors, Heroes, Sages, Beauties, lie.[52]

The medal's human trait of fidelity is shown to its 'charge': the burden of knowledge and inspiration that it carries inviolate through the ages, as did the ships through 'the vast seas of time' in Bacon's metaphor.[53] This 'charge of fame' is not merely referred to but displayed; the final line, with its sense of an opening out of abundant variety and richness, has this effect. The line unfolds before us a whole hierarchy, ranging down from the divine to the spheres of human action, reflection and beauty. Pope's amplification at this point is in marked contrast to the diminution effect carried out in the previous paragraph; with the line 'And little Eagles wave their wings in gold' the turning-point of the epistle has been passed, the possibility of *translatio imperii* and *translatio studii* has been asserted and accounted for, and one would expect Pope to devote the remainder of his poem to the unfolding of a new Augustan Age to counterbalance the old.

This expectation is fulfilled – one of the strengths of the epistle is its sense of deliberate procedure and controlled form – but not before Pope has turned his attention to one serious obstacle to such a rebirth: the uncritical adulation of antiquity for its own sake.

With sharpen'd sight pale Antiquaries pore,
Th'inscription value, but the rust adore;

[51]*Iconologia: Or, Moral Emblems*, (London, 1709), Preface, n.p. Cf. Evelyn, *Numismata*, p. 66. The writer of this preface also may have remembered the more eloquent statement of the power of the visual image in Thomas Blount's *The Art of Making Devices* (see n. 49 above), pp. 13–14: '*Bargagli* saith with good reason, That a *Devise* is nothing else, but a rare and particular way of expressing ones self; the most compendious, most noble, most pleasing, and most efficacious of all other that humane wit can invent. It is indeed most compendious, since by two or three words it surpasseth that which is contained in the greatest Volumes. And as a small beame of the Sun is able to illuminate and replenish a Cavern (be it ever so vast) with the rayes of its splendor: so a *Devise* enlightens our whole understanding, & by dispelling the darknesse of Errour, fills it with a true Piety, and solid Vertue. It is in these Devises as in a Mirrour, where without large Tomes of Philosophy and History, we may in a short tract of time, and with much ease, plainly behold and imprint in our minds, all the rules both of Morall and Civill life; tending also much to the benefit of History, by reviving the memory of such men, who have rendred themselves illustrious in all sorts of conditions, and in the practice of all kinds of Vertue.' In his Epistle Dedicatory, Blount claimed to be the first writer on this subject in English, except for a 'small parcell of it in Camden's Remaines', but he had forgotten, or did not know, Samuel Daniel's translation of the dialogue of Paulus Jovius (see n. 49 above).
[52]Ll. 31–4; *Poems*, VI, p. 203. Cf. Addison, *Dialogues*, I; *Miscellaneous Works*, II, p. 284.
[53]See n. 21 above.

This the blue varnish, that the green endears,
The sacred rust of twice ten hundred years!
To gain Pescennius one employs his schemes,
One grasps a Cecrops in ecstatic dreams;
Poor Vadius, long with learned spleen devour'd,
Can taste no pleasure since his shield was scour'd;
And Curio, restless by the Fair-one's side,
Sighs for an Otho, and neglects his bride.[54]

The rust upon medals was indeed, in some cases, prized by antiquaries; Addison's Philander is afraid of being laughed at for taking it seriously, but Jobert, in *La Science des Médailles*, is quite unashamed to do so.[55] Rare medals, likewise, were coveted more than common ones. An image of Augustus was more likely to inspire emulation of antiquity than an image of Otho, Pescennius Niger or the entirely mythical Cecrops, yet these were most highly prized collectors' pieces.[56] The last line of the passage sharply juxtaposes such antiquarianism with the real world; its utterly dead and unproductive character is the more stressed by the mention of the neglected bride. This characteristic, comically presented, is the very opposite to that for which medals should rationally have been valued: an accession of inspiration and knowledge. Medals, in short, are to be prized for what they convey, not for their actual antiquity or rarity. The 'sharpen'd sight' of the antiquaries is thus ironical on the level of metaphor, though literally true; they cannot discern wherein lies the true value of antiquities, and where there is no discrimination there can be no new growth.

And Build Imaginary Rome Anew

In a letter to the Emperor Charles IV Petrarch conjures up the Genius of Rome to plead for help in reviving her ancient importance and glory; in Canzone VI ('Spirto gentil . . .'), addressed to Cola di Rienzo, his pleading was animated by genuine belief that the moment for such a revival was at hand – that the revival was indeed beginning.[57] Du Bellay, as we have seen, deviated from his dominant theme of mutability to take note of the enduring spirit of Rome and its capacity for self-renewal.[58] These references mark out the tradition in which Pope is writing in the passage from *An Essay on Criticism* already quoted –

Rome's ancient *Genius*, o'er its *Ruins* spread,
Shakes off the *Dust*, and rears its rev'rend Head![59]

[54]Ll. 35–44; *Poems*, VI, pp. 203–4. It was this passage that Warburton used to justify the inclusion of *To Mr. Addison* in the *Moral Essays* group (see n. 6 above).

[55]Addison, *Dialogues*, I; *Miscellaneous Works*, II, p. 291; Jobert, *The Knowledge of Medals*, pp. 129–30. Pope mocks a similar, though more eccentric attitude, in the slapstick comedy of the *Memoirs of . . . Martinus Scriblerus*, Ch. III. Cf. also *The Dunciad*, IV, pp. 347–96; *Poems*, V (Revised Edition), pp. 377–81.

[56]*Poems*, VI, p. 207; ll. 39, 40 and 44n. Medals of Pescennius are mentioned by Patin as particularly rare: 'Je donnerai icy l'example de la plus rare Medaille de bronze qui soit au monde. Elle represente *Pescennius Niger*, dont le regne fut si court, & la demeure si eloignée de l'Italie, qu'il ne faut pas s'estonner si les Medailles en sont si rares en tous metaux' (p. 180), and Jobert notes that '. . . the Latin *Otho* of the large size in Copper is inestimable . . .' (p. 15).

[57]*Epistolae De Rebus Familiaribus et Variae*, ed, cit. II, pp. 60–2; see in this Canzone stanzas 1–3 and 7–8 especially.

[58]See n. 40 above.

[59]Ll. 699–700; *Poems*, I, p. 319.

– and in the last part of the present epistle, where he heralds the advent of a new Augustan Age in England. It is therefore necessary to the plan of Pope's poem that he should clearly distinguish Addison's estimation of medals from that of the blind antiquaries.

> Theirs is the Vanity, the Learning thine:
> Touch'd by thy hand, again Rome's glories shine,
> Her Gods, and god-like Heroes rise to view,
> And all her faded garlands bloom a-new.
> Nor blush, these studies thy regard engage;
> These pleas'd the Fathers of poetic rage;
> The verse and sculpture bore an equal part,
> And Art reflected images to Art.[60]

The distinction necessary to Pope's purpose is made in the first line; the marked antithesis brings learning and vanity into full contrast, the one both outward-looking and critical, the other inward-looking and without thought. The allusion in the next line is specific; Philander in the *Dialogues* (who is for all intents and purposes Addison himself) had described how a medal might be redeemed from harmful varieties of rust. The 'skilful Medallist . . .'

> will recover you a Temple or a triumphal Arch out of its rubbish, if I may so call it, and with a few reparations of the graving tool restore it to its first splendour and magnificence. I have known an Emperor quite hid under a crust of dross, who after two or three days cleansing has appeared with all his Titles about him as fresh and beautiful as at his first coming out of the Mint.[61]

Just as, in the first half of the epistle, Rome was seen to shrink to a coin, so here the cleaning of the coin assists in Ambition's 'vast design' and is a prelude to the swelling act of new Augustanism. It is the peculiar character of the writing on numismatics at this period that so great a concept should be linked to so mundane and precise an action as (for example) the application of 'Vinegar, or the Juice of Lemons' for the removal of rust from medals.[62] The emphasis on the possibility of new life and growth, expressed in the words 'rise' and 'bloom a-new' culminates in the final couplet of the passage. Pope alludes here to Philander's contention, in the *Dialogues*, that the medals, sculpture and poetry of the ancient world had much in common, and that medals might therefore assist in elucidating the obscurities and heightening the appreciation of the ancient poets.[63] To clean a medal, then, is not only to reveal an object in itself a thing of beauty and an emblem of antiquity; it is also to help clear away the 'rust' from the literature of antiquity, to reveal it as it would have been understood at the time of its composition. In this way medals demonstrate the fundamental affinity, and possibility of cross-fertilization, between the visual and

---

[60]Ll. 45–52; *Poems*, VI, p. 204.
[61]Addison, *Dialogues*, I; *Miscellaneous Works*, II, pp. 291–2.
[62]Louis Jobert, *The Knowledge of Medals*, p. 130; see n. 55 above.
[63]Addison, *Dialogues*, I; *Miscellaneous Works*, II, pp. 293–9; and the whole of *Dialogue II*. Cf. also *Dialogue I*; *Miscellaneous Works*, II, p. 285 and n. 47 above for further discussion of medals and painting.

literary arts – a cross-fertilization which can give birth to stirring visions. It is significant that the last line quoted anticipates a similar line in the Epistle *To Mr. Jervas* – 'While images reflect from art to art' – expressive as the later line is of a dialogue between poet and painter which leads on to 'Rome's pompous glories rising to our thought', 'And builds imaginary *Rome* a-new'.[64]

The final paragraph of the epistle opens with a stirring call to Britain to rise to the challenge of ancient achievement. Here too, as Warburton was right to note, there is a specific allusion to Addison. In his *Guardian* paper No. 96, which was reprinted in 1715 with the revised English translation of Jobert's *La Science des Médailles*, Addison had contended that the modern world should adopt the Roman practice of circulating medals as popular currency.[65] 'This Method', wrote Addison,

> published every noble action to advantage, and in a short space of time spread through the whole *Roman* Empire. The *Romans* were so careful to preserve the memory of the great events upon their coins that when any particular piece of money grew very scarce, it was often re-coined by the succeeding Emperor, many years after the death of the Emperor to whose honour it was first struck.[66]

Addison continues that 'This is one of those Arts of Peace which may very well deserve to be cultivated, and which may be of great use to posterity'. He then appends a proposal, purporting to be the work of a friend, and about to be put into execution. It urges that English farthings and halfpennies be recoined as currency of the now united kingdoms of England and Scotland; that they commemorate 'all the most remarkable parts of her Majesty's reign'; that a society be established to advise on subjects, inscriptions and devices; and that no coins be stamped without approval of this society or, perhaps, authority of the Privy Council. From these proposals it may be seen how far the literary ideal of a new Rome could reach into the commercial life of modern society where, as under Augustus, currency was a means of influencing and spreading a nation's idea of itself.

> By this means, Medals, that are at present only a dead treasure, or meer curiousities, will be of use in the ordinary commerce of life, and, at the same time, perpetuate the Glories of her Majesty's reign, reward the labours of her greatest subjects, keep alive in the people a gratitude for publick services, and excite the emulation of posterity. To these generous purposes nothing can so much contribute as Medals of this kind, which are of undoubted authority, of necessary use and observation, not perishable by time, nor confined to any certain place; properties not

---

[64]Ll. 20, 24, 32; *Poems*, VI, pp. 156–7.

[65]Addison, *Works*, 1721, IV, pp. 135–7. The same argument occurs in *Dialogue III* (*Miscellaneous Works*, II, pp. 380–1) and Patin had drawn attention to the same point (*L'Histoire des Médailles*, pp. 45–6). Pope's allusion here would seem to be primarily to the *Guardian* paper, since only this contains a definite proposal that Britain should adopt the Roman practice. Addison does, however, perhaps allude to his own *Guardian* paper when, in *Dialogue III*, Eugenius is made to say: 'I have often wondered that no nation among the moderns has imitated the ancient *Romans* in this particular. . . . But where Statesmen are ruled by a spirit of Faction and interest, they can have no passion for the glory of their country, nor any concern for the figure it will make among posterity . . .' and Cynthio replies: 'We shall think . . . you have a mind to fall out with the Government, because it does not encourage medals.' (*Miscellaneous Works*, II, p. 380.)

[66]Addison, *Works*, IV, p. 136. Cf. Louis Jobert, *The Knowledge of Medals*, p. 110.

to be found in books, statues, pictures, buildings, or any other monuments of illustrious actions.[67]

This is more than the expression of regret that 'no nation among the moderns has imitated the ancient Romans in this particular' which we find in the *Dialogues*.[68] It is a specific and practical proposal, the 'Society' mentioned in clause three being a copy of the French *Académie des Inscriptions et Belles Lettres*, of which Racine and Boileau had been members.[69] Addison is here quite seriously advocating that Britain should adopt the Roman practice. He is not, however, proposing an imitation of the ancients merely for its own sake, but for good reasons; by the means proposed Britain would attain a heightened awareness of the quality of her own civilization; and would at the same time discharge an obligation to posterity. It is an assumption which seems to underlie much of the writing on medals at this time that it is a mark of civilization to leave records, a characteristic of barbarism to leave none.[70] Hence Philander's observation in Dialogue III:

> We ought to look on Medals as so many monuments consigned over to Eternity, that may possibly last when all other memorials of the same Age are worn out or lost. They are a kind of Present that those who are actually in Being make over to such as lie hid in the depths of Futurity.[71]

Little advancement of learning and civilization could be hoped for in a world which had lost its past. It is significant that Addison likens the destruction of coins to 'the burning of the *Alexandrian* Library' and that Pope was to include this latter event in the *Dunciad*, Bk III, as a sign of the triumph of Dulness.[72] These are the issues to which Pope seeks to give poetic expression in the final section of his epistle.

---

[67]Addison, *Works*, IV, p. 137.

[68]See n. 65 above.

[69]Addison alludes to the French *Académie* in *Dialogue III* (*Miscellaneous Works*, II, p. 390): 'One might expect, methinks, to see the Medals of that nation [France] in the highest perfection, when there is a society pensioned and set apart on purpose for the designing of them.' See L.-F. Alfred Maury, *L'Ancienne Académie des Inscriptions et Belles-Lettres*, (Paris, 1864), pp. 28–9, 428, 449, and Frances Yates, *The French Academies of the Sixteenth Century*, (London, 1947), pp. 301–3. The academy was officially constituted in 1701 under the title of 'L'Académie royale des inscriptions et médailles.' It was laid down that '. . . L'Académie s'appliquera à faire des médailles sur les principaux événements de l'histoire de France; elle travaillera à l'explication de toutes les médailles, medaillons, pierres et autres raretées antiques et modernes, du cabinet de Sa Majesté, comme aussi à la description de toutes les antiquitez et monuments de la France.' (Maury, p. 28).

[70]Cf. Patin, *L'Histoire des Medailles*, pp. 111–13, especially the following: 'Ces barbares se contenterent de fair courir pour Monoye, des pieces malfaites, dont on ne peut expliquer les caracteres & les types. Ils se servoient mesme d'or tres-bas, & il n'y avoit pas quelquefois le quart de fin. C'est sans doute grand dommage que leur nonchalance nous ait fait ignorer leur histoire, par le peu de monumens que nous en avons, & qui ne suffisent pas pour nous en informer. La ruine de l'Empire Romain a fait l'establissement des Monarquies d'aujourd'huy, & nous scaurions toutes les particularitez de leurs origines, si on avoit continué de faire des Monoyes & des Medailles, comme dans les six Siecles precedens.'

[71]*Miscellaneous Works*, II, p. 389.

[72]Ibid., II, p. 379; *The Dunciad* (1729), III, ll. 71–4 and note; *Poems*, V, p. 156.

Oh when shall Britain, conscious of her claim,
Stand emulous of Greek and Roman fame?
In living medals see her wars enroll'd,
And vanquished realms supply recording gold?
Here, rising bold, the Patriot's honest face;
There Warriors frowning in historic brass:
Then future ages with delight shall see
How Plato's, Bacon's, Newton's looks agree;
Or in fair series laurell's Bards be shown,
A Virgil there, and here an Addison.[73]

These and the concluding lines counterbalance the broad vista of Rome in its ruins, at the beginning of the Epistle, and complete the symmetrical structure of the poem. The tone, set by the phrase 'conscious of her claim' in the first line, is one rather of confidence than aspiration. The argument assumes that Britain is already in a position to sustain comparison with Rome. She has her patriots, warriors and philosophers; she can afford to measure herself by the standard of antiquity, which is what adopting the Roman usage of medals would mean. In keeping with this assumption, and the confident tone, the passage moves to a recognition of Britain's duty to the distant future, which can best be fulfilled by the adoption of Addison's proposals. The swift movement of 'Plato's, Bacon's, Newton's . . .' grandly overleaps the mere hiatus of the Middle Ages, and ranges Newton and Bacon with Plato, as in a single series of medals laid out before some antiquary of the far future.[74] The very marked antithesis and balance of the line: 'A Virgil there, and here an Addison' (contrasting with the swift connected movement of the line just discussed) is even more expressive of a new Augustan confidence; the weighing of one age against the other, and the resultant equipoise, is here specifically enacted by the verse. In the same way Pope, in his Horatian epistles, was to print Horace's Latin and his own English opposite to one another on facing pages, as though to invite comparison and assert a balance; in the same way, in the 1739 edition of Jobert's *La Science des Médailles*, the profiles of 'Divus Augustus' and 'Lodovicus Magnus Novus Augustus', side by side, are to be found engraved.[75]

[73]Ll. 53–62; *Poems*, VI, p. 204.

[74]Pope imagines a series of medals devoted to great philosophers, just as different series were devoted to consuls, cities, kings, emperors, deities and so forth. The jump from Plato to Bacon derives some of its boldness from its confident departure from the conventional categories of 'Ancient' and 'Modern' in contemporary numismatics – this, says Jobert, 'is the first Notion of the Art, on which depends their [i.e. the medals'] esteem and value. The Ancients are all those that were coined within the Third and Ninth Age of Jesus Christ; the Modern which have been made within these last Three Hundred Years: For, as for those we have after Charlemagne till that time, the Curious will not vouchsafe to collect them . . .' (*The Knowledge of Medals*, p. 3).

[75]At the head of the Preface de l'Edition de 1715; p. xxxv. It may be thought surprising that Pope's exalted compliment to Addison should have been retained after the estrangement between the two men in 1715. Pope probably wished to seem well-affected to the new government, but the main reason is that the *idea* of a modern counterpart to an Augustan original is of more importance to the poem than the name itself. *To Mr. Addison* is a poem of ideas not personalities; it would not, by its nature, have demanded revision in the light of personal developments. The compliment, nevertheless, seems exaggerated and implausible to modern ears. It would not have done so to a contemporary. Addison's reputation, not only as a writer of prose but also as a poet in Latin and English, could not well have stood higher at this time. In addition to this, Addison had recently held the Secretaryship of State for the Southern Department, one of the highest political offices in the

At this point, according to Pope's own testimony, the epistle was once concluded.[76] To have ended with 'A Virgil there, and here an Addison' would certainly have been to impress the reader with a fine, bold note of finality, almost a note of triumph. Yet it would perhaps have been abrupt. By adding the ten lines in tribute to his and Addison's friend, the statesman James Craggs (1686–1721), Pope has been able to improve the poem in several ways. Firstly he is able to sustain and expand his imaginary insight into the future, thus imparting fuller and more satisfying symmetry to the range through time which has been the theme of the epistle. Secondly he is able to expand upon the moral and human qualities which seem to him to merit the term Augustan. Thirdly he is able, to the great advantage of the poem, to take up and develop the circle imagery which was so important a part of the first half of the epistle.

> Then shall thy CRAGS (and let me call him mine)
> On the cast ore, another Pollio shine;
> With aspect open, shall erect his head,
> And round the orb in lasting notes be read,
> 'Statesman, yet friend to Truth! of soul sincere,
> In action faithful, and in honour clear;
> Who broke no promise, serv'd no private end,
> Who gain'd no title, and who lost no friend,
> Ennobled by himself, by all approv'd,
> And prais'd, unenvy'd, by the Muse he lov'd'.[77]

That the Whig statesman, whose profile is thus imagined eternized upon a medal, should be compared to the Consul Pollio of Virgil's Fourth Eclogue is of the highest significance. Not only is this a part of the conscious procedure by which Augustan figures are given modern counterparts, but Pollio in Virgil's Eclogue, and, by analogy, Craggs in the present epistle, is associated with the return of the Golden Age.[78] The Fourth Eclogue, by virtue of its very date and

---

land. He thus exemplified in his own person that close alliance of political power and literary excellence (Augustus's patronage of Virgil and Horace) which has always been an important part of the conception of an Augustan Age. Both these points are well demonstrated by contemporary reactions to Addison's promotion to high office, in 1717: 'who would have expected to have seen the Head of the Poets a Secretary of State? However, he has the character of an incorrupt man, which is no little matter now a days.' The French Ambassador commented: 'Mr. Addison un homme d'esprit est tres poli mais imaginéz vous ce qu'on auroit dit en France si l'on eut fait Mr. Racine Secretaire d'Etat.' (Peter Smithers, *The Life of Addison*, (Oxford, 1954), p. 367.)

[76] *Poems*, VI, p. 205.

[77] Ll. 63–72; *Poems*, VI, p. 204.

[78] It may be that at some stage Pope and Addison looked to Craggs to implement the proposal on medals in *Guardian*, No. 96, and that they envisaged the offices of the monarch's Secretaries of State being recorded on coins, just as those of the Roman consuls had been. See, however, E.H. Gombrich, 'Renaissance and Golden Age', *Journal of the Warburg and Courtauld Institutes*, XXIV, pp. 306–9, for traditional use of the concept of the Golden Age in Renaissance dedication and panegyric. Pope had of course published his own version of Virgil's Fourth Eclogue in 1712 (see n. 15 above). James Craggs is, indeed, here paid a compliment almost as exalted as that to Addison. There are several reasons why Pope may have thought this appropriate. First, Craggs had succeeded Addison as Secretary of State; the last lines of the epistle were almost certainly composed when he was in office. Secondly, Addison's collected *Works*, in which the *Dialogues* together with Pope's poem were to make their first official appearance, was to be dedicated to Craggs. (Though both Addison and Craggs died before publication, the dedication was retained.) Thirdly, Craggs had not

subject, unavoidably suggests the identity of the Augustan Age with a returning Age of Gold, recurring on the completion of a cycle of ages or the Platonic Year. It is obvious that such an identification would be attractive to Renaissance minds, eager as they were to hail the dawn of a new Augustan Age. Pope, by comparing James Craggs to Pollio at this point in the epistle, makes it very clear that Augustan and Golden Ages are associated in his own mind.[79] Addison indeed had discussed the Golden Age, in his *Dialogues*:

> The person in the midst of the circle is supposed to be *Jupiter*, by the Author that has published this Medal, but I should rather take it for the figure of Time. I remember I have seen at *Rome* an antique Statue of Time, with a wheel or hoop of marble in his hand . . . and not with a serpent as he is generally represented . . . As the circle of marble in his hand represents the common year, so this that encompasses him is a proper representation of the great year, which is the whole round and comprehension of Time . . . To sum up therefore the thoughts of this Medal. The inscription teaches us that the whole design must refer to the Golden Age which it lively represents, if we suppose the circle that encompasses *Time*, or if you please *Jupiter*, signifies the finishing of the great year; and that the *Phoenix* figures out the beginning of a new series of time. So that the compliment on this Medal to the Emperor *Adrian*, is in all respects the same that *Virgil* makes to *Pollio*'s son, at whose birth he supposes the *annus magnus* or platonical year run out, and renewed again with the opening of the Golden Age.[80]

This discussion, which Pope cannot but have had in mind when he compared Craggs to Pollio, helps to disclose the relevant meanings of the line in which the symbol of the orb is once more introduced. In the first place it is clear that the same levels of meaning discovered in the word 'orb' earlier in the poem are to be found here; most obviously the orb is the medal which will bear the features of James Craggs and whose Legend will bear witness to his virtues; on the next level it is the world itself, and here the word 'round' does not refer to the Legend which runs round the circumference of the medal but rather suggests that medals will convey the fame of James Craggs 'round the world'.[81] It is when we

---

only a frank and pleasing personality, which won him good opinions from all sides, but also a genuine desire to help men of letters and to promote the arts. He had offered Pope a pension of £300 a year, which the poet refused (Spence, *Anecdotes*, I, p. 99, item 229). Addison's own tribute, from the letter which was to become the dedication of his *Works*, is perhaps the most telling: 'I have no time to lay out in forming such Compliments as would but ill suit that Familiarity between us, which was once my greatest pleasure and will be my greatest Honour hereafter. Instead of them, accept of my hearty Wishes, that the great Reputation you have acquired so early may increase more and more; and that you may long serve your Country with those excellent Talents, and unblemished Integrity, which have so powerfully recommended you to the most gracious and amiable Monarch that ever filled a Throne. May the Franknesse and Generosity of your Spirit continue to soften and subdue your Enemies, and gain you many Friends, if possible, as Sincere as your self.' (*The Letters of Joseph Addison*, ed. Walter Graham, (Oxford, 1941), pp. 406–7.) Pope expressed a high opinion of Craggs in his letters; and his friend Robert Digby, in a letter probably written on 30 July 1720, playfully suggested that Pope's intimacy with Craggs heralded a return of 'the figurative moral golden-age' and 'a revival of the polite arts' (Pope, *Correspondence*, II, pp. 73 and 51).

[79]Cf. Dryden, *Astraea Redux*, ll. 292–322, and *Absalom and Achitophel*, ll. 1026–31; *Poems*, ed. James Kinsley, I, pp. 23–4, 243.

[80]*Miscellaneous Works*, II, pp. 316–17.

[81]'Therefore we shall call only those words the Legend which go round the Medal, and which serve to explain the Figures that are upon the Field.' Jobert, *The Knowledge of Medals*, p. 79.

come to the original third level of meaning (the orb as a symbol of eternity) that we realize a new complication has been introduced. The reference to Pollio now prompts us to think of eternity as that cycle of ages which periodically renews itself with the return of the Age of Gold, and the 'orb' as that encompassing circle which, in Addison's words, is 'the whole round and comprehension of Time'. It is significant that Dryden used the word to express this meaning, in his translation of the Fourth Eclogue.

> The last great Age, foretold by sacred Rhymes,
> Renews its finish'd Course, *Saturnian* times
> Rowl round again, and mighty years, begun
> From their first Orb, in radiant Circles run.[82]

It would thus appear that Pope is not thinking of eternity as a simple concept of timelessness, but rather as a recurrent series of new Augustan Ages which as yet, in Addison's words, 'lie hid within the depths of Futurity', but to which his own age may communicate by medals just as the spirit of Rome's original grandeur has been communicated to him. In the future, as in the past, a medal may conquer time. To all this the phrase 'lasting notes' lends an appropriate suggestion of harmony, and the qualities for which Pope now proceeds to celebrate James Craggs are not inappropriate to the rule of justice, concord and peace with which the Golden Age has traditionally been associated.

The Achievement of the Poem

The purpose of the foregoing analysis has been twofold: firstly to investigate in Pope's poetic practice his concept of Augustanism at this period of his career; secondly to display the structure and working of one of his most accomplished yet commonly neglected epistles.

Under the first head, I have tried to show that *To Mr. Addison* has a major subject: one which is central to an understanding of Pope's conception of his own age and its relation to classical antiquity. *To Mr. Addison* is a poem about Augustanism. It demonstrates that Pope's concept of the Renaissance and his concept of an Augustan Age were integrally related to one another, and that both Renaissance and Augustan Age, in his view, draw their vitality from the proper understanding and the inspiration of man's past achievement. This pattern of beliefs, as the poem clearly shows, depends for its cogency upon the particular conception of time that the poet holds. Man cannot afford to lose touch with his past, yet the ravages of time threaten his heritage. It is notable that, at the beginning of *To Mr. Addison*, time is presented as a destructive power, and it is in this connection that Pope so movingly evokes the theme of mutability as it has descended to him from Jerome through Du Bellay and Spenser. At the end of the epistle, on the other hand, the 'all-devouring years' have been set in the wider perspective of a cyclical theory of time: the revolutions of the Platonic Year which regularly bring round again the age of gold, a new Augustan era to emulate and counter-balance the old. This evolution in the Epistle expresses Pope's confidence in man's capacity to transcend the destruc-

---

[82]*The Fourth Pastoral. Or, Pollio*, ll. 5–8; *Poems of John Dryden*, ed. Kinsley, II, p. 887.

tion of time, and in his civilized and civilizing duty to do so; it is as much man's effort as it is providence that brings round the new Augustan Age. At the very centre of this complex of ideas lies the study of antiquities and in particular of medals. What Spence was later to speak of to Pope as 'so dry a study as Antiquities' stands out, in this poem, as alive with the promise and excitement of a revelation: a new access of spirit and power.[83] This is the significance of the medal; it is devised by providence for man's active use in perpetuating his achievements, for preserving his heritage. In this poem Pope is not, I believe, using the medal primarily as a symbol; its wide import is nevertheless abundantly clear and is comparable to that of the bee in Swift's *Battle of the Books*; both stand out against ignorance, against man's capacity for self-satisfied isolation from the past and the future: the forces of darkness evoked by Pope in his *Dunciad*.

Under the second head, I have tried through an exposition of the subject of *To Mr. Addison*, and the manner in which it is expressed, to set out the evidence upon which the poem must be judged as a work of art. On the basis of this evidence it is clear that the raw materials of this poem – the ideas and even many of its phrases – are of an entirely traditional kind. Pope is here very obviously an eclectic; the artistic merit of the Epistle lies, if anywhere, in the way traditional concepts, sentiments and phrases have been put together. It is in this respect that the poem is a triumph of artistry. The perfect adjustment of form to theme renders the Epistle outstanding. On the most obvious level the poem is lent form by its logical procedure: a problem is stated, a solution proposed, and then pressed through to a successful conclusion. This elementary pattern is reinforced by the expanding and contracting of the focus of attention throughout the poem. At the beginning the focus is at its widest; we behold Rome's ruins through the wastes of time. Then gradually it narrows as, with sight almost as sharpened as the antiquary's, we concentrate more and more upon the medal itself: the one means by which Rome's past glory may be transmitted through the dark ages into the future. Finally the focus widens once more as Pope hails a new Augustan Age to equal the old, and even looks forward to successive Augustan eras in the far future. This narrowing-down and broadening-out effect is the peculiar form of the Epistle. It is admirably suited to a poem which seeks to comprehend, in its subject, two widely separated Augustan Ages and the expanse of time between them. The structural pattern of the poem thus enacts the historical pattern with which it deals. And just as the medal was the centre of the complex of *ideas* elucidated above, so here it is at the centre of the total pattern of the Epistle: at that pivotal point where the focus is at its narrowest:

And little Eagles wave their wings in gold.[84]

The poem is further shaped and unified, its dominant form elegantly complicated, by the circle symbolism which runs throughout. This has an almost decorative effect; but it is very far from being merely decorative since it arises from the very heart of Pope's subject: his concern with medals against time, and

---

[83]Spence, *Anecdotes*, I, item 550.
[84]L. 30; *Poems*, VI, p. 203.

serves, in a way a less widely employed symbol could never have done, to sustain a number of relevant meanings simultaneously in the mind of the reader.

To Mr. Addison, then, is a poem with a great subject; further, Pope has seldom succeeded in shaping the flexible poetic kind of the epistle into so brilliantly appropriate an expressive form. Does this make it a major poem? Perhaps not, because the actual poetry, though never ineffective, has often a certain thinness about it. The poem triumphs in its design, and for the rest one feels a little too readily that 'Expression is the *Dress* of *Thought*'.[85] This appears perhaps most obviously in one of the culminating lines of the poem:

A Virgil there, and here an Addison.[86]

The line is in thought entirely consistent and of a piece with the rest of the epistle, and its clear balance well expresses the thought. Yet there is a starkness about it which springs not from restraint but from a lack of verbal and poetic inventiveness. This lack is, I believe, less obvious in the rest of the poem, and I do not find it at all in the vivid lines with which Pope carries out his spectacular diminution-effect from *Orbis Romanus* to the narrow round of the surviving medal.[87] Taking the epistle *To Mr. Addison* as a whole, however, the reader coming to it from the later poetry is likely to miss the richness, energy and imperious strength with which Pope, at the end of *To Burlington* (1731), affirms the Augustan ideal –

Bid Harbors open, public Ways extend,
Bid Temples, worthier of the God, ascend;
Bid the broad Arch the dangerous Flood contain,
The Mole projected break the roaring Main;
Back to his bounds their subject Sea command,
And roll obedient Rivers through the Land;
These Honours, Peace to happy Britain brings,
These are Imperial Works, and worthy Kings.[88]

[85] *An Essay on Criticism*, l. 318; *Poems*, I, p. 274.
[86] L. 62; *Poems*, VI, p. 204.
[87] Ll. 23–30; *Poems*, VI, p. 203.
[88] Ll. 197–204; *Poems*, III – ii, p. 151.

XI Pope's Imitations of Horace: 1733–5

I cough like *Horace* . . . .
(Pope's Epistle *To Dr. Arbuthnot*, l. 116)

'Consider', says Belarius to Guiderius and Arviragus in the mountains of Wales, 'That it is place which lessens and sets off' (*Cymbeline*, III, iii, 13). We may learn from Belarius. There is something to be said for thinking in a barren landscape of Horace's Satires and Epistles, and of Pope's *Imitations* of them. Any reader will recall such a scene. By contrast with the bare grandeur of such regions and the poverty of land that hardly supports the subsistence farmer, we can apprehend better the intensely social world of Horace (its thronging life and luxury so often countered by the poet's reflectiveness and indeed his awareness of the labour and fruits of the land) as the product of a long evolution. From the produce of land and sea only society and wealth arise. Approaching Horace and Pope as most of us do from the satisfactions, obligations and importunities of our own complex society, we are in danger of ignoring the concentrated human interest of their worlds. Horace was of course aware of the emergence of the *polis*, the megalopolis, indeed Rome and the World City. He sought and built into his life the strong contrast and difference of perspective afforded him by his familiarity with Rome on the one hand, and the possession of his Sabine farm on the other, as is well known. Less commented on is the place in *Sat.* I, iii, where, having alluded not for the first time to the death of the singer Tigellius, and named several other contemporary people, Horace can throw his reflections into sharp relief by opening up a long perspective upon human development:

Cum prorepserunt primis animalia terris . . . .

Horace here draws upon Lucretius (*De Rerum Natura*, V, 925ff.) to offer a picture of primitive man. Against this background the familiar contemporaneity of his Satires is the more striking, yet a notion of *aequabilitas* and of *aequalitas* link the two (ll. 9, 104–12). This is, at the very least, a major *motif* in the Satires and Epistles of Horace and of Pope's *Imitations*. It will be the major theme of this chapter. For in Pope's *Imitations of Horace* we have arrived at the culmination of the English tradition of literary imitation − certainly of a series of central Augustan texts. And the practice of imitation, as is by now well understood, is not synonymous with copying, or even with the imaginative recreation of an ancient or foreign text in modern or native terms, though this must always be a powerful creative drive behind it. Imitation at its most intelligent and creative seeks points of significant difference as well as identification: only in this way can the artistic intelligence take the measure of the huge historical and cultural gulf between ancient and modern times. Only when difference is recognized can the moments of identity be appreciated as the cultural opportunities they are: the medal faithful to its charge of fame opening out a world which is at once old and new. Not all, but much of the diversity of thought about Augustus and Augustan Rome that has been explored in the foregoing chapters can be accommodated within the imitation of Horace as Pope handles it, and the recognition of sameness in difference, the dialectic that can sometimes arise in the drama of a poem between identity and distinctness, form a new 'balance of the mind' achieved by the imitator but absent, by definition, from the imitated.

Sat. II, i

We have it on Pope's own anthority that he first rendered Horace into English several years before the *Imitations*. It was *Sat*. I, i, and done in 'quite a different manner . . . much closer and like a downright translation'.[1] The first surviving Horatian imitation, though it is only a fragment, is his *HORACE, Satyr 4, Lib.l. Paraphrased*, first published in the *London Evening Post* (22-5 January 1731/2). It arises out of the immediate reception of the Epistle *To Burlington* (December 1731), including the attempt to identify 'Timon' with the Duke of Chandos, and has all the marks of an angry and immediate response on Pope's part. The word 'Paraphrased' in the title stresses that freedom from the original which distinguishes imitation from translation, while the quotation of the corresponding lines from the Latin text (ll. 81-5) and the system of cross-reference between that and the English passage anticipate the rationale of the *Imitations*. This is that the reader should be able to hold both texts in his mind, noticing the points of identity and difference, and registering the relation between them. Here Pope does not so much deviate from Horace as expand and particularize a series of general maxims.[2] From this episode a truth may be recognized which is simple, though not so obvious that it has never been denied. It is that when Pope wished to publish a swift, pointed and public riposte to the gossip about his poem *To Burlington* his immediate reaction was to write '*An Answer from* Horace'.[3] He could have composed lines entirely his own. He must have felt that an answer from Horace would be more effective. He can neither have thought himself, nor expected others to think, that the Horatian rôle was that of the sycophant.[4] For though these lines were published anonymously at first, it was obvious that they were a specific defence of Pope's position even before they were incorporated (immediately before the Sporus Portrait) into the Epistle *To Arbuthnot* (1734/5).[5]

---

[1] Joseph Spence, *Observations, Anecdotes, and Characters of Books and Men*, ed. J.M. Osborn (Oxford, 1966), I, p. 144 (item 322).

[2] *The Poems of Alexander Pope*, VI, pp. 338-40.

[3] *Poems*, IV, p. 3 (Pope's phrase from the Advertisement to his *Imitations*).

[4] H.D. Weinbrot, *Augustus Caesar in 'Augustan' England* p. 141, uses this term. Still less can Pope have associated Horace with 'lies and collaboration' (ibid., p. 217). However Weinbrot argues that 'Horace did not indelibly become the collaborator until about the middle of the 1730s' (p. 148). See my 'Satire and Self-Portrayal', *Wolfenbütteler Forschungen*, ed. Walther Killy (Munich, 1981), pp. 153-71, for further discussion of this and connected arguments.

[5] *Poems*, IV, pp. 116-17: the lines are 289-304. From their placing in *To Arbuthnot* immediately before the Sporus Portrait (ll. 305-33) Pope may be thought to imply that they were aimed at Lord

This little poem is no doubt the significant background to that occasion, recounted by both Pope and Bolingbroke, when Bolingbroke suggested that Pope imitate an Horatian satire.[6] Each account has its own salient points, Bolingbroke declaring that Pope sent the new poem'hastily to the press, and Pope, recording that it was *Sat*. II, i of which Bolingbroke observed 'how well that would hit my case, if I were to imitate it in English'. Each agrees that Pope's version was completed in about two days. And this, concluded Pope, 'was the occasion of my imitating some other of the Satires and Epistles afterwards'. This crucial episode has great significance for the reputation of Horace among opposition writers at this time. Bolingbroke had been conspicuous in his use of the Tacitean view of Augustus against George II and the Whig hegemony. That he did not think Horace, by this token, a sycophantic court poet, is made as plain as it could be by his recommending Pope to imitate Horace – and in particular *this* poem of Horace, which happens to focus on the relation of poet and prince. I shall discuss these imitations firstly in the order of their composition.[7]

The First Satire of the Second Book of Horace Imitated (published 15 February 1732/33) takes us at once into the heart of society: what it is said people say, whether it is credible that they say it, whether what they say is true. Like *Sat*. I, iv and x it is a defence of satire, and this involves judging the situation of the poet's judgement in society: opinion, the moral rights and wrongs, sensible advice, the legal situation, and what can only be described as 'the human realities' –

Laws are explain'd by Men – so have a care (l. 144).

Horace's brilliant dialogue-satire involves four people: firstly the two participants, Q. Horatius Flaccus, author of a controversial book of satires, and C. Trebatius Testa, the successful and established *iureconsultus* to whom Cicero had once addressed letters; secondly the two men they chiefly refer to, Caesar Augustus, and the earlier Roman satirist Lucilius. In recreating the part of Trebatius Pope, we know,[8] thought of his friend William Fortescue, his neighbour, legal adviser, MP, friend of Sir Robert Walpole and supporter of the court party. Unlike Trebatius, however, he is not named in the poem, though, possibly in line with Pope's last wishes, brought into its subtitle in the 1751 edition of the *Works*. In each poem a good deal of comedy arises from the rôle played by the lawyer. Horace, unlike Pope (ll. 8–10) does not specify that he seeks legal advice: that this is partly what he wants is implicit in its being Trebatius he approaches. But what does this valuable legal advice amount to? A bit of worldly common-sense, followed up by a little jocularity on the individual traits of the two men: from Trebatius a characteristic recommendation to swim

Hervey, and that Pope had persuaded himself, perhaps correctly, that it was Hervey who had attempted to point Timon's Villa in *To Burlington* against Lord Chandos. The collocation of the two passages may work by association, just as the direct naming of Addison (l. 192) is immediately followed by the Atticus Portrait, based on Addison.

[6]Spence, *Anecdotes*, I, pp. 143–4 (items 321, 321a).

[7]My general approach to the imitations of Horace and Donne follows that sketched out in my short edition of Pope, *Horatian Satires and Epistles* (Oxford, 1964).

[8]Pope to Fortescue, 18 February, 1732/33; *The Correspondence of Alexander Pope*, ed. George Sherburn (Oxford, 1956), III, pp. 350–1.

and have plenty to drink before bedtime,[9] from Pope's lawyer some witty byplay about wives and medicines. There's an exquisite realism in all this, especially in Horace: you come for a very special consultation only to be told not to work so hard and take more exercise. Each lawyer at first evades the moral and legal issues by advising his poet with equal terseness: 'Quiescas' (l. 4). 'I'd write no more' (l. 11). Pope's lawyer, however, though laconic to begin with, is made rather more talkative than Trebatius, and as the drama of the dialogue develops allows himself to be prompted and led on by the poet. Several commentators on Pope have noticed his agile and telling expansions of the Horatian text which, as in all Pope's *Imitations of Horace*, was printed on the facing page.[10] Thus the idea of a poetry expressing esteem for the ruler, the serious object of Horace's careful apologia is delightfully laughed at in Pope. Trebatius's word about winning a reward through praise of Caesar is expanded in Pope to 'a *Knighthood*, or the *Bays*', a reference full of latent irony which Pope's ensuing parody of Sir Richard Blackmore's epic style – 'rumbling, rough and fierce' – fully brings out. But then the lawyer himself joins in the parodic game, and matches Pope's mock-sublime 'Thunder' with the mock-lovely mellifluence of court-compliment. Trebatius has nothing like 'Lull with *Amelia*'s liquid Name the Nine' (l. 31), but instead makes the substantial point that if Horace must write, and will not write epic, he might praise Caesar's character (ll. 16–17). However, in l. 22 Horace gives Trebatius a sonorously empty line; and as if in response Pope, at the end of his poem, does something similar and makes his lawyer pad out the couplets with legal abbreviations –

> Consult the Statute: *quart.* I think it is,
> *Edwardi Sext.* or *prim. & quint. Eliz*:
> See *Libels*, *Satires* – here you have it – read.[11]

and we have here a brief vignette of the two men poring together over the Statutes of England.[12] Pope's lawyer retains Trebatius's rôle of worldly adviser, but while the one-time protegé of Cicero is absolutely brief and straightforward in his references to Caesar Augustus, Fortescue is drawn into the joke against the court poetry of the time and, implicitly, against the court itself. The consequences of this for the poem as a whole can best be seen when we have considered the rôle of the satirist himself in the two poems.

When Trebatius advises Horace to praise the character of Caesar (ll. 16–17), Horace replies:

[9]Eduard Fraenkel, *Horace* (Oxford, 1957), p. 147. André Dacier, whose commentaries on Horace Pope knew and approved of (*Correspondence*, I, p. 492) observed that Cicero's letters showed Trebatius to have been a master of raillery (André Dacier, *Remarques Critiques sur Les OEvres D'Horace Avec une nouvelle Traduction* (Paris, 1687–1700), VII, pp. 21–2.

[10]R.A. Brower, *Pope: The Poetry of Allusion* (Oxford, 1959), pp. 286–7; Thomas E. Maresca, *Pope's Horatian Poems* (Columbus, Ohio, 1966), pp. 57–9; John M. Aden, *Something Like Horace: Studies in the Art and Allusions of Pope's Satires* (Vanderbilt, 1969), pp. 8–13. Aden catches the relation between Pope and the lawyer particularly well.

[11]Ll. 147–9; *Poems*, IV, p. 19.

[12]As Aden points out; *Something like Horace*, pp. 12–13.

Haud mihi deero,
Cum res ipsa feret. Nisi *dextro tempore* Flacci
Verba per attentam non ibunt *Cæsaris* aurem;[13]

Originally Pope wrote something closer to the Latin: 'I'll take the first occasion,
I declare'[14] but nothing of the kind was admitted into his published poem. This
remark of Horace links with his last word: 'Esto, siquis *mala*; sed *bona* siquis /
Judice condiderit laudatur *Caesare*' (ll. 83–4) and constitutes, with a careful
indirection and inconspicuousness, his intimation to Trebatius that he may
already have the approval of the *princeps*.[15] The implication, be it noted, is not
that Horace may write what Augustus wants, but that Augustus may approve of
those freedoms taken by Horace in the First Book of Satires, mostly written
before the consolidation of the principate. While Pope's substitution for the
quoted lines (17–19) is the scarcely wounding observation that the Hanoverian
court cannot bear its laureate and that George II looks to history not poetry for
praise, this deviation from Horace is a salient one, affecting as it does the whole
question of the relation of the artist with the ruler. Nor is this Pope's only striking departure from Horace. It was W.J. Courthope (one of the best critics of
Pope) who in 1881 saw that while at l. 62 *et seq.* Horace defended himself by
pointing to the greater courage and freedom of the earlier satirist Lucilius, Pope
at the corresponding point assumes the rôle of Lucilius himself: 'What? arm'd
for *Virtue* when I point the Pen . . .' (l. 105). As Courthope pointed out, 'fine as
[Pope's] declamation is, it is much more in the manner of Juvenal than of
Horace'.[16] This was a crucial observation. And while, as Brower has rightly said,
the Horatian original from Horace's 'Quid? cum est Lusilius ausus . . .' down
to Trebatius's 'Equidem nihil hinc diffindere possum' does itself reach towards
a Juvenalian mode,[17] still the way Pope makes the mode his own (while
substituting Boileau and Dryden for the precedent of Lucilius) provides a bolder
and more combative crescendo to the poem than the reasonably arguing
Horace. This is the first really notable point in Pope's *Imitations* which shows
that the English poet may, while basing himself in the Horatian original, still
wish to produce poetry that can combine Horatian with Juvenalian, and
something like Persius.[18] Later in the imitations we shall see the same thing.

Pope's 'Lucilian' passage is perhaps especially notable for its sense of moral

[13]Ll. 17–19; *Poems*; IV, p. 6. I refer throughout to the text of Horace which Pope printed on the
facing pages of his *Imitations*, and which now appears there in *Poems*, IV, 'I will not fail myself
when the occasion itself prompts. Only at an auspicious moment will the words of a Flaccus find
with Caesar entrance to an attentive ear' (the Loeb translation by H. Rushton Fairclough; *Horace:
Satires, Epistles and Ars Poetica* (London 1926; reprint of rev. edn, 1955), p. 129).

[14]*The Works of Alexander Pope*, ed. Rev. Whitwell Elwin and W.J. Courthope (London,
1871–89), III, p. 291 n.l.

[15]See Fraenkel, *Horace*, pp. 148–9, for the *laudes Caesaris* in *Sat.* II, i. One may only differ by
suggesting that the approval of the *princeps* is hinted at by the poet rather than stated. 'To be sure, in
case of ill verses. But what if a man compose good verses, and Caesar's judgement approve?' (Loeb
edn, p. 133).

[16]*The Works of Pope*, ed. Elwin and Courthope, III, pp. 297–8.

[17]Brower, *Pope: The Poetry of Allusion*, pp. 287–8.

[18]Pope is likely to have agreed with Dryden when, in his 'Discourse Concerning Satire', the earlier
poet argued that the 'Majestique way of *Persius* and *Juvenal*' (ll. 2356–7) should be taken into
account in a true definition of satire (*The Poems of John Dryden*, ed. James Kinsley (Oxford, 1958),
II, pp. 660–1).

and psychological liberation. It is not that we find him here at grips with evil, as in the Sporus Portrait in *To Arbuthnot*, or in tragic confrontation with the prospect of a degraded Britain, as at the end of Dialogue I of the *Epilogue to the Satires*. The note here is closer to one of exhilarating self-assertion. Partly Pope, following Donne as well as Horace,[19] is defying the constraints of social rank. He does so in the service of Virtue, and it is actually his use and placing in the poem of this abstract noun which contributes to the dramatic sense of freedom which he imparts. Pope's imitation, still more than Horace's satire, is studded with proper names, '*Peter*', '*Chartres*', 'Lord *Fanny*', '*Celsus*', 'C*Æ*SAR', 'Sir *Richard*', 'GEORGE', 'BRUNSWICK' and so forth. Each exerts its sometimes small but always telling pressure on poet and reader. Each, with its reminder of resentment, or menace, or ridiculousness, or reassurance, or authority, joins the rest to form the network of a society specifically apprehended. Through much of his poem each poet weaves an unpredictable way amidst these social landmarks. By contrast with these very specific names the abstract noun when, later in Horace than in Pope, it is reached, discloses the poet's ultimate orientation. Pope extends and heightens the emotion at this stage of the poem by allowing 'What? arm'd for *Virtue* . . .' to anticipate 'TO VIRTUE ONLY and HER FRIENDS, A FRIEND' (l. 121) – and by printing Horace's corresponding line (l. 70), on the facing page, in great capitals.[20] The sense of freedom he thus conveys is the recognition that by comparison with this loyalty no danger or allurement of all-surrounding society can matter at all.

Yet while thus differing from Horace Pope is also, and in perhaps a deeper way, faithful to him. Fraenkel, in discussing the presentation of Lucilius in *Sat.* II, i, says that 'Horace now knows that to speak of the fighting spirit of Lucilius is not the same thing as to give an idea of the mind of Lucilius as mirrored in his writings. What appeared in these writings was something immeasurably wider, something . . . unique in ancient literature.' C.O. Brink later observed, with a differing emphasis, that 'Lucilius figures in the poet's defence because, like Horace, he could not help writing and writing honestly. Hence his life is in his writings. But in each case it is the life of a fighter. The poet belongs to a pugnacious border-race . . .'.[21] What has interested modern commentators on this satire of Horace was there in the eighteenth century writ large in the Latin text for Pope to see. This is the self-presentation of the individual mind and its associated way of life in all its miscellaneous particularities. Perhaps the greater part of Horace's response to censure, in *Sat.* II, i, lies in his admiration for the autobiographical openness of Lucilius's writing:

> quo fit ut omnis
> Votiva pateat veluti descripta tabella
> Vita senis.[22]

[19]Cf. l. 116 with Donne, *Satyre IV*, ll. 160–5 (*Poems*, IV, pp. 17, 42). This is a crucial echo, the poet's affirmation forming a prelude to the climax of Pope's as of Donne's poem.

[20]Pope possibly remembered here the fragment of Lucilius on Virtue printed at this point in at least one seventeenth-century edition of Horace, namely Quincti Horatii Flacci, *Opera Omnia: Cum nouis Argumentis* Ex Officina Plantineana, Raphelengii (1608), p. 209.

[21]Fraenkel, *Horace*, p. 151; see also Gordon Williams, *Tradition and Originality in Roman Poetry* (Oxford, 1968), pp. 448–50. C.O. Brink, *Horace on Poetry: Prolegomena to the Literary Epistles* (Cambridge, 1963), p. 174.

[22]Ll. 32–4; *Poems*, IV, p. 8. 'So it comes that the old poet's whole life is open to view, as if painted on a votive tablet' (Loeb edn, p. 129).

Pope had thus the opportunity to strengthen his rôle as an attacking satirist (as distinct from the less combative rôle of Horace) because the attacking vein could be presented as but part of this Lucilian openness. He is able to respond generously to the ideal of a wider candour:

> P. Each Mortal has his Pleasure: None deny
> *Scarsdale* his Bottle, *Darty* his Ham-Pye;
> *Ridotta* sips and dances, till she see
> The doubling Lustres dance as fast as she;
> F[ox] loves the *Senate*, Hockley-Hole his Brother
> Like in all else, as one Egg to another.
> I love to pour out all myself, as plain
> As downright *Shippen*, or as old *Montagne*.
> In them, as certain to be lov'd as seen,
> The Soul stood forth, nor kept a Thought within;
> In me what Spots (for Spots I have) appear,
> Will prove at least the Medium must be clear.
> In this impartial Glass, my Muse intends
> Fair to expose myself, my Foes, my Friends;
> Publish the present Age, but where my Text
> Is Vice too high, reserve it for the next:
> My Foes shall wish my Life a longer date,
> And ev'ry Friend the less lament my Fate.
>   My head and Heart thus flowing thro' my Quill,
> Verse-man or Prose-man, term me which you will,
> Papist or Protestant, or both between,
> Like good *Erasmus* in an honest Mean,
> In Moderation placing all my Glory
> While Tories call me Whig, and Whigs a Tory.[23]

[23] Ll. 45–68; *Poems*, IV, pp. 9–11. Maresca has interesting remarks on Horace's *votiva tabella* and what Pope makes of them (*Pope's Horatian Poems*, pp. 41–3). He argues that Pope saw the writing of Lucilian *saturae* as 'an almost sacramental self-revelation and confession'. This is hardly true of the pre-Augustinian Horace, as Fraenkel had warned (*Horace*, pp. 152–3). But Pope, influenced perhaps by Christianizing commentaries on Horace, might be supposed to have introduced a sacramental meaning in his Imitation. It is an interesting test-case of the extent to which Pope reads and produces a 'Christian' Horace. His chief stress appears not to be sacramental confession but, like Horace, openness. Maresca's argument thus becomes contextual in the most extreme form. It is that, despite appearances to the contrary in both poets, the tradition of Christian commentary was so strong that Pope could not avoid reading Horace in this way, and took it for granted that his own readers would likewise see sacramental confession in his own 'impartial Glass'. However, of the four editions of Horace certainly known to Pope, those by Daniel Heinsius (1629), Louis Desprez (1695), Richard Bentley (1711) and Alexander Cunningham (1721), only one, Desprez, comments on the votive tablets in *Sat.* II, i, his purpose being straightforward and explanatory (Q. Horatii Flacci, *Opera, Interpretatione, Notis et Indice illustravit, Ludovicus Desprez* (Amsterdam, 1695), pp. 616, 24). Dacier has more to say on the point, but he too lays chief stress on the open nature of the votive tablets. In commenting on the Roman practice in the Fifth Ode of the First Book he relates it to that of 'les premiers Chretiens' and even to those of his own time, but not in such a way as to impute a potentially Christian meaning to Horace (*Remarques Critiques*, VII, p. 34; I, pp. 91–3). Pope certainly introduces Christian expressions and tone into the *Imitations* at times, but this example shows that Christian commentary on Horace was not a consistent and comprehensive system. Pope was influenced but not imaginatively imprisoned by it. (For Pope's Horaces, see Lillian Bloom, 'Pope as Textual Critic: A Bibliographical study of His Horatian Text', Maynard Mack, ed., *Essential Articles for the Study of Alexander Pope* (Hamden, Conn. 1964), pp. 495–506. For a fuller version of the present argument, see my 'Satire and Self-Portrayal' (see n. 4 above), pp. 167–8).

Well known and attractive as these lines are, with their repudiation of political labels and apparent affirmation of the middle way, they do raise certain problems. If we accept the lines: 'I will, or perish in the gen'rous Cause' (l. 117) and: 'In Moderation placing all my Glory' (l. 67) in the same poem is it not because Pope's fluent affirmative vein is sweeping us along too easily? Or, to be more specific, if this poem is as carefully aimed at the government of Walpole and the court of George II as Maynard Mack has convincingly suggested[24] how can Pope make such light play with 'Whig' and 'Tory'? Surely his stand in the poem is unmistakably Tory, and he is disingenuous to pretend otherwise?

Pope is certainly disingenuous at times. Yet it is doubtful whether he is here, since the two sides of what he is doing are in fact so strangely and challengingly brought together. As so often in Pope it is illuminating to consider the names. The line: 'As downright *Shippen*, or as old *Montagne*' is a case in point. Each name is there to exemplify forthrightness and candour. At a glance, the whole passage is about being yourself, not about being political. Yet William Shippen (1673–1743), political poet in his younger days and now prominent in the considerable party of parliamentary Jacobites, was one of the most committed political figures of his time. Known for his outspoken Jacobitism, he was once committed to the Tower for refusing to retract the statement that George I 'was a stranger to our language and Constitution'.[25] The name may now be seen to unfold its implications into the poem. Praise of Shippen strengthens its anti-Hanoverian bias. But to strengthen it in a Jacobite way ran against the official line of Bolingbroke's Tory Opposition, which had formally repudiated Jacobitism.[26] Reference to Shippen takes Pope out of the weekly Toryism of *The Craftsman* into a broader alliance of anti-Hanoverian feeling, while at the same time reminding us that Bolingbroke himself wished to see party divisions laid aside in a form of renewed constitutional and patriarchal monarchy. The roots of Pope's political sensibility are diverse, but he certainly was among those who saw the opposition to Walpole's government as a movement considerably deeper in its importance than the urge of those who were 'out' of office to be 'in'.[27] If we now look at the second name of the line, '*Montagne*', we may see that it expresses the other half of what Lucilius meant to Pope, and to Horace. Here the reference is quite unpolitical. It was Montaigne's secluded self-examination, his candid reflectiveness, his self-presentation, which Pope admired; and we know that he had been reading the Essay *On the Inconstancy of Our Actions* for his Epistle *To Cobham, On the Characters of Men* (to be published in January 1733/4). Further, Pope is concerned with what an individual human mind may make of religious as well as of political claims. It is in this context that 'Moderation' and the 'honest Mean' of Erasmus have their chief force. In the Epistle *To Bathurst* (January 1732/3) Pope used the Aristotelian idea of the mid-point as the point for virtue to structure his poem; in this

[24]Maynard Mack, *The Garden and the City: Retirement and Politics in the Later Poetry of Pope, 1731–43* (London, 1969), pp. 174–87.

[25]See Courthope's apposite citation, *The Works of Alexander Pope*, III, p. 193, n. 3.

[26]See Bolingbroke's *Letter to Sir William Wyndham* (1717) and Letter VI of the *Dissertation on Parties* (1733–5); *Works of . . . Lord Viscount Bolingbroke* (London, 1754), I, pp. 3–106; II, pp. 118–24.

[27]See Dialogue II of the Epilogue to the Satires, ll. 122–5, where Pope anticipates and (for the moment) refutes the suggestion of more superficial motivation (*Poems*, IV, p. 320).

Horatian imitation he gives us a more flexible and intimate analysis, still concerned with the great public issues, yet more attentive to the movement and honesty of the individual mind. Pope, by implication, distinguishes between the Mean and 'an honest Mean'. Where the soul stands forth is not necessarily at the exact centre of any ethical, political or religious range. It may still express the balance of the mind, be a considered rather than a mindlessly conformist or mindlessly impetuous view. This, it seems to me, is where Pope takes the full measure of Horace's praise of Lucilius. Thus it is that the third major aspect of Pope's poem, candid self-presentation, integrally relates with the other aspects, outright comedy and heroic attack, and is in some ways the psychological ground from which they arise. Certainly the art of each poem consists in the transitions and balance – this special *aequalitas* – between such different moods and modes.

Niall Rudd has called Horace, *Sat*. II, i 'the most brilliant piece of shadow-boxing in Roman literature'. He speaks of 'a playfulness almost amounting to farce'.[28] The little drama of Horace's poem does raise great issues, but rather in glancing ways than in frontal engagement; the Horatian comedy is faithful to the irrational shifts and reiterations of familiar conversation. Both Horace and Pope end their poem on a note not of defiance but of laughter. Now, in keeping with Pope's taking to himself the Lucilian rôle, the concluding laughter of the later poem has a satirical charge: Walpole stands in place of Caesar, as the Latin on the facing page reveals, and the very quiet admission of the possible approval of the *princeps* gives way to a recognition that 'Laws are explain'd by Men' and may be bent by ministers. At the same time, too much stress has in recent years been laid on Pope's high heroic rôle in this poem. Pope had once been on personal terms with Walpole. Some humour lies in the fact that in the fiction of the poem the poet's reference to Sir Robert *might* not be ironical; the lawyer might reasonably infer that Pope had got clearance for what he was doing from the most powerful man in Britain – in which case the foregoing kindly advice from this informal representative of 'the great man' has been all for nothing. Another aspect of the poem's comic equivocality at the end is the distinction Pope makes between '*Libels* and *Satires*! lawless Things indeed!' and 'grave *Epistles*, bringing Vice to light' (ll. 150–1). Horace, punning it is true on *malum*, had distinguished between *bona* and *mala carmina*, and suggested that Augustus might place his *saturae* in the former category. Pope mockingly condemns libels and satires while actually imitating a satire. At this point Pope follows his master in shadow-boxing. But, thinking now of the poem as a whole, how well has Pope taken the measure of Horace? R.A. Brower, who of recent commentators on Pope seems to me to have shown most intimacy with Horace's poetry, says of Pope's imitation of *Ep*. I, i that 'Pope gives a good equivalent for Horace's playful balancing of loyalties, but he makes us feel less keenly the *span* between the contrasting positions'.[29] This crucial observation applies to Pope's handling of the lawyer, in the imitation of *Sat*. II, i, as compared with Horace's handling of Trebatius. The poem narrows in human range as a result of the *adversarius* being drawn so readily into Pope's mockery of the court. What we must ask ourselves, however, is whether this loss is not compensated for by the

---

[28]Niall Rudd, *The Satires of Horace: A Study* (Cambridge, 1966), pp. 128–9.
[29]Brower, *Pope: The Poetry of Allusion*, p. 290.

greater range of the poet's own idiom within the fiction of the poem, and whether it was not just this range that Horace admired in Lucilius?

Five days after the appearance of Pope's imitation of the Trebatius satire the First Epistle of *An Essay on Man* was anonymously published. This was followed on 29 March and 8 May by Epistles II and III. There could hardly be a greater contrast than that between the intensely social and specific character of the imitation of Horace and the cosmic generality of *An Essay* with its abundant natural imagery. The very closeness of publication dates might have been contrived to suggest that such different poems could only be the work of different authors.[30] When, six months later, Pope brought out the next of the *Imitations*, this too was anonymous. *The Impertinent, Or a Visit to the Court, A Satyr. By an Eminent Hand* (5 November 1733) first appeared anonymously, no doubt, because Pope had never before used his art of poetry to assail the court so strongly, and wished first to test the public reaction. The prosecution Pope may have feared did not take place, and in 1735 this poem was admitted into Pope's *Works* under the altered title of *The Fourth Satire of Dr. John*. The fact that Pope turned to the imitation of Donne so soon after the version of Horace, *Sat.* II, i has not, perhaps, been sufficiently noticed. Pope's versions of Donne were certainly not an afterthought in the composition of the *Imitations*. There were good reasons why his Horatian imitation should have now pointed Pope to Donne's *Satyre IV*. The brief echo of Donne in the earlier poem:

Shall I, none's slave, of high-born or rais'd men
Fear frowns . . .?

And I not strip the Gilding off a Knave,
Un-plac'd, un-pension'd, no Man's Heir, or Slave?[31]

is of interest because at corresponding points of each satire the poet is building up to a climax that is to give expressive form to the whole poem, and because Pope echoes Donne while playing the part of Lucilius. It is right to remember that when Dryden, in his 'Discourse Concerning Satire,' came to speak of the satires of Donne he did so in terms closely resembling some of those applied by Horace to Lucilius.[32] The way was already open to any poet, exploring a possible parallel between himself and Horace, to think of Donne as an English Lucilius. Dryden's remark, however, referred only to wit and numbers. Horace, *Sat.* II, i took Pope to the other side of Horace's tribute to Lucilius: the praise of his freedom and courage. When, therefore, Pope came to acknowledge *The Impertinent, Or a Visit to the Court* as an imitation by Pope of Donne, he chose an epigraph which, taken from yet another poem of Horace (*Sat.* I, x, 56–9), would serve to link Donne with the Horatian and Lucilian values (not the same, yet intimately connected) which he had just set forth. A detailed exploration of Pope's poem in relation to Donne's satire has been offered in an earlier chapter, but two general points should be made here. First, Pope's linking of Donne with himself, Horace and Lucilius demonstrates his resolve to use not only Horace but the tradition of Horace in the varieties of its later development. Secondly

[30]This point has been well made by Simon Varey in 'Rhetoric and *An Essay on Man*', Howard Erskine-Hill and Anne Smith, eds., *The Art of Alexander Pope* (London, 1978), p. 141.

[31]*Poems*, IV, pp. 42, 17.

[32]Ll. 102–5; Dryden, *Poems*, II, p. 603.

(and the point is closely related) Pope had found a way of some delicacy by which he could imitate Horace in the light of Christian awareness. 'To rest, the Cushion and soft Dean, invite, / Who never mentions Hell to ears polite', Pope wrote in his Epistle *To Burlington* (ll. 149–50). This was a natural allusion for Pope to make. At the same time it points to some of the problems when a poet of a Christian civilization sets out to imitate the pre-Christian Horace. On the one hand he may heavily Christianize his versions of the pagan texts; on the other, he may try to confine himself to a more or less historical reconstruction of the pagan milieu. Pope was writing poetry for his own time and country, so the second alternative was out of the question. But for him Horace was visible beyond the Christian commentators; Pope had enough historical sense to recognize and value the poet of Augustan Rome. Pope's versions, therefore, often develop Christian nuances (we have already noticed some and shall find others). They do so lightly and with much sensitivity. In *Satyre IV* Donne had achieved an altogether bolder transformation of Horace: through a moment of tragic soliloquy he had indeed linked the comedy of Horace with a vision of Hell. In imitating Donne Pope allowed a tradition of Christian satire to speak for him, without cutting himself off from the Roman Horace, and without violating that possibility of a closer identification with the Augustan poet which he felt to be available to him. This is another reason why Pope wanted the following full title to be included in the *Imitations*: *The Fourth Satire of Dr. John Donne, Dean of St. Paul's, Versifyed*.

Sat. II, ii

The next of the *Imitations*, *The Second Satire of the Second Book of Horace Paraphrased*, was published on 4 July 1734. Although it follows serially in the Book of Horace's Satires Pope had already begun to imitate, Pope's subsequent procedure in the choice of Horatian originals makes it likely that this poem was chosen with a particular eye to its subject and character. It is in marked contrast to the imitation of *Sat*. II, i and even more, perhaps, to *The Impertinent, Or a Visit to the Court*. Each of those poems had thrown down a challenge to court and government, though the real comedy of each, and especially of the former, had mitigated the intensity of that challenge. In his imitation of *Sat*. II, ii Pope draws back. Partly this is because culinary self-indulgence is a safe subject for satire, and there is a good deal about rare food in Horace's poem and Pope's imitation. Partly the reason is that Pope now sought to offset his combative and dangerous rôle as satirist with a more intimate and kindly self-presentation. To put an important point simply, this is the first poem in which we see Pope at home.

This is achieved by a structural change comparable to that effected by Pope in *Sat*. II, i, when he himself assumed the rôle of Lucilius. *Sat*. II, ii is divided into two parts. In the first part Horace recounts the opinions of the farmer Ofellus on plain living. In the second part, with an effective dramatic heightening, Ofellus is made to address the reader directly. Pope rearranges this pattern. After a short introduction in which he announces the subject of the satire ('What, and how great, the Virtue and the Art / To live on little with a cheerful heart . . .') be brings forward 'A Doctrine sage, but truly none of mine' and, within eleven lines, allows Hugh Bethel (his Ofellus) to speak directly. The first part of the poem is thus not Pope's but 'Bethel's Sermon' (l. 9). In the second part of the poem, Bethel's sermon is formally concluded ('Thus Bethel spoke . . .' – l. 129), and where in Horace Ofellus concluded the poem in direct speech, Pope now addresses Bethel (and his readers) *in propria persona*. This change has all kinds of implications. Once again Pope exploits a flair for dramatic self-presentation, though here it is not fearless self-expression but a truly-judging hospitality that he celebrates. Again, Pope's substitution of an eighteenth-century landed gentleman (Bethel) for a Roman tenant-farmer (implying that Pope had to draw Horace's poem up the social scale) is effectively counter-balanced by the fact that in Pope's poem what really happens is that Ofellus–Bethel's precepts on plain living are answered by Ofellus–Pope's account of his life at Twickenham. This turns a carefully modulated *sermo* into a simple dialogue (Horace, *Sat.* II, i and Pope's imitation were also dialogues, we note), and balances Ofellus–Bethel with the case of Pope who, like Ofellus, really had once lived on his own, that is, his father's land, but now, like Ofellus, was only a tenant. This is a highly expressive alteration of Horace – though it does nothing to bring Pope closer to Juvenal. The true criterion by which luxury and self-indulgence can be judged is use, and nothing throws the principle of use into relief so much as the contrast between use and possession. Thus the shift from the landowner Bethel's precepts on temperance, to the tenant Pope's practice of hospitality, is more striking than anything to be found in the original poem.

It has sometimes troubled Horace's readers that the teaching of *Ofellus rusticus* should be so conversant with the culinary luxury of wealthy and fashionable Rome. The problem is not too grave, since it is clear that in this part of the poem Horace, in the guise of saying what Ofellus thinks, is really applying the farmer's wisdom to what the poet and his readers know. Still, Pope avoids this slightly uneasy act of mediation: Bethel speaks directly of what Bethel directly knew. It is sometimes said, I think justly, that Pope's *Imitations* differ from Horace in their heartiness and wit.[33] Whether or not Pope recognized this as a problem, it is well resolved in the present poem, uncommonly bluff and blunt as it is. This is the manner assigned to Bethel.

> 'Tis yet in vain, I own, to keep a pother
> About one Vice, and fall into the other:
> Between Excess and Famine lies a mean,
> Plain, but not sordid, tho' not splendid, clean.
> *Avidien* or his Wife (no matter which,
> For him you'll call a dog, and her a bitch)
> Sell their presented Partridges, and Fruits,
> And humbly live on rabbits and on roots:
> One half-pint bottle serves them both to dine,
> And is at once their vinegar and wine.[34]

In Horace's satire, only the link between the two parts of the poem appears personal to the poet: Horace's memory from his youth of Ofellus on his farm. This gives Pope his cue to speak of himself, but he continues to do so now to the

[33]Brower, *Pope: The Poetry of Allusion*, pp. 290–2, is close to this view.
[34]Ll. 45–54; *Poems*, IV, pp. 57–9.

poem's end. I have written in detail elsewhere on this passage, as describing the practicable embodiment for Pope of his country house ideal.[35] Suffice here to say that the candid, sensitive and evocative idiom of this part of the poem could hardly have been given a more effective foil than 'Bethel's Sermon'. We notice how Pope takes all opportunities to seem to *reply* to Bethel –

> *But* ancient friends, (tho' poor, or out of play)
> That touch my Bell, I *cannot* turn away . . . .
>
> Fortune not much of humbling me can boast.[36]

thus drawing the poem in the direction of dialogue. Indeed this move is further developed by the entry of a third figure, Swift, whose views on property contrast with Pope's own.

Swift's interruption brings forward the final point about this poem. It concerns the evolution of a poetic autobiography. Before the publication of this poem Pope had (save some passing allusions) never written in verse about his own life. Horace, on the other hand, whatever subtle rôles and guises he adopted from time to time, and in different degree, was famous for his having written of his own mind, his day-to-day life and his personal history. There is clear historical content and circumstance, as opposed to pure literary convention, in many of the poems in which he speaks of himself. It is also notable that when Pope imitates a poem of Horace, he does not imitate the text of that poem alone. Thus, for example, Pope introduces into his imitation (l. 131) the idea of a balance or equality of mind. There is no such reference in *Sat.* II, ii. Yet it is an immediately recognizable Horatian *motif*.[37] Pope not only copies Bethel's 'equal mind' where he can; in Pope's hands the poem itself becomes a balance between the vigour of precept, and the sensitivity of practice. But the more conspicuous example of this capacity of Pope to concentrate salient Horatian characteristics into a single text is the fact that Pope now does that very Horatian thing – talk about himself – in imitating an original where, as it happens, Horace hardly does it at all. Pope allows himself to allude, for the first time in any of his poems, to the disabilities suffered by Roman Catholics during his lifetime:

> Tho' double-tax'd, how little have I lost? (l. 152)

and he undoubtedly means to use autobiography, in an Horatian form, to bring various contrasts to the mind of the reader. While Horace acquired his lands and farm under the new political order of the principate, Pope and his father lost theirs with the coming of the Hanoverians. Like Ofellus Pope can face his loss with resolution, and even find happiness, loyal still to 'ancient friends', in the face of an alien order.

[35] *The Social Milieu of Alexander Pope*, pp. 310–16.
[36] Ll. 139–40, 151 my Italics; *Poems*, IV, pp. 65–7. Dacier noted that Ofellus had not been so fortunate as Virgil, in preserving his property at the time when Augustus was settling his veterans on the land (*Remarques Critiques*, VII, pp. 134–5). Pope would have been well aware of the political history behind Horace's satire.
[37] Cf. *Sat.* I, iii, 9; *Ep.* I, xviii, 111–12. Dacier saw the present satire of Horace as offering a mean between Epicurean and Stoic (*Remarques Critiques*, VII, p. 85).

Sat. I, ii

Pope's next imitation of Horace, the *Sober Advice from Horace To the Young Gentlemen about Town*, was published on 28 December 1734. It is as different from *Sat*. II, ii as that was from *The Impertinent* and *Sat*. II, i, being neither politically combative nor decent and autobiographical. It is the earliest of Horace's satires and epistles to be imitated by Pope, and marks an attempt to strike out into the realm of the comedy of sexual appetite. In effect Pope takes the idea of the Mean which in different ways has been central in *Sat*. II, i and II, ii and, following Horace, produces outrageous variations upon it. The *Young Gentlemen about Town* are, in effect, advised neither to slum, nor be over-ambitious, but go like B[athurs]t for a clean, willing, moderately-priced whore. The only begetter of the *Imitations*, Bolingbroke, considered that Pope 'chose rather to weaken the images than to hurt chaste ears overmuch' but noted that 'the Rogue has fixed a ridicule upon me, which some events of my life would seem perhaps to justify him in doing'.[38] Despite Bolingbroke's view, Pope manages to be more scandalous than Horace in more than one place. Ll. 31–4, for example, now have the special advantage of a Christian context:

> My Lord of *L[ondo]n*, chancing to remark
> A *noted Dean* much busy'd in the Park,
> 'Proceed (he cry'd) proceed, my Reverend Brother,
> ''Tis *Fornicatio simplex*, and no other:
> 'Better than lust for Boys, with *Pope* and *Turk*,
> 'Or others Spouses, like my Lord of – [York][39]

Pope is if anything more pointedly obscene than Horace, and more licentious in allusions to particular people. The poem has been described as 'fairly nasty',[40] but the predominant tone is perhaps naughty rather than nasty: a physical comedy issuing in farce and wit:

> Suppose that honest Part that rules us all,
> Should rise, and say – 'Sir *Robert*! or Sir *Paul*!
> 'Did I demand, in my most vig'rous hour,
> 'A Thing descended from the Conqueror?[41]

In Horace it is the *mind* that asks the question. Pope rises with added exaggeration and bawdy wit to the extraordinary tumult with which Horace's poem explodes to its conclusion:

> No furious Husband thunders at the Door;
> No barking Dog, no Household in a Roar;
> From gleaming Swords no shrieking Women run;
> No wretched Wife cries out, *Undone! Undone!*[42]

---

[38]Bolingbroke to Swift, 27 June – 6 July, 1734 (*Correspondence of Alexander Pope*, III, pp. 413–14.

[39]Ll. 39–44; *Poems*, IV, p. 79.

[40]Brower, *Pope: The Poetry of Allusion*, p. 293.

[41]Ll. 87–90; *Poems*, IV, p. 83.

[42]Ll. 167–70; *Poems*, IV, p. 89.

One might think that Pope, in imitating *Sat*. I, ii, would have drawn on Rochester, and there are a few Rochesterian moments. But the general feeling is totally different. Whoring is a mere pastime here, if dangerous and undignified; there is nothing of Rochester's libertine ecstasy, nor his as frequent loathing of the physical. To that extent, at least, Pope is closer to Horace.

The *Sober Advice* was never candidly owned by Pope. He denied his authorship of it equivocally to the pious but shrewd Caryll,[43] and when in 1738 he admitted it into his collected works it was under the title of *The Second Satire of the First Book of Horace. Imitated in the Manner of Mr. Pope*. While Pope may have shown some caution on account of this poem's licentiousness, there is no reason to suppose that he regretted writing it, no reason to doubt that it expressed for him a further side of Horace's achievement. The fact that it is little known, and under-valued,[44] is largely the result of its exclusion from the Warburton and Elwin-Courthope editions of Pope's works. It was, however, also excluded from the important second volume of Pope's collected *Works*, published in April 1735. It is to this volume that we should turn to see Pope's first thoughts on the arrangement of the *Imitations*. Here we find a simple and symmetrical grouping: first *The Satires of Horace Imitated*, II, i then II, ii; then *The Satires of Dr. John Donne, Dean of St. Pauls's*, Satire II (first written in 1713 but now much changed and expanded),[45] then Satire IV, the two pairs linked by the epigraph from Horace *Sat*. I, x, 56–9, suggesting the interrelations between Pope, Donne and Horace through the image of Lucilius. At this stage the concept of the *Imitations of Horace* is connected with Satires only.

To Dr. Arbuthnot

In this second volume of Pope's *Works*, however, there was printed among the Epistles a poem which had been first published only a month or two earlier. This was *An Epistle from Mr. Pope, to Dr. Arbuthnot* (2 January 1734/5). Described by Pope as 'a Sort of Bill of Complaint, begun many years since, and drawn up by snatches, as the several Occasions offer'd',[46] the poem goes back at least as far as to the early version of the Atticus Portrait (of Addison), written but not published in 1715.[47] Other notable passages which had been written earlier are the lines beginning 'Did some more sober Critic come abroad?' (ll. 157–72) which formed a preamble to the Atticus Portrait in 1727; the imitation of Horace, *Sat*. I, iv, 81–5 which we have already noted as the very beginning of Pope's surviving imitations of Horace (ll. 289–304); and ll. 406–19 which conclude the epistle with a prayer concerning Pope's care of his ageing mother, and which had been enclosed by Pope in a letter to Aaron Hill on 3 September 1731.[48] What precipitated the writing of the Epistle was certainly the dangerous illness of Pope's old literary friend Arbuthnot in the summer of 1734 (he was to die next spring), together with Arbuthnot's letter of last wishes to Pope (17 July

---

[43]Pope to Caryll, 31 December, 1734; *Correspondence*, III, p. 447.

[44]But see Aden's discussion, *Something Like Horace*, pp. 59–68.

[45]For Pope's version of Donne's *Satyre II*, see Ch. IV, p. 91; and my *Social Milieu of Alexander Pope*, pp. 246–9.

[46]Advertisement, ll. 1–2; *Poems*, IV, p. 95.

[47]*Poems*, VI, pp. 142–5.

[48]*Correspondence*, III, pp. 226–7.

1734) concerning the writing of satire. This coincided with an unusually relaxed few weeks at Southampton with the Earl of Peterborough, 'our way of life quite Easy, & at liberty . . . I study, write, & have what Leisure I please', as Pope put it to Arbuthnot himself.[49] In these circumstances Pope had the opportunity to reflect upon his literary and personal career, in the light of Arbuthnot's 'Last Request':

> that you continue that noble *Disdain* and *Abhorrence* of Vice, which you seem naturally endu'd with, but still with a due regard to your own Safety; and study more to reform than chastise, tho' the one often cannot be effected without the other.[50]

This advice reads like a direct response to some of Pope's most recent poems, and especially the Lucilius passage in Pope's version of *Sat.* II, i; the first part of the 'Request' is couched very much in the idiom of those lines, with the emphasis at once on moral dedication and on naturalness. Pope is asked to be true to Virtue by being himself. The reference to Pope's 'own Safety' is most obviously to be construed as a political warning, and is appropriate to that increasing tendency to challenge government and court which *To Bathurst*, the imitation of *Sat.* II, i and *The Impertinent* all display. The last part of Arbuthnot's advice may be thought to deal chiefly with Pope's motivation. Since reforming without chastising is so hard, Arbuthnot seems to be speaking of Pope's moral goal, and to be quietly warning against a love of chastisement for its own sake.

  Pope replied to this letter on 2 August 1734. What he said has a special importance since the MS has survived, whereas Arbuthnot's letter descends to us only in the form found in the 1735 Edition of Pope's *Correspondence* printed by Curll from Pope's covert supply of copy.[51] Thus it appears from this reply of Pope that while the version of Arbuthnot's letter published by Pope spoke of there not having been any 'little Suspicions or Jealousies' between the two men, Arbuthnot had in fact spoken of there having been 'scarcely any . . . suspicions or jealousyes' – and we find Pope quibbling over 'scarcely' in his reply to his friend. Again, it appears that Arbuthnot's letter had specified that Pope should 'manifest' his 'Disdain & abhorrence of Vice' in his 'writings'.[52] Arbuthnot had been even more concerned with Pope's publications than Pope's slightly amended version of his own letter allows. There is no doubt, however, that Arbuthnot's advice immediately raised in Pope's mind the question of general against particular satire. The linked aims of chastising and reforming almost certainly attached themselves in Pope's thinking, while he studied at ease and liberty with Lord Peterborough, to the attacks upon him in 1733 by Lady Mary Wortley Montagu and by Lord Hervey. That he had brought these assaults on himself by being particular in his satire, and that he now inclined, rather than retreat into generality, to retort with even greater particularity, were certainly thoughts that now passed through his mind. And in his reply to Arbuthnot he declared:

---

[49]Pope to Arbuthnot, 2 August, 1734; *Correspondence*, III, p. 424.
[50]Arbuthnot to Pope, 17 July, 1734; ibid., III, p. 417.
[51]*Correspondence*, I, pp. xii–xiv.
[52]*Correspondence*, III, p. 423.

General Satire in Times of General Vice has no force, & is no Punishment: People have ceas'd to be asham'd of it when so many are join'd with them; and tis only by hunting one or two from the Herd that any Examples can be made. . . . And in my low Station, with no other Power than this, I hope to deter, if not to reform.[53]

Although this letter was a speedy and personal reply to Arbuthnot, which Pope had no special reason to think would ever be published, he meets Arbuthnot's advice in terms of a general debate about the age in its relation to literature. There is no mention, though there must have been acute awareness, of personal wounds.

This letter was not, however, Pope's only reply to Arbuthnot. It formed the basis of a much longer letter, published and probably written after the publication of the Epistle *To Arbuthnot* in January 1735, and after Arbuthnot's death in February of that year. Pope has here used his actual exchange with his friend as the basis for a formal statement of purpose in his writing of satire. It is a letter meant for the public. Pope uses the original personal and historical occasion, here an exchange of letters with his dying friend, to take a strong hold upon the public's imagination. The letter is indeed one of Pope's most powerful statements of personal motive and artistic purpose, and certainly a central critical document in his later life. At the same time it is moving, its fictionality (Pope's later expansion of the historical letter of 2 August 1734) not falsifying but serving to bring out an underlying principle. It is designed, as Pope said, 'to shew you my whole heart on this subject'.[54] Setting aside the paragraphs of greeting and farewell at the beginning and end, the letter divides into three parts. First, a section which expands and makes more eloquent Pope's 'Disdain & abhorrence of Vice' and resolve to continue writing particular satire. Pope's idiom seems now even closer to the Lucilius passage of the version of *Sat*. II, i: 'But sure it is as impossible to have a just abhorrence of Vice, without hating the Vicious, as to bear a true love for Virtue, without loving the Good . . . To attack Vices in the abstract, without touching Persons, may be safe fighting indeed, but it is fighting with Shadows. General propositions are obscure, misty, and uncertain . . . Examples are pictures, and strike the Senses, nay raise the Passions, and call in those (the strongest and most general of all motives) to the aid of reformation.' The second section takes up Arbuthnot's warning about safety. Pope allows himself to be more particular here – 'I can guess', he says, 'what occasions it at this time'. It seems likely that he has Lord Hervey in mind, an influential political figure as well as a man of dangerous talent. 'Some Characters I have drawn are such', Pope now says, 'that if there be any who deserve 'em, 'tis evidently a service to mankind to point those men out . . .'. By the time of the publication of this letter Pope had, of course, published his verse Character of Hervey as Paris (later Sporus). His earlier attacks on Hervey had been flying hits. It is notable that in this section of the letter Pope actually touches on the possibility of assassination.[55]

The third section of the letter is prompted only implicitly by what Arbuthnot had said. Pope here turns to those Roman parallels, comparisons and contrasts which underlie the writing of imitations of Horace. Coming as it does in the

[53]Ibid., III, p. 423.
[54]Ibid., III, pp. 419–20; Sherburn here calls it 'Pope's best defence in prose of his satire'.
[55]Ibid., III, p. 419–20.

midst of the period when Pope was engaged with his *Imitations*, the paragraph must be considered direct evidence of Pope's intentions in this group of poems.

> It is certain, much freer Satyrists than I have enjoy'd the encouragement and protection of the Princes under whom they lived. Augustus and Mecœnas made Horace their companion, tho' he had been in arms on the side of Brutus; and allow me to remark it was out of the suff'ring Party too, that they favour'd and distinguish'd Virgil. You will not suspect me of comparing my self with Virgil and Horace, nor even with another Court-favourite, Boileau: I have always been too modest to imagine my Panegyricks were Incense worthy of a Court; and that I hope will be thought the true reason why I have never offer'd any. I would only have observ'd, that it was under the greatest Princes and best Ministers, that moral Satyrists were most encouraged; and that then Poets exercised the same jurisdiction over the Follies, as Historians did over the Vices of men. It may also be worth considering, whether Augustus himself makes the greater figure, in the writings of the former, or of the latter? and whether Nero and Domitian do not appear as ridiculous for their false Taste and Affectation, in Persius and Juvenal, as odious for their bad Government in Tacitus and Suetonius? In the first of these reigns it was, that Horace was protected and caress'd; and in the latter that Lucan was put to death, and Juvenal banish'd.[56]

Pope's words endorse no simple view of the relation of himself and Horace. If anyone supposes that Pope thought himself an achieved eighteenth-century replica of Horace, here in the third sentence is Pope's recognition of an important difference between Horace and himself. It is not just diffidence and modesty that leads him to repudiate the likeness, but consciousness that he had not, since the death of Anne (Pope says 'never'), offered praise to the ruling prince. His own relation with the centre of power in his country is quite different from that of Horace in Augustan Rome. Again, if anyone supposes that Pope looked on Horace as a flatterer, and collaborator, here is clear evidence that Pope considered him a free moral satirist.[57] If anyone thinks that Pope considered Augustus a tyrant, here is the plain evidence that, on the contrary, when Pope chose to write a public letter on the relation of satire to government, he included Augustus and Maecenas among 'the greatest Princes and best Ministers'. He appears to draw the quite traditional distinction between Augustus on the one hand, and Nero and Domitian on the other.[58] The free moral satirist Horace evidently praised the great Augustus and the good Maecenas. That Pope should make these points is notable, since though they

---

[56]Ibid., III, p. 420.

[57]Cf. Weinbrot, *Augustus Caesar in 'Augustan' England*, p. 217. The passage is briefly acknowledged by Weinbrot, and seems just to have prevented him from reading Pope's Advertisement to his Epistle *To Augustus* as 'ironic' (p. 189).

[58]Weinbrot, ibid., pp. 63, 231, quotes Pope's remark to Henry Cromwell, 10 May 1711, that Augustus as a proscriber was a 'severe & barbarous' tyrant. What Pope wrote in full was: 'Who cou'd have imagin'd, that He [Atticus] who had escapd all the Misfortunes of his Time, unhurt even by the Proscriptions of Antony and Augustus, shoud in these days find an Enemy: more severe & barbarous than those Tyrants [,] and that Enemy, the gentlest too, the bestnatu[rd] of Mortalls, Mr. Cromwell? whom I must in th[is] compare once more to Augustus; who seem'd not more unlike himself in the Severity of one part, & the Clemency of the other part of his Life, than You?' (*Correspondence*, I, p. 116. The words 'severe & barbarous', which have a striking effect in Weinbrot's argument, appear quite different in their original context. Pope has simply strung together two standard features of Augustus (barbarity as a proscriber, clemency as *princeps*) in order to banter his friend Cromwell.

were certainly traditional, they were no more universally held in the eighteenth than in the seventeenth century. Pope had precedents for taking a very different view.[59] There are other points worth noting. It is rather surprising that Pope is content to see follies as the special province of poets, and vices of historians, and interesting that he associates Juvenal and Persius with ridicule rather than rage. Most interesting is Pope's stress upon Horace's having been in arms on the side of Brutus, and 'of the suff'ring Party'. Plainly enough, Pope likens his own original position in Britain (his inheritance from his father of a Roman Catholic and Jacobite background which caused him to share with other Papists the disabilities of a 'suff'ring party') to the early position of Horace. In short, Pope does not claim to be comprehensively like Horace. His political situation is different. Further, while Horace, Persius and Juvenal are all, in his view, chiefly concerned with folly, Pope's poetry, as he has just affirmed to Arbuthnot, is to be concerned with vice also. Pope does not praise Augustus in the highest moral terms. He speaks of his greatness, but is silent as to his goodness. He is not, however, singled out for 'bad Government' like Nero and Domitian, and he has whatever qualities it takes to encourage and protect a free moral satirist, and make him his companion. Even Horace's original political opposition had not deterred the *princeps* from this. Pope's letter shows no bland and uncritical Augustanism. It does show the possibility of a sustained and intelligent sympathy with Horace on Pope's part, and it does show that the example of Augustus could be used by Pope as a positive standard in the relations of writing to rule.[60]

These letters between Pope and Arbuthnot form the immediate context of the Epistle *To Arbuthnot*. Since this poem is not in the precise sense an imitation of Horace (it is not a modern version of an Horatian original), and since it was not originally included among the *Imitations* – a point to which I shall return at the end of the final chapter – it is worth asking how Horatian, how Augustan, is the Epistle *To Arbuthnot*?

Where in the Epistle are we made to think of Horace? He is named only twice – both comic and disavowing moments:

> There are, who to my Person pay their court,
> I cough like *Horace*, and tho' lean, am short,
> *Ammon*'s great Son one shoulder had too high . . .[61]

and the lines on Bufo:

> Fed with soft Dedication all day long,
> *Horace* and he went hand in hand in song.[62]

We need only recall *An Essay on Criticism* to think how Pope could write glowing tributes to the Ancients (including Horace): here, with the independence and

[59]See Ch. IX, pp. 250–1.

[60]It is worth noting that this public letter may have been based, not only on Pope's 'authentic' letter to Arbuthnot of 2 August 1734, but on subsequent conversation with him (*Correspondence*, III, p. 434).

[61]Ll. 115–18; *Poems*, IV, p. 104.

[62]Ll. 233–4; ibid., p. 112.

rueful self-knowledge of maturity Pope can measure his distance and mockingly repudiate the identification. ('Go on, obliging Creatures, make me see / All that disgrac'd my Betters, met in me' (ll. 119–20). The allusion is there, along with those to Alexander the Great, Ovid, Virgil and Homer, as a sign of sceptical detachment. So is the recognition that Horace's name can be a mere counter in the game of flattery. Pope is determined to be true to himself. Only his cough is like Horace. Yet this very moment is an example of highly sophisticated double-take, because it is also highly Horatian. The whole situation of the poet and man of sense being pestered by impertinents, poetasters, climbers, would-be sycophants is classic in the Horatian satiric tradition, and goes back to *Sat.* I, ix which Pope had so recently imitated through the medium of Donne.[63] As Donne had expanded on Horace's concise comedy of situation in *Sat.* I, ix, so Pope much expands the same basic situation into a ruefully comic account of his own literary life. The urban encounter, immediately familiar from Horace –

> No place is sacred, not the Church is free,
> Ev'n *Sunday* shines no *Sabbath-day* to me:
> Then from the *Mint* walks forth the Man of Ryme,
> Happy! to catch me, just at Dinner-time.[64]

– is developed into a masterly refashioning of that exquisite comedy in which the poet, despite his good judgement, fame and established position, or rather because of these advantages, simply cannot shake the impertinent off:

>   Bless me! a Packet. – ' 'Tis a stranger sues,
> 'A Virgin Tragedy, an Orphan Muse.'
> If I dislike it, 'Furies, death and rage!'
> If I approve, 'Commend it to the Stage.'
> There (thank my Stars) my whole Commission, ends,
> The Play'rs and I are, luckily, no friends.
> Fir'd that the House reject him, 'Sdeath I'll print it
> And shame the Fools – your Int'rest, Sir, with *Lintot.*'
> *Lintot*, dull rogue! will think your price too much.
> 'Not Sir, if you revise it, and retouch.'
> All my demurrs but double his attacks,
> At last he whispers 'Do, and we go snacks.'
> Glad of a quarrel, strait I clap the door,
> .Sir, let me see your works and you no more.[65]

Like Horace Pope plays on false hopes that he has got rid of the nuisance (his 'whole Commission' does not, after all, end at l. 59) and like Donne he finally breaks free with the mention of money. However, it is a detail typical of Pope's more outwardly assertive manner that he eventually gets ground for a quarrel and turns the impertinent out. Nearly the first third of the Epistle is occupied with variations on this Horatian situation. If it is said that he lacks the last art of Horatian comedy, knowing when to stop, we must appreciate that all this time Pope, like Donne in *Satyre IV*, is building up through something Horatian to

---

[63]See Ch. IV, pp. 76–83 above.
[64]Ll. 11–14; *Poems*, IV, pp. 96–7.
[65]Ll. 55–68; ibid., IV, p. 100.

something very different. Those risings of impatience, those bursts of anger ('*Lintot*, dull rogue . . .') are the gradual and still humorous beginnings of such a surge of emotion as the poetic epistle had scarcely managed before. But since the early part of the Epistle rests, as we have seen, on an Horatian paradigm, it is right to search for other signs of an Augustan position, and to register their absence if it is conspicuous. The name of 'Horace', we have noted, has been appropriated into shallow flattery. So have those of Virgil and Ovid. What about Augustus? There is 'great GEORGE' (l. 222), uninterested in poets and ignoring (excusably enough Pope would consider) 'a Birth-day Song'. What about Maecenas? Here, in response to Pope's now vehement self-questioning ('Why did I write?', 'But why then publish?') a number of Maecenases (noblemen of power, good judgement and generous disposition) appear in the roll-call of those men who first encouraged the poet. '*Granville* the polite', 'The Courtly *Talbot*, *Somers*, *Sheffield*', 'mitred *Rochester*' and, '*St. John*'s self' all urged him on in his poetic career. It is to be noted that of these six lords, three, Granville, Sheffield and Rochester, had been committed Jacobites and therefore of 'the suff'ring party', one, St John, had had at least one conspicuous Jacobite episode, and two, Talbot and Somers, were prominent Whigs. The implication is plainly that Pope was encouraged from all political quarters. He does not, perhaps, want us to notice that the Jacobites just outnumber the Whigs, or that Atterbury and St John were the two men who continued to mean most to him, even though their names are at the climax of the list.

To pursue a little further the question of civil strife and the attitude of the prevailing power towards writers, we must now consider the Atticus Portrait which occupies the central area of the Epistle. What we are concerned with here is the magnanimity which can recognize talent on the opposing side, as Pope told Arbuthnot Augustus had recognized Horace. Pomponius Atticus, described by Addison's friend Budgell as 'one of the best Men of ancient *Rome*' who 'amidst the Civil Wars of his Country when he saw the Designs of all Parties equally tended to the Subversion of Liberty, by constantly preserving the Esteem and Affection of both the Competitors, found means to serve his Friends on either Side' (*Spectator*, No. 385), and by Pope's Roman Catholic friend Edward Blount as 'engaged in no party, but . . . a faithful friend to some in both', had shown that genuine impartiality during civil war upon which a magnanimous victor might build after the establishment of peace.[66] Addison's name is put into the reader's mind just before the Atticus Portrait (l. 192) and the two names do, of course, resonate. Many readers would recognize the Atticus Portrait as a revised version of Pope's satire on Addison. At the personal level the portrait expresses Pope's sense of a deceptive friendship. At the literary and political level – one is tempted to say at the level of civilization – it is concerned with a man who had all the qualities to transcend personal ambition and party rivalry, and who comported himself as if such was precisely his aim, yet who used those marks of moderation and civility as means to the opposite end. Hence 'One whose fires / True Genius kindles, and fair Fame inspires' can 'Damn with faint praise, assent with civil leer . . .' (ll. 193–4, 201). At the numerical centre of the Epistle (l. 209[67]) Addison, like his own Cato, gives laws to his little Senate. It is

[66]*The Spectator*, ed. D.F. Bond (Oxford, 1965), III, pp. 446–7; and see n. 58 above.
[67]See Alastair Fowler, *Triumphal Forms: Structural Pattern in Elizabethan Poetry* (Cambridge, 1970), Ch. 4: 'Numerology of the Centre'.

not an heroic last stand of liberty against the new dictatorship of the Julian House – behind the trappings of republican idealism lurk the motives of the oriental despot (l. 198). The littleness of Cato's senate marked the courage of his resistance to Caesar. The littleness of Addison's is the relative insignificance of a coffee-house, and of mean and petty motives. 'Had Cato bent beneath the conqu'ring Cause', Granville the polite had written in 1690, 'He might have liv'd to give new Senates Laws.' But Granville at that time refused to serve under a usurper.[68] The Whig Addison had hardly seemed to civilize the winning side. In reality he was a false Atticus, and it is notable that the *topos* of laughing and weeping satire which we have already discussed in relation to Donne's Satires III and IV reappears in the last couplet of the Atticus Portrait, where satire trembles on the brink of tragedy:

> Who but must laugh, if such a man there be?
> Who would not weep, if *Atticus* were he?[69]

Pope's references to Horace, his exploitation of *Sat.* I, ix, his tribute to his Maecenases and his brilliant use of the name and ideal of Atticus show that Horace and Augustus are important within the Epistle. Indeed the poem arises from a well known situation in Horace. But by the time we have reached the mid-point, where in an image of trivial triumph Cato–Addison presides over his senate, it is already clear that Pope is moving in a strongly independent direction. It is Horatian only in so far as Lucilian openness was admired by Horace. The satire on Addison was in existence eleven years before it was published by Pope, and six years before it was printed.[70] Now, with the Lucilian ideal in mind, Pope is prepared to open out, as if on a votive tablet, 'my Motives of writing, the Objections to them, & my answers.'[71] He thus develops further that form of autobiographical poem which he had already begun to learn from Horace through imitating *Sat.* II, i and II, ii. It is not just that Pope has now found a form in which circumstantial self-portrayal may be appropriate. We may also sense the removal of long-customary restraints. Pope now speaks out about Addison, in the full context of a poem about himself. 'Three thousand Suns went down on *Welsted*'s Lye' (l. 375), he proclaims, hyperbolically. Three thousand, but not a day more! The subtle internal dialogue which introduces the Sporus Portrait – a dialogue which Arbuthnot's remonstrations may well have activated in his mind – only increases this feeling:

> 'Who breaks a Butterfly upon a Wheel?'
> Yet let me flap this Bug with gilded wings . . .[72]

and the poetry here rises to a metaphorical articulation of personal, political and theological Evil – Christian satire if ever Christian satire has been written – which is unlike anything in Horace for all Horace's variety. It is at this

---

[68]*Poems*, IV, p. 111, 209n; Elizabeth Handasyde, *Granville the Polite* (Oxford, 1933), Ch. 2.
[69]Ll. 213–14; Poems, IV, p. 111.
[70]In the meantime Pope published his laudatory Epistle *To Mr. Addison*.
[71]Pope to Arbuthnot, 25 August, 1734; *Correspondence*, III, p. 428. See too the letter of 3 September; ibid., III, p. 431.
[72]Ll. 308–9; *Poems*, IV, p. 118.

point that we must think again about the way in which Pope has learnt to shape his epistles emotionally. The first appearance of miscellaneousness (though true to the original Roman sense of the word *satura*) is quite deceptive. Here, just as in the imitation of *Sat*. II, i and II, ii, the exertion of greatest poetic energy has been held back until the second half of the poem, and involves a heightened dramatization of the poet in *propria persona*. The Sporus Portrait is the emotional climax of the Epistle.[73] The Atticus Portrait is, in its concern with literary judgement and literary affairs, connected with the Horatian comedy of the early part of the poem, yet is also marked off from what has gone before as constituting a new stage of seriousness:

> Peace to all such! but were there One whose fires. . . .[74]

Even here we have the sense of such assured control, such nicely judged restraint, as hold it back from the climactic. Pope's use of conditional forms has much to do with this: 'were there One', 'Shou'd such a man', 'if such a man there be' – these have a distancing effect. Only at the end, with a delicacy and restraint worthy of Addison at his best, is the conditional form mingled with an emotional appeal ('Who would not weep, if *Atticus* were he!'). In the Sporus Portrait the procedure is far different. 'Let *Sporus* tremble' is a much more direct beginning, and while the terms of the Atticus Portrait hardly take their subject out of the social world (Atticus could be dramatized in a comedy of manners) the terms of the Sporus Portrait manage to combine unmistakable contemporaneity ('His Wit all see-saw between *that* and *this* . . .') with something ancient and surreal ('A Cherub's face, a Reptile all the rest . . .'). Sporus could never be dramatized. Or rather the drama has become the immediate writing of the poem. And after that extraordinary exertion is complete, in one of the most conclusive phrases that could be created from the history of Satan ('Pride that licks the dust'), comes the moment when Pope turns to his own devotion to very different ideals, and begins, still for the moment with great energy, that long, protracted diminuendo which is going to take us down through domestic retrospect to the contrasting final words of the poem: not, now, 'Pride that licks the dust' but 'the rest belongs to Heav'n'.

In these last eighty-five lines of the Epistle the poet's affirmation of loyalty to 'Virtue' has an added power if we compare it with the Lucilius passage in the imitation of *Sat*. II, i. There the very abstractness of the word 'Virtue' contrasted with the web of proper names which stretched across the poem. That is true also here; but the abstract words are more affected than others by their poetic position. The Sporus Portrait is full of horrible movement: the movement proper to each metaphor, and the movement from metaphor to metaphor. By the time it has ended in the dust we long for something plain and steady: to use a word which Pope now uses, something 'manly' (l. 337). Hence the enhanced effect of an affirmation such as this:

> That not for Fame, but Virtue's better end,
> He stood the furious Foe, the timid Friend,[75]

[73]See Howard Erskine-Hill and Anne Smith, eds., *The Art of Alexander Pope*, p. 11.
[74]L. 193; *Poems*, IV, p. 109.
[75]Ll. 342–3; ibid. IV, p. 120.

The Epistle now seems to wind backwards. Having spoken out and exposed 'furious Foe' and 'timid Friend', Pope tells how he was himself duped (ll. 368–9), how he has forgiven offences, how patient with poetasters for so long, he held his tongue – and that (l. 382) leads us to the example set him by his parents, and thus to the poet's own origins (cf. ll. 127–8). The lines in praise of his father form an Horatian *topos* quite as well known as that of the poet trying to shake off the impertinent.[76] Nobody could read this passage of Pope's Epistle without being reminded of Horace, *Sat.* I, vi, 45–99, in which the poet with an impressive dignity and directness spoke of his freedman father, a poor man, and a tax-collector, who yet gave his son a good education and a virtuous start in life. Pope, like Horace, is aware of disparaging comments having been made on his father's humble station; each poet pays his filial and moral tribute: 'Nil me paeniteat sanum patris huius . . .' (l. 89); 'Oh grant me thus to live, and thus to die!' (l. 404). Taken on its own Pope's passage is not only shorter, but less circumstantial and impressive than Horace's, much more a general tribute. But in this poem it could only have a more subordinate function than Horace's passage has in *Sat.* I, vi, where it is the heart of the subject. Pope is now going to do something further, at once true to Horace's autobiographical vein and yet remarkably extending it. For it is now that Pope introduces the lines on his care of his ageing mother, an early version of which he had sent to Aaron Hill on 3 September 1731. Their placing here shows not only Pope's firm understanding of the autobiographical possibilities of the Horatian form he was using, but also his sure sense of the thematic and emotional shaping of his Epistle. A personal, even confessional poem, comes to rest with allusion to an unusual circumstance of Pope's life: his own unmarried position and his mother's great age. It is a situation as peculiar to him as Horace's having a freedman father was to the Roman poet. But how much more effective it is as a conclusion than the tribute to Pope's father would have been! That tribute can be regarded not only as (now) an Horatian convention, but as conventional in content. Further, it takes us back to a time of Pope's life before the Sporus Portrait developed from Pope's experience of Lord Hervey. The Sporus Portrait was not a retrospective satiric summary, but satire in action, engagement with the present. Pope's stress upon immediacy throughout the Epistle now demanded that the last lines should set forth not a retrospect but a continuing action.[77] At the same time it should complete the cathartic arc of the emotions which Pope has traced, up from the exasperated comedy of the early sequences, through the intense satiric combat of the Sporus Portrait, to loyalty, tenderness and peace at the end, in which all but loving emotion should be laid to rest, and that finally submitted to heaven. At the end of the poem, two people close to death, Pope's mother and Arbuthnot, are joined together as the objects of Pope's loyalty and love.

[76]Cf. Horace, *Sat.* I, vi and I, ix. While alert to verbal echoes of Horace in *To Arbuthnot*, the Twickenham Edition in *Poems*, IV has ignored the larger Horatian paradigms which Pope is refashioning in his epistle.

[77]Thus, while Arbuthnot was still alive when the poem came out, the fiction of the poem feigns that Pope's mother is alive also.

XII Pope's Imitations of Horace: 1737–8

> A Voice there is, that whispers in my ear,
> ('Tis Reason's voice, which sometimes one can hear). . . .
>
> > *(To Bolingbroke*, ll. 11–12)

Carm. IV, i

It is the subject of love we next encounter. Since Pope was willing to use Horatian imitation to write poetry often personal in its implications, the sheer unexpectedness of his next version of Horace, *The First Ode of the Fourth Book of Horace, To Venus* (9 March 1737), suggests an autobiographical origin. Here Pope turns from the *sermones* to the *carmina* of Horace, from social to purely personal – and to the experience of love. Some lines early in the poem:

> I am not now, alas! the man
> As in the gentle Reign of My Queen *Anne*.
> Ah sound no more thy soft alarms,
> Nor circle sober fifty with thy Charms[1]

recall Pope's elegant but sad farewell to Windsor Forest in 1716, a poem which is clearly also a farewell to love.[2] Plainly enough, the loved ones at that time were Martha and Teresa Blount.[3] A year before the publication of the *Ode to Venus*, however, Pope had brought out the last of the *Epistles to Several Persons, To a Lady*, addressed to Martha Blount. That poem, while putting the author's relation with the lady on terms of friendship and deep affection, had in it little of love. The Epistle seemed to set a seal on the relationship. Pope avowed it and at the same time clarified it as friendship. The *Ode to Venus* shows that the Epistle's formal tribute was not to be the last word. This *is* a love poem, written soon after Martha Blount had been staying near Pope, at Fortescue's house.[4] To clinch the point, the unauthorized first edition (in *The Whitehall Evening Post*, 26 February – 1 March, 1737) gives for:

> But why? ah tell me, ah too dear!

> But why, ah PATTY, still too dear![5]

---

[1]Ll. 3–6; *Poems*, IV, p. 151.
[2]*Poems*, VI, p. 194.
[3]See Maynard Mack, 'Pope: The Shape of the Man in His Work', *Yale Review* (Summer 1978), pp. 509–10.
[4]Pope to Fortescue, 21 Sept. 1736; *Correspondence*, IV, p. 34.
[5]*Poems*, IV, p. 153.

Patty being the affectionate familiar name for Martha Blount. Pope follows the plan of Horace's poem faithfully. The prayer to Venus to spare him, the central section of the ode which seeks to redirect her attentions to someone more worthy, and the conclusion in which the ageing man is not spared the longing of love, is common to each poet. Only in detail is Pope's imitation different from Horace. Thus, where Horace referred to the reign of his mistress Cinara, Pope nicely returns the metaphorical to the literal, with his 'gentle Reign of My Queen *Anne*' (l. 4). This expresses the period of Pope's youth and hope for the love of women, and hints, perhaps, at his relatively affectionate attitude towards that monarch. She was also his 'Queen *Anne*' in that she figured in two of his celebrated poems, *Windsor Forest* and *The Rape of the Lock*. Since the Georges came in Pope had been a different poet and a different man. Again, for Horace's Paullus Fabius Maximus, a handsome and accomplished young member of the wealthy nobility, Pope proposes a young man, William Murray, who fits the part in every respect except riches. Fraenkel notes the one detail in Horace's ode which seems not to fit its being a love-poem: Paullus Maximus is an eloquent defender of anxious clients, and he argues that this first Ode of Horace's new book thus prepares us for the series of public portraits which is to follow. In this light it is interesting that, in less than a year's time, Pope was to publish his imitation of the Sixth Epistle of the First Book of Horace, a strongly public poem addressed to Murray. Finally, of course, Pope has substituted love of a woman for Horace's love of the boy Ligurinus. When Jonson imitated this Ode, as we have seen, he took Horace's 'sequor / te' from ll. 39–40 and made it the end of his poem, laying the stress on his endless search for a receding love. Pope chooses the other course, and places the verb early in his expanded closing sequence:

> Thee, drest in Fancy's airy beam,
> Absent I follow thro' th'extended Dream,
>   Now, now I seize, I clasp thy charms,
> And now you burst, (ah cruel!) from my arms,
>   And swiftly shoot along the Mall,
>   Or softly glide by the Canal,
>   Now shown by Cynthia's silver Ray,
> And now, on rolling Waters snatch'd away.[6]

Pope has made the dream a good deal more excited, active, and demonstrative, and greatly weakened the effect of 'iam captum teneo' in the process. But his use of a Restoration amatory style accords quite well with the place-names of fashionable London which he contrasts with the Campus Martius in Horace. The addition of a third shorter line (l. 47) modifies the regular stanza pattern to draw out the enchantedly elusive glimpses of the loved one, silvered finally by moonlight, and in Pope the 'rolling Waters', which in Horace's dream carried Ligurinus away as they might well do in real life, yield a more mysteriously dream-like and little less effective conclusion.

---

[6]Ll. 41–8; *Poems*, p. 153.

Ep. II, ii

The movement from Pope's version of Horace, *Sat*. II, i through *Sat*. II, ii to *To Arbuthnot* and the *Ode to Venus* shows the development of the self-expressive impulse towards a form of poetic autobiography. That Pope recognized this is strongly suggested by his choice of his next poem of Horace to imitate, the Second Epistle of the Second Book which, as Fraenkel points out,[7] contains the one piece of formal autobiographical narrative in all Horace's writings. In the *Imitations* so far produced Pope had given a kind of portrait of his mind; in *To Arbuthnot* he had given (among other things) a personal and literary autobiography. What he had not yet done in any poem was to speak of the political and religious character of his early life. Allusions in his version of *Sat*. II, ii –

Tho' double-tax'd, how little have I lost?

– led him in this direction, but the otherwise very full autobiographical content of *To Arbuthnot* did not touch this wound. The subject is exposed in Pope's imitation of Horace, *Ep*. II, ii, first published on 28 April 1737.

> Bred up at home, full early I begun
> To read in Greek, the Wrath of Peleus' Son.
> Besides, my Father taught me from a Lad,
> The better Art to know the good from bad:
> (And little sure imported to remove,
> To hunt for Truth in *Maudlin*'s learned Grove.)
> But knottier Points we knew not half so well,
> Depriv'd us soon of our Paternal Cell;
> And certain Laws, by Suff'rers thought unjust,
> Deny'd all Posts of Profit or of Trust:
> Hopes after Hopes of pious Papists fail'd,
> While mighty WILLIAM's thundring Arm prevail'd.
> For Right Hereditary tax'd and fin'd,
> He stuck to Poverty with Peace of Mind;
> And me, the Muses help'd to undergo it;
> Convict a Papist He, and I a Poet.
> But (thanks to *Homer*) since I live and thrive,
> Indebted to no Prince or Peer alive . . .[8]

As in the final section of *To Arbuthnot* the content, however mediated and shaped, is unequivocally autobiographical. Not only is Pope able to liken his own situation to that of Horace in having been one of 'the suff'ring Party', but he brings forward the anti-catholic legislation which has determined the character of his life. He thus acknowledges himself one of a small minority within eighteenth-century Britain, far smaller than those who opposed the Julian house in Rome, or the establishment of William and Mary on the throne of Britain. We see too that the character of Pope's father, formulated rather generally in *To Arbuthnot*,

[7]*Horace*, p. 7.
[8]Ll. 52–69; *Poems*, IV, pp. 167–9.

> Stranger to Civil and Religious Rage,
> The good Man walk'd innoxious thro' his Age. . . .
> Nor dar'd an Oath. . .

is now filled out. The laws deprived him and his family of his home; he and his son were denied posts of profit and trust; it was for 'Right Hereditary' that he was punitively taxed. Thus the hint in *To Arbuthnot* that he was a non-juror is expanded, and the plain interpretation of l. 64 is that he was a Jacobite in principle.[9] Connected with this is the nature of the reference to William III. Though the tone is not accusing, the clear implication is that Williams prevailed by force not right, and it is interesting to recall what is probably Pope's early lampoon (and earliest published verses) on the allegedly hollow conquests of William and Mary.[10] The bitterly contemptuous style has now quite gone from the reference; the language is almost the language of tribute, and only the prose-sense contrasts might with 'Right Hereditary'. Line 60 is even more a triumph of tone: 'by Suff'rers thought unjust' disarms the reader by the sheer precision and modesty of its reproach. Indeed the whole paragraph seems tonally more complex than its Horatian parallel. If Horace's tongue is half-way to his cheek when he says that poverty drove him to poetry, his account is otherwise a candid admission of the violence of events which like a wave snatched him up, flung him into war, and as suddenly left him high and dry after the defeat at Philippi. He implies no criticism of Augustus.[11] In Pope the historical process seems more humanly controlled, 'Depriv'd' and 'Deny'd' being the important verbs. The hopes of pious papists are amusingly paralleled with Horace's inexperience in arms, and the relation of these hopes (in the faltering rhythms of their line) to military victory (in the long majestic march of the next line) is correspondingly different. The muted and sorrowful wit of the passage is allowed just a touch of triumph as, near the end, popery and poetry are allied, and one beautiful point of autobiography (his profits from his Homer translations) enables Pope to pull the whole paragraph together, make more of Horace's allusion to the *Iliad*, and subtly imply that, deprived as he has been, he has survived through cultivation of what was originally given him in his lost home.

Aubrey Williams has rightly pointed out the dominance of the idea of theft in the first third of this poem.[12] The hypothetical tale with which the poem opens is modified from Horace so as to focus on the word 'steal' (l. 20). The anecdote about Sir Godfrey Kneller which Pope then interpolates (it has no basis in Horace) is explicitly concerned with theft. Horace's tale of the soldier of Lucullus who, desperate at having been robbed, captured a fort is the first part of the Latin poem to bear upon theft, and Pope retains it accordingly. Indeed he does more, for one of his modulations of Horace's tale implies that the great

[9]Cf. *To Arbuthnot*, l. 397. The significance of l. 64 is not noted by the Twickenham editor, but see my *Pope: Horatian Satires and Epistles*, p. 159, and Maresca, *Pope's Horatian Poems*, pp. 137–8.

[10]David Nokes, 'Lisping in Political Numbers', *Notes and Queries*, N.S. 24 (June 1977), pp. 228–9.

[11]'Il fait icy un aveu sincere de son malheur, & de la misere qui l'avoit obligé à faire des vers; & il le fait d'autant plus volontiers que cet aveu tourne à la gloire d'August' (Dacier, *Remarques Critiques*, IX, p. 487).

[12]Aubrey L. Williams, 'Pope and Horace: The Second Epistle of the Second Book', *Restoration and Eighteenth-Century Literature* (London, 1963), pp. 309–21, especially 312–15.

modern commander he parallels with Lucullus is Marlborough, known for his parsimony and grand style. Pope, in contrast with the insinuatingly genteel sales-talk of the opening tale, attacks this tale with an extraordinarily derisive *brio*:

> 'Prodigious well!' his great Commander cry'd,
> Gave him much Praise, and some Reward beside.
> Next pleas'd his Excellence a Town to batter;
> (Its Name I know not, and it's no great matter)
> 'Go on, my friend (he cry'd) see yonder Walls!
> 'Advance and conquer! go where Glory calls!
> 'More honours, more Rewards, attend the Brave' —[13]

We need only recall Pope's attitude to conquest in *Windsor Forest* and *The Temple of Fame*, and the Tory attitude to Marlborough, to preceive that in Pope's hands the tale now deals with robbery twice over: the original robbery of the soldier only fuels the grandiose and magniloquent robbery urged by the 'great Commander'; and the paths of glory are but theft on theft. What has not been sufficiently noted, even in Aubrey Williams's brilliant essay, is the very feeling drama with which Pope can now turn from his lofty external view of conquest ('Next pleas'd his Excellence a Town to batter; / (Its name I know not . . .'), through the allusion to Achilles, to the inward and suffering experience of one who undergoes deprivation by conquest. Nothing marks the greatness of this poem more than the way it has thus penetrated historical process to express its cost in personal experience.

As Williams says, the metaphor of theft rises to its 'meridian'[14] with the appearance in the next paragraph of Time itself as 'This subtle Thief of Life' (l. 76). Pope thus returns to his starting-point (his friend's request for verses) with the offer of a more comprehensive understanding to his reader. At its deepest level, Pope's answer to his friend's request is that time has so changed his life that it has come near to stealing him from himself, taking from him his peculiar happinesses, skills and fame, changing his identity. This does not now strike the reader as a mere figure of speech because Pope, as he has refashioned Horace, has led us upward in almost meditative fashion through more concrete examples of deprivation so that the feeling prompted by these may be brought to the understanding of time's deprivation, which is the most dire of all. What is of such interest in Horace's poem and in Pope's, what strikes one as so humanly authentic, is that while each poet pleads that he cannot be expected to produce more verse, each views with dismay at the very least the prospect of losing his capacity to write. Horace allies his poems with mirth, love, feasting and play ('jocos, venerem, convivia, ludum'), while Pope, in another autobiographical moment, does not make a statement but asks a question, and raises the issue of identity:

What will it leave me, if it snatch my Rhime?[15]

---

[13]Ll. 42–8; *Poems*, IV, p. 167.
[14]'Pope and Horace', p. 315.
[15]L. 77; *Poems*, IV, pp. 170–1.

So far is each poet from merely saying (though of course each does say it): 'don't ask me for poetry; I have better things to do now.' But Pope's expansion of Horace's famous passage is more than poignant:

> If ev'ry Wheel of that unweary'd Mill
> That turn'd ten thousand Verses, now stands still.[16]

We note the backward glance at Pope's *Homer* (his most arduous and pro-longed poetic activity, already referred to); the subtle poising of the word 'turn'd' which carries the sense both of the genteel knack of 'turning a verse' and the ceaseless productivity of the mill, a metaphor which has itself a trace of shame in its self-deprecating modesty; above all we feel the steady, prolonged, enjambed rhythm: eight uninterrupted iambic beats, brought up short, almost at the end of the couplet, by the emphatic deferred pause, and the lonely contrast of the final three words. What is there which can fill that sudden silence?

With 'But after all what wou'd you have me do?' (l. 80) Pope relaxes his manner, and leads us from that unnerving silence almost thankfully back into the world of folly. He follows Horace, and the appropriate Horatian vein, into the city of impertinents and poetasters, the noisy, mindless metropolis. Here, as Aubrey Williams says,[17] we may see in literal detail how time may take a man from himself:

> In Palace-Yard at Nine you'll find me there –
> At Ten for certain, Sir, in Bloomsb'ry-Square –
> Before the Lords at Twelve my Cause comes on –
> There's a Rehearsal, Sir, exact at One. –[18]

If the city is not for poetry-writing, neither perhaps is the seclusion of Oxford (where, Pope has just told us, he was prevented from matriculating, and was, perhaps, not much the worse for it). While the logic of both Horace's and Pope's poems may be that, if a man just emerged from retreat is a laughing-stock, a poet cannot write amidst tumult, what sticks in the mind in each case is the image of a man suddenly transformed by a shift of environment: stolen from himself. By comparison the delusions of the world of professional folly appear less alarming. The mutual compliments of the lawyers, the poetic rôle-playing of the poetasters, facile games by which men try to seem better than they are, are ways of their growing worse, all the same:

> 'My dear *Tibullus*!' if that will not do,
> 'Let me be *Horace*, and be *Ovid* you.'[19]

It is a fascinating moment for Pope since Horace, though he also mocks this kind of self-complimentary rôle-playing, uses the names of Callimachus and

---

[16]Ll. 78–9; ibid., IV, p. 171.
[17]'Pope and Horace', pp. 316–17.
[18]Ll. 94–7; *Poems*, IV, p. 171.
[19]Ll. 143–4; ibid., IV, p. 175.

Mimnermus, writers of elegy. Pope, on the other hand, is not only using an Horatian form, but even imitating one of his poems. Is *he* not saying, in effect, 'Let me be *Horace*'? Here is another paradox of identity. Our need to resolve it brings us up the more forcibly against the discipline of truth and self-knowledge.[20] The following discourse on the pains and self-denial required to create poetry that will defy time makes it clear that the imitation is no facile playing of parts. The stringent judgement prescribed by Horace must be applied to the imitation of Horace. No fashionable favour can be allowed to soften that judgement, and Pope's glancing reference to the court replaces a somewhat obscure allusion in Horace (l. 114), to contrast the established taste of their two ages. The whole paragraph, as has been observed,[21] is couched in terms of law and love; judgement of poetry here is meant to recall earlier and unmetaphorical references to the laws and judges of the kingdom. The view that the law of poetry is completed by love rests on the line: 'In downright Charity revive the dead' (l. 164), but we should be very cautious before we discover here an image of how poetry, 'divinely strong' (l. 172), may enter into a Christian love which resurrects the dead. These images of law and love are muted; we must attend to the tone as well as the content of the lines. 'Downright Charity' is a rueful sarcasm: if there were no other reason to draw on the past one might do it to avoid inflicting so much modern rubbish on the future. This is not to deny the presence of a Christian pattern behind the lines, but only to note how this is overlain by a contemporary and secular tone, so that the reader is not at once and irresistibly reminded of the raising of Lazarus.[22]

The paragraph on the discipline of true poetry comes to an end with a multiple allusion. The lines of Horace which the concluding couplet parallels provide the epigraph of the imitation: 'Ludentis speciem dabit & torquebitur' while Pope is at the same time quoting from *An Essay on Criticism* (ll. 362–3). In Pope's text of Horace on the facing page 'Ludentis' and 'torquebitur' are picked out by different type. Once again Horace is helping Pope to be himself and reveal himself. Horace leads Pope to quote himself quite naturally. At the same time the juxtaposition of 'learning to dance' (not very painful) and 'being on the rack' (very painful) gives us pause. In the wider context of this poem, in which Pope following Horace has spoken of his early deprivations and sufferings, the idea of being on the rack while seeming to be at ease is even more expressive. If the Muses impose their rigorous requirements on the true poet, Pope's learning to dance, that is, learning to be a poet, has helped him to 'undergo' (l. 66) the pains of his personal situation, and to move with apparent ease in a society bitterly opposed to men of his own background. Poetry has both bound him and freed him.

The next tale of the poem takes up its central theme of identity. The deluded 'Patriot' who hears, notes and answers in the empty Chamber is another and

---

[20]It may be argued that here Pope wishes to dissociate himself from the *example* of Horace. It would be consistent with the position of those who have contended that in the Epistle *To Augustus* and elsewhere Pope uses his imitation to reject Horace and even satirize him. The argument is implausible because Horace, Tibullus and Ovid, poets of Augustan Rome, are not the only names mentioned: Homer, Milton, Dryden and Otway are there too. What Pope is attacking is the shallow imitation of *any* good model.

[21]Maresca, *Pope's Horatian Poems*, pp. 125–8.

[22]Ibid., pp. 126–7.

more striking example of the self-deception which Pope has already more lightly alluded to in the case of the poetasters. However gratifying to the vanity it is a delusion which must be abandoned. In Pope's poem, though not Horace's, this delusion is political: Pope's madman thinks he is in parliament not the theatre. It would be a little surprising, in context, if this had no implication for Pope himself, and the whole passage may be considered as one of those movements of withdrawal from political engagement which Pope, seeking all the time to assert the balance of his mind, renders in his poetry. We are prompted to look ahead to the imitation of the First Epistle of the First Book (7 March 1737/8):

> Sometimes a Patriot, active in debate,
> Mix with the World. . . .
> Sometimes. . . .
> Back to my native Moderation slide. . . .[23]

The difference is that here the movement by which the poet recovers himself is not a grateful relinquishment but a harsh awakening. The present poem sharply poses the question of identity. Thus Pope, again following a characteristic Horatian movement away from the noisy capital and towards retirement and personal concern, seeks to apply the harmonies of his art to his own mind and to the ethical course of his own life.

> To Rules of Poetry no more confin'd,
> I learn to smooth and harmonize my Mind,
> Teach ev'ry Thought within its bounds to roll,
> And keep the equal Measure of the Soul.[24]

These lines express an even closer growing together of art and life than the poem has hitherto exposed. This is to propose an even harder form of integrity: not just that of the true poet as against the poetaster, but that of the true poet and good man. The notion of a balance or harmony of the individual mind has never been so comprehensively introduced in the *Imitations*. And as recent commentators have rightly observed, it is here that time is re-introduced in its larger sense, as the force against which integrity of life must be opposed.[25] A life saved from political deprivation, from the vanity of the poetasters and perhaps from the delusions of political engagement, must oppose some kind of ethical pattern against the imperfections of human law, and a harmonized self-knowledge against 'the waste and onrush of the years'[26] and approach of death. Yet the attempt to read the conclusion of the poem as a kind of *ars moriendi*, a preparation for a holy death, does not seem to catch the quality of Pope's awareness.[27] It is certainly the hunger for possession and power which threatens to unbalance the soul, and Pope proceeds to a meditation on use as opposed to possession, delivering a series of heavy satirical sideswipes on the way. It is true, too, that he wishes to draw his poem closer to a Christian viewpoint. As in the case of the

[23]Ll. 27–8, 31, 33: *Poems*, IV, p. 281.
[24]Ll. 202–5; ibid., IV, p. 179.
[25]Maresca, *Pope's Horatian Poems*, p. 131.
[26]Aubrey Williams, 'Pope and Horace', p. 318; Maresca, *Pope's Horatian Poems*, p. 128.
[27]Maresca, *Pope's Horatian Poems*, pp. 145–7.

passage on use and possession in the imitation of *Sat*. II, ii, the letter to Bethel of 9 August 1726 with its quotation from Thomas à Kempis, lies just beneath the surface of the poem: 'I am but a *Lodger* here: this is not an abiding City. I am only to stay out my lease, for what has Perpetuity and mortal man to do with each other?':

> The Laws of God, as well as of the Land,
> Abhor, a *Perpetuity* should stand[28]

Horace's line (l. 173) with its use of a legal and secular sense of prayer has been adroitly transformed. At the same time, all the integrity and wisdom that the poet can oppose to the massive 'earthslide of Time and its inevitable changes'[29] appear quite frail and secular. So strongly has Pope developed Horace's lines on mutability that his list of false values ('Gold, Silver, Iv'ry . . .') and his remarks on moral contraries in human nature, even his allusion to the 'God of Nature' (ll. 280–81) with its clear recognition (not in Horace) of the freedom of the will, seem to constitute a return to a smaller human world. But this is certainly the logic of the end of the epistle. Briefly reiterating some of its leading motifs ('a Tyrant gone', the 'Avarice of Pow'r', and 'the black Fear of Death, that saddens all'), Pope follows Horace in leading his poem down into the everyday and domestic:

> Pleas'd to look forward, pleas'd to look behind,
> And count each Birth-day with a grateful mind?. . . .

> Has Age but melted the rough parts away,
> As Winter-fruits grow mild e'er they decay?[30]

This image, which (it has been suggested) may allude to Shakespeare and have arisen from Sanadon's commentary on the parallel lines in Horace,[31] is extraordinarily felicitous, expressive as it is of something less than the full strength of 'ripeness' in *Lear* and the corresponding 'maturity' which Sir Thomas Elyot found in Augustus. Pope recommends no more than mildness and prudence; the possible Christian suggestiveness of 'Lenior & Melior' is not brought out. Certainly Pope is concerned with measure and harmony before death, but it seems wrong to suggest that the last lines 'gather great strength and solemnity from their correspondence to the final steps of the *ars moriendi* tradition . . .'.[32] The metaphor of the stage (Horace speaks of a feast) is not introduced by Pope for its possible solemnity; it has none of the resonance of its use by More in *Utopia* or Shakespeare in *The Tempest*. Despite the human range of the poem, its gravity, sadness and acknowledgement of suffering, Pope at last brings it firmly back into the world of fools:

---

[28]Ll. 246–7; *Poems*, IV, p. 183. Maresca (pp. 143–4) aptly cites Leviticus, 25, 23.
[29]Aubrey Williams, 'Pope and Horace', p. 320.
[30]Ll. 314–15, 319–20; *Poems*, IV, p. 187.
[31]Aubrey Williams, 'Pope and Horace', p. 320.
[32]Maresca, *Pope's Horatian Poems*, p. 146. Dacier, by contrast, stresses a wise but worldly aim: 'Horace ne songe pas a rendre Florus sage, mais a le rendre moins malheureux' (*Remarques Critiques*, IX, p. 535).

Walk sober off; before a sprightlier Age
Comes titt'ring on, and shoves you from the stage:

One wonders whether the metaphor is meant to recall (among other things) the last words of Augustus.[33] At all events the deprivations dealt with by the poem here assume their least daunting form. This challenge can be met on the level of social deportment, and no more need be said.

Ep. II, i

Pope's celebrated version of Horace, *Ep*. II, i, his Epistle *To Augustus*, was composed at Southampton (Lord Peterborough's) in Spring and Autumn 1736, and published in May 1737.[34] The character of Horace's poem presented Pope with a challenge and an opportunity. The challenge was that this poem, unlike others that Pope had imitated, squarely confronted him with the problem of how to write about Augustus. The *princeps* is no longer the subject merely of passing allusion, as in *Sat*. II, i where he is paralleled with Walpole, or *Ep*. II, ii where he is paralleled with William III. Augustus had, as we have seen, recently begun to be used in his Tacitean aspect in the Tory attack upon George II, Walpole and the Whig hegemony. Writing in *The Craftsman*, 220 (19 September 1730), St John compared the 'Usurpation of *Augustus*' unfavourably with the 'glorious *fourth* and *fifth Centuries* of the Republick of *Rome*' and referred his opponent to 'Mr. *Gordon*'s excellent Discourses, prefix'd to his Translation of *Tacitus*; in which He will find his favourite *Augustus* set in a true light, and prov'd to be an infamous Tyrant, though somewhat more artful than his Successors'.[35] Pope, if he did not already know Gordon's work, must have followed up the reference of his 'Guide, Philosopher, and Friend' to find, amongst much hostile criticism of Augustus, the following passage:

> The Renown of AUGUSTUS was also notably blazon'd by the Historians and Poets of his time; men of excellent wit, but egregious flatterers. According to them AUGUSTUS had all the accomplishments to be acquired by man, the magnanimity of Heroes, the perfections and genius of a Deity, and the innocence peculiar to the primitive race of men. After so many instances of his cruelty, revenge, selfishness, excessive superstition and defect in courage; after all the crying calamities and afflictions, all the oppression and vassalage, that his ambition had brought upon his Country and the globe, one would think that such praises must have pass'd for satyr and mockery: but *nihil est quod credere de se non possit cum laudatur Diis aequa potestas*. Ambition, successful ambition is a credulous passion; or whether he believed such praises or no, he received them graciously, and caress'd the Authors. Hence so much favour to VIRGIL and HORACE, and to such other wits as knew how to be good Courtiers: and hence every admirer of those charming Poets, is an admirer of AUGUSTUS, who was so generous to them, and is the chief burthen of their Panegyricks.[36]

[33]Ll. 324–5; *Poems*, IV, p. 187. See Ch. I, p. 23 above.

[34]Pope, *Correspondence*, IV, p. 33 and 56n.

[35]*The Craftsman. By Caleb D'Anvers*, bound edn of Nos. 1–511, 1726–36 (London, 1731–7), VII, p. 36.

[36]Thomas Gordon, *The Works of Tacitus. . . . To which are prefixed, Political Discourses* (London, 1728–31), I, p. 49. For a hint at irony in Horace's addresses to Augustus, see Shaftesbury, *Advice to an Author: Characteristics of Men, Manners, Opinions and Times* (London, 1711; rev. edn, 1714), I, pp. 269–70, III, p. 21. For Pope's own views of Augustus, see his *Correspondence*, I, p. 116, and III, p. 420, discussed in Ch. XI, pp. 308–9 above.

It seems likely that in this passage, and especially its third sentence, we have one source of Pope's decision to compose an *ironical* epistle to *Augustus*. If there were a current fashion, especially in Tory circles, to disparage both the Emperor Augustus and George Augustus of Britain, the genuine idealism of Virgilian and Horatian panegyric could not be allowed to be dismissed as egregious flattery. '*An Answer from* Horace' would not only reassert the Augustan ideal in its civilized splendour, but, by its necessary application to contemporary Britain, would demonstrate how a clear-eyed idealism might be *converted* to 'satyr and mockery', that is to irony, by fallen reality itself.

The opportunity was to write a poetic essay in familiar and specific terms on the values and development of English poetry. *An Essay on Criticism* may have aroused in Pope the desire to write a poem of this kind, but there the general nature of his scheme restrained him. The conversations with Spence show the pleasure Pope took in comments and discriminations on English writers, and in a broad sense an imitation of *Ep*. II, i might share with Dryden's Epistle '*To Mr. Congreve*' that awareness of a special vantage-point from which literary and political achievement might be measured: 'Venimus ad summum fortunae. . . .'; 'Well then; the promis'd hour is come at last. . . .'.[37] The special art of Horace's epistle is its integration of diverse observations into a total cultural view; it is not an opening and closing address to a ruler with a sequence of literary criticism in between. The *princeps* is addressed throughout; to remember him is to remember the relation of Rome to Greece; history, society, manners, writing, religion and rule are in the easiest and most familiar way taken up into the idiom of the epistle.

Pope's opinion of the poem is found in short form in his letter of 21 September 1736 where he calls it 'the finest [epistle] in Horace'.[38] If the poet who three years later was to condemn the third *Georgic* for gross flattery of Augustus considered Horace guilty of similar flattery, it seems unlikely that he would give Horace's poem such praise at the very time he was imitating it.[39] Condemnation of one passage in Virgil does not imply condemnation of Augustan poetry in general. Pope's view of the *laudes Caesaris* of Horace's epistle may be seen from relating his public letter to Arbuthnot (26 July 1734) with his Advertisement to the Epistle *To Augustus*. The two are consistent with one another, and evince a qualified admiration for Augustus on Pope's part. Each speaks of Augustus as a great prince; each credits him with the intelligence to recognize the best poets of his time; each notes that he was ready to encourage freedom in satire. Neither document charges Augustus with corruption, but the Advertisement notes that Horace painted 'His Prince' 'with all the great and good Qualities of a Monarch, upon whom the *Romans* depended for the Encrease of an *Absolute Empire*'; Pope by comparison will 'add one or two of those Virtues which contribute to the Happiness of a *Free People*'.[40] The need for this reservation shows

---

[37]Horace, *Ep*. II, i, 32; 'To Congreve', l. 1; *Poems*, ed. Kinsley, II, p. 852.

[38]Pope to Fortescue, 21 September 1736; *Correspondence*, IV, p. 33. C.O. Brink's judgement of the poem should be recalled here: 'It is a command performance executed with great candour and skill. It is also a personal poem designed to give voice to some of Horace's most cherished convictions as to the relation of poetry and society. The two features are not mutually exclusive' (*Horace on Poetry: Prolegomena to the Literary Epistles* (Cambridge, 1963), p. 191.

[39]Spence *Anecdotes*, ed. J.M. Osborn, I, p. 229 (item 543).

[40]*Poems*, IV, p. 191. Dacier had noted, in discussing the opening of Horace's Epistle, that allu-

that both letter and Advertisement are to be read at their face value (not ironically). Pope required as telling and famous a positive example as he could find; he
directs his focus upon those positive aspects of Augustus's achievement which it
is hardest to deny and which reflected most damagingly upon George Augustus
of Britain: his political greatness, his intelligence, his concern with the civilization of Rome and with the best in its literature. Pope's use of Augustus is to this
extent like Jonson's in *The Poetaster*. Despite the fact that two views of
Augustus were widespread in the earlier eighteenth century, each finding
expression within Pope's own literary and political circle, and that a clever
manoeuvre of patrician Tory propaganda sought to link George Augustus with
a Tacitean Augustus – corrupt with corrupt as it was alleged – Pope's own
contemporary statements plainly show that he needed the positive example of
Augustus, and felt that it had a sufficient basis both in history and the minds of
his readers for him to use it with conviction in a major poem. Whether this
corresponded fully with his personal view of the historical Augustus may be
another question.

Let us for a moment set aside the well known opening and end of Pope's
Epistle, which critics of his satire have been most eager to discuss, and consider a
passage from the 'literary' part of the poem.

> On Avon's bank, where flow'rs eternal blow,
> If I but ask, if any weed can grow?
> One Tragic sentence if I dare deride
> Which Betterton's grave Action dignify'd,
> Or well-mouth'd Booth with emphasis proclaims,
> (Tho' but, perhaps, a muster-roll of Names)
> How will our Fathers rise up in a rage,
> And swear, all shame is lost in George's Age!
> You'd think no Fools disgrac'd the former Reign,
> Did not some grave Examples yet remain,
> Who scorn a Lad should teach his Father skill,
> And, having once been wrong, will be so still.
> He, who to seem more deep than you or I,
> Extols old Bards, or Merlin's Prophecy,
> Mistake him not; he envies, not admires,
> And to debase the Sons, exalts the Sires.
> Had ancient Times conspir'd to dis-allow
> What then was new, what had been ancient now?
> Or what remain'd, so worthy to be read
> By learned Cricks, of the mighty Dead?
>   In Days of Ease, when now the weary Sword
> Was sheath'd, and *Luxury* with *Charles* restor'd;
> In every Taste of foreign Courts improv'd,
> 'All, by the King's Example, liv'd and lov'd.'
> Then Peers grew proud in Horsemanship t'excell,
> New-market's Glory rose, as Britain's fell;
> Then Soldier breath'd the Gallantries of France,

sions to Augustus's sole power would not, Horace knew, displease the *princeps*; and he is sensitive
and alert to the *laudes Caesaris* as acceptable to a monarch. These are the points where Pope, in his
own version, mounts his irony (*Remarques Critiques*, IX, pp. 310–12, 434).

And ev'ry flow'ry Courtier writ Romance.
Then Marble soften'd into life grew warm,
And yielding Metal flow'd to human form:
Lely on animated Canvas stole
The sleepy Eye, that spoke the melting soul.
No wonder then, when all was Love and Sport,
The willing Muses were debauch'd at Court;
On each enervate string they taught the Note
To pant, or tremble thro' an Eunuch's throat.
But Britain, changeful as a Child at play,
Now calls in Princes, and now turns away.
Now Whig, now Tory, what we lov'd we hate;
Now all for Pleasure, now for Church and State;
Now for Prerogative, and now for Laws;
Effects unhappy! from a Noble Cause.[41]

By this point in the Epistle Pope is well advanced in his argument for a discriminating assessment of earlier English literature, and a relatively favourable assessment of the modern achievement. It is surprising, perhaps, from the poet of the 1729 *Dunciad*: what has happened is that Horace's defence of modernity (and he had a better case to press than Pope) has called forth in Pope his awareness of a modern self-confidence, justified if not in regard to the Ancients yet in regard to the earlier literature of England. Though Pope, when he came to Horace's 'venimus ad summum fortunae', added a little special ridicule of his own times, he nevertheless makes us feel throughout the poem a kind of *summum sapientiae*: the learning, the long views and the leisure to make fair judgements. That is the balance of mind and the authentically Augustan note of this Epistle. We should now ask to whom Pope's eminently reasonable observation on Shakespeare is addressed: who, specifically, stands between the poet and the ordinary reader? The nature of Pope's discourse, like that of Horace, implies in his reader intelligence, reasonableness, judgement; he is not writing as he writes when he apostrophizes stupidity and vice.[42] Is he not (as Pope's readers must have asked when the poem first appeared) addressing the King? Doubtless he is, at many points. But, as many points in the poem recognize, George was not interested in poetry, while Pope is in the midst of a most detailed literary discourse, involving Shakespeare, Jonson, *Gammer Gurton's Needle*, Sidney, 'Sprat, Carew, Sedley, and a hundred more'. Formally speaking the Epistle may be addressed to the reigning 'Augustus' but in the fiction of the poem a greater Augustus stands behind the Hanoverian monarch, not just because the *princeps* had shown appreciation of poetry, but because, as was well known to Horace and as Suetonius recorded, he was an admirer of the old Roman literature.[43] Horace's whole defence of the new literature is delicately addressed to the amendment of this view, and for Pope to follow Horace's literary argument, as he does, involves him in the recreation of the implied literary personality of Augustus.

---

[41] Ll. 119–60; *Poems*, IV, pp. 205–9.
[42] Cf. for example his mode at the end of *Dunciad*, III, or of Dialogue I of the Epilogue to the Satires.
[43] Fraenkel, *Horace*, p. 396 (citing Suetonius, Divus Augustus, 89).

For the educated reader of Pope's poem, 'How will our Fathers rise up in a rage' (l. 125) would recall the original Augustus. Line 126, on the other hand, complicates the relation of poet and addressee: here Pope momentarily appears to be defending 'George's Age' as Horace had that of Augustus – just for a moment the complicity of amiable and reasonable discourse reaches out to include King George II. But the line sets a trap for the reader including (if conceivable) Pope's unwary monarch. What follows can be given an entirely literary significance, but the pointedly singular case of 'Reign' (l. 127), followed by the statement of the next line signals a sudden turn into anti-Hanoverian satire, and it has been convincingly suggested that behind Pope's general observation on the relation of young and old is a reflection upon the bad relations between George II as Prince of Wales and George I, now repeated in the bad relations between Prince Frederick and George II.[44] Pope thus adroitly blends Horace's defence of the modern in literature with a pat on the back for Prince Frederick as one current focus for opposition to the ruling monarch. This train of thought, however, leads back to literature by the end of the paragraph.

The next paragraph registers a further subtle shift in position. One strategy for an opposition poet writing an Epistle To Augustus would have been to have pretended to praise George's reign while bestowing unequivocal praise upon that of one of his Stuart predecessors. Atterbury, as we have seen, might have nominated the reign of Charles II as the English Augustan Age;[45] Pope's Jacobite friend, Mrs Charles Caesar, would certainly have done so, and so would Bevil Higgons.[46] For Pope to have adopted this strategy would have entailed some realignment of Horace's argument, but no more than we often find in the *Imitations*. What Pope actually does here is subtle. First he aligns an earlier English reign, that of Charles II, with the Greeks in Horace, though later on in the Epistle the Greeks are paralleled with the French. Secondly, he describes this period as though it were a sort of Renaissance – compare:

Then Marble soften'd into life grew warm,
And yielding Metal flow'd to human form . . .

with his lines on the Renaissance from *An Essay on Criticism*:

The *Sculpture* and her *Sister-Arts* revive;
Stones leap'd to *Form*, and *Rocks* began to *live*. . . .[47]

Pope here adapts a programmatic description of the Renaissance for purposes which blend praise with satire. The choice and placing of the word '*Luxury*' (l. 140) gives the reader his cue (it could easily have been another word – 'Liberty' perhaps) and Pope strikes a remarkable balance in recognizing

---

[44]Manuel Schoenhorn, 'The Audacious Contemporaneity of Pope's *Epistle to Augustus*, *Studies in English Literature, 1550–1900*, VIII, no. 3 (Summer, 1968), pp. 431–43.

[45]See Ch. IX above, pp. 236–7, 244–8.

[46]The Journal of Mrs Charles Caesar, 1724–41 (Bodleian MS Film 740), Vol. III: 'Much is said of Augustus's Reign, but sure Nothing Ever Like King Charl's. for as Falstaf says. He Had Not Only Wit Him self – but Caus'd Wit in Other men, For then how it Abounded. Now in this Poor Unhappy Isle . . .'. For Higgons, see Ch. IX, pp. 248–9.

[47]Ll. 701–2; *Poems*, I, p. 319.

a genuine growth in sophistication and expressiveness going hand in hand with superficiality and licence. Another marvellously poised word is 'melting' (l. 150): on the one hand a movement of the spirit, part of the '*animated* Canvas' (my italics), on the other leading on to 'Love', 'Sport' and debauchery. This 'Augustan Age' which should have combined vigour with form, flowed prematurely into decadence. As Dryden seemed to imply in his poem *To Congreve*, the Restoration failed to find and hold the all-important Augustan meridian, the *summum fortunae*, between Renaissance and decadence. Pope responds to this with a wonderful blend of admiration, affection and asperity. It is a superb portrait of an age, and one which allows Pope to hold to Horace's defence of the modern: implicitly 'George's Age' seems again to be commended. But once again the literary leads artfully into the political. Self-indulgent Britain, changeful as a child, 'Now calls in Princes, and now turns away'. The present tense is most adroit. Britain called back the Stuarts in 1660, and turned them away in 1688. It called in the Prince of Orange. It called in George I. Some had tried to call in the Pretender. The poem gives no assurance that the process of calling in and turning away is over. Charles's reign lacked the controlled strength of an Augustan age, 'George's Age' lacks the stability. George has been warned.

In the corresponding lines Horace ascribed the restless self-indulgence of the Greeks to peace and good fortune. Pope ascribes the political restlessness of Britain, through an allusion to Prior,[48] to the 'Noble Cause' of the love of liberty. This departure from Horace still stays within the terms of the Horatian debate in his Letter to Augustus. As Fraenkel observes, Horace somewhat simplifies both his picture of the self-indulgent Greeks and of the hardworking early Romans: he requires a sharp contrast, and draws it repeatedly. Time and again he turns back to pictures of primitive vigour, of 'Agricolæ prisci'.[49] Such passages might be thought to appeal to the Roman conservatism of Augustus; Horace uses them to depict, without rancour or contempt, an industrious narrowness; his plea is that the civilization of Augustus, and particularly its literary civilization, must combine the traditional Roman with the modern Greek, and it must combine vigour with sophistication. This is the ideal of art which Horace finally offers to Augustus in this Epistle. Neither in his rendering of the passage of Horace, nor in his imitation of the Epistle at large does Pope dissent from this view. He ascribes the instability of Britain to too much liberty rather than too much ease, but it is the union of the same opposites which constitutes his ideal of civilization.[50] Sturdy freedom must ally with regularity and sophistication. Pope's is an alertly shifting address, sometimes turning, amiably or warningly, to George II, sometimes reaching beyond to the original Augustus, whose position and taste shape the larger outlines of Pope's argument as they do also in Horace. Between the two Augustuses move Pope and his ordinary reader, affirming, modifying, distinguishing: tacking and falling off before the wind. The poem's judgement is nothing if not mobile.

The passage quoted is representative of the whole epistle. The poem has no single chronological progression. Five times it turns back to the Restoration, to

---

[48]*A Letter to M. Boileau Despreaux*, l. 194; *The Literary Works of Matthew Prior*, I, p. 226.
[49]Fraenkel, *Horace*, pp. 389–90, 391–2; Horace, *Ep.* II, i, 139.
[50]*An Essay on Criticism*, ll. 711–22; *Poems*, I, pp. 322–3, expresses what is still Pope's ideal here.

comment on some merit or deficiency of its 'Ease'. Repeatedly, too, it follows Horace in recalling the virtues and limitations of less 'civilized' times. Here Pope effects a signal departure from Horace, for in the later poem the growth of a chastizing but constructive satire surviving into the present time is traced back to 'Our rural Ancestors, with little blest,': this is a point where primitive vigour bestows a necessary quality and practice upon the present. Pope's added stresses, in the account of how invective was restrained by law, are worth noticing: 'But Times corrupt . . .' (l. 251) and (after the intervention of law) 'Most warp'd to Flatt'ry's side . . .'; finally Pope parallels with Horace's generalized 'benedicendum, delectandumque' (italicized by Pope on the facing page) his own couplet:

> Hence Satire rose, that just the medium hit,
> And heals with Morals what it hurts with Wit.[51]

Pope's letter to Arbuthnot makes clear that this, though not what Horace wrote, was not out of the Horatian character, nor in Pope's view, the kind of writing frowned on or feared by Augustus. What is offered here to the understanding of the equal-minded reader, could have been offered, in Pope's view, to the original Augustus. With George Augustus and his ministers, Pope's 'Augustus', the case is altered. Here Pope behind his vein of politeness and praise plays a dangerous game of political warning. For Horace and Augustus the sturdiness of old Rome was an essential component of civilization. For Pope the 'Noble Cause' of the lover of liberty is a part of old England, and equally indispensable for civilization in his time. His account of the growth and use of satire links back with, and explains, the lines in praise of Swift, for which Pope, as once before at the time of the Atterbury Plot,[52] was in danger of arrest and examination.

> Let Ireland tell, how Wit upheld her cause,
> Her Trade supported, and supply'd her Laws;
> And leave on SWIFT this grateful verse ingrav'd,
> The Rights a Court attack'd, a Poet sav'd.[53]

In a modification of Horace similar to what he has effected in *Sat*. II, i and II, ii, Pope has the modern poet not just tell of noble deeds and pass on famous examples, but perform such a deed, and become such an example. What is so remarkable in the main body of Pope's imitation of this poem is the way it can blend a friendly, confident and intelligent manner – one appropriate to an Augustan Age in the positive sense of that term – with the sense of a political and cultural crisis. He can put the case for contemporary literature – praising among other things a play by Colley Cibber – while yet making the political and cultural point:

> Old Edward's Armour beams on Cibber's breast![54]

[51]Ll. 261–2; *Poems*, IV, pp. 216–17.
[52]George Sherburn, *The Early Career of Alexander Pope* (Oxford, 1934), pp. 223–5. Mrs Caesar's Journal (see n. 46 above) also throws light on Pope's danger at this moment.
[53]Ll. 321–4; *Poems*, IV, pp. 213–15 (and note to ll. 221–8).
[54]L. 319; *Poems*, IV, p. 223.

But this is done lightly, as a 'jest' (l. 318); it is no savage attack.

> . . . Now calls in Princes, and now turns away:

how lofty and assured the observation, how light and glancing the touch, yet how serious the political content!

Hence the need for the famous irony at the opening and conclusion of the Epistle. There can be few more significant moments in the history of the Augustan idea in England. Here we must see these lines in relation to the poem as a whole. We have noted that the body of the poem demands, not just an intelligent auditor or reader, but one holding certain views concerning literature and civilization which have definite value but which still need to be expanded and amended. By implication the original Augustus behind George Augustus has been recalled. The remarkable opening of Pope's last paragraph, its sculptural image recalling the several earlier points in the poem where sculpture betokened the nature of a civilization, has nothing decadent about it, and nothing extravagant:

> Not with such Majesty, such bold relief,
> The Forms august of King, or conqu'ring Chief,
> E'er swell'd on Marble; as in Verse have shin'd
> (In polish'd Verse) the Manners and the Mind.[55]

Like the Doric and Corinthian columns of Congreve's literary temple, in Dryden's poem, this image of verse brings together the strength and the grace, the vigour and the polish, which form the ideal of civilization Horace offered to Augustus at the end of his Epistle. It is an ideal as valid for Pope's time as for Horace's, and may remind us not only of the *Aeneid*, but of Dryden's *Aeneid* – and indeed Pope's Homer. If this, however, were to be the only, or the predominant vein of the concluding paragraph, the next three lines ('Oh! could I mount on the Mæonian wing . . .') might make the reader a little uneasy. The imperiously managed syntax of ll. 390–3 is not further strengthened by the rather easy exclamatoriness of the next line; the word 'Repose' is a definite warning either that something is going wrong, or that the poetic purpose is more complex than at first appeared. It is no adequate parallel to the strong lines in which Horace praises Augustus for bringing peace in the world and closing the gates of the Temple of Janus. The words 'dearly bought!' go further; they would be sufficient, if the reader knew nothing of England under George II and Walpole, to raise the question whether this passage could really be praise; they would send the reader from the poem to its world for an answer. From this point we can see that Pope is now engaged in a kind of descending poetic strategy similar to that found in Dryden's *Mac Flecknoe*. Opening with a high ideal of poetry, forcefully expressed, it descends through slackening rhythms, easy verbal patterns, pointed equivocations, through an almost *Dunciad*-like vision –

> How, when you nodded, o'er the land and deep,
> Peace stole her wing, and wrapt the world in sleep[56]

[55]Ll. 390–3; ibid., IV, p. 229.
[56]Ll. 400–1; ibid., p. 229.

– to the low world of flattery and ephemeral literature, and the 'rails of Bedlam and Sohoe' at the end. In executing this descent, Pope gives blunt enough un-Horatian warnings as to his real purpose – ' "Praise undeserv'd is scandal in disguise!" '; 'And when I flatter . . .' – so that we may mark the difference between Horace's including Augustus among other Romans who would be embarrassed at an unskilful portrait or inept praise, and Pope's speaking of what was and was not actually deserved. Fraenkel speaks of the end of Horace's poem as 'a steady diminuendo' until the reader is dismissed with a smile;[57] Pope has made of this a moral descent.

The opening lines of Pope's Epistle, to turn finally to what is first and best known in the poem, start at once into equivocation and irony. Without corresponding words in Horace, '. . . open all the Main' alludes to all those moments in Stuart and Cromwellian panegyric which make maritime supremacy a part of a vision of expanding power. It could mean 'give peace to the seas'; it could, in 1737, glance at a Britain which had long neglected its traditional policy of naval strength, and opened the seas to damaging rivalry from other powers. The couplet holds up in contrast the original Augustus, who could without exaggeration be said to rule the lands and seas of the world, and the ruler of Britain, whose government now failed to assert even its own maritime advantage. The irony of the equivocation, in this case, does not rest on the *princeps* having been a benevolent so much as a powerful and efficient ruler. It is an irony relying on contrast. As with the concluding paragraph of the poem, one notices a certain trend to easy overstatement:

> How shall the Muse, from such a Monarch, steal
> An hour, and not defraud the Publick Weal?[58]

Once again the tone departs from the Horatian. Horace is only reluctant to detain the *princeps* from his affairs of state too long; Pope says that even an hour would defraud the public, and at once sounds more exaggerated and unctuous. He also echoes Waller's *Panegyric to My Lord Protector*, thus drawing on the central English tradition of panegyrical comparison with Augustus, and possibly implying a rather unwelcome comparison between George II and Cromwell.[59] A little later, still pursuing Horace's *laudes Caesaris* motif, Pope adds a highly hyperbolical couplet –

> Great Friend of LIBERTY! in *Kings* a Name
> Above all Greek, above all Roman Fame:

which sounds more inflated than Horace's higher praise of the *princeps*:

> Nil oriturum *aliàs*, nil ortum tale *fatentes*[60]

and Pope's rendering: '. . . like whom, to mortal eyes / None e'er has risen, and none e'er shall rise.' (ll. 29-30). Pope is managing to do several things here. He

---

[57]Fraenkel, *Horace*, p. 399.
[58]Ll. 5-6; *Poems*, IV, p. 195.
[59]Ll. 17-18; ibid., IV, p. 195 (and note to ll. 15-16).
[60]Ll. 25-6; ibid., IV, pp. 196-7.

generally recreates the very high praise Horace offers Augustus, as in the line quoted above, while imparting to it a more exaggerated tone. 'Wonder of Kings!' really says no more than some of Horace's lines imply (save that of course Horace never calls the *princeps* a king) but sounds more like high-wrought flattery. Pope must transpose Horace's literal meaning when he says that altars are raised to Augustus even during his lifetime, but his transposition –

> Whose Word is Truth, as sacred and rever'd,
> As Heav'n's own Oracles from Altars heard[61]

is praise so extreme that the reader is forced (and especially after some of the equivocal phrases already remarked) to the conclusion that it cannot be meant at face value. As of course it is not. 'Great Friend of LIBERTY', further, picks up the reservation which Pope has expressed in his Advertisement: he has added to Horace's picture 'one or two of those Virtues which add to the Happiness of a *Free People . . .*' (ll. 7–8).

While not having restructured his original as he had *Sat.* II, i and II, ii, Pope has thus freely deviated from Horace in tone. His un-Horatian irony is directed. Can its exaggerated and hyperbolical idiom be meant to reflect upon Horace's *laudes Caesaris* as well as upon George Augustus, or is it intended to throw into 'bold relief' the salient differences between George Augustus and the original Augustus?[62] One consideration is that satiric irony working through contrast is more sharply effective as well as more amusing than that which works through similarity. It is wittier and more characteristic of Pope to praise George Augustus as an Augustus if the latter represents a positive standard for princes. It is thus made to seem George Augustus's own failing rather than the satirist's overt attack which constitutes the judgement. ' "Praise undeserved is scandal in Disguise" ': the King is condemned by his own nature. It is less striking and amusing if Pope, in seeming to praise George Augustus, praises him as a Nero or a Domitian. That would be approximately the effect if we assumed that Pope considered Augustus to have been, for the purposes of his poem, a monster or masked tyrant. The portrayal of Addison as the Cato of his little senate, in *To Arbuthnot*, would be far less effective if it were supposed that Cato had had the same deficiencies as Addison. That is one argument for the traditional interpretation of the Epistle. Pope, of course, need not necessarily have wanted to take the cleverer and more effective course, but the probability that he did is much strengthened by his willingness, in the public letter to Arbuthnot, to use Augustus as the example of the wise prince prepared to encourage the freedom of the satirist. A further consideration is that Pope's poem not only alludes to Augustus's good intentions to the best poets, but to his ability to recognize them, to his intelligence, and to his political power – all features of the *princeps* which even his detractors would have been hard put to it to deny. Finally, we have seen how Pope's whole style of address, in the body of the poem, presupposes in the person addressed not only intelligence, judgement and a concern with the qualities of civilization, but the known taste of the original

---

[61]Ll. 27–8; ibid., IV, p. 197.
[62]The argument of Weinbrot, *Augustus Caesar in 'Augustan' England*, Ch. 6.

Augustus for the older literature. Pope was not obliged to follow Horace in this respect, and George Augustus was not, after all, *more* interested in 'Christ's Kirk o' the Green' or 'beastly Skelton' than, say, in Addison. Every argument points to the fact that what Pope is doing in the Epistle *To Augustus* is taking a traditional type of the good prince – such a type as could most effectively be used as a weapon against George Augustus – and familiarizing and naturalizing it by means of his easy English manner of discourse. And while Pope's poem is more complicated in its operation than that of Horace, Pope was certainly assisted in his task by the remarkable way in which Horace offers the highest praise to Augustus while yet addressing him in a manner appropriate to one Roman citizen conversing with another. The idiom of the Epistle brings poet and ruler together in one sustained, serious, amusing and familiar act of communication. This is true of both poems. But in Pope's Epistle the false ruler is, at the beginning and end, thrust out of this ideal dialogue into bold relief by the obtrusion of an extravagant and un-Augustan irony.

Ep. I, vi

The version of Horace, *Ep.* I, vi (23 January 1738), the shortest of Pope's pentameter imitations, is addressed to the youngest of all the known addressees of these poems. A poem written to review the diverse goals and satisfactions at which men aim in their lives, it is appropriate to a man successfully launched in his career, but with the greater part of his life ahead of him. This was the situation of William Murray, a Scot of a noble Jacobite family, educated at Westminster School, and now a lawyer of rising fame, as a result of his pleading at the bar of the House of Lords on Scotch appeals. Pope was right to detect exceptional promise in him, for he was to become Solicitor-General, Attorney-General, and a famous Lord Chief Justice (1756–88). On 26 August 1736 the poet wrote that 'He is one of the few people whom no man that knows, can forget, or not esteem.[63] Some fifteen months after the appearance of the poem, Pope included Murray with Lord Cornbury, Lord Polwarth, and some others 'with whom I would never fear to hold out against all the Corruption of the world'.[64] Between these two dates Murray was to play a key rôle in Britain's declaration of war against Spain, and the subsequent fall of Walpole, by representing at the bar of the House of Commons the case of the English merchants molested by the Spaniards. It is entirely reasonable to suppose that different political parties were eager to secure Murray's support, and that Pope's poem was in part designed to win him for the Boy Patriots and the opposition to Walpole.[65] Whether Murray continued a Jacobite sympathizer at this time is an interesting question, and one not entirely irrelevant to Pope's poem. Certainly some time after Pope's death, and the 1745 Rebellion, Murray was accused of Jacobitism in the most explicit terms by Charles Churchill:

> What if to that PRETENDER's foes,
> His greatness, nay, his life, he owes,
> Shall common obligations bind,

---

[63]*Correspondence*, IV, p. 29.
[64]Pope to Swift, 17–19 May 1739; Ibid., IV, p. 178.
[65]John M. Aden, *Something Like Horace*, pp. 69, 74.

And shake his constancy of mind?
Scorning such weak and petty chains,
Faithful to JAMES he still remains,
Tho' he the friend of GEORGE appear . . .[66]

As Pope refashions Horace, the poem familiarly acknowledges its literary status in the opening lines, a translation among other translations, though faithful to the 'Plain Truth' of its original. The literal English translation ' "Not to Admire" ' arrests the attention by its apparent paradox, for the more usual sense of the word was current when Pope wrote.[67] The poem's stress on 'Plain Truth' – morally appropriate no doubt in addressing an orator 'Grac'd. . . . with all the Pow'r of Words' (l. 48) – is wittily underlined by the pun in 'very words', and indeed the opening is full of conscious wordplay. Then Pope launches out in a vein most resembling parts of his *Essay on Man*, dealing with cosmic subjects in a familiar way. This idiom is used to make the early sequence of the poem both more providential and political than Horace. Not feeling fear at the cosmos in Horace, becomes trusting 'the Ruler with his Skies' in Pope, and the verbal bow to God is so phrased as just to remind us of earthly rulers, an effect which is not dispelled by the words 'Stars that rise and fall'.[68] This motif, so delicate at first, is strongly developed as Pope expands on Horace, and by the time he has completed the argument that if it is possible to view the cosmos with philosophic calm it should be possible to resist the allurements of the world, he is writing political satire:

Admire we then what Earth's low entrails hold . . .
Or Popularity, or Stars and Strings?
The Mob's applauses, or the gifts of Kings?
Say with what eyes we ought at Courts to gaze,
And pay the Great our homage of Amaze?[69]

Political satire – but so firmly based on the philosophic view of the opening lines that it is not overtly partisan. All the same, 'homage of Amaze' belongs to the vocabulary of inflated praise at the beginning and end of *To Augustus*. It is hard to say whether the sense of amusement or of moral independence is uppermost in the expression.

An important part of Horace's argument, that deprivation of worldly satisfactions is as much a threat to the thinking self as possession of them, is concisely rendered, and then Pope moves off again in another long expanded section, which asks Murray not to lose his judgement in the pursuit of professional success. This sequence reaches upwards through scenes of worldly activity, and of rejection by a loved one, to the intrinsic merit of Murray

[66]*The Ghost*, ll. 1843–9; *The Poetical Works of Charles Churchill*, ed. Douglas Grant (Oxford, 1956), p. 189; and Aden, *Something Like Horace*, p. 70.
[67]Cf. *To Augustus*, l. 275, and the present poem, l. 41; *Poems*, IV, pp. 219, 239. Dacier comments on the two senses of 'admire' in connection with *Ep*. I, vi – one signifying what Plato called the Mother of Wisdom (*Remarques Critiques*, VIII, pp. 291–2).
[68]L. 6; *Poems*, IV, p. 237. Dacier connects Horace's sentiment with those of Lucretius against the fear of death from superstition (*Remarques Critiques*, VIII, p. 297).
[69]Ll. 11, 14–17; *Poems*, IV, p. 237.

himself, '. . . whom Nature, Learning, Birth, conspir'd / To form, not to admire, but be admir'd' (ll. 40–1 – note here how the two senses of 'admire' are juxtaposed), and thence to the idea of fame, admirable yet transient:

> And what is Fame? the Meanest have their day,
> The Greatest can but blaze, and pass away.
> Grac'd as thou art, with all the Pow'r of Words,
> So known, so honour'd, at the House of Lords;
> Conspicuous Scene! another yet is nigh,
> (More silent far) where Kings and Poets lye;
> Where MURRAY (long enough his Country's pride)
> Shall be no more than TULLY, or than HYDE![70]

In the superb compliment Pope pays his younger friend the trajectory of the long verse-paragraph curves downward; the faint anti-climax on 'House of Lords' (marvellously felicitous if an imperfect rhyme), the Abbey standing nearby, and the famous names of Roman and English history echoing away into silence.

At this point attention should be paid to three of the proper names Pope is using: Tully, Hyde and Cornbury. The comparison of Murray with Cicero is of course a compliment to the former's oratorical genius. Lord Chancellor Clarendon is not so obvious, unless Pope here wished to prophesy the high office to which Murray might attain. There is, however, a contemporary political flavour to these names. Pope had urged his friend Atterbury, the Jacobite leader, to 'Think of Tully, Bacon, and Clarendon' at the time when he faced trial, and probable exile or death. The Jacobite *True Briton* had also made much of the comparison of Atterbury with Cicero.[71] Apart from the general point that each had fallen from power, it may be relevant to note that all three could be regarded as proscribed, that Cicero had exposed and survived conspiracies, and that Clarendon had brought Charles II back from exile at the Restoration. Since Murray was not, like Atterbury, suffering a fall from high office, these latter allusions may be to the point. They would certainly have been welcome to one who, like Pope, had a Jacobite background.[72] There is, however, a further allusion. Pope refers not only to the famous Hyde, Clarendon, but also to his contemporary, Cornbury, great-grandson of Clarendon. And Cornbury was not only a young man noted for his resistance to political corruption but, as we now know, one who had undertaken a mission to the Pretender at Rome in connection with the Jacobite initiatives of 1731. It may seem improbable that Pope was unaware of this bid by a new Hyde to bring about a new Restoration, and end the long proscription of Tories from office.[73]

With Horace's reference to virtue being more than words as a forest is more than firewood (l. 31) Pope follows him off onto a new tack, again giving the

---

[70]Ll. 46–53; ibid., IV, pp. 239–41.

[71]Pope to Atterbury, 20 April 1723; *Correspondence*, II, p. 167. See the poem in *The True Briton*, No. 43 (28 October 1723); *The Life and Writings of Philip Late Duke of Wharton* (London, 1732), II, pp. 380–2. Aden, *Something Like Horace*, p. 70, stresses the links with Cicero.

[72]Ibid., p. 70.

[73]Eveline Cruickshanks, *Political Untouchables: The Tories and the '45* (London, 1979), pp. 12, 4–7.

stark philosophic terms of the Latin a Christian and political flavour. This is done by substituting a church that is more than bricks and stones for Horace's forest, and by alluding to the deist Matthew Tindal, 'Who Virtue and a Church alike disowns' (l. 65). A renegade Roman Catholic, later an extreme Whig and anti-Jacobite pamphleteer, Tindal was one in whose life Pope could reasonably connect a rejection of revealed religion with political timeserving.[74] This paragraph depicts desire uncurbed by religious or moral restraint. It shows the wildness, the absurdity, and finally the terrible restlessness of desire –

Still, still be getting, never, never rest[75]

– with an interesting reference en route to a 'German Prince', 'proud of Pedigree' but 'poor of Purse' (ll. 83–4). The allusion to the amount of the Prince of Wales's income, a current parliamentary issue, reflects back upon the apparent avarice of the court and government to which he was opposed. And now, still displaying the forms of immoderate desire, Pope turns directly, for the first time, to the pursuit of political power. Though he brilliantly expands and naturalizes what he finds in Horace, the essence of what he gives is there in his original, and it is dramatic: not just an allusion but a little scene from contemporary power-seeking. It has a distinct whiff of electioneering, which Pope fully brings out:

> But if to Pow'r and Place your Passion lye,
> If in the Pomp of Life consist the Joy;
> Then hire a Slave, (or if you will, a Lord)
> To do the Honours, and to give the Word;
> Tell at your Levee, as the Crouds approach,
> To whom to nod, whom take into your Coach,
> Whom honour with your hand: to make remarks,
> Who rules in Cornwall, or who rules in Berks;
> 'This may be troublesome, is near the Chair;
> 'That makes three Members, this can chuse a May'r.'
> Instructed thus, you bow, embrace, protest,
> Adopt him Son, or Cozen at the least,
> Then turn about, and laugh at your own Jest. [76]

The poem has already considered genuine fame. In the theatre of the world which the poem sketches, the 'congregated Ball', the shades of Tully and Hyde look down on this little drama of corrupt politics. Again Pope arrests by literalness of translation; Horace's straightforward reference to a slave, like his praise of Augustus, means something different in a different culture, registering here the social absence and moral presence of slavery in eighteenth-century Britain. Of course it is pointed by Pope's added parenthesis, and is one of his most telling images for a corrupt and decadent land, which is to be accorded full imaginative expression in the Epilogue to the Satires and the later *Dunciad*. Pope is unerring in his particular shafts (Cornwall was full of rotten boroughs) and Timon showing off rare editions in his study –

[74] *Poems*, IV, pp. 389–90.
[75] L. 96; ibid., IV, p. 243.
[76] Ll. 97–109; ibid., IV, pp. 243–5.

> To all their dated Backs he turns you round

– has not more immediacy of dramatic life than this great man, as all his instructed gestures of courtesy and kinship are made hollow by his own self-congratulatory laughter. This is not King George;[77] kings do not study electioneering in such detail, nor (of course) could Murray aspire to power and place of that kind. It is rather a corrupt politician maintaining himself in power, modelled, if on any, on Walpole. The last lines of the portrait are gathered into a most effective triplet – which makes 'your own Jest' seem a more superfluous valediction than ever – and it is interesting from the point of view of the architecture of the poem to note that there is a kind of moral symmetry in the distribution of its three triplets (ll. 11–13, 60–62, and 107–9), with the tribute to the youthful and virtuous Cornbury at the centre.

Following the course marked out by Horace, the imitation now plunges downward into animal appetite, 'Circæan Feasts' (l. 122). The political thread is woven in with the allusion to the disgraceful Tory and sometime Jacobite Earl of Kinnoull (ultimately a placeman of Walpole like Tyrawley[78]) and it is possible that ll. 124–5 is partly inspired by the extraordinary libertine career abroad of another Jacobite Pope now disapproved of: the celebrated and brilliant Duke of Wharton.[79] Certainly the life of the uncontrolled libertine is in Pope's focus at the end of his imitation, as the allusion to Rochester shows. The well known passage from *Artemisia in the Town* . . . serves Pope well, for it suggests that only the fragile positive value of love remains to make life worth living. But as an alternative, Pope quotes Swift to suggest that there might be even less: just the *bagatelle*. Each writer, thus briefly evoked, is an example of one who has looked through life and found, or claimed to find, little worth living for. In each case the reductive affirmation is the consequence of having taken the world with a painful seriousness. Pope himself, however, does not stand fully behind these final precepts of the poem. With Horace in so far as he advocates rationality in living (live for whatever you think best in life), he nevertheless adds the saving couplet, to which nothing in Horace corresponds:

> – if this advice appear the worst,
> E'n take the Counsel which I gave you first:[80]

which points the reader back to the earlier parts of the poem. Rochester and Swift, as here cited, hardly express Pope's ultimate ideal, even though they might possibly be thought to represent the amorous reign of Charles II and the laughter-loving reign of Anne. Rather we are meant to recall the meaning of the opening precept: do not let anything lead you to abandon your sense of judgement; and, that having first been understood, our attention is redirected to Cicero and Clarendon, noble examples of patriotism, and to the young Cornbury, who has the secret to be 'blest', 'Virtuous' and 'happy'. In all the calls and pleasures of the world, where the judgement may be paralysed and the

---

[77]As apparently argued by Aden, *Something Like Horace*, pp. 82–3.
[78]Ibid., p. 83.
[79]See Pope's Epistle *To Cobham, On the Characters of Men*, ll. 174–207; *Poems*, III-ii, pp. 28–31.
[80]Ll. 130–1; *Poems*, IV, p. 246.

self overwhelmed, wisdom lies above all in retaining the balance of the mind. Both Pope and Horace insist on this, and it is quite wrong to suggest that Horace's philosophy of detachment is a mere screen for Pope's subtler poetry of commitment. Pope, no doubt, wished to win Murray and his other readers for what he judged to be the cause of true patriotism in his time. It is perfectly true that he develops Horace's poem in a way not only historical and political, but Tory and even possibly crypto-Jacobite. This is, however, a branch from the parent tree. Political commitment cannot be commended unless it comes from independent judgement, and the foundation of such independent judgement is, in brief, 'Not to Admire . . .'.

Ep. I, i

Pope's poem to Henry St John, Viscount Bolingbroke (the version of the First Epistle of Horace's First Book) has been often cited as showing a bolder and deeper hostility to court and government than he had yet expressed, a development that was to culminate in the writing, the following year, of The Epilogue to the Satires.[81] An essay on Pope the political poet can excerpt certain lines from the imitation and show this to be so.[82] Yet this is far from the whole truth that balanced literary criticism must acknowledge. Single-minded focus upon the political defiance of the poem relegates its other aspects to masks of gentility, or passages where Pope is otherwise less than true to himself. In the first place, at least, the poem deserves to be explored as a total work of art.

Though St John had been Pope's regular visitor and companion from his return from exile in 1723, he had withdrawn to France in 1735, and was not at hand to attend on the composition and publication of the poem that is dedicated to him. For the first two years of St John's absence Pope had published no poems; then, as we have seen, the retrospective version of the poem to Florus appeared, to be rapidly followed by the poem *To Mr. Murray*. This second wave of the composition of the *Imitations of Horace* suggests a period of taking stock between 1735 and 1737, and a deliberate and independent return to a kind of poetry which St John had originally suggested to him. The opening paragraph of the poem (though 'S**' did not become 'ST JOHN' until the first revision a few months later) must certainly allude either to his intention to revisit Britain after three years, or to his explicit encouragement of Pope to write further. Like Horace Pope at once acknowledges the rôle of his Maecenas in urging him on to write, as also his own individuality and reluctance. Of course the casting of Lord Bolingbroke as Maecenas was not only an act of striking personal loyalty at a time when this politician was in nobody's good books, the opposition he had helped to create fragmenting and turning against him; it also prompted the question which *To Augustus* had more obviously asked: what are the qualities of Augustus? Can they now be found?

The poem, which is as a whole Pope's answer to Bolingbroke's invitation, is quite as much one of personal wisdom as of political attack. Vice in society and evil at court are indeed assailed, but only as part of a drama of the self which

---

[81] E.g. Weinbrot, *Augustus in 'Augustan' England*, pp. 234, 246.

[82] As I have done in my 'Pope: The Political Poet in His Time', *Eighteenth-Century Studies*, XV, 2 (Winter 1981-2), pp. 123-48.

may in the end be termed tragi-comic. In its concern with the achieving of an equality and harmony of the self this epistle may have more in common with *Ep*. II, ii than with the poem to Murray. It opens and closes with what the poet is, would like to be and should be as a man. This is very much more than a formal frame: the long opening sequence, containing some of the most thoughtfully inflected and pausing verses Pope ever wrote, makes this clear:

> ST. JOHN, whose love indulg'd my labours past
> Matures my present, and shall bound my last!
> Why will you break the Sabbath of my days?
> Now sick alike of Envy and of Praise.
> Publick too long, ah let me hide my Age!
> See modest Cibber now has left the Stage:
> Our Gen'rals now, retir'd to their Estates,
> Hang their old Trophies o'er the Garden gates,
> In Life's cool evening satiate of applause,
> Nor fond of bleeding, ev'n in BRUNSWICK's cause.[83]

The atmosphere of the passage is extraordinary, dignity and affection in the tribute mingling with the sense of exhaustion after achievement, open and indeed emotional appeal ('ah let me hide my Age!') no sooner made than mixed with a shared amusement ('See modest Cibber . . .'), the notion of the Sunday of a single life continued in 'Life's cool evening'. 'Our Gen'rals', supplanting Veianius the gladiator in Horace, lends a very faintly political air to the passage; such trophies were likely to recall the wars of Anne or William but are now as domestic as the garden gates. The pacific policy of Walpole under the not universally admired succession of Brunswick is a criticism no more than hinted. The generals had won their trophies and, more to the point, the poet whose own battles are implicitly compared with theirs has real achievement to his name too. Though it is not in Horace, a deeply and recognizably Augustan note is struck by Pope's words 'Matures my present . . .' – why must his Maecenas urge him to yet further effort when he at least had earned his Augustan peace?

> A Voice there is, that whispers in my ear,
> ('Tis Reason's voice, which sometimes one can hear)
> 'Friend Pope! be prudent, let your Muse take breath,
> 'And never gallop Pegasus to death. . . .[84]

It has been well said that this is 'almost more Horatian than Horace'.[85] Horace does not formally identify the voice though he implies the identity. Pope speaks of 'Reason' and immediately, in 'sometimes', qualifies the claim with exquisitely amusing human self-knowledge: it could hardly be more true to an Horatian spirit.

> But ask not, to what Doctors I apply?
> Sworn to no Master, of no Sect am I:

---

[83]Ll. 1–10; *Poems*, IV, p. 279.
[84]Ll. 11–14; ibid., IV, p. 279.
[85]See Frank Stack, 'Pope's Epistle to Bolingbroke and Epistle I, i' in Howard Erskine-Hill and Anne Smith, eds., *The Art of Alexander Pope*, p. 174.

As drives the storm, at any door I knock,
And house with Montagne now, or now with Lock.
Sometimes a Patriot, active in debate,
Mix with the World, and battle for the State,
Free as young Lyttelton, her cause pursue,
Still true to Virtue, and as warm as true:
Sometimes, with Aristippus, or St. Paul,
Indulge my Candor, and grow all to all;
Back to my native Moderation slide,
And win my way by yielding to the tyde.[86]

Like Horace to Maecenas, Pope candidly confesses his own freedom to St John. The patron-friend is thus candidly reminded of the limits of his influence, and the reader learns this too. If the poet responds to the expected call from his Maecenas, it will be because he chooses to respond. Maecenas encouraged a discriminate endorsement of the new principate. St John as all readers would realize played a very different part in the state: the very equation of the one with the other was a recognition of the very different situations of Rome under Augustus and Britain under George Augustus. What St John wished of the poet was to be 'a Patriot, active in debate': a spirited opponent of 'the present happy establishment'. Because St John did not enjoy in the Britain of that time the position of Maecenas, the relation between Pope and St John could somewhat resemble that between Horace and Maecenas. Pope thus acknowledges resemblance in difference. But he will not be a patriot to order. The rôle is only part of his life, as it is only part of the present larger and more subtle poem. It is because the independent if not necessarily consistent mind of the poet has been so firmly established in the first fifty or sixty lines of the poem that such drastic things can be said in such bold, confident and often humorous ways later on:

Yet every child another song will sing,
'Virtue, brave boys! 'tis Virtue makes a King.'. . . .
And say, to which shall our applause belong,
This new Court jargon, or the good old song?
The modern language of corrupted Peers,
Or what was spoke at CRESSY and POITIERS?[87]

Once again martial heroism resounds in the moral background.

If such a Doctrine, in St. James's air,
Shou'd chance to make the well-drest Rabble stare;
If honest S[chut]z take scandal at a spark,
That less admires the Palace than the Park;
Faith I shall give the answer Reynard gave,
'I cannot like, Dread Sir! your Royal Cave;
'Because I see by all the Tracks about,
'Full many a Beast goes in, but none comes out.'
Adieu to Virtue if you're once a Slave:
Send her to Court, you send her to her Grave.[88]

[86] Ll. 23–34; *Poems*, IV, p. 281.
[87] Ll. 91–2, 97–100; *Poems*, IV, pp. 285–7.
[88] Ll. 112–19; ibid., IV, p. 287.

Pope avails himself of Horace's beast fable, but gives it a very different point. Horace did not turn it against court and *princeps*, but Pope does – writing with an almost contemptuous wit and brevity. The following passage, on the lust for gain, has a cynicism and intensity all Pope's own, and nothing like Horace. At such moments it is entirely right to say that Horace was not a sufficient model for what Pope wanted to do, though his earlier identification with an Horatian idiom and Horatian concerns helps him (by contrast) to make his present attack more telling.

But the tone must lighten again. The poem must return to the self from which it began, and that self cannot be seen candidly without the recognition of inconsistencies and fallings short. The focus thus shifts to the vain and volatile, the aimless energies of society that signify nothing. It is all ridiculous, but Horace and Pope have a trick in hand, for when laughter is actually mentioned it is the laughter of Maecenas–St John at the poet himself, who is only too plainly at one with the world.

> You laugh, half Beau half Sloven if I stand,
> My Wig all powder. . . .'[89]

Cruel – that the man who loves him and who has matured his art should, in that world of fashion and everyday carelessness, mock the outward muddles of his life, and ignore the inner contradictions:

> Careless how ill I with myself agree;
> Kind to my dress, my figure, not to Me.
> Is this my Guide, Philosopher, and Friend?
> This, He who loves me, and who ought to mend?
> Who ought to make me (what he can, or none,)
> That Man divine whom Wisdom calls her own;
> Great without Title, without Fortune bless'd,
> Rich ev'n when plunder'd, honour'd while oppress'd,
> Lov'd without youth, and follow'd without power,
> At home tho' exil'd, free, tho' in the Tower.
> In short, that reas'ning, high, immortal Thing,
> Just less than Jove, and much above a King,
> Nay half in Heav'n – except (what's mighty odd)
> A Fit of Vapours clouds this Demi-god.[90]

Pope here makes a good deal more of his ending than the quick human joke against the Stoics with which Horace finishes his own epistle:

> Ad summam, *Sapiens* uno minor est Jove! Dives!
> Liber! honoratus! pulcher! –
> 　　　　　　　　　　　　– Rex denique regum!
> Præcipue sanus –
> 　　　　　　　　– Nisi cum pituita molesta est.[91]

---

[89]Ll. 161–2; ibid., IV, p. 291. Dacier had stressed the comedy of human inconstency in Horace's epistle (*Remarques Critiques*, VIII, p. 23.)

[90]Ll. 175–88; *Poems*, IV, p. 293.

[91]Ll. 103–6; ibid., IV, p. 292. Dacier commented on the way Horace directed 'raillerie' and 'ridicule' against the Stoics, at the end of the poem (*Remarques Critiques*, VIII, p. 123).

The later poet follows the same anti-climactic contour: here the Man of Reason suffers 'A Fit of Vapours' – wonderful slang of the genteel everyday eighteenth century! – as in Horace the Wise Man is to be envied in everything, except that he still gets 'flu. In Horace the humour lies partly in the speed with which the verse rattles off the incredible advantages of wisdom; Pope extends Horace's analysis of Maecenas's attitude to him into the final summary, greatly magnifies it and makes of it something at once more historical and more personal. More historical and personal, because the marks of the Man of Reason as recited in the lines in apposition to 'me' beginning 'Great without title' could apply so aptly to several of Pope's most admired friends and patrons: men of the calibre that are recalled early in the Epistle *To Arbuthnot*. St John himself could be said to have been followed without power since his return from exile in 1723. Like St John, Pope's admired friend Atterbury suffered exile: unlike St John this was for good. Lord Oxford and Lord Granville – names much honoured in Pope's earlier verse – each spent time in the Tower when under political suspicion. Some of the epithets Pope uses could apply to himself as well as others – 'honour'd while oppress'd' perhaps. Pope's character of the Man of Reason thus has something of an historical and autobiographical cast to it: it seeks to unite him with the noble characteristics of those he has admired. No doubt there is a stronger personal appeal from Pope to St John than there is from Horace to Maecenas, but this is another passage, worthy of Horace, that is subtle in its variety of tone. 'That Man divine whom Wisdom calls her own' can (or could) be straightforward. The build-up of the next four lines may in its panegyrical manner seem to leave the world a little far behind: the next line completely takes off in fluent hyperbole, and with 'Just less' and 'Nay half in Heav'n' the diction makes the warning lights of irony shine more and more brightly. The parenthesis '(what's mighty odd)' blows the truly noble but insubstantial conception away – the brilliantly chosen word 'clouds' reaches after it yet is involved in the 'Vapours' – and we are back in the world of muddle, half-success and headaches.

It is tragi-comedy. What makes it so savingly Horatian (while yet doing things Horace did not do) is the warm self-knowledge that can link Reason and Wisdom with the poem's bitter and brave assault on court and society, an assault which contemporary readers would have certainly supposed was enjoined by St John, but then so disarmingly disclaim the achievement of Reason and Wisdom at the end. Humanly authentic too is the serene early statement of the poet's independence: 'Sworn to no Master, of no Sect am I' compared with the urgent desire at the end that St John should take him and make him into the Wise Man. Yet, surely, the recognition of all this in the 'impartial Glass' of the present poem is the balance of the mind which is also the freedom of the poet. Here, we may think, the deepest demand of Horace and Pope: that they should be given back to themselves –

> So slow th'unprofitable Moments roll,
> That lock up all the Functions of my soul;
> That keep me from Myself . . .[92]

---

[92]Ll. 39–41; *Poems*, IV, p. 281.

– is answered: answered in the unmistakable implication that an active concern with the world can return a man to himself, though not always with dignity. The other side of the poem's dialectic is the establishment of the self in personal and introspective as well as public terms. Relentless attack, long sustained, falls into monotony and in the end fails to carry conviction. As W.J. Courthope once remarked of Marston, 'What can be an easier form of satire than to suppose one's age a seething mass of corruption, and one's self inspired by hatred of villainy to unmask the shows and hypocrisies by which one is surrounded.'[93] Horace helped Pope avoid the temptation of routine attack. Attack Pope did, with a courage and eloquence that, as a matter of record, put him in danger from the state.[94] With Lucilius, Persius, Juvenal and Donne in mind, Pope often mounted from a situation faithfully and feelingly imitated from Horace a challenge to society and its established powers more powerful than Horace ever wrote. That does not make Horace incidental or subordinate in Pope's *Imitations of Horace*. The example of Horace inspired Pope to do something as rewarding and more difficult: to convey a familiarity, intimacy, awareness of the flexible and moving mind, a sense of the detail of place and everyday life, a candid exploration of ethical values, an awareness of some possible accommodation with his own time that at least allowed him to be at home and be himself in a society that often seemed menacing or alien. 'Horace belongs to the company of those whose poetic world is as diverse as it is harmonious, and whose poetic personality while unmistakably present defies easy identification', C.O. Brink has written.[95] Contemporary political experience sometimes led the English Augustans to oversimplify the character and situation of Horace. The Dryden of the 'Discourse Concerning Satire' shows signs of this. Pope has resisted this pressure. Horace allowed Pope to take the whole measure of his life, even its love. This is what is Augustan about *Ep*. I, i and the other *Imitations*.

The Epilogue to the Satires

With the imitation of *Ep*. I, i we come to the end of Pope's *Imitations of Horace* proper. But by 1738 it is probable that he was already giving tentative thought to the arrangement of the *Imitations* as a group, and evidence of this is to be found in the appearance and titles of Pope's two last efforts in the genre of formal satire: *One Thousand Seven Hundred and Thirty Eight. A Dialogue Something like Horace* (May 1738), and *One Thousand Seven Hundred and Thirty Eight. Dialogue II* (July 1738), both designated *Epilogue to the Satires. Written in 1738. Dialogue I* and *Dialogue II* in the revised edition of 1740. In this two-part Epilogue to the Satires the present chapter on Pope's *Imitations* of Horace may find its own epilogue. The subtitle of the first poem '*Something like Horace*' raises the question of their status as Horatian, while the later joint title invites discussion of their place in a wider group of poems.

---

[93]W.J. Courthope, *A History of English Poetry* (London, 1895–1910), III, p. 73.
[94]See nn. 52 and 53 above.
[95]The reader is urged to consult C.O. Brink's wide-ranging discussion of Horace at the end of *Horace on Poetry*, II (Cambridge, 1971), pp. 449–57. He will then wish to read the study of Horace's Epistles to Florus and to Augustus in *Horace on Poetry*, III (Cambridge, 1982).

Something like Horace, the original subtitle of the first but not the second dialogue, demands to be linked with the discussion of Horace between the Poet and the Friend, which seizes our attention early in the poem. It is a passage that has been much discussed as, in recent years, the Epilogue to the Satires has deservedly come to be thought among the most powerful of Pope's poetic achievements.[96] It offers a certain view of Horace, one markedly in keeping with a Tacitean view of Augustus extended to include the poets of that age:

> But *Horace*, Sir, was delicate, was nice;
> *Bubo* observes, he lash'd no sort of *Vice*:
> *Horace* would say, *Sir* Billy *serv'd the Crown*,
> Blunt *could do Bus'ness*, H[u]ggins *knew the Town*,
> In *Sappho* touch the *Failing of the Sex*,
> In rev'rend Bishops note some *small Neglects*,
> And own, the *Spaniard* did a *waggish thing*,
> Who cropt our Ears, and sent them to the King.
> His sly, polite, insinuating stile
> Could please at Court, and make AUGUSTUS smile:
> An artful Manager, that crept between
> His Friend and Shame, and was a kind of *Screen*.
> But 'faith your Friends will very soon be sore;
> *Patriots* there are, who wish you'd jest no more –[97]

First, this account of Horace is not the fantasy of the 'Friend' but a view for which, on one occasion at least, Horace's own precepts lend support, and which Pope probably took from Dryden's 'Discourse Concerning Satire' where the older poet also drew on Tacitus's view of Augustus.[98] Secondly, Pope does not give this account of Horace in his own person but puts it into the mouth of the pusillanimous and time-serving 'Friend' whose opinions in the poem he seeks to refute and ridicule almost all down the line. Bubo's judgement of Horace does not inspire confidence, and that of Juvenal might be preferred when, denouncing the corruptions of Rome, he said: 'Such Villanies rous'd *Horace* into Wrath.'[99] Pope calls our attention, in a footnote, to the passage from Persius, I upon which ll. 21–2 are modelled. If we turn to this, and to Dryden's version which Pope also used, we find that Horace is not there condemned as time-serving and servile, but appreciated for the subtlety of his means. Dryden's version distinguishes Horace only in 'method' from the old fearless Lucilius who 'lash'd the City'.[100] What then is Pope's intention here? He cannot be said to endorse the 'Friend's' view. But neither, as it happens, does he refute it, though he rejects all the other opinions and advice of the 'Friend'. This image of Horace is meant to stand in Pope's Dialogue as a warning. Neither endorsed nor rejected, it serves to show how in corrupt times Horace could be read superficially and easily traduced. Look again at the passage. It has a Horatian subtlety in

[96]Maynard Mack, *The Garden and the City: Retirement and Politics in the Later Poetry of Pope, 1731–1743* (London, 1969), pp. 221–3; Aden, *Something Like Horace*, pp. 19–26; Weinbrot, *Augustus in 'Augustan' England*, pp. 137–41.

[97]Ll. 11–24; *Poems*, IV, pp. 298–9.

[98]Cf. Horace, *Sat*. I, iii, 49–54. Dryden, Discourse, ll. 1988–2075; *Poems*, II, pp. 651–3.

[99]Juvenal, I, 78 in Dryden's version; Dryden, *Poems*, II, p. 673.

[100]Ibid., II, p. 748.

itself: how mordant is its touch! Horace in Dryden's Persius 'Laugh'd at his Friend, and look'd him in the Face'. Pope says (talking of Walpole in the present Dialogue):

> Come, come, at all I laugh He laughs no doubt,
> The only diff'rence is, I dare laugh out.[101]

But laughter and the mordant touch are no longer enough. This passage from Dialogue I does not constitute a moral or political condemnation of the Augustan poet Pope has so often imitated; it does suggest that Horace is no longer an adequate model for the kind of poetry Pope now felt he must write. If Horace was able to draw closer to the principate as time went on, Pope, by contrast, registers a greater sense of estrangement from court, government and indeed the whole national scene. A further sign of estrangement from an Augustan stance is his comment on Virgil: 'To *Cato*, *Virgil* pay'd one honest line' (Dialogue II, l. 120); while, as Malcolm Kelsall points out, complete alienation from his age seems to be expressed by his playing *ultimus Romanorum* – Brutus or Cato – at the end of the same poem.[102] What the 'Friend' makes of Horace is a way of acknowledging this difference of situation, and of warning the reader to expect new poetic developments.

And what the reader finds is a genuine development from the *Imitations of Horace* rather than a rejection and wholly new start. Those places in the *Imitations* where Pope seemed to press Horace towards Juvenal, or where the tones of John Donne, Dean of St Paul's, as an English Lucilius, could be blended with the Augustan satirist, or where in general and subtle ways Pope's Christian sensibility entered into his recreations of his classical original, all now release a further power and intensity in the *Epilogue to the Satires*. Pope no longer chooses a specific Horatian text to follow. Neither does he follow a text of Juvenal or Persius, though his handling of satiric dialogue is close to Persius. He is thus free in the sense that he was in *To Arbuthnot* and that freedom retains a very great deal that is still Horatian in manner and art. The peculiar aesthetic achievement of the Epilogue to the Satires may well seem Pope's development of what is virtually a drama between Horatian and Juvenalian, or, better perhaps, between the man of the world and the 'Priestess Muse'. The extraordinary density of social reference, which the example of Horace seems to have encouraged in Pope, is still present: writer and reader alike seem entangled and entrapped in the social web, the verse twisting and turning amidst a hundred instances, specific or typical. There is much local Horatian wit, much plain speech too –

> Ev'n *Peter* trembles only for his Ears.
>   *Fr*. What always *Peter*? *Peter* thinks you mad,
> You make men desp'rate if they once are bad:
> Else might he take to Virtue some years hence –

---

[101]Ll. 35–6; Poems, IV, p. 300.
[102]Malcolm Kelsall, 'Augustus and Pope', *Huntington Library Quarterly*, XXXIX, 2 (February 1976), pp. 127–30. His whole discussion is of great interest.

P. As S[elkir]k, if he lives, will love the PRINCE.
Fr. Strange spleen to *Selkirk*!

                              P. Do I wrong the Man?
God knows, I praise a Courtier where I can.[103]

– but each of the Dialogues seems to be reaching for a period of releasing eloquence, such as the 'arm'd for *Virtue*' passage in the version of *Sat*. II, i, or for a commanding prospect from which to see as a whole and to transcend the condition of the nation. The tension of these two Dialogues is not like that of *Sat*. II, i and *To Arbuthnot*, something which finds release early in the second half of the poem, so as to allow for a concluding jest, or a long devoted *diminuendo*. Rather it builds up in anger, disgust and fear, through a series of possible releases which only lead down again into the thickets of society, to achieve, with maximum drama, a highly un-Horatian release and transcendence deferred to the very end. This is the rôle of the superb Juvenalian prospect of a corrupted Britain at the end of Dialogue I. And this is the rôle of the extraordinary late crescendo of Dialogue II, which is sacred, rather than secular and historical as in Dialogue I. It is a vision of the last things, in which the truth-telling poet, fame-bearer through a darkening world, is vindicated by Heaven whose 'whole Chorus' only just seems to outsing the howl of Envy, whose incense only just seems to overwhelm the flattery of society. It is in these ways that the Epilogue to the Satires may be described by the subtitle of Dialogue I: 'Something like Horace'.

It will be right to add a word about the arrangement of Pope's *Imitations of Horace*. We have followed the poems here in the order of composition, but it is by no means clear that Pope, at the end of his life, wished them to be read in this order. In the case of the four *Epistles to Several Persons* (*To Cobham*, *To A Lady*, *To Bathurst*, *To Burlington*) which Pope took from a larger group of epistles and published together at the end of his life, it can be shown that he wanted them to be read in a non-chronological order.[104] With the *Imitations of Horace* we run up against the problem of how far Pope's first editor, Warburton, preserved in the complete 1751 Edition of the *Works* the latest wishes of the poet. What Warburton did was to print all the imitations proper, not in chronological but formal order: that in which they are to be found first in the Satires and then the Epistles of Horace. The rationale of such an arrangement would have suggested that the two imitations of Donne should be brought together, in their formal order, after the Horatian imitations, and this is what Warburton did. The two Dialogues written in 1738 were printed at the end as an *Epilogue to the Satires*. The Epistle *To Dr. Arbuthnot* opened the volume, with the new subtitle: 'Being the Prologue to the Satires'. It was also designated 'An Apology for himself and his Writings'. Warburton devoted a whole volume to this group of Pope's poems, which is notable for certain exclusions and inclusions. Warburton did not include, either in this or in any volume of the *Works*, the version of *Sat*. I, ii: *The Sober Advice from Horace*. The imitation of the *Ode to Venus*, and the two imitations in octosyllabic verse, *Sat*. II, vi and *Ep*. I, vii, were printed not in the volume containing the major Imitations but in the

---

[103]Ll. 57–63; *Poems*, IV, pp. 315–16.
[104]See Pope to Swift, 16 February 1732/33; *Correspondence*, III, p. 348.

volume of *Minor Poems*. But Warburton did include with the major Imitations Thomas Parnell's version of Donne's *Satyre III*, and he appended, as an envoy to the whole volume, Pope's lovely occasional poem *On receiving from the Right Hon. the Lady Frances Shirley a Standish and Two Pens*, which is surely a comment on the Epilogue to the Satires. While he retained 'Imitations of Horace' as running title of the six Imitations Warburton designated the whole volume: *Satires*, thus specifying the reference of 'Epilogue to the Satires' and 'Prologue to the Satires'.

Pope may have sanctioned these arrangements but we cannot prove it. We can only ask whether any features of the volume can be traced to Pope's known decisions or probable wishes. One of them can. As already noted, the collective title of the two 1738 Dialogues appeared in Pope's lifetime in the 1740 edition of his *Works*. Whether the term 'Satires' did not carry for Pope some reference to work earlier than the *Imitations of Horace* is hard to say, but its chief reference is likely to be to them. The *Epilogue* is most appropriately an epilogue to *them* because it reconsiders Horace as a model for formal satire. If Pope thus envisaged a sequence of satirical Horatian imitations concluded by an Epilogue, it is a fair hypothesis that he planned a Prologue too. We know that Warburton added the subtitle 'being the Prologue to the Satires' to *To Arbuthnot* at the last minute.[105] But the placing of *To Arbuthnot* at the head of the sequence was not done at the last minute, and both the new rôle and subtitle of this epistle seem in keeping with the nature of all the poems involved and with Pope's probable wish. As an astonishing blend of Christian and classical, of Horatian and Juvenalian satire, *To Arbuthnot*, written during the period of the *Imitations of Horace*, is a marvellous opening of the sequence. As for Warburton's other decisions, the exclusion of *Sober Advice . . . Imitated in the Manner of Mr. Pope*, which had never been formally acknowledged, may have been what Pope wished. Of the exclusion from the volume of the *Ode to Venus* and of the Swiftian imitations nothing can be said. The inclusion of Parnell's version of Donne's *Satyre III* was probably unwarranted.

It seems likely that at the end of his life Pope had begun to think about his *Imitations* of Horace as a group, to consider them as 'The Satires' (thus allowing the inclusion of his two versions of Donne to look more consistent), and to ponder the idea of giving a certain shape to the sequence. The formal order had some advantages for him over the chronological. It observed a certain principle of alternation and combination evident in some of the poems themselves, and in epistles such as *To Burlington* and *To Bathurst*.[106] The predominantly public *Sat.* II, i (*To Fortescue*) is succeeded by the much more domestic *Sat.* II, ii (*To Bethel*), and this by *Ep.* I, i (*To St. John*) which in its blend of personal and public is also, in a sense, more philosophical. *Ep.* I, vi (*To Murray*) is again largely public, while *Ep.* II, i (*To Augustus*), in its blend of political with literary critical, offers a quite new combination. *Ep.* II, ii (*To Colonel –*) is personal, retrospective and historical, introducing the experience of being a papist poet in Pope's time, a theme picked up by the two succeeding versions of Donne. The placing of these at the end of the sequence of imitations proper has the merit of displaying a Christian succession in thé tradition of Horace, which in turn has

[105]See John Butt's summary of the evidence, *Poems*, IV, pp. 93–4.
[106]See my *Social Milieu of Alexander Pope,* pp. 294–309.

implications for what Pope does in *To Arbuthnot* and the *Epilogue to the Satires*. The sequence as thus envisaged is bounded by three poems in which Pope asserts his own character as man, poet and satirist with particular force. It is in these poems that we are most aware of the embattled satirist, and only after we have penetrated these strong and splendid outworks, do we see the poet in a more free and intimate setting. It is as if Pope has presented us with the anatomy of himself, his defiant and heroic aspect facing outward upon the world, his more subtly personal and familiar qualities more fully expressed by the poems of the inner sequence of the group.[107]

In Pope's *Imitations of Horace* we have a poetic text which brings more to the recreation of a text of Augustan Rome than any other work in English literature.

[107]A point I first suggested in my edition *Pope: Horatian Satires and Epistles* (Oxford, 1964), p. 19. It was there too that I first attempted a sketch of the delicate relationships between the modes of Horace, Lucilius, Juvenal and Persius, in Pope's *Imitations of Horace*, which I have now explored more fully.

Epilogue

Flux and Reflux

> There shall be sung another golden Age,
>   The Rise of Empire and of Arts,
> The Good and Great inspiring epic Rage
>   The wisest Heads and noblest Hearts.
>
> Not such as *Europe* breeds in her decay;
>   Such as she bred when fresh and young
> When heav'nly flame did animate her Clay,
>   By future Poets shall be sung.
>
> Westward the Course of Empire takes its Way,
>   The four first Acts already past.
> A fifth shall close the Drama with the Day;
>   Time's noblest Offspring is the last.
>
> (George Berkeley, *Verses on the Prospect of
> Planting Arts and Learning in America* – February
> 1726)

'Virtue is now no Treason, nor no man wisheth the Reign of Augustus, nor speaketh of the first Times of Tiberius', said the Speaker of the House of Commons to James I in 1604. Waller, in his poem *On St. James's Park*, saw Charles II ruminating 'Of rising kingdoms, and of falling states', his vision of the ebb and flow of political fortune just suggesting a Bodinian perspective in which republics must expect to be supplanted by monarchies. Each of these tributes conveys intimations of political mortality, however, and in the eighteenth century many writers wrote of Augustus and 'Augustan' with a sense of decline and fall very much in mind. As Shaftesbury put it in his *Characteristics*, just when the arts had come to their perfection in Rome the failure of liberty began their decay.[1]

Pope's *Dunciad*, which received into its ironical synthesis many of the pane-gyrical gestures – 'This, this is he . . .!' – associated with the acclaiming of a new Augustan Age, is if anything more memorable for its historical prospects of a falling empire and failing civilizations:

> Lo! where Mæotis sleeps, and hardly flows
> The freezing Tanais thro' a waste of snows,

---

[1] Shaftesbury, *Characteristics of Men, Manners, Opinions, Times* (2nd edn, 1714), I, pp. 219–22.

The North by myriads pours her mighty sons,
Great nurse of Goths, of Alans, and of Huns!
See Alaric's stern port! the martial frame
Of Genseric! and Attila's dread name!
See the bold Ostrogoths on Latium fall;
See the fierce Visigoths on Spain and Gaul!
See, where the morning gilds the palmy shore
(The soil that arts and infant letters bore)
His conqu'ring tribes th'Arabian prophet draws,
And saving Ignorance enthrones by Laws.
See Christians, Jews, one heavy sabbath keep,
And all the western world believe and sleep.[2]

Bolingbroke's writings in the 1730s, calling for a revival of Patriotism and *virtù*, also had the effect of making men think about irreversible decline. 'It may be said, that governments have their periods, like all things human; that they may be brought back to their primitive principles during a certain time, but that when these principles are worn out in the minds of men, it is a vain enterprise to endeavour to renew them . . .'.[3] Such fears lay behind *The Dunciad*. It is also probable that they compelled the imagination far backward and forward in time, so that the real and alleged ills of the present age could be seen in a longer and loftier perspective. This was the rationale of Pope's *Brutus* project, which was to have drawn on Geoffrey of Monmouth's *Historia Regum Brittanicae*, to trace the original 'Imperial Works' of Britain. By drawing perspectives longer even than those of *The Dunciad*, Pope sought to show the creative as well as destructive periods in the pattern of history, and from them regenerate a faith in providence and the positive values of civilization by which men should live. The creative endeavour of this Brutus, the mythological founder of Britain, began with his learning wisdom from Egypt and from the court of Evander in Italy, proceeded with his gathering together the dispersed descendants of the Trojan exiles, and ended with his liberation of the native British from superstition and tyranny to implant a new civilization. Pope's introduction to the plan of his blank verse epic on *Brutus* may be seen as a stage or two beyond the political thought of the Epilogue to the Satires:

How came the Arts & Civility he [Brutus] introduced into Britain to be lost again?

A Prophecy delivered to him by an Old Druid that the Britons should Degenerate in an age or Two, and Relapse into a degree of Barbarism, but that they shou'd be Redeemd again by a Descendant of his Family out of Italy, Iulius Caesar, under whose successors they shou'd be Repolish'd, and that the Love of Liberty he had introduced, the Martial spirit, and other Moral Virtues shoud never be lost. With observations upon the Impossibility of any Institution being Perpetual and without some Changes.[4]

The same capacity to think in terms of a pattern of civilizations, though with a

[2]*The Dunciad* (1743), III, ll. 87–100; *Poems*, V, p. 324. The passage was the same in substance in 1729.
[3]*A Letter on the Spirit of Patriotism* (1736); *The Works of Henry St. John Viscount Bolingbroke* (London, 1754), III, p. 16.
[4]BL MS Egerton 1950, f. 4 (1st column).

very different feeling and purpose, may be seen in Joseph Warton. In his *Essay on the Life and Genius of Pope*, where he also defined his idea of an Augustan Age, Warton specified the 'five ages of the world, in which the human mind has exerted itself in an extraordinary manner; and in which its productions in literature and the fine arts have arrived at a perfection, not equalled in other periods'. The first age was the age of Philip and Alexander; the second that of Ptolemy Philadelphus in Egypt; the third that of Julius Caesar and Augustus; the fourth that of Popes Julius II and Leo X; and the fifth that of Louis XIV in France, and King William and Queen Anne in England.[5] From what we have seen before of Warton's discussion it is plain that he is thinking of a pattern of Augustan Ages.

On 24 November 1774, Horace Walpole brought together the two features of Warton's discussion which we have noticed, using the idea of an Augustan Age to acknowledge the failure of his own time while thinking half humorously of the possibility of new Augustan ages across the Atlantic and in future periods of the world. In a letter to Sir Horace Mann which is of extraordinary interest for its allusion to recent political events, to archaeological investigation, and to Horace, Voltaire and Rousseau, Walpole begins with a mention of the General Congress in America, and then turns to the new developments in France:

> The old French Parliament is restored with great éclat. Monsieur de Maurepas, author of the revolution, was received one night at the opera with boundless shouts of applause. It is even said that the mob intended, when the King should go to hold the *lit de justice*, to draw his coach. How singular it would be if Wilkes's case should be copied for a King of France! Do you think Rousseau was in the right, when he said that he could tell what would be the manners of any capital city, from certain given lights? I don't know what he may do on Constantinople and Pekin – but Paris and London! I don't believe Voltaire likes these changes; I have seen nothing of his writing for many months: not even on the poisoning Jesuits! For our part, I repeat it, we shall contribute nothing to the *histoire des moeurs*, not for want of materials, but for want of writers. We have comedies without novelty, gross satires without stings, metaphysical eloquence, and antiquarians that discover nothing.

> *Boetum in crasso jurares aere natos*!

> Don't tell me I am grown old and peevish and supercilious – name the geniuses of 1774, and I submit. The next Augustan age will dawn on the other side of the Atlantic. There will perhaps be a Thucydides at Boston, a Xenophon at New York, and, in time, a Virgil at Mexico, and a Newton at Peru. At last some curious traveller from Lima will visit England and give a description of the ruins of St Paul's, like the editions of Balbec and Palmyra – but am I not prophesying contrary to my consummate prudence, and casting horoscopes of empires like Rousseau? Yes; well, I will go and dream of my visions.[6]

Before he closes his letter Walpole refers to 'the rebellion of the Province of Massachusetts'. Plenty of change but no geniuses is Walpole's complaint. Archaeological finds and stirring events on both sides of the Atlantic combine to produce a relativistic vision of empires. Like the philosopher Berkeley's poem on his project to found a university in the Bermudas, Walpole envisions a new era of civilization across the Atlantic. Like Pope he sees the new world launch

[5]Joseph Warton, *An Essay on the Genius and Writings of Pope* (3rd edn, 1772), I, p. 190–2.
[6]*The Yale Edition of Horace Walpole's Correspondence*, ed. W.H. Lewis, XXIV (Oxford, 1967), pp. 61–2.

forth to seek the old: an old world not in maturity but ruin. It is possible that the 'rebellion of the Province of Massachusetts' prompts him to cast horoscopes of empires in this way. Certainly, after the Seven Years War, well described as the First World War,[7] and during the coming century which was to see such dramatic expansion of the European powers into all regions of the world, this relativistic vision of empires was to prove a way of thinking about history that was both chastising and inspiring.

It was not confined to poetry and *belles lettres*. Ideas so important as this usually penetrate the transactions of government. As James I had been hailed in Parliament as an Augustus, it was in Parliament, speaking on 2 April 1792 in support of Wilberforce's motion for the abolition of the slave trade, that William Pitt the Younger drew on a relativistic view of empire similar to that of Horace Walpole. What is more, the idea of ancient Britain was as important to Pitt's speech as it had been to Pope's *Brutus* project. Challenging the opinion that Providence never intended Africa 'to rise above a state of barbarism; that Providence has irrevocably doomed her to be only a nursery for slaves, for us free and civilized Europeans,' Pitt continued:

> Allow of this principle, as applied to Africa, and I should be glad to know why it might not also have been applied to ancient and uncivilized Britain. Why might not some Roman senator, reasoning on the principles of some hon. gentlemen, and pointing to British barbarians, have predicted with equal boldness, 'There is a people that will never rise to civilization; there is a people destined never to be free; a people without the understanding necessary for the attainment of useful arts; depressed by the hand of nature below the level of the human species; and created to form a supply of slaves for the rest of the world.' . . . .we have almost forgotten that we were once barbarians; we are now raised to a situation which exhibits a striking contrast to every circumstance, by which a Roman might have characterized us, and by which we now characterize Africa. . . . had other nations applied to Great Britain the reasoning which some of the senators of this very island now apply to Africa, ages might have passed without our emerging from barbarism; and we, who are enjoying the blessings of a British civilization, of British laws, and British liberty, might at this hour, have been little superior, either in morals, in knowledge, or refinement, to the rude inhabitants of the coast of Guinea.[8]

The rhetorical thrust of Pitt's argument doubtless has the effect of over-idealizing Rome, but the idea of Rome, as so often before, has prompted crucial insights into the movements of history.

It is always suspicious if a new century seems to establish a new cultural character. In such cases the craving for periodization has probably falsified the historical experience. And if the end of the eighteenth and beginning of the nine-teenth centuries were marked by major continental wars and political events of an unprecedented kind, which in many ways really did change the aspect of things, it was not these which put an end to literature on the model of Virgil and Horace. Indeed it is not clear that major literature of this kind did come to an end. The eighteenth century itself had been too civilian to sustain even Virgilian epic; mock-epic had been largely played out by the later eighteenth century,

---

[7]Paul M. Kennedy, *The Rise and Fall of British Naval Mastery* (London, 1976), p. 98.
[8]*Cobbett's Parliamentary History of England*, (London, 1806-20), XXIX, cc. 1155-6.

while nothing had been produced to match the literary imitation as practised by Pope and Johnson. Taste was changing restlessly, well ahead of the great political events of the times. Yet in several ways the legacy of an admiration for the Augustan Age lived on in nineteenth-century culture in modified and diffused forms. There is first of all the notable case of Byron, whose *Hints from Horace* and *English Bards and Scotch Reviewers* certainly draw on the miscellaneous Horatian *sermo* on literary subjects, and whose *Vision of Judgement* relates to and extends the eighteenth-century and late seventeenth-century mock-epic. There is a real sense in which *A Vision of Judgement* releases an evident comic resource of this form to relegate monarchy – the 'poor Kings' of Hume's 1760 letter – into unimportance. The laughter of Byron's poem may be thought to be directed against a restored *ancien régime* as well as against Southey's panegyrical poem on the death of George III. Byron's masterpiece, *Don Juan* itself, with its volatile blend of grave and gay, its capacity to dismiss with a laugh, and its idiom of spontaneous self-portrayal, may be thought to have taken more than a hint from Horace.

At the same time eighteenth-century Georgic poetry, which Dr. Michael Meehan has well designated as a moderating influence in the eighteenth-century debate for and against the Augustan Age,[9] developed so as to help shape much 'Romantic' poetry of landscape. Wordsworth's *Tintern Abbey* and *The Prelude*, place-poetry on a small and on a large scale, view human life and destiny in the matrix of nature. Nor does the Georgic tradition affect only poetry; its influence is seen strongly in the work of Constable and other painters of rural life and labour. Again, the architectural heritage, descending from Vitruvius, Palladio and Inigo Jones – all celebrated together in Pope's Epistle *To Burlington* and continued by among others Burlington himself – was finally diffused into a mode of urban and rural architecture which spread throughout the country and is everywhere visible and graceful to this day. The Georgic landscape and the 'Georgian' house thus became characteristic features of English life.

Study of the Augustan Age of Rome, on the other hand, now took place in a developing academic scholarship increasingly occluded from the major trends of nineteenth-century life and thought. The experience of empire, it may be, now swelled beyond the point where the drawing of Roman parallels to understand the nature of history was an interesting and attractive task. For the moment (we may speculate) the immediate and immersing experience of expanding world empire actually made the great classical precedent of Rome seem more rather than less remote. The plotting of the rise and fall of states, the casting of the horoscopes of empires in the manner of Horace Walpole, is nevertheless to be found in the new century, among others in Macaulay, Melville and Conrad, and is the theme of the final pages of this book. It is significant, perhaps, that it was not modern empire but the institution of the Papacy which prompted Macaulay to cast his horoscope, while the national origins of Melville and Conrad may possibly have given them that measure of inner detachment from imperial experience now necessary to afford a relativistic view and, in the

---

[9]See Michael Meehan's notable review article of Weinbrot's *Augustus Caesar in 'Augustan' England*: 'The Waning of the Augustan Age', *Southern Review*, XII, 3 (November 1979), pp. 294–5.

case of Conrad, to deploy a Roman parallel to understand the processes of history more fully.

At all events the Augustan idea, whether as ideal or warning, may now seem to have been subsumed once again in the general idea of empire, of which Rome itself was no more than a part. The ruins of London and the movement of peoples, flux and reflux, were the ideas that laid hold of the imagination in three final literary examples. Macaulay, reviewing Von Ranke's *History of the Popes* in 1840, stressed the Roman Catholic Church's power of survival, and using a figure almost the same as that used by Horace Walpole, speculated whether she would not 'still exist in undiminished vigour when some traveller from New Zealand shall, in the midst of a vast solitude, take his stand on a broken arch of London Bridge to sketch the ruins of St Paul's'.[10] In Macaulay's essay this chastising scene was opposed to notions of general progress in the world, and to the idea that such progress would be bound to favour Protestantism against Roman Catholicism. Responding to its subject, Macaulay's essay shows the same wide-ranging vision of history we have noted in Horace Walpole and Pitt: it is a view that can look beyond the latest and most obvious developments. Nine years later a writer from that side of the Atlantic on which Horace Walpole had predicted, in his 'horoscopes of empires', 'the next Augustan age', drew his romantic and discursive fiction to an end through a political allegory in which the United States and Great Britain, Europe and America can with other countries plainly be recognized. In the same chapter of Melville's *Mardi* which acknowledges the institution of slavery in the great and free continent of Kolumbo, America 'last sought last found', the philosopher Babbalanja predicts the ebb and flow of peoples and the rise and fall of states:

. . . what Vivenza [the United States] now is, Kanneeda [Canada] soon must be . . . The thing must come. Vain for Dominora [Britain] to claim allegiance from all the progeny she spawns. As well might the old patriarch of the flood reappear, and claim the right of rule over all mankind as descended from the loins of his three roving sons.

' 'Tis the old law – the East peoples the West, the West the East; flux and reflux. And time may come, after the rise and fall of nations yet unborn, that, risen from its future ashes, Porpheero [Europe] shall be the promised land, and from her surplus hordes Kolumbo people it.'[11]

And the new World launch forth to seek the Old[12] – once again.

In a later chapter it is prophesied specifically that 'The eagle of Romara revives in your own [America's] mountain bird and once more is plumed for her flight.[13]

As the idea of an old and new Augustan Age gave birth to works of art, so this broader view of the rise and fall of empire and the migration of peoples was to shape some major fiction of the nineteenth century. Melville's own *Benito*

[10]*The Complete Works of Lord Macaulay: Essays and Biographies*, III (London, 1897), p. 288. See Anthony Trollope's interesting expansion of the idea in his *The New Zealander*, ed. N. John Hall (Oxford, 1972), pp. 3–6. *The New Zealander* was completed in 1856.

[11]*Mardi and A Voyage Thither*, ed. Harrison Hayford, Hershel Parker and G. Thomas Tanselle (Evanston and Chicago, 1970), Ch. 157, p. 512.

[12]Pope, *Windsor Forest*, l. 402; *Poems*, I, p. 191.

[13]Ch. 161; ed. cit. p. 527.

Cereno (1855), with its encounter between representatives of a new American republic, an old European empire, and an enslaved people blindly seeking a return east to their native continent, might have been born out of Chapter 157 of *Mardi*. '*Follow your leader*'! That legend, chalked by the mutinous slaves beneath the figurehead of the old Spanish ship: the figurehead which had been 'the image of Christopher Colon, the discoverer of the New World' but was now the skeleton of the Spanish gentleman and slave-owner, Don Alexandro Aranda, poses the moral question invited by a broader vision of human history, in which empire and the memory of a civilization grown to maturity can no longer be accepted as ends in themselves. What are the ends aimed at? What are the motives of action? Is the real leader hope, slavery or death? In his speech for the abolition of the slave trade, Pitt the Younger had spoken confidently of the light of civilization, laws, liberty, morals, knowledge and refinement, and imputed to Rome the same values he now urged Britain to adopt towards Africa. For him those were the values that should lead. Britain did abolish the slave trade. In October 1892 the explorer Stanley, on being given the freedom of the town of Swansea, quoted from Pitt's speech, including most of the sentences cited above. This was in turn published in *The Times* on 4 October that year. In one of many valuable suggestions as to the origins of Conrad's fiction, Norman Sherry has pointed out how this speech, with its relativistic vision of empire, appears to have shaped the brilliant opening scene of *Heart of Darkness*, written by 1899 though not published until 1902:

The sea-reach of the Thames stretched before us like the beginning of an interminable waterway. In the offing the sea and the sky were welded together without a joint, and in the luminous space the tanned sails of the barges drifting up with the tide seemed to stand still in red clusters of canvas sharply peaked, with gleams of varnished spirits. A haze rested on the low shores that ran out to sea in vanishing flatness. The air was dark above Gravesend, and farther back still seemed condensed into a mournful gloom, brooding motionless over the biggest, and the greatest, town on earth. . . .

Forthwith a change came over the waters, and the serenity became less brilliant but more profound. The old river in its broad reach rested unruffled at the decline of day, after ages of good service done to the race that peopled its banks, spread out in the tranquil dignity of a waterway leading to the uttermost ends of the earth. We looked at the venerable stream not in the vivid flush of a short day that comes and departs for ever, but in the august light of abiding memories. . . . The tidal current runs to and fro in its unceasing service, crowded with memories of men and ships it had borne to the rest of home or to the battles of the sea. . . . It had borne all the ships whose names are like jewels flashing in the night of time, from the *Golden Hind* returning with her round flanks full of treasure, to be visited by the Queen's Highness and thus pass out of the gigantic tale, to the *Erebus* and *Terror*, bound on other conquests – and that never returned. It had known the ships and the men. They had sailed from Deptford, from Greenwich, from Erith – the adventurers and the settlers; kings' ships and the ships of men on 'Change; captains, admirals, the dark 'interlopers' of the Eastern trade, and the commissioned 'generals' of the East India fleets. Hunters for gold or pursuers of fame, they all had gone out on that stream, bearing the sword, and often the torch, messengers of the might within the land, bearers of a spark from the sacred fire. What greatness had not floated on the ebb of that river into the mystery of an unknown earth! . . . The dreams of men, the seed of commonwealths, the germs of empires. . . . .

It is the storyteller Marlow who makes the switch of perspective that was the crux of Pitt's argument:

> 'And this also,' said Marlow suddenly, 'has been one of the dark places of the earth.'
>
> '. . . . darkness was here yesterday. Imagine the feelings of a commander of a fine – what d'ye call 'em, trireme in the Mediterranean, ordered suddenly to the north; run overland across the Gauls in a hurry; put in charge of one of these craft the legionaries. . . . used to build. . . . Imagine him here – the very end of the world, a sea the colour of lead, a sky the colour of smoke, a kind of ship about as rigid as a concertina – and going up this river with stores, or orders, or what you like. Sand-banks, marshes, forests, savages, precious little to eat fit for a civilised man, nothing but Thames water to drink. . . . Here and there a military camp lost in a wilderness. . . .'[14]

Conrad's Thames differs from the personified Thames of Jonson's 1604 Entry, and of Pope's *Windsor Forest* not only in the artistic convention through which it is portrayed – seascape in an originally Dutch tradition (the tanned sails of the barges) replacing an allegorical idiom. It differs also because Conrad's purpose is not just to contrast the past and present of the great river. As Africa is now, Pitt had argued, Britain was then. And as Britain and the Thames were then, so the fiction of *Heart of Darkness* suggests, Africa and the Congo are now. Once again a Roman parallel is proposed as a way of understanding the present, but while barbarism and civilization were always implicitly involved in earlier comparisons with Rome, a received idea 'that the world is constantly becoming more and more enlightened' (Macaulay's words)[15] is the object of special scrutiny in this tale. For the question implicit in Melville's '*Follow your leader*' is asked here too – and only the first of several answers within the fiction is the familiar Conradian judgement that the enterprise is carried through for its own sake. 'Did it very well, too . . . without thinking much about it' – the verdict on the Roman naval commander sailing his ship up the Thames.

Conrad at the beginning of *Heart of Darkness*, like Pope at the end of *Windsor Forest*, is stirred into unashamed eloquence by historical grandeur. Like Pope he is morally alert without needing or wishing to be ironical. 'Hunters for gold' is balanced by 'pursuers of fame', but 'bearing the sword' not quite balanced by 'and *often* the torch' (my italics). If historical endeavour and the impulse to empire are not totally humane, that does not mean they must be the object of cynicism. *Benito Cereno* and *Heart of Darkness* both deal with civilization, savagery and servitude. In each tale these ideas challenge each other, but none can dissolve the others and incorporate them into itself. In *Windsor Forest* conquest and empire may seem to go hand in hand, but Pope can still envision an empire of peace in which conquest shall cease 'and Slav'ry be no more'. *Heart of Darkness* in its presentation of empire may be thought to pose in extreme form those problems of idealism and historical knowledge which have run through this book. The expression of an ideal and the longing for a better time may in some measure reach beyond experience into the utopian and

[14]Joseph Conrad, *Youth: A Narrative and Two Other Stories* (London, 1902), pp. 51–6; Norman Sherry, *Conrad's Western World* (Cambridge, 1971), pp. 119–21.

[15]See n. 10, p. 355 above.

other-worldly. But ideals cannot long subsist without being seen in some degree to be grounded in experience. History is drawn on to show that an ideal has known at least partial fulfilment. The selective art of the panegyrist projects from the historical record what is most admirable and relevant to the present need. The *princeps* as long-awaited bringer of peace; the principate and Julian House as guarantors of the world hegemony won by the Republic; the *pax Augusta* as providential preparation for the coming of Christ; recognition by the *princeps* of the greatest talent and best promise in the arts of peace; civil freedoms between ruler and writer; the architectural transformation of Rome; the mature intelligence of the ruler hastening slowly in the world's ways; the use of unparalleled power to maintain rather than expand a world state – all these features of Rome's Augustan Age were remembered as ideals of civilization: the torch rather than the sword.

Nobody, however, who found in that period the fulfilment of an ideal supposed it to have been total fulfilment, or the whole historical truth. Seneca, in his *De Clementia* one of the first writers of a later age to find in the principate an ideal for the edification of his own time, was quite clear that the whole career of Augustus was far from praiseworthy. Innocent Gentillet insisted on the same thing: critical appraisal must precede the selection of positive features for use as example in panegyric. For Orosius, Augustus was not less in the hand of Christian providence because he crucified 6,000 slaves. Pope made it clear which aspects of the Augustan principate he thought 'seasonable to the present Times'. From the time of Seneca to the eighteenth century it was taken quite for granted that there was a dark side of Augustus; that the principate which did so much good had partly arisen from wrong and probably led to further wrong. To many, a monarchy that established civil peace and stability for so long still seemed worth the cost. The torch that was borne by the sword was a torch nevertheless. Horace, though no soldier after Philippi, would not have been read fifteen centuries later in Western Europe had it not been for the sword of Rome, Republic and Empire alike. Nor, perhaps, would the architectural traditions of Greece, in the hand of Vitruvius, have shaped the buildings of the world.

Conrad's story, and Melville's too, remind us of another thing. Not only did the civilization of Rome rest on the sword and the wealth which the sword won; it rested in part on the institution of slavery. The existence of slavery in the ancient world offered an ever-present analogy for other relationships within the state. Not for nothing did Augustus repudiate the title *dominus*, redolent as it was of the mastery of slaves; and not for nothing did Tacitus later charge that Augustus had established *dominatio* over a hitherto free people. No civilization but is bought at a price. Only as civil peace and stability came to be taken for granted in eighteenth-century France and Britain did the record of Tacitus begin to persuade people that the price had been too high: for now the whole populations of nation states began to reach for those freedoms enjoyed at Rome only by the patrician Republic. This too, when it was eventually achieved, was to be paid for at a price: once again a positive political evolution, in this case representative not monarchical government, was purchased by wealth won by the sword and founded, in part, on that very slavery against which the Younger Pitt so eloquently appealed. At a time when the educated public was aware of slavery and the slave-trade as an issue, Jane Austen quietly included in her fiction a connection between the prosperity of Mansfield Park and estates in the West Indian island of Antigua (Ch. 3).

A critical balance and some humility of judgement is therefore required. Sir Thomas Bertram is in the end a better man than Kurtz and so is Benito Cereno. The freedoms and amenities we ourselves enjoy have been bought, at least in part, by the sufferings of those who have known neither. The relativistic perspectives of a Horace Walpole, Pitt or Conrad prompt us to see some analogy between our own time and the *summum fortunae* of the Augustan Age. If the legacy of ancient empire is not yet exhausted, as surely it is not, it is still too soon to weigh the effects of modern empire. If civilization survives long enough it may be that Macaulay's vision will come true, and travellers from New Zealand, Nigeria and Bangladesh will come to gaze at the ruins of London and New York. It is even more likely, in that case, that some future Tacitus, looking back to the good fortunes of our age, will diagnose in our failures the seeds of a new decline.

Bibliography of Principal Primary Sources

At the end of each section items marked with a dagger are works which express an anti-Augustan view. The order is otherwise broadly chronological, listing authors by the date of their earliest work cited.

I Classical Sources

P. Vergili Maronis *Opera*, ed. R.A.B Mynors (Oxford, 1969)

Q. Horati Flacci *Opera*, ed. E.C. Wickham and H.W. Garrod (Oxford, 1912)

P. Ovidii Nasonis *Metamorphoses*, ed. W.S. Anderson (Leipzig, 1977)
Amores, Medicamina Faciei Femineae, Ars Amatoria, Remedia Amoris, ed. E.J. Kenney (Oxford, 1961)
Tristivm Libri Qvinqve Ex Ponto Libri Qvattvor, ed. S.G. Owen (Oxford, 1915)

M. Vitruvius Pollio, *De Architectura*, ed. and tr. Frank Granger (London, 1931)

Octavianus Caesar, *Res Gestae Divi Augusti*, ed. P.A. Brunt (Oxford, 1967)

C. Vellei Paterculi *Ex Historiae Romanae Libri Duobus*, ed. C. Stegmann De Pritzwald (Stuttgart, 1965)

Velleius Paterculus, *The Tiberian Narrative*, ed. A.J. Woodman (Cambridge, 1977)

L. Annaei Senecae, *De Beneficiis Libri VII, De Clementia, Libri II*, ed. Carolus Hosius (Leipzig, 1914)

C. Svetoni Tranqvilli *Opera*, ed. Maximilian Ihm (Stuttgart, 1908). The *Historie of the Twelve Caesars* was translated by Philemon Holland, 1606; intro. Charles Whibley, Tudor Translations Series (London, 1899)

Cassius Dio, *Roman History*, ed. and tr. Ernest Cary (London, 1917).

Plutarch, *Lives*
The Lives of the Noble Grecians & Romanes . . . Translated by James Amyot: and . . . Thomas North was published first in 1579. Dryden lent his name to a collaborative translation published in 1684–8, contributing a life of Plutarch.

†C. Cornelius Tacitus, *Annals*, ed. F.R.D. Goodyear (Cambridge, 1972). The *Histories* and *Agricola* of Tacitus were first translated into English in 1591 by Henry Saville; the *Annals* and *Germania* by Richard Grenaway in 1598. John Dryden and others put together a translation in 1698 (partly drawing on Saville). Tacitus was translated again in the eighteenth century by Thomas Gordon, 1728–31.

II Patristic and Medieval Sources

Eusebius Pamphilius, *Ecclesiastical History* (including the Apology of Melito of Sardis) in J.P. Migne, ed. *Patrologia Graeco-Latina*, XX.

Demonstratio Evangelica, in Migne *Patrologia Graeco-Latina*, XXII.
Meredith Hanmer's translation of Eusebius's *Auncient Ecclesiasticall History* . . . was first published in 1577.

Q. Septimius Florens Tertullianus, *Apologeticus adversus gentes* in Migne, *Patrologia Latina*, I. An English version, *Tertullian's Apology* . . ., by H[enry] B[rown] appeared in 1655.

Paulus Orosius, *Historia adversus paganos*, in Migne, ibid. XXI.
The Old English Orosius, ed. Janet Bately (London, 1980), EETS, is a refashioning of the work produced by an anonymous member of the circle of King Alfred.

Dante Alighieri, *De Monarchia*, ed. E. Moore and W.H.V. Reade (Oxford, 1916); *Dantis Alighierii Epistolae*, ed Paget Toynbee (Oxford, 1920; rev edn, 1966)

Dante Alighieri, *Monarchy and Three Political Letters*, ed. Donald Nichol and Colin Hardie (London, 1954)

The Chester Nativity Drama, *The Chester Plays*, ed. Herman Deimling (Oxford, 1892)

†*Caesar Augustus*, *The Towneley Plays*, ed. George England and A.W. Pollard (London, 1897)

†S. Aurelii Augustini, *De Civitate Dei Contra Paganos Libri XXII*, ed. J.E.C Welldon (London, 1924). *The Citie of God . . . Englished by J[ohn] H[ealey]* appeared in 1610.

III Renaissance Sources

Sir Thomas Elyot, *The Boke Named the Governour*, ed. H.H.S. Croft (London, 1880)

Jean Bodin, *Les Six Livres de la République*, 1576 (Paris, 1583). *The Six Bookes of a Commonweale. . . . done into English by Richard Knolles* was published in 1606.

Innocent Gentillet, *Discours, Svr Les Moyens De Bien Gouuerner vn Royaume, Contre Nicholas Machiavel Florentin* . . . (Geneva, 1576). Simon Patricke's English version, *A Discourse Vpon The Meanes of VVel Gouerning and Maintaining in Good Peace, a Kingdome* . . . was published in 1602.

John Donne, *Satyres* I and IV, in John Donne, *The Satires, Epigrams and Verse Letters*, ed. W. Milgate (Oxford, 1967)

Ben Jonson, *The Poetaster*, in *Ben Jonson*, ed. C.H. Herford and Percy and Evelyn Simpson (Oxford, 1925–50), IV.
Part of *The King's Entertainment*; ibid. VII.

John Nichols, ed. *The Progresses, Processions and Magnificent Festivities of King James the First* . . . (London, 1828)

William Shakespeare, *Julius Caesar*, ed. T.S. Dorsch, Arden Series (London, 1955)
Antony and Cleopatra, ed. R.H. Case and M.R. Ridley, Arden Series (London, 1964)
Cymbeline, ed. J.M. Nosworthy, Arden Series (London, 1955)

Ben Jonson, *Poems*; *Ben Jonson*, VIII.

William Drummond of Hawthornden, *Poetical Works*, ed. W.B. Turnbull (London, 1586)

Thomas Carew, *Poems, With His Masque Coelum Britannicum*, ed. Rhodes Dunlap (Oxford, 1949)

Pierre Corneille, *Cinna: Ou La Clemence d'Auguste*; *Théâtre Complet*, ed. G. Couton and M. Rat (Paris, 1960–67)

Robert Herrick, *Poetical Works*, ed. L.C. Martin (Oxford, 1956)

Andrew Marvell, *Complete Poems*, ed. E.S. Donno (Harmondsworth, 1972)

Edmund Waller, *Poems*, ed. G. Thorn Drury (London, 1901)

Musa Ruralis [Alexander Huish], *In Adventum Augustissimi Principis & Monarchiae, Carolus II . . .* (London, 1660)

†Nicolo Machiavelli, *Tutte Le Opere* . . . (1550). The first work of Machiavelli to be translated into English was *The Art of Warre . . . set forthe in Englishe by Peter Whitehorne*, 1560; intro. W.E. Henley, Tudor Translations Series, (London, 1905). *Machiavels Discourses* . . . tr. E[dward] D[acres] appeared in 1636. *Nicholas Machiavel's Prince*, also by Dacres, With Some Animadversions Noting and Taxing His Errors, was published in 1640. *The Works of the Famous Nicholas Machiavel . . . newly and faithfully Translated into English* [by Henry Neville] was published in 1675.

IV Restoration and Eighteenth-Century Sources

John Dryden, *Poems*, ed. James Kinsley (Oxford, 1958), containing the 'Discourse concerning Satire', and all other prose works connected with the poems

Edmund Waller, *Poems*, ed. G. Thorn Drury (London, 1901)

John Ogilby, *The Relation of His Majestie's Entertainment . . .* (London, 1661) *The Entertainment of His Most Excellent Majesty Charles II . . .* (London, 1662)

John Milton, *Poems*, ed. John Carey and Alastair Fowler (London, 1968)

Nathaniel Lee, *Gloriana, Or The Court of Augustus*; in *Works*, ed. T.B. Stroup and A.L. Cooke (New Brunswick, 1954)

Francis Atterbury, Preface to the Second Part of Mr. Waller's Poems, Printed in the Year 1690; in Waller, *Poems*, I. *Sermons and Discourses on Several Subjects and Occasions* (London, 1723)

John Dennis, *The Advancement and Reformation of Poetry*, 1701; in *The Critical Works of John Dennis*, ed. E.N. Hooker (Baltimore, 1939–43)

Matthew Prior, *Literary Works*, ed. H. Bunker Wright and Monroe K. Spears (Oxford, 1959)

Nicholas Rowe, *Ulysses: A Tragedy*, 1706; in *Three Plays*, ed. J.R. Sutherland (London, 1929)

Alexander Pope, *Poems*, general ed. John Butt, The Twickenham Edition, (London, 1939–61); *Correspondence*, ed. George Sherburn (Oxford, 1956); Conversation, in Joseph Spence, *Observations, Anecdotes and Characters of Books and Men*, ed. J.M. Osborn (Oxford, 1966)

Joseph Addison, 'Dialogues Upon the Usefulness of Ancient Medals', in *The Works of Joseph Addison* (London, 1721)

Tamworth Reresby, *A Miscellany of Ingenious Thoughts and Reflections* (London, 1721)

Leonard Welsted, *Epistles and Odes, &c . . .* (London, 1724)

Richard Savage, *Poetical Works*, ed. Clarence Tracy (Cambridge, 1962)

Bevil Higgons, *Historical and Critical Remarks on Bishop Burnet's History . . .* (2nd edn: London, 1727)

Samuel Boyse, *The Olive: An Heroic Ode*, 1736/37; in *The Works of the English Poets*, ed. Alexander Chalmers (London, 1810)

John, Baron Hervey of Ickworth, *Some Materials Towards Memoirs of the Reign of King George II*, ed. Romney Sedgwick (London, 1931)

Joseph Spence, *Polymetis* (London, 1747)

Joseph Warton, *An Essay on the Genius and Writings of Pope* (3rd edn: London, 1772, 1782)

Thomas Sheridan, *The British Education: Or, The Source of the Disorders of Great-Britain* (London, 1756)
Complete Dictionary of the English Language (London, 1780)

David Hume, *The History of Great Britain* (Edinburgh, 1754–7)
The Letters of David Hume, ed. J.Y.T. Greig (Oxford, 1932)
Oliver Goldsmith, *Enquiry into the Present State of Polite Learning in Europe*, 1759;
An Account of the Augustan Age of England, *The Bee*, 24 November 1759;
both in *The Collected Works of Oliver Goldsmith*, ed. Arthur Friedman (Oxford, 1965)
The Roman History from the Foundation of the City of Rome to the Destruction of the Western Empire (London, 1769)

George, Baron Lyttelton, *Dialogues of the Dead* (London, 1760)

Vicessimus Knox, *Essays Moral and Literary* (London, 1778)

William Godwin, *The Enquirer. Reflections on Education, Manners, and Literature* (Dublin, 1797)

Samuel Taylor Coleridge, *Essays on His Times*, ed. David Erdman, Bollingen Edition, (London, 1978)

†Thomas Gordon, *The Works of Tacitus . . . To which are prefixed, Political Discourses* (Edinburgh, 1728–31)

†Henry St John, Viscount Bolingbroke, *Craftsman* Paper, 19 September 1730; *The Craftsman*, 1726–36 (London, 1731–7), VII, p. 36.

†Thomas Blackwell (and John Mills), *Memoirs of the Court of Augustus* (London, 1753–63)

†Edward Gibbon, *Essai sur l'étude de la litterature* (c. 1758–9), in *Miscellaneous Works*, ed. John, Lord Sheffield (London, 1814); *Critical Observations on the Sixth Book of the Aeneid*, 1770, in *The English Essays of Edward Gibbon*, ed. Patricia B. Craddock (Oxford, 1972)
The History of the Decline and Fall of the Roman Empire, 1776–91, ed. J.B. Bury (London, 1896; rev. edn, 1909)

†John Gordon, *Occasional Thoughts on the Study and Character of Classical Authors* (London, 1762)

Index

In the following index entries have been made for the chief proper names in text and footnotes, but names of works have been listed under names of authors only. Subject entries have been added where they seemed especially important to the chief themes of the book.